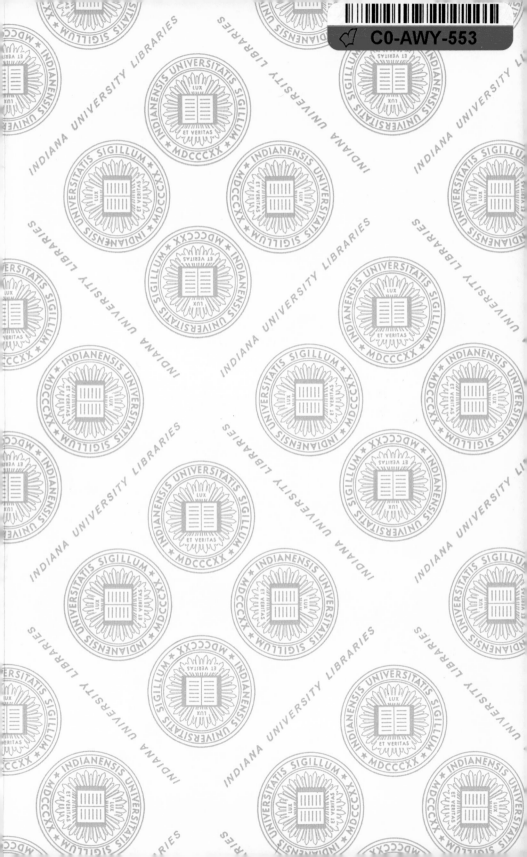

Child Development and Personality

DISCARD

UNDER THE EDITORSHIP OF
GARDNER MURPHY

W. Eugene Sm[...]

Child Development and Personality

Paul Henry Mussen
University of California, Berkeley

John Janeway Conger
University of Colorado School of Medicine

Harper & Brothers: New York

Library of Congress catalog card number: 56–6094

Contents

Preface

In the course of teaching classes in child psychology and personality development, the writers began to feel the need for a text which would meet several requirements. It should trace child development chronologically in order to enable the reader to gain a feeling of continuity from one stage of development to the next. The various aspects of growth —physical, intellectual, social, and emotional—should not be considered as unrelated phenomena. An attempt should be made to present a comprehensive view of the child at each stage of his growth, with the main focus being on the ways in which various factors influence the development of personality. Furthermore, the vast body of data of child development should be integrated—in so far as is possible at our present stage of knowledge—with general behavior theory. In our view, concepts derived from research on learning, from clinical psychological investigation, particularly psychoanalysis, and from sociological and cultural anthropological studies appeared most relevant for this purpose.

The present book is the result of a joint effort by the writers to achieve these objectives. It has been a thoroughly coöperative venture. The book was jointly planned and carried out. In the actual writing, chapters by one author were often extensively revised, as a result of suggestions by the other. Because of this extremely close collaboration, the order of names on the title page is purely a matter of chance.

A number of individuals have played an important role in the development of the general thinking reflected in this book. Among those who have influenced us most strongly, through their teaching or writing, are David P. Ausubel, Irvin L. Child, John Dollard, Leonard W. Doob, Glen Heathers, Neal E. Miller, Seymour B. Sarason, Robert R. Sears, and John W. M. Whiting.

The following individuals have read all or part of the manuscript, and have made many helpful suggestions: Irvin L. Child, Linda Hassel,

Jerome Kagan, Marvin Kahn, Gardner and Lois B. Murphy, Harry Mussen, Robert Rainey, Philburn and Mildred Ratoosh, Alvin Scodel, and Judith Worrell. Our greatest single debt of gratitude is to Irvin L. Child of Yale University for his unflagging interest in our efforts and his extensive criticisms of the entire manuscript.

In addition, we are grateful for the stimulation received from students on whom earlier versions of the manuscript were inflicted. Our research assistants, Donald Payne, Joseph Rychlak, and Ted Nelson, have been particularly helpful.

For aid in typing the manuscript or in preparation of tables and illustrations we are indebted to: Jessie Greensley, Mabel Oakley, Roberta Kuhn, Mildred Waddell, Virginia Brevort, Marcille Goss, Katharine J. Conger, Raymond S. Patterson, Henry L. Janeway, and Glen Mills.

For their constant encouragement and support throughout this venture, we wish to thank Herbert S. Gaskill, Gardner Murphy, John Benjamin, Julian Rotter, Robert Stubblefield, and our more than tolerant wives, Ethel Mussen and Trista Conger.

P. H. M.

J. J. C.

Denver, Colorado
January, 1956

Child Development and Personality

Chapter I

INTRODUCTION

In common with other fields of psychology, child psychology is concerned with the accurate description, explanation, and prediction of behavior. The field is not unique and cannot be considered independent of other areas of psychology. Basic general principles pertaining to learning, perception, motivation, and interpersonal relations are as applicable to child psychology as they are to other branches of the science. In fact, many aspects of children's behavior remain incomprehensible without an understanding of these generalizations.

For this reason, child psychology draws heavily upon the knowledge and resources of the entire realm of psychology. But it also makes many contributions to the total discipline of which it is a part. Many of the principles of psychology have been derived largely from laboratory experimentation with animals or with human beings in highly artificial, contrived situations. Consequently, it is often difficult to evaluate their importance as general explanations of behavior. If, however, these principles can be shown to apply to children's behavior, their usefulness is substantially increased. Thus the area of child psychology provides a proving or testing ground for determining the generality of psychological principles.

In addition, scientific study of children may be extremely important from a theoretical point of view. Findings from systematic observations or studies of children may suggest certain generalizations which extend beyond the area of child psychology. For example, an investigation of children's social relationships may lead to conclusions about interpersonal relations, social groupings, communication, and leadership which are also applicable to adults. Of course, the scientific psychologist must withhold his judgments about the broader applicability of principles derived from the study of children until he does further research with other groups. Nevertheless, it is often true that what he learns from children is extremely useful in pointing out directions for further study. The ideas and concepts which are suggested by work in child psychology may have value in stimulating research in other areas.

THE PRACTICAL IMPORTANCE OF CHILD PSYCHOLOGY

In addition to its theoretical importance, there are three substantial practical reasons for studying child psychology.

Understanding Individual Children

The first is to make the individual child's behavior more comprehensible and meaningful. Through systematic investigation of psychological development and social adjustment, research workers learn what is "average" for children of a given age. This knowledge may be employed in evaluating individual children. Are they progressing as they should be? Are they average, below average, or superior in some respects? Does this particular youngster learn to walk before, after, or at the same time the average child learns to walk? Does he know as many words as the average child his age? Can he answer as many and as difficult intelligence test items? Is his emotional control as adequate as other children's? Does he participate in social activities which are typical of children his own age or of younger or older children? Having standards or norms of development to which children may be compared is often of great help in diagnosing problems arising in these areas.

Child psychology includes the study of the child's heredity, physical constitution (biological, chemical, and physiological processes within his body), and environmental forces to which he is exposed. All these, working together, affect his physical and intellectual growth, psychological health, and social adjustment. Understanding these factors and their interrelationships may aid in the solution of the kinds of behavior problems which bring children to the attention of juvenile courts, social welfare agencies, psychologists, and psychiatrists.

For example, a child eight months old may be brought to a well-baby clinic or to a doctor's office because his parents do not feel that he is progressing as rapidly as other children. They report that he seems generally unresponsive, uninterested in people or in the environment. Developmental scales (cf. pp. 180–182) may demonstrate that, according to the norms or standards of performance for his age group, he is retarded in motor and sensory development. While it is almost impossible to make an accurate diagnosis of intellectual status in a child this young, these findings suggest, very tentatively, the possibility of mental deficiency.

If, in addition to his retardation in sensory and motor development, the child is very small for his age, a thorough medical checkup may be advised. This examination may reveal that the child is suffering from a thyroid deficiency. Previous research has shown that in a special kind of mental defect known as *cretinism*, there is an intimate connection between iodine deficiency in thyroid secretion and intellectual and physical retardation. Treatment by the administration of thyroid is, in many cases, highly effective in stimulating both physical growth and psychological development, particularly if the condition is detected early.

In this case, comparison of this child's ability with norms of motor and sensory development made it clear that the child was retarded in those areas. Facts derived from previous research showing the relationships among psychological retardation, physical size, and thyroid deficiency were useful in prescribing therapy. In short, the norms served as a basis for suggesting a diagnosis and knowledge of the interactions among these factors was valuable in suggesting a method of treatment.

Another illustration of the practical utility of the data of child psychology may be drawn from the field of juvenile delinquency. A 10-year-old boy has been stealing bicycles from other children in his neighborhood and is therefore brought to a juvenile court. His delinquency may be thought of as evidence of social retardation; that is, even though he knows the rules of acceptable social behavior, he does not conform to them. Research in this field has shown that delinquent behavior often has its roots in the child's deep feelings of rejection and insecurity in his home. Knowing the results of such scientific investigations, the court psychologist has some notion of how to proceed with the case. He will be alert to possible feelings of rejection in this boy; if he finds them, he can then look for their sources and work toward alleviating them.

In this connection, techniques of psychological treatment (psychotherapy) may be used with the delinquent child. The aim of such treatment is to allow the child to express his feelings freely and to learn to understand the factors involved in his socially unacceptable behavior. If he can gain insight (emotional understanding) and release his emotional tensions, the child may be able to reconstruct his emotional attitudes and behavior.

The psychologist may attempt to modify the child's environment if this is possible. By working with the delinquent's family, he may be able to help reduce conflict and stress in the home. The child may perceive the changed home situation as less rejecting, and hence there may be less motivation for him to commit delinquent acts. In this case, scientific findings about the relationship between home environment and personality problems could be applied in attempting to modify the child's behavior and to make it more socially acceptable.

Understanding Adult Behavior

Studying the psychology of childhood provides us with a background for a more thorough understanding of adult behavior. Clinical data from case histories of criminals and patients at psychiatric clinics reveal that personal and social maladjustments among adults almost always have their beginnings in early life experiences. It was Sigmund Freud, the father of psychoanalysis, who called attention to the importance of childhood events most forcefully. Through his penetrating analyses of the patients with whom he worked, he made abundantly clear the truth of the poet's statement, "the child is father to the man."

Generally speaking, the origins of adult unhappiness, maladjustment, feelings of inadequacy, and insecurity must be sought in the individual's childhood. Therefore, in order to understand the adult's psychological problems with any degree of sophistication, we must learn about his early developmental history.

This does not imply that it is only abnormal behavior that has its origins in childhood. It seems safe to say that most of the normal adult's important personality characteristics and behavior patterns can be traced back to factors in his earlier life. A man may be shy and withdrawn or friendly and outgoing; generous or stingy; independent in his actions or dependent on others; lazy or ambitious; tense or relaxed; passive or aggressive. All these characteristics are the outcomes of his entire unique history of personality development, but particularly of the intimate experiences of his childhood. Similarly, the broad lifetime goals and over-all philosophy of the individual—his choice of vocation and the satisfactions he will seek from it, the kind of person he will want to marry, and his expectations with regard to his children—become fully understandable only in the light of his entire developmental history.

Understanding Social Problems

Still another major reason for much of the current interest in child psychology is the increasing evidence that many crucial social problems are closely related to individual personality structure and its determinants. Systematic investigations have shown that conflict between groups is often a reflection of the personal tensions of the individuals in these groups (cf. pp. 441–447). It has also become apparent that vital social attitudes—such as attitudes toward other nations and toward minority groups, toward democracy and fascism—and political activity or disinterest are directly connected with personality development and structure. For example, while children's and adults' anti-minority group feelings are undoubtedly learned from others, they have their roots in, and derive much of their strength from, early resentments and hostilities toward parents (cf. pp. 441–445). Investigations of this sort provide impressive evidence of the pervasive and enduring effects of childhood influences.

THE PURPOSE OF THIS BOOK

Stated most generally, we propose to trace the process of development of the total, integrated personality of the child. More specifically, we shall attempt to bring together the pertinent data relating to such challenging questions as: Why and how does the child become the kind of individual he is? What are the innate, constitutional, and environmental sources of his habits, feelings, emotions, and attitudes? How are certain aspects of his personality learned? What are the origins of neuroses and maladjustments in children? It has already been hinted—and will become increasingly obvious—that many factors, operating in complicated ways and in varied combinations, are involved in the answers to any of these questions.

Personality development may be viewed as a continuous, highly complex process, involving the interaction of a biological organism with its physical, psychological, and social environment. No two individuals will ever develop identical personalities, since no two people ever encounter quite the same patterns of developmental influences. For one thing, except in the case of identical twins, no two people have identical hereditary endowments. Furthermore, as development proceeds, differences between people become magnified as a consequence of individual variations in maturational factors and in prenatal and postnatal experiences.

Because of the highly complex nature of the developmental process, physical, emotional, intellectual, and social development cannot be viewed as separate, independent components of development. All these aspects are functionally related to one another. For example, emotional factors may affect aspects of physical health, while emotional malad-

justment may influence intellectual performance. Our emphasis throughout this book will be on connections of this sort.

In order to provide background for understanding the interrelationships, it will often be necessary to isolate one or another aspect of personality and discuss it separately. When this occurs, the reader should keep
in mind that this abstraction is made for convenience of exposition only.
The developing personality is a vast, unified network of interrelated
segments, and fundamentally, the parts cannot be separated from one
another. However, just as one of the organ systems of the body can be
made to stand out from the rest of the animal's anatomy by the use of
special dyes in a fluoroscopic examination, one aspect of personality may
be highlighted by focusing attention on it. In each of these cases the
basic unity of the entire structure—the biological organism in one case
and personality in the other—cannot be overlooked, even though a part
of it can be isolated temporarily for more thorough examination.

Consideration of separate aspects of development may also have utili-
tarian value. Thus, as we have seen, studies of single segments of growth
and development, such as motor ability, yield background information
and provide standards which may be applied in assessing a child's developmental status. But an evaluation of one segment of development cannot
be meaningful unless other aspects and other factors in the child's environment are considered simultaneously.

For example, in a particular case, retarded physical development itself
may not be a crucial determinant of the child's psychological adjustment.
However, parental attitudes toward the child may be influenced by his
physical size. Whether they realize it or not, adults may treat him as a
younger or inferior child because he is smaller than most children his
age. The child's attitude toward himself will be derived largely from the
attitudes of others toward him, and he may begin to have feelings of
inferiority and inadequacy. This, in turn, will affect his general social
and emotional adjustment. Thus it is often true that the influence of a
single factor in the child's development, e.g., physical status, can be
understood only in terms of the total context of forces impinging upon
him.

PLAN OF THE BOOK

The general plan of this book is to follow personality development
chronologically. Development is a continuous process, starting with conception. The chapters of the book center attention on various periods of
the child's life in chronological order. However, this arbitrary division

has been made for purposes of exposition only. In the process of development, one period follows the next in unbroken order.

Working within this organizational framework, we will make use of what we have labeled a "crucial events" approach. Scientific research and theory strongly suggest that certain occurrences in the individual's history have widespread ramifications for personality development. Examples of such important events are birth itself, early feeding experiences, toilet training, birth of a sibling, starting school, achieving rewards in school, joining neighborhood groups, and rejection by parents or peers. Events such as these will be stressed, and their broad implications for the child's subsequent adjustment will be examined.

Throughout the book, each aspect of personality development and each crucial event will be analyzed in terms of antecedents and consequents. That is, the child's behavior, interests, attitudes, and feelings will be discussed from the points of view of: (1) factors in the child's background (biological, psychological, or social) leading up to and influencing the development of these characteristics, and (2) the importance of these characteristics for the child's future development. In short, we must look backward in our efforts to understand the many factors (antecedents) which underlie the child's present behavior. Conversely, a forward look is necessary to see how his present characteristics and behavior may influence his personality later on (consequents).

Only part of the data required to understand the infinitely complicated process of personality development comes from psychology itself. For this reason, modern child psychology draws from many disciplines. Some knowledge of genetics is required to understand how heredity operates. Medical science, particularly the specialized field of pediatrics, has contributed considerable data on differences in biological structure and functioning and their consequents. Psychiatry has yielded a vast body of facts and theories about the relationship of childhood events to subsequent maladjustment. Anthropological and sociological research have provided extremely valuable information on the influences of membership in particular ethnic groups, social classes, castes, or minority groups within or outside American culture. A thorough science of personality development requires contributions from all these fields. In our opinion, comprehensive understanding can emerge only from the integration of many kinds of data.

We must acknowledge that child psychology is still a young science. Although facts and theories in the field are accumulating at a rapid rate, there are still tremendous areas about which we know practically nothing. A multidisciplinary approach, making use of the best each discipline has to offer, seems to be the best route to scientific progress and maturity.

PRESCIENTIFIC CHILD PSYCHOLOGY

Philosophical Writings

Although scientific child psychology is a relatively recent development, writers in all periods of history have been interested in children's behavior. Plato recognized the importance of early childhood training in the determination of the individual's later vocational aptitudes and adjustments. In his *Republic,* he discussed inherent differences among individuals and recommended that steps be taken to discover each child's outstanding aptitudes so that specific education and training along the lines of his particular talents might begin early.

Late in the seventeenth century, the English philosopher, John Locke, published his essay, *Some Thoughts Concerning Education.* He maintained that infants have minds which are blank tablets (*tabulae rasae*) at birth and they are therefore receptive to all kinds of learning. The object of all education, according to Locke, is self-discipline, self-control, and the "power of denying ourselves the satisfaction of our own desires, where reason does not authorize them" (8). He felt that the best way to achieve these goals was to begin instructing children in self-denial "from their very cradles." The teaching techniques advocated by Locke resemble quite closely the methods of what we now call "formal education."

Jean Jacques Rousseau, a French philosopher, writing in the latter half of the eighteenth century, believed that the child is born with an innate moral sense. In *Emile* (12) he spoke of the child as a "noble savage" with intuitive knowledge of what is right and wrong. Restrictions imposed on the child by adult society thwart him and force him to become less virtuous. For the general improvement of the individual and society, Rousseau advocated a back-to-nature movement which would eliminate social conventions and encourage the unrestrained expression of original, inherently noble impulses.

There is, of course, no scientific evidence to substantiate Rousseau's assumption that children are inherently "good" or "noble." Nevertheless, his views have been tremendously influential in education, especially in the establishment of "progressive" schools which stress spontaneity and freedom of expression. Parenthetically, it is interesting to note that Rousseau considered the experiences of the first few years of life the most influential ones in the individual's development, thus anticipating much present-day psychological thinking.

Plato, Locke, and Rousseau were only three of the many philosophers who were implicitly or explicitly interested in children and their development. Their writings often reflected penetrating, but untested, philosophical thinking. In contrast to the methods of contemporary psychology, these philosophers' theories, ideas, and hunches were not checked by systematic or careful observations. Nevertheless, their speculations have been stimulating, and their writings have had profound influences upon psychological and educational theory, practice, and research.

Baby Biographies

Beginning late in the eighteenth century, a few curious and courageous individuals attempted to learn about children by the novel procedure of actually observing them. In 1774, a Swiss named Pestalozzi published notes based on the careful observation of the development of his 3½-year-old son (10). Thirteen years later, Tiedemann published a book (13) tracing the sensory, motor, language, and intellectual growth of a single infant during the first two and a half years of life.

In the nineteenth century, a series of "baby biographies" began to appear. Typically these were accounts of the development of the author's own child, niece, or nephew. Among the writers of such biographies were Charles Darwin, the famous biologist, (A Biographical Sketch of an Infant, 1877) (4) and Bronson Alcott, the father of Louisa May Alcott, the author of Little Women, who entitled his biography Observations of the Vital Phenomena of My Second Child (1).

Biographies of this sort do not provide good scientific data for several reasons. Often the observations were unsystematic, and made at irregular intervals. Moreover, the observers were usually proud parents, uncles, or aunts, and were probably biased and "selective" in their perceptions; that is, they saw primarily the positive, praiseworthy aspects of early development, and neglected other, negative factors. Finally, since each account is based on only one case, it is almost impossible to make generalizations from any of them.

Nevertheless, like the earlier philosophical works, these biographies had some value, for they contained some information, and many hypotheses about the nature of development. In fact, the conclusions drawn from the "baby biographies" were not nearly so important as their influence in delineating major problems of child psychology and exciting widespread interest in the scientific study of children.

Beginnings of Modern Child Psychology

Toward the end of the nineteenth century, systematic study of larger groups of children began. A pioneer in such study in the United States was G. Stanley Hall, president of Clark University, who was interested in investigating "the contents of children's minds" (7). For this purpose, he devised a new research technique, the questionnaire, consisting of a series of questions designed to obtain information about children's and adolescents' behavior, attitudes, and interests. Hall collected written responses to questionnaires from both children and parents.

In a sense, Hall's work, which continued into the twentieth century, marks the beginning of systematic child study in the United States. By present-day standards, his work would not be considered controlled or highly objective. The problems with which he was concerned have been investigated with much greater scientific sophistication in recent years. Nevertheless, he did employ large numbers of subjects in an effort to obtain representative data, and attempted to determine the relationships among personality characteristics, adjustment problems, and background experiences. For these reasons, Hall's approach to child psychology certainly represents a distinct advance methodologically over the philosophical and biographical approaches discussed above.

THE NATURE OF SCIENCE

Throughout this book, emphasis will be placed on the most important empirical findings and basic principles which have been derived from scientifically conducted studies in child psychology and personality development. But before we begin to discuss the actual content of the field, it is important to consider briefly the nature of science and scientific investigation. Our aim is to clarify the major differences between scientific child psychology, with which we are concerned in this book, and nonscientific child psychology, exemplified by the earlier works of the philosophers and baby-biographers.

If asked, "What is science?" and "How does the scientist work?" most people would immediately think of the dramatic achievements of physical and biological scientists working in laboratories and applying their findings to practical problems. The most publicized products of scientific endeavor are more and better mechanical devices, improved industrial and agricultural techniques, and more effective methods of preventing and curing disease. In the minds of the few, we may be living in the "age of anxiety," but to most, it is the "atomic era." The power of physical science is now virtually unquestioned. The image of the scientist as a long-haired, absent-minded, and usually impractical laboratory doodler, has been largely replaced by that of the powerful, dynamic, efficient, atomic scientist, self-assuredly working in the midst of a welter of flashing lights and high-voltage sounds.

But many doubt whether scientific methods are applicable to the social sciences, such as child psychology, where the focus of attention is human beings and their relationships to one another. In these areas, every bartender, cab driver, and congressman still feels that he is his own expert. To the layman, the problems of these fields seem to be infinitely complex. He is likely to conclude, often correctly, that they cannot be solved through what he thinks of as the scientific method, namely, the rigorous laboratory experimentation characteristic of much physical research. Consequently, he is likely to be suspicious of the social scientist's claims that these areas are amenable to scientific investigation. In our opinion, the fundamental problem here is a misconception on the part of the layman as to the true nature of science.

If we lay aside for the moment the conception of a scientist as a white-coated laboratory technician, manipulating atomic reactors or test tubes, and actually make a survey of the fields generally accepted as scientific, we find that a wide range and variety of subject matters are covered. Many different methods and techniques are used in the research programs of these varied fields of study. Although geology, meteorology, taxonomic biology, and astronomy are generally classified as scientific disciplines, they involve little laboratory experimentation. It seems clear, therefore, that laboratory experimentation is not the sole criterion of what is or is not science. Rather, such experimentation must be considered only one of many methods employed by scientists in their pursuit of knowledge.

Since each branch of science deals with its own particular phenomena, it must devise its own techniques, apparatus, and measuring instruments for solving its problems. Science cannot be defined in terms of any specific concrete techniques such as the use of specialized laboratory equipment or methods of measurement. Rather, it is a way of doing things which involves certain basic general principles and procedures. All scientists, regardless of their area of inquiry, adhere to these fundamental methods.

An examination of the elements common to all fields of scientific inquiry, may provide deeper insight into the broad objectives, processes, and principles of science. It will also enable us to see how the social sciences generally, and child psychology in particular, fit into the scheme of activities generally regarded as scientific.

STEPS IN SCIENTIFIC INVESTIGATION

D. G. Marquis, a psychologist at the University of Michigan, has said that what is common to all science is "a system of logically interrelated concepts, derived from experiment or observation, from which specific predictions can be derived and verified by further experiment or observation" (9, 411). To make this statement more concrete and applicable to social science, he reviewed the actual processes of accumulating scientific knowledge and arriving at scientific generalizations. He concluded that: "It is possible to distinguish a sequence of six steps which can be identified in any complete research" (9, 411).

These steps can serve as a kind of idealized model or paradigm of the scientific process. They are summarized here because, taken together and in sequence, they constitute the essential pattern or working procedure which has been extremely effective in advancing physical and biological science. The plan seems equally applicable to the investigation of problems in social science and child psychology.

Step 1. Research begins with the statement of a problem (*problem formulation*). The source may be simply scientific curiosity. Often, however, it is some practical situation such as an individual health problem or a social problem. When a previously unidentified disease strikes, questions about its origin arise. If a 10-year-old child of normal intelligence cannot read, his difficulty requires further psychological investigation. When juvenile delinquency increases at an alarming rate, people begin to wonder about the underlying factors in delinquency. All these situations present pragmatic problems which must be solved in the interests of the general welfare. However, they are general problems, and more precise formulation is necessary before scientific investigation can proceed. Thus, the question, "What causes juvenile delinquency?" is a broad one and must be broken down into specific questions before it becomes capable of scientific solution. Such questions might be, "What are the personality characteristics of juvenile delinquents?" "What kinds of homes do these children come from?" "What is the influence of intelligence on a child's proneness to commit delinquent acts?"

Step 2 is "*Review of knowledge*—of what has been learned or said by others about the topic" (9, 412). This step involves a thorough survey of relevant earlier scientific work as well as speculative writings. It is at this stage that philosophical treatises and records such as the baby biographies mentioned earlier might be reviewed to learn something about earlier thinking and investigations of the problem. In the case of a subject like juvenile delinquency, writings, research studies, and accounts of experiences by juvenile court personnel (judges, psychiatrists, psychologists, and social workers) might give leads for attacking some of the problems formulated in Step 1.

Step 3 is called *preliminary observation.* Intensive scientific work begins with this step, for observation is the fundamental operation, the *sine qua non,* of all scientific research. At this stage, the emphasis is on collection of facts and descriptions of the phenomena which may be important in the solution of the problem.

For example, if the personality structures of juvenile delinquents are to be investigated, preliminary observation might consist of informal interviews, covering a wide range of background information, with a group of delinquent children. From the data obtained, the researcher might form some tentative impressions of the specific characteristics of delinquents which are related to antisocial behavior.

From these preliminary interviews (a particular kind of observation), the most important concepts to be used in the next steps are derived. For example, there may be indications that delinquents are similar to other children in some aspects of personality, but differ in others. The concepts used in further investigations will deal with those characteristics in which delinquent children deviate from normal.

Step 4 is *hypothesis* or *theory construction.* The scientist is now ready to offer his hypothesis (best guess, tentative suggestion, or conjecture) regarding the problem stated in the first step of the scientific process. This hypothesis (or hypotheses) will be founded on previous work by others and the scientist's own preliminary observations. Generally it involves "tentative explanations," stated in terms of relationships between variables, e.g., the relationship between the volume and pressure of a gas, between personality variables and delinquency, or between socioeconomic background and intelligence. When these "explanations," or statements of relationship, are formulated in more comprehensive and abstract terms and bring together several hypotheses, they are called theories.

In studying the relationship between personality and juvenile delinquency, the investigator might hypothesize that the outstanding distinctive characteristics—or most important underlying factors—involved in juvenile delinquency are feelings of inadequacy and rejection. Until the hypothesis is tested, however, the scientist cannot either accept it or reject it. This means that the hypothesis must be stated in a testable form.

Step 5 consists of the testing or *verification of the hypothesis* (or hypotheses) formulated in Step 4. Scientific hypotheses always imply predictions. A hypothesis will be supported or refuted, depending on whether or not the predictions made from it are found to be true.

In our illustration, the investigator's hypothesis regarding personality factors related to juvenile delinquency may lead to the specific prediction that feelings of rejection and inadequacy will be more common among delinquents than among nondelinquent children. This prediction may be tested by giving psychological tests and intensive psychiatric interviews to groups of delinquents and nondelinquents of the same age, sex, intelligence, and socioeconomic status. If analyses of the test and interview data reveal that delinquent children actually do show more feelings of rejection and inadequacy than the others, the prediction—and therefore the hypothesis—is supported and verified. If there are no differences between the two groups, the hypothesis must be rejected and a new one, taking account of these findings, must be constructed. This hypothesis, in turn, must be tested before it can be accepted. The process of building up scientific knowledge requires continuous formulation of theory, checking of theory, reformulation of theory, and rechecking. In this way, increasingly satisfactory theories—that is, theories which will account for more and more observed facts—are constructed.

Step 6 is the *application of the verified theory* or putting the tested hypothesis to work. If the predictions derived from the hypothesis prove to be correct, the scientist feels quite confident that the hypothesis is valid and that he can make practical use of it. Let us assume that there is support for the hypothesis that the delinquent's feelings of rejection and worthlessness are the most important factors underlying his antisocial behavior. This information could be used in planning the psychological treatment of individual delinquent children. Furthermore, the findings could be taken into account in organizing parent-participation programs for the reduction of juvenile delinquency.

CHILD PSYCHOLOGY AND THE SCIENTIFIC PROCESS

The steps outlined above represent an idealized program for the establishment of scientific knowledge. The whole sequence has actually been carried out most adequately in highly developed sciences such as mathematical physics. In general, the social sciences, being newer and generally dealing with more complex and involved phenomena, have not yet achieved this level of scientific sophistication. Research in these fields seldom follows the full pattern of scientific inquiry. As Marquis points out, "current social science is deficient not so much because it violates any of the steps but rather because it fails to complete the necessary sequence of steps" (9, 413).

An examination of the present status of child psychology from the point of view of this six-step procedure lends support to Marquis' statement. Problems in this field have always been considered vital, and problem formulation therefore has a long history. Questions have been rephrased and brought up to date, but as we have seen, even the ancients were aware of many basic problems which still concern child psychologists. Moreover, new problems are constantly being uncovered. Since scientific progress is continuous, new problems and questions will arise as new data and theories accrue.

A vast amount of information about child psychology has been accumulated, particularly since 1900. As a result, innumerable articles, general treatises, textbooks, and handbooks have been published. Carrying out Step 2, review of knowledge, has thus become a difficult, scholarly task. Nevertheless, most investigators are conscientious in searching the literature for earlier writings pertinent to their research problems. Thorough reviews of empirical findings, as well as of theoretical and speculative contributions, reveal the methodological shortcomings of existing studies and point up aspects of problems which have previously been neglected or inadequately explored. For these reasons, recent studies do not merely repeat older ones. They avoid the errors of earlier research workers, use fresh approaches, and hence contribute new data for the solution of the problems formulated in Step 1.

A survey of the literature of child psychology reveals that the major emphasis to date has been placed on Step 3, preliminary observation. The majority of articles and books stress empirical data such as norms of physical, intellectual, emotional, and social development. Until recently, relatively few research studies were designed specifically to test or verify hypotheses.

This does not mean that Step 3 has been overemphasized. All scientific research must begin with careful observation of natural phenomena. As new problems are formulated or old ones rephrased, new preliminary observations become necessary. At present, the amount of basic data available is limited. Moreover, the validity of many conclusions is questionable, for techniques of measuring important psychological variables are often not precise enough to yield more than suggestive results.

Progress in child psychology is intimately related to progress in other branches of the field. Increased precision of methodological tools, better techniques of observation and experimentation, and optimal use of statistical techniques will lead to greater scientific sophistication in all areas of psychology, including child psychology.

Data collected in the preliminary observation stage may have immediate utility in providing norms or standards for evaluative purposes. In addition, analyses of such data may uncover previously unsuspected relationships among variables, and thus suggest important hypotheses which can be tested later.

Theory in Child Psychology

Child psychology, and the social sciences generally, have been quite deficient in Step 4, theory construction. The value of a scientific theory may be judged on the basis of two criteria. The first is its utility in integrating and explaining different kinds of facts. Thus Einstein's theory of relativity was extremely useful in bringing together gravitational and electromagnetic phenomena, which had previously seemed unrelated.

The second criterion for evaluating a theory is its fruitfulness as a source of scientifically testable hypotheses. A good theory gives rise to many predictions which may then be tested. In brief, the best theory is the one which brings together many data and generates many verifiable hypotheses.

At present there is no single comprehensive theory encompassing the vast body of information which child psychology has accumulated. Two kinds of theory have been extremely useful, however, from the points of view both of integration of data and stimulation of research. The first of these, psychoanalytic theory, began with Freud's monumental work, and is concerned with personality development, and more particularly, with the development of emotional problems and neuroses. The concepts and hypotheses of psychoanalysis have been derived largely from clinical experience.

The psychoanalysts' therapeutic activities made them keenly aware of the tremendous impact of the child's early environment in paving the way for adult maladjustment. From their investigations of their patients' backgrounds, the analysts derived many hypotheses about the consequents of infantile and childhood experiences on later personality. The major contributions of psychoanalytic theory to child psychology have been its stimulation of hypotheses about personality development and its delineation of crucial areas in need of scientific investigation. Later on, we will discuss more explicitly some concepts and hypotheses of psychoanalysis.

A second kind of theory which is extremely valuable for child psychology is known as learning theory. The most important aspects of behavior are learned: "precisely that behavior which is widely felt to characterize man as a rational being or as a member of a particular nation or social class is learned rather than innate" (5, 25).

There are many facts and theories about the nature of the learning process and the conditions under which learning occurs most effectively. As we shall see, learning begins to influence the child's development early in life. Thus, learning theory seems indispensable in understanding the individual's development from complete helplessness and dependence on others to maturity and independence. The basic principles of learning will be elaborated in detail in Chapter 5, and we shall refer to them often throughout this book.

Psychoanalytic and learning theories are the primary ones on which we will draw throughout this book. However, other theories, growing directly out of the study of child behavior and dealing with somewhat more limited aspects of behavior, have also contributed a great deal to our understanding of child psychology. For example, much of our knowledge of the role of maturation in behavior change comes from the empirical research and developmental theories of Arnold Gesell. A Swiss psychologist, Jean Piaget, has formulated and tested many ingenious and useful hypotheses about the development of moral standards and moral behavior which we shall also discuss.

The Experimental Method

A number of techniques are available for verification of hypotheses, the fifth step in scientific procedure. As we noted earlier, the experimental method is only one of many methods used by scientists in testing their predictions, but since it has many advantages, it is generally considered the most desirable. In physical science, experimentation is the method most frequently employed in Step 5. Although it is applied whenever suitable in child psychology, as in many areas of social science, there are many problems for which it is not appropriate or practical.

In its simplest form, the experimental method consists of holding constant all but one of the variables presumably related to a given phenomenon. This particular variable is then manipulated by the experimenter as he sees fit. The purpose of the experiment is to test whether, and how, something else changes as the variable being manipulated by the experimenter (referred to as the independent variable) is changed. To cite a simple example, Boyle's hypothesis about the compression of gases stated that the volume of a gas is "inversely proportional to the pressure." From this hypothesis, it may be predicted that as the pressure applied on a gas is doubled, its volume will be halved. To test this prediction, and thus the hypothesis, the experimenter manipulates and varies the pressure exerted on the gas (independent variable) and then measures its volume (dependent variable). Other relevant variables which are known to influence the volume of a gas, such as temperature, must be controlled; that is, these factors must be held constant during the experiment, because the hypothesis is concerned only with the relationship between pressure and volume. By controlling all other relevant variables, the experimenter can be certain that pressure alone varies and he can therefore be sure that changes in volume are related *only* to changes in pressure.

In a similar way, the psychological experimenter attempts to control all the relevant variables except the one with which he is particularly concerned. He systematically manipulates the independent variable in order to determine its consequents. Suppose, for example, the experimenter wants to test the hypothesis that competitive situations will stimulate better performance on arithmetic tests. His specific prediction is that a competing group of children will do better in these tests than a group working without competition.

The prediction may be tested experimentally by setting up two groups of children, one called the *experimental group* and one called the *control group*. Ideally, the experimenter would start with a large group of children and assign half of them, chosen at random, to the experimental group and half to the control group. Under these conditions of assignment, there is little likelihood that the two groups will be significantly different in any variable. However, further to assure comparability of the two groups, the experimenter might also equate them on all variables likely to affect performance in arithmetic, e.g., age, grade placement, arithmetic ability, intelligence, sex, and health. Thus he could feel confident that the two groups were alike at the beginning of the experiment.

In the experiment proper, the two groups would be subjected to different treatments. A competitive situation could be set up in the experimental group by informing them that the student getting the highest grade on an arithmetic test would be given a prize. In the control group, no such competitive situation would be created. Both groups would then be given the same arithmetic test, and the difference between the performances of the two groups would be determined. If the competing group did better than the other group, the prediction and the hypothesis would be considered verified.

Here the independent variable was competition, and it was regulated by the experimenter. Other important variables were controlled by initial random assignment of children to the two groups and by matching the groups on variables considered likely to affect performance in arithmetic. Therefore we can be fairly certain that the obtained differences between the two groups must be due to the introduction of competition in one group and its absence in the other.

These two examples, one drawn from physical science and the other from social science, make clear the unique advantage of experimental method, namely, the direct demonstration of relationships between variables. Without the use of experimental procedures, we cannot be sure which factors may be most important in determining a particular outcome.

As long as we depend on the observation of occurrences not involving our assistance, the observable happenings are usually the product of so many factors that we cannot determine the contribution of each individual factor to the total result. The scientific experiment isolates the factors one from the other; the interference of man [that is, the experimenter] creates conditions in which one factor is shown at work undisturbed by the others . . . (11, 97).

It is obvious that the experimental method cannot always be used in psychology even though it has great advantages, and is therefore highly desirable. For example, suppose a psychologist has an hypothesis that one of the consequents of rejection is greater proneness to delinquency. He could hardly expect parents to reject their children for experimental purposes. However, the investigator might be able to study a group of children known to have been rejected and a control group of non-rejected children. He would attempt to control for the effects of other possibly relevant variables by equating these two groups as closely as possible in factors such as age, intelligence, sex, health, and socioeconomic status. It would then be possible to compare the occurrence of delinquency in the two groups and hence to determine whether significantly more rejected than non-rejected children commit antisocial acts. If there is actually more delinquency among rejected children, he may conclude that his hypothesis is supported, i.e., that rejection is, in fact, related to delinquent behavior.

The study cannot be considered an experiment in the usual sense, because the experimenter did not manipulate the independent variable, rejection. However, his study was as close to the ideal of an experiment as was possible under the circumstances.

Nevertheless, it must be recognized that the relationship between rejection and delinquency has not been demonstrated as clearly as the relationship between competition and performance on arithmetic tests in the experiment cited earlier. There is still the possibility that some factor not controlled by the experimenter is also an effective determinant of delinquent behavior. For example, rejected children often come from homes where there is a great deal of friction between the parents. In such cases, it is possible that delinquency represents the child's reactions to interparental tensions, rather than to rejection. This is only a possibility, of course, but it illustrates that other factors associated with rejection, rather than rejection itself, may account for the observed differences in the delinquency rates of the rejected and non-rejected groups. In the experiment on the effects of competition, on the other hand, we feel more confident of the meaning of the findings. The observed differences between the experimental and control groups must have resulted from the experimenter's manipulation of competition, since all other factors were controlled.

To summarize, the experimental method can be considered the ideal procedure, or method of choice, in the step of verification of hypotheses. It permits the most direct demonstration of relationships between variables. For this reason, it should be employed whenever and wherever it seems feasible. However, under some circumstances, and for some kinds of research problems, the method is not practical, and in these cases, other methods must be used. Other available techniques will be described later in the book in connection with specific studies in which they have been used.

Application of Scientific Findings

The sixth step in the scientific process, *application,* can be carried out legitimately only after the first five steps have been satisfactorily completed. Nevertheless, in many instances, hypotheses have been applied, although there is little scientific evidence to support them. As a matter of practical necessity, pressing social and personal problems must often be tackled, and solutions attempted before there is a substantial body of pertinent verified principles or facts. For example, educators and clinicians working with disturbed children are frequently forced to use their best judgments in mapping out plans or giving concrete advice about treatment. In such cases, they are often forced to depend on common sense, their own experience, and any theory that seems applicable, even though it may not have been adequately tested. As scientists, however, child psychologists are interested only in the application of verified hypotheses about children.

Most scientists sincerely hope that eventually the results of their endeavors will be useful in advancing human welfare. But they realize that this broad objective can be achieved only by applying knowledge which is derived from sound basic research.

TWO APPROACHES TO UNDERSTANDING CHILDREN

Ordinarily, psychologists are interested in discovering regularities in human behavior, formulating general principles, exploring interrelationships among variables, or establishing norms of development. To accomplish these purposes, they usually study large groups of subjects, thus employing what Allport has called the *nomothetic approach* (2). Almost all systematic investigations in psychology and social science, such as those to be reported in this book, are *nomothetic*.

Certainly there are characteristics common to all members of the species and general laws which apply to all. Yet no two human beings are exactly alike. As psychologists, or as interested laymen, our ultimate concern is usually with individual human beings. The psychological practitioner or educator must center his attention on a particular individual and attempt to understand him thoroughly. This cannot be done simply on the basis of nomothetic knowledge. Complete comprehension of the individual case requires more than an understanding of general principles of growth and development and the uniformities of human behavior.

Studies such as case histories and biographies which stress the individuality of personality are examples of what Allport has labeled the *idiographic*, or individual clinical approach (2). A good case study depicts the individual in all his natural complexity. Idiographic knowledge involves understanding the unique organization of a particular personality, the complex relationships of the individual's heredity and life experiences, and the interactions of his nature and endowments with the specific environment in which he has grown up. "In the human realm we have to *particularize* our nomothetic knowledge before it is of any value and it must be particularized . . . in the light of concrete existing circumstances" (2, 58; italics ours). In other words, generalizations, norms, and verified nomothetic hypotheses demonstrate their value most graphically when they are applied to individual cases.

Both idiographic and nomothetic approaches are necessary and useful in child psychology. A simple illustration may clarify the way in which the two approaches supplement each other. Suppose all the children in a certain school are given an intelligence test. Ten children in the school are found to be mentally retarded, that is, they obtain scores which place them in the lowest 2 percent of all children their age. The norms (nomothetic data) supply the basis for the diagnosis. But if we are to understand or help any of these children, we must shift from a nomothetic to an idiographic, individual approach. We must ask ourselves: "What are the specific factors underlying this particular child's retardation?"

Again, nomothetic generalizations may provide some leads in the search for the etiology of any particular case. For example, certain physical conditions, such as vitamin deficiency, thyroid or other glandular dysfunctions, may be contributing factors. Brain trauma, high fever, or infection of the nervous system sometimes lead to mental deficiency. Studies have shown that emotional problems often handicap the performance of capable children in tests of intelligence. Children from lower-class homes generally are not so highly motivated to do well in school or in intelligence tests as their middle-class peers. Any one—or any combination—of these factors may be involved in a particular case of mental retardation.

Employing an idiographic approach, that is, studying each individual clinically, enables us to determine the underlying factors in each case and thus to make concrete plans for care or treatment. The combination of nomothetic and idiographic methods makes possible a more complete scientific investigation of single personalities; it enhances the understanding and prediction of individual behavior.

It is obvious that in the present state of psychology the idiographic approach poses many more problems than the nomothetic. As we noted earlier, almost all the studies and experiments reported in this book are based on groups of subjects; that is, they are nomothetic studies. This is at least partially attributable to the fact that there are as yet few idiographic studies in psychology. Scientific traditions in the field have emphasized experimentation with groups, objective measurement, statistical manipulation, and the discovery of relationships between characteristics.

In short, methods for dealing with groups and group data are readily available, whereas methods for dealing with the individual case scientifically are not.

Recently, however, there has been some shift in emphasis and a growing trend toward a psychology which endeavors to understand the individual as a unique personality (3, 6). Psychoanalytic and other personality theories, as well as increased clinical work with both normal and abnormal subjects, have been extremely influential in stimulating scientific interest in the individual case.

Generally speaking, the clinician uses nomothetic norms and generalizations primarily as standards for evaluating the child's observable characteristics. They may also give *suggestions* as to the nature of the major factors underlying these characteristics. Only through the use of an individualized, clinical approach, however, can we specify the many complex forces which have produced the unique personality being studied.

REFERENCES AND ADDITIONAL READING

1. Alcott, B., Observations of the vital phenomena of my second child, cited in D. McCuskey, *Bronson Alcott, teacher.* New York: Macmillan, 1940.
2. Allport, G., *The use of personal documents in psychological science.* New York: Social Science Research Council, 1942.
3. Barker, R. G., and Wright, H. F., *One boy's day. A specimen record of behavior.* New York: Harper, 1951.
4. Darwin, C., A biographical sketch of an infant. *Mind* (1877), 2:285–294.
5. Dollard, J., and Miller, N., *Personality and psychotherapy.* New York: McGraw-Hill, 1950.
6. Evans, J., *Three men.* New York: Knopf, 1954.
7. Hall, G. S., The contents of children's minds on entering school. *Ped. Sem.* (1891), 1:139–173.
8. Locke, J., *Some thoughts concerning education; 1690 Sections 38 and 40.* London: Cambridge University Press, 1913.
9. Marquis, D. G., Scientific methodology in human relations. *Proc. Am. phil. Soc.* (1948), 92:411–416.
10. Pestalozzi, G., A father's diary, 1774, cited in R. De Guimps, *Pestalozzi, his life and work.* New York: Appleton, 1906.
11. Reichenbach, H., *The rise of scientific philosophy.* Berkeley: University of California Press, 1951.
12. Rousseau, J. J., *Emile: or concerning education. 1762, Book 2.* New York: Dutton, 1938.
13. Tiedemann, D., *Beobachtungen über die Entwickelung der Seelenfahigkeiten bei Kindern.* Altenburg: Bonde, 1787.

PART I

The Prenatal Period

Chapter 2

GENETIC FACTORS IN DEVELOPMENT

When one human being is puzzled by the behavior of another, the question he is most likely to ask is, "How did he get that way?" In a sense, that is the question that we shall be attempting to answer throughout this book. Obviously, this attempt can be only partially successful, for we are only beginning to break ground in our efforts to erect a broad science of human behavior.

Nevertheless, as we shall see, some progress has been made. We know enough, for example, not to resort to easy and superficial explanations of behavior. We know that people do not do puzzling things only because "they were born that way," because "their mothers spoiled them," or because they are foreigners, or underprivileged. Any of these things may be true of a particular individual and may help to determine his behavior.

But no man, despite the bias of specialists, is only a genetic man, a physiological man, or a sociological and psychological man. Every man is the result of a complex and unique combination of all these kinds of forces. Development depends on the existence of a living, reacting organism, and the interaction of this organism with its environment—physical, psychological, and social.

BEGINNINGS OF LIFE

The life of each individual begins when a sperm cell from the father penetrates the wall of an ovum, or egg, from the mother. As we shall see in some detail in Chapter 3, the fertilization of an ovum by a sperm sets in motion an intricate maturational process, called *mitosis*. In this process the original fertilized ovum divides and subdivides until thousands of cells have been produced. Gradually, as the process continues, the resulting cells begin to assume special functions, as parts of the nervous,

27

skeletal, muscular, or circulatory systems. The embryo, which at first resembles a gradually expanding ball, begins to take shape, and the beginnings of head, eyes, trunk, arms, and legs appear. Approximately nine months from the time of fertilization the embryo, which by this time we call the fetus, is ready for birth.

HEREDITARY TRANSMISSION

Thus life begins at conception. But what of the forces that, throughout the individual's existence, will influence his development? When do they begin? The answer, again, is at conception. For at the moment that the tiny sperm penetrates the wall of the ovum, it releases 24 minute particles called *chromosomes*. At approximately the same time, the nucleus, the inner core of the ovum, breaks up, releasing 24 chromosomes of its own.

This process is of great interest to us because it has been established through painstaking research, that these *chromosomes,* which are further subdivided into even smaller particles called *genes,* are the carriers of the child's heredity. All the child's physical heritage from his father and his mother is contained in these 48 chromosomes.

What is Transmitted?

Long before the geneticists established the existence of chromosomes and genes, scientists were convinced that many characteristics of a child's parents were transmitted to the child at conception. People have, however, differed about what was transmitted and how. For example, one school of thought, dating back to Lamarck, a French zoölogist who published a book called *Philosophie zooligique* in 1773, long maintained a doctrine known as the inheritance of acquired characteristics. Lamarck felt that individuals improved or weakened their own physical capacities through experience or training, and that the effects of such changes could be transmitted to their offspring. Thus, by developing a diseased lung or poor digestion, a prospective parent would be hurting his child's chances of being healthy. People began to postulate such notions as that the giraffe acquired his long neck because his ancestors had spent a great deal of time reaching into trees for food, or that the snake lost his legs as a result of his forebears' propensity for creeping through crevices (27, 40).

Nor were such speculations confined only to obvious physical characteristics. Many people believed that a mother could influence her child's chances of being born with a talent for singing, if she had, in her youth, carefully cultivated her own voice. Or that if a father had previously developed an interest in mathematics, this interest was likely to be inherited by his son.

However, such early theories as these, and the inferences based upon them, were dealt a hard blow by Weismann in 1889 (47). He presented evidence suggesting that while the rest of the body may change with increasing age or through exercise, illness, or injury, the germ cells (chromosomes and genes) which an individual harbors, and which are passed on to his children at their conception, do not ordinarily change.

In the main, subsequent research has tended to support Weismann's position. However, it has since been determined that under exceptional circumstances, genes may change or be killed, as for example, through direct radiation from x ray or from atomic blasts. Nevertheless, genes are not subject to any of the usual influences that either build up or break down our bodies or improve our minds. Thus the genes that a sick, but well-educated man of 50 possesses, are no different from those that he possessed as a healthy, but untutored youth of 17. In short, changes in the rest of the body do not affect the genetic characteristics of the germ cells which are passed on to our children. Hence there is no reason for believing that we can affect our children's biological destinies by engaging in physical education or self-improvement campaigns.

The Mechanisms of Hereditary Transmission

One of the things that must have puzzled parents in prescientific days was why two children of the same parents should be so different physically. The answer lies in the mechanics of hereditary transmission.

If each child received all of both parents' genes, we could not explain individual genetic differences between them, since all the children would then have identical heredities. The fact, however, is that each child inherits only half of each parent's genes. Moreover, different children in a family may inherit different combinations of their mother's and father's genes. Thus individual differences between them become possible.

The way in which this happens will become clear as we proceed. It will be recalled that the original fertilized ovum contains 48 chromosomes. As this cell divides to form two new cells, each of its 48 chromosomes also divides in half, by splitting lengthwise down its center (see Figure 1). Through a process known as *polarization*, the halved chromosomes then go to opposite sides of the cell. Thus, when the cell itself

1. Original cell. (Only four chromosomes shown, for simplification.)

2. Each chromosome splits in half, lengthwise.

3. The halved chromosomes go to opposite sides and wall forms between them as cell begins to divide.

4. The halved chromosomes grow to full size, resulting in two cells, each a replica of the original.

FIGURE 1.   How a fertilized egg cell multiplies. (From A. Scheinfeld, *The New You and Heredity*. Philadelphia: Lippincott, 1950.)

divides down the center, the new cells will each contain the same 48 chromosomes as the original cell.

This process is repeated again and again as development proceeds. Even in the completed human being, when the myriad cells of the body have by this time taken on their special functions as tissue, bone, blood, and muscle, each cell still contains a replica of the original 48 chromosomes of the fertilized ovum.

Germ Cells

But if this is true, why don't the sperm and ovum, which go to make up a new individual, also contain 48 chromosomes each, since certainly they too are cells? It will be recalled that the new individual receives only 24 chromosomes from each parent.

The answer, stripped of genetic complexities, is actually quite simple. The adult organism contains, not one, but two kinds of cells—body cells which go to make up bone, nerves, muscles, and organs; and germ cells, from which the sperm and ova are derived. While the process of chromosome and cell division described above applies to the somatoplasm (the body cells), it does not apply completely to the germ cells. Throughout most of their evolutionary history, the latter develop just as the body cells do. But at the time of their final division into recognizable sperm or ova, the pattern varies. At this point, the germ cells split, but the chromosomes do not. Instead, the 48 chromosomes, which in reality are 24 pairs of similar chromosomes—one pair-member from each parent—simply

 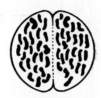

1. Germ cell containing 48 chromosomes.

2. The paired chromosomes separate, going to opposite sides of the cell, and the cell divides.

3. There are now two half-cells, with only 24 single chromosomes in each.

4. The chromosomes mass together, and part of the cell contents forms a sheath around them.

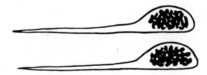

5. The sheath shapes the chromosomes into a tightly packed mass forming the head. The rest of the cell contents is squeezed out behind to form the tail.

FIGURE 2. How sperms are produced. (From A. Scheinfeld, *The New You and Heredity.* Philadelphia: Lippincott, 1950.)

divide into two groups. One member of each pair goes to one of the resulting sperm or egg cells, and one to the other (see Figure 2). Thus the ova and sperm have only 24 chromosomes each and the new individual obtains a total of only 48.

We can see, too, why it is that the children of the same parents do not all have to be alike. As may be seen from Figure 3, if Sperm A unites

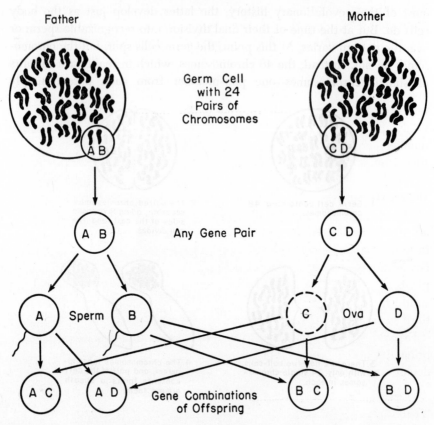

FIGURE 3. Schematic diagram showing possible gene combinations of off-spring resulting from gene pairs of parents.

with Ovum D, the new individual will possess a different set of chromosomes than if Sperm B unites with it. (Ovum C is indicated in dotted lines since ordinarily at any one conception only one ovum from the mother is ready for fertilization. The same of course is not true of sperm. At any one mating millions of sperm are released—as many as a hundred million in one drop of seminal fluid, any one of which might potentially fertilize the receptive ovum).

Is Identity Possible?

We have seen how it is possible for individuals in the same family to be different in their genetic make-ups. But is identity between siblings possible? The answer, for all practical purposes, is *no*, except in the case of identical twins who actually develop from the same fertilized ovum and only later split into two individuals.[1] If the 48 chromosomes in the germ cells always divided the same way, with one combination going to one sperm or ovum and the rest to the other, identity would be possible. In fact, it could be anticipated frequently. But these 48 chromosomes do not divide in this way. Except that one member of each of the 24 pairs goes to one sperm or ovum and the other member to the other, the pattern is pretty much random. In other words, the way one pair of chromosomes splits does not determine the way another pair will split. Thus the number of possible combinations of chromosomes contained in the fertilized ovum, instead of being confined to four, is almost infinite.

The Mendelian Laws

The elementary principles of gene interaction were first worked out by an Austrian monk, Gregor Mendel, in the privacy of his monastery garden in 1857. Mendel worked with two strains of peas, red-flowering and white-flowering. He found that if he mated plants of a pure red strain with plants of a pure white strain, in the second generation all the offspring would be red. But if he then mated these offspring with each other, the third generation would average three red-flowering peas to one white.

Experiments such as this led Mendel to derive a number of general principles about hereditary transmission, often referred to as the "Mendelian laws." These principles have been summarized by Scheinfeld.

1. The inherited characteristics are produced by genes (called by Mendel "factors") which are passed along *unchanged* from one generation to another.
2. In each individual these genes are found in pairs, and where the two genes in a pair are different in their effects, one gene *dominates* the other so that it might be referred to as a "dominant," the other as a "recessive." [In the above example of the two strains of peas, red genes dominate white, so that when both are present in a gene pair, the pea flower will be red.]
3. When seeds are formed in any individual, the members of each pair of genes *segregate out*, independently of the other pairs, *with just one of every two mated genes* going from each parent to *each offspring* (*40*, 51–52).

Mendel's results were largely ignored during his own day. It was not until 1900, sixteen years after the brilliant monk's death, that his work, first published in 1865, was rediscovered, and serious attack on the problems of genetic transmission begun. Subsequent work by many geneticists (*14, 16, 29, 40, 42*) tended to confirm and vindicate Mendel's theories.

---

[1] For an interesting and simple discussion of the way in which identical and fraternal twins are produced, the reader is referred to Scheinfeld (*40, 41*). Somewhat more technical discussions will be found in general texts by Stern (*44*) and Gates (*13*).

Their work also demonstrated, however, that the mechanisms of heredity were often a good deal more complex than they had originally appeared.

For example, they showed that genetic prediction is often complicated by the fact that many characteristics depend on complex combinations of gene pairs, rather than on a single pair. In addition, they found that genes do not simply behave dominantly or recessively but in numerous other ways also, and that their effects may vary under different conditions. A discussion of these complexities is not necessary for our purposes. It is enough to say that it would be much easier to weigh the relative importance of hereditary and other factors in determining human characteristics if all these characteristics were as simple in their hereditary aspects as blossom color and other characteristics studied by Mendel in the pea plant. Some, such as eye color, hereditary baldness in men, some forms of diabetes, and certain kinds of night blindness, are almost as simple; but most are not. Eye color, for example, is determined primarily by a combination of one gene from each parent. Certain types of mental deficiency, on the other hand, seem to depend on a number of pairs of genes being present in a particular combination.

THE NATURE-NURTURE CONTROVERSY

This leads us to the age-old heredity-environment, or nature-nurture controversy (33). In general, it is a controversy that has generated more heat than light.

What human characteristics are due to heredity, what to environment, and what to a combination of the two? Or, stated in more dubious, if more popular fashion, "Which is more important, heredity or environment?"

Apparently, there is some room for confusion about these questions, as the challenging statements of the following scientists reveal.

Heredity and not environment is the chief maker of man. . . . Nearly all

PEANUTS®   **By Schulz**

TITLE—Peanuts, Reg. U. S. Pat. Off.

FIGURE 4. The nature-nurture controversy. (Cartoon by Shulz. Copyright, 1955, by United Features Syndicate. Reproduced by permission.)

the misery and nearly all the happiness in the world are due *not* to environment. . . . The differences among men are due to differences in the germ cells with which they are born (*1*, 102–103).

Compare this statement with the following:

Give me a dozen healthy infants, well formed, and my own specified world to bring them up in and I'll guarantee to take any one at random and train him to become any type of specialist I might select—doctor, lawyer, merchant, chief, and yes, even beggar-man and thief, regardless of his talents, peculiarities, tendencies, abilities, vocations, and race of his ancestors. There is no such thing as an inheritance of capacity, talent, temperament, mental constitution, and characteristics (*1*, 103). *Watson*

The statements of both these gentlemen seem rather naïve. To maintain the positions described above, the first author at least would have to deny the possibility of *learning* as a determinant of human behavior, to say nothing of the effects of specific influence from physiological and physical aspects of the environment, such as illness, injury, or malnutrition. And the other gentleman, it seems to us, would almost have to deny that man was a *biological organism* at all—at least one that could vary in its structure and function from one individual to the next.

Actually, the general question of which is more important, heredity or environment, is a rather meaningless one, as many observers have pointed out. The question of which is more important cannot be answered at all except in specific terms. We must define the characteristic with respect to which the question is asked. Is it eye color, baldness, intelligence? The relative contributions of heredity and environment may differ markedly from one characteristic to another.

We must also ask under what conditions the characteristic is being manifested. This is particularly important in the case of behavioral characteristics. Take, for example, the task of determining the hereditary and environmental antecedents of illiteracy. As Haldane (*15*) has pointed out, the answer need not always be the same.

632

. . . among adults in England under 40 years of age, illiteracy is probably most often due either to mental deficiency or to blindness. But among adults in Elizabethan England, or in India today, illiteracy may be attributed primarily to the lack of educational opportunity. (*17*, 583). *Haldane*

Obviously, under these differing conditions the relative contributions of heredity and environment to illiteracy will not be the same.

Or take another example, closer to the concerns of this book. Suppose that a child fails a reading-readiness test, of the type given children prior to admission to the first grade in school. If the child is suffering from cerebral sclerosis, a form of mental deficiency which is dependent on the coexistence of two specific recessive genes, heredity could reasonably be called the "more important" contributor to his failure. No amount of superior medical care, and no amount of desperate training by his mother or teacher could overcome the disabling effects of the disease. On the other hand, if the child shows no evidence of specific hereditary deficiency, but has lived an isolated mountain life with illiterate parents, and later with proper training passes the test, environment would obviously be the more important determinant of his original failure.

In other words, it is impossible to make general statements, such as "People are 60 percent the result of heredity, and 40 percent the result of environment." However, at the level of specific cases such as those just described, it is often possible to answer, at least partially, questions about the relative importance of hereditary and environmental factors. "The question of the relative importance of nature and nurture has no general answer, but . . . a very large number of particular answers" (15).

But even when we make such statements of relative importance in specific instances, we are never saying that either heredity or environment is unimportant.

The hereditary "determiners" or genes cannot function unless the various aspects of the environment play their necessary roles. On the other hand, the influence of environmental factors is subject to very definite limitations, for (to cite one example) no normal environmental force can change an individual with chromosomes of one species into an individual with the characteristics of another species (17, 583).

PUTTING GENETIC DETERMINANTS IN PERSPECTIVE

We can probably set the whole problem of genetic factors in human behavior in the most helpful perspective by reviewing the original contention of this book, namely, that an individual becomes the person he does through the continuing interaction of his biological make-up and his total environment. An individual's inherited gene structure is an important determinant of the kind of biological potential with which he starts life, and it will continue to play a part in determining his biological characteristics as maturation proceeds. Thus, through their purely biological effects, genetic forces can help to determine the kind of person that develops.

To cite a few simple examples, genetic forces determine whether an individual is a man or a woman; [2] they help to determine whether he is tall or short, fat or thin, handsome or ugly, sluggish or high-strung. They may influence his resistance to various diseases, and set limits beyond which his intelligence cannot develop.

Since heredity acts *directly* only upon the individual's *biological* characteristics, it cannot itself produce a child's jealousy of its mother or an enthusiasm for space guns and rocket ships. These attributes, necessarily depending in part upon learning through interaction with particular objects in the environment, cannot be entirely and simply determined by heredity. Heredity may play a role, however, since it helps to produce the kind of individual who is doing the learning. For example, it may help to determine whether an individual becomes a racing-car driver, or a tea taster, through its influence on the speed of his reaction time—the racing car driver with a slow reaction time would neither be successful nor have a great life expectancy. On the other hand, slow reaction time is probably no great disadvantage to the tea taster.

Determining the Extent of Genetic Influences

By and large, we cannot directly observe the tiny genes in action. Instead, we are forced to infer their presence from their effects, just as Mendel inferred the presence of red-flowering and white-flowering genes from the colors of the blossoms which were produced.

Sometimes this is relatively easy. Let us take the case of a degenerative disease of the nervous system like Huntington's chorea. This disorder strikes in generation after generation of the same family. Its frequency can be predicted by genetic principles, and thus far no one has discovered any environmental variation, either physical or psychological, which can affect its course. Under the circumstances, we can say that the disorder is determined pretty exclusively by genetic factors—in this case, a single dominant gene.

In other cases, however, the situation is by no means so clear. In many instances, a characteristic may be the result either of hereditary or environmental influences, or both. To go back for a moment to the matter of reaction time. Some newborn babies have faster reaction times than others, and it seems likely that these variations may be due to genetic factors. (For purposes of this illustration, let us ignore the possibility

[2] For a discussion of the genetic mechanisms determining sex, see Scheinfeld (40), and Parshley (32).

that prenatal influences [cf. pp. 61–75] also play a part.) However, it has been found that when people are anxious and under psychological stress, their reaction times also speed up. Certain drugs have the same effect. Thus, only through an intensive review of a particular individual's history may we be able to sort out the relative effects of drugs, genetic factors, or psychological influences on his reaction time.

Actually, since we must infer the importance of both genetic and environmental factors from their effects on the individual, the only sure way of determining whether either set of factors plays an important role in a specific condition, is to find some way of holding one constant while varying the other. If the condition then also varies, we know that the factor we have varied plays an important role.

For example, in a number of studies, identical twins have been used to control as much as possible for genetic factors. Since they have identical hereditary background, any differences between them may be attributed to environmental influences, e.g., different experiences. Newman, Freeman, and Holzinger (30) have used this method to study the effects upon personality of rearing children in different home environments. Some of this work will be discussed in a moment.

In other studies, particularly those with animals (where by controlled mating it is possible to experiment on genetic factors), the physical and psychological environments are held as constant as possible, and the effects of varying heredity are noted (31). In cases where we are unable to hold most of the factors constant, we can only make, at best, intelligent guesses concerning the relative importance of genetic or environmental influences.

RESULTS OF HUMAN GENETIC RESEARCH

As a result of the difficulties inherent in much genetic research with humans, there are large gaps in our knowledge of the role of heredity in human development. Nevertheless, progress is being made. A brief summary of the findings from some of the more pertinent studies in this area will be presented here.

Much of this research has employed the so-called twin-study method. In this type of approach, an attempt is made to control environmental influences, thus making it possible to note whether genetic factors alone will produce variations in the phenomenon under study. In the case of intelligence, for example, the performances of identical twins on intelligence tests may be compared with those of fraternal (nonidentical) twins or other siblings. The assumption here is that the environments of fraternal twins or other siblings are as similar as those of identical twins. In this way, the possible effects of environmental factors on I.Q. are considered to be controlled. Consequently, if identical twins are found to resemble each other more closely in I.Q. than fraternal twins or other siblings, it is concluded that genetic factors affect intelligence. The greater similarity in the I.Q. scores of the identical twins is considered to be due to the fact that these twins have exactly the same heredity, whereas fraternal twins and other siblings do not.

However, a word of caution about this type of approach is necessary. It should be readily apparent to the reader that the environmental influences to which two children are exposed will differ somewhat, even though they are both raised in the same family. Furthermore, it appears that these environmental influences may differ, at least in some respects, more for fraternal twins or other siblings than for identical twins.

Several studies have shown that identical twins spend more time together, enjoy more similar reputations, are more likely to be in the same classrooms, have more similar health records, and in many other respects share a more common physical and social environment than that ordinarily experienced by fraternal twins (17).

Thus the assumption in twin studies like the one described above, that the possible effects of environment have been adequately controlled for, may not always be justified. In a few studies, an attempt has been made to avoid this problem by comparing identical twins reared apart with fraternal twins or other siblings reared together. If, in this instance, identical twins still resemble each other more closely than fraternal twins or other siblings, we can be confident that genetic factors are playing a role. It would be highly improbable in such a case that the environments of the identical twins would be more similar than those of the fraternal twins; hence environmental similarity could not account for the closer resemblance of identical twins. Thus findings of greater similarity among identical twins must be considered the result of genetic rather than environmental factors.

In evaluating the results of many of the twin studies which follow, the possibility that environmental variations may be accounting for some of the differences observed must be considered. It is also true that in several of these studies, the number of subjects used was quite small; and final judgment should be withheld until an adequate number of cases have been accumulated.

Physical Features

An individual's physical features depend heavily upon his heredity. Birth injury may alter the shape of his face, disease may whiten his hair. But the color of a person's eyes; the shape of his nose; the pigmentation of his skin; the color, curliness, and stiffness of his hair, are typically a direct function of the genes he has inherited. Some features, such as eye color, depend upon quite simple combinations of genes. Others, such as skin color, are more complex.

For the most part, variations in physical features within the American population bear little relation to an individual's biological ability to adapt to the demands of living. An individual with brown eyes can see as well as one with blue. An individual with fair skin may have greater difficulty with sunburn than an individual whose skin has more pigment to protect it. But the principal effects of variation in physical features upon the individual's adjustment are not biological, but social and psychological. People do not always treat a person with one skin color the same way that they would treat another of a different hue. Nor do they always respond similarly to people with hooked noses and straight noses. The ugly duckling and Snow White have different crosses to bear. Knowledge of the ways in which people with different features are often treated in our society is essential to a proper understanding of personality development, as we shall see later.

Anatomical Traits

Although body form and structure are more subject to nonhereditary influences—such as nutrition, climate, exercise, and even occupation—than are physical features, there is evidence to suggest that hereditary factors are also of great importance. For example, in their classic study of twins, Newman, Freeman, and Holzinger (30) found that among twins who were raised together, identical twins were consistently more alike than nonidentical twins on measures of height, weight, hand length, and hand width. They also found that, except in the case of weight, identical twins reared in different environments resembled each other more than nonidentical twins reared together.

On the other hand, environmental factors may also be important in determining growth patterns. For example, it has been found that within one generation, the children of Jewish and Japanese immigrants grew to an average height of two inches greater than their parents (3). Recent studies (5, 6, 7, 8) also indicate that obesity may be more frequently the result of dietary problems than of glandular disorders or hereditary factors. What is more, the antecedents of overeating appear to be intimately related to such psychological factors as "parental overprotection . . . and to deprivation of satisfying outlets and contacts so that for the child, food intake assumes inordinate importance" (45, 276).

Physiological Traits

There is an intimate relationship between physiological and psychological processes. For example, while fear and anger generally elicit rises in blood pressure, dryness of the throat, and increases in pulse rate, there are wide individual differences in the intensity of these reactions. For example, equally disturbing psychological events may have more severe —and perhaps more persistent—effects on a person with a highly reactive nervous system than on a person with a less reactive one. It is therefore important for the student of personality development to know the extent to which differences in physiological and neurological functioning are genetically determined.

Various investigators have used the twin-study method to investigate the role of growth factors in determining physiological and neurological functioning. They have, for example, been able to show that while environmental influences are important in determining such physiological functions as blood pressure and pulse rate, genetic factors are important too. In one study (26), the average difference in blood pressure (expressed in millimeters of mercury) between identical twins was 5.1, as compared with 8.4 for nonidentical twins. Similar findings were obtained for the pulse rate. The closer correspondence between the blood pressures and pulse rates of identical twins suggests that heredity may play a role in determining these characteristics.

In a more elaborate setting, Jost and Sontag (18) studied the similarities in seven neurological and physiological measures, using pairs of identical twins, pairs of "unrelated siblings" (i.e., singletons with the same parents) and pairs of unrelated children. These measures included such factors as breathing rate, blood pressure (systolic and diastolic), salivation, perspiration, and pulse rate. All the measures were combined into one score, an *index of autonomic stability.*

They then correlated [3] the paired individuals in the three groups on the various measures. The scores of each twin were correlated with those

[3] Mathematically, a correlation coefficient of zero means that there is no relationship between two sets of measures. A coefficient of 1.0, on the other hand, indicates a one-to-one, or perfect, relationship. Partial relationships are expressed by coefficients ranging from zero to 1.0.

of his partner, those of each child with those of his siblings, and those of the unrelated children were correlated with each other.

In three studies, conducted between 1940 and 1942, the scores of identical twins were consistently much more closely related than those of siblings. Sibling scores in turn were more alike than those of unrelated children. The results are shown in Table 1. As in the study above, the finding that of all the groups, identical twins resemble each other most

TABLE 1.   Correlations of Twins, Siblings, and Unrelated Children on Indices of Autonomic Stability [a]

Year	Correlation	N
1940		
Twins	0.434	5
Siblings	0.255	10
Unrelated	0.164	361
1941		
Twins	0.470	5
Siblings	0.406	19
Unrelated	0.017	364
1942		
Twins	0.489	6
Siblings	0.288	25
Unrelated	0.080	300

[a] From (*18*). With permission of *Psychosomatic Medicine*.

closely on these measures suggests "that there is a genetic factor in autonomic nervous system functioning" (*18*).

The authors feel that the results of such studies may help to explain the development of a number of so-called "psychosomatic conditions." For example, under psychological stress, some individuals become hypertensive (develop high blood pressure), while others do not react this way. The findings of Jost and Sontag suggest that genetic factors may be involved in predisposing some individuals to such conditions.

AGE OF FIRST MENSTRUATION.   Another physiological trait which seems to be partly a function of heredity, and which has considerable psychological significance, is age of first menstruation (*44*). It should be obvious that delay in menstruation, or premature menstruation, relative to her contemporaries, would have important implications for the girl's psychological adjustment (cf. pp. 479–480). In one study (*38*), it was found that the average difference in age of menstruation was 2.8 months for identical twins, 12 months for nonidentical twins, 12.9 months for non-twin siblings, 18.4 months for mother and daughter, and 18.6 for unrelated women. Of course, as in most genetically influenced characteristics, environmental forces also play a role in age of menstruation.

LONGEVITY. Longevity is, of course, conspicuously influenced by all sorts of environmental factors, including accidents; but even here, genetic influences seem to play a part. One team of investigators (23), studied the intrapair differences in the life span of deceased twins who died after the age of 60. They found an average difference in the life span of 36.9 months for identical, and 78.3 months for nonidentical twins. The number of subjects used in this study was small, but the results are at least suggestive.

Motor Ability

Several investigators (4, 28, 44, 46) have found that the height which twins could jump (at age 4 to 4½), as well as the ages of first beginning to sit up and of first walking, were all much more similar for identical twins than for nonidentical twins. Again the number of subjects in these studies was too small to permit a final conclusion, but the results are suggestive. In another study, it was found that the eye movement patterns used in reading were significantly more alike in identical twins than in fraternal twins (44).

Physical Defect and Disease

In such conditions as certain types of diabetes, hemophilia (inability of the blood to clot properly when an individual is cut), and some types of visual and hearing defects, hereditary factors have been shown to be highly important. In other conditions, however, the question of hereditary predisposition is the subject of much controversy, although there is little concrete evidence. Such conditions include various allergies, high blood pressure, some kinds of cancer, stomach ulcers, and tuberculosis. It seems probable that there are many physical diseases which are dependent on a complex combination of hereditary and environmental factors.

Mental Disorder

The role of genetic factors in the production of mental disorder has also been and continues to be a source of much heated controversy in the field of psychiatry. There is general agreement that certain forms of mental disorder such as general paresis (syphilis of the central nervous system), are caused by infection or similar agents attacking the body from without. Some other rather rare forms of mental illness (such as Huntington's chorea) result from definite genetic factors, usually quite simple in their genetic structure.

There is considerably less agreement when it comes to the vast majority of cases of mental disorder, those falling into the two categories of (1) "the functional" psychoses (severe mental disorders without known organic cause) and (2) the psychoneuroses (the milder forms of mental disorder and maladjustment). Some experts (*19, 21, 22, 24*) tend to view these disorders as primarily genetic in origin. Others tend to view them as almost entirely dependent on environmental factors, usually early life experiences.

Why is there so little agreement? In order to provide a concrete basis for discussion, let us consider one of the commonest forms of functional psychosis, namely, *schizophrenia* or *dementia praecox,* as it is sometimes called. This illness, manifested by severe defects in logical thinking and in emotional responsiveness, probably comes closest to the average person's idea of what it means to be "crazy." It accounts for the occupancy of more hospital beds in the United States than any other form of illness, mental or physical.

Schizophrenia has been attributed exclusively to hereditary defects by some authors, and exclusively to disturbances in early parent-child relationships by others (*2*). Most psychiatrists consider schizophrenia a total reaction of a biological organism to its environment, although they may differ widely as to the relative importance of hereditary and environmental influences in its determination.

There are several reasons for this. For one thing, the diagnosis of most mental disorders, including schizophrenia, is based upon a rather vague constellation of behavioral symptoms. One cannot apply any simple test (as for example, one can in the case of tuberculosis) in order to determine the presence or absence of the disorder. As a result, it is often difficult to make a diagnosis of schizophrenia, and disputes over diagnosis are not uncommon, particularly when the presenting symptoms are not severe (*12*).

There is no simple explanation applicable to all cases of schizophrenia. Kallmann (*20*) has used the twin-study method to investigate genetic factors in schizophrenia. Using 794 patients, who had twin siblings available for examination, Kallmann then studied the relative incidence of schizophrenia among the patient's relatives. His results indicate that schizophrenia may be expected in about 2 percent of the step-siblings of schizophrenic patients; in 2 percent of their marriage partners; in 7 percent of half-siblings; 9 percent of their parents; 14 percent of their full siblings; 15 percent of their nonidentical twins; and in 86 percent of their identical twins. In brief, the more closely one is related to a schizophrenic, the greater one's chances are of developing the disorder. According to Kallmann, this demonstrates that "the predisposition to schizophrenia—that is, the ability to respond to certain stimuli with a schizophrenic type of reaction—depends on the presence of a specific genetic factor which is probably recessive . . ." (20).

While Kallmann's findings seem to be impressive, his studies have been subjected to criticisms, relating particularly to his neglect of the possible role of early environment (10, 34). Despite the relevance of these criticisms, the work does suggest that genetic factors may be of importance in at least some cases of schizophrenia.

Certainly there is need for further intensive psychological and genetic research on the origin of schizophrenia. Even Kallmann's data suggest the importance of environmental factors. For example, he found that the monozygotic (identical) twins of schizophrenic patients developed the disorder also in about 91 percent of the cases when the twins were raised in the same general environment; and in only 78 percent of cases when raised in different environments.

Similar investigations of genetic factors in manic-depressive psychosis have been made by a number of authors (22). This disorder, which is marked by (either or both) an acute press of activity and excitement (mania) or by an unreasonable melancholia (depression) (24), accounts for about 12 percent of the entire resident population of mental hospitals (as compared with 45 percent for schizophrenics) (24).

A summary (22) of the findings of a number of twin studies of manic depressive psychosis suggests that genetic factors may be involved in predisposing an individual to this disorder. These studies have also been subjected to considerable criticism, however.

More precise knowledge of the role of genetic and other factors in various mental disorders must await future research. Probably the most generally accepted opinion among psychiatrists at present is that genetic factors may play a role, at least in some cases of schizophrenia and manic depressive psychosis, but that other factors, physiological, psychological, and social are also of vast importance.

Considerably less systematic research has been devoted to the role of genetic factors in the psychoneuroses. Furthermore, most work that has been done has yielded equivocal results. However, in one recent study

(*11*), 25 identical and 25 fraternal twins were compared for incidence of a "neurotic personality factor." Finding that the identical twins tended to be more alike on this factor than fraternal twins, the authors concluded that genetic factors play a major role in the development of neurotic traits. The possible effects of environmental forces do not appear to have been completely controlled in this study, however, and thus the conclusions are open to question. In general, it is felt by most psychiatrists that genetic factors are less significant in the development of the psychoneuroses (the milder forms of adjustment difficulties) than in the more severe functional psychoses.

Intelligence

We shall discuss the meaning and measurement of intelligence later in this book (cf. pp. 367–380). For the present, we would simply like to summarize a few of the studies which are most pertinent to demonstrating the operation of genetic factors in intelligence.

A number of studies have compared the levels of performance on intelligence (I.Q.) tests of identical and fraternal twins (*17*). In the Newman, Freeman, and Holzinger study (*30*), there was an average difference in I.Q. of 9.9 points for pairs of fraternal twins, and of 5.9 points for pairs of identical twins. Other studies have also found that identical twins are more alike in I.Q. than fraternal twins (*30, 39, 43*).

As Jones (*17*) points out, such results would be expected if twin similarities were primarily genetic, but we must also take into account the possibility of a greater degree of environmental as well as genetic similarity for the identical twins. It will be recalled (cf. p. 49), that in several studies, identical twins have been shown to lead more similar lives and to be exposed to more common experiences than fraternal twins.

More definitive findings regarding the role of genetic factors in determining intellectual status may be expected from comparisons between fraternal twins reared together and identical twins reared apart. Newman, Freeman, and Holzinger (*30*) found a higher correlation between the I.Q.'s of identical twins raised in different environments (.76) than between those of nonidentical twins reared together (.63). In other words, since it seems highly unlikely that the relevant features of the environments of identical twins reared apart were as similar as those of fraternal twins reared together, one is forced to the conclusion that heredity is one of the important determiners of intellectual performance.

Still another approach to the problem of genetic factors in intellectual performance is through the study of children in foster homes. We may compare the resemblance between foster children's intelligence and that of their foster parents with the resemblance between true parents' intelligence and that of their own children (brought up by them). If we find that the latter correlation is higher than the former, we may infer that hereditary factors account for the difference.

In one such study, Burks (9) obtained the I.Q.'s of 204 school-age foster children, all of whom had been placed in foster homes before 12 months of age. In addition she obtained the I.Q.'s of the children's foster parents.

A control group of children who were living with their true parents

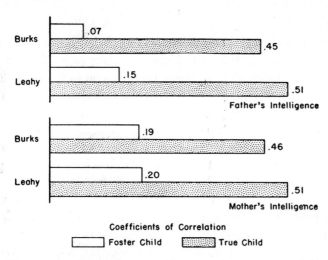

FIGURE 5. A comparison of foster and true parent-child correlations. (After H. E. Jones, "Environmental Influence on Mental Development" in L. Carmichael (ed.), *Manual of Child Psychology*. New York: Wiley, 1946.)

was then also set up, and the I.Q.'s of these "true" children and their parents were also obtained. Thus Burks was able to compare the correlations in I.Q. between foster parents and their children, with those between true parents and their children. A similar approach was used by Leahy (25). Figure 5 shows the results of both these studies.

The relationships between children and their own fathers and mothers were higher than those between children and their foster parents. The differences in correlation might be expected to be even higher were it not for the fact that "when placement officers have knowledge of the cultural circumstances of the true parents, this is likely to influence their choice of foster homes" (17). In other words, when adoptive agencies can estimate the intelligence of the child's true parents, they are likely to try to place the child with a foster family of similar intellectual status. This practice tends to increase the correlation between the I.Q. of children and their foster parents. Despite this, the true parent-child correlations were higher than those between foster parents and their foster children.

While environmental factors may be important (as we shall see later) in raising or lowering a child's level of intellectual performance, these studies demonstrate quite clearly that they can only do so within definitely prescribed limits. These limits appear to be set by heredity.

Personality

Probably largely because of the technical difficulties involved, less work has been done in the area of genetic effects on personality (as distinct from mental illness) than in any other area of human genetics (37).

In one study, Pearson (35) found that the average correlation between siblings for traits such as vivacity and temper was .52. These family resemblances in personality traits were comparable to those which he found for physical traits, such as height, eye color, and hand movement. According to Pearson, "We are forced to the conclusion that the physical and psychical characteristics in man are inherited within broad lines in the same manner and with the same intensity" (35). To this conclusion, however, Jones notes the important objection that "a given degree of resemblance may (theoretically) be obtained not only through the influence of a common heredity, but also through the effects of living in a common environment . . ." (17).

Since it was impossible to separate out the effects of these two types of influence in this study, no immediate inferences can be drawn as to causal factors (5).

In another study, an attempt was made to separate out the effects of variations in heredity from those of environment. Using the twin-study method, Newman, Freeman, and Holzinger (30) found that on a number of tests of personality and temperament "the correlations of identical twins are but little higher than those of fraternal twins" (30). Since in the same study, these authors found considerably higher correlations for the identical twins on physical traits (and to a lesser extent on intelligence), they conclude: "These seem to indicate that inheritance is a greater factor relatively in producing likeness or difference in some traits than in others" (30).

In brief, there is at present little evidence that genetic factors are directly related to the development of specific personality characteristics. On the other hand, despite the embryonic state of child psychology, we have already learned much about the impact of environmental influences on the individual's personality development and adjustment. This will be demonstrated repeatedly throughout this book.

REFERENCES AND ADDITIONAL READING

1. Allport, G., *Personality: a psychological interpretation.* New York: Holt, 1937.
2. Bellak, L., *Dementia praecox or the group of schizophrenics.* New York: International University Press, 1950.
3. Boas, F., *Changes in bodily form of descendants of immigrants* (U.S. Senate Document 208). Washington: Gov't. Printing Office, 1911.
4. Bossik, *Proc. Maxim Gorki med-biol. res. institute.* 3 (1934), cited in Stern, C., *Principles of human genetics.* San Francisco: W. H. Freeman, 1949.
5. Bronstein, I. P., Wexler, S., Brown, A. W. and Halpern, L. J., Obesity in childhood. *Am. J. Dis. Child* (1942), 63:238–251.
6. Bruch, H., Studies in obesity in childhood: I. Physical growth and development of obese children. *Am. J. Dis. Child.* (1939), 58:457–484.
7. Bruch, H., Studies in obesity in childhood: III. Physiologic and psychologic aspects of the food intake of obese children. *Am. J. Dis. Child.* (1940), 59:739–781.
8. Bruch, H., Obesity in relation to puberty. *J. Pediat.* (1941), 19:365–375.
9. Burks, B. S., The relative influence of nature and nurture upon mental development: a comparative study of foster parent-foster child resemblance and true parent-true child resemblance. *27th Yearbook. Nat. Soc. Stud. Educ.,* Part I, 1928, pp. 219–316.
10. Cameron, N., and Magaret, A., *Behavior pathology.* Boston: Houghton Mifflin, 1951.
11. Eysenck, H. J., and Prell, O. B., The inheritance of neuroticism; an experimental study, *J. ment. Sci.* (1051), 97:441–465, cited in *Annual review of psychology,* Vol. 6. Stanford, Calif.: Annual Review, Inc., 1955.
12. Fenichel, O., *The psychoanalytic theory of neurosis.* New York: Norton, 1945.
13. Gates, R. R., *Human genetics,* Vol. II. New York: Macmillan, 1946.
14. Goldschmidt, R. B., Theory of the gene. *Science Monthly,* Mar. 1938.
15. Haldane, J. B. S., *Heredity and politics.* New York: Norton, 1938.
16. Jennings, H. S., *Genetics.* New York: Norton, 1935.
17. Jones, H. E., Environmental influence on mental development in L. Carmichael (ed.), *Manual of child psychology.* New York: Wiley, 1946, pp. 582–632.
18. Jost, H. and Sontag, L. W., The genetic factors in autonomic nervous-system. *Psychosomatic Medicine* (1944), 6:308–310.
19. Kallmann, F. J., *The genetics of schizophrenia.* New York: Augustin, 1938.
20. Kallmann, F. J., The genetic theory of schizophrenia. *Am. J. Psychiat.* (1946), 103:309–322.

21. Kallmann, F. J., Genetic aspects of psychosis. In *The history of mental health and disease.* New York: Hoeber, 1952, pp. 283–298.

22. Kallmann, F. J., *Heredity in health and mental disorder.* New York: Norton, 1953.

23. Kallman, F. K., and Sander, G., Twin studies on aging and longevity. *J. Hered.* (1948), *39*:349–357.

24. Landis, C., and Bolles, M. M., *Textbook of abnormal psychology.* New York: Macmillan, 1947.

25. Leahy, A. M., Nature-nurture and intelligence. *Genet. Psychol. Monogr.* (1935), *17*:235–308.

26. Malkova, N. N., *Proc. Maxim Gorki med.-biol. res. institute.* 3 (1934), cited in Stern, C., *Principles of human genetics.* San Francisco: Freeman, 1949.

27. McGraw, M. B., Motivation of behavior, in L. Carmichael (ed.), *Manual of child psychology.* New York: Wiley, 1946, pp. 332–369.

28. Minerva, *Proc. Maxim Gorki med-biol. res. institute,* 3 (1934), cited in Stern, C., *Principles of human genetics.* San Francisco: Freeman, 1949.

29. Morgan, T. H., *Scientific basis of evolution.* New York: Norton, 1932.

30. Newman, H. H., Freeman, R. N., and Holzinger, K. J., *Twins: a study of heredity and environment.* Chicago: University Chicago Press, 1937.

31. Parker, M. M., Experimental studies in the psychology of temperament in the adult albino rat. *Abstr. doct. Diss.* Ohio State University, No. 30, 1939.

32. Parshley, H. M., *Science of human reproduction.* New York: Norton, 1933.

33. Pastore, N. *The nature-nurture controversy.* New York: King's Crown Press, Columbia University, 1949.

34. Pastore, N., The genetics of schizophrenia: a social review. *Psychol. Bull.* (1949), *46*:286–302.

35. Pearson, K., On the inheritance of mental and moral character in man, and its comparison with the inheritance of physical character. *J. Antrop. Inst.* (1903), *33*: 179–237.

35. Pearson, K., On the inheritance of mental and moral character in man, *Biometrika* (1904), 3:131.

37. Penrose, L. S., Heredity, in J. McV. Hunt, (ed.), *Personality and the behavior disorders,* Vol. I. New York: Ronald, 1944, pp. 505–525.

38. Petri, *Zeitschr. Morph. u. Anthropol.* 33 (1934), cited in Stern, C., *Principles of human genetics.* San Francisco: Freeman, 1949.

39. Rosanoff, A. J., Hardy, L. M., and Plesset, J. R., The etiology of mental deficiency with special reference to its occurrence in twins. *Psychol. Monogr.* (1937), *48*:No. 4.

40. Scheinfeld, A., *You and heredity.* New York: Garden City Publishing Co., 1939.

41. Scheinfeld, A., *The new you and heredity.* Philadelphia: Lippincott, 1950.

42. Stockard, C. R., *Physical basis of personality.* New York: Norton, 1931.

43. Stocks, P., and Karn, M. N., A biometric investigation of twins and their brothers and sisters. *Ann. Eugen.,* (1933), 5:1–55.

44. Stern, C., *Principles of human genetics.* San Francisco: Freeman, 1949.

45. Thompson, H., Physical growth, in L. Carmichael (ed.), *Manual of child psychology*, New York: Wiley, 1946.
46. Verschuer, *Ergeb. inn. Med. u. Kinderheilk.*, *31*, 1927, cited in Stern, C., *Principles of human genetics*. San Francisco: Freeman, 1949.
47. Weismann, A., *Essays upon heredity and kindred biological problems*. New York: Oxford, 1889.

Chapter 3

PRENATAL DEVELOPMENT

It is a rather curious fact that while we recognize that the new individual's life begins at conception, we reckon his age from the moment of birth. It would almost seem that we were implicitly saying that the events in a person's life prior to birth are of little importance in determining the future course of his development. This attitude is especially likely to apply to our conceptions of *psychological* development. And yet the environment in which the unborn child grows can be of tremendous importance in influencing later patterns of growth, not only physically, but psychologically as well.

The Chinese have traditionally been somewhat more realistic in their age computations.

Each of their babies is given at birth a full year's credit on the reckoning of its age. They know, of course, that the span of our prefatory existence is actually only nine months long, but fractions are a bother, and in China every man claims one more year of age than does the European born of the same day and the same year (3, 1).

In view of the magnitude of the growth processes occurring during the prenatal period, the Chinese approach to age reckoning appears somewhat more appropriate than ours.

HOW CONCEPTION OCCURS

Conception occurs when a sperm from the male pierces the cell wall of an ovum or egg from the female. The occasions on which such mating is possible are strictly limited physiologically, and are quite independent of the vagaries of human impulse. Figure 6 shows a schematic diagram of the female reproductive system. Once every 28 days (usually around the middle of the menstrual cycle) an ovum ripens in one of the two ovaries, is discharged into the corresponding fallopian tube, or oviduct,

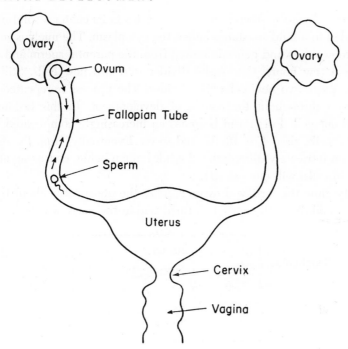

FIGURE 6. Schematic diagram of female reproductive system, showing how conception occurs.

and begins its slow journey toward the uterus, propelled by small hair-like cilia which line the tube. In most cases, it takes from 3 to 7 days for the ovum to reach the uterus (*16*). If the ovum has not been fertilized in the course of this journey, it disintegrates in the uterus after a few days, "and its remains, which are less than a grain of dust, disperse unnoticed" (*3*).

If, on the other hand, a mating has taken place, one of the many millions of tiny sperm released by the male may find its way up into the oviduct during the time the ovum is making its descent. There it may unite with the ovum and the conception of a new individual may result.

THE EARLIEST PERIOD OF EMBRYONIC DEVELOPMENT

At the moment of conception, the ovum, the largest cell in the human body, is still very small—only about $1/175$ inch in diameter (*3*). Once it has been fertilized however, it begins to grow. The first of the three stages of prenatal development, *the period of the ovum*, has begun.

At first the fertilized ovum, or *zygote*, consists of only one cell. It is surrounded by a thin membrane and contains in its center a solid nucleus suspended in a fluid substance called the cytoplasm. The nucleus contains the chromosomes and genes inherited from the parental sperm and ovum.

After a few hours, the zygote divides into two new cells. Still later, each of these two new cells also divides. The process is repeated again and again throughout the course of development. In this fashion, the original one-celled organism becomes an increasingly complicated being, first of 2 cells, then 4, 8, 16, 32, and so on. Eventually, from the original zygote an intricately differentiated adult human being, consisting of some 26 billion cells, will emerge (9).

By the time the fertilized ovum reaches the uterus, it is about the size of a pinhead. A small cavity is formed within the mass of cells, resulting

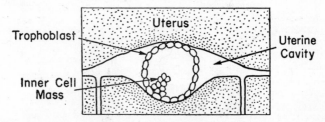

FIGURE 7. Schematic representation of ovum at early state of implantation in uterine wall.

in an outer and a separated inner cluster of cells (see Figure 7). The outer layer, called the *trophoblast*, will ultimately develop into accessory tissues which protect and nourish the embryo. The inner cluster of cells will become the embryo itself.

While these developments are taking place, small burrlike tendrils have begun to grow around the outside of the trophoblast. It is by means of these tendrils that in a few more days (around 10 days after fertilization), the ovum will attach itself to the uterine wall.

In the meantime, however, the uterus itself has begun to undergo changes in preparation for receiving the fertilized ovum (called a *blastocyte* at this stage). At the time of implantation (attachment of the ovum to the uterine wall), the tendrils from the trophoblast burrow into the receptive mucous membrane of the uterus. Extensions of the tendrils reach into the blood spaces which have formed within the maternal tissue. At this time, the period of the ovum comes to an end, and the second phase of prenatal development, the period of the embryo begins. The new individual has ceased to be an independent, free-floating organism and has established a dependent relationship with the mother.

THE PERIOD OF THE EMBRYO

Once the growing egg has been successfully lodged in its new home, development is rapid. Its *inner* cell mass, which will become a recognizable embryo, begins to differentiate itself into three distinct layers:

1. *The ectoderm* (outer layer), from which will develop the epidermis or outer layer of the skin, the hair, the nails, parts of the teeth, skin glands, sensory cells—and the nervous system.

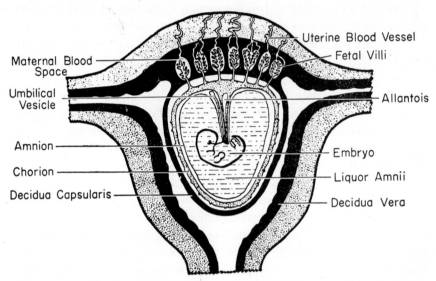

FIGURE 8. Diagram representing the relationship between the uterus, the membranes, and the embryo during early pregnancy. (From L. Carmichael, "Origin and Prenatal Growth of Behavior," in C. Murchison (ed.), *A Handbook of Child Psychology*, 2nd ed. Worcester: Clark University Press, 1933, p. 50. By permission of the publisher.)

2. *The mesoderm* (the middle layer), from which will develop the dermis or inner skin layer, the muscles, skeleton, and the circulatory and excretory organs.

3. *The endoderm* (inner layer), from which will develop the lining of the entire gastrointestinal tract, the Eustachian tubes, trachea, bronchia, lungs, liver, pancreas, salivary glands, thyroid glands, and thymus (9, 16).

While the inner cell mass is being differentiated into a recognizable embryo, the outer layers of cells are giving rise to the fetal membranes— the *chorion* and *amnion*. These two membranes, together with a third membrane derived from the uterine wall of the mother (the *decidua capsularis*), extend from the wall of the uterus and enclose the developing embryo (see Figure 8). They form a sac which is filled with a watery fluid (*liquor amnii*) which acts as a buffer to protect the embryo from shocks experienced by the mother. It also helps to provide an even temperature for the embryo and serves to prevent adhesions between the embryo and the amniotic membrane (*24*).

Simultaneously, other fetal sacs are formed, the most important of which becomes the umbilical cord. It extends from the embryo, and is attached at its opposite end to the section of the uterine wall where the uterus and the chorion are joined. This area is called the *placenta*.

The umbilical cord might well be referred to as the lifeline of the embryo. Through it, two arteries carry blood from the embryo to the placenta, and one vein carries blood to the infant from the placenta. However, the relationship between the child's blood stream and the mother's is not a direct one. Both the child's and the mother's blood streams open into the placenta. But the two systems are always separated by cell walls within the placenta. These cell walls consist of semipermeable membranes—that is, they function as extremely fine meshes, large enough to permit the passage of gases, salts, and other substances of small molecular size; but too small to allow blood cells to get through.

We still lack a precise knowledge of all the substances which can get through a normal placenta. However, various nutrient substances from the mother's blood—chiefly sugars, fats, and some protein elements—are known to permeate it. Waste products from the infant, primarily carbon dioxide and other metabolites, can also pass through the placenta. In addition, some vitamins, drugs (including nicotine and alcohol), vaccines, and a few disease germs (notably those of diphtheria, typhoid, influenza, and syphilis) may also get through (*3, 6, 27*) and affect the embryo's development (cf. pp. 62–70).

It should be noted that aside from the exchange system existing between the maternal and embryonic blood streams, there are no means of communication between mother and child. There is no connection between their nervous systems.

Not a single nerve fiber crosses the placental barrier; there is no channel for the transmission of feelings or intentions, moods, memories, or ideas. The infant is in fact completely shut off from its mother save for the exchange of simple chemical nutrients and wastes through a screen so fine that it will pass nothing but the smaller molecules of matter (*3, 53*).

In other words, there is no physiological basis for the kinds of superstitious notions about prenatal influences which were once common. A child does not spend his life reeling and staggering because his mother saw a drunken man reeling in the street during her pregnancy; nor do children develop harelips because their mothers encountered rabbits while the children were in the womb.

Development of the Embryo

Much of our knowledge of prenatal development has been derived from the intensive study of embryos and fetuses which, for medical reasons, had to be surgically removed from the womb.

During the period of the embryo, development is extremely rapid. By eighteen days, the embryo has already begun to take some shape. It has established a longitudinal axis and its front, back, left, and right sides,

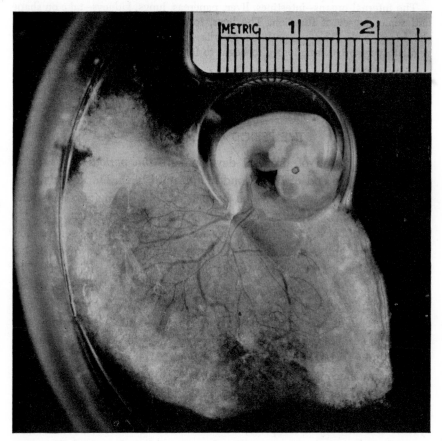

FIGURE 9.   Human embryo at 8 weeks. (From M. E. Davis and C. Carmon, *De Lee's Obstetrics for Nurses*. Philadelphia: Saunders, 1951. With permission of the author and publisher.)

and a head and tail are discernible. By the end of the third week a primitive heart has developed and has begun to beat (*10*).

At the end of the first month the embryo is about ⅕ inch long. It has the beginnings of a mouth region, of a gastrointestinal tract, and of a liver. The heart is becoming well developed, and the head and brain regions are becoming more clearly differentiated. At this stage, the embryo is still a very primitive organism. It has as yet no arms or legs, no developed features, and only the most elementary of body systems.

By 8 weeks, however, the picture has changed markedly (see Figure 9). The embryo is now about an inch long. Face, mouth, eyes, and ears have begun to take on fairly well-defined form. Arms and legs and even hands and feet with stubby fingers and toes have appeared (*9*).

The internal organs—intestines, liver, pancreas, lungs, kidneys—take on shape and some degree of function. The liver, for example, begins to manufacture red blood cells. The sympathetic ganglia and nerves which will some day regulate vegetative functions also begin to form (*9, 28*).

Well-defined neuromotor activity (activation of the muscles by impulses from the nerves) is still absent at this stage, however.

THE PERIOD OF THE FETUS

The third period of prenatal development, *the period of the fetus,* extends from the end of the second month until birth. During this time, the various body systems, which have been laid down in rudimentary form earlier, become quite well developed, and begin to function. Up until about 8½ weeks, the fetus has led a relatively passive existence, floating quiescently in the amniotic fluid. At this time, however, it becomes capable of responding to tactile (touch) stimulation (*24*). The trunk flexes, and the head extends. From this point on, motor functions become increasingly more differentiated and complex.

By the end of the third month, the fetus is about 3 inches long and weighs about ¾ ounce. It has definitely begun to resemble a human being, though the head is disproportionately large (see Figure 10). Muscles are becoming well developed, and spontaneous movements of the arms and legs may be observed. Eyelids and nails have begun to form, and the fetus' sex can now be distinguished easily. The nervous system is still very incomplete, however. During the next four weeks, motor behavior becomes more complex. Gesell has described the status of motor behavior in the fetus during these weeks:

He moves his upper lip. When a little more mature he moves his lower lip. Later he moves both lips in unison. Still later he opens and closes his mouth. He swallows with closed mouth, but at times he also swallows amniotic fluid. His tongue moves. . . . He may also rotate his head in association with the "oral reflex"; for complex patterns of feeding behavior are in the making. Peristaltic waves sweep over his lengthening digestive tube.

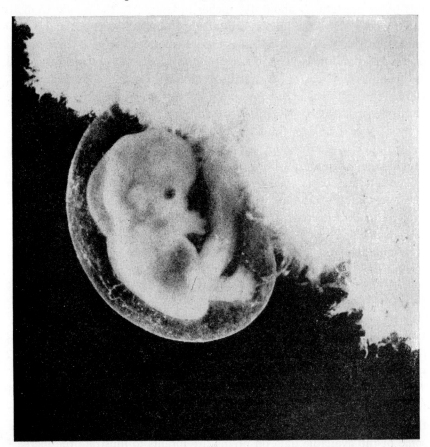

FIGURE 10. Human fetus at 3 months. (From A. Gesell, *The Embryology of Behavior*. New York: Harper, 1945, p. 29.)

Arms and legs occasionally move in diagonal alternation in a manner which suggests locomotion, whether aquatic or terrestrial—small movements which may, however displace the position of the fetus. But human arms and hands are ultimately meant for manipulation as well as locomotion, and the fetus accordingly foreshadows long in advance the patterns of a higher order. He elevates the upper arms, he extends his drooping hands. Elbows formerly fixed are mobile. He deploys his hands in the median plane: sometimes they almost touch the mouth. His movements are less stilted than they were in the previous month, when his palms assumed a stiff pat-a-cake attitude or were retracted far apart. He now rotates his forearm medially. He opens and closes his hands. He moves his thumb independently, or curls it fist-like under the conjoint digits, a token of later opposibility (9, 68).

By the end of 16 weeks, the mother can feel the fetus' movements. At this point the fetus is about 4½ inches in length. In the period from 16 to 20 weeks, the fetus increases to about 10 inches in length and 8 or 9 ounces in weight (16). It becomes more human-looking and hair appears on the head and body. The mouth becomes capable of protrusion, as well as opening and closing—a precursor of later sucking movements (9). Blinking of the eyes occurs, although the lids are still tightly fused. The hands become capable of gripping in addition to closing.

By 24 weeks of age, the fetus is capable "not only of spaced exhalations, but of true inspirations and expirations, and of a thin crying noise should he be prematurely born" (9, 71).

The fetal age of 28 weeks is an important one. It demarcates the zone between viability (the ability to live if born) and nonviability. By this age, the child's nervous, circulatory, and other bodily systems have become sufficiently well structured to stand a chance of being able to function adequately in the extrauterine environment, although, of course, special care is required. At this point, reactions to changes in temperature approximate those of the full-term infant. Experimental studies of infants born at this age indicate that basic tastes, such as sweet, salt, sour, and bitter can be differentiated by the fetus (2). So can basic odors. Visual and auditory reactions also occur, though not as clearly as in the full-term infant. On the other hand, sensitivity to pain seems to be relatively absent in the premature infant.

The period from 28 weeks to birth at full-term (40 weeks) is marked by further development of the basic bodily structures and functions. In the outline which follows, Watson and Lowrey (35) have employed some of the available data on premature infants to illustrate the increasingly elaborate behavior which develops between 28 weeks and normal birth.

Fetus at 28–32 weeks
Movements meager, fleeting, poorly sustained
Lack of muscular tone
Mild avoidance responses to bright light and sound
In prone position turns head to side
Palmar stimulation elicits barely perceptible grasp
Breathing shallow and irregular

Sucking and swallowing present but lack endurance
No definite waking and sleeping pattern
Cry may be absent or very weak
Inconstant tonic neck reflex

Fetus at 32–36 weeks

Movement sustained and positive
Muscle tone fair under stimulation
Moro reflex (startle reaction) present
Strong but inadequate response to light and sound
In prone position turns head, elevates rump
Definite periods of being awake
Palmar stimulation causes good grasp
Good hunger cry
Fairly well-established tonic neck reflex

Fetus at 36–40 weeks

Movements active and sustained
Muscle tone good
Brief erratic following of objects with eyes
Moro reflex strong
In prone position attempts to lift head
Active resistance to head rotation
Definite periods of alertness
Cries well when hungry and disturbed
Appears pleased when caressed
Hands held as fists much of time, good grasp
Tonic neck reflex more pronounced to one side (usually right) than to the
    other
Good, strong sucking reflex (35, 37)

PRENATAL ENVIRONMENTAL INFLUENCES

Thus far, we have been discussing what might be called "normal" or typical patterns of prenatal development. But such patterns can only occur when the organism itself and its environment fall within what might be thought of as normal limits.

The chapter on genetic mechanisms emphasized that hereditary factors can affect the individual's development in important ways. We also noted, however, that no trait or characteristic of an individual is entirely hereditarily determined. Heredity may make important contributions to many of the individual's potentialities or limitations, but most of his characteristics are the consequents of complex interactions between genetically transmitted factors and environmental influences. The growth and development of the individual's inherent potential may be actualized, facilitated, and enhanced—or thwarted, mutilated, and limited—depending on the kind of physical, social, and psychological environment he encounters. "The important point to understand . . . is that the same genes may be influenced to express themselves differently and to have different end effects as a consequence of the different environments in which they function" (20, 151).

Ordinarily we think of the prenatal environment as constant and similar for all fetuses. Certainly, the fetus' surroundings are relatively simple in comparison with the complex world he will encounter after birth. Nevertheless, there are many variations in prenatal environment, and the pressures to which one fetus is subjected may differ greatly from those exerted on another. Recent research suggests that the mother's physical and emotional status (and consequently the prenatal environment she provides) may exert important influences on the course of fetal development and the subsequent health and adjustment of the child. Some of the more important prenatal environmental factors which have been investigated will be discussed in the following sections.

Maternal Malnutrition

The expectant mother should have an adequate diet if she is going to maintain her own general good health during her pregnancy and deliver a healthy infant. This appears entirely reasonable when we remember that the growing fetus' food supply comes ultimately from the mother's blood stream, via the semipermeable membranes of the placenta and the umbilical cord. In one experimental investigation of the consequents of malnutrition during pregnancy, the subjects were 210 pregnant women attending a clinic at the University of Toronto (7, 8). All of them had inadequate diets during their first 4 or 5 months of pregnancy. In the later phases of pregnancy, the diets of 90 of the women were supplemented and made adequate from a nutritional standpoint. The other 120 maintained their nutritionally deficient diets throughout their pregnancies. By comparing these two groups, the investigators could systematically study the influence of good and poor maternal diets upon the course of pregnancy and the condition of the infant during the first few months of life.

The "good-diet" mothers were in better health throughout their pregnancies. Complications such as anemia, toxemia, threatened and actual miscarriages, premature births, and stillbirths were much more frequent in the "poor-diet" group than in the "good-diet" group. On the average, women in the latter group were in labor five hours less than the women with inadequate diets.

Compared with the infants born to "poor-diet" mothers, the babies of "good-diet" women had better health records during the first two weeks of postnatal life. They also had a much smaller incidence of major illnesses (pneumonia, rickets, tetany, anemia) and minor diseases (colds, bronchitis) during the entire first six months.

Another investigator (33) demonstrated that stillbirths, prematurities, and deaths in early infancy were less common among the babies of mothers with nutritionally adequate diets than among those whose mothers had less adequate diets. These data also indicated that a regimen of six small meals a day, at approximately three-hour intervals, decreased the prospective mother's nausea and vomiting and helped to reduce fatigue and other symptoms associated with energy depletion. The findings "support the ideas that the fetus obtains its nutritional requirements prior to the maternal organism and draws upon maternal storages. When these storages are depleted to a point of deficiency in the mother, the baby will fail to obtain the necessary elements" (33, 380).

Drugs

As we mentioned earlier, narcotics may permeate the maternal blood stream and be transmitted to the fetus, affecting its development. Although there is no evidence of permanent harm to the fetus or infant as the result of its mother's use of narcotics, temporary dysfunctions have been noted. Neonates whose mothers have been given barbiturate drugs or other preparations during labor may show signs of oversedation and respiratory difficulties. Electroencephalograms (records of cortical electrical activity) of 20 infants whose mothers had been given doses of seconal sodium while in labor showed depressed cortical activity for two days following birth (15). During this time the infants seemed sluggish and drowsy. By the third day, however, these symptoms of mild sedation had worn off and no residuals were noted. Nevertheless, it seems reasonable to believe that a heavy dosing of the mother with drugs "may so overload the fetal blood stream as to produce asphyxiation of the fetus at birth, with permanent brain damage of such a kind as to lead to mental impairment" (20, 162).

The pregnant mother's smoking may affect the fetus because the nicotine from her cigarette may be transmitted to him through the placenta. Fetal heart rate is often, but not invariably, accelerated following the mother's smoking, although there is no evidence of enduring heart or circulatory system impairment (*31*).

Irradiation

Radium or Roentgen (x-ray) irradiation of the pelvis may be therapeutically necessary for the pregnant woman with a pelvic or ovarian tumor or cancer. Small amounts of this irradiation, such as those used in x-ray photography, are not known to damage the fetus, but large therapeutic doses may be injurious or precipitate abortions.

Over one-third of a group of 75 full-term infants whose mothers had therapeutic irradiation during pregnancy manifested mental or physical abnormalities which could not be attributed to any source other than the treatments. Twenty had severe disturbances of the central nervous system, 16 of them being microcephalic. (Microcephaly is a clinical type of feeble-mindedness, in which there is an abnormally small, pointed skull and a very small brain). Eight others were extremely small, physically deformed, or blind (*21, 22*).

Maternal Diseases

There appears to be an effective barrier between the embryo and most of its mother's virus or germ organisms. Hence fetal infection from maternal disease is infrequent. In some rare cases, however, infants have been born with smallpox, measles, chickenpox, or mumps, transmitted from the mother (*12*).

On the other hand, infection with syphilitic spirochetes from the mother is not infrequent. One investigator (*6*) found spirochetes in 16 fetuses taken from a group of 67 syphilitic mothers—an incidence of 24 percent. These spirochetes may produce abortion or miscarriage. Or, if the child survives, he may be born weak, deformed, or mentally deficient. In some cases, the child may not manifest syphilitic symptoms until several years later. Since fetuses under 18 weeks of age are apparently not susceptible to the disease, transmission of the spirochetes may be prevented if treatment of a syphilitic mother begins early in her pregnancy.

Rubella (German measles) contracted by the prospective mother in the first 3 or 4 months of pregnancy may damage the fetus considerably, producing deaf-mutism, cardiac lesions, cataracts, or various forms of mental deficiency. There does not appear to be any direct relation between the severity of maternal infection and the degree of fetal involvement. Mild attacks produce fetal malformations as grave as those suffered when the mother is ill from 7 to 14 days.

Rh Factors

If there are genetically determined differences between the blood types of the fetus and its mother, they may be biochemically incompatible. For example, the child's red blood corpuscles may contain a substance which makes his blood agglutinate or "clump" in response to a specially prepared serum, while his mother's blood may lack this substance. In this case, the child, like 85 percent of the white American population, is "Rh positive"; his mother is "Rh negative" (19).

The Rh positive fetus produces certain substances called antigens, which enter into the mother's circulation through the placental barrier. Toxic substances (antibodies) are then manufactured in her blood and passed back into the fetus' circulatory system. They may do a great deal of damage there, destroying his red blood cells and preventing them from distributing oxygen normally. There may be tragic consequences, including miscarriage, stillbirth, or death shortly after birth from erythroblastosis (destruction of red blood corpuscles). Or, if the child survives, he may be partially paralyzed or mentally deficient, possibly as a result of brain damage from inadequate oxygen supply during a crucial developmental period (20).

Fortunately, these disastrous consequences do not occur in every case of mother-child Rh incompatibility. Erythroblastosis occurs only in about one out of every 200 pregnancies (20). First-born children are not usually affected, since it takes time for the mother to develop the antibodies, but subsequent offspring are more likely to suffer if their Rh blood types differ from their mother's.

There are medical techniques now available which, if applied early, minimize the consequences of this incompatibility. "Every (woman) planning marriage should consult her physician to find out the Rh types both of herself and her prospective husband. There are various ways in which the evil factors of clashing Rh factors may be partially averted if doctors know about them beforehand" (20, 166).

Age of Mother

Advances in medical science have made pregnancy and birth much less dangerous and difficult than they ever have been previously. The total incidence of infant and maternal mortality, regardless of the age of the mother, has become very low. There is some evidence, however, that these mortality rates are higher if the mothers are below 23 or above 29 than if they are between these two ages. This may be due to the inadequate development of the reproductive system in some younger women and to progressive decline in the reproductive functioning in some older ones (20).

Women who deliver their first infant when they are 35 or over are also more likely than younger women to experience illnesses during pregnancy and longer and more difficult labor (17). Furthermore, they are also more likely to require operative delivery and caesarian sections. The older the woman, the greater the likelihood that these problems will arise. However, the absolute incidence of serious complications is small.

Mongolism, a condition of severe mental retardation associated with certain physical features (oblique, slit eyes and disordered growth of the skull bones) is found more frequently among children born to older than to younger mothers (18). However, the condition occurs infrequently, probably not more than once in a thousand births.

Maternal Emotional States

Despite the fact that there are no direct connections between the mother's and the fetus' nervous systems (cf. pp. 55–56), the mother's emotional state can influence fetal reactions and development. This is true because emotions such as rage, fear, and anxiety bring the mother's autonomic nervous system into action, liberating certain chemicals (acetylcholine and epinephrene) into the blood stream. Furthermore, under these conditions the endocrine glands, particularly the adrenals, secrete different kinds and amounts of hormones. Cell metabolism is also modified. In brief, the composition of the blood changes, and new chemical substances are transmitted through the placenta, producing changes in the fetus' circulatory system (32).

Sontag (29, 30, 31) working at the Fels Research Institute in Yellow Springs, Ohio, showed that these changes may be irritating to the fetus. He noted that bodily movements of fetuses increased several hundred percent while their mothers were undergoing emotional stress. If the mother's emotional upset lasted several weeks, fetal activity continued at an exaggerated level throughout the entire period. When these upsets were brief, heightened irritability usually lasted several hours.

According to this investigator, prolonged maternal emotional stress during pregnancy may have enduring consequents for the child (30). Emotionally disturbed women give birth to babies who weigh less than average. Apparently they have reduced by increased exercising without adding to their food intake. Moreover, infants born to upset, unhappy mothers have high activity levels.

Such an infant is from the beginning a hyperactive, irritable, squirming, crying child, who cries for his feeding every two or three hours, instead of sleeping through his four-hour feeding period. Because his irritability effects control of his gastrointestinal tract, he empties his bowels at unusually frequent intervals, spits up half his feedings and generally makes a nuisance of himself. He is to all intents and purposes a neurotic infant when he is born—the result of an unsatisfactory fetal environment. In this instance, he has not had to wait until childhood for a bad home situation or other cause to make him neurotic. It has been done for him before he has even seen the light of day. In certain instances of severely disturbed maternal emotions which we have observed—for example, one in which the father became violently insane during his wife's pregnancy—the infant's bodily functions were so disturbed that a severe feeding problem resulted. The child was unable to retain food and became markedly emaciated and dehydrated. Experience with other similar cases suggests that many of the feeding problems which pediatricians experience with young infants arise from an abnormal fetal environment (30, 4).

Sontag also found that extreme maternal fatigue, unusual abdominal pressure, and violent and repeated sounds may produce strong fetal movement responses. If these stimuli are prolonged, they may elicit reactions similar to those that follow maternal emotional distress.

In summary, it appears that maternal anxiety and emotional tension may affect the developing fetus adversely and handicap the newborn infant in his adaptation to life outside the womb. The long-time consequences are difficult to evaluate, however, since it is often impossible to determine whether prenatal or very early postnatal conditions play the more important role in the young infants' reactions and adjustments.

Maternal Attitudes

The expectant mother's attitude toward her pregnancy may be reflected in her emotional state during that period. A woman who resents being pregnant is more likely to be emotionally disturbed than one who is happy about the prospect of having a child.

The mother's attitudes toward her pregnancy are intimately related to her emotional maturity, past and present happiness, and personal adjustment. For example, one team of investigators concluded that "marital conflict, whatever its cause, was the major factor in the acceptance or rejection of pregnancies" (13). They also noted that in some instances failure to adjust to pregnancy was related to the mother's emotional immaturity and her continued desire to return to the dependent status she enjoyed as a child.

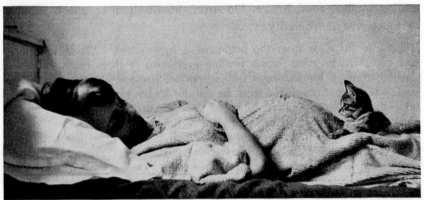

Elliott Erwitt

In a more extensive systematic study (5), one hundred middle-class women who were anticipating their first baby were asked to answer lengthy questionnaires about their backgrounds, marital adjustments, and general health during pregnancy. Attitudes toward pregnancy were assessed on the basis of answers to questions relating to: desire to postpone pregnancy; feelings of depression; wish to be pregnant again; fears of labor and confinement; and concern with changes in their own body structure during pregnancy.

In order to determine which factors were related to favorable and unfavorable attitudes toward pregnancy, the investigator compared the responses of the 25 women with the most positive attitudes and the responses of the 25 who were least favorably disposed to having a child. Nausea and prolonged periods of vomiting occurred with greater frequency in the unfavorable-attitude group, indicating that psychological factors may be important determinants of these symptoms. Generally speaking, those who were favorable toward pregnancy were well adjusted in marriage, felt financially secure, and were sexually and socially compatible with their husbands. In addition, more of these women had siblings, especially brothers, and experienced close family relationships during childhood. On the other hand, poor marital adjustment, emotional impoverishment during childhood, absence of close relationships with the mother during childhood, poor sex education, and being forced to take care of younger siblings were associated with unfavorable attitudes toward pregnancy.

Such maternal attitudes may affect the course of fetal development. Thus a mother's resentment of her pregnancy may be related to premature birth of the child (13). In some cases, abortion and stillbirth seem to be associated with the mother's frigidity, concern about the sex of the baby, or frustration over her career (32).

Furthermore, there appears to be a relationship between maternal reactions to pregnancy and the infant's subsequent adjustment. In one investigation (34), one hundred women responded to anonymous questionnaires concerning the nature and extent of their psychosomatic reactions (e.g., nausea, vomiting, backaches) during pregnancy, their general adjustment, and the development of their infants during the first six months. The presence of many psychosomatic complaints was used as a criterion of negative attitudes toward pregnancy, since other studies have shown that such complaints are related to resentment about having a child (cf. p. 68). Among women with two children, unfavorable attitudes toward pregnancy were associated with six kinds of disturbance in their infants: irregular eating, many bowel movements, gas pains, inability to sleep at night, too much crying, and unusual needs to be held.

These relationships did not hold for mothers having only one child. The authors feel that this inconsistency may be partially attributable to the fact that during their first pregnancy, women are likely to receive decidedly greater indulgence and solicitude from their husbands and others than during later pregnancies. Hence, even those who are basically rejecting of their pregnancy may feel compensated, and consequently may not become emotionally upset.

Although the results of this study are suggestive, the conclusions may not be entirely valid or definitive. For one thing, all the data came from mother's reports. It is quite possible that the mother's complaints about both her psychosomatic conditions and the baby's disturbances are related to a third, more basic factor—the mother's emotional adjustment. An emotionally maladjusted woman might complain more about her own health and her baby's behavior, even though a more objective observer might not judge them to be unusual. Furthermore, the authors' assumption that the physical disturbances reflect negative attitudes toward pregnancy may not be justified in all cases.

Nevertheless, it is interesting to note that the negatively disposed mothers had infants who manifested the kinds of problems also found to be characteristic of children whose mothers were emotionally upset during pregnancy (30). Apparently unfavorable attitudes and emotional disturbances during pregnancy may have similar consequences for the infant, possibly because the prospective mother's unfavorable attitudes are reflected in emotional distress. In the case of the rejecting woman who is expecting her first child, the compensations involved may neutralize or counteract the resentment she otherwise might feel toward her child. Thus real psychological upset may be avoided.

Further research will be needed before the consequents of the mother's emotional adjustments and attitudes for the child can be precisely evaluated. Conclusions based on studies such as those cited here must be considered tentative since they were often based on few cases and employed only gross measurements. Moreover, in many cases, the "problems" of the neonate may be attributable to his early postnatal handling rather than to prenatal environmental conditions.

Nevertheless, all these studies agree in suggesting that various aspects of the mother's personality, attitudes, and adjustment influence the prenatal environment of the child and thus affect his subsequent well-being. Such findings, if confirmed in further studies, would point up the importance of the expectant mother's psychological status during her pregnancy for the health and emotional stability of her progeny.

THE BIRTH PROCESS AND ITS CONSEQUENTS

Birth has been viewed by a number of psychoanalysts and others as an event of tremendous psychological as well as physical significance. Birth involves ejection from the warm, calm, quiet, and peaceful womb into the cold, intensely stimulating, "blooming, buzzing confusion" of the outside world. Some analysts regard birth as the first danger the infant experiences, hence providing a prototype or model for all later anxieties (25).

Rank, a student of Freud's, went to greater extremes than his teacher and other analysts in his thinking about the "birth trauma." In his view, birth represents the loss of paradise—"The pleasurable primal state is interrupted through the act of birth" (25). He felt that the shock is so profound, both physiologically and psychologically, that it creates a reservoir of anxiety, parts of which are released all through life. "All neuroses stem from severe birth anxieties, and all later anxiety can be interpreted in terms of birth anxiety—not merely as a model, but as the source itself" (1, 3).

In the form in which it is stated, Rank's hypothesis is probably untestable, and in our view, its validity is highly questionable. However, Rank's theories have led some investigators to postulate that an unusually severe birth process might adversely affect the later emotional development of the child.

In order to test this hypothesis one investigator correlated the amount of crying of newborn infants with the severity of their birth experiences (26). His subjects, 66 infants aged 1 to 8 days, were carefully observed in a hospital nursery. The amount of time spent in crying was considered to be a measure of the infant's distress. On the assumption that longer labor means a more difficult birth, the time interval between the mother's admission to the hospital and the birth of the baby was used as a criterion of the severity of the birth process. There was no significant corre-

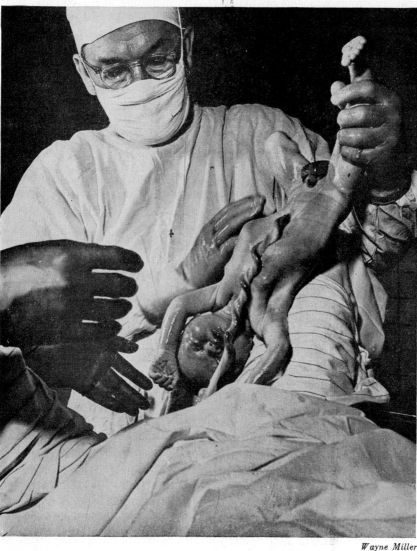

Wayne Miller

lation between the two measures; i.e., there was no evidence in this study that difficult birth produced great distress in the child.

In another study (36) of the relationship between instrumental or operative delivery and later personality, 380 children who were born spontaneously were compared with 120 who were assisted by instrumental or operative methods, i.e., had more severe birth experiences. There were no significant differences between the two groups with respect to intelligence. The major problem manifested by the instrumental delivery group was general hyperactivity, including motor activity, restlessness, and irritability. However, aggressiveness (rages, tantrums, pugnacity), submissive behaviors (fears, unhappiness, fantasy), tics, nail biting, food fads, school difficulties, and sibling conflicts were more frequent among the spontaneously born children. The investigators feel that hyperactivity and restlessness are probably related to pressures involved in protracted instrumental delivery, but they conclude that "birth trauma, in the Rankian sense, has comparatively little meaning in the light of the behavior exhibited by our two groups" (36, 333). The results of this study cannot be regarded as conclusive, however, because there was no control of factors such as family size, ordinal position, and parental behavior which contribute significantly to personality development.

Consequents of Birth Injury

The evidence thus far presented certainly does not permit us to make any definite statements about the relationship between severity of the birth process and later personality characteristics. However, there is a great deal of data showing how specific *birth injury* may affect the child's physical and intellectual status permanently. Instrumental delivery, abnormally difficult labor, obstetrical mishandling, asphyxia, and cerebral hemorrhage occurring at birth may produce central nervous system impairment with consequent motor and mental defect. Cerebral palsy, "a motor defect present or appearing soon after birth, and dependent on pathological abnormalities in the brain" (37), often stems from birth injuries. Many victims of cerebral palsy are mentally, as well as physically, defective.

Before, during and immediately after birth the child is subject to the danger of anoxia or asphyxiation (prolonged loss of oxygen), which may produce degenerative changes in the brain cells, and hence mental deficiency. In one clinical study, 132 children whose fetal development had been normal but who had suffered serious anoxia at the time of birth, 35, or 26 percent, of the subjects were found to be dull or subnormal in intelligence, while 97 were in the range of normal or superior intelligence (23). Nevertheless, it was the investigator's clinical impression that anoxia had damaged the central nervous system of every child in some way, seriously affecting his subsequent behavior. According to her observations, those who experienced a lesser degree of anoxia exhibited extreme excitability and hyperactivity. As infants, these children responded vigorously to many stimuli, cried a great deal, and slept little. Later they were inconsistent in their thinking, learned slowly, and could not conform to any group. In adolescence, they developed into highly aggressive, independent personalities.

On the other hand, it was her impression that children who had experienced greater degrees of anoxia showed extreme apathy. In infancy and early childhood, they slept a great deal, moved slowly, and seemed to be highly frustrated. As adolescents, they developed submissive, dependent personalities.

Both hyperactive and apathetic children of normal intelligence learned to stand, walk, and speak at the usual ages. However, their behavior was considered troublesome at home and in school, and half of them were rejected by their parents. The children, in turn, shunned social contacts. Two-thirds of them expressed "no liking for anybody" and were said to be disliked by others.

Although the results of this study are provocative, they cannot be considered definitive for several reasons. For one thing, most of the data were informal clinical impressions rather than controlled observations. Moreover, the subjects who suffered anoxia were not compared with any control group. Hence, it is impossible to separate the influences of anoxia from the influence of other important factors, e.g., parental treatment.

Consequents of Premature Birth

During the birth process, the organism is subjected to extreme pressures and is deprived of its accustomed sources of support and nourishment. For the child who is born prematurely, the event may be considered even more traumatic, since the organism is extremely fragile, inelastic, and physically not ready for birth. Moreover, premature births are often cataclysmic, unduly prolonged or precipitate, thus subjecting the infant to unusual stress. If such birth conditions affect the child's psychological development adversely, we would expect more evidence of personality disturbances among children prematurely born than among those born at full term. Shirley noted that:

. . . prematurely born infants usually experience an initial arrest or delay in development during the early weeks after birth, but thereafter they resume growing at an accelerated rate that enables them eventually to overtake their full-term contemporaries in weight, height, and other physical features and in intellectual attainment. When they catch up with their birth age, they are likely to vanish into the general child population and the fact of their premature birth is no longer regarded as particularly significant in their behavioral development (28, 115).

Nevertheless, there is a possibility that premature birth may have lasting physical and emotional consequences.

Shirley and her co-workers (28) observed the mannerisms and the emotional responses of 95 prematurely born children in standard intelligence tests and play situations. Sixty-five of the children were 6 to 30 months of age, and 30 of them were between 3 and 6 years old. Their reactions were compared with those of a group of full-term children of the same age, sex, and ordinal position in the family. On the basis of this comparison, Shirley concluded that there are a group of traits which may be tentatively labeled as a "prematurity syndrome." Children who had been born prematurely displayed more of the following characteristics than the full-term children: highly developed auditory and visual acuity or interest; speech difficulties (baby talk, mispronunciation); poor motor coördination, awkward movements; activity extremes (tendency to be either hyperactive or sluggish); difficulties in sphincter control; shyness, dependence upon mother; tendency to be either extremely flighty and distractible or extremely persistent in work; high level of esthetic appreciation and desire to be artistically creative.

However, these characteristics may not be attributable to premature birth alone. Unfavorable prenatal environment or birth injuries may account for some of the premature child's personality difficulties; but it is more likely that postnatal environment and experiences are more important influences. Early in his life the premature child may be overprotected and isolated. Since the parents may be afraid of harming the extremely delicate organism, they may not stimulate the child sufficiently. Later, they may become overstimulating in their attempts to help the child overcome the discrepancies between him and his contemporaries. Understimulation followed by pressure may lead to various kinds of maladjustment. Hence it may be concluded that "the family environment of the premature child's early years is quite adequate to account for most of the social and emotional difficulties of the prematures" (28, 127).

Intelligence and personality tests administered to 22 children ages 8 to 19, who had been born prematurely, revealed that prematurity itself did not permanently affect intellectual development but was often associated with emotional maladjustment (14). Thus 12 of the 22 prematures had below-average adjustment according to personality tests. Fourteen children were feeding problems as infants, and 7 were still enuretic (bedwetters) at 4 years of age. Eight showed unusual aggressive tendencies, while 12 of the 22 had extremely submissive, passive characteristics. Five were so severely disturbed that their family physicians recommended psychological treatment. These emotional maladjustments often prevented the optimal use of the children's intellectual abilities. It seems likely that overprotectiveness and anxiety on the part of parents, rather than prematurity itself, may account for the development of these symptoms of maladjustment.

From this summary of studies on the influence of difficult birth, birth injury, and premature birth, it is apparent that final conclusions cannot yet be drawn. It is difficult to assess the consequences of these variables accurately, for many other obvious and subtle factors which may contribute to personality development after the child is born cannot be controlled. This problem was illustrated most clearly in the studies of prematurely born children, where observed differences between the prematures and full-term children could as easily be ascribed to parental treatment and family relations as to prematurity itself.

REFERENCES AND ADDITIONAL READING

1. Blum, G., *Psychoanalytic theories of personality*. New York: McGraw-Hill, 1953.
2. Carmichael, L., The onset and early development of behavior, in L. Carmichael (ed.), *Manual of child psychology*. New York: Wiley, 1954.
3. Corner, G. W., *Ourselves unborn; an embryologist's essay on man*. New Haven: Yale University Press, 1944.
4. Despert, J. L., Anxiety, phobias, and fears in young children with special reference to prenatal, natal, and neonatal factors. *Nervous Child* (1946), 5:8–28.
5. Despres, M. A., Favorable and unfavorable attitudes toward pregnancy in primaparae. *J. genet. Psychol.* (1937), 51:241–254.
6. Dippel, A. L., The relationship of congenital syphilis to abortion and miscarriage, and the mechanisms of intrauterine protection. *Am. J. Obst. and Gynec.* (1944), 47:369–379.
7. Ebbs, J. H., Brown, A., Tisdall, F. F., Moyle, W. J., and Bell, M., The influence of improved prenatal nutrition upon the infant. *Canad. M.A.J.*, 1942, pp. 6–8.
8. Ebbs, J. H., Tisdall, F. F., and Scott, W. A., The influence of prenatal diet on the mother and child. *The Milbank Memorial Fund Quarterly* (1942), 20:35–36.

9. Gesell, A., *The embryology of behavior*. New York: Harper, 1945.
10. Gesell, A., and Amatruda, C. S., *Developmental diagnosis*. New York: Hoeber, 1941.
11. Gesell, A., and Amatruda, C. S., *Developmental diagnosis; normal and abnormal child development*. New York: Hoeber, 1947.
12. Goodpasture, E. W., Virus infection of the mammalian fetus. *Science* (1942), *95*:391–396.
13. Hall, D. E., and Mohr, G. J., Prenatal attitudes of primapirae: a contribution to the mental hygiene of pregnancy. *Mental Hygiene* (1933), *17*:226–234.
14. Howard, P. J., and Worrell, C. H., Premature infants in later life: a study of intelligence and personality of 22 premature infants at ages 8 and 19 years. *Pediatrics* (1952), *9*:577–584.
15. Hughes, J. G., Ehemann, B., and Brown, U. A., Electroencephalography of the newborn. *Am. J. Dis. Child* (1948), *76*:626–633.
16. Hurlock, E. B., *Child development*. New York: McGraw-Hill, 1950.
17. Kuder, K., and Johnson, D. G., The elderly primipara. *Am. J. Obst. and Gynec.* (1944), *47*:794–807.
18. Malzberg, B., Some statistical aspects of mongolism. *Am. J. ment. Deficiency* (1950), *54*:226–281.
19. McCurdy, R. N. C., *The rhesus danger: Its medical, moral and legal aspects*. London: Heinmann, 1950.
20. Montagu, M. F. A., Constitutional and prenatal factors in infant and child health, in M. J. E. Senn (ed.), *Symposium on the Healthy Personality*. New York: Josiah Macy, Jr. Foundation, 1950, pp. 148–175.
21. Murphy, D. P., The outcome of 625 pregnancies in women subjected to pelvic radium roentgen irradiation. *Am. J. Obst. and Gynec.* (1929), *18*: 179–187.
22. Murphy, D. P., *Congenital malformation*, 2nd ed. Philadelphia: University of Pennsylvania Press, 1947.
23. Preston, M. I., Late behavioral aspects found in cases of prenatal, natal and postnatal anoxia. *J. Pediat.* (1945), *26*:353–356.
24. Rand, W., Sweeny, M., and Vincent, E. L., *Growth and development of the growing child*. Philadelphia: Saunders, 1946.
25. Rank, O. *The trauma of birth*. New York: Harcourt, Brace, 1929.
26. Ruja, H. J., The relation between neonate crying and length of labor. *J. genet. Psychol.* (1948), *73*:53–55.
27. Scheinfeld, A., *The new you and heredity*. Philadelphia: Lippincott, 1950.
28. Shirley, M. M., A behavior syndrome characterizing prematurely-born children. *Child Develop.* (1939), *10*:115–128.
29. Sontag, L. W., The significance of fetal environmental differences. *Am. J. Obst. and Gynec.* (1941), *42*:996–1003.
30. Sontag, L. W., War and fetal maternal relationship. *Marriage and Family Living* (1944), *6*:1–5.
31. Sontag, L. W., and Wallace, R. F., The effect of cigarette smoking during pregnancy upon the fetal heart rate. *Am. J. Obst. and Gynec.* (1935), *29*:3–8.

32. Squier, R., and Dunbar, F., Emotional factors in the course of pregnancy. *Psychosom. Med.* (1946), 8:161–175.
33. Tompkins, W. T., The clinical significance of nutritional deficiencies in pregnancy. *Bull. New York Acad. Med.* (1948), *24*:376–388.
34. Wallin, R., and Riley, R., Reactions of mothers to pregnancy and adjustment of offspring in infancy. *Am. J. Orthopsychiat.* (1950), *20*:616–622.
35. Watson, E. H., and Lowrey, G. H., *Growth and development of children.* Chicago: Year Book Publishers, 1954.
36. Wile, I. W. and Davis, R., The relation of birth to behavior, *Am. J. Orthopsychiat.* (1941), *11*:320–334.
37. Yannet, H. Mental deficiency, in A. G. Mitchell and W. E. Nelson (eds.), *Textbook of pediatrics,* 5th ed. Philadelphia: Saunders, 1951.

PART II
The First Two Years

Chapter 4

BIOLOGICAL CHANGES IN THE FIRST YEAR

Birth brings enormous changes in the life of the developing child. With his sudden exposure to the wider world outside his mother's womb, the forces which can affect his development increase markedly. Before this, only hereditary factors and limited intrauterine conditions could influence him. After birth, the number of environmental stimuli impinging on the infant and affecting his status is multiplied many times.

Moreover, birth marks the passing from a completely parasitic dependence on the mother physiologically to a position of some independence. Whereas previously his mother's body took care of all the fetus' bodily needs, the infant must now satisfy some of these needs at least partially by himself.

The interruption and cessation of circulatory relations with the maternal organism mean that no more nutrient materials ready for assimilation are available to the child. Henceforth, it must take food, digest it, excrete, egest, and maintain a relatively uniform body temperature despite variations in its thermal environment (52, 216).

It is a major theme of this book that learning, which in large measure begins after birth, is of central importance in personality development. Principles of human learning will be elaborated in the next chapter. As we shall see, the starting points of learning are the infant's biological needs, his ability to notice environmental stimuli, and his response capacities. Certain responses seem to depend almost exclusively on physical maturation (i.e., neuromuscular development) and physiological changes in the organism, since they emerge regardless of whether or not the infant has opportunities for practice.

However, most behavior with which we will be concerned in this book is learned, i.e., develops as a consequence of specific experiences. But even these responses cannot be learned until the essential neuromuscular mechanisms are "ready."

The maturation of neural tissues sets certain limits for children's behavior. No amount of parental effort is sufficient to enable the three-month-old infant to talk in sentences. Neural development is too limited at this age for such complex behavior (68, 84).

In this chapter, we shall examine the neonate's (newborn's) basic ✓ equipment for learning—his innate needs, capacities for receiving information and responding—and the ways in which these develop during the first year. A survey of the important modifications in body size and proportions will be followed by discussions of primary needs and sensorimotor capabilities.

BODY GROWTH

In view of the vast variations among infants in size at birth and in rate of growth, averages or norms can give only a general picture of development. On the average, full-term male babies, who are slightly larger in all body dimensions than females, are about 20 inches tall and weigh 7½ pounds at birth. It should be noted, however, that the range of "normal" birth heights and weights is large. For example, Negro babies are generally smaller, weigh less, and grow more slowly than whites (2, 3, 4); and neonates from poverty-stricken environments, although similarly proportioned, tend to be smaller in all dimensions than those from more favorable environments (3).

The first year of the child's life brings remarkably rapid and extensive growth changes. Body length increases over one-third, and weight almost triples, so that by the age of one, the average baby is about 28 or 29 inches tall and weighs about 20 pounds.

In addition, there are vast modifications in body proportions and in skeletal, neural, and muscular structure. Detailed technical discussions of these developments are beyond the scope of this book, but a condensed description of the major changes follows.

Body Proportions

Since "the body does not grow as a whole and in all directions at once" (69, 299), the infant's overall body proportions change rapidly, partic-✓ ularly during the second half of the first year. The differential growth rates of the legs and face illustrate the way in which body proportions change. At birth, the infant's legs are about one-fifth as long as they will be when he is an adult, but from about 8 weeks of age they grow at an accelerated rate. In contrast to this, the head and face grow more slowly than the body as a whole, although skull size and shape become significantly modified. The total length of the head and face of the 3-month-old fetal infant is about one-third of his total body length; at birth this height is less than one-fourth; in adulthood, about one-tenth (69) (see Figure 11).

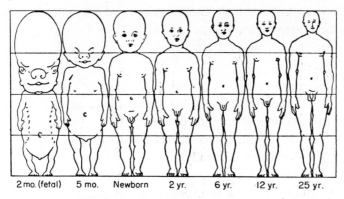

2 mo. (fetal)   5 mo.   Newborn   2 yr.   6 yr.   12 yr.   25 yr.

FIGURE 11.   Changes in form and proportion of the human body during fetal and postnatal life. (From C. M. Jackson, "Some Aspects of Form and Growth," in W. J. Robbins, S. Brody, A. F. Hogan, C. M. Jackson, and C. W. Green, *Growth*. New Haven: Yale University Press, 1928, p. 118.)

Skeletal Development

At birth, the infant's skeletal system differs in many ways from that of the adult. The neonate has 270 bones, but these consist largely of cartilage, containing more water and fewer minerals than adults' bones. They are therefore softer, more pliable, more reactive to muscular pull and pressure, and more susceptible to deformity. Fortunately, they are also less subject to breakage. In the process of ossification (bone development), these early bone units calcify and become firmer, grow in length and width, and assume different shapes. They also gradually fuse, or make firmer and more closely knit connections with other bones.

Additional bones of the body appear at different times and mature and assume definite shape at different rates. For example, while wrist bones are seldom present at birth, they begin to appear in an orderly fashion soon afterward. By the end of the first year most children have developed 3 of their total (i.e., adult) complement of 8 wrist bones. In a similar way, the skull of the newborn infant has 6 soft spots (fontanelles) which ossify gradually and disappear by the age of 2. Other bones develop still later (69).

As in other aspects of development, there are marked individual differences in rates of ossification and skeletal growth. Sex differences favoring girls are present at birth and increase with age. Hereditary factors undoubtedly affect the rate of development, while illness, allergies, and gastrointestinal upsets may produce disturbances of bone structure. In general, minor fluctuations in bone development are not serious and tend to be self-corrective (6).

Teeth

Tiny beginnings of the deciduous or "baby" teeth are present in the fetus from the age of 10 weeks, but there is a great deal of individual variability in the time of eruption of the first tooth. Some infants are born with one or more teeth, others do not have any until after they are a year old. The first tooth, generally a lower front tooth, erupts at an average age of 6 or 7 months. By the time the average child is a year old, he has 6 teeth, but the range is from zero to twelve (25).

Muscles

Although the neonate has all the muscle fibers he will ever have, they are small, delicate, and infirm in their attachments to bones. However, there is continuous growth in length, breadth, and thickness until, in adulthood, the weight of the muscles is about 40 times what it was at birth. The striped or skeletal (voluntary) muscles of the body are not yet completely under control during the first year. Although they fatigue rapidly, they recover easily in the early stages of the development of voluntary responses such as sitting and walking (69).

BASIC NEEDS

The infant is born with a number of basic physiological drives or needs which must be satisfied if he is to survive. Most of these are usually taken care of in a self-regulatory manner, without any active participation by the infant. However, two drives, hunger and thirst, are not gratified (reduced) automatically. For this reason, as we shall see later, they are crucially involved in the infant's earliest learning.

Need for Oxygen

Within the first few days of postnatal life, respiration is stabilized on an adultlike level (49). Reflex mechanisms (regulated by the saturation of oxygen and carbon dioxide in the blood) operate to assure the neonate an oxygen supply adequate for his needs. Consequently, the drive for oxygen rarely becomes high or intense.

Irregular and shallow breathing in the neonate is usually normal, not a sign of inadequate functioning of the respiratory mechanisms. However, noisy breathing that begins suddenly may be a symptom of croup, asthma, or other infection and requires immediate medical attention (64).

Temperature Regulation

Before birth, the child's temperature is likely to remain fairly stable, since he is protected by the surrounding amniotic fluid. Once outside the womb, however, his temperature is much more likely to vary in response to changes in the environment. The newborn infant may be exposed to drafts and to changes in the weather. He may kick off his blankets and become cold; or more likely, according to pediatricians, he may be bundled up too snugly by his anxious parents and become too hot. He is much more subject to fever-producing infections than he was before birth.

Within limits, the child's need to maintain a relatively constant temperature is fulfilled by automatic physiological mechanisms. When these limits are exceeded, however, as in the above examples, the temperature regulation drive becomes intensified, and the child requires external assistance in bringing his temperature back to normal. In short, he needs parents to open or shut windows, add or remove blankets, and, if indicated, to administer proper drugs.

Need for Sleep

At present, there is no completely satisfactory physiological theory to account for the need for rest. Sleep seems to be another device by which the body regulates itself, maintains equilibrium in its chemical constitution and physiological processes, and thus preserves the organism's energy for later activity.

The proportion of time spent in sleep decreases as the child grows older. Neonates on the average spend 80 percent of their time asleep and 20 percent awake, while 1-year-olds on the average are awake as much of the time as they are asleep (9).

The rhythms and depth of sleep also change rapidly during the first year. For the first three or four weeks, the average infant takes seven or eight short naps a day, but the number is reduced to between two and four longer periods of sleep by 6 weeks of age. By 28 weeks, most children will sleep through the night, and from then until they are about a year old, will require only two or three daytime naps (23). Night sleep also becomes less broken as the child matures—to the considerable relief of weary mothers.

There are great individual differences in sleep needs, and any particular child's requirements may vary from time to time. Many factors influence the quality and quantity of sleep. During the earliest months, intestinal upsets, and later on, wetness, bodily discomfort, noise, or emotional factors (violence, excitement, etc.) may interfere with sound rest. The infant's need for sleep or rest seldom becomes intense, since he will ordinarily sleep as much as is necessary and wake when he is rested. Later on, he will have to learn the culturally approved patterns of sleep and wakefulness, but this is not an important problem during the first year.

Need for Elimination

When the neonate's bowel is full, the anal sphincters open reflexively and the contents are expelled. In the same way, when the bladder is swollen, the urethral sphincter is automatically released. These processes are entirely involuntary in early infancy, since the neuromuscular equipment necessary for voluntary control has not yet matured.

There are major alterations in patterns of elimination during the first year. While there are wide individual differences, bowel movements are generally frequent and sporadic during the first few weeks, but by the time the infant is 4 weeks old, the number generally falls to three or four evacuations daily, ordinarily associated with waking. By 8 weeks of age, the average infant usually has only two bowel movements daily, one upon waking and one close to, or during, a feeding. By 16 weeks, a definite interval between feeding and evacuation has usually been established (23).

During the first few weeks of postnatal existence, the average infant urinates frequently, but gradually the number of micturitions decreases and their volume increases. By 28 weeks of age, intervals of dryness may be as long as one or two hours. At the end of the first year, the baby may still be dry after a long nap and will likely begin to be intolerant of wet diapers.

Learning to withhold elimination until the proper—that is, socially approved—place and time requires the inhibition or suppression of responses which initially occur automatically. In toilet training, voluntary control must be substituted for reflex actions. This presents a complex and difficult learning problem which requires a great deal of skill and patience in handling, as we shall see later.

Hunger and Thirst

These two drives are confounded, i.e., are not easily differentiated, in young infants and hence will be discussed together. From a psychological and social point of view, they are the most important of the neonate's basic drives, for their satisfaction depends on someone else's help, rather than on automatic, reflex activities. If the infant's hunger and thirst are not reduced soon, tensions mount, become severe, and provoke a great deal of bodily activity. For this reason, these drives play an important role in the infant's earliest learning. Here we shall review briefly the changes in physiological hunger needs and feeding patterns during the first year. Discussion of the broader social learning implications of the feeding situation, the infant's first interpersonal relationship, is reserved for Chapter 6.

Data on American newborn infants on self-demand schedules (feeding whenever the baby is hungry) indicate that, on the average, they take seven or eight feedings per day. By 4 weeks of age, the number has been reduced to five or six. At this time, the average infant's food intake is between 18 and 25 ounces, but this rises to about 35 ounces when he is 6 to 8 weeks old. Within the next few weeks, the number of feedings is further reduced, although total food intake does not change significantly (23).

In our culture, solid foods are often introduced into the infant's menu when he is about 20 weeks of age, and by 40 weeks, cereals and vegetables may form a regular part of his diet. By the time the American child is a year old, the three-meal regime has probably become stabilized and he may manifest marked food preferences. The time and manner of weaning the infant to solid foods varies from culture to culture (cf. pp. 162–163).

SENSORY DEVELOPMENT

The infant cannot learn unless he receives information from his environment. He does this through his senses—vision, audition, taste, smell, and touch. There have been numerous attempts to investigate sensory functioning at birth, but there are considerable difficulties in such research. Consequently, our knowledge of the neonate's sensory capacities is still limited. In this section, we will review briefly some of the fairly well-established facts and "best guesses" regarding neonatal and first year sensory development.

Vision

Although the essential neural mechanisms begin to appear in the second or third week of prenatal life, the neuromuscular apparatus involved in vision is still not perfected when the infant is born. For example, the optic nerve is not fully developed, and the ciliary muscles are not mature enough to permit accommodation (adjustment of the thickness of the lens of the eye) which brings the light rays into proper focus on the retina. Hence the neonate probably does not perceive clear-cut images.

However, the structure and functioning of the eyes improve and become perfected rapidly after birth. The nature of the infant's visual sensitivity can be determined only by observing his responses to visual stimuli.

1. The *pupillary reflex* (contraction of the pupil in response to light), observed even in premature infants, reveals that the neonate is sensitive to differences in the *intensity* of visual stimuli. Although the response is somewhat sluggish at birth, it becomes perfected during the first few days of postnatal life (51, 52). At first, it can be elicited only by strong stimuli, but with increasing age, less intensity is required.

2. *Visual pursuit movements* (following a stimulus with the eyes) in response to moving colored spots projected on an overhead screen demonstrate that infants as young as 15 days can discriminate colors. Moving visual stimuli such as lights may also evoke pursuit responses (12).

3. According to the best available data (43), *coördination and convergence* of the two eyes, both essential for fixation and depth perception, are absent at birth, but appear in rudimentary form a few hours afterwards.

Real convergence or binocular fixation first occurs at about seven or eight weeks. It is initially accomplished by a series of jerking movements which are gradually eliminated, and replaced by smooth, continuous convergence. One investigator concludes that "the oculomotor responses of the human infant are among the earliest complex behavior patterns to become organized and functional in the infant's adaptation to his environment. By the end of the first month the infant is able to fixate an object in the direct line of his vision with active, intense, and well-sustained regard. By the end of the second month binocular fixation with convergence begins to appear. Thus, long before the infant is able to assume command of his trunk and extremities, he is already busily exploring and apprehending his environment with his eyes" (43, 272).

Hearing

Although the auditory mechanism is sufficiently well developed to be functional at birth, neonates may have relatively poor hearing during the early postnatal days—possibly as a consequence of mucus in the middle ear or an obstruction of the external auditory canal. In general, they respond strongly to variations in the intensity (loudness) and duration of sounds, but not to differences in pitch. Thus loud stimuli provoke more bodily movements, more eyelid closing, and changes in respiratory rates. Moreover, sounds lasting 15 seconds elicit more bodily movement, and faster respiratory rates than those of 1 second duration (65). On the other hand, stimuli of longer duration—5 minutes, for example—may inhibit activity. Apparently, "the auditory stimulus first releases certain overt responses and thereafter, if the stimulus persists, overt activity subsides and there is less movement than would occur in a period of no experimental stimulation" (52, 237).

Although low tones may produce some decrease in bodily activity, neonates do not ordinarily react to differences in tones. In general, pitch discrimination does not become well developed until after the first few months. Genetic factors may partially account for early observed individual differences in pitch sensitivity.

Olfaction

Some investigators report differential responses to markedly pleasant and unpleasant odors (i.e., sucking in response to pleasant odors such as anise oil; and facial grimaces and turning away of the head to unpleasant ones such as ammonia). However, these differences are slight and highly variable. The neonate seems to show little or no discrimination of weak or less distinctive odors. However, the presence of odors may provoke more activity than clear air, and greater saturations of odors may stimulate greater activity (19, 53).

Gustation

Neonates do not react differentially to solutions of salt, sugar, citric acid, quinine, and distilled water (as a control) applied to their tongues, thus demonstrating that they have little taste sensitivity. Apparently this sensitivity develops rapidly, however, for within the first two weeks they begin to make pronounced positive (sucking) responses to sugar and negative (grimacing) responses to quinine and citric acid (53).

One experimenter observed that newborn infants would suck when given milk, glucose, acid milk, and sterile water, but would inhibit this response when given salt solutions. Moreover, he noted that the "moderately full baby is a better discriminator than the very hungry infant" (40).

Thermal Sensitivity

The neonate's activity level is elevated when the atmosphere is cold and reduced when it is warm. Experimental studies indicate that infants respond to temperature changes of 5 or 6 degrees in objects contacting their legs (cylinders which can be heated or chilled from a neutral point of 33°C) (15). Cold stimuli (average temperature, 11 or 12 degrees centigrade) applied to the legs elicited extension and flexion, while head movements, acceleration in breathing, and irregular pulse followed cold stimulation of the forehead (53).

Early thermal sensitivity is also reflected in the finding that most infants squirm and suck irregularly if their milk is warmer than 50°C or colder than 23°C (40). There are, of course, large individual differences in sensitivity to warmth and cold.

Static-Kinaesthetic Sensitivity

Neonates are highly sensitive to changes in the spatial position of the body. If the baby falls from a sitting position, is held upside down, or jarred, he will make generalized postural adjustments. Body rotation or prone placement on a table may stimulate nystagmus (oscillation of the eyes) or head movements. Newborn infants make alternate "stepping" movements when they are held upright with their feet resting upon a flat surface. These important responses, which subsequently become involved in maintaining upright posture and walking, reveal that the infant reacts to stimulation from sense organs located in his muscles and semicircular canals of the ear (the organs involved in maintaining balance).

Pain

Sensitivity to pain is present to some degree at birth and becomes sharper during the first few days of postnatal life. For example, between birth and 8 days, there is a substantial decrease in the number of pain stimuli (pin pricks) necessary to instigate withdrawal of the stimulated area (the original response to pain) (57, 58).

Data from systematic studies indicate that there are constitutional differences among infants in pain sensitivity (57). As we shall see later, pain may play an important role in the child's learning, particularly in acquiring fears and anxiety. These basic variations in pain sensitivity, detectable early in life, may partially account for the wide individual differences in susceptibility to fear which become apparent subsequently.

RESPONSE CAPABILITIES

Since the infant's sensory development can be evaluated only by observing his overt responses to various kinds of stimuli, we have inevitably discussed some of the neonate's response capabilities in the preceding section. Hence the reader is already aware that even at birth, the infant can make many complex sensory and motor responses. It may reasonably be assumed that these behavior patterns are unlearned, i.e., that they emerge in spite of the lack of opportunities to learn or practice them. Apparently they are the consequents of biological changes in the organism: increased size and complexity of the central nervous system and general anatomical and physiological growth. For example, although fetuses do not suck to obtain nourishment, almost all infants make sucking movements when their lips or cheeks are stimulated. The neonate's pupils contract in response to bright lights and flashes, although he has never experienced these stimuli prenatally.

Here we shall list merely a few responses drawn from the neonate's astonishingly extensive behavior repertoire. Complete reviews and classifications have been made by Dennis (16) and summarized by Munn (48) and Thompson (68).

Many of the neonate's responses—pupillary and sucking reflexes, head-mouth orientation movements ("searching" movements in response to stimulation), swallowing, opening and closing the eyes, crying, coughing, vomiting and rejecting foods, turning away the face when it is irritated, and assuming resting and sleeping positions—have "survival value." That is, they facilitate the infant's physical adjustment in his new environment, keep him healthy, and to some extent, remove him from damaging or noxious stimuli.

In addition to these, there are many other localized responses. These include: (1) *shuddering* in response to bitter taste; (2) *head balancing* instigated by changes in bodily position; (3) *arm flexion* when the hand is pricked with a pin or slapped; (4) the *grasp reflex* (closing the hand tightly—usually stimulated by contact or pressure on finger or palm) which is very strong at birth, but weakens after the first few weeks; (5) *knee jerk, flexion* and *extension* of the leg; (6) the *Babinski reflex* (extension of the big toe and fanning out of the other toes when the sole of the foot is stroked); (7) in the male, *penis erection and raising the testes,* elicited by irritation of the inner thigh.

Coördination of many parts of the body is involved in the newborn infant's more generalized responses including: (1) *trunk movements* (squirming, twisting, arching the back, and drawing in the stomach); (2) *body jerks;* (3) *shivering, trembling;* (4) *creeping movements;* (5) the *startle* response, consisting of throwing arms apart, and head back, and extending legs, which may be a response to loud noises, falling, and applications of hot or cold.

General Responsiveness

In any group of newborn infants, there are wide individual differences in general activity level. In one study (28), body movements during the first 10 days were recorded both instrumentally and by trained observers. Some infants were five times as active as others during the first day; and extreme, but consistent, individual differences were noted throughout the observation period.

Within a few days after birth, neonates can be rated reliably as "very active," "moderately active," and "quiet" (20). Differences in activity patterns may be attributed to hereditary factors, or to differences in prenatal experiences. A follow-up study of a group of infants showed that relative activity levels remain fairly stable for the first three years, although environmental variations may produce changes.

The importance of the child's early activity level should not be underestimated, for it may exert a profound influence on his subsequent learning and personality development.

The development of behavior . . . depends upon the responsiveness of the growing organism. An active, irritable infant participates in a wider environment than does a quiet, phlegmatic one, and he invites different reactions from those who share the environment with him. The baby who turns, reaches, and kicks restlessly in his crib; who cries, smiles, or coos a great deal; or who nurses actively and long, inevitably exposes himself to situations which differ from those which the placid, unreactive child encounters. What these differences in reactivity may mean for the infant's behavior organization is also importantly determined, of course, by the needs and attitudes of his parents and of the others who respond to him. An exuberant, accepting family may welcome noisy activity in its newest member which quieter, more restrictive parents would consider irritating, frightening, or bad (10, 22).

MOTOR DEVELOPMENT IN THE FIRST YEAR

In addition to the responses present at birth, numerous new motor activities are added to the infant's inventory of abilities during the first year. Many of these emerge independently of learning, i.e., without the benefit of any previous teaching or practice. Apparently the infant becomes capable of these responses and makes them as a consequence of the maturation of certain neural tissues, expansion and increased complexity of the central nervous system, and growth of bones and muscles. In many instances, these seemingly unlearned behavior patterns improve and become better coördinated, more precise, and more accurate after practice.

We will make no attempt to review the whole vast array of responses of the first year. Complete surveys may be found in the works of Gesell and Amatruda (22) and McGraw (46). In this chapter, we will emphasize only developments in locomotion, reaching, and grasping.

Locomotion

SITTING. The response repertoire of the neonate does not include any reflex sitting posture, but the ability to sit develops early (5, 17, 22, 59). On the average, babies are able to sit for a minute, with support, at the age of 3 or 4 months, and by 7 or 8 months, they can do this without support. Once sitting is achieved, there is rapid improvement, so that by nine months babies can sit independently for 10 minutes or longer (22).

CRAWLING AND CREEPING. Ames (1) analyzed motion pictures of crawling and creeping in 20 infants and concluded that there are 14 stages in the development of these activities (see Figure 12). There are great individual differences in the ages at which infants reach the various stages, but practically all infants go through the same sequence.

The first stage, thrusting one knee forward beside the body, appeared in half the infants at 28 weeks or younger. The median age for crawling (i.e., moving with the abdomen in contact with the floor) was 34 weeks. At this age, the muscles of the trunk, arms, and legs are not sufficiently strong or coördinated to maintain the body weight. The infants began to creep on hands and knees, which requires new coördination and equilibrium, at a median age of 40 weeks, while creeping on hands and feet, the final stage of prone progression, was attained by a median age of 49

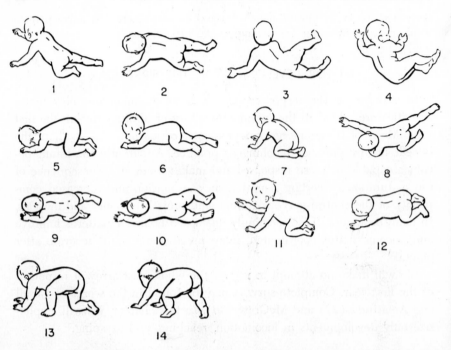

FIGURE 12. The fourteen stages of prone progression. (Described by L. B. Ames in "The Sequential Patterning of Prone Progression in the Human Infant." *Genet. Psychol. Monogr.* (1937), *19*:409–460).

weeks. Infants may skip one or two stages of development, but all of them progress through most of the steps (*1*).

WALKING. The ability to walk independently also matures gradually, after a series of preliminary achievements. As in other aspects of development, there is a wide range of ages at which the various stages are attained. The median ages for standing while holding on to furniture, walking when led, pulling up to a stand, standing alone, and walking alone were 42, 45, 47, 62, and 64 weeks, respectively, according to Shirley's data on 25 children (*60*) (see Figure 13). The transition from one developmental step to the next is not always smooth and "never does the infant pass completely and irretrievably from one stage into another. There is always a merging of patterns and parts of patterns both in the degree of perfection of the action and in the frequency of occurrence. There are often regressions to the less mature response" (*45, 69*).

There is considerable evidence (*17, 45, 46, 58*) that growth changes and maturation of the neural and muscular systems—rather than environmental conditions, experiences, or practice—determine when the child

FIGURE 13.   The development of posture and locomotion in infants. (From M. M. Shirley, *The First Two Years, a Study of Twenty-Five Babies:* Vol. II, *Intellectual Development. Inst. Child Welfare Monogr. Ser. No. 8.* Minneapolis: University of Minnesota Press, 1933. With permission of the University of Minnesota Press.)

will sit, stand, and walk. For example, Dennis (17) kept a pair of female twins on their backs for the first nine months of their lives, thus preventing any practice in sitting or standing. Despite these restrictions, they were only slightly retarded in these activities, the most marked retardation being in sitting. When they were given their first opportunities to sit alone at the age of 37 weeks, the restricted twins were not able to do so. Several weeks later, however, they were able to sit alone. Although most children can support their body weight while standing with help by the time they are 40 weeks old, the twins were not able to do this at 52 weeks, when they were given their first opportunity to do so. Within three days, however, both infants could stand with help for at least two minutes. One twin suffered no retardation in crawling, walking when led, or standing or walking independently. Apparently these behaviors develop without any special practice or teaching by adults.

In order to determine whether there are any enduring consequents of early restriction of motor activity, Dennis (18) studied locomotor progress in Hopi Indian babies. Most of these children are bound to cradle-boards almost immediately after birth and kept this way almost all the time for the first three months of their lives. After this, the time spent on the board is gradually reduced. However in two Hopi villages cradle-boards are no longer used. Yet the children from these two villages do not walk any earlier than cradled Hopi children. Apparently, early restrictions of movement do not impede later locomotor progress. Moreover, as we shall see later, special training and practice at an early age do not affect the acquisition of locomotor skills such as stair climbing (cf. p. 172).

Manipulation

Like locomotion, manipulative ability evolves through a series of stages. Analysis of motion pictures of infants reaching for and grasping cubes showed that those under 20 weeks of age do not actually reach for objects, although they may follow them with their eyes. Some infants 20 weeks old stretch their arms in the general direction of the object, making slow, awkward, and angular reaching movements, involving primarily shoulder and elbow action. With increased age, the approach becomes more direct, and the wrist and hand participate. By 60 weeks of age, the infant reaches for attractive objects without superfluous movements (26, 27).

There are ten stages in the development of prehension, according to Halverson (26). The neonate's grasp reflex disappears by the time he is

4 months old. Sixteen-week-old infants make no real contact with an object, but by 20 weeks, they can touch and squeeze things in a primitive way without taking hold firmly. Grasping becomes more successful and unnecessary movements decrease as the child matures. Thus by 28 weeks of age, he uses his palm smoothly in closing in on a cube, but his thumb and fingers are not involved. The forefinger begins to play a part in grasping at about 36 weeks. In the final stages of the development of prehension, thumb and forefinger function together, and other fingers are also used precisely in securing a cube. By the time the child is 60 weeks of age, his grasp is much like an adult's (see Figure 14).

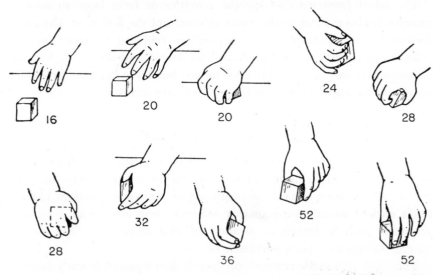

FIGURE 14. The development of prehension. (From H. M. Halverson, "An Experimental Study of Prehension in Infants by Means of Systematic Cinema Records." *Genet. Psychol. Monogr.* (1931), *10*:107–286. With permission of The Journal Press.)

Developmental Trends

First-year sensory and motor developments reflect several general directional trends. The *cephalocaudal* or head to foot trend, is illustrated in the relatively early accomplishment of head movements, visual fixation, and eye-hand coördination, and the relatively late appearance of standing and walking. The limbs and muscles of the upper part of the body become functionally effective before the lower limbs. In walking, appropriate coördination of the arms precedes that of the legs.

The principle is well illustrated in the behavior characteristics of the twenty week old infant. His trunk is still so flaccid that he must be propped or strapped in a chair to maintain a sitting posture. When he is so secured, however, his eyes, head, and shoulders exhibit heightened activity and intensified tonus. The pelvic zone and the lower extremities at 20 weeks are, in comparison, very immature (21, 341).

Progress in the development of motor responses during the first year also follows a roughly *proximodistal* direction, i.e., from the central to the peripheral segments of the body. Thus, in reaching, the shoulders and elbows are used before the wrist and fingers. In both prone and erect locomotion, the upper arm and upper leg are brought under control before the forearm, foreleg, hands and feet.

The trend *from mass to specific* activities or from large to smaller muscles is also evident in the motor advances of the first year. The gross awkward movements of early grasping are replaced by more precise, refined movements of the thumb and forefinger. Locomotion is initially accompanied by excess bodily movements, but these decrease gradually until only the appropriate muscles and limbs are involved.

LANGUAGE DEVELOPMENT

The laryngeal and respiratory organs involved in vocalization are ready to function before birth, but the mechanisms are not used until the birth cry, a reflex accompanying the beginning of normal respiration. The infant's earliest sounds are primarily reflexive, associated with automatic responses such as breathing, swallowing, and hiccoughing. He has no specific sounds to express particular needs.

The most systematic research on speech development in early infancy has been conducted by Irwin and his associates at the University of Iowa (13, 14, 30, 31, 32, 33, 34, 35, 36, 37, 38, 39). They recorded phonetically the speech sounds made by 40 infants during the first ten days of life. The vowel sounds uttered were i (as in bit), e (as in bet), a (as in bat) or u (as in but), a being the one all infants made. The aspirate h (as in house) was the most frequently used consonant, and w and k were also noted occasionally. The consonants m, l, and b were not heard during this period.

Throughout infancy, there are marked changes in the nature and number of sounds produced. In a 30-month longitudinal (follow-up) study of speech development, Irwin (30, 31, 32, 33, 36, 37) phonetically transcribed monthly samples of the speech sounds uttered by 95 infants during a short test period (30 breaths). Speech development was measured in terms of phoneme types (elemental speech sounds listed in the

International Phonetic Alphabet) and phoneme frequency (the number of times each of the types is used by the infant).

The data revealed rapid and far-reaching expansion in the infant's speech catalogue during the first year. As early as "the second quarter of the first year of life infants produce most of the vowel elements and about half of the consonants" (44, 507). The average baby under 2 months of age has 7 phonemes in its speech repertory; at 6 months he has 12, and at a year, 18. (Adult American speech includes 35 phonemes.) The number of sounds uttered also multiplies rapidly during this period. During the first 2 months, infants vocalized an average of 63 sounds (counting all repetitions) in the test period, but at 6 months, the average number rose to 74, and at a year it was about 90 (30, 36, 37).

Throughout the first year, the number of vowel types used exceeds the number of consonant types. The vowel-consonant ratio is 5:1 during the first month, but this discrepancy becomes reduced gradually until after the first year, consonants predominate. Adults have a consonant-vowel ratio of 1.4:1 (33).

About 90 percent of the earliest consonant sounds made by the infant are glottals (aspirate *h* or stops and catches made in the throat), but by the end of the first year, these sounds constitute only about 30 percent of the infant's consonants. Labials (for example, *p, b, m, w, wh*) and labiodentals (*f* and *v*) and postdentals (*t, d, n*) are practically non-existent in the neonate's repertory, but they become quite frequent during the first year (31, 32).

The regularity of trends in sound production provides some evidence that early sound patterns are dependent primarily on maturation and changes in anatomical, neuromuscular systems. For example, the postural change involved in sitting "must affect the shape of the oral cavity, especially by affecting the normal position of the soft palate, which undoubtedly accounts at least in part for the forward movement of the control of muscles involving the later-appearing consonants" (44, 513).

Moreover, children of all nationalities seem to go through the same sequence of speech development. "Children who are hearing only English use German [vowel] sounds, French guttural r, and a wide variety of sounds they will not be able to produce as English speaking adults" (47, 146) .

A child cannot learn verbal responses until he is old enough and mature enough to learn them. Maturation sets the pace. With a normal environment the child's speech awaits a step by step unfolding of the growth process. Consequently we find a succession of developmental stages that are quite similar in all children. By manipulating the language environment of the child we can modify or delay the development but we shall never teach a baby to utter prepositional phrases before he begins to babble. The successive stages of language development are similar in all normal children (47, 141).

Environment and Language

Even at these early ages, however, environmental factors may play an important part in language development. For example, babies under 6 months of age living in unstimulating orphanage environments are often retarded in both phoneme type and frequency (cf. pp. 157; 178).

Once the elementary speech sounds are acquired, progress in speech consists of using them in a variety of ways and in different combinations. Individual differences in the rates of speech development are apparent from earliest infancy.

Shirley (59) recorded all the language responses of her 25 infant subjects during testing sessions, and found that the first distinct syllable sound was uttered at the median age of 8 weeks, while two-syllable sounds were recorded at a median age of 13 weeks. Cooing and babbling appeared by the third month and continued until about the end of the first year. According to these data, "talking" to a person, singing tones, and expressive sounds were observed at median ages of 25, 32, and 38 weeks, respectively. Infants' speech sounds are less precise and definite than those of adults, but during the babbling period, syllables become sharper and more distinct.

Imitation of sounds generally begins after nine months. "Most present day psychologists seem to agree . . . that new sounds are not learned by imitation of the speech of others, but rather that they emerge in the child's spontaneous vocal play as a result of maturation, and that the child imitates only those sounds which have already occurred in its spontaneous babblings. This view holds that imitation of the speech of others serves only to call attention to new combinations of sounds already used" (44, 517).

It is difficult to determine when the child actually says his first meaningful word. Parents, anxiously anticipating their offspring's accomplishments, may jump to the conclusion that their baby has begun to talk if he happens to utter a sound vaguely resembling a word. On the basis of systematic observations, different psychologists have reached different conclusions regarding the average age of the onset of talking. When mothers' reports are used as basic data, the appearance of the first word is found at an average age of 11 months (9, 11). While there is a great deal of individual variation, data indicate that the average child generally says his first word sometime around the end of the first year. Gifted children often do this at an earlier age, some of them as early as 8 months (67).

Since much of the child's early babbling consists of repetitions of identical or similar syllables, the first words uttered are usually reduplicated monosyllables such as bye-bye, mama, or dada. The first word spoken is characteristically a noun or interjection but often functions as a whole sentence. For example "momma" may mean, *where is mother* or *I want mother*, or *there is mother*, depending upon the inflection and accompanying behavior.

Most normal children begin to walk before they begin to talk, but there are many exceptions, especially among intellectually precocious children. Several investigators report that progress in linguistic development may slow down or even cease while new motor skills are being mastered. For example, one investigator (60) found that children's vocalizations decreased in frequency during periods when they were beginning to reach for objects, to sit alone, or to walk. Apparently, "speech development is held in abeyance at the time when motor progress is most rapid" (44, 597).

EMOTIONAL DEVELOPMENT

Many of the neonate's responses—crying, grimacing, withdrawing, smiling—are at least overtly similar to older children's and adults' "emotional" responses. Despite these superficial resemblances, however, it is doubtful that young infants experience complex emotional states such as joy, anxiety, fear, elation, or disgust. By and large, these emotions develop somewhat later, as we shall see.

In the late 1920's, J. B. Watson, the behaviorist, theorized that there are three distinct unlearned or primary emotions, each with its own characteristic patterns of behavior and each evoked by specific environmental stimuli (70). According to his theory, fear reactions consisting of breath-catching, blinking of the eyelids, and crying, are instigated by loud sounds or sudden loss of support. Rage, the second primary emotion, involves stiffening of the body, slashing of the arms and legs, breath-holding, and crying, and is exhibited whenever the infant's movements are restrained. Love, the third unlearned emotion, characterized by stretching, cooing, and extension of the arms, is the response to stroking sensitive areas (genitals, lips, legs), rocking, and petting.

Subsequent research failed to support Watson's claim that emotional states in the infant can be differentiated by observing their overt responses. Contrary to his beliefs, trained adults (psychology graduate students, medical students, and nurses) could not differentiate these "primary emotions" from each other on the basis of the baby's overt behavior. Unless they were aware of the stimulating conditions, these observers disagreed among themselves more frequently than they agreed about the emotions being expressed. For example, infants' pain reactions (following needle pricks) were variously labeled discomfort, fear, hunger, or colic. Apparently, "differentiation of emotions is based on a knowledge of the character of the stimulating circumstances rather than upon differences in overt behavior" (55).

Furthermore, other investigators (55, 56, 66) found that specific stimuli such as loud noises, dropping, restriction of bodily activity, or stroking, did not universally instigate the responses Watson reported. Strong, sudden stimulation often produced much generalized, aimless muscle activity, including crying, but there were no consistent patterns of response following what Watson called "fear" and "rage" stimuli. Hence, it may be concluded that those conditions which Watson described do not initiate constant pattern responses in all infants.

Nevertheless, many aspects of emotional response are unlearned. Crying, flushing, thrashing about, and withdrawal of head and face—all involved in the expression of anger, fear, and rage—develop regardless of the child's experiences, as do smiling and laughing. The physiological, visceral concomitants of emotional excitement also appear to be unlearned. Infants as young as 3 months manifest the galvanic skin reflex (the sweat response which indicates decreasing skin resistance in emotional tension) following mild pain stimulation and loud sounds. This aspect of emotional response is functional in young infants, but it becomes more intense and is more easily aroused with increasing age (41).

Maturation of the child's sensory capacities also plays a role in emotional development, enabling him to discriminate stimuli such as smiling and frowning faces, pleasant and unpleasant voices, and friendly and angry gestures. Thus it has been found that babies between 2 and 6 months of age smile indiscriminately in response to nodding faces or masks, regardless of whether the facial expression is pleasant or unpleasant from an adult point of view. However, by the second half of the first year, infants usually show evidence of discrimination among people by smiling at those they know and perhaps acting shy with strangers (63).

Variations in constitutional factors may also influence the child's emotional reactivity. Neonates differ markedly from one another in susceptibility and responsiveness to all kinds of emotional stimulation, as they do in general activity level (cf. p. 92). Research indicates that children who are fearful and irritable immediately after birth often maintain these characteristics throughout early infancy (61). There are also vast individual differences among young infants in autonomic nervous system functioning and intensity of physiological changes during emotional episodes. Such stable differences in sensitivity, probably attributable to a combination of hereditary and prenatal influences, may well affect subsequent emotional development.

Even cursory observation shows that with advancing age, emotional response patterns become more varied, differentiated, and recognizable. Moreover, as the study of smiling in young infants indicates, emotional displays become more appropriate to the situation—at least as judged by adult standards. Bridges (8) suggests that specific emotions emerge from a general state of excitement or agitation in a rather definite and orderly developmental sequence. At about 3 weeks of age, distress, characterized by muscular tension, crying, and checked breathing, can be distinguished. Delight, manifested by smiles and cooing while being nursed or patted, becomes differentiated at 3 months, and laughter occurs at about 4 months.

At about 4 or 5 months of age, distress becomes further differentiated into behaviors indicative of fear (withdrawal, trembling, crying, rapid heart beat), disgust, or anger (see Figure 15). No distinct pattern of visceral responses corresponding to these different emotions has been detected.

Most observers agree with Bridges that as the infant matures, fear and anger responses become easier to differentiate and identify. Parents report that routine care such as dressing and bathing, deprivation of attention, and minor physical discomforts are frequent antecedents of anger in infants under a year of age.

The effectiveness of specific stimuli in eliciting anger and fear responses varies with duration and intensity of the stimuli, as well as with the child's physiological state and activity at the moment. For example, when frustrated by having their bottles withdrawn, infants who have consumed a great deal of milk react more slowly than those who had only a small amount (54). Infants are less likely to be startled by loud noises when they are being held securely than when they are alone in a strange situation.

From our point of view, changes in emotional responses are products

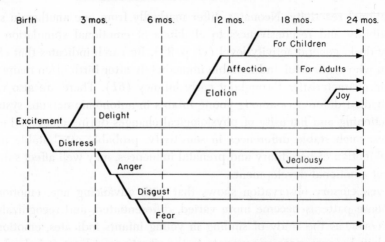

FIGURE 15.   Differentiation of emotions during the first two years. (After Dashiell in *Fundamentals of General Psychology*. Boston: Houghton Mifflin, 1949. From K. M. B. Bridges, "Emotional Development in Early Infancy." *Child Develop.* (1932), 3:324–341. With permission of Society for Research in Child Development.)

of complex interactions of maturation and learning. The child's ability to manifest increasingly differentiated emotional responses, such as delight, is at least partly dependent on physical maturation. On the other hand, the kinds of stimuli which become associated with these responses, and which tend to arouse them, will be greatly influenced by the child's learning experiences. Thus neonates do not manifest fear reactions in response to darkness, animals, or strangers, while many infants a few months old do. After noting that fear of snakes was characteristic of older children, but not of young infants, Jones and Jones concluded that "fear arises when we know enough to recognize the potential danger in the situation but have not advanced to the point of complete comprehension and control of the changing situation" (42, 143). Apparently infants must learn the significance of "strangeness" or snakes before these stimuli become effective in eliciting emotional responses. Detailed discussion of the role of learning in the development of basic emotions such as fear, affection, aggression, and anxiety is reserved for later chapters (cf. pp. 124–125; 206–207).

REFERENCES AND ADDITIONAL READING

1. Ames, L. B., The sequential patterning of prone progression in the human infant. *Genet. Psychol. Monogr.* (1937), 19:409–460.
2. Bakwin, H., and Bakwin, R. M., Body build in infants: II. The proportions

of the external dimensions of the healthy infant during the first year of life. *J. clin. Invest.* (1931), *10*: 369–375.

3. Bakwin, H., and Bakwin, R. M., Growth of thirty-two external dimensions during the first year of life. *J. Pediat.* (1936), 8:177–183.

4. Bakwin, H., and Patrick, T. W., Jr., The weight of Negro infants. *J. Pediat.* (1944), *24*: 405–407.

5. Bayley, N., The development of motor abilities during the first three years. *Monogr. Soc. Res. Child Develop.*, 1935, No. 1.

6. Breckenridge, M. E., and Vincent, E. L., *Child development. Physical and psychological growth through the school years.* Philadelphia: Saunders, 1949.

7. Bridges, K. M. B., *The social and emotional development in the pre-school child.* London: Kegan-Paul, 1931.

8. Bridges, K. M. B., Emotional development in early infancy. *Child Develop.* (1932), *3*:324–341.

9. Buhler, C., *The first year of life* (Trans. by Greenberg and Ripin). New York: Day, 1930.

10. Cameron, N., and Magaret, A., *Behavior pathology.* Boston: Houghton Mifflin, 1951.

11. Cattell, P., *The measurement of intelligence of infants and young children.* New York: The Psychological Corporation, 1940.

12. Chase, W. P., Color vision in infants. *J. exp. Psychol.* (1937), *20*: 203–222.

13. Chen, H. P., and Irwin, O. C., Infant speech: vowel and consonant types. *J. Speech Disorders* (1946), *11*:27–29.

14. Chen, H. P., and Irwin, O. C., Development of speech during infancy: curve of differential percentage. *J. exp. Psychol.* (1946), 36:522–525.

15. Crudden, C. H., Reactions of newborn infants to thermal stimuli under constant tactual conditions. *J. exp. Psychol.* (1937), *20*: 350–370.

16. Dennis, W., A description and classification of the responses of the newborn infant. *Psychol. Bull.* (1934), *31*:5–22.

17. Dennis, W., Infant development under conditions of restricted practice and of minimum social stimulation. *Genet. psychol. Monogr.* (1941), *23*: 143–191.

18. Dennis, W., and Dennis, M. G., The effect of cradling practices upon the onset of walking in Hopi children. *J. genet. Psychol.* (1940), 56:77–86.

19. Disher, D. R., The reactions of newborn infants to chemical stimuli administered nasally. *Ohio State Univer. Stud., Contr. Psychol.*, No. 12, 1934, pp. 1–52.

20. Fries, M. E., and Lewi, B., Interrelated factors in development: a study of pregnancy, labor, delivery, lying-in period, and childhood. *Am. J. Orthopsychiat.* (1938), 8:726–752.

21. Gesell, A., The ontogenesis of infant behavior, in L. Carmichael (ed.), *Manual of child psychology,* 2nd ed. New York: Wiley, 1954, pp. 335–373.

22. Gesell, A., and Amatruda, C. S., *Developmental diagnosis: normal and abnormal child development.* New York: Hoeber, 1941.

23. Gesell, A., Halverson, H. M., Thompson, H., Ilg, F. L., Costner, B. M.,

Ames, L. B., and Amatruda, C. S., *The first five years of life: a guide to the study of the preschool child.* New York: Harper, 1940.

24. Gesell, A., and Thompson, H., Learning and growth in identical infant twins: an experimental study by the method of co-twin control. *Genet. Psychol. Monogr.* (1929), 5:1–124.

25. Gesell, A., and Thompson, H., *The psychology of early growth.* New York: Macmillan, 1938.

26. Halverson, H. M., An experimental study of prehension in infants by means of systematic cinema records. *Genet. Psychol. Monogr.* (1931), 10: 107–286.

27. Halverson, H. M., Complications of the early grasping reactions. *Psychol. Monogr.* (1936), 47:47–63.

28. Irwin, O. C., The amount and nature of activities of newborn infants under constant external stimulating conditions during the first ten days of life. *Genet. Psychol. Monogr.* (1930), 8:1–92.

29. Irwin, O. C., Proximo-distal differentiation of limbs in young organisms. *Psychol. Rev.* (1933), 40:467–477.

30. Irwin, O. C., Development of speech during infancy: curve of phonemic frequencies. *J. exp. Psychol.* (1947), 37:187–193.

31. Irwin, O. C., Infant speech: consonantal sounds according to place of articulation. *J. Speech Disorders* (1947), 12:397–401.

32. Irwin, O. C., Infant speech: consonant sounds according to manner of articulaton. *J. Speech Disorders* (1947), 12:402–404.

33. Irwin, O. C., Infant speech: development of vowel sounds. *J. Speech Hearing Disorders* (1948), 13:31–34.

34. Irwin, O. C., Infant speech: the effect of family occupational status and of age on sound frequency. *J. Speech Hearing Disorders* (1948), 13: 320–323.

35. Irwin, O. C., Infant speech: speech sound development of sibling and only infants. *J. exp. Psychol.* (1948), 38:600–602.

36. Irwin, O. C., Speech development in the young child: 2. Some factors related to the speech development of the infant and young child. *J. Speech Hearing Disorders* (1952), 17:269–279.

37. Irwin, O. C., and Chen, H. P., Infant speech: vowel and consonant frequency. *J. Speech Disorders* (1946), 11:123–125.

38. Irwin, O. C., and Chen, H. P., Development of speech during infancy: curve of phonemic types. *J. exp. Psychol.* (1946), 36:431–436.

39. Irwin, O. C., and Curry, F., Vowel elements in the crying vocalization of infants under ten days of age. *Child Develop.* (1941), 12:99–109.

40. Jensen, K., Differential reactions to taste and temperature stimuli in newborn infants. *Genet. psychol. Monogr.* (1932), 12:363–479.

41. Jones, H. H., The galvanic skin reflex in infancy. *Child Develop.* (1930), 1:106–110.

42. Jones, H. E., and Jones, M. C., Fear, *Childhood Educ.* (1928), 5:136–143.

43. Ling, B. C., I. A genetic study of sustained visual fixation and associated behavior in the human infant from birth to six months. *J. genet. Psychol.* (1942), 61:227–277.

44. McCarthy, D., Language development in children, in L. Carmichael (ed.), *Manual of child psychology*, 2nd ed. New York: Wiley, 1954, pp. 492–630.
45. McGraw, M. B., *Growth: a Study of Johnny and Jimmy*. New York: Appleton-Century, 1935.
46. McGraw, M. B., Maturation of behavior, in L. Carmichael (ed.), *Manual of child psychology*. New York: Wiley, 1946, pp. 332–369.
47. Miller, G. A., *Language and communication*. New York: McGraw-Hill, 1951.
48. Munn, N. L., *Psychological development: an introduction to genetic psychology*. Boston: Houghton-Mifflin, 1938.
49. Pinneau, S. R., A critique of the articles by Margaret Ribble. *Child Develop.* (1950), *21*:203–228.
50. Pratt, K. C., The effects of repeated auditory stimulation upon the general activity of newborn infants. *J. genet. Psychol.* (1934), *44*:96–116.
51. Pratt, K. C., The effects of repeated visual stimulation on the activity of newborn infants. *J. genet. Psychol.* (1934), *44*:117–126.
52. Pratt, K. C., The neonate, in L. Carmichael (ed.), *Manual of child psychology*, 2nd ed. New York: Wiley, 1954, pp. 215–291.
53. Pratt, K. C., Nelson, A. K., and Sun, K. H., The behavior of the newborn infant. *Ohio State Univer. Stud., Contr. Psychol.*, No. 10, 1930.
54. Sears, R. R., and Sears, P. S., Minor studies of aggression: V. Strength of frustration-reaction as a function of strength of drive. *J. Psychol.* (1949), 9:297–300.
55. Sherman, M., The differentiation of emotional responses in infants: I. Judgments of emotional response from motion-picture views and from actual observation. *J. comp. Psychol.* (1927), 7:265–284.
56. Sherman, M., The differentiation of emotional responses in infants: II. The ability of observers to judge the emotional characteristics of the crying of infants and of the voice of the adult. *J. comp. Psychol.* (1927), 7:335–351.
57. Sherman, M., and Sherman, I. C., Sensori-motor responses in infants. *J. comp. Psychol.* (1925), 5:53–68.
58. Sherman, M., Sherman, I. C., and Flory, C. D., Infant behavior, *Comp. Psychol. Monogr.* (1936), *12*:No. 4.
59. Shirley, M. M., *The first two years, a study of twenty-five babies:* Vol. I. *Postural and locomotor development. Inst. Child Welfare Monogr. Ser. No.* 6. Minneapolis: University of Minnesota Press, 1933.
60. Shirley, M. M., *The first two years, a study of twenty-five babies:* Vol. II. *Intellectual development. Inst. Child Welfare Monogr. Ser. No. 8.* Minneapolis: University of Minnesota Press, 1933.
61. Shirley, M. M., The first two years, a study of twenty-five babies: Vol. III. Personality manifestations. *Inst. Child Welfare Monogr. Ser., No. 8.* Minneapolis: University of Minnesota Press, 1933.
62. Smith, M. E., An investigation of the development of the sentence and the extent of vocabulary in young children. *Univer. Iowa Stud. Child Welfare* (1926), *3*:No. 5.
63. Spitz, R. A., and Wolf, K. M., The smiling response: A contribution to the ontogenesis of social relations. *Genet. Psych. Monogr.* (1946), *34*:57–125.

64. Spock, B., *The pocket book of baby and child care.* New York: Pocket Books, 1950.

65. Stubbs, E. M., The effect of the factors of duration, intensity, and pitch of sound stimuli on the responses of newborn infants. *Univer. Iowa Stud. Child Welfare* (1934), 9, No. 4, pp. 75–135.

66. Taylor, J. H., Innate emotional responses in infants. *Ohio State Univ. Stud. Contr. Psychol.*, 1934, No. 12, pp. 69–81.

67. Terman, L. M., et al., *Genetic studies of genius: Vol. I. Mental and physical traits of a thousand gifted children.* Stanford University: Stanford University Press, 1925.

68. Thompson, G. G., *Child psychology: growth trends in psychological adjustment.* Boston: Houghton Mifflin, 1952.

69. Thompson, H., Physical growth, in L. Carmichael (ed.), *Manual of child psychology*, 2nd ed. New York: Wiley, 1954, pp. 292–334.

70. Watson, J. B., *Psychology from the standpoint of a behaviorist.* Philadelphia: Lippincott, 1924.

Chapter 5

LEARNING

In previous chapters we have traced the development of the individual from conception to birth. We have seen how the genetic inheritance and the intrauterine environment of the child can affect his biological structure and functioning as he progresses from fertilized ovum to embryo, to fetus, and finally to infant.

The neonate, as we have seen, is already a highly complex organism, but in comparison with the adult or adolescent, he appears relatively simple. The arm flexion of the neonate is a pretty gross, undifferentiated response in comparison with the highly skilled operations of the telegrapher. The visual pursuit capacities of the infant are quite different from those of the airplane spotter. And the needs of the infant—for food, for water, for warmth—appear refreshingly simple. He has none of the subtle and often conflicting needs that may drive adults to pursue such goals as social status, professional or artistic accomplishment, the welfare of other human beings, or even self-destruction.

The development of such needs and response skills may be influenced or limited by hereditarily determined forces of maturation, but they are not the direct result of such forces. They must be learned. Thus while some persons may have more native aptitude than others for becoming good telegraphers, because of superior neuromuscular organization, no amount of aptitude will take the place of systematic training in telegraphy. Similarly, a child with a hereditarily determined slow growth rate may be at a greater disadvantage in athletic competition than the large, well-developed child. Thus he may be more likely to develop a need for intellectual success to compensate for his lack of athletic skill. But this need is nevertheless a learned one.

We shall be particularly concerned with learned needs throughout this book. They are among the most important sources of motivation in human beings, and are of great significance in determining the child's chances for satisfaction and effectiveness, or for ineffectiveness and neurotic misery. In our society most individuals are able to satisfy their basic needs for food, for rest, even for sexual outlet. Finding satisfaction for their varied and often conflicting learned needs is likely to be a more difficult matter. It is often easier to satisfy the physiological hunger for food than the learned hunger for love and affection, or to find rest for one's body than to find peace of mind in the face of learned anxieties.

It becomes necessary, then, to gain some understanding of the ways in which learning occurs if we are to understand a major segment of human behavior.

WHAT IS LEARNING?

Learning has been defined by Hilgard (7) as "The process by which an activity originates or is changed through training procedures (whether in the laboratory or in the natural environment) as distinguished from changes not attributable to training."

A child who was previously unable to skip rope, but who became able to skip after being trained in this socially useful bit of behavior by an older brother, may be said to have demonstrated learning. Obviously, however, all behavior changes are not the result of learning: "If a behavior sequence matures through regular stages irrespective of intervening practice, the behavior is said to develop through maturation and not through learning" (7). As we have already seen (cf. pp. 94–96), such aspects of development as beginning to walk are relatively unaffected by practice (i.e., will occur whether or not the child gets any kind of special training). Thus, they are primarily the result of maturation rather than learning.

As these two illustrations suggest, "growth is the chief competitor of learning as a modifier of behavior" (7). At times, it is quite easy to determine whether a particular modification of behavior is primarily due to growth or to learning. Changes in behavior stemming directly from change in the child's musculoskeletal structure are readily attributable to the effects of maturation. On the other hand we can be equally sure that a child has *learned* to play hopscotch or to recite a poem.

There are other types of behavior, however, in which the relative importance of growth and environment are more difficult to determine. In some cases, only carefully controlled observation or experiment will tell us whether a particular change is primarily the result of maturation or of learning. The child's development of walking, discussed in the last chapter, provides a case in point (cf. pp. 94–96).

The extent to which this behavior is dependent on previous practice or on "maturational permission" is not immediately obvious. Only by comparing children who have been allowed to develop normally with those whose opportunities for practice have been restricted can the relative contributions of learning and maturation be determined. It will be recalled that Dennis found that the Hopi babies who had been bound to their cradleboards almost from birth walked as soon as those who had been allowed more freedom of movement. This suggested that the major determinant of this type of behavior is maturation.

On the other hand, some activities, often thought to be due to maturational factors alone, are actually learned. For example, recent research by Davis, Sears, et al. (4) suggests that the human infant's need to suck may be largely the result of learning. Until recently, many psychoanalysts and child psychologists have considered the need to suck to be primarily a physiologically determined need, arising in the course of maturation.

A knowledge of the relative importance of normal growth factors, as contrasted with learning experience, is often of considerable practical importance. As we shall see later, the problem of toilet training (cf. pp. 193–202) not infrequently produces a crisis in the relations between mother and child. Because of cultural pressures—or deep-seated personal needs for cleanliness, not to mention a realistic aversion to washing diapers—the mother may want to toilet train her child early. If her efforts meet with little success, she may become angry at the child for his apparent refusal to coöperate, and a deterioration of the relationship between mother and child may result.

In a number of cases, such crises could have been prevented if the mother had been aware that the child was not physiologically ready to assume control of his bladder or bowels. The argument that other children have been trained by a certain age does not rule out the possibility that a particular child may not be sufficiently mature, since there are great individual differences in the ages at which the child becomes Spock physiologically ready to assume this control (22). For example, while most babies are not physiologically mature enough to assume bladder control before about 15 months of age, an occasional baby, usually a girl, may be ready at 10 months. An occasional child, most likely a boy, may as late as not be ready until nearly 2 years of age (22).

WHEN DOES LEARNING BEGIN?

While most of a child's learning follows birth, it is probable that some learning does occur in the prenatal period. The difficulty of investigating learning in the fetus is obvious, and has served to discourage many investigators, but some progress has been reported. In an ingenious experiment, Spelt (20) has reported some success. He observed that fetuses between the age of 6½ and 8½ months responded with vigorous movements if a clapper was sounded near the mother's body. On the other hand, they did not respond if a vibrator was applied to the mother's abdomen. In an effort to determine whether the fetus could be taught to respond to this vibration, he repeatedly presented the stimulus of vibration, followed 5 seconds later by the sound of the clapper. By the time he had presented 100 such paired stimuli, he found that the infant was responding to the tactile vibration alone. Since the effect of the vibrator in producing the movement responses "originated through training procedures," learning may be said to have taken place, though of course of a simple sort.

While it has proved difficult to obtain evidence of fetal learning, there are clear indications that the neonate is capable of rudimentary learning even when only a few days old.

Mothers often report signs of learning within a week or so after birth. For example, a hungry, crying baby only a few days old may cease his crying as soon as he is picked up and held in his mother's arms, whereas previously he became quiet only when actually fed. Now the preparatory steps, being picked up and held, produce quiet. Thus, it might appear that the response of becoming quiet when he was picked up was learned. However, ". . . it is possible that the experience of being picked up and held would at the later age have had a great effect in itself, even if not previously associated with the experience of being fed" (10). In other words, the change in behavior might conceivably be the result of maturation rather than learning.

More conclusive evidence of very early learning in relation to feeding is reported by Marquis (13). Working with 10 infants between 2 and 9 days of age, she sounded a buzzer in their presence 5 seconds prior to each feeding. Within 5 days after the beginning of training, 8 of these infants began to exhibit sucking and mouth opening responses as soon as they heard the buzzer. She also noted that the sound of the buzzer tended to reduce crying and general activity. Four control infants who had also been subjected to the sound of the buzzer, but who were not fed immediately afterward, did not manifest these behaviors in response to the buzzer.

The controlled nature of this experiment rules out maturation as an explanation of the behavior change, for while both groups of infants were continuing to mature at the same rate, only the group that was given training learned to respond to the buzzer.

PRINCIPLES OF LEARNING

Learning has long been one of the primary concerns of psychologists. Before child psychology had begun to develop as an independent discipline, psychologists were hard at work attempting to understand how people and animals learn.

As a result, a tremendous body of empirical information and theoretical explanation has been developed over the years. It is only fair to point out to the student, however, that despite the magnitude of the work performed to date, there are still many troublesome questions. In the discussion which follows we have attempted to stress those concepts which at present seem to us most useful in understanding and predicting human learning.

Miller and Dollard (15) maintain that for an individual to learn something, four fundamental conditions are required: The individual must want something, notice something, do something, and get something. Or, in more technical language, there must be: (1) a drive, or need, (2) a distinctive stimulus, or cue, (3) a response, whether it be a motor act, a thought, or a physiological change, (4) a reward, or reinforcement.

At the beginning of Marquis' experiment, the cue of the buzzer did not provoke the response of sucking. At the end of the experiment, however, this cue did tend to provoke the response. The learning consisted of the establishment of a connection, or association, between the cue and the response. If the stimulus of the buzzer had not been presented, or if it had not been sufficiently distinctive to be noticed, and if the response had not been made, learning obviously could not have occurred. This example of learning illustrates the role of cue and response as essential requirements of the learning situation.

But what about the other two postulated essentials of learning, drive or need, and reward? At least in this particular situation these conditions were also satisfied. The child had a drive, hunger, and a subsequent reward, food. This example, of course, does not demonstrate that learning always requires the presence of a need and a subsequent reward. There may be some kinds of learning which can occur without them (16). This possibility will be discussed later. At the moment, however, it is enough to state our conviction that need and reward are essential to the development of most social learning. For this reason, it seems important to discuss the meaning of these terms in greater detail before proceeding.

Drive

For our purposes, drives [1] may be defined as states of tension resulting from conditions of deprivation or disequilibrium within the individual, whether physiological or psychological in nature. Often these states of tension lead to activity aimed at satisfying the individual's needs. Thus the hungry person may end up by making a restless midnight pilgrimage to the icebox. However, such is not always the case. An adolescent, for example, may vaguely feel the tensions of unsatisfied sexual needs, but may not respond with acts aimed at satisfying them.

Simple examples of drive include hunger, thirst, sex, and pain. All these drives may be aroused because of the way people are constructed. For this reason such drives are referred to as innate drives, or more commonly *primary drives*.

There are, of course, other drives besides primary ones. There is nothing innate about the need for social status, for security, for love from one's mother, for acceptance as one of the gang. Such drives are in themselves learned. In common with primary drives, however, *learned* drives may serve as the motivating conditions of future learning.

Reward

Reward or reinforcement is defined in terms of drive reduction. If something produces a reduction in existing drives (satisfies a need), it is said to have reward value. Thus food may be said to have reward value if a person is hungry. Once a person has eaten his fill, however, food will no longer constitute a reward. Neither will food serve as a reward if the person happens to be only thirsty or cold or tired.

Such things as food, water, or sleep are called *primary rewards* when they lead to the reduction of primary drive. But just as there are learned drives, there are also learned rewards. Money has no reward value for a

---

[1] In our discussion, the words drive and need will be used interchangeably. Theoretically, however, a distinction may be made between the two terms. When an individual needs something in order to maintain his physiological or psychological balance, a strong state of drive almost always occurs. Thus when an individual's existence is threatened by a need for food, strong stimuli are set in motion which serve as warnings, and lead the person to act. Drives in most cases act as built-in safety devices to protect the individual from the effects of unsatisfied needs. This is not always true, however, as in the case of carbon monoxide poisoning. The individual needs oxygen but since this need does not produce warning drive stimuli, the individual may simply become comatose and die. Fortunately for the continued existence of the human race, however, most needs produce increases in drive.

baby, or for an Amazonian head hunter. Such reward values have to be learned.

Perhaps a few examples will help to illustrate these principles. A newborn child is hungry. The drive of hunger impels him to action, and guided by the mother, and aided by the sucking reflex, he begins to make sucking responses. These lead to the ingestion of milk and a consequent reduction in hunger drive. Learning has begun. Association between the cues of the sight and feel of the mother's breast and responses of seeking the breast and sucking have started to develop.

Or let us consider another example, toilet training. Motivated by a learned need for his mother's approval, a child may with a little coaching begin to associate the cues of a full bladder with the complex series of responses which are necessary to guide him to the bathroom. Although initially accidents are likely to occur, the child will soon learn to respond unerringly to bladder cues with a successful trip to the bathroom.

Other sources of motivation, such as pain, may lead to learning in the young child. For example, a young child in the course of exploratory crawling about the living room floor may discover an electric outlet and try putting his finger in it. As a result, he gets a painful shock. He quickly draws his hand away and he is rewarded by a rapid reduction in pain. The cue of the sight of the electric outlet quickly tends to become associated with the response of *withdrawing* his hand. In a similar fashion, the child eventually learns to avoid rather than to approach such other household dangers as hot stoves and steaming radiators (*15*).

One fact, however, becomes rapidly apparent when we consider such examples of learning, namely, that learning is not an all-or-none affair. In all the above examples the learning takes place gradually. The infant becomes increasingly more proficient in pursuit of the mother's breast. The older child begins to make fewer errors in his toilet training, and to get shocked less frequently by the electric outlets. A number of additional principles of learning are necessary to account for the gradual nature of learning, as well as for related phenomena such as unlearning (i.e., the disappearance of learned responses). A number of these principles will be discussed.

PRINCIPLE OF REINFORCEMENT. The strength of the bond between a cue and a response (i.e., habit strength—the likelihood that the cue will elicit the response) varies as a function of the amount of reward (*15*). The total amount of reward, can, of course, be increased in several ways. For one thing, the individual can be given a greater number of trials in which the response is rewarded. Or he can be given a greater amount of reward on each trial. (It should be pointed out in this connection that the amount of reward it is possible to give on any one trial will be a function of the strength of the drive operating at the moment. For example, if a person is only hungry enough for a glass of milk, we cannot increase the amount of reward by giving him a gallon of milk to drink. After the first glass, he will no longer be hungry, and future glasses will have no rewarding value because there is no drive left to be reduced.)

A related principle, referred to as the *gradient of reinforcement* (9) states that the more immediately the reward follows the response, the stronger will be the bond between the cue and the response.

Let us assume that we want to teach a child to look both ways before crossing the street. In accordance with the principles just discussed, we should then reward the response of looking as soon as it occurs (gradient of reinforcement), and we should repeat this procedure many times, making sure each time that the reward is a really satisfying one to the child (amount of reward).

If such a procedure is followed, the child's chances of learning always to make the correct response will be much greater than if we only occasionally reward the child for looking; use a trivial reward; or delay giving the reward until after the child is through playing and has come into the house.

EXTINCTION. A corollary of the principle of reinforcement is the principle of extinction. As Miller and Dollard phrase it, "reinforcement is essential to the learning of a habit; it is also essential to the maintenance of the habit. When a learned response is repeated without reinforcement the strength of the tendency to perform that response undergoes a progressive decrease. This decrement is called . . . extinction" (15). In other words, if the making of a learned response ceases to be rewarded, it will be unlearned.

The child in the above example may appear to have learned a stop-look-and-listen response quite thoroughly. But without occasional later reward from the mother, he is likely eventually to become neglectful and to fail to make the response.

Like learning, extinction is for the most part a gradual process. The number of unrewarded responses required to produce extinction will be a function of the strength of the original learning. If, in the above example, the child's stop-and-look-training has been of the recommended type, he will be much more resistant to extinction than if his training had not followed these principles. Extinction will also be slower when the drive involved is high. If the drive in this case is a need for maternal approval, the child who is more concerned with such approval at the moment is less likely to forget to stop and look than a child who is less concerned about his mother's reactions.

GENERALIZATION AND DISCRIMINATION. When a child has been trained to avoid one hot radiator, he will, fortunately, also tend to avoid other similar radiators. This tendency to make the response learned to one stimulus to another similar stimulus without specific reinforcements is called *stimulus generalization* (9, 15). The tendency to generalize is a highly useful one, since no two stimulus situations are ever quite the same. Unless we generalized, we could hardly ever profit from past experience. Of course, generalization can have its negative side also. For example, if a child has learned to respond to a particular teacher with hatred because she has been cruel and rejecting toward him, he is then likely to generalize this response to all other teachers, regardless of whether hatred of these teachers is justified or not.

Initially generalization is likely to be extensive. A child who has learned to attach the label *dog* to the family pet is likely to extend this label to cover all four-footed animals he meets. Thus the first cow or horse or cat he meets is likely also to be called *dog*. However, the child is likely to find that the response *dog* to the sight of actual dogs is consistently rewarded, while the generalized response *dog* to cows, horses, and cats, is not rewarded. As a result, the extent of the generalization will gradually decrease until finally it is (correctly) limited only to dogs. This learned correction to overgeneralization is called *discrimination* (15) and is, of course, based on extinction of incorrectly generalized responses.

ANTICIPATORY RESPONSE. In the Marquis experiment, as a consequence of the pairing of the buzzer and food, the response of sucking became attached to the cue of the buzzer and would occur before the infant received any food. Originally these responses would occur only at the time food was presented. What happened in the course of the experiment was that the responses of sucking and ceasing crying began to appear earlier in the response sequence—to become anticipatory. The occurrence of these *anticipatory responses* (15) is common to many examples of learning. The child learning to ride a bicycle originally may lean to one side only after almost falling on the other. Gradually, however, he will learn to lean slightly in an opposite direction as soon as the bicycle begins to fall. The rewarded responses to the stimuli of falling way over will tend to generalize to the similar stimuli of falling slightly, and hence will become anticipatory. All anticipatory responses however, are not so useful—as for example, the case of a child learning to dive. Originally, the child will close his eyes only after he has been struck painfully by the water. Gradually, however, this response is likely to become more and more anticipatory until the child goes to the end of the board, closes his eyes, and hopes.

The applicability of the basic conditions of learning, and of the supplementary principles described above, to the problem of understanding the child's psychological development will be stressed throughout the book.

Response Hierarchies

In discussing various instances of learning, psychologists are likely to use such terms as *innate, initial,* and *resultant response hierarchies* (15). Since we will be dealing with these concepts later in the book, their meaning should be explained. This can best be done through a series of examples.

Let us take the case of the young child who is to be toilet trained. Before this training, the cue of a full bladder is most likely to lead to prompt urination, with little regard for the social amenities. It may, of course, also lead to other responses—perhaps squirming, or general restlessness. It almost certainly will not lead to a trip to the bathroom. As Miller and Dollard point out, we may arrange such pretraining responses "in the order of their probability of occurrence, and call this the *initial hierarchy* of responses" (15).

After successful toilet training, however, this order of responses will be changed. The cue of a full bladder will now be much more likely to lead to trips to the bathroom than to immediate urination. "The new hierarchy produced by learning may be called the *resultant hierarchy*" (15).

"Usually the order of responses in an initial hierarchy is the resultant of previous learning in similar situations. In the cases in which the order of response is primarily determined not by learning, but by hereditary factors, the initial hierarchy may be called the *innate hierarchy*" (15). As we shall see in the following chapter, some sounds (e.g., *i* as in bit) occupy a higher position in the infant's innate hierarchy than others (e.g., *b*). Thus it is much easier for the infant to learn to respond to various cues (for example, the sight of its mother's face, or the approach of its bottle) with certain sounds than with others.

The changed order of responses between the *initial* and *resultant hierarchies* is an evidence of learning. It is an indication that some of the responses in the initial hierarchy have been rewarded more than others, and thus have become better learned (i.e., have acquired greater "habit strength"), and are more likely to occur.

The concept of *hierarchy of response* has numerous practical implications, as we shall see later in the book. We shall give but one example here. A child of 5 may have learned that the most frequently rewarded method of attracting his parents was by asking questions. Thus this response became high in his hierarchy of responses in this situation. However, his parents may suddenly have become too busy to answer his questions for some reason (possibly because they are busy with a new baby, or because they are preoccupied with their own worries). They may then cease to reward the response of asking questions. As a result, this learned response may become weaker and fall to a lower position in the child's response hierarchy. Older responses, which have been rewarded earlier in life, such as crying or temper tantrums, may eventually become the strongest in the response hierarchy, and the most likely to occur. Such phenomena as the above may be noted frequently in everyday life, and are referred to by psychologists and psychoanalysts as *regression*.

LEARNING IN THE NEONATE

As we have already seen, the neonate is a considerably simpler individual than the adult. The number of responses he can learn to attach to cues are many fewer than the adult's. In some instances he has not matured enough to be physically capable of a particular response. In other instances, he may be unable to make a response because he lacks the proper groundwork for it. Many complex behaviors require prior training in simpler, but related behaviors—training that the neonate will not have had. For example, before one can learn to write, he must have previously learned to control the movement of his arms in space and to grasp and hold objects in his hands.

Furthermore, there is evidence that his ability to distinguish among incoming stimuli is considerably less developed than in the adult. For example, as we saw in the previous chapter, color vision appears to be considerably less well developed in the infant than in the adult. The same thing appears true of the gustatory or taste sense and to some degree of audition and pain.

In contrast to the adult, the neonate's motivational repertoire is limited to such primary drives as hunger, thirst, pain, fatigue, air hunger, thermal stimulation, defecation, and urination. Beginning with these basic needs, he must go on to develop the numerous *learned drives and rewards* which play such a dominant role in the determination of later childhood and adult behavior. We have already seen several examples of the ways in which learning may occur through the reinforcement of primary drive. Now let us turn our attention to the ways in which learned needs and rewards develop.

LEARNED NEED AND REWARD

Earlier we defined drives as states of tension arising in the individual as a result of internal conditions of deprivation or disequilibrium. This does not mean, however, that we are always able to identify the nature of the deprivation when we use the term *drive*.

Let us take the case of hunger. What steps do we actually go through in arriving at the concept of hunger as a primary drive? We observe that a person has been without food for a long period of time; that as the period of deprivation increases, the person becomes restless; that if he encounters and eats food, he ceases being restless, and may even lie down and take a nap. In order to account for this sequence of events, we postulated or inferred the existence of a state of tension, or drive, stemming from food deprivation. While a primary drive such as hunger, because of its obviously physiological nature and because of our own subjective feelings under conditions of deprivation, seems very real to us, no one has actually observed or measured it.

Drive is simply a useful scientific construct, similar to the concept of force in physics, "a hypothetical process, the occurrence of which is imagined in order to account for certain objective and subjective facts" (17). This becomes more apparent when we turn our attention to the learned drives (such as anxiety or the need for affection) and learned rewards (such as money or parental praise). The concept of learned drive has been implicit in the thinking of men for a long time. Literature is filled with speculation about the kind and number of learned drives that are important as determinants of man's behavior. The arguments among various authors as to man's most important needs provide ample proof of their inferential character.

Oddly enough, the importance of motivation received more recognition for a long time from literature than from psychology. The early philosopher-psychologists, such as John Locke, were too busy trying to construct laws explaining how one thought became connected to another, to pay much attention to the role of people's needs as a determinant of their behavior (*1*).

Although most psychologists today are impressed with the importance of drives or needs, there is still considerable disagreement about how to *Classification* categorize man's important needs. On the one hand, there are the ortho- *schemes* dox psychoanalysts, who feel that man's truly basic needs are few and that most other apparent needs are really derivatives of these basic needs.

On the other hand, we have some extreme individuals who postulate great numbers of drives, inferring them directly from overt behavior. Such persons are likely to speak of drives for chocolate candy, for western movies, or even for a certain kind of cornflakes. There is little question that these are examples of acquired appetites, and hence drives. But the extent of their importance in trying to understand the individual as a whole, and the practicability of including them in lists of important needs seems open to serious question.

The problem of the list maker, it seems to us, is a two-sided one: (1) he must concentrate on needs or drives which are sufficiently important and basic in the individual personality to serve as an explanatory and unifying principle for a variety of specific behaviors. This is what the psychoanalysts have tried to do. But, (2), he must also insure that these needs are sufficiently specific and diverse so that the behavioral data to which they are intended to apply do not have to be unduly tortured in order to make them fit an oversimplified list of needs.

Such a problem obviously has no definitive solution. There is no ultimately perfect list of learned needs waiting to be discovered. But there can be lists which are of greater or less utility. The practical problem of making such lists is further complicated, however, by the general perversity of human personality. The dictum of psychoanalysis that the needs behind behavior are not always what they seem to be has by now been pretty well accepted by most psychologists.

It has often been found in the child guidance clinic, for example, that the child who protests the loudest his great love for his mother may actually be concealing unconscious feelings of hostility toward her. It is as though he were protecting himself and others from the realization of his unacceptable hostile feelings by saying, "How could I possibly hate my mother? Just look at how much I am doing to show that I love her; see how worried I am that something might happen to her." Freud recognized the principle that one feeling or need may actually conceal its opposite, and labeled the process *reaction formation.*

Man is also often incredibly ingenious in inventing socially acceptable reasons for behavior which may actually have been motivated by quite different needs. Few people will say that they want to become president of a club simply to gain power over others. They will be more likely to say that they want to be able to serve their fellows. Similarly, many parents will not admit to spanking a child because he has made them angry. They will say that they are doing it "for his own good."

In the above examples, both the acceptable and unacceptable reasons may actually have been involved. The point is that in conceptualizing our motivations to ourselves and others, we tend to focus only on those which are socially or personally acceptable, ignoring those which are not. This process has been labeled _rationalization_ by Jung (*11*) the Swiss psychoanalyst.

By penetrating the surface of behavior, psychoanalysis has convincingly demonstrated that man may be little aware of some of his principal needs. Indeed, the function of many of the so-called defense mechanisms postulated by the psychoanalyst—such as rationalization, reaction formation, and others—is largely to protect the individual from becoming painfully aware of some of his own needs. In short, we have to recognize that (1) a person may have needs which he himself cannot recognize (i.e., unconscious needs), as well as conscious needs that he can recognize; and (2), that he is capable of resorting to many ingenious subterfuges in his conscious thinking and overt behavior, in order to protect himself from becoming aware of the nature of these unconscious needs. Both of these facts sometimes make it difficult to infer a person's drives from what he says or does.

A USEFUL SYSTEM OF NEEDS

It is probably no coincidence, therefore, that the most helpful classifications of needs which have been proposed thus far have come from psychologists who have been trained in scientific methodology and who are also experienced in the complexities of psychotherapy—the "window of the higher mental life" (*5*). Having watched the development of behavior "from the inside looking out" such psychologists are not likely to accept a superficially reasonable explanation of behavior. At the same time, because of their scientific training, they are likely to insist on precision and meaningfulness in their definitions.

One such writer, Henry Murray (*17*) until recently director of the Harvard Psychological Clinic, has proposed a list of needs which is useful in trying to understand why people behave as they do.

Some of these needs, such as respiration (breathing), water, food, sex, lactation, urination, heat avoidance, cold avoidance (i.e., needs to avoid hot and cold) are called *viscerogenic*. We call them primary drives. Others, which we would call learned drives, are included by Murray under the title of *secondary* or *psychogenic* needs. Some examples are:

n [i.e., need] Acquisition (acquisitive attitudes). To gain position and property. To grasp, snatch, or steal things. To bargain or gamble. To work for money or goods.

n Order (orderly attitude). To arrange, organize, put away objects. To be tidy and clean. To be scrupulously precise.

n Superiority (ambitious attitudes). This has been broken up into two needs. The n Achievement (will to power over things, people, and ideas) and the n Recognition (efforts to gain approval and high social status).

n Dominance (dominative attitude). To influence or control others. To persuade, prohibit, dictate. To lead and direct. To restrain. To organize the behavior of a group.

n Deference (deferent attitude). To admire and willingly follow a superior allied person. To cöoperate with a leader. To serve gladly.

n Affiliation (affiliative attitude). To form friendships and associations. To greet, join, and live with others. To cöoperate and converse socially with others. To love, to join groups.

n Nurturance (nurturant attitude). To nourish, aid or protect a helpless person. To express sympathy. To "mother" a child.

n Succorance (succorant attitude). To seek aid, protection or sympathy. To cry for help. To plead for mercy. To adhere to an affectionate, nurturant parent. To be dependent.

n Aggression (aggressive attitude). To assault or injure an individual. To murder. To belittle, harm, or blame, accuse or maliciously ridicule a person. To punish severely. Sadism.

n Abasement (abasive attitude). To surrender. To comply and accept punishment. To apologize, confess, atone. Self-depreciation. Masochism.

In attempting to describe an individual's need system, it is important not only to point out the kinds of needs or drives that seem particularly important for him, but also the kinds of stimuli that arouse these needs, and the kind of rewards that satisfy them. Thus it is of little value simply to say that an individual has strong needs for dominance and succorance. It would make a great deal of difference in a child's personality adjustment whether the need for dominance was primarily aroused by other boys and men and satisfied primarily in competition with them, while the need for succorance was primarily aroused by women; or whether the reverse was true.

ANXIETY—AN EXAMPLE OF LEARNED DRIVE

Fear, or anxiety as it is often called when its source is not immediately apparent (*14*), will serve as a useful illustration of the way in which drives are learned. It has been the subject of more experimental investigation than other learned drives, and is of great importance as a determiner of human behavior. It is the one learned drive which is most likely to conflict with the satisfaction of other drives, both primary and learned, since, above all, it is the drive which restrains us. A child wants to jump off a diving board like the other children, but he is afraid to. He would like to tell his parents how angry their "unreasonable" demands make him, but he fears retribution. Life would be much easier for him if he could admit to himself the way he sometimes secretly feels about his mother or father or older brother, but even *thinking* such thoughts would produce too much anxiety. He learns to avoid these acts and thoughts because avoiding them is rewarding (i.e., leads to a reduction in the anxiety aroused by them).

How does anxiety begin? What produces the feeling of acute discomfort, the pounding heart and rapid pulse, the sinking feeling in the stomach, the perspiration, the trembling, the exaggerated startle, the dryness of the throat and mouth and other indicators of fear? Objectively, as these illustrations show, the potential for becoming anxious must exist within the physiology of the individual. It is not the nature of the anxiety response itself that leads us to speak of anxiety as a learned drive. It is the *arousal* of the response that is learned: "Fear is called learnable because it can be learned as a response to previously neutral cues; it is called a *drive* because it can motivate the learning and performance of new responses in the same way as hunger, thirst, or other drives" (*14*).

Pain as a Determinant of Anxiety

As we pointed out earlier, if learning is to take place—if a new bond between a cue and a response is to be formed, we must somehow find a way of eliciting the response in the first place.

In the opinion of a number of psychologists, one of the stimuli which may innately produce fear is pain (*7, 14*). In such case, it is not hard to see how anxiety may get started even in infancy. Infants often experience pain, no matter how solicitous their mothers. The infant may be burned, he may become intensely hungry—and experimental evidence tends to support the common observation that hunger pangs rise to greater heights in infants than in adults (23)—he may nearly suffocate from an illness or from smothering his head in a pillow, he may be stuck by pins, he may suffer the acute anguish of colic.

It seems quite possible that other stimuli besides pain may innately produce anxiety, though we know all too little at this point about their nature. Some psychologists argue that mere suddenness of intense stimulation may produce fear. Others hypothesize that specific kinds of psychological experiences may innately engender fear (6, 14). At any rate, it seems clear that regardless of the original stimuli which may produce fear, the great majority of human anxiety responses, and the ones which are most likely to be crippling to an individual's attempts to adjust to his environment, are learned.

An Example of Learned Fear

Let us assume that an infant's older brother, understandably jealous of the attention that this pint-sized intruder into the family circle is receiving, walks up to the crib in which the baby is playing and jabs it with a pin. If the baby's visual perception is sufficiently mature, the visual stimuli (cues) presented by his brother will be discriminably different from those of his mother, father, and other nonjabbers. If so, the chances are that future appearances of his older brother's face at the side of the crib will provoke fear.

The learning paradigm in this case may be analyzed as follows: A stimulus (pain) which is innately capable of arousing the response of fear is paired with a neutral one (the sight of the older brother's face). As a result of this pairing, one might expect the sight of the older brother's face alone to produce fear in the future if drive reduction has occurred also. But what, one may ask, were the drive and reward?

According to Miller (14), the drive in this case would be pain resulting from the pinprick, and the reward would be a reduction in pain following its cessation.

Experimental evidence of this kind of learning comes from a number of classic experiments on conditioning, such as one by Watson and Raynor (24). They found that an infant could be taught to fear a previously unfeared white rat, if they produced a frighteningly loud noise (by striking a steel bar) every time the infant reached for the rat. After seven such experiences, the infant displayed fear when the rat was presented alone.

All authors, however, would not agree that the learning of such conditioned responses as fear necessarily involves reward. A number of learning theorists such as Skinner (19) and Mowrer (16) feel that there are some kinds of learning which do not require drive reduction, but only contiguity (i.e., just the occurrence of the response in the presence of the cue) (21).

In other words, some learning theorists maintain that one factor, drive reduction, is an indispensable factor in all learning. Others feel that the factor of drive reduction is necessary for some kinds of learning, but that other kinds of learning depend only on the factor of contiguity without accompanying drive reduction.

One-Factor Versus Two-Factor Theories of Learning

Mowrer's opinion, referred to as a two-factor theory of learning, is that skeletal-muscle activities, such as riding a bicycle, going to the bathroom, or playing hopscotch—or what are often referred to as examples of *instrumental conditioning*—require drive reduction to be learned. However, he feels that "emotional [i.e., classical] conditioning involving responses controlled by the autonomic nervous system," such as anxiety, does not (21). Stated in the simplest terms, he feels that learned responses involving "doing" something require drive reduction, while learned emotional responses such as increases in blood pressure when frightened by an animal and secretion of the gastric juices when confronted with a tenderloin steak, do not.

While the difference in viewpoint between the one-factor and two-factor learning theorists is interesting, and a fruitful subject for continued research, the problem presents no crucial issues for our purposes. Most instances of human learning seem to us best understood by accepting the drive-reduction hypothesis, and even if some, such as anxiety, perhaps do not, they still follow in other respects the same general principles of learning (14). Thus, in the example discussed above, anxiety will become more strongly attached to the cue of the older brother's face with repeated jabbings. Similarly, anxiety will tend to *extinguish* if further appearance of the older brother's face ceases to be accompanied by painful jabbing. The concept of *generalization* is just as applicable to anxiety as it is to motor responses. A child whose reactions to one policeman consist of an increase in anxiety, and violent running away, will tend to generalize both these responses to other policemen even, perhaps, to other tall, broad, dark-haired Irishmen.

MONEY, AN EXAMPLE OF LEARNED REWARD

Just as primary drives may serve as the basis for learned drives, so may primary rewards, such as food and water, serve as the basis for learned rewards. An obvious example is money. In our culture, at least, money certainly qualifies as an example of learned reward. The extent of its use as a reinforcement in learning is attested by the popular expression that "Money is the root of all evil."

Nevertheless, in many cultures money has no reward value. Explorers have long since found that with some tribes, bright-colored beads, matches, and other objects are of much more use in eliciting native cooperation than money. Thus the reward value of money is obviously learned. How?

Interesting examples of how money may acquire reward value even with animals are cited by Wolfe (25), and Cowles (3). Actually, for convenience they used poker chips, but the principle is, of course, identical. The results of their experiments have been summarized by Miller.

In order to give reward value to the tokens (poker chips) Cowles first trained hungry chimpanzees to insert them into a vending machine which delivered a raisin with each token inserted. As a preliminary test, and as a further means of establishing the reward value, he repeated Wolfe's procedure of requiring a chimpanzee to work for the chip by pulling a handle against a weight. First the animals were allowed to change the chip immediately for a raisin; then by stages were forced to accumulate 20 chips before they could spend them.

In order to determine whether or not the poker chips could serve as a learned reward, he took the animals into another room where they were confronted with two boxes. If they opened the one to the left they found a token, if they opened the one to the right they found nothing. They quickly learned to open the box on the left in spite of the fact that they were not allowed to exchange the tokens for food until the end of the day's session. The next day they were taught to select the box on the right.

In later experiments they were taught a variety of more complicated habits. In some of these experiments the possible innate reward value of the token was controlled by giving the animal the token that had been associated with food if he performed the correct response, and a different-colored token, that the animal had learned could not be exchanged for food, if he performed the incorrect response. The *learning of the correct response under these circumstances shows that the reward value of the token depended on its previous association with the primary reward of receiving food when hungry* [italics ours] (*14*, 454).

Money acquires its reward value for children in much the same way as with these chimpanzees. Only after a child has discovered that his father's nickels and dimes may be exchanged for such primary delights as ice cream cones, candy bars, and bubble gum, does money itself acquire reward value. It might also be observed that it was probably no harder to teach the chimpanzee to accumulate 20 chips before spending them than it is to teach a child to hold on to his dimes and nickels until he has enough "to buy something he really wants."

Once money has acquired reward value, it may be successfully employed as reinforcement not only for such responses as opening boxes, but other, perhaps more useful ones, such as making beds, sweeping sidewalks, or delivering newspapers. It may even serve as some encouragement to "being a good boy." In the case of adults, it keeps innumerable people busy building cars, walking tightropes, and selling shoes. An implicit recognition of the fact that learned needs like money derive their ultimate reward value from primary needs is revealed by the common reference to one's source of income as his "bread and butter."

Other examples of learned reward in our culture are numerous. Medals, cups, high grades in school, pats on the back, use of the family car, promotions—all may have reward value. Of course, a particular object cannot function as a reward unless there is a drive operating at the moment which will be reduced by receipt of the object. This is obvious in the case of primary rewards. No one thinks of offering food to a thirsty individual, or sexual objects to one who is hungry, in order to reward him.

This principle is not always readily apparent in the case of learned rewards. For example, with children we often assume that there is something intrinsically rewarding about objects simply because they serve as rewards for most children. Since children have different kinds of learning experiences, no two of them will have exactly the same needs. Consequently, they will not always be equally reinforced by the same rewards. For example, while praise may well serve as a reward for children who are in need of social approval, it is not likely to serve well for a boy whose overwhelming need is to convince himself and others that he's a "tough guy," not a "mamma's boy." In the same way, one can hardly expect a rich boy who needs love and acceptance to learn something by offering him money as a reward. It is impossible to get an adolescent farm boy who has no curiosity about what is going on in the next county to join the Navy by promising him the delights of travel and adventure. At the level of cultures, it is probably unreasonable to expect that one could convert a starving Indian or Chinese to the American way of life by pointing out the blessings of freedom of speech, religion, and the press. To be rewarding, an object must always be able to reduce, at least to some degree, a drive (or drives) operating at the moment.

LEARNED DRIVE AS A BASIS FOR FURTHER LEARNED DRIVE

Once a previously neutral stimulus has acquired the ability to arouse anxiety, it may serve as a basis for learning other anxieties. If a little boy has once learned to fear his father, he may later come to fear objects associated with the father, such as the father's friends. Thus, a learned drive, such as fear of the father, may serve as a basis not only for learning new instrumental acts but also for acquiring new learned drives.

A learned need for money may originally have been developed because the acquisition of money led to the reduction of primary drives such as hunger, thirst, avoidance of cold, and the like. In its turn, however, the learned need for money may serve as the basis (or part of the basis) for further learning of other drives, such as the need for social approval. A child may find out that his parents will give him his allowance only if he has been a "good boy." Or the adolescent may find out that he can get a job only if he is well liked by his prospective employer. In situations like these, the learned need for money may help to develop the need for social approval.

Love for the mother may originally have developed because of her role in meeting primary needs through such acts as providing warm bottles, changing diapers, removing safety pins, and adding blankets on cold nights. Once developed, however, this need may serve as part of the basis for further complex needs. For example, if the mother gives love only if the child is being orderly and conscientious, the child may develop needs for orderliness and conscientiousness which will be manifested even when the mother is not around. He may even learn to do many complex acts, such as always putting his toys away carefully, never getting his clothes dirty, washing his hands frequently, and always doing what he is told, in order to satisfy these needs.

The kinds of learned needs that children tend to develop, the ages at which they are likely to emerge, and the circumstances which may lead to their emergence, will be discussed repeatedly throughout the book.

HEREDITY AND LEARNED DRIVE

In our discussion of primary drives in the neonate, we mentioned that some primary drives, such as hunger, may rise to greater heights in infants than in adults. As we shall see later, there are others, such as sex, which become stronger as development proceeds. It also appears that there are individual differences in the maximum height and in the periodicity of these drives. Such differences may affect learning. And since they are probably due primarily to hereditary factors, we can see easily how differences in heredity may influence learning. For example, experimental evidence suggests that individuals differ in their susceptibility to pain. A child who is more susceptible to pain than another is more likely to develop strong anxiety and to attach it to more cues than a less susceptible child. A child whose hunger drive is capable of rising to greater heights than another's is likely to learn more ways of behaving and more social needs that center around reducing hunger, and to learn them more strongly, than is the child with weaker drive.

There are of course, certain ways that heredity can affect the development of learned drives and acts besides producing individual differences in the strength of primary drives. The obvious fact that heredity determines whether a child is a boy or a girl means that heredity influences the kinds of needs and skills the child will learn. In our society boys and girls are treated quite differently, and because they are so treated they learn different patterns of response. For example, girls are more likely to develop esthetic interests, boys political interests. Girls are more likely to develop overt needs to nurture others, boys to be dominant. Boys are more likely to be interested in sports and mechanics and in general acting more or less like daddy. Girls are more likely to be interested in dolls, baby carriages, tea parties, and wearing mother's old shoes and dresses. The influence of sex typing, which plays such an important role in the socialization of the child, will be discussed at length later in the book.

Since heredity plays a role in determining an individual's intellectual potential, it can strongly influence the kinds of needs and acts for which he will be rewarded by the society, and consequently which he will learn. The child who is below average in intelligence is not likely to be rewarded for trying to be a good student or for wanting to become a doctor, or a lawyer, or a teacher. Nor is he likely to be rewarded for efforts to write for the school paper, or to play for the chess club, or to orate for the debating society. He is more likely to gain acceptance as a follower than as a leader.

Heredity can affect physical strength, stability of the autonomic nervous system, and susceptibility to disease. It can even help to determine whether an individual meets our society's momentary notions about beauty or ugliness of appearance. All these factors may significantly influence the future development of the individual's learned needs and characteristic ways of responding.

LEARNED DRIVE AND ENVIRONMENT

While heredity is involved in determining the kinds of learned drives and acts that an individual develops, environmental forces also play crucial roles, as we shall see repeatedly throughout this book. Factors of culture, class, caste, role, and parental attitudes—all play important parts, chiefly in determining many of the kinds of responses for which the individual is or is not rewarded. In one family, a child's inquisitive, aggressive responses may lead to social approval: "He's a regular boy," we hear some admiring parents say, "Always into something." Equally often, however, we hear other parents complain, "That kid's always into something. Honestly, he's going to drive me crazy. I caught him with his father's tool chest this afternoon, and had to spank him and send him to bed." Negro children in the rural south tend to be rewarded for submissive responses to figures of authority, and to be punished severely for aggressive responses. With white children, particularly boys, the reverse is likely to be the case (18). Americans generally are rewarded for assertive behavior. The Zuni Indian, on the other hand, is genuinely shocked at such behavior and certainly does not reward it in his children (2). In pioneer New England, where climate and topography combined to frustrate man in the satisfaction of his primary needs, the development of aggressive behavior was encouraged. In some tropical countries, where food and shelter present few problems, aggressive behavior is little rewarded, at least in part because it is not so necessary for the satisfaction of primary drives (8). Environmental factors such as these, and their influences on the individual's psychological development, will be emphasized throughout the book.

IMITATION—AN EXAMPLE OF LEARNING

As a child grows older, many of the responses he adopts to reduce *model* primary and learned drives are the result of imitation. It is largely through this process that the little girl learns to dress up like her mother, to "take care" of her doll, or to play at housekeeping. Imitation also accounts largely for the boy's attempts to smoke his father's pipe, or to play at driving the family car.

Obviously some understanding of imitation is essential to the study of children's psychological development. Miller and Dollard point out that, in general, there are two sorts of imitation: "matched-dependent behavior," and "copying" (15). The process of learning in the two cases is somewhat different.

1. In *matched-dependent behavior*, the follower makes the same responses as the leader, because in the past making such responses has more often been rewarding than not. For example, an older child in a family may see a telephone truck passing his home, announce that he is going to watch the telephone repairman, and run for the door. His two-year-old younger brother who has no idea even what a telephone repairman is, may nevertheless immediately run along after his brother. In this case, the older brother's *cue* is the sight of the repair truck. He responds to this cue by running after the truck, since in the past he has found such responses to be rewarding.

For the younger brother (the imitator), however, the *cue* is his brother's running response. In turn, he also runs, because making responses like his older brother's has been rewarded in the past in a variety of ways. Perhaps on one occasion, it resulted in being given an ice cream cone by a neighbor; and in another by being allowed to play a game. This type of imitation is called *matched-dependent* because the follower's responses are *matched* to the leader's, and are also *dependent* upon the occurrence of the leader's responses, since these serve as cues for the follower (15).

2. In *copying*, the imitation process is somewhat more complex. Here the follower is not originally able to make the same response as the leader, but eventually learns to do so. In the example of matched-dependent behavior described above, the younger brother already knew how to make running responses like his older sibling. But in the case of a little girl who is trying to cook or sew like her mother, or a little boy who is trying to play ball or saw wood like his father, the response itself must be learned by copying.

According to Miller and Dollard (15), copying depends essentially on trial-and-error behavior on the part of the follower. When a "same" response is made, it is then rewarded. When a "different" response is made it is punished. The reward and punishment may stem either from the subject himself or from the person being imitated. For example, in the case of a little boy trying to copy his art teacher's drawing, the reinforcement may be self-imposed. The child may tell himself, "That's fine," whenever he makes a line that is the same as his teacher's drawing; and,

"That's lousy," whenever he makes a different line. However, in the case of a boy being taught to play baseball by his father, the reinforcement may come from the father. Thus, every time the boy happens to swing the bat correctly, the father congratulates him. When he swings it incorrectly, the father admonishes him.

As might be anticipated, all people are not equally likely to evoke imitative responses on the part of others. If imitating another is not rewarding, the tendency to imitate him will extinguish in the same fashion as any other type of learned response. Because imitating certain kinds of persons in our culture has more frequently been rewarding than imitating others, people generally are more likely to follow them. Thus American children as well as adults are more likely to imitate intelligent people than they are the unintelligent, and those of superior social or professional status than those of lesser status (15). One possible explanation in all these cases is that imitating these people has proved more likely to lead to personal rewards.

Innumerable examples of the role played by imitation in the child's psychological development will occur throughout this book—in relation not only to parents, but to teachers and other adults, and to peers.

SUMMARY

Learning may be defined as the process by which an activity originates or is changed through training procedures, as distinguished from changes not attributable to training. The primary determinants of behavior are growth and learning. Both play an important role in the development of most behavior. While some learning may occur in the prenatal period, most learning occurs after birth. Most kinds of learning require the presence of a drive, a cue, a response, and a reward. Some kinds of learning may require only the pairing of a cue and a response, but this is not clear. However, regardless of whether all instances of learning require drive reduction, all follow certain other general principles, such as generalization, discrimination, extinction, and anticipatory response.

The initial learning of the infant is based upon the satisfaction of primary drives, such as hunger, thirst, pain, fatigue, air hunger, defecation, urination, and thermal stimulation. Primary drives and rewards may serve as the basis for learning not only such responses as acts and thoughts but also other drives and rewards, called learned drives and learned rewards. Anxiety may be considered an example of learned drive, money an example of learned reward. Learned drives, once they have been acquired, may serve as the basis for acquiring further learned drives.

Heredity may affect the development of learned needs and responses through its role in determining many characteristics of the individual. These include the strengths of his primary drives, his sex, intelligence, susceptibility to disease, the stability of his autonomic nervous system, and his physical appearance.

The development of learned needs and behavior may also be affected by such environmental factors as culture, class, caste, role, climate, topography, and population density.

Imitation is an example of learning, and follows the same principles as other types of learning. It is an important process because much of an individual's psychological development is dependent upon imitation.

Applications and illustrations of the principles brought out in this chapter will occur throughout the book.

REFERENCES AND ADDITIONAL READING

1. Allport, G., *Personality: a psychological interpretation*. New York: Holt, 1937.
2. Benedict, R., *Patterns of culture*. New York: Penguin, 1946.
3. Cowles, J. T., Food tokens as incentives for learning by chimpanzees. *Comp. Psychol. Monogr.* (1937), *14*:No. 5.
4. Davis, H. V., Sears, R. R., Miller, H. C., and Brodbeck, A. J., Effects of cup, bottle and breast feeding on oral activities of newborn infants. *Pediatrics* (1948), 3:549–558.
5. Dollard, J., and Miller, N. E., *Personality and psychotherapy: an analysis in terms of learning, thinking and culture*. New York: McGraw-Hill, 1950.
6. Freud, S., *The problem of anxiety*. New York: Norton, 1936.
7. Hilgard, E. R., *Theories of learning*. New York: Appleton-Century, 1948.
8. Honigman, J. J., *Culture and personality*. New York: Harper, 1954.
9. Hull, C. L., *Principles of behavior: an introduction to behavior theory*. New York: Appleton-Century. 1943.
10. Jersild, A. T., *Child psychology*. New York: Prentice-Hall, 1947.
11. Jones, E., *The life and work of Sigmund Freud*. New York: Basic Books, 1953.
12. Jones, H. E., and Jones, M. C., Fear. *Childh. Educ.* (1928), 5:136–143.
13. Marquis, D. P., Can conditioned responses be established in the newborn infant? *J. genet. Psychol.* (1931), 39:479–492.
14. Miller, N. E., Learnable drives and rewards, in S. S. Stevens (ed.), *Handbook of experimental psychology*. New York: Wiley, 1951, pp. 435–472.
15. Miller, N. E., and Dollard, J., *Social learning and imitation*. New Haven, Yale University Press, 1941.
16. Mower, O. H., On the dual nature of learning—a reinterpretation of "conditioning" and "problem-solving." *Harvard educ. Rev.* (1947), *17*:102–148.

17. Murray, H. A. *et al.*, *Explorations in personality.* New York. Oxford, 1938.
18. Myrdal, G., *An American dilemma.* New York: Harper, 1944.
19. Skinner, B. F., *The behavior of organisms.* New York: Appleton-Century, 1938.
20. Spelt, D. K., The conditioning of the human fetus in utero. *J. exp. Psychol.* (1948), 38:338–346.
21. Spence, K. W., Theoretical interpretations of learning, in S. S. Stevens, (ed.), *Handbook of experimental psychology.* New York: Wiley, 1951, pp. 690–729.
22. Spock, B., *The pocket book of baby and child care.* New York: Pocket Books, 1946.
23. Taylor, R., Hunger in the infant. *Am. J. Dis. Child* (1917), 14:233–257.
24. Watson, J. B., and Raynor, R., Conditioned emotional reactions. *J. exp. Psychol.* (1920), 3:1–4.
25. Wolfe, J. B., Effectiveness of token rewards for chimpanzees. *Comp. Psychol. Monogr.* (1936), 12:No. 60.

Chapter 6

SOCIAL LEARNING IN THE FIRST YEAR

As we noted earlier, the most important aspects of personality are acquired, rather than inherited. Personality development and socialization, our major interests throughout this book, are primarily phenomena of learning. Socialization refers to "the whole process by which an individual, born with behavioral potentialities of enormously wide range, is led to develop actual behavior which is confined within a much narrower range—the range of what is customary and acceptable for him according to the standards of his group" (9, 655). In brief, it is the process by which the individual learns to be a member of his social group.

In Chapter 4, we reviewed the primary needs, sensory capacities, and response capabilities of the infant. These are the raw materials of learning, the foundation stones for the more complex motor, emotional, and social behaviors that characterize the child and adult.

In the last chapter, the basic principles of learning were described. In this chapter, we shall examine more concretely how these principles operate during the first year of the child's life, producing dramatic behavior changes and affecting the course of his subsequent development in many ways.

It will be recalled that the first prerequisite for learning is heightened drive. However, most of the newborn's primary drives (needs for oxygen, temperature regulation, sleep, elimination) are reduced automatically in a self-regulatory manner (cf. pp. 83–87). They do not produce any sustained tensions, and therefore they cannot ordinarily serve as a basis for learning.

The Hunger Drive

The situation is different with respect to hunger and thirst, the child's most urgent, most incessant, and most activity-producing drives. As we pointed out earlier, it is difficult to differentiate these two needs in infants, since both may be reduced by drinking milk. Therefore, for purposes of simplifying our discussion, we will refer to them together as hunger.

The infant is almost completely dependent upon someone else's participation for gratification of this need. Hunger tensions cannot be relieved without help. If there is a delay between the first twinges of hunger (internal stimuli) and their relief, tensions may mount considerably. Since such delays are practically unavoidable and occur frequently, hunger is the primary drive most likely to reach a high level of sustained stimulation. Hence much of the child's earliest learning will be built on the basis of this drive.

Feeding as a Social Learning Situation

Feeding constitutes the child's earliest experience in social participation. His mother is his first and most important social contact (8). The kind and degree of satisfaction obtained in the feeding situation may be important determinants of his future reactions to other people and to social relationships generally. If the mother feeds the child in a relaxed and comfortable way, she becomes associated with satisfactory drive-reducing, relaxing experiences. The feelings of pleasure that come with hunger reduction and relief of tension become attached to her personally, and she begins to have considerable learned reward value for the child. Her mere presence (the visual and auditory cues she presents) becomes capable of eliciting feelings of well-being. In short, the child learns to love his mother.

As the mother satisfies her infant's needs, he begins to depend upon her. Whiting (66) has presented a detailed description of the development of the dependency drive among infants of a New Guinea tribe, the Kwoma.

Kwoma infants are cared for almost exclusively by their mothers. For approximately the first three years of life a Kwoma infant sits in the lap of his mother during the day and lies by her side at night. It is the Kwoma mother's duty to care for all the needs of her child during this period. When, despite this constant care, Kwoma infants suffer frustration, crying is the response which becomes most firmly fixed. A Kwoma mother, whenever her infant cries, does her best to comfort him. If he is hungry, she feeds him; if he is cold, she warms him; if he is sick or in pain, she tries to soothe him. Thus by removing the source of frustration or pain the Kwoma mother rewards crying as a response to these conditions. Toward the end of infancy, when the child begins to talk, he responds to frustration or pain by asking for help, and his mother complies with his request whenever it is possible for her to do so. Thus during infancy a frustration-dependence sequence is established (66, 141).

Of course, Kwoma mothers have closer relationships with their children and care for them for longer periods than mothers in some other societies, including our own. Nevertheless, the general pattern of development of dependency is probably similar in all groups in which the mother takes care of the young infant.

This early learning has broad implications for the child's subsequent social adjustment. In early infancy his mother is practically all the child knows of society. Further, his ability to discriminate the mother from other individuals is extremely limited. Thus, in the child's vague perceptions, she is the representative of the world at large. If the mother-child relationship is a rewarding one, the infant's positive responses to her will tend to generalize to other people. Thus, learning to love the mother early in life facilitates the establishment of warm, friendly relations with others in the future.

On the other hand, if the feeding situation is not a satisfactory one, the infant may develop negative "attitudes" toward the mother. A mother who handles her baby in a routine, impersonal, or nervous, agitated manner may make feeding a frustrating and unpleasant experience. For example, if she holds him tensely or in strained, awkward positions, pain or discomfort may become associated with hunger reduction as well as with the mother's presence. In this case, the child will be in conflict whenever he feels hungry. He needs and desires food to relieve his hunger pangs. However, he has learned that such relief is likely to be accompanied by discomfort. His reactions to his mother also involve conflicts. She has become associated with the pleasant feelings of hunger reduction, on the one hand, and with the pain and discomfort of poor handling on the other. If the latter feelings occur with great frequency, the mother may come to be regarded as a kind of pain stimulus, and the child may react to her as he does to pain, i.e., by withdrawing or turning his head away.

If the infant is not fed soon after he becomes hungry, hunger contractions become severe and painful. He may learn to fear his own hunger, for experience teaches him that early hunger twinges are followed by greater contractions and pain. In extreme cases, the pain may become so great that eating may produce gastric upset or nausea, rather than reduction of hunger. In this instance, too, unpleasant sensations may become associated with the mother who gave the food. Withdrawal reactions toward the mother may be generated in this way.

These responses, learned on the basis of early experiences with the mother, may generalize to others in the same way that positive attitudes do. Lack of social feeling, suspiciousness, mistrust of people, and resentment and hostility towards society may have their deepest roots in the mother's inept handling of the feeding situation (8, 12).

METHODS OF HANDLING INFANT FEEDING

Obviously, there are many possible ways of handling the infant's hunger drive. At different times, within the relatively recent past, child specialists have recommended diametrically opposite feeding procedures. For example, in the late 1920's and early 1930's, the writings of John B. Watson (64, 65), the behaviorist, were influential. He recommended strict, cold, and impersonal treatment. Loving, cuddling, and displays of affection were to be practically eliminated. According to Watson, the child should be forced to comply with parents' wishes and rules of conduct. As one aspect of this, he must learn to conform with a rigidly controlled feeding schedule right from the start.

Adaptation to a Schedule

Is it possible for neonates to learn such conformity? D. P. Marquis experimentally investigated the problem of adaptation to (i.e., learning) a feeding schedule within the first ten days of life (42). She measured the bodily activities (restlessness) of two groups of infants who were on different feeding schedules. Daily changes in restlessness were used as the criterion of adaptation. One group, consisting of 18 infants, was on a four-hour feeding schedule throughout the ten-day period. Sixteen other infants were on three-hour schedules for the first eight days of their lives, but were shifted to four-hour schedules on the ninth day.

After a few days, the infants' bodily activities rose sharply immediately before their next scheduled feeding, the increase being greater and more abrupt in the four-hour group. This provides some evidence that this group had learned to wait four hours for food.

On the day the "three-hour schedule" infants were shifted to the four-hour schedule, there were marked changes in their activity patterns. At the end of three hours, their habitual feeding time, body movements increased abruptly and reached the highest level recorded during the study. Apparently this group had learned to respond to hunger cues at the end of three hours. Failure to receive food at this time produced extreme restlessness and activity. It may be concluded that infants just a few days old can modify their behavior in accordance with external demands such as feeding schedules. Watson maintained that it is desirable to begin this kind of training immediately after the child's birth.

Warm Mothering in Feeding

There are, however, other points of view about infant feeding practices. The fact that infants *can* learn to adapt to feeding schedules does not mean that it is *advisable* to force them to conform to such schedules. Aldrich, another writer on child-rearing practices, recommends procedures which differ radically from Watson's. He advocates a "warm-mothering" relationship in which the child is breast fed on demand and is often cuddled, loved, and played with affectionately (*2, 3*). Many of his ideas about these matters are related to psychoanalytic theories regarding important factors in the care of infants.

The Oral Phase

Freud called the first stage of personality development (the first 12 or 18 months) the *oral phase*, and according to his theory, the infant's earliest intense pleasures come from sucking activities. Successful adjustment at this period requires not only hunger reduction, but satisfaction of the desire (drive) to exercise the mouth and lips.

It was Freud's hypothesis that the lips and mouth become erotogenic, i.e., capable of giving pleasurable sensations when stimulated, as a result of the association of sucking with food taking (*55, 124*). In other words, because of its association with hunger reduction, excitation of the mouth area soon acquires secondary reward value and becomes gratifying in itself.

Freud cited the familiar observation that infants often suck their thumbs as evidence that sucking involves pleasures not directly related to the satisfaction of hunger needs. Moreover, if the infant's nonnutritive sucking is interfered with, he appears to become frustrated, cries, and thrashes about.

The Sucking Drive

According to psychoanalytic theory, sucking represents the initial expression of sexuality. For the infant, the satisfactions derived from stimulation of the mouth and lips may be compared to those the adult derives from genital stimulation (5, 16).

One of the implications of Freud's hypothesis is that sucking is not merely a _reflex_ which may be activated for the purpose of getting food, but a _need_ or _drive_. Since almost all infants indulge in nonnutritive sucking, some of Freud's followers concluded that the sucking need is innate or instinctual. There is some good evidence, however, that it is a drive which is at least in part learned through association with satisfaction of the primary hunger drive.

A group of investigators (11) compared the oral activities (responses to a sucking test and spontaneous mouth and lip exercise) of neonates who were fed in different ways. Their subjects were three groups of 20 infants each, one breast fed, one bottle fed, and the third cup fed. Cup feeding, of course, involves less sucking activity than does either breast or bottle feeding, while breast feeding requires longer and more vigorous sucking than bottle feeding. The investigators reasoned that if oral (sucking) drives are secondary or learned, cup-fed babies, having had less opportunity to associate sucking with hunger reduction, should manifest less sucking drive than the other infants. On the other hand, if sucking is simply an inherent, biologically given drive, the opposite results would be expected, i.e., cup-fed babies would show more nonnutritional sucking, since they may not have adequate opportunities to reduce their sucking drives during feeding.

As a test of nonnutritional sucking activity, a nipple-covered finger was held in the infant's mouth for a period of time each day for the first ten days of his life. The amount of time he would suck this finger served as the criterion of strength of sucking drive. During the 10-day period, the breast-fed group showed consistent increases in responsiveness to the test, while the other two groups did not change. At the end of ten days, breast-fed infants had stronger sucking responses than those fed by bottle or cup. Their high oral drives may be attributed to frequent experiences in which vigorous mouth activities were accompanied by hunger reduction. In brief, sucking had acquired great habit strength and had become gratifying in its own right through strong primary reinforcement. On the basis of these findings, the investigators concluded that this drive is at least partially learned.

Once the drive has developed, however, its tensions can be relieved only by performing the secondary goal response appropriate to it, in this case, sucking. Thus nursing infants were found to be more prone to crying and to disturbances of appetite than cup-fed babies. Presumably, since these infants had stronger sucking drives, they were more likely to suffer frustration and hence to manifest more vigorous frustration reactions (such as crying, restlessness, and appetite disturbances) when the drive was not adequately satisfied.

A more direct test of the psychological consequents of different amounts of rewarded practice in sucking is reported by Sears and Wise (55). These investigators were concerned with the relationships between age at weaning (change from breast or bottle to cup feeding) and the amount of disturbance displayed at this time. The weaning process involves interference with the reduction of the sucking drive. It may be inferred that the amount of disturbance associated with weaning may be an index of how much frustration of oral drive the child suffers in this process.

The subjects were three groups of children aged 2 to 10 years: (1) the early weaned group, weaned before they were 2 weeks old. had little rewarded sucking experience; (2) the middle weaned group, weaned at between 2 weeks and 3 months, had a medium amount of rewarded sucking experience; and (3) the late weaned group, weaned after 4 months, had a great deal of rewarded sucking experience. All data were obtained from interviews with the children's mothers. The degree of weaning disturbance was rated on the basis of their statements about the child's reactions to the change in feeding method.

Children with a great deal of sucking experience had the greatest number of frustration reactions to weaning. Also, the incidence of thumb-sucking (a manifestation of oral drive strength) was slightly greater in this group. Apparently, the late weaned infants, i.e., those whose sucking had been rewarded most frequently, had the strongest oral drives. Consequently, they reacted most violently when deprived of the opportunity to make the sucking responses capable of reducing that drive.

The two studies just cited demonstrate that oral or sucking needs are at least partially learned and become stronger if there is frequent rewarded practice in breast or bottle feeding. These findings support Freud's original hypothesis that the pleasure and gratification from stimulation of the mouth and lips grow out of the association between this stimulation and securing nourishment.

Even casual observation attests that most infants have strong oral drives. This is what we would expect on the basis of learning theory, for in most cases, sucking responses are frequently made and rewarded during early infancy.

INFLUENCES OF EARLY ORAL EXPERIENCES ON PERSONALITY DEVELOPMENT

The Psychoanalytic Hypotheses

Freud was much impressed with the possible persisting or permanent consequents of frustration or satisfaction of infantile oral drives. Many psychoanalytic writers (1, 15, 16, 17), as well as psychologists and pediatricians, have maintained that satisfaction of these drives is essential for the development of a secure, healthy personality. Prolonged nursing (in preference to artificial feeding), self-demand feeding (rather than rigid, time-regulated schedules), and gradual (rather than abrupt) weaning have been recommended as means of promoting optimal oral experience.

ORAL FIXATION. According to classical psychoanalytic theory, these infantile feeding techniques play a role in determining the kind of person a child will become. If the infant is excessively frustrated or deprived in his feeding and sucking experiences, or if he is excessively gratified or overindulged, he becomes fixated at the "oral stage" (develops an "oral fixation"). This means that he fails to progress normally from the first or "oral phase" of personality development and continues to be overly concerned, even in later childhood and adulthood, with oral gratifications. "Oral matters continue to have for him an actual or potential importance greater than they would have for someone who had not had these experiences" (67, 129). Under these circumstances, psychological and emotional maturation may be thwarted.

THE ORAL PERSONALITY. According to the analytic hypotheses concerning oral fixation, certain kinds of personality characteristics are common among individuals who had been frustrated or overindulged in their infantile feeding experiences. For example, Fenichel (15), an outstanding psychoanalytic writer, links oral indulgence in infancy to later feelings of optimism and self-assurance, provided that the external environment does not threaten the individual's security. Moreover, the theory maintains that early oral deprivation frequently manifests itself later in an *oral character*, a constellation of personality traits. These include general dissatisfaction, pessimism, suspiciousness, impatience, passivity, and strong cravings and demands for sympathy, support, and protection from others. Murphy (44) describes the *oral character* as a "tagger-on," "leaner," "parasite." "He is dependent because the supreme value is the dependency relationship" (44, 746).

Since they are still concerned with "oral" matters, many such individuals might also be expected to overemphasize activities such as eating, smoking, and drinking and to display "oral symptoms" (nailbiting, thumbsucking, speech disorders). In general, they might be expected to be more neurotic and maladjusted than individuals who had experienced optimal oral gratification in infancy. Is there any evidence to support such notions as these concerning the relationship of early oral experience and later personality and behavior—either in childhood or at maturity?

Oral Experiences and Childhood Personality

Studies dealing with the consequents of variations in feeding practices on the child's personality and behavior may be divided into several groups—those dealing with specific behaviors, such as thumbsucking and nailbiting; those dealing with general adjustment; and those dealing specifically with so-called oral personality traits. Each will be discussed in turn.

THUMBSUCKING. In the light of its obvious physical similarity to sucking in the original feeding situation, habitual thumbsucking might reasonably be regarded as a consequence of early oral frustrations. In fact, there is some empirical evidence that this behavior (which is often considered a "problem") in children may be a reaction to oral deprivation. Levy (37) obtained information about the infantile feeding experiences and thumbsucking of 122 children by interviewing their mothers. Of the total group, 28, or 25.4 per cent, had done some thumbsucking, most of them starting before they were 3 months old. None of the 20 children who were allowed to use pacifiers became thumbsuckers.

Analysis of the background data revealed that as infants, the fingersuckers had less opportunities than other children for adequate sucking-drive reduction. For example, they had fewer, more widely separated, and briefer nursing periods. Hence, the author concluded that there is a definite relationship between oral deprivation in infancy and subsequent thumbsucking.

In order to study this problem experimentally, this same investigator (38) divided a litter of six puppies into three pairs having different amounts of sucking experience. One pair, the long feeders, were fed with a bottle with a small-holed nipple and allowed unrestricted opportunity to suck on a nipple-covered finger after each meal. The second pair, short feeders, were fed with a large-holed nipple and had no additional sucking experiences. The third pair were left with the mother and breast fed. During the 20 days of the experiment, the long feeders sucked for an average of more than an hour a day, while the short feeders spent only about 20 minutes a day in feeding activities. Between meals, the latter pair chewed and sucked at each other's bodies and at a proffered finger more frequently than the long feeders did. The breast-fed puppies showed no interest in nonnutritional sucking.

The findings from both of these studies are, of course, consistent with the hypothesis that, once sucking needs have developed, inadequate opportunity to suck in connection with feeding may be an important antecedent of nonnutritive sucking. While the findings of experimental animal studies are suggestive, they cannot be considered definitive for our purposes. Since the subjects studied were of another species, generalization to humans may not be valid.

Further research with children has yielded more evidence that thumbsucking may be a consequence of inadequate sucking experiences in early infancy. Another investigator (51) compared 15 thumbsuckers with 15 non-thumbsucking (control) children. The majority of a group of the thumbsuckers had been allowed feeding periods averaging less than 70 minutes per day for the first 7 or 8 months of their lives. All 15 controls fed for at least 90 minutes a day during this period. Among children who averaged more than 130 minutes of feeding time daily until they were 8 months old, there were no thumbsuckers. In several of the thumbsucking cases, the habit began immediately after the infant's feeding time had been reduced. The investigator therefore concluded that the findings confirm the hypothesis that restricted sucking experience in infancy is an important determinant of habitual thumbsucking.

Other evidence, however, suggests that oral deprivation may not be the *only* important antecedent of this habit. Thus, one investigator found 5 thumbsuckers in a group of 26 children who had been breast fed on self-demand schedules and allowed to nurse as long as they wanted (57). Since these 5 children had developed the habit in spite of apparently adequate gratification during infantile feeding, the investigator concluded that "whatever the cause or cure of thumbsucking, self-regulated feeding times without limit in nursing time are no panacea" (57, 184).

GENERAL ADJUSTMENT. Studies of the relationship between early feeding experiences and general adjustment in childhood are more difficult to evaluate, and have yielded more conflicting results than those dealing specifically with thumbsucking. For example, according to one investigation of an American clinic population, artificially fed children were physically and mentally inferior to those who were breast fed (32). In another study, 109 London clinic children were observed from birth until the age of 7. Those who had been artificially fed in infancy had a higher incidence of feeding difficulties, poor health, and restlessness than those who had been breast fed. At the age of 7, a greater proportion of the bottle-fed group manifested poor appetites, poor sleep, enuresis, fears, nervousness, and poor school records (52).

Another interesting study (33) of the relationship between the degree and quality of self-regulation in infantile feeding and subsequent adjustment of normal children made use of the technique of standardized play interviews. The child was brought into a room containing a doll house, miniature furniture, and dolls representing important people in his life (father, mother, siblings). As he played with this equipment his behavior was observed and recorded.

The major assumption underlying the use of this technique was that the child revealed himself through his play, expressing his deep-seated feelings and emotions and his attitudes toward others in his environment. Clinical research and experience have suggested that certain kinds of play (e.g., recognizing the materials and using them imaginatively but appropriately) are generally indicative of good adjustment. Other kinds of play (e.g., completely inappropriate and fantastic use of equipment) may be diagnostic of emotional maladjustment.

The investigator was concerned with testing the hypothesis that babies who were gratified in early feeding became better adjusted emotionally than those who suffered oral frustrations. According to the hypothesis, the latter would be more maladjusted and would indulge in more play reflecting this maladjustment.

The subjects were 17 highly intelligent young children, 8 boys and 9 girls between the ages of 3 and 5. Their behavior in play was scored in terms of the amount of time spent in activities reflecting good adjustment and the amount spent in play indicative of maladjustment. Data on degree of self-regulation in infantile feeding and duration of nursing were obtained from interviews with the subjects' mothers.

The author's hypothesis was substantially supported by her data. There was a significant positive correlation ($+.78$) between ratings on feeding self-regulation and play reflecting emotional stability. In contrast, self-regulation and play indicative of poor adjustment were highly negatively correlated ($-.80$). In other words, self-demand feeding appeared to be associated with good adjustment, while scheduled infantile feedings (low degree of self-regulation) and poor adjustment were related. Duration of breast feeding was found to be positively correlated with "well-adjusted" play scores ($+.59$), implying that longer nursing periods are conducive to later emotional stability. Unfortunately, the number of subjects involved was too small to permit broad generalization from this study. Nevertheless, the findings suggest that infants who are nursed for a long period of time and fed on self-demand are likely to achieve psychological health subsequently.

While the data of the last three studies reviewed are generally supportive of hypotheses relating early oral experiences to later general adjustment, not all investigations yield similar findings. In one study, the duration of nursing was correlated with children's personality characteristics at nursery school and preadolescence (47). Mothers supplied information about early feeding, while nursery school teachers rated the children on affection, cheerfulness, confidence, kindness, resistance, social apprehensiveness, aggressiveness, cruelty, jealousy, quarrelsomeness. Personality tests and inventories were administered to the same subjects when they were preadolescents. All the correlations derived were statistically insignificant, leading the authors to conclude that "there is no relation between duration of breast feeding and child personality at the nursery school level, nor with adjustment at the preadolescent stage" (47, 65).

A more recent study attempted to relate three aspects of infantile feeding behavior—type of feeding (breast or bottle), nature of the feeding schedule (demand or regular), nature of the weaning process (sharp or gradual)—to adjustment in childhood (56). The subjects of this study were 162 rural Wisconsin 5- and 6-year-olds who came from middle-class, native American families. Data on feeding, behavior problems, oral symptoms (nailbiting, thumbsucking, stuttering), and general personality adjustment were derived from intensive interviews with mothers, personality tests, and teachers' ratings. There were no significant relationships between infantile feeding experiences (presumably related to early oral gratification or frustration) and later oral symptoms or general adjustment.

It is our feeling that taken together, available studies relating feeding practices to general adjustment neither clearly support nor contradict the hypothesis that oral deprivation in infancy produces poor general adjustment in childhood. In some cases, the information dealing with the feeding practices employed is open to serious question. This is particularly true in studies in which the data were obtained from mothers long after their children were weaned. Mothers' recollections of most of the procedures they employed in early infant care are probably subject to considerable error (4). In addition, in many cases, the measures of personality (tests, rating scales, inventories) were inadequate, either because of test invalidity or lack of clinical skill of the raters.

Many of these studies are also subject to the criticism that many relevant variables which might affect the results have not been adequately controlled. Thus we cannot determine whether the personality and adjustment differences between orally deprived children and those not so deprived are actually attributable to variations in feeding experiences. As one reviewer (46) has pointed out, in many of the studies there is little or no relevant information about other characteristics of the subjects. The two groups of children may have differed, not only in their feeding experiences, but in other important respects such as social-class background or parental attitudes, discipline procedures, or psychological adjustment. It is quite possible that differences in these extraneous factors may be more important than the specific feeding experiences in determining the personality differences observed.

DEPENDENCE. Several investigators have attempted to avoid some of the methodological problems mentioned above by concentrating their attention on careful and detailed study of a limited number of personality variables presumed to be related to variations in oral experience. An excellent study of the antecedents of aggression and dependency by Sears and his colleagues (54) may serve as an illustration of this approach. As we saw earlier, the infant soon learns that when he is frustrated or faces an insoluble problem, dependency reactions, e.g., crying, bring rewards and thus acquire great habit strength (cf. pp. 137–138). The child who encounters a greater number of frustrations is therefore likely to manifest more dependency responses and to have these responses reinforced. Hence he will develop the strongest dependency reactions. On the basis of this reasoning, the investigators predicted that "degree of early infant frustration will vary positively with later overt dependency behavior" (54, 187). This is exactly what would be predicted on the basis of psychoanalytic theory, although the theoretical rationales involved in the two approaches are different.

In order to test this hypothesis, the investigators interviewed the mothers of 40 nursery school boys and girls about their child-rearing practices. These data provided a basis for rating many aspects of the mother's behavior, including her weaning and scheduling techniques. Total nursing and weaning frustration scores were derived from these ratings.

Nursery school teachers evaluated each child on scales constructed to measure various kinds of aggressive and dependent behavior. *Total aggression ratings* were obtained by summing ratings on such items as: attacking other children; destroying property of the other children; quarreling or fighting with others; threatening teacher or other children; derogating others; displaying undirected aggression. *Dependence on teachers* and *dependence on other children* were assessed separately from scales of the frequencies of the child's seeking help, physical contact, praise, approval, or attention. Taken together, these yielded a *total dependency rating.*

Moreover, each child was observed by a trained observer for 15-minute periods on 16 occasions. The number of instances of dependent behavior and aggression manifested during these periods constituted the *total observed dependency* and *total observed aggression* scores.

As was predicted, severe frustrations in nursing and weaning were associated with high dependency during the preschool years. For example, severe weaning was related to *high total dependency* (*total rated* plus *total observed dependency*) in both girls and boys (correlations of +.54 and +.40, respectively). Rigid scheduling of feeding was also associated with high total dependency in girls (correlation of − .38 between degree of self-demand in feeding and *total dependency*). The authors state that "the best overall statements of the relation between infant feeding frustration and dependency . . . are the correlations of .55 (girls) and .35 (boys) between the combined scales (i.e., total infantile feeding frustration) and the total ranking of dependency" (*54*, 184). There were no significant relationships between any of the measures of infant feeding frustration and measures of aggressiveness in preschool.

Consequents of Infantile Feeding Experience on Adult Personality

Research data relevant to the notion that early feeding experiences may have important bearing on adult personality structure are even more difficult to obtain and evaluate than data on children's personality. This may be due partly to the fact that in most studies of adults, the dependability of the available information on early feeding practices is even more suspect. Furthermore, the measures of personality employed are often more superficial and of questionable validity. In addition, the adult has been subjected to many more experiences in the intervening years since his contacts with early feeding practices—experiences that may serve to mask or modify the personality consequents of these practices.[1]

At any rate, research studies on this problem yield varying results. In

---

[1] Many of these problems are difficult to overcome except through detailed and expensive long-term studies of personality development. Such studies are now in progress at a number of centers and may ultimately help to provide us with more dependable information.

one study, it was discovered that college students who had been breast fed a medium amount of time during infancy were more _insecure_ (according to a security-insecurity inventory) than those who had experienced brief or prolonged periods of nursing (*43*). This result is obviously inconsistent with the hypothesis that short periods of nursing are related to poor subsequent emotional adjustment. It is also in disagreement with the findings of studies of patients at children's clinics (cf. pp. 145–147). However, the adequacy of the feeding information and the validity of the measure of insecurity used in this study are open to question. Hence the findings of the study must be interpreted cautiously.

As we pointed out earlier, the term _oral personality_ refers to a specific constellation of personality characteristics rather than to general adjustment, security, or insecurity. Direct testing of these analytic hypotheses therefore requires investigation of the relationships between early feeding experiences and these particular "oral" traits.

In one study of 91 college men, mothers were asked to supply information on three aspects of their sons' feeding training (duration of nursing, total sucking time, and age of weaning) (*63*). The subjects' personality structures, particularly the so-called oral characteristics, were assessed by means of the Thematic Apperception Test (TAT). In this test, the subject is instructed to make up a story about each of a series of pictures showing various kinds of people and situations. It is assumed that in telling these stories, the subject, without realizing it, describes his own characteristics, feelings, and desires. In short, we learn about the storyteller from the stories he creates. On the basis of his story characters and their activities, each subject was given a score on each of a number of _oral personality_ characteristics (e.g., dependence, pessimism, talkativeness, suspiciousness). Analysis of the data revealed no significant correlations between any of the oral characteristics and the measures of feeding gratification or frustration.

Another study of the relationship between early feeding experiences and adult personality yielded different results, however. An English researcher devised a series of 19 self-administering verbal rating scales corresponding to the oral traits described in psychoanalytic literature (*26, 27, 28, 29*). From these she derived measures of _oral pessimism_ (made up of _oral personality_ characteristics) and _oral optimism_ (corresponding to descriptions of adults who were orally gratified in infancy). One hundred adults rated themselves on the scales, while their mothers supplied information about age of weaning.

There were small but significant relationships between early weaning (at four months or earlier) and *oral pessimism* ($+.27$) and between late weaning (after nine months) and *oral optimism* ($+.31$). According to these data, shortening the nursing period was associated with the development of the oral characteristics or *oral pessimism*. However, long periods of breast feeding did not necessarily lead to overgratification, fixations, or later *oral personality*. Although these findings are somewhat supportive of the analytic hypotheses, the size of the correlation leads the author to conclude that "there are other factors [in addition to duration of breast feeding] involved in oral pessimism which account for it to a greater extent, and which still await investigation" (29, 168). In this connection she states that nursing may be "only a symptomatic manifestation of more fundamental factors, such as the attitude of the mother, the constitution of the child, and the interaction of both" (29, 169).

In general, the studies reviewed here give little support to the analytic theory concerning the origins of pessimism, dependency, suspiciousness, and impatience in adults. However, in fairness to the theory, we must acknowledge that the inconsistencies in the findings may be attributable to methodological shortcomings, specifically the inadequacies of measurement techniques or research design discussed above (cf. p. 147). On the other hand, it is quite possible that early oral experiences, considered apart from other variables, do not in fact have an overriding influence in shaping adult personality. The available empirical evidence does not allow us to choose between these alternative explanations. It seems entirely reasonable, however, to conclude that hypotheses about direct one-to-one connections between specific aspects of feeding experiences and subsequent personality structure are oversimplified. As we noted earlier, there may be indirect relationships between infantile oral gratification and adult adjustment. For example, in many cases, nursing, self-demand feeding, and gentle gradual weaning reflect the mother's wish to establish a close warm relationship with her child. It may be primarily this general attitude toward the child, rather than the specific practices employed, which makes the feeding situation rewarding.

It is our hypothesis that gratification in infantile feeding may generate feelings of satisfaction, relaxation, and security in relationships with the mother, and these may generalize to other social situations. The infant who has learned to associate social interaction with gratification, rather than with tension, is likely to approach later interpersonal relationships confidently, to handle them adequately, and to derive further satisfactions from them. Consequently, his feelings of social ease and adequacy will be further reinforced and become stronger. Thus early learning of a sense of security may start the child on the path which facilitates the development of good social adjustment and emotional health.

CONSEQUENTS OF "GOOD MOTHERING"

On the basis of these considerations, we would expect the general quality of early mother-child relationships to exert an important influence on the child's later adjustment. Actually, there is a great deal of evidence to support this expectation, and most modern child specialists recognize the importance of establishing strong and satisfying emotional mother-child relationships very early in life. For example, Erik Erikson, a psychoanalyst who works primarily with children, believes that the child's basic trust in himself and the world stems from the oral stage of development. He argues that gratification of oral needs is important in the establishment of these feelings of self-esteem and confidence that the world is pleasant. However, he feels that "the amount of trust derived from the infantile experience does not depend on absolute quantities of food or on demonstrations of love, but rather on the quality of the maternal relationship" (14, 221).

One of the outstanding advocates of "adequate mothering" treatment, Margaret Ribble, says "the psychological care of the infant is fully as important for his emotional, intellectual, and social development as is careful feeding for adequate nutrition and good digestive functioning" (50, 622). The child's need for love is described as "elemental," stemming "directly out of the factors connected with the maintenance of life itself during the period of infancy" (50, 627).

Specific training techniques as well as subtle attitudinal factors are involved in the establishment of emotional bonds between mother and child. According to Ribble, three kinds of sensory gratifications—tactile, kinaesthetic (or sense of body position) and sound—contribute to strengthening the attachment. Holding, fondling, and rocking the baby provide him with a great deal of kinaesthetic and tactile pleasure, while speaking softly or singing to him is soothing and relaxing. Since the infant's oral needs are prominent, good mothering "includes allowing the child unrestricted opportunities for pleasurable sucking." While it is our contention that the infant *learns* to love and depend upon his mother, Ribble believes that there is "an *innate* need for contact with the mother, and that the mother who supplies this contact unstintingly fosters her child's development" (50, 628, italics ours).

Ribble observed 600 infants over a long period of time, focusing her attention on the nature of infant-mother interactions and their influence on the child's physical and emotional health, particularly the development of anxiety or tensional states. Unfortunately, this research work, although challenging, is of questionable scientific value for several reasons. There is a strong propagandistic flavor in Ribble's writings. Statistical data are inadequately reported, observational techniques are not described, and fact and opinion are not clearly differentiated. Thus the observations on which her conclusions are based may be biased. Nevertheless, her ideas and observations will be summarized here because they are thought-provoking and have had considerable influence on many pediatricians and psychologists.

Ribble maintains that the child's physical and psychological welfare is dependent upon "good mothering." Adequate maternal care fosters nervous integration, "energy for mental growth," and "feelings of well-being and a sense of security in the child." In addition, the infant's biological well-being is affected by his mother's behavior. For example, 180 of the neonates she observed suffered from generalized, exaggerated muscular tensions. In each case, these tensions disappeared when the infant was allowed to suck at his mother's breast or was put into close contact with her body. However, if deprivation of this kind of experience continued, the infant manifested persistent muscular tension, inadequate breathing, and gastrointestinal disorders.

"Good mothering" techniques, personal care, and massage are also recommended for the restoration of the child's appetite, alertness, and reflex excitability, for the reduction of exaggerated mouth movements and nervous tension, and for the relief of constipation. According to Ribble, adequate sucking experiences are essential for good breathing and digestion and are also important in the structural development of the face and jaws and in the stimulation of mental alertness. At least one writer (48) has challenged Ribble's conclusions about the relationship between the mother's behavior and the neonate's physiological functioning. For example, he maintains that adequate breathing begins reflexly, regardless of the mother's method of handling the child.

Ribble also asserts that women who are emotionally disturbed or reject their children cannot provide "adequate" mothering for them. This generally results in one of two extreme types of reaction. One is *negativism*, which is characterized by refusal to suck, loss of appetite, hypertension, rigidity of body muscles, breath holding, shallow breathing, and constipation. The other reaction, *regression*, is marked by depressive quiescence, lack of interest in food, stuporous sleep, loss of muscle tone and reflex excitability, pallor, irregular breathing, and gastrointestinal disturbances such as vomiting and diarrhea. The extreme form of this regressive reaction, _marasmus_, is a malady of "wasting away," involving extreme lethargy and lack of interest, deterioration of body reflexes, increase of pallor, and muscular flabbiness.

"It seems clear from these reactions that inadequate mothering is an actual privation which may result in biological, as well as psychological, damage to the infant's organism. It is in no case a casual matter of sentiment" (50, 635).

Consequents of Impersonal Care and Institutionalization

Other researchers who have been more systematic in their investigations generally corroborate Ribble's conclusions about the adverse consequents of extremely unfavorable treatment during infancy. Spitz (58, 59, 60) studied children from two institutions where they had been raised since birth. One was a foundling home where each infant was attended by a nurse who had charge of from eight to twelve other children; hence it may be inferred that these infants were handled impersonally. In the other institution, a nursery, each child was cared for by his own mother. Both institutions offered adequate nutrition, high levels of hygienic and sanitary conditions, good medical care, and excellent housing. They appeared to differ significantly in only one factor, the presence or absence of emotional interchange between mother and child. This factor was considered by the author as the independent variable accounting for the observed differences between the two groups.

Infants at both institutions were observed and tested over a period of two years. Hetzer-Wolf Baby Tests were used to measure six aspects of development (perception, bodily functions, social relations, memory and imitation, manipulative ability, and intelligence) and to give a developmental quotient (D.Q.) comparable to the I.Q. In the first four months at the institution, the average D.Q. of the foundling home children was 124, while the average for the nursery children was only 102. However, at the end of the first year the foundlings' average D.Q. declined to 72, while on the average, nursery children maintained their original level (see Figure 16). The downward trend of the foundling home children's D.Q. scores continued until the end of the second year, when their average D.Q. was only 45.

Spitz maintains that the absence of emotional interchange with the mother was responsible for this reversal of developmental trends.

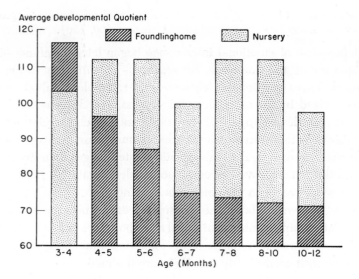

FIGURE 16. Comparison of development in nursery and foundling-home children. (Personal communication from Dr. René A. Spitz, reproduced with his permission. See also [60].

While the children in "Nursery" developed into normal, healthy toddlers, a two-year observation of "Foundling-home" showed that the emotionally starved children never learned to speak, to walk, to feed themselves. With one or two exceptions in a total of 91 children, those who survived were human wrecks who behaved in a manner of agitated or apathetic idiots (60, 149).

The two groups also differed strikingly in physical health and mortality rates. Despite excellent hygienic conditions, foundling-home children very early showed extreme susceptibility to all kinds of infection and illness. In a two-year period, there were no deaths among the nursery children, but 37 percent of the foundlings died in a measles epidemic. Since both institutions maintained adequate precautions against contagion, Spitz feels that the high mortality rate of the foundlings was a consequence of their complete physical and psychological decline stemming from emotional starvation. Among the foundling-home survivors, *marasmus* (cf. p. 154), also referred to as *hospitalism*, and hyperexcitability were common conditions.

Spitz concludes that:

. . . regularity in the emergence of emotional response, and subsequently of developmental progress, both physical and mental, is predicated on adequate mother-child relations. Inappropriate mother-child relations [as in the foundling home] resulted regularly either in the absence of developmental progress, emotional or otherwise, or in paradoxical responses (60, 150).

If deprivation of emotional interchange began later in infancy—in the third quarter of the first year, for example—*anaclitic depression* often developed. This condition, which somewhat resembles adult depression, is characterized by intense sullenness, sadness, and displeasure, coupled with arrested development. If favorable mother-child relations were reëstablished within three months, the normal course of development was resumed. However, if the deprivation lasted longer than five months, the child did not improve but continued to deteriorate (61).

Spitz's work has been extremely challenging and his findings provide impressive evidence about the consequences of unfavorable mother-infant relationships. Unfortunately, the author does not specify which variables are of major importance in "emotional interchange." From our point of view, it seems likely that these are the factors involved in learning positive or negative responses to the mother. We shall elaborate this argument after reviewing studies of enduring consequents of poor mother-infant interactions.

Later Consequences of "Inadequate Mothering"

Ribble and Spitz studied only newborn and very young infants, but another investigator, Goldfarb (18, 19, 20, 21, 22, 23, 24, 25), focused his attention on later development of children who experienced impersonal infant care ("inadequate mothering"). In a series of investigations, he compared orphans who had been reared in an institution for the first 3 years of their lives with others (matched in age, sex, and years of dependency) brought up in foster homes. Subjects were drawn from four age groups, averaging approximately 3½, 6½, 8½, and 12 years. There were extensive case studies and test data (intelligence, educational achievement, personality, motor coördination, social maturity, and language ability) on all the children.

Despite the fact that their true mothers were superior in terms of vocational competence, an approximate measure of intelligence, the institution children in all the age groups studied were inferior to the foster children on all tests of intelligence. Their greatest weaknesses were in the areas of concept formation, reasoning, and abstract thinking. As late as adolescence, institution-reared children had difficulty with tests involving learning songs, rhymes, and stories, recalling the past clearly or anticipating the future. According to the investigator, the test results reflect the general apathy, intellectual passivity, and impoverishment of children who spend their early lives in institutions.

Many of the institution children were subsequently adopted into foster homes which were intellectually and emotionally more stimulating than the institution. Despite this, they continued to be retarded in mental growth. The author therefore concluded that extensive psychological deprivation in infancy may exert long-lasting influences on the child's intellectual performance.

Moreover, specific language and speech difficulties, often noted among institution children (7), persisted long after the child left the institution. Apparently the early lack of stimulation resulted in restricted capacity for language development which was not overcome in spite of long periods of ordinary school, family, and community experience (19, 23).

Behavior problems, overt expressions of anxiety (restlessness, hyperactivity, inability to concentrate), aggression (temper tantrums, impudence, destructiveness, antagonism, and cruelty), and emotional impoverishment were much more frequent among the institution-reared than among the foster-home children. Personality tests revealed that, long after they had been placed with families, institution children were still less mature, less self-controlled and self-critical, more passive and apathetic, less persistent in goal-directed activities, and less willing to conform to social customs. Case records supported these test results, showing that children reared in institutions were generally insecure and made insatiable demands for attention. Most of them did not develop strong or affectionate personal attachments, but remained emotionally cold and isolated, capable of only the most superficial interpersonal relationships. According to the author, these social and emotional difficulties, which persisted into adolescence, were related to the deprivations experienced in infancy when "strong anchors to specific adults were not established" (18, 19, 22, 23).

There were, of course, a few institution children who achieved good adjustments subsequently in foster homes. Analysis of the case histories of these children revealed that they had originally been placed in institutions at an average age of 11 months and had remained there an average of only 25 months. On the other hand, adolescents described as maladjusted in foster homes had been placed in institutions at significantly younger ages (6 months on the average) and were there for longer periods of time (an average of 34 months) before being transferred to foster homes.

The impersonal care, coldness, and isolation of the institutional program left permanent marks on the children. The author therefore concluded that predisposition to poor adjustment is "fixed" in the course of the infantile experiences involving deprivations. Moreover, the earlier the age at which this experience is initiated and the longer its duration, the greater is the extent of maladjustment likely to be manifest (23, 24).

The works of these three investigators—Ribble, Spitz, and Goldfarb—demonstrate the pervasive and long-lasting consequences of poor infantile care and inadequate parent-child relationships. Despite the different techniques and populations used in these studies, they all agree that consistently warm, personalized attention and contact with an adult in the role of a parent are necessary for subsequent good adjustment. Care which is directed solely at satisfying the child's minimum biological needs and keeping him physically healthy may lead to an utter lack of emotional responsiveness and inability to develop close interpersonal relationships.

LEARNING THEORY AND EARLY MOTHER-CHILD RELATIONSHIPS

Learning theory helps us to understand the broad significance of the child's earliest relationships. The number of stimuli (cues) in the child's environment is relatively small. During his first year, his social interactions are normally restricted to his parents, particularly his mother. If

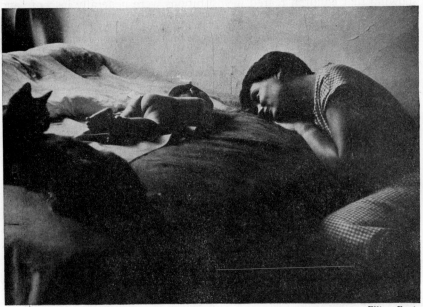

Elliott Erwitt

the mother responds to the child's needs, she becomes associated with tension-reducing, i.e., rewarding, experiences. Subsequently, she herself acquires reward value, and the need for the mother, i.e., dependence on her, becomes a secondary or learned drive. Moreover, the greater the proportion of pleasant, rewarding experiences with the mother, the greater the likelihood that her presence will evoke feelings of relaxation, well-being, and security in the child. The woman who practices "adequate mothering" is often a tension reducer and satisfier; hence positive reactions toward her are elicited frequently and acquire great habit strength.

It is important to remember that at this time in the infant's life, his mother is practically the sole representative of the larger social group. Through the behavior mechanism of generalization, reactions to her spread to others. If the mother is seen as gratifying, warm, relaxing, and tension-reducing, other people are more likely to be regarded similarly. In other words, the feelings (reactions) originally attached to the stimuli presented by the mother may generalize to cues presented by other people.

Under conditions of "inadequate mothering" or impersonal care, as in institutions, the child is not likely to have pleasant, tension-reducing experiences with his mother. On the contrary, he may be handled carelessly, held in uncomfortable positions, and fed at specified times whether he is hungry or not. The pain and displeasure elicited by such care may become associated with the stimuli present at those times, including his mother or the nurse feeding him. Negative attitudes toward this person may develop and these may generalize to others, resulting in widespread withdrawal and avoidance of people, and, consequently, social maladjustment.

The findings from the studies of Ribble, Spitz, and Goldfarb supply vivid demonstrations of these basic social learning principles. Their "inadequately mothered" foundling home and institutional subjects displayed restricted responsiveness to people, difficulty in interpersonal relationships, and emotional isolation. These socially maladaptive general reactions may be viewed as outgrowths of the dissatisfaction, discomfort, and frustration experienced originally during infantile care and feeding. After these feelings became associated with the mother or nurses attending them, they were generalized to other people.

Goldfarb's findings concerning the enduring consequences of early impersonal care underscore the vast implications of the child's early learning with respect to interpersonal relationships. It may be assumed that the institution subjects developed negative attitudes toward social relations in general after they found that interactions with others (nurses) were often accompanied by unpleasant feelings and sensations. In the course of their random activities, these children probably discovered that the responses of turning away or avoiding social contacts were sometimes tension-reducing (rewarding) since they removed them from distressing situations. In the institutional setting such social withdrawal responses were probably rewarded frequently and hence acquired great habit strength. Therefore they were carried over to other situations, such as the foster home, and could be extinguished only with great difficulty.

Furthermore, to make their wants known, babies in an institution may often be forced to resort to attention-getting mechanisms such as temper tantrums, destructiveness, or extreme restlessness. Since these reactions are likely to bring attention and satisfaction of needs, they are learned and transferred to other situations. Thus some "behavior problems" of maladjusted adopted children are in all probability simply continuations of previously rewarded responses.

It will be recalled that, in general, the children who showed the poorest adjustments in foster homes were those who had been admitted to the institution earliest and stayed longest. These children had many more opportunities to get reinforcement for their withdrawal and attention-getting responses. Having thus gained great habit strength, these responses were repeated and were not eliminated even though they were maladaptive in the foster home. Among the children who had not been in the institution as long, these reactions were not rewarded so frequently and hence did not acquire such great habit strength. Therefore, they could be extinguished more readily, and new responses, more suitable for foster-home adjustment, could be rewarded and learned, and eventually could replace the older maladaptive ones.

To summarize, early learning may be built on the basis of hunger drives and experiences associated with feeding. As Marquis' experiment (cf. pp. 139–140) demonstrated, neonates can learn to respond with restlessness to simple internal cues such as a certain degree of hunger (time elapsed since last feeding). Responses to external and more complex cues, such as those involved in interpersonal relations, are also learned in early infancy. The feeding situation is basically a social one in which fundamental attitudes toward the mother are formed. These may be positive or negative—or a conflictful combination of the two—depending on the amount of reward and discomfort ordinarily associated with food getting. Initial reactions toward other people may be generalizations of attitudes learned in the child's earliest social interactions.

Learning theory also helps us to understand how specific feeding practices may influence the child's later adjustment. Certain feeding procedures are probably more likely to insure that feeding experiences will be tension-reducing. For example, nursing may be preferable to artificial feeding because it maximizes the pleasurable aspects of the feeding situation and thus helps strengthen the mother-child attachment. In breast feeding, the mother is afforded an excellent opportunity to hold the child closely and thus give him feelings of support, relaxation, and comfort. These feelings may also accompany bottle feeding *if* the child is held securely during the process, "talked" to, and played with; but not if his bottle is propped up and accompanying ministrations are lacking. Moreover, the infant's early learned oral drives are most likely to be satisfied in the relatively long sucking periods involved in breast feeding.

Halversen (30) has shown that signs of contented feeding (steady, rhythmic sucking and swallowing movements, steady gripping, infrequent changes of body position) generally accompany nursing or feeding from a nipple from which milk is easily obtained. Signs of discomfort and frustration (strong sporadic sucking, rejection of the nipple, general restlessness, increased bodily and muscular tension) are elicited by interrupted nursing or feeding from a nipple from which milk can be obtained only with difficulty. Apparently holding the infant comfortably during uninterrupted nursing, or feeding him from a relatively easy nipple (especially if he is given an opportunity to suck a pacifier afterwards), can satisfy oral needs and evoke feelings of satisfaction.

Demand feeding may be a desirable practice because it prevents the building up of painful hunger tensions. Regular scheduling in early infancy, on the other hand, may mean that the child is sometimes fed before he desires food, while at other times he eats only after his hunger pangs have become intense. As noted earlier, under either of these conditions, eating may be uncomfortable.

Of course, there are situations where the mother cannot feed her child on a strictly demand schedule because of the pressures of family or work duties. If she attempts to do so, she may become irritable and inadvertently handle the child roughly, thereby making the feeding situation unpleasant. Since babies soon develop fairly regular schedules of their own, a modified demand-feeding regimen may provide a good compromise. Under such a system, the mother can anticipate approximately the proper time to feed her child. Even though he may not be fed immediately when he cries for food, his hunger tensions will not become intense.

In weaning, the child must learn to like new foods and to eat in a new way. If this is accomplished too abruptly, the child may have inadequate opportunities to satisfy his oral drives in the accustomed way, receive inadequate amounts of nourishment (i.e., insufficient hunger reduction), or have difficulty in digesting the new food. Any of these conditions, which make weaning unpleasant or frustrating, can be avoided if weaning is accomplished gradually. For this reason, a gradual weaning process is preferable to an abrupt one.

From our theoretical standpoint, specific feeding training practices assume their major importance because they are embedded in the matrix of mother-child relationships. If the practices employed make the feeding situations pleasant and rewarding, the child's attachment to his mother will be strengthened, and warm, friendly feelings toward her will increase. If these feelings generalize to others, as they are likely to, the child will be started on the road to good future social and emotional adjustment.

FACTORS INFLUENCING THE MOTHER'S CHOICE OF FEEDING PRACTICES

A mother can obviously choose from many alternative techniques for handling her infant's hunger: "warm mothering" or impersonal treatment, breast or bottle feeding, regular scheduling or demand feeding, abrupt or gradual weaning. Since, as we have seen, the feeding procedures employed may exert powerful influences on the infant's developing personality, it is important to understand the factors involved in the mother's selection of her particular method.

Cultural Factors

Throughout this book we will stress the fact that child-rearing techniques vary from one culture to another. Whiting and Child (67) found a very wide variety of feeding practices in 51 cultural groups for which they had data. The Marquesans, for example, do not indulge their children, and nurse them only a short time. Marquesan mothers, fearing disfigurement of their breasts, generally wean their infants within the first year. At the other extreme, the Chenchu tribe of India allow their children to nurse until they are 5 or 6. The Lepcha of India ordinarily wean their children by the age of 3, but youngest children are occasionally allowed to nurse until puberty.

There are also great cultural differences in the severity of the weaning process. Thus, among the Baiga, weaning is accomplished entirely by techniques of punishment, whereas the Kurtatchi attempt a gradual build-up of the child's satisfactions in eating like an adult, without actively discouraging him from nursing.

Subgroups within our own culture employ different feeding practices with their children. About 12 or 15 years ago, Davis and Havighurst (10) studied the child-rearing practices of lower- and middle-class white and Negro mothers. Their data, obtained from intensive interviews with 200 women, showed that permissive feeding and weaning treatment was more characteristic of lower-class than of middle-class mothers. More lower-class children were fed only by breast, nursed for longer periods of time and on self-demand schedules, and allowed to use pacifiers. Negro mothers tended to be more lenient than whites in their feeding procedures, nursing their children longer, feeding on demand, and weaning more gradually.

Research done about 10 years later challenges these findings on the greater permissiveness of lower-class parents. A staff of investigators at the Laboratory of Human Development at Harvard University conducted interviews with 198 upper-middle and 174 upper-lower class mothers in the Boston area (41). They found few differences between the social classes in infant-feeding practices. Middle-class mothers breast fed somewhat more frequently, and scheduled feedings slightly more rigidly, but neither of these differences was significant.

There are obviously major differences in the findings of these two studies. These may be explained partially in terms of the ten years which elapsed between the two investigations. During this time, middle-class mothers, having become educated about the value of more permissive feeding practices, may have adopted more of them.

Education About Child-Rearing Practices

Education may be an equalizer as far as feeding practices are concerned. In one study, questionnaires were completed by 229 lower-, middle-, and upper-class mothers who had been taught a philosophy of flexible, permissive child care (35). The data showed that, in this group, women from different social classes did not differ in their use of self-demand scheduling or duration of breast feeding.

Perhaps different segments of American society traditionally had their own standards of feeding training. Hence the techniques chosen by a particular mother depended, in part, on her social-class membership. However, it appears that special education may become more influential than social status in influencing the feeding practices employed.

Advice from doctors may have the same consequents as special parental education. At present, psychiatrists and pediatricians generally advocate greater leniency in infant disciplinary procedures. Advice from pediatricians is probably becoming more influential, since more mothers —especially of the middle class—consult them now. Breast feeding, self-demand scheduling, and gradual weaning will probably become more common if these doctors continue to advocate permissiveness.

Widely circulated writings may have far-reaching influence. Watson's book *Psychological Care of Infant and Child* (65), published in 1928, enjoyed a great deal of popularity for a number of years. Many mothers followed Watson's teaching, employing "impersonal" procedures, like those discussed earlier in this chapter, in child rearing. Unfortunately, these techniques do not appear to provide a substantial foundation for good mental health later in life. Clinicians are well acquainted with children and young adults whose mothers accepted Watson's ideas completely, and neglected to attend to many of their children's important psychological and social needs.

In contrast to this kind of approach, recent popular literature, reflecting pediatric thinking, stresses flexible, permissive child-rearing procedures and the establishment of warm, intimate mother-child relationships. An excellent example is Spock's well-known book *Infant and Child Care* published in 1946 in both regular and pocket-book editions (62).

Obviously there are many fads in child-rearing techniques. As we have seen, there is good evidence that warm, close parent-child relationships foster good adjustment in children. But it is not yet possible to make adequate evaluations of some of the specific child-rearing practices currently being recommended. Moreover, it is highly improbable that parents will ever be able to depend on rules of thumb, applied in a mechanical fashion, in rearing their children. If parents are to avoid the errors of Watson's followers, they should probably be guided by their own creative intelligence and a broad general understanding of the factors influencing personality development.

Mothers' Attitudes

As we would expect, the personality of the mother strongly affects her relationship with her child and the specific training techniques she employs. An extremely orderly, rigid, compulsive mother will find strict scheduling of activities, including feeding, consistent with her general way of doing things. On the other hand, a flexible, easygoing, and affectionate mother will, in all probability, establish an intimate relationship with her infant, holding him a great deal, loving and cuddling him.

Maternal rejection may be reflected in the mother's refusal to nurse her child. The subjects of one psychiatric study were 200 children, patients at a New York child-guidance clinic (40). Half of them had been nursed one month or less, while the other 100 children had had 12 months or more of breast feeding. According to the investigator, half the children in the short-fed group were "rejected," while two-thirds of the children in the long-fed group were "overprotected" by their mothers. From this he concluded that "in general, all factors favoring rejection of the child tend to shorten, all factors favoring overprotection tend to lengthen, the breast feeding act." This generalization does not seem to be valid for all groups, however. A pair of investigators working with normal nursery children and their mothers in Ohio found that "duration of breast feeding is not related to maternal rejection and cannot therefore be taken as an index of rejection" (47, 65). (For further discussion of rejection, see pp. 331–335.)

Two recent studies call attention to the relationship between maternal attitudes and nursing behavior. In one study, 91 mothers were interviewed just after they had delivered their babies (45). On the basis of their responses, attitudes toward breast feeding were classified as positive, doubtful, or negative. The course of lactation and nursing during their confinement in the hospital were also studied.

Although there were no differences in volume of milk secretion at the time of delivery, mothers with positive attitudes gave more milk on the fourth day (average of 59 grams at each feeding) than those with doubtful or negative attitudes (averages of 42 and 35 grams, respectively). Among the women with positive attitudes, 74 percent were successful breast-feeders, i.e., had enough milk by the fifth day to make supplementary feeding unnecessary. Significantly fewer women with doubtful and negative attitudes (35 percent and 26 percent, respectively) were successful by this criterion. Abortive breast feeding (abandonment of the effort to breast feed within a few days) occurred in only 2 percent of the women with positive attitudes, but in 18 percent of those with doubtful attitudes and 30 percent of the negative-attitudes group. Very few women with positive attitudes complained that their babies had difficulty in sucking or refused the breast. The investigators felt that women

with negative attitudes did not allow their babies to suck enough to stimulate an easy flow of milk. The study emphasized the facilitating effects
of positive attitudes toward breast feeding in promoting an abundant
supply of milk.

In another study, 1251 prospective mothers at a prenatal clinic were
asked if they preferred the usual nursery care or a rooming-in plan for
their babies immediately after delivery (36). In the rooming-in plan, the
neonate is kept in the same room as its mother, thus giving her an opportunity to observe and care for him continuously from birth. The majority
of women who preferred this plan also expressed a desire to nurse their
babies. Among those who favored nursery care, the majority wished to
bottle-feed. It may be concluded that more mothers who wish to establish
close relationships immediately with their babies choose breast feeding.

Of course, there are no one-to-one relationships between variables such
as social class, maternal attitudes, and child-rearing practices. Numerous
other factors may be involved in the determination of the kinds of feeding training techniques employed. For example, a mother who is in poor
health or has breast infections may not be able to breast-feed her child
regardless of her attitudes toward this practice. For physiological reasons,
milk supply may not be adequate for long periods of nursing. Working
mothers and those with many children may be forced to employ regular
schedules even though they would prefer self-demand feeding. The research work reported above, however, does make it clear that the following maternal variables tend to be associated with permissive feeding
training and nursing: education in a philosophy of lenient child-rearing
practices; warm, accepting personality; favorable attitudes toward nursing; and desire for early intimate contact with the infant.

REFERENCES AND ADDITIONAL READING

1. Abraham, K., *Selected papers on psychoanalysis*. London: Hogarth, 1927.
2. Aldrich, C. A., The advisability of breast feeding. *J. Am. med. Assn.*
   (1947), *135*:915–916.
3. Aldrich, C. A., and Hewitt, E. W., A self-regulating feeding program for
   infants. *J. Am. med. Assn.* (1947), *135*:340–342.
4. Benjamin, J. D., Methodological considerations in the validation and
   elaboration of psychoanalytic personality theory. *Am. J. Orthopsychiat.*
   (1949), *19*:342–350.
5. Blum, G. S., *Psychoanalytic theories of personality*. New York: McGraw-
   Hill, 1953.
6. Brodbeck, A. J., The effects of three feeding variables on the nonnutritive
   sucking of new-born infants. *Am. Psychologist* (1950), *5*:292–293.

7. Brodbeck, A. J., and Irwin, O. C., The speech behavior of infants without families. *Child Develop.* (1946), *17*:145–165.

8. Cameron, N., *The psychology of behavior disorders*. Boston: Houghton Mifflin, 1947.

9. Child, I. L., Socialization, in G. Lindzey (ed..), *Handbook of social psychology*. Cambridge: Addison-Wesley, 1954.

10. Davis, A., and Havighurst, R. J., Social class and color differences in child-rearing. *Am. sociol. Rev.* (1946), *11*:698–710.

11. Davis, H. V., Sears R. R., Miller, H. C., and Brodbeck, A. J., Effects of cup, bottle, and breast feeding on oral activities of newborn infants. *Pediatrics* (1948), *3*:549–558.

12. Dollard, J., and Miller, N. E., *Personality and psychotherapy*. New York: McGraw-Hill, 1950.

13. English, O. S., and Pearson, G. H. J., *Emotional problems of living*. New York: Norton, 1945.

14. Erikson, E., *Childhood and society*. New York: Norton, 1950.

15. Fenichel, O., *The psychoanalytic theory of neuroses*. New York: Norton, 1945.

16. Freud, S., Three contributions to the theory of sex, in A. A. Brill (ed.), *The basic writings of Sigmund Freud*. New York: Modern Library, 1938, pp. 553–629.

17. Glover, E., Notes on oral character formation. *Int. J. Psychoanal.* (1925), *6*:131–154.

18. Goldfarb, W., Infant rearing and problem behavior. *Am. J. Orthopsychiat.* (1943), *13*:249–266.

19. Goldfarb, W., The effects of early institutional care on adolescent personality. *J. exp. Educ.* (1943), *12*:107–129.

20. Goldfarb, W., The effects of early institutional care on adolescent personality (graphic Rorschach data). *Child Develop.* (1943), *14*:213–225.

21. Goldfarb, W., Effects of early institutional care on adolescent personality: Rorschach data. *Am. J. Orthopsychiat.* (1944), *14*:441–447.

22. Goldfarb, W., Infant rearing as a factor in foster home placement. *Am. J. Orthopsychiat.* (1944), *14*:162–167.

23. Goldfarb, W., Effects of psychological deprivation in infancy and subsequent stimulation. *Am. J. Psychiat.* (1945), *102*:18–33.

24. Goldfarb, W., Psychological privation in infancy and subsequent adjustment. *Am. J. Orthopsychiat.* (1945), *15*:247–255.

25. Goldfarb, W., and Klopfer, B., Rorschach characteristics of "institution children." *Rorschach Res. Exch.* (1944), *8*:92–100.

26. Goldman, F., Breastfeeding and character formation. *J. Personality* (1948), *17*:83–103.

27. Goldman, F., Breastfeeding and character formation: II the etiology of the oral character in psychoanalytic theory. *J. Personality*, (1950), *19*: 189–196.

28. Goldman-Eisler, F., The problem of "orality" and of its origin in early childhood. *J. ment. Sci.* (1951), *97*:765–782.

29. Goldman-Eisler, F., Breastfeeding and character formation, in C. Kluck-

hohn and H. A. Murray (eds.), *Personality in nature, society and culture.* New York: Knopf, 1953, pp. 146–184.

30. Halverson, H. M., Infant sucking and tensional behavior. *J. genet. Psychol.* (1938), 53:365–430.

31. Hartley, E. L., and Hartley, R. E., *Fundamentals of social psychology.* New York: Knopf, 1952.

32. Hoefer, C., and Hardy, M. C., Later development of breast fed and artificially fed infants. *J. Am. med. Assn.* (1929), 92:615–619.

33. Holway, A. R., Early self-regulation of infants and later behavior in play interviews. *Am. J. Orthopsychiat.* (1949), 19:612–623.

34. Irwin, O. C., Infant speech: the effect of family occupational status and of age on use of sound types. *J. Speech Hearing Disorders* (1948), 13: 224–226.

35. Klatskin, E. H., Shifts in child care practices in three social classes under an infant care program of flexible methodology. *Am. J. Orthopsychiat.* (1952), 22:52–61.

36. Klatskin, E. H., Lethin, A. G., and Jackson, E. B., Choice of rooming-in or newborn nursery. *J. Pediat.* (1950), 6:878–889.

37. Levy, D. M., Fingersucking and accessory movements in early infancy: an etiological study. *Am. J. Psychiat.* (1928), 7:881–918.

38. Levy, D. M., Experiments on the sucking reflex and social behavior of dogs. *Am. J. Orthopsychiat.* (1934), 4:203–224.

39. Levy, D. M., Primary affect hunger. *Am. J. Psychiat.* (1937), 94: 643–652.

40. Levy, D. M., *Maternal overprotection.* New York: Columbia University Press, 1943.

41. Maccoby, E. E., Gibbs, P. K., and the Staff of the Laboratory of Human Development, Harvard University, Methods of child-rearing in two social classes, in W. E. Martin and C. B. Stendler (eds.), *Readings in child development.* New York: Harcourt, Brace, 1954, pp. 380–396.

42. Marquis, D. P., Learning in the neonate. The modification of behavior under three feeding schedules. *J. exp. Psychol.* (1941), 29:263–282.

43. Maslow, A. H., and Szilagyi-Kessler, I., Security and breast feeding. *J. abnorm. soc. Psychol.* (1946), 41:83–85.

44. Murphy, G., *Personality,* New York: Harper, 1947.

45. Newton, N. R., and Newton, M., Relationship of ability to breast feed and maternal attitudes toward breast feeding. *Pediatrics* (1950), 5:869–875.

46. Orlansky, H., Infant care and personality. *Psychol. Bull.* (1949), 46:1–48.

47. Peterson, C. H., and Spano, F. L., Breast feeding, maternal rejection, and child personality. *Character and Personality* (1941), 10:62–66.

48. Pinneau, S. R., A critique of the articles by Margaret Ribble. *Child Develop.* (1950), 21:203–228.

49. Ribble, M., *The rights of infants.* New York: Columbia University Press, 1943.

50. Ribble, M., Infantile experience in relation to personality development, in J. McV. Hunt (ed.), *Personality and behavior disorders.* New York: Ronald, 1944, pp. 621–651.

51. Roberts, E., Thumb and finger sucking in relation to feeding in early infancy. *Am. J. Dis. Child.* (1944), 68:7–8.

52. Rogerson, B. C. F., and Rogerson, C. H., Feeding in infancy and subsequent psychological difficulties. *J. ment. Sci.* (1939), 85:1163–1182.

53. Sears, R. R., *Survey of objective studies of psychoanalytic concepts.* Bulletin 51, New York: Social Science Research Council, 1943.

54. Sears, R. R., Whiting, J. W. M., Nowlis, V., and Sears, P. S., Some child-rearing antecedents of aggression and dependency in young children. *Genet. Psychol. Monogr.* (1953), 47.

55. Sears, R. R., and Wise, G. W., Relation of cup-feeding in infancy to thumb sucking and the oral drive. *Am. J. Orthopsychiat.* (1950), 20:123–138.

56. Sewell, W. H., and Mussen, P. H., The effects of feeding, weaning, and scheduling procedures on childhood adjustment and the formation of oral symptoms. *Child Develop.* (1952), 23:185–191.

57. Simsarian, F. P., Case histories of five thumbsucking children breast fed on unscheduled regimes, without limitation of nursing time. *Child Develop.* (1947), 18:180–184.

58. Spitz, R. A., Hospitalism: an inquiry into the genesis of psychiatric conditions in early childhood. In A. Freud, *et al.* (eds.), *The psychoanalytic study of the child.* Vol. I. New York: International Universities Press, 1945, pp. 53–74.

59. Spitz, R. A., Hospitalism: a follow-up report on investigations described in Vol. I., 1945. In A. Freud *et al.* (eds.), *The Psychoanalytic study of the child.* Vol. II. New York: International Universities Press, 1946, pp. 113–117.

60. Spitz, R. A., The role of ecological factors in emotional development in infancy. *Child Develop.* (1949), 20:145–156.

61. Spitz, R. A., and Wolf, K. M., Anaclitic depression; an inquiry into the genesis of psychiatric conditions in early childhood, II. In A. Freud *et al.* (eds.), *The Psychoanalytic study of the child.* Vol. II, New York: International Universities Press, 1946, pp. 313–342.

62. Spock, B., *The pocket book of baby and child care.* New York: Pocket Books, 1946.

63. Thurston, J. R., and Mussen, P. H., Infant feeding gratification and adult personality. *J. Personality* (1951), 19:449–458.

64. Watson, ·J. B., *Psychology from the standpoint of a behaviorist.* Philadelphia, Lippincott, 1924.

65. Watson, J. B., *Psychological care of infant and child.* New York: Norton, 1928.

66. Whiting, J. W. M., The frustration complex in Kwoma society, *Man,* 1944, pp. 140–144.

67. Whiting, J. W. M., and Child, I. L., *Child training and personality.* New Haven: Yale University Press, 1953.

Chapter 7

DEVELOPMENT AND SOCIAL LEARNING IN THE SECOND YEAR

Throughout childhood physical growth and learning go on simultaneously. As we shall see presently, both contribute significantly to the new developments of the second year. New responses obviously cannot occur until the infant is physically ready to make them; that is, until the basic skeletal and neuromuscular equipment has developed. Once the child is capable of a response, however, learning factors become important in determining how, when, and where it will be used. Many new behaviors become manifest, are rewarded, and acquire great habit strength during the second year.

GENERAL PHYSICAL DEVELOPMENT

In general, physical development in the second year proceeds rapidly, although more slowly than in the first year. For example, the average infant grows about 4 inches and gains 3 to 5 pounds during the second year, as opposed to height increases of 8 or 9 inches and weight gains of 14 or 15 pounds during the first. At 2, the average child is 32 or 33 inches tall and weighs approximately 25 pounds (82).

Skeletal Structure

The infant's skeletal structure also changes. Bones increase in size and number and become modified in texture. Although the 2-year-old still has a great deal of cartilage, he has many more calcified bones than the 1-year-old. The fontanelles, or soft membrane spots in the skull, generally close (i.e., the bones become hardened and fused) somewhere between the ages of 18 and 24 months, and most of the child's temporary teeth erupt during the second year (82).

Body Proportions

It will be recalled that, compared with adult body proportions, the newborn infant is top-heavy. His head is too large for his body, and his cranium is out of proportion to his face, his arms are too long, and his legs, hands, and feet are too short (see Figure 11, p. 83). Differential rates of development of the various body parts during the first 2 years produce a body build more like the adult's. For instance, the head grows a good deal more slowly than the rest of the body and assumes more adultlike proportions as the facial skeleton becomes relatively larger. Between birth and 2 years of age, both the arms and legs develop rapidly, the former becoming comparatively longer.

Muscular and Nervous Systems

The child increases markedly in strength during the second year, as his muscles develop more, accounting for a greater proportion of body weight. His potential for making new, finer, and more precise movements is also increased as his nervous system develops. His brain becomes heavier, increasing from an average of 350 grams at birth to about 1000 grams, three-quarters of its total adult weight, at age 2. The rest of his nervous system also becomes more complex and more highly differentiated. Immature nerve fibers which previously have not been entirely separated become insulated from one another by developing protective fatty shields. This process is called *myelinization*.

MOTOR DEVELOPMENT

Walking

As the child's general physical status advances, his motor response capacities become correspondingly enlarged. The locomotor phases preceding independent walking—sitting, crawling, creeping, standing, walking with support—were discussed in Chapter 4. Apparently neuromuscular maturation, rather than specific practice, is the chief antecedent of these responses. Available evidence suggests that this holds true of independent walking, too. As we pointed out earlier, Hopi Indian babies, bound to cradleboards, suffer a great deal of movement restraint during their first year. Nevertheless, they walk independently as early as infants who have had considerable previous practice in locomotion (18). In other words, it again appears that physical maturation—or more specifically, changed body proportions, advanced neural development, and increased muscle strength—is far more crucial than practice in determining the child's progress from one locomotor stage to another.

By 12 months of age, the average child is able to pull himself to a standing position and walk with support. By 14 months he can stand alone, and by 15 months he walks awkwardly and cautiously, but unassisted. These, of course, are normative, average data, and there are wide individual differences among perfectly normal children. Some children walk independently as early as 10 months; others not until they are almost 2 years old. In general, severe illness during the first 2 years may delay the onset of creeping and walking slightly (79). There is no evidence to support the popular opinion that "heavier types of infants are later sitters, standers, or walkers than lighter ones" (66, 38).

According to one large-scale investigation, the average child can walk up and down stairs with help at about 20 months, and without assistance by the end of the second year (7). Like other locomotor activities, the initial ability to climb stairs seems to be more influenced by maturation than by learning experiences. Gesell and Thompson (33) demonstrated this experimentally, using the method of co-twin control. One of a pair of identical twins (T) was given 6 weeks of daily practice sessions in stair climbing beginning at the age of 46 weeks. The other twin (C) had no contact with stairs until she was 53 weeks old. At this time, however, she was given a brief 2-week training course in stair climbing. After 2 weeks of practice, twin C climbed more rapidly and efficiently than her sister. "The climbing performance of twin C at 55 weeks was far superior to the climbing performance of twin T at 52 weeks, even though twin T had been trained seven weeks earlier and three times longer. The maturity advantage of three weeks of age must account for the superiority" (33, 116).

These studies demonstrate that locomotor skills do not emerge until the child's neuromuscular apparatus is sufficiently mature. Until this time, efforts to "teach" him these responses are bound to meet with failure. Under normal conditions, the child will make these responses once he reaches the required maturation level, even though opportunities for learning are restricted. After he becomes capable of these basic locomotor responses, however, practice brings improvements. For example, in walking and stair climbing, coördination improves; waste movements are eliminated; steps become longer, straighter, and more rapid.

Other Motor Skills

Physical developments in the second year set the stage for a vast expansion in other motor skills, too. There are marked improvements in such activities as reaching, grasping, block building, eating, self-feeding, and handling objects. Some samples, taken from Gesell's research (30), illuminate the range of activities and the progress made during this year. The average 15-month-old can build a stable tower of 2 cubes, insert a pellet into a bottle, and place a round block correctly in a formboard, although at 12 months he could do none of these. At 18 months, he can throw a ball and construct a tower of 3 blocks (see Figure 17). The 2-

1. Walks alone; seldom falls
5. Fills cup with cubes
9. Hurls ball
2. Seats self in small chair
6. Dumps pellet from bottle
10. On command puts ball on chair
3. Turns pages two or three at a time
7. Imitates stroke
11. Walks into ball
4. Builds tower of three
8. Identifies one picture
12. Pulls toy

FIGURE 17. The child at eighteen months. (From A. Gesell and C. S. Amatruda, *Developmental Diagnosis: Normal and Abnormal Child Development.* New York: Hoeber, 1941.)

year-old can kick a ball, turn the pages of a book, insert 3 blocks into their proper places in a formboard, and build a column 6 or 7 cubes high.

Gesell and Thompson (33) have shown that these tasks, like locomotion, can be mastered only after the child has achieved sufficient neuromuscular maturation. The twin subjects of the stair-climbing experiment, C and T, also participated in a controlled study of cube manipulation. For a period of 6 weeks, twin T was given training in building towers with cubes. Twin C had no such practice. Yet, at the end of the training period, the twins did not differ in ability to manipulate the cubes. The authors feel that T's failure to demonstrate marked improvement as a result of special training was due to her physical immaturity. "There is no conclusive evidence that practice and exercise even hasten the actual appearance of types of reaction like . . . tower-building. The time of appearance is fundamentally determined by the ripeness of the neural structures" (33, 114). Again it must be emphasized that once the initial components of a response are made, practice leads to improved performance.

LANGUAGE DEVELOPMENT

Basic Speech Sounds

In Chapter 4 we traced language development during the first year. Like progress in locomotion and manipulation, progress in language in the second year is the consequence of both maturation and learning. It will be recalled that most of the earliest sounds emerge in the child's spontaneous vocal play without special training (cf. pp. 97–99). These originally meaningless utterances constitute the elements from which true speech develops.

During the second year, the infant's repertoire of basic sounds (phonemes) grows. On the average, 1-year-olds can pronounce 18 phonemes; by 23 months, the average is 25. Throughout the first year, vowel sounds predominate in the infant's babbling, and vowel types of phonemes outnumber consonant types. After the first year, however, the vowel-consonant ratio becomes reversed. By 23 months, the number of vowel types in the baby's repertoire has increased to about 11, the number of consonant types to about 14 (43, 44).

Among the consonants, the proportion of nasals increases, while the proportion of fricatives (e.g., f, v, s, z) drops considerably. Sounds made with the forward parts of the mouth (postdentals, dentals, and labials) become more frequent, while glottals decrease. As McCarthy points out in her comprehensive and thoughtful review of language development, these changes are largely attributable to physical maturation.

Two other changes [affecting language development] which follow shortly in the last quarter of the first year of life, are the experience with solid food, which stimulates chewing and exercises jaw muscles, and dentition. As chewing activity increases and nursing and sucking activity decreases, the sucking pads in the cheeks of the infant become absorbed, which again alters the shape of the oral cavity. He also acquires front teeth, usually 4 upper and 4 lower ones by the end of the first year, which give a new front wall to the oral cavity and make possible dental and postdental consonant sounds. It is only after respiration has been satisfactorily established, after the child has assumed the erect posture, has ceased to be nursed, has begun to use solid food, and after the frontal incisors have erupted, that the onset of true speech is observed (56, 513).

Vocabulary Growth

While the ability to vocalize specific sounds depends on physical maturation, the child must *learn* to use language in communication and thought. Real progress comes through combining sounds into words and understanding the speech of others.

It is difficult to overestimate the importance of language in modern life. In addition to being the basis of all social communication, language is essential for almost all "higher learning" and "higher mental processes" such as planning, thinking, reasoning, attention, memory, and judgment. In short, when the child learns to use language, he encounters "a host of dramatic new possibilities" (64, 84) for psychological growth.

Second-year development is marked by swift and dramatic improvements in verbal ability. The child begins to use words meaningfully; his comprehension of questions and commands increases; and his speech becomes more comprehensible. He begins to respond to simple commands at about 10 months. The first word—generally a single or duplicated syllable such as bye-bye, mama, or dada—is spoken sometime around the first birthday, on the average.

Following the appearance of the first word, vocabulary grows slowly for a while. This may be related to the fact that at this time the infant's attention is devoted largely to mastering locomotion. However, language development generally advances rapidly once skill in independent walking has been acquired, usually around 18 months.

By the age of 2, the average child in one investigation had spoken 37 different words in the presence of an examiner (76). There were marked individual differences, the range being from 6 to 126 words. These are hardly accurate estimates of the children's verbal achievements, however, for the data are based only on *spontaneous* talk during periodic routine examinations.

In another study, the investigator tested the total effective vocabulary (defined as the ability to speak *or* to understand the test words) of 154 children below 2 years of age. She found that word knowledge increased tremendously during the second year. The average vocabulary of the 1-year-old, according to these tests, was 3 words. By 15 months, the average was 19; by 18 months, 22 words; by 21 months, 118; and by 2 years, 272 words (78).

Analysis of young children's talk reveals that their early vocabularies are made up mostly of nouns and interjections. There is a stage of asking and repeating the names of objects in the environment, and object naming constitutes about half of the speech of 18-month-olds (55, 56). At this age, one word may function as a whole sentence, but 6 months later two or three words may be combined into simple sentences (76, 78). Gifted children may use 4-, 5-, and 6-word sentences at this age.

Learning and Language Development

Most studies of language development have dealt primarily with age norms rather than with the process of learning language. Unfortunately, we have little exact knowledge of the factors influencing the acquisition of verbal responses in infancy. However, there have been at least two notable theoretical contributions to this problem, one by Miller and Dollard and one by Mowrer. Both theories employ fundamental learning concepts, such as secondary reward value and generalization, and stress the role of imitation in verbal learning.

In discussing the development of comprehension and speech, Miller and Dollard say:

At the same time that the child is practicing his own crying responses, he is learning to respond to the voices of others. Adults who are feeding, fondling, and otherwise caring for infants usually talk to them; thus certain tones of the human voice acquire a reward value and may later be used to soothe the fretful child. It seems possible that this acquired reward value of the sounds in the language generalizes to sounds which the child makes while he is babbling and helps to reinforce his babbling behavior.

In general, a child's first contact with the more formal aspects of language is in learning to use words spoken by other people as cues for his responses. A sharp "No!" is followed by punishment, which can only be escaped by stopping or retreating. Eventually, stopping becomes anticipatory and occurs to the word "No" spoken sharply, without the punishment. At the same time, "No" is acquiring an anxiety-arousing value, so that any response which brings an escape from a torrent of "Noes" is rewarded. Exactly which verbal cues a child will learn to respond to and how he will learn to respond to them depends, of course, upon his learning capacity at the particular age and upon what his parents try hardest to teach him.

At the same time that the child is being rewarded for making more responses to words as cues, he is gradually learning another aspect of language, namely, how to make the response of uttering words. If a cooky is out of reach, the response pattern of pointing at it with the body and eyes and reaching for it with the hand is often rewarded by inducing some older person to give the child the cooky. If this gesture is accompanied by a sound, it is more likely to be rewarded. If the sound seems to be some appropriate word, such as "look-at," reward is still more likely. Eventually, the more effortful parts of the gesture drop out, and the verbal response, which is least effortful and most consistently rewarded, becomes anticipatory and persists. The mechanism of reward gradually differentiates language from its original matrix of other, more clumsy, overt responses. The child learns to talk because society makes that relatively effortless response supremely worthwhile.

The child is given meticulous training in connecting words to objects and connecting acts to words. He is also given careful training in connecting words to other words, in combining words into sequences of stimulus-producing responses (62, 81).

On the basis of his study of "The psychology of talking birds," Mowrer suggests a "tentative hypothesis"—in some respects similar to that of Miller and Dollard—relating verbal behavior to the mother-child relationship.

It is very generally agreed, in all human societies, that a good mother is one who is loving and attentive to the needs of her child, and it is also a common expectation that mothers will coo and make other gentle noises when caring for their young. These two practices—loving care combined with vocalization—presumably create in the infant a predisposition to react with emotional satisfaction, first to the vocalizations of others and later to his own vocalizations. Since the sound of the mother's voice has often been accompanied by comfort-giving measures, it is to be expected that when the child, alone and uncomfortable, hears his own voice, it will likewise have a consoling, comforting effect. In this way it may be supposed that the infant will be rewarded for his own first babbling and jabbering, without any necessary reference to the effects they produce on others.

Gradually, from what the infant probably perceives as an inarticulate murmuring or warbling on the part of the mother, certain specific, recognizable words emerge which are especially welcome and reassuring, so that when, in the course of random vocalization, the child hits upon a sound that is recognizably like a sound which the mother (or possibly the father) makes, the child is motivated to reproduce that noise over and over and to try to perfect it, since a perfect reproduction of it is more satisfying than is an imperfect one.

If one wishes to call this a kind of self-contained trial-and-error learning, there can be no objection, provided we remember that it has been preceded by important emotional conditioning and that the success of the infant's efforts at vocalization is not necessarily dependent upon the reactions of others. *It is the child's own reactions to the sounds he makes which seem all-important at this stage.*

In suggesting that the utterance of word-like noises occurs first on a purely autistic basis, I mean, specifically, that when a child or a bird is lonely, frightened, hungry, cold, or merely bored, it can comfort and divert itself by making noises which have previously been associated with comfort and diversion. These sounds have become "sweet music"; and they are reproduced, not because of their social effectiveness, but because of the intrapsychic satisfaction they provide. Later, once particular sounds have been learned on this autistic basis, the stage is set for them to function instrumentally, in connection with the child's (or bird's) interactions with the external world; but this appears to be a second stage in language learning, not the first one (63, 699).

A number of studies yield evidence consistent with these hypotheses. For example, one researcher (51) demonstrated that, with increasing age, infants' imitations of adult sounds become progressively more accurate. In explaining these modifications and improvements in imitation, McCarthy makes use of learning-theory concepts similar to those of Miller and Dollard and of Mowrer.

When the child accidentally, and later purposefully, reproduces sounds which he himself has made, the adults in the environment usually say a real word which the child's sounds appear to approximate. This tends to give auditory reinforcement to the sounds the child has just made, at the same time making for more precise perception and rendition of the approved sound groups. Thus there occurs a progressive elimination of errors and a selection of movements which give the best approximation to the real word heard in the speech of adults. Continued practice thus results in the fixation of the sound groups, which come to be uttered habitually (56, 518).

Other empirical data support Mowrer's hypothesis that affectionate parent-child relationships contribute a great deal to the child's early verbal progress. As we noted in Chapter 4, institutionalized infants under 6 months of age who do not have close relationships with adults are inferior to children living with their families, both in frequency of vocalization and in number of phoneme types used. The retardation persists and may become more marked as the children become older (35). Freud and Burlingham (27, 28) also noted that children under two who were separated from their families were backward in speech development.

The relationship between speech retardation and lack of emotional stimulation in the home was demonstrated in a clinical study comparing

50 children who were delayed in speech with 50 who talked at the normal age (9). The children in the delayed-speech group tended to be isolated, frightened children who played alone, cried easily, and did not seem to want attention.

All these findings indicate that, as learning theorists would predict, "severely neglected children and those whose attachments to adults are interrupted and infrequent . . . are slow in learning to speak and may remain retarded in speech throughout their lives" (12, 288).

Group Differences In Language Development

SEX DIFFERENCES. In our culture, boys and girls are likely to be rewarded differentially for specific accomplishments. For example, boys are more likely to be highly rewarded for motor activities and hence to devote greater attention to manipulative and motor tasks than to language. Girls, on the other hand, are more likely to be reinforced for verbal accomplishments. Therefore, on the basis of learning theory, it would be predicted that girls will make more progress in language development than boys. Data from several studies confirm this prediction. Even in infancy, girls surpass boys in all aspects of language: onset of speech, vocabulary size, length and complexity of sentences, comprehensibility of speech, number of phoneme types used (43, 44).

SOCIAL-CLASS DIFFERENCES. Verbal achievements are probably more highly prized and rewarded in middle- and upper-class than in lower-class homes. Hence, we might predict that children from upper classes will make more rapid progress in language and achieve higher levels of verbal performance than lower-class children. Again, available data confirm this prediction. One investigator discovered that infants under a year old from professional and business families vocalize more and use more phonemes than those from working-class homes (42). Another study indicated that, on the average, children with delayed speech come from less well-educated families and families of lower occupational status than those who talk at the normal age (9).

INTELLECTUAL DEVELOPMENT

As a consequence of maturation and learning, and the interaction between them, the child makes tremendous strides in his ability to behave adaptively (intelligently) during the first 2 years. Piaget, the Swiss psychologist, made many interesting observations of intelligent behavior in his own children. On the basis of these observations, he delineated six successive stages in the development of intelligent behavior in infancy (67). At each stage, the infant becomes capable of new types of behavior and learns more about the world around him. A brief review of these stages can serve as a vivid illustration of the nature of the infant's progress in adaptive behavior during the first 2 years.

In the first or *neonatal stage,* the infant makes only reflex and random, diffuse, mass reactions. In the second stage, infants develop reactions that initiate and prolong certain types of activities which are already in their repertoire (e.g., thumbsucking, grasping, and sucking objects). In the third stage, the infant repeats a simple action which previously produced an interesting result (for example, kicking his legs to make a toy suspended in the crib swing). According to Piaget, during the fourth stage (*means-end behavior*) the child becomes able to use some of his already established behavior to obtain goals. For example, at 7½ months, Piaget's son knocked down a pillow to obtain a desirable object hidden behind it.

During the fifth developmental stage, the infant appears to be interested in *active experimentation,* i.e., he tries out new variations of behavior. Modifications of old behavior patterns become apparent, and curiosity and exploration are characteristic. The infant uses overt trial and error to solve simple problems such as obtaining an object that is out of reach. In the sixth step, which occurs at about 18 months of age, the infant manifests a number of elements of more complex intellectual processes: memory (imitating a model no longer present), planning, pretending, and insightful solutions to problems (e.g., using a stick as a tool to obtain objects out of reach) (67).

Obviously these latter abilities are in a rudimentary state at this age. Nevertheless, Piaget's careful observations suggest that by the age of 2, the infant has developed the beginnings of many important intellectual skills. There is, of course, no satisfactory way of determining how much of this progress stems from maturation and how much from specific learning experiences, but both sets of factors are clearly involved.

Infant Intelligence Tests

There are a number of scales designed to evaluate infant intelligence, e.g., California Preschool Mental Scale, Cattell Intelligence Scale for Infants and Young Children, Merrill-Palmer Scale, Minnesota Preschool Scale, the Gesell Developmental Schedules (see Figure 18). These tests, however, tap functions which are vastly different from those sampled

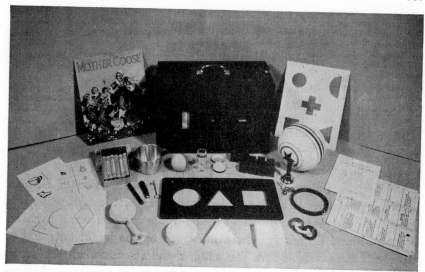

FIGURE 18. Materials used with the Gesell Developmental Schedules. (With permission of The Psychological Corporation.)

in measuring the intelligence of school-age children (cf. pp. 369–372). At these later ages, intelligence tests are heavily weighted with items dealing with abstract thinking, reasoning, and memory. However,

We cannot test a one-year-old on abstract thinking; we don't even know if he is doing it at this age. We cannot test the three-year-old on complex reasoning, because he has not developed adequate sustained attention and understanding of directions to attempt the problem. Investigators have concentrated on those aspects of behavior which can be identified objectively in the young child (13, 167).

For this reason, most infant intelligence tests are made up primarily of sensorimotor tasks.

In order to study mental growth during the first 3 years, Bayley (6, 7) assembled 185 items taken from a number of widely used infant intelligence scales. She drew particularly heavily from the Gesell and Amatruda Developmental Schedules which test four major areas: motor; "adaptive intelligence"; language; and personal-social behavior. Bayley's own "mental series includes tests of adaptability or learning and tests of sensory acuity and fine motor (manual) coördinations" (7, 90). The following, taken from Bayley's scale, illustrate the kinds of items used in infant tests. Numbers in parentheses refer to the age placement (months) of the items.

Says two words (12.9)
Spontaneous scribble (13.2)
Tower of 2 cubes (13.5)
Throws ball (15.8)
Tower of 3 cubes (16.3)
Puts cover on box (17.5)
Places pegs in holes in 38 seconds (18.2)
Turns doorknob (20.0)
Builds tower of 6 cubes (21.3)
Points to 5 pictures (23.1)

The child's score is based on his performance on these items.

In Bayley's follow-up studies, children were examined at frequent intervals beginning in early infancy. During the first few years her own 185-item scale was used, and at 6 and 7 the subjects were given the Stanford-Binet. Correlations between scores on the infant tests and on later tests were insignificant. The writer therefore concluded that "scores made before 18 months are completely useless in the prediction of school age abilities" (7, 100).

Moreover, test performance at 21 months gives a negligible prediction of success on the Stanford-Binet at 6 or 7 years (38). These findings all emphasize "the impossibility of making an accurate prognosis of the future ability of a child on a single mental test before the age of two" (3, 355).

While these scales have little predictive value for the population at large, they may help to identify cases of gross sensorimotor or language retardation. On the basis of extensive clinical experience, Escalona concludes that these tests "can succeed in detecting the mentally deviant at a very early age, often before pathology becomes manifest through pediatric or neurological examinations" (24, 120).

In view of the immense methodological difficulties in infant testing, it has been recommended that children under 2 years should not be tested "except in those cases where the pediatrician may wish to supplement his clinical observations with more objective information about the infant's sensorimotor abilities" (81, 403).

SOCIAL LEARNING IN THE SECOND YEAR

The physical, manipulative, intellectual, and language advances of the second year form the foundation for further socialization training. Since the child is more mature physically and mentally, he will be expected to substitute a certain measure of independence and self-reliance for the complete dependence of the first year. With improved verbal ability, he can make his needs known more directly. He can help more in feeding and in dressing himself. When he wants something, he is more likely to be able to get to it and obtain it. During the second year, cleanliness (toilet) training is to be initiated and perhaps completed; and certain cultural taboos are to be learned.

The child's social world is still a limited one, however. Contacts with persons outside his family constellation are few, infrequent, and, as we shall see, not very meaningful. Fundamentally, social learning at this period consists of learning *within* the family circle.

In the last chapter we discussed the vast and enduring consequents of mother-infant interactions during feeding. As we pointed out there, the child's first social learning experiences may set him on the path toward good or poor social adjustment.

But learning obviously does not stop when weaning is completed. The experiences of the next few years—particularly parental reactions to the child—"may go far toward counterbalancing the ill effects of an unsatisfactory infancy, or to undermine the first security that has resulted from satisfying experiences" (65, 655). Moreover, "changes in the environment or parent security may operate . . . to change the total balance of childhood experience" (65, 656).

Dependency

Although the child is expected to exhibit some small degree of independence, he is still highly dependent during the second year. Looking to the mother for assistance and signaling her for help have been rewarded frequently in the past, and these dependent behaviors have acquired great habit strength. Unless the child was extremely deprived, his mother's learned reward value has become firmly established by the end of the first year. Her mere presence, quite apart from her function as a supplier of food and warmth, has become associated with comfort, satisfaction, and lack of tension.

In studying the development of the dependency drive during the first 2 years, Robertson and Bowlby, British psychiatrists, found that the very young infant was concerned only with food and comfort.

In the next stage, however, which began somewhere between three and six months, a new element entered in. He began to take notice of his mother as an individual and not just as a giver of food and comfort. His eyes would search for her and light up when she came his way; a bond of feeling was developing which had grown to great intensity by his first birthday. *If we look at him now that he is 18 to 24 months old, we see a little human of some individuality who is at the peak of dependency on his parents—particularly on his mother.* He is by no means content to be fed and tended by anyone, but appreciates his mother as a particular person and has a hunger for her love and presence which is as great as his body's hunger for food. He has been weaned from the breast, but he is still unweaned from complete dependence on the protection and love of this one person. His attachment is fiercely possessive, selfish, utterly intolerant of frustration (69, 137).

Freud and Burlingham (27) concur with these views.

The personal attachment of a child to its mother [which started with her providing for his bodily needs] in the first year of life, comes to its full development in the second one. It was said before that the child is attached to its mother; it can now be safely said that it loves her. The feelings for her which it is able to experience acquire the strength and variety of adult human love (27, 49).

In brief, despite the fact that the child in his second year is capable of greater independence than he was earlier, his relationships with his mother are still of critical importance. In our culture, she remains his chief source of security, the provider of basic satisfactions, and an outstandingly important "representative of the whole outer world" (27).

REACTIONS TO SEPARATION FROM THE MOTHER. Since the infant's dependency drives are strong, it may therefore be expected that separation from the mother, the primary satisfier of these drives, will be extremely frustrating to him and will elicit reactions indicative of emotional upset. Investigations of American and European children's reactions to separation from their mothers offer impressive evidence that this is true. One group of studies involved children whose home life was disrupted, either by World War II or other events necessitating their removal from their own families. For example, Freud and Burlingham (27, 28) worked with young children at the Hampstead Nurseries in London, where children lived while their parents were in service or employed. Those between 1 and 2 years of age reacted most violently to parting from the mother.

The child feels suddenly deserted by all the known persons in its world to whom it has learned to attach importance. Its new ability to love finds itself deprived of the accustomed objects, and its greed for affection remains unsatisfied. Its longing for its mother becomes intolerable and throws it into states of despair which are very similar to the despair and stress shown by babies who are hungry and whose food does not appear at the accustomed time (27, 50).

Emotional upsets in children this age are likely to be reflected in disturbances in physical health. During World War II, a substantial proportion of English children under two did not "make satisfactory progress on admission to a day nursery, as judged by their weight gains in three monthly periods" (57, 500). This was true in spite of the fact that, compared with children remaining at home, those in nurseries had almost double rations and dietetically better-balanced meals. Their failure to gain weight adequately may therefore be attributed to emotional upset stemming from separation from the mother.

The disruption of routines and generally upset environmental conditions associated with war do not distress youngsters of this age nearly so much as separation from the mother does. John (48) studied a large group of children housed at an evacuation center where they were accompanied and attended by their mothers. Under these conditions, few children under 2 gave evidence of emotional disturbance (e.g., increased irritability, peevishness, temper tantrums, timidity, fears, disturbances of appetite and sleep), while many older children were unable to adjust satisfactorily. Apparently the mother is the basic source of satisfaction for the young infant, and if she is present, disruptions of family life are not likely to produce maladjustment. However, older children have learned to associate security and satisfaction not only with their mothers, but also with others and their homes and neighborhoods. Hence, they became distressed when they were removed from familiar surroundings.

Two research teams, one French and one British, working under the auspices of the International Children's Center, a United Nations project, have made detailed observations of infants' reactions to separation from the mother (69, 71). Their subjects, all of whom were between the ages of 1 and 2, were in public hospitals or nurseries for short periods (usually about two weeks) because of the mother's illness or pregnancy. During this time, they were attended by people who were strangers to them and their physical surroundings, eating routines, and clothing were all unfamiliar.

The French group, observing babies between 12 and 17 months of age, described three major types of reactions to separation (71). The first, *intense distress*, is characterized by crying, moaning, screaming, lack of interest, ignoring of adults, and apathy. Children with this reaction had learned to associate need gratification with their mother's presence, and her absence was therefore upsetting.

The second, *easy adjustment*, is displayed by children who seem friendly, active, independent, happy, relaxed, playful, and even-tempered at the time they arrive in the wards. However, "no child can maintain this type of adjustment; they all come to a point where they suddenly break down and show overt distress, or more progressively develop more signs of maladjustment" (71, 70).

Moreover, children who were able to adjust easily were

. . . those who have already been able to acquire a certain independence and security. They all seem to belong to a rather poor social group and to be accustomed to being taken care of by genuinely warm neighbors during the daily absences of the mother. Their well-integrated play, their friendly relationship with strange adults, remind of the play of a baby kept by a friendly stranger and perfectly confident that the mother will be back. It seems that this previous social experience, combined with a rather loose, but positive tie with the mother delays their awareness of being abandoned (71, 72).

Apparently these children had already learned that their needs could be gratified in situations involving strangers and strange surroundings. For them, the new nursery or hospital settings were similar to others to which they had been exposed and in which they experienced tension reduction.

Most children in this survey manifested the third type of reaction, *partial or precarious adjustments*, manifesting varying degrees and qualities of maladjustment. Symptoms of this third type of reaction included mournful, strained expressions; difficulties in relationships with adults, such as disinterest, ignoring or rejecting them, demanding attention from them; and generalized signs of emotional disturbance including stereotyped and impoverished behavior.

The authors concluded that the main problem of mother-separated children is their inability to establish and maintain relationships with the adults who cared for them. "This seems to be the core of their disturbances at this age, when they are still entirely dependent on their mother and when their mother is the only person with whom they have so far been able to establish a satisfactory relationship" (71, 72).

The English research team (69), working with babies between 18 and 24 months of age, concluded that when separated from their mothers they are "under considerable mental stress, and have many features quite unusual in the small child, which, if persistent, bode ill for the future development of . . . personality" (69, 131).

These investigators described three phases of emotional response to separation. The first consists of *protest*, i.e., crying loudly, expecting, on the basis of their previous learning, that their mothers will respond. When the child discovers that his mother will not answer his cries, he shows his *despair* by crying monotonously and becoming dull, apathetic, docile, and withdrawn. In the final stage, *denial*, he either transfers his attachments (i.e., dependency) to anyone who will satisfy his physical needs or ceases to show any feelings toward others. Apparently at this stage the child has learned that previously reinforced dependency reactions toward his mother are no longer rewarded. Hence the acquired dependency responses may become partially extinguished (i.e., he becomes indifferent to everyone). Alternatively, he may learn to associate others' presence with tension reduction and comfort and so transfer his dependency reactions.

A few children did not protest separation from their mothers. The researchers maintained that these children already had a low degree of attachment (dependency) as a result of "inadequate previous experience of maternal care." "None of these children behaved in a way typical of the normal family child whose dependency on the mother is at a peak at this age" (69, 133).

Perhaps these children, like Spitz's foundling-home infants and Goldfarb's institution-reared children (cf. pp. 154–158) were seldom rewarded for dependency and hence had not developed strong or extensive dependency responses or drives. Thus they were less vulnerable to frustration. While such children may appear to have more independence than others of this age, this is achieved at the cost of adequate personal interactions. It will be recalled that those children who never learned to form attachments to others often remained disinterested or avoided subsequent social relationships.

All these studies indicate that most youngsters under 2 become upset when they are separated from their mothers, i.e., when their acquired dependency needs are not gratified. Their disturbances are manifested in maladaptive responses such as crying, peevishness, apathy, and withdrawal. These reactions are, of course, incompatible with more adaptive ones. It might therefore be predicted that more mature, adaptive, independent responses are more likely to occur—and hence to be reinforced and repeated—in the mother's presence than in her absence.

INFLUENCE OF THE MOTHER'S PRESENCE ON REACTIONS TO NEW SITUATIONS. In order to study the influence of the mother's presence or absence on the child's reactions, Arsenian (4) placed 24 children (between 11 and 30 months of age) in a new "insecure" situation, specifically, a strange room. Some of them were accompanied by their mothers; others were alone. Each child spent 11 five-minute periods in the strange room, which was attractively decorated and contained many toys and pictures.

The behavior of each child at each session was observed through a one-way vision mirror. The child's reactions were classified as adaptive or goal-directed (e.g., playing, locomotion, talking) or emotional, mal-adaptive and nongoal-directed (e.g., crying, autistic gestures, thumb-sucking, fingering parts of body, waving arms, stamping feet). Security in the situation was also rated on the basis of the type of response made (withdrawal and crying, agitated movement, retreat, attack, play, free approach).

It may be hypothesized that if the child's security is dependent on his mother's presence, he should manifest few symptoms of fear and anxiety, i.e., he should behave adaptively, when she is in the room with him. However, if he is placed there alone or if his mother leaves the room, the child should become distressed and behave maladaptively. On the other hand, a child who becomes disturbed when he is alone in the unfamiliar room should feel more secure, and behave more adaptively, when his mother accompanies him there later.

Arsenian's findings generally confirmed these hypotheses. Children who were left alone for the first few sessions spent most of their time crying and making autistic gestures. On the other hand, the majority of the children who faced the "insecure situations" accompanied by their mothers were secure from the start. During the first session they displayed three times as much adaptive behavior, and only one-third as much emotional behavior, as children who were left alone in the room. On the average, the mother-present group was rated as more secure in the *initial* session than the mother-absent group was in its *final* trials (after they had presumably become accustomed to the strange room). In summary, the mother's presence elicited positive, adaptive responses, while her absence brought out immature, maladaptive responses.

Subjects whose mothers were present *only* during the first few sessions became much less secure during later sessions when their mothers were absent. Apparently personal security in this situation, as in the English wartime evacuation centers or nurseries, was based on the mother's presence. Hence, her absence evoked responses indicative of insecurity.

The children who experienced early mother-absent sessions and later mother-present sessions became only slightly more mature and adaptive in their responses when their mothers accompanied them. The author concluded that

. . . the behavior of [this] group points to the difficulty of increasing the security of the child in a situation where he has been permitted to become truly insecure. Children who were accompanied by an adult from the outset were immediately or rapidly secure in the strange situation but children who were allowed to become insecure before the adult arrived did not respond rapidly to the new source of protection (4, 203).

In summary, most 1- and 2-year-olds do not react adaptively in new situations if they face them alone. Under these circumstances, insecurity responses are frequently manifested. The mother's presence—and the implied availability of dependency-need gratification—ordinarily reduces the insecurity and anxiety and hence enables the child to react adaptively. When more mature responses are made, they become reinforceable. If reinforced, these responses will be repeated and will acquire great habit strength. Thus, the mothers' presence may be a crucial variable conducive to most children's making and learning socially mature responses.

PARENTAL ATTITUDES AND THE DEVELOPMENT OF INDEPENDENCE

Mature responses will not be made while the child is emotionally upset. At the same time, independent responses cannot acquire greater habit strength unless they are reinforced. Parental attitudes toward the child's early independent, self-reliant responses will to a large extent determine how early and rapidly he will progress in the direction of independence.

As we have seen, physical and mental maturation during the second year, together with prior learning, prepare the child for increased self-reliance. Under normal conditions, the child will want to exercise his new powers and abilities.

The earliest manifestations of the child's locomotor, manipulative, and language skills are generally praised and rewarded. First steps are usually greeted enthusiastically by the parents and the child is thus encouraged to further attempts at walking. When he can get around without assistance, the child's world expands tremendously and he takes advantage of the situation. Soon he discovers new things he has not seen before. In short, he begins to explore independently.

Permissiveness

The mother who is permissive and easygoing provides a social setting conducive to learning independent behavior. She rewards new responses and thus encourages her offspring to continue his exploration. If his self-initiated responses are rewarded, he learns that it is permissible to be curious and to try out new responses. Experiences of this sort foster the development of self-confidence and spontaneity. Since exploration and self-expression are frequently rewarded in a permissive family situation, they acquire reward value, and become learned drives.

The youngster who is rewarded for learning new responses becomes motivated to learn more. With greater freedom of movement, increased self-confidence, and a willingness to be spontaneous and creative, he will allow himself to encounter many new situations and to experiment with new solutions to problems. As he does this, his learning opportunities increase. For example, the child who has achieved success (been rewarded) in riding his kiddie car is more likely to attempt to ride a tricycle than one whose earlier efforts met with failure or punishment. Obviously the behavior and skills involved in tricycle riding cannot be rewarded and learned unless they are tried. If the child finds that "trying things out" is discouraged, he will not make the attempts.

Some interesting animal experiments by Harlow (37) provide us with further evidence that successful learning experiences facilitate further learning. Animals that had learned to make responses in previous experiments learned new, unrelated tasks much more quickly than tame naïve

Courtesy, United Nations.

First steps.

animals that had not participated in other experiments. Apparently the animals had "learned to learn." In the same way, we would anticipate that children who have been rewarded frequently for attempting new activities will be more likely to try out other new responses in the future. For them, learning itself has become rewarding.

Ordinarily we would expect the mother who has given her child warm mothering experiences when he was an infant would continue to be permissive when he is in the early locomotor stage. If the mother expresses pleasure at her child's new activities, she may again become associated with feelings of gratification, pleasantness, relaxation, and well-being. If the mother-child relationship has previously been positive, it becomes strengthened.

Rejection

Some rejecting mothers actually facilitate their children's learning of independent responses. For example, if a mother rejects her child from earliest infancy, he may never develop strong dependency reactions. Such a child is likely to learn independent responses relatively early. Thus, as the observation of young children separated from their mothers showed (cf. pp. 185–186), children who were inadequately cared for by their mothers did not become so upset as others when separated from them. In this sense, these children appeared independent. It should be pointed out, however, that this kind of independence—or lack of dependence— may be achieved at the cost of good social adjustment, as Spitz's and Goldfarb's studies demonstrated (cf. pp. 154–158).

The mother who has been rejecting in her earlier treatment of the child may give him more reward and approval during later periods. She may welcome the signs of independence which, with further development, will free her from many burdensome child care duties. Her child may learn independence easily, because the mother rewards such behavior directly or because, by behaving independently, he can obtain some gratifications himself, e.g., he can secure candy or cookies. If the mother's early rejection has been severe, this child may never become socially outgoing (i.e., his withdrawal from his mother may generalize widely), but he will become independent. If his earlier relationship with his mother was unsatisfactory, although not too severe, her more accepting, satisfying behavior at this time may improve its quality. The child's new feelings about her may help to overcome emotional disturbances stemming from earlier frustrations (65).

Other kinds of rejecting mothers who have frustrated their children in early infancy face even greater problems and become more rejecting as their children manifest more independence. A child who is walking, running, climbing, and jumping all over the house may be even more burdensome to such a mother than he was as a nursing infant. If this is true, the mother may find it most convenient to restrict the child's activities by punishing him whenever he goes anywhere outside a limited area (perhaps a playpen) or touches anything except his own toys.

Overprotection

In some cases, mothers who have generously satisfied all the child's earliest needs frustrate them as soon as they show any signs of independence. Levy (50) demonstrated that "overprotective" mothers, who are highly permissive with their infants (breast-feed for a long time, cuddle them, etc.) may actually retard their acquisition of mature responses. These mothers use two techniques, "infantilization" and "prevention of independent behavior," to maintain close, dependent infant-mother relationships (50). The overprotective mother sees the child's growing independence as a threat to her domination and possession of him. Hence she attempts to restrict independent activities such as exploration and experimentation as soon as they appear. Thus she minimizes her youngster's opportunities to learn new responses.

Overmeticulousness

Like some rejecting, overprotective mothers, women who are overly concerned about order and neatness in the house may inhibit their children's spontaneous activities. If the youngster is spanked or scolded every time he explores outside a designated area or grabs something which is not his, pain and punishment become associated with such responses. Subsequently unfamiliar areas and objects become capable of eliciting fear and anxiety, and the child learns to avoid them in order to escape these tensions.

Obviously children must learn to keep away from places and objects which are dangerous, valuable, or fragile. But if the child is continually restricted or repeatedly rebuked for his independent exploratory behavior, he may become extremely inhibited. Fear of punishment will keep the child from practicing and perfecting his newly developed skills, such as walking, and thus may contribute to his becoming an awkward, poorly coördinated individual.

Moreover, anxieties attached to the practice of locomotor and manipulative responses may generalize and become pervasive fears of attempting anything new. A child with such fears appears to be lacking in self-confidence. Having been punished so frequently for displaying curiosity or for experimenting, he is reluctant to venture out, to have novel experiences, or to try to do anything he has not done before.

Such a child is afraid to act in any way that does not meet his parents' standards precisely or does not bring specific parental approval. He is likely to experience difficulties in social adjustment, since he has never learned to deal adequately with new problems (ones for which he does not have ready-made answers) as they arise.

TOILET TRAINING

Cleanliness, or toilet, training is one of the main problems of this period and one of the touchiest from the point of view of parent-child relationships. In many families it represents the first major source of conflict between the child's needs and the wishes of the parents—the first of many conformity demands that must be met in the process of growing up and becoming socialized. But although mastery of bowel and bladder control is a minimum prerequisite for social acceptance in any culture or in any class or caste group, it is not always easily achieved. The mother's role in relation to the child shifts. She becomes a "teacher," expecting him to assume some independence and responsibility for his own care.

During feeding training,

She acts in a supportive manner, giving, providing, bringing to him. In toilet training her role is quite different. She does nothing *for* the child, only *to* him. He has no initial desire to use the potty; her putting him on it is not a reward, as is her giving him food. Only gradually does he learn to *want* to have approved toilet habits, and the desire comes at the end of the mother's training activity; it is not there while she is teaching. Thus, toilet training fills no need, satisfies no initial drive; it is nothing but a modifier of behavior, a frustration, mild under the best procedure and dreadful under the worst (*74, 187*).

The child who has been the recipient of all bounties of the home . . . now confronts a considerable change in his environment. Now, instead of being the receiver, he is asked to begin to be the giver. Now, instead of being contributed to, he is asked to make a contribution. Now, instead of being in the position of irresponsibility, he is asked to assume a responsibility in relation to himself (*23, 44*).

One of the major difficulties in toilet training stems from the fact that it requires substitution of voluntary control for what is initially an involuntary reflex process. Originally, when the bladder and bowel are full, strong tensions are produced and urethral and anal sphincters are automatically released, expelling the urine or feces.

To meet cultural demands this sequence must be rearranged. The connection between bowel stimulus and the evulsion response must be weakened. The child must learn to suppress the evulsion response to the bowel drive stimulus alone. It must then insert other responses in the sequence. At first it must learn to call to the parents. It must later learn to insert walking, unbuttoning, and sitting on the toilet chair while it is still suppressing the urgent evulsion response. Only to a new pattern of cues—the bowel stimulus, the cues of the proper room, the sense of freedom of clothes, the pressure of the toilet seat on the child's thighs—may the evulsion response occur without anxiety.

In short, this response occurs not only to the pressure of the primary drive involved but also to the complex stimulus pattern just named. If one can once get the child to order the responses correctly, the strong tension reduction produced by defecation will reinforce the responses to the pattern of cues enumerated. The real problem, therefore, is getting the child to suppress the naive evulsion response and to insert a considerable series of responses into the sequence before evulsion (21, 137).

Techniques of Toilet Training

A survey of sociological and anthropological literature on toilet training reveals that there exists, as in the case of feeding training, a tremendous diversity of practices. Cultures vary greatly in age at which toilet training is begun and in the degree of severity or permissiveness with which it is managed. Extreme indulgence in training is illustrated by the practices of the Siriono of South America, who never punish the child even if he urinates or defecates on his parents. In this society, the mother makes almost no effort to train her child in habits of cleanliness until he can walk. Even then he is taught gradually, with a great deal of help, and without punishment.

The Tanala of Madagascar, on the other hand, are extremely severe in their cleanliness training practices. These people make no use of diapers, and anal training is begun at the age of 2 or 3 months. The child is expected to have gained control by the age of 6 months, and he is severely punished for accidents after that time.

In their comparison of the toilet-training practices of 20 cultures, Whiting and Child (84) found that the American middle-class group was quite extreme in severity. They were using the data from Davis and Havighurst's study of child-rearing practices in white and Negro families of the middle and lower class (17) (cf. p. 163). The findings of these researchers indicated that there were great differences in toilet-training practices among social classes and racial groups within American culture.

Thus bowel and bladder training were found to be initiated relatively early in white and Negro middle-class children. Comparison of the two racial groups revealed that, on the average, training for bowel and bladder control was begun and completed earlier in Negro than in white children.

A more recent study has yielded substantially different results (52). According to the data of this study, there were no significant differences between white upper-lower and upper-middle classes with respect to age of initiation of toilet training, but the lower-class group tended to be more severe in the process. The discrepancies between the findings of the two studies may be at least partially attributable to changes in middle-class practices between the times of the two studies. (The earlier one was conducted in the early 1940's, the later in the early 1950's.) It is also possible that there were differences in the specific lower- and middle-class samples examined in the two studies.

Time of Initiation of Training

Child experts (23, 32, 39) generally agree that training should be delayed until the child is "ready" for it, i.e., until his neuromuscular apparatus is mature. He should be able to sit up comfortably and to understand and communicate signals. This means that any real learning of bowel and bladder control is not ordinarily possible until the child is about 18 months old.

If the child is burdened with so complicated a set of coordinations as those involved in the voluntary control of bowel movements before his neuromuscular development has reached the stage that he can cope with such a task, it puts too great a burden on him from the physiological point of view (39, 306).

Psychoanalytic Theory: the Anal Phase

Freud maintained that the handling of training for cleanliness is of critical importance and has many ramifications for the child's subsequent personality development. It will be recalled that psychoanalytic theorists describe the first stage of personality development, lasting about a year, as the *oral phase*. During this time, the child derives his greatest pleasures from activities involving the mouth and lips, such as sucking.

According to psychoanalytic theory, the second phase of personality development, beginning sometime during the second year, is the *anal stage*. The anal zone becomes the major source of the infant's pleasure in his own body. In the first part of this period, the expulsive phase, the child's major pleasurable sensations are derived from the stimulation of mucous membranes involved in excreting feces. In the later part, the retentive phase, pleasure is associated primarily with retaining, rather than expelling, feces.

THE ANAL CHARACTER. As in the case of the oral phase of development, excessive indulgence or extreme deprivation during the anal period may lead to fixation. Freud suggested that three traits characterized the *anal character* or individual fixated at the anal stage. These have been called the three P's: parsimony (frugality), petulance (obstinacy), and pedantry (orderliness) (*10*).

As an adult, the *anal character* is likely to remain retentive not only in regard to defecation, but in many aspects of his life. Physically, for example, he may suffer from constipation. Psychologically, he may exhibit his retentiveness in other ways, such as hoarding money, or becoming extremely miserly. Obstinacy may also be considered a continuation of a childish desire to retain and to defy the parents' wishes that he defecate when they want him to. The *anal character* is likely to become compulsive, i.e., excessively concerned with orderliness, tidiness, punctuality, meticulousness, and propriety. According to psychoanalytic theory this compulsiveness stems from, and is an extension of, the child's compliance with his parent's wishes in regard to expulsion. Cruelty and aggression are also likely to be important components of the anal personality and are believed to arise partly as a consequence of the frustrations involved in severe toilet training (*10, 25*).

Toilet Training as a Learning Situation

Since bowel and bladder control must be learned, reinforcement learning theory may also provide a framework for understanding the process. On the basis of this theory, we can make some predictions about effective and ineffective methods of training and about the immediate and long-time consequences of various types of procedure.

For example, it seems clear that in the early phases of training, it is necessary "to attach anxiety responses to the defecation drive, so that they will win out over the immediate evulsion response. These anxiety responses also motivate and cue off the next responses in the series, such as calling the parents, running to the bathroom, unbuttoning clothes, and the like" (*21*, 138). If these responses are to be repeated, they must be rewarded when they occur.

By watching for signs that the child needs to urinate or defecate, and taking him to the bathroom immediately, the parent has the opportunity to reward the child for using the toilet. If this is done frequently, the connections between the pattern of internal cues (bowel and bladder tensions) and the external cues (the bathroom) and the responses of excretion become strengthened. On subsequent occasions, the child is likely to withhold elimination until he gets to the bathroom. If the child is able to talk or signal his needs in some other way, the learning process will be easier.

As we saw earlier, responses are more likely to be strong if they are greatly rewarded. It could therefore be predicted that the mother who has previously established close relationships with her child will have less difficulty than others in training her child, since her approval has become an important type of reward for him.

The principles of learning theory may also be used to make predictions about the consequences of premature or severe, overly punitive toilet training. It could be predicted, for example, that training which is initiated too early will be unsuccessful and may have unfortunate consequents for the child's later adjustment. A response can be rewarded and learned only after it is made. If the child is not physiologically ready to assume voluntary control he cannot make voluntary evulsion responses at the appropriate time and place. Moreover, he is likely to become frustrated and upset by the pressures exerted upon him.

Severe punishment during the training, even if the child is more mature, may also have unfortunate consequences both for the success of training and for the child's subsequent development. Feelings of pain and discomfort elicited in the training situation may generalize to the toilet, to the bathroom, or to defecation itself. If this is the case, the child may try to inhibit defecation as long as he can. When he does this, bowel and bladder tensions mount, and loss of control, which must inevitably follow, is rewarding (tension-reducing). Thus the responses which are being reinforced, and therefore those which will tend to be repeated, involve "losing control." This, of course, makes the subsequent learning of cleanliness behavior more difficult. Thus premature initiation or poor handling of toilet training may actually interfere with the easy acquisition of socially approved toilet habits.

Furthermore, the fear, anxiety, and hostility generated in stressful, punitive toilet training may become attached to the parents who enforce it. Subsequently their presence may become capable of eliciting anxiety, and the child may attempt to avoid interactions with them. Such reactions to the parents, developed during toilet training, may then generalize and may affect the child's subsequent interpersonal relations adversely.

Dollard and Miller (21) have pointed out that excessive timidity and overconformity may also stem from unduly severe toilet training. If the child is punished too frequently, he will feel that it is safe to make responses *only* when he is *certain* that they are correct, i.e., conform with what his parents or society expect from him. Like the child whose locomotor and manipulative activities are often punished, he becomes inhibited, timid, and afraid to attempt responses which are not specifically approved by his parents.

Two other far-reaching possible consequents of punitive procedures in cleanliness training may be mentioned. The first relates to the development of the child's feelings about himself. The youngster may not discriminate between his parents' reactions to his lack of cleanliness and to him as an individual. That is, he may interpret their disappointment with his lack of cleanliness as disapproval of him. Since the parents' reactions toward the child are, to a great extent, the sources of his attitudes toward himself, he may come to think of himself as a dirty, unworthy, or insignificant individual.

Another possible outcome of punitive training involves the individual's sexual functioning. At this age, the child may not differentiate clearly between the process, organs, and products of elimination. Fears and anxieties which arise in connection with elimination may generalize to the organs of elimination. The physical proximity of genitals, urethra, and anus makes it easy for these reactions to generalize further to the sex organs and sexual activities. "In other words, some of the emotion that is engendered at this period over bowel and bladder functioning spreads out and encompasses sexuality, since the organs of sexual functioning and excretion are the same" (23, 46). If anxieties connected with sexuality persist, the individual may find it extremely difficult to make mature sexual adjustments later on.

In short, on the basis of learning principles, it would be predicted that punishment of the child or impatience with him during the training period may have devastating consequences for later development. In contrast, it might be predicted that the mother who creates a sympathetic, permissive, relaxed environment while her child is undergoing toilet training would be more likely to complete the training without unduly upsetting the child. It is apparent that in many cases, the predictions derived from learning theory closely parallel those derived from psychoanalysis.

Research on the Consequents of Various Toilet Training Procedures

Hypotheses about toilet training, derived either from psychoanalysis or learning theory, if valid, would appear to have broad practical implications. Unfortunately, however, there are only a few studies which attempt to test these hypotheses directly. Some of the psychoanalytic hypotheses are inherently difficult to test. For example, it is obviously difficult to determine whether or not young infants find retention of feces or evacuation pleasurable. It is clear, however, that they are just as interested in their feces as they are in other objects or in parts of their bodies. Many infants will at some time do a "smearing job," playing with their feces and spreading them over themselves, the furniture, and the nearby walls. There is no "natural revulsion" against excreta; the feeling that they are loathsome, disgusting, and filthy must be learned.

From a methodological point of view, it is more feasible to study such matters as the validity of the concept of *anal character* or the consequents of various training practices. For example, Sears (73) showed that among male college students, the so-called anal personality traits of frugality, obstinacy, and orderliness do indeed seem to form a personality pattern or syndrome (i.e., the three are positively correlated with each other). However, Sears made no attempt to relate these traits to childhood training.

Hypotheses on the consequences of frustration during the anal period (severe toilet training) are potentially testable, but even when correlations between training practices and personality are discovered, it is difficult to interpret them. For example, as in the case of oral experiences (cf. pp. 143–151), it is almost impossible methodologically to separate the consequents of the training itself from the consequents of other important variables such as general familial attitudes and parent-child relationships.

INFLUENCE OF TYPE OF TRAINING ON THE ACQUISITION OF VOLUNTARY CONTROL. A number of studies appear to confirm the prediction that too early imposition of training may actually delay the acquisition of control. Thus, in one study of a large group of normal children, "it was found that the long continued enuretic [bedwetting] patterns occurred most often in boys who were slow maturing, both physiologically and intellectually, and whose training by energetic mothers was started too early, maturationally, to be followed by success" (53, 84).

One investigator has presented some evidence confirming the prediction that if the parent is calm, and easygoing in toilet training, control may be achieved with a minimum of upset (19). In the group she studied, mothers who held the child securely rather than placing him on a pot on the floor were found to be most successful in toilet training. This procedure gave the child physical support and simultaneously reassured him of his mother's close presence. According to the investigator, this technique was most likely to be used by mothers who had close relationships with their children and had no distaste for toilet training. These women were able to prevent unnecessary tensions and to create a satisfactory emotional atmosphere. As might be anticipated, under these conditions, children achieved control more easily, with less resistance, and with less tendency to relapse, provided the training had not been attempted earlier than neuromuscular maturation would permit (19).

INFLUENCE OF SEVERE TRAINING ON SUBSEQUENT ADJUSTMENT. A study of 213 problem children between 1 and 13 years of age yielded data relevant to the hypothesis that premature or severe toilet training may elicit maladaptive responses immediately, and may affect the child's subsequent adjustment adversely (39, 40). The subjects had been referred to a child guidance clinic because they manifested symptoms of maladjustment such as: conduct disorders; motor disturbances (restlessness, tics, body manipulation, speech disturbances); physical symptoms of functional origin; and emotional symptoms, like pathological fear or school failure despite adequate intelligence.

Analysis of the case histories of these children indicated that in over half of the cases bowel training had been started "prematurely," completed "too early," or had been accomplished by coercive methods (marked use of shame, or suppositories, rigidity of toilet schedule, unduly frequent placement on toilet). The majority of these children reacted to the training immediately in ways which were considered "undesirable from the point of view of ultimate health" (e.g., constipation, fear, negativism, diarrhea, rage, excessive cleanliness, guilt) (39).

Similarly, 68 percent of the group were started in their bladder training too early. Moreover, half the group had achieved complete dryness by 2 years of age, which is very early according to Gesell's standards, and about 30 percent of the cases had been trained coercively (with use of physical punishment, restraint, forcing child to wear wet clothes, scolding, thwarting, shaming).

A great majority (63 per cent) of the prematurely or coercively trained children reacted immediately with one or more of the following symptoms of emotional distress: continuation of wetting, fear of the toilet, defiance, anger, aversion to urine, wetness, stickiness, overconcern with cleanliness. Fifty-eight percent of the children were still enuretic (bed wetters) after they were 3 years old. In speaking of these reactions, the author says that they are

. . . a seed-bed of psychopathology. Most if not all of them fall in the category of anxiety . . . , and anxiety in childhood is the starting point in the genesis of much of the psychopathology observed in later life. By some psychiatrists, it has been aptly described as "the nucleus of neurosis" (40, 261).

Unfortunately there was no matched control group of normal children with whom to compare the problem cases in this study. Hence, although the frequency of histories of coercive training among the maladjusted seems very high, we cannot be confident of the investigator's conclusion that this factor itself is an important determinant of personality disturbance. The findings are suggestive, however, especially since they indicate, as would be predicted on the basis of either psychoanalytic or learning theory, that severe practices are often followed by temporary emotional upset and problem behavior. It seems likely that, once begun, severe maladaptive reactions may be maintained for a long time.

Evidence presented in one recent study indicates that children who were severely toilet-trained tended to become highly compulsive, aggressive, and fearful in later childhood (85). Clinical data from another study also indicate that children who were trained too early revealed rigid behavior and mildly compulsive characteristics (19). Other investigators have also presented evidence supporting the hypothesis that severe toilet training is related to a high degree of aggression in boys (74) and to negativism (a combination of resistance to pressure and self-assertion) (53).

Such findings suggest that severe or premature toilet training *may* have unfortunate consequences for the child. However, they do not establish that there are any invariant relationships between specific techniques and specific symptoms. As with feeding practices, it appears quite likely that toilet-training disciplines employed are not ordinarily of critical significance in themselves. Of course, they may be important in terms of their intimate connection with parent-child relationships in general. As we pointed out earlier, cleanliness training is a learning situation in which these relationships may be strengthened or may deteriorate, thus facilitating or handicapping subsequent healthy emotional and social adjustment.

Recent evidence indicates that there is generally little relationship between the mother's permissiveness in one aspect of socialization training (e.g., feeding) and in later aspects (e.g., toilet training) (75). Many mothers who were permissive in feeding practices, thus fostering a close relationship with their children at that time, may become quite strict during toilet training, and may undermine the child's earlier established security. On the other hand, the mother who failed to provide adequate gratification during the child's first year may handle his cleanliness training adeptly. Feelings of dissatisfaction, insecurity, and hostility, based on very early experiences, may be overcome if a more positive mother-child relationship is established at this stage.

EARLY EMOTIONAL DEVELOPMENT

While the child is learning that certain responses are likely to bring rewards and that others lead to punishment, he is continuing to develop what adults label "emotional" responses. As we have already noted, dependency needs and reactions are probably the first socially learned emotional responses. During the second year, especially during toilet training, other emotional responses of extreme importance become more clearly defined. Among these are anger, aggression, and fear. Although these emotional responses have physiological and neurological bases, they are subject to the laws of learning.

The Development of Anger and Aggression

Manifestations of anger consist of vigorous reactions which exist from earliest infancy: crying, kicking, thrashing, screaming, tense facial expression, striking. When these responses are effective in bringing maternal aid, and hence gratification or relief from tension, they are reinforced and tend to be repeated. Anger and aggressive acts "may acquire learned reward value by association with the more primary rewards secured by the aggression" (21, 84). Thus the expressions of these emotions may be regarded as learned responses, while the emotions themselves may be considered learned drives (that is, they can motivate behavior, and their reduction can reinforce the learning and performance of new responses).

Dollard and Miller present an excellent description of the development of these emotions.

Reinforcement is the selective agent in the learning which produces . . . habits of aggression. It seems probable that a more detailed analysis of social conditions will indicate that there are two sets of circumstances in which the responses involved in the anger pattern are likely to be rewarded. In one, habits motivated by a drive and leading to a reward are blocked by the intervention of another individual. Under these circumstances, responses of aggression are likely to cause the other individual to get out of the way and thus allow the reward to be secured. Another condition is that in which a motivated response usually leading to reward is prevented by some sort of a physical obstacle, such as a sticking door. Both of these conditions will be recognized as the type of situation usually referred to as a frustration (21, 83).

Aggression, which may be defined as "an act whose goal response is injury to an organism" (20, 9), also

. . . develops because the child discovers that he can secure compliance with his wishes, i.e., rewards from the social environment, by hurting. As his knowledge of others' motivation increases, he becomes more and more skilled at utilizing this method of control. The devices he learns are a function of what the parents and others respond to, and the extent or degree to which he develops such a motive is a function of their rewarding responsiveness when he behaves injuriously—i.e., aggressively (74, 179).

Anger and aggression may be expressed in many diverse ways. During the individual's life, certain aspects of the original anger responses are rewarded and repeated, while others are punished and eliminated. New responses (such as swearing, name calling, feelings of jealousy or hate) may be inserted into the pattern of angry and aggressive behavior.

EARLY MANIFESTATIONS OF ANGER. Goodenough's study of anger in young children demonstrates how the expression of this emotion is modified through learning in the early years (36). She collected data from 45 mothers who recorded a total of 1878 instances of anger outbursts in their children (aged 7 months to 8 years) during a period of one month. The precipitating conditions and environmental factors involved were also noted. Within the first two years, the greatest share of the boys' and girls' outbursts consisted of displays of "undirected energy."

Such apparently unserviceable acts as those of screaming, kicking, or holding the breath may have proved themselves to be the most effective means for getting one's own way. On later occasions, therefore, such devices may have been more or less deliberately adopted by the child as methods of accomplishing his purposes (36, 53).

The data indicated that motor and language responses soon begin to play a part in the expression of anger. Thus, while motor or verbal resistance constituted only 14 percent of the anger responses of children under one, 56 percent of the outbursts of those between ages 1 and 2 fell into these categories. Since such behavior is more likely to be accepted and rewarded, or even encouraged, among boys, they manifested this kind of response more frequently than girls.

Peevishness, whining, and sulking became more common expressions of anger as children grew older, and displays of simple undirected energy decreased in frequency. "With advancing age the forms of behavior displayed during anger become more definitely directed toward a given end, while the primitive bodily responses of the infant and young child are gradually replaced by substitute reactions commonly of a somewhat less violent and more symbolic character" (36, 69).

Infants under 1 year of age had relatively long anger outbursts (median duration about 10 minutes) as compared with the older ones (median duration of about 3 minutes). Apparently, prolonged displays of anger are less likely to be rewarded after the first year; consequently the child gains "self-control," i.e., learns to shorten their duration.

The findings that the overt manifestations of aggression change in form and duration do not necessarily indicate that the learned aggressive drive is more easily reduced in older children. More likely, the older child has learned that vigorous aggressive outbursts lead to punishment; hence he withholds this kind of expression and substitutes others. For example, few children (13 percent) under 2 had "after-effects," while 31 percent of the outbursts of the older children were followed by sullenness, resentment, or brooding. Apparently, overt expressions of anger are somewhat inhibited by older children (reduced violence and shorter duration of outbursts) while internal nonviolent responses become more frequent.

From the parents' reports, Goodenough was also able to determine the circumstances under which anger arises. Among children under 2 years of age, restricting clothing, toilet training (being forced to remain on the toilet in order to induce evacuation), and being forced to go to bed were important precipitators of anger outbursts. Protests following refusal of permission to carry out some desired activity, either by verbal or physical restraint, occurred most frequently among children between the ages of 1 and 2, accounting for 20 percent of their total outbursts. Disagreements between playmates accounted for only 10 percent of the anger manifestations at this age.

Having visitors in the home or living in a family of several adults were among the social situational factors conducive to frequent expression of anger. These are conditions which often entail frustrations for the child. Thus, when there are visitors in the home, he may be deprived of some of his accustomed attention and sources of satisfaction. If there are several adults in the home, they are likely to restrict the child's activities and prevent him from obtaining some things he desires.

Almost all these are situations in which "habits motivated by a drive and leading to a reward are blocked by the intervention of another individual" (21, 83). These are the kinds of situations in which aggressive responses were probably rewarded in the past. Hence these responses are repeated whenever the child encounters interference.

Goodenough found that greater irritability and proneness to anger outbursts were also associated with: restless sleep or bed wetting during the previous night; colds, constipation, or frequent illness; hunger; fatigue. Whether the source of the child's frustration is intrinsic or extrinsic, he reacts in a way which he has learned may overcome interference, i.e., with anger and aggression (36).

In general, boys were more likely than girls to manifest temper in response to restraint. It is probable that even very young boys are rewarded for unhampered physical activities more frequently than girls. Hence free movement acquires greater habit strength among boys, and restriction of movement is regarded as more of an interference for them. Moreover, in our culture, boys are more likely to be rewarded for aggressive expression, and girls are likely to be rewarded for *inhibiting* aggression.

It is interesting to note that problems of self-help often provoke aggression among older children but account for only a small percentage of the temper outbursts of children between the ages of 1 and 2. At this age independent self-help responses cannot have acquired much habit strength; hence interference with this behavior will not be seen as very frustrating at this age. Later, when habits of self-help are firmly established through frequent rewards, blocking them may be viewed as real frustration, and hence will elicit anger responses.

Parents tried many ways of handling their children's outbursts. Ignoring attitudes, spanking or slapping, removal of the source of trouble, diversion of attention, and coaxing were used frequently to control the anger outbursts of children under two. Scolding, threatening, and isolation were more typically used by the parents of older children. The number of different techniques attempted during the course of a single outburst depended on the duration and violence of the child's behavior.

The methods which appeared to be most useful in bringing the outburst to an end often included removal of interferences with motivated activities—for example, granting the child's desire—removing the source of trouble, diverting the child's attention, providing a substitute activity, ignoring the outburst, and isolation. Coaxing, soothing, reasoning, scolding were effective only if employed in conjunction with other methods. As would be predicted on the basis of learning principles, "giving the child his own way" led to more frequent temper displays subsequently. In other words, if the child finds that his aggressive responses are rewarded, i.e., get him what he wants, he will repeat them.

On the basis of her investigations and appraisal of the children's total home situation, Goodenough concluded that:

> The control of anger in children is best achieved when the child's behavior is viewed with serenity and tolerance, when the standards set are within the child's ability to achieve, and when the standards are adhered to with sufficient consistency to permit the child to learn through uniformity of experience, without such mechanical adherence to routine that the child's emotional and physical well-being is sacrificed to the demands of an inflexible schedule. However, when departures from the established schedules are made, they should be determined by a recognition of the needs [i.e., taking into account the motivated, previously rewarded habits] of the child and not simply by the convenience or mood of the adult in charge. Self control in the parents is, after all, likely to be the best guarantee of self control in the child (36, 248).

Fears

In Chapter 5 we discussed the learning of fear and anxiety. The physiological responses involved in this emotion, such as changes in heart rate and blood pressure, trembling, crying, and retreat, are not learned, but innately determined. But the attachment of these responses to previously neutral cues (i.e., stimuli which do not originally elicit the response) is learned.

Fear responses may be innate reactions to pain. The child *learns* to fear the individual who inflicts pain or punishment on him. The sight (visual cues) of the punisher comes to elicit the fear responses originally connected with pain. Similarly, as we saw earlier, a child may begin to fear objects which he did not fear originally (such as white rats), if these are frequently associated with painful, unpleasant, or frightening stimuli (e.g., loud noises).

Certain stimuli seem capable of eliciting fear responses in infants more readily than others. Moreover, as Jersild has pointed out, "at all age levels . . . children differ decidedly in their susceptibility to fear" (45).

The origins of these differences in susceptibility to fear are not completely understood. Innate factors, similar to those underlying individual differences in the amount of activity displayed by neonates, may be involved. There is also evidence (cf. p. 90–91) that very young infants differ in susceptibility to pain. Dollard and Miller also suggest that "there could be individual differences in the capacity of the mechanism producing fear so that people would differ in the strength of their maximum fear responses just as they differ in the strength of grip. The strength of the innate connections between pain and fear could also differ so that fear would be more readily elicited in some people than it would be in others" (21, 70).

Jersild and Holmes (46, 47) have made extensive studies of children's fears. Their data came from standardized forms on which parents recorded all situations in which their children displayed fears during a 21-day observation period. Information was available on 136 children, ranging in age from 3 to 97 months.

During the first year, fear occurred most frequently in response to noises and events previously associated with them, falling or displacement, sudden or unexpected movement, flashes of light, persons or objects previously associated with pain, animals, and strange persons, objects, and events.

In the second year, fear reactions were elicited primarily by noises, strange events, and falling or danger of falling. Sudden movements and flashes of light were less frightening than they were previously, but fears of animals and persons or objects associated with pain increased. Some children in the second year were afraid of the dark or of being alone, although they had not shown these fears earlier. While data on the origins of these fears are not available, it seems possible that many of these children's most prominent fears may have been learned on the basis of association between the feared object and painful, unpleasant stimuli.

Reduction of Fear

Since most fears are probably learned, they are potentially subject to unlearning. In a logical follow-up of the study in which an 11-month-old infant was conditioned to fear a white rabbit (cf. p. 125), Jones (49) showed how such a fear can be eliminated. Peter, her subject, had learned to fear rabbits and other soft furry objects (e.g., fur coat, cotton). In an attempt to eliminate this fear, the experimenter brought Peter to a playroom with three other children who were unafraid of rabbits. A rabbit was always present during a part of the play period, and Peter became progressively less frightened of the animal.

In the course of the study, Peter accidentally relearned to fear the animal. At this point, the experimenter decided to use another method of reducing fear—*direct conditioning*. The rabbit was presented in a wire cage while the child was eating food which he liked. "Through the presence of a pleasant stimulus (food) whenever the rabbit was shown, the fear was eliminated gradually in favor of a positive response" (*49*, 312). In the last stage of the study, Peter displayed a genuine fondness for the rabbit and his fears of other soft furry animals were also reduced.

Arsenian's study, reported earlier (cf. pp. 187–189), also suggests that frightening stimuli, such as strange rooms, can become associated with pleasant feelings, if the child approaches them in the company of an individual with whom he feels secure. On the basis of observational data, others have reached similar conclusions.

At any age level, in case of the *same* child, the circumstances that elicit fear are likely to be . . . complex. A given noise, for example, may provoke no fear if the child is with a familiar adult or is already engaged in noisy horse play; but a similar noise may elicit fear in a different setting (such as when the child is in the company of an unfamiliar person or if he is suddenly startled) (*46*, 335).

After repeated experiences in which feared objects are associated with relaxation and pleasantness, the child may begin to react constructively, rather than in an upset, diffuse way when he encounters them. In short, learned fears, like other learned responses, can be eliminated, and fear reactions can be replaced by more positive ones.

SOCIAL RESPONSES AT AGES ONE AND TWO

Generally speaking, coöperative social activity does not begin until children are of at least nursery school age (cf. pp. 275–283). Youngsters under 2 or 3 are generally content to play parallel to, and alongside, others without interacting with them.

Research on social development in very young children is limited. In an early, inadequately controlled study, the interactions between pairs of infants in the first year of life were observed (*11*). Children below 6 months of age did not seem to be aware of each other. Beginning at this age, however, they initiated contacts by touching, cooing, and interfering with the other child's activities. Later in the first year, there were tendencies to take away or offer toys, inhibit the other's movements, ward off attacks, or "coöperate" in play. Generally, the older of the two children, probably because of superior motor coördination, was dominant in social situations (*11*).

In a more extensive study, 92 children, aged 6 to 25 months, were observed in standard play situations, each with a partner of the same age (*54*). In some test periods, the partners were without playthings; in others a toy was given to each child; in still others only one toy was available for the two.

Babies between 6 and 8 months of age neglected the social aspects of the situation, paying little specific attention either to each other or to the playthings. Between 9 and 13 months, they responded primarily to the playthings and little to the other child. However, when only one toy was present, the partner was sometimes perceived as an obstacle to obtaining it, and aggressive responses (fighting for the toy, watching tensely, hitting, biting) resulted. However, according to these researchers, these represented general reactions to the frustrations presented by the playmate, rather than any specific hostility toward him. Friendly and aggressive contacts occurred with equal frequency when there was no competition, i.e., both had toys or neither child had one. Coöperative and social uses of play materials were also occasionally observed among the children at this age.

The investigators described the period 14 to 18 months as a transitional stage in the development of social responsiveness. Children of this age were generally friendly to each other in noncompetitive situations. Fighting for materials decreased, while coöperative behavior, paying attention to the partner, and social use of the material increased (54).

From 19 months on, the children were primarily socially oriented. Interest in the playmate generally superseded concern with the material, and most interactions were cordial. Coöperative play occurred as commonly as more primitive friendly reactions such as smiling and touching. Respect for the other child's property seemed to increase, for at this age, children did not ordinarily try to take the partner's toys.

These nomothetic studies provide basic data about the "typical" social behavior of children of various ages, but reveal little about critical factors related to social responsiveness. Buhler (11) maintains that even in the first year, there are marked individual differences in aggressive and passive behavior in social situations. Moreover, many personality characteristics, such as friendliness or unfriendliness, self-assurance, intimidation, and rivalry, may be apparent even at this time.

In accordance with learning principles, we would expect that children who have received the most frequent gratifications in their social relationships within the family group would be the most socially oriented. On the other hand, lack of gratification in early interpersonal relations with his mother and others at home might lead to withdrawal, and this, too, could generalize to other social interactions outside the family. Research data bearing directly on the problem of earliest familial relationships as antecedents of the very earliest social reactions are not available.

It may also be inferred that children who make their first social contacts when they are secure (e.g., when accompanied by their mothers) will be less frightened and make more outgoing, adaptive responses in other social situations. Moreover, those who have established habits of independence and self-confidence will behave more adaptively than children who have not developed such habits.

REFERENCES AND ADDITIONAL READING

1. Ames, L. B., The sequential patterning of prone progression in the human infant. *Genet. Psychol. Monogr.* (1937), *19*:409–460.
2. Ames, V. C., and Flory, C. D., Physical growth from birth to maturity. *Rev. educ. Res.* (1944), *14*:427–437.
3. Anderson, J. E., The limitations of infant and preschool tests in the measurement of intelligence. *J. Psychol.* (1939), 8:351–379.
4. Arsenian, J. M., Young children in an insecure situation. *J. abnorm. soc. Psychol.* (1943), *38*:225–249.
5. Bayley, N., The development of motor abilities during the first three years. *Monogr. Soc. Res. Child Develop.*, 1935, No. 1.
6. Bayley, N., Mental growth during the first three years: a developmental study of sixty-one children by repeated tests. *Genet. Psychol. Monogr.* (1933), *14*:No. 1.
7. Bayley, N., Mental growth during the first three years, in R. G. Barker, J. S. Kounin, and H. F. Wright (eds.) *Child behavior and development.* New York: McGraw-Hill, 1943, pp. 87–106.
8. Bayley, N., and Davis, F. C., Growth changes in bodily size and proportions during the first three years: a developmental study of sixty-one children by repeated measurements. *Biometrika* (1935), *27*:26–87.
9. Beckey, R. E., A study of certain factors related to retardation of speech. *J. Speech Disorders* (1942), 7:223–249.
10. Blum, G., *Psychoanalytic theories of personality.* New York: McGraw-Hill, 1953.
11. Buhler, C., The social behavior of children, in C. Murchinson (ed.), *A handbook of child psychology*, 2nd ed. Worcester: Clark University Press, 1933, Chapter IX, pp. 374–416.
12. Buxbaum, E., The role of a second language in the formation of ego and superego. *Psychoanal. Quart.* (1949), *18*:279–289.
13. Cronbach, L. J., *Essentials of psychological testing.* New York: Harper, 1949.
14. Davenport, C. B., Post-natal development of the head. *Proc. Am. Phil. Soc.* (1949), *83*.
15. Davenport, C. B., Post-natal development of the human extremities. *Proc. Am. Phil. Soc.* (1944), *88*:375–455.

16. Davenport, C. B., and Drager, W., Growth curve of infants. *Proc. Nat. Acad. Sci.* (1936), 22:639–645.
17. Davis, A., and Havighurst, R. J., Social class and color differences in child-rearing. *Am. social Rev.* (1946), 11:698–710.
18. Dennis, W., and Dennis, M. G., The effect of cradling practices upon the onset of walking in Hopi children. *J. genet. Psychol.* (1940), 56:77–86.
19. Despert, J. L., Urinary control and enuresis. *Psychosom. Med.* (1944), 6:294–307.
20. Dollard, J., Doob, W., Miller, N. E., Mowrer, O. H., Sears, R. R., et al., *Frustration and aggression.* New Haven: Yale University Press, 1939.
21. Dollard, J., and Miller, N. E., *Personality and psychotherapy.* New York: McGraw-Hill, 1950.
22. English, H. B., Three cases of conditioned fear response. *J. abnorm. soc. Psychol.* (1929), 24:221–225.
23. English, O. S., and Pearson, G. H. J., *Emotional problems of living.* New York: Norton, 1945.
24. Escalona, S., The use of infant tests for predictive purposes, in W. E. Martin and C. B. Stendler (eds.), *Readings in child development.* New York: Harcourt, Brace, 1954, pp. 95–103.
25. Fenichel, O., The psychoanalytic theory of neurosis. New York: Norton, 1945.
26. Francis, C. C., and Werle, P. P., The appearance of centers of ossification from birth to 5 years. *Am. J. Phys. Anthrop.* (1939), 25:323–331.
27. Freud, A. and Burlingham, D. T., *War and children.* New York: Medical War Books, 1943.
28. Freud, A., and Burlingham, D. T., *Infants without families.* New York: International Universities Press, 1944.
29. Gesell, A., The ontogenesis of infant behavior, in L. Carmichael (ed.), *Manual of child psychology,* 2nd ed. New York: Wiley, 1954, pp. 335–373.
30. Gesell, A., and Amatruda, C. S., *Developmental diagnosis: Normal and abnormal child development.* New York: Hoeber, 1941.
31. Gesell, A., and Ames, L. B., The ontogenetic organization of prone behavior in human infancy. *J. genet. Psychol.* (1940), 56:247–263.
32. Gesell, A., Halverson, H. M., Thompson, H., Ilg, F. L., Costner, C. S., *The first five years of life: a guide to the study of the preschool child.* New York: Harper, 1940.
33. Gesell, A., and Thompson, H., Learning and growth in identical infant twins: an experimental study by the method of co-twin control. *Genet. Psychol. Monogr.* (1929), 6: 1–124.
34. Glass, N., Eating, sleeping, and elimination habits in children attending day nurseries and children cared for at home by mothers. *Am. J. Orthopsychiat.* (1949), 19:696–711.
35. Goldfarb, W., The effects of early institutional care on adolescent personality. *J. exp. Educ.* (1943), 12:106–129.
36. Goodenough, F. L., Anger in young children. *Inst. Child Welf. Monogr. Ser., No. 9.* Minneapolis: University of Minnesota Press, 1931.

37. Harlow, H. F., The formation of learning sets. *Psychol. Rev.* (1949), 56:51–65.
38. Honzik, M. P., The constancy of mental test performance during the preschool period. *J. genet. Psychol.* (1938), 52:285–302.
39. Huschka, M., The child's response to coercive bowel training. *Psychosom. Med.* (1942), 4:301–308.
40. Huschka, M., A study of training in voluntary control of urination in a group of problem children. *Psychosom. Med.* (1943), 5:254–265.
41. Irwin, O. C., Infant responses to vertical movements. *Child Develop.* (1932), 3:167–169.
42. Irwin, O. C., Infant speech: The effect of family occupational status and of age on use of sound types. *J. Speech Hearing Disorders* (1948), 13:224–226.
43. Irwin, O. C., and Chen, H. P., Infant speech: Vowel and consonant frequency. *J. Speech Disorders* (1946), 11:123–125.
44. Irwin, O. C., and Chen, H. P., Development of speech during infancy: curve of phonemic types. *J. exp. Psychol.* (1946), 36:431–436.
45. Jersild, A. T., *Child psychology*, 4th ed. New York: Prentice-Hall, 1954.
46. Jersild, A. T., and Holmes, F. B., Children's fears. *Child Developm. Monogr.*, 1935, No. 20, pp. 358.
47. Jersild, A. T., and Holmes, F. B., Some factors in the development in children's fears, *J. exp. Educ.* (1935), 4:133–141.
48. John, E. M., A study of the effects of evacuation and air raids on children of preschool age. *Brit. J. educ. Psychol.* (1941), 11:173–182.
49. Jones, M. C., A laboratory study of fears. *J. genet. Psychol.* (1924), 31:308–315.
50. Levy, D. M., *Maternal overprotection*. New York: Columbia University Press, 1943.
51. Lynip, A. W., The use of magnetic devices in the collection and analyses of the preverbal utterances of an infant. *Genet. Psychol. Monogr.* (1951), 44:221–262.
52. Maccoby, E. E., Gibbs, P. K., and the Staff of the Laboratory of Human Development, Harvard University, Methods of child-rearing in two social classes in Martin, W. E., and Stendler, C. B. (eds.) *Readings in child development*. New York: Harcourt, Brace, 1954, pp. 380–396.
53. Macfarlane, J. W., Allen, L., and Honzik, M. P., A developmental study of the behavior problems of normal children between twenty-one months and fourteen years. *University of California Publications in Child Development*, Vol. II, Berkeley: Univ. of Calif. Press, 1954.
54. Maudry, M., and Nekula, M., Social relations between children of the same age during the first two years of life. *J. genet. Psychol.* (1939), 54:193–215.
55. McCarthy, D., Language development of the preschool child. Chap. VII in R. G. Barker, J. S. Kounin, and H. F. Wright (eds.) *Child behavior and development*. New York: McGraw-Hill, 1943, pp. 107–128.
56. McCarthy, D., Language development in children, in L. Carmichael,

(ed.), *Manual of child psychology,* 2nd ed. New York: Wiley, 1954, pp. 492–630.

57. Menzies, H. F., Children in day nurseries with special reference to the child under two years old. *Lancet.* (1946), *251*:499–501.

58. Meredith, H. V., Physical growth from birth to maturity. *Rev. educ. Res.* (1939), 9:47–49.

59. Meredith, H. V., Order and age of eruption for the deciduous dentition. *J. dent. Res.* (1946), *25*:43–66.

60. Miller, G. A., *Language and communication.* New York: McGraw-Hill, 1951.

61. Miller, N. E., Studies of fear as an acquirable drive: I. Fear as motivation and fear-reduction as reinforcement in the learning of new responses. *J. exp. Psychol.* (1948), *38*:89–101.

62. Miller, N. E. and Dollard, J., *Social learning and imitation.* New Haven: Yale University Press, 1941.

63. Mowrer, O. H., On the psychology of "talking birds"—a contribution to language and personality theory. *Learning theory and personality dynamics.* New York: Ronald, 1950, pp. 689–707.

64. Mowrer, O. H., and Kluckhohn, C., Dynamic theory of personality, in J. McV. Hunt (ed.), *Personality and the behavior disorders.* New York: Ronald, 1944, pp. 69–138.

65. Murphy, L. B., Childhood experience in relation to personality development, in J. McV. Hunt (ed.), *Personality and the behavior disorders,* Vol. II. New York: Ronald, 1944, pp. 652–690.

66. Peatman, J. G., and Higgons, R. A., Relation of infants' weight and body build to locomotor development. *Am. J. Orthopsychiat.* (1942), *12*:234–240.

67. Piaget, J., *The origins of intelligence in children,* trans. by Margaret Cook. New York: International Universities Press, 1952.

68. Rand, W., Sweeney, M. E., and Vincent, E. L., *Growth and development of the young child,* 4th ed. Philadelphia: Saunders, 1946.

69. Robertson, J., and Bowlby, J., Responses of young children to separation from their mothers. II. Observations of the sequences of response of children aged 18 to 24 months during the course of separation. *Courrier,* (1952), 2:131–142.

70. Robinow, T. F., Richards, T. W., and Anderson, M., The eruption of deciduous teeth. *Growth* (1942), 6:127–133.

71. Roudinesco, M., David, M., and Nicholas, J., Responses of young children to separation from their mothers. I. Observations of children aged 12 to 17 months recently separated from their families and living in an institution. *Courrier* (1952), 2:66–78.

72. Sandler, H. C., The eruption of the deciduous teeth. *J. Pediat.* (1944), 25:140–147.

73. Sears, R. R., Experimental studies of projection. I. Attribution of traits. *J. soc. Psychol.* (1936), 7:151–163.

74. Sears, R. R., Whiting, J. W. M., Nowlis, V., and Sears, P. S., Some child-

rearing antecedents of aggression and dependency in young children. *Genet. Psychol. Monogr.* (1953), 47:135–234.

75. Sewell, W. H., Mussen, P. H., and Harris, C. W., Relationships among child training practices. *Am. sociol. Rev.* (1955), 20:137–148.

76. Shirley, M. M., *The first two years, a study of twenty-five babies:* Vol. II. *Intellectual development. Inst. Child Welf. Monogr. Ser.,* No. 8. Minneapolis: University of Minnesota Press, 1933.

77. Shirley, M. M., *The first two years, a study of twenty-five babies:* Vol. III. *Personality manifestation. Inst. Child Welf. Monogr. Ser.* No. 8. Minneapolis: University of Minnesota Press, 1933.

78. Smith, M. E., An investigation of the development of the sentence and the extent of vocabulary in young children. *Univer. Iowa Stud. Child Welf.* (1926), 3:No. 5.

79. Smith, S., Influence of illness during the first two years on infant development. *J. genet.·Psychol.* (1931), 39:284–287.

80. Sontag, L. W., Snell, D., and Anderson, M., Rate of appearance of ossification centers from birth to the age of five years. *Am. J. Dis. Child* (1939), 58:949–957.

81. Thompson, G. G., *Child psychology: growth trends in psychological adjustment.* Boston: Houghton Mifflin, 1952.

82. Thompson, H., Physical growth, in L. Carmichael (ed.), *Manual of child psychology,* 2nd ed. New York: Wiley, 1954, pp. 292–334.

83. Watson, J. B., *Psychology from the standpoint of a behaviorist.* Philadelphia: Lippincott, 1924.

84. Whiting, J. W. M., and Child, I. L., *Child training and personality.* New Haven: Yale University Press, 1953.

85. Wittenborn, J. R., *The development of adoptive children.* New York: Russell Sage Foundation. In press.

PART III

The Preschool Years

Chapter 8

PERSONALITY DEVELOPMENT
IN THE PRESCHOOL YEARS

PHYSICAL DEVELOPMENT

The nursery school years are exciting ones in the young child's development. Impressive advances in height and weight, in physical strength, in motor skills, in language, and in general intellectual ability occur during this period. These changes enable the child to enter into, and to profit from contact with, a much broader world of social experience. .

Before surveying the kinds of psychological and social influences to which the preschool child is subject, and their consequents, we will review briefly the changes which are taking place in the child's physical and intellectual capacities.

Physical Growth

By age 3, the average boy stands about 38 inches tall and weighs about 33 pounds. The average girl is almost as tall (37.6 inches), and nearly as heavy (32.5 pounds) (86). Figure 19 shows the average yearly gain in pounds and inches of boys and girls from birth to 5 years of age.

As a result of gradual increases, the average 5-year-old boy has attained a height of 43.6 inches and a weight of 42.8 pounds. As at age 3, the average girl's measurements are roughly comparable, though again the boy is slightly taller and heavier (86).

Along with these increases in height and weight, the child's body form becomes more mature. As the upper parts of the body begin to approximate adult size, their growth slows down and eventually stops, giving the lower extremities a chance to catch up by continued growth. Thus, during the preschool years, head growth is slow, limb growth is rapid, and trunk growth is intermediate (84). By the time the child reaches his sixth birthday, his body proportions are a great deal more like those of an adult than they were at age 2 (88).

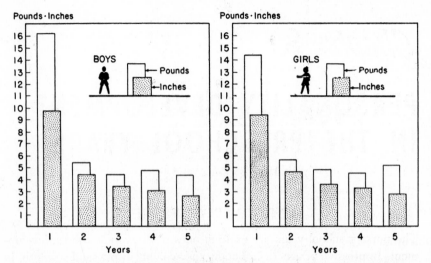

FIGURE 19. Average gain in height and weight of boys and girls from birth to five years. (After E. H. Watson and G. H. Lowrey, *Growth and Development of Children*. Chicago: Year Book Publishers, 1954.)

Along with these changes in body proportions, the child's skeletal, muscular, and nervous systems are becoming more mature. More and more of the cartilage in the child's skeletal system is becoming replaced by bone; the size and number of bones in the body increase, and they become harder. Between 2 and 3, the child's set of temporary teeth is generally completed, and he is adequately equipped to eat adult food.

Significant changes in muscular development also occur during this period. Up until about 4 years of age, growth in the muscular system is roughly proportional to the growth of the body as a whole. Thereafter, the muscles develop at a faster rate, so that about 75 percent of the child's weight increase during the fifth year can be attributed to muscular development (*84*). Throughout this period, however, the larger muscles remain better developed than the small, fine muscles—partly accounting for the fact that the young child is more skillful in activities involving large movements. Needless to say, individual differences in strength and muscular development will depend on many factors, such as the child's constitution, general health, and habits of eating, sleeping, and activity.

Other physiological changes also increase the child's endurance and enable him to participate in more strenuous activities. During this period, respiration becomes deeper and slower; heart rate also slows down and becomes less variable; conversely blood pressure increases steadily (*84*).

The nervous system grows rapidly in the nursery school years. For example, the child's brain has reached 75 percent of its adult weight by the end of the second year; by age 6 it has increased to 90 percent of its adult weight (45). Myelinization of the nerve fibers (cf. p. 171), which has already been nearly completed in the lower portions of the body, is generally completed in the higher brain centers during this period.

PSYCHOMOTOR DEVELOPMENT

The progressive maturation of the preschool child's neuromusculature lays the foundation for increased skill in psychomotor activities. Learning plays an increasingly greater role in these improvements, but as with younger children, expansion of the repertoire of motor skills must await neuromuscular development.

By age 3, the persisting traces of infancy in the child's motor behavior have about disappeared (31).

He runs with more smoothness, accelerates and decelerates with greater ease, turns sharper corners, negotiates sudden stops. Can go upstairs unaided alternating his feet. He can jump down from the bottom tread with both feet together, whereas the child aged two leaps down with one foot leading. Three can jump upward with both feet as much as twelve inches . . . he can stand on one foot for a precarious second or more (30, 41). . . . In the eyes of the three-year old child himself, his psychomotor development has one especially significant ramification—he is now ready for a tricycle, instead of a "mere kiddy-car with its primitive propulsion" (30, 42).

There are other indications of the average 3-year-old's expanding psychomotor development. He can build a tower of 9 or 10 cubes as opposed to the 2-year-old's 6 or 7. In drawing, his strokes are becoming better defined, less diffuse, and less repetitive. He can fold a piece of paper vertically or horizontally, but still not diagonally, even with the aid of a model (31).

By 4, the child's psychomotor skills have increased still further. He can run more smoothly, and is better able to break up the regular rhythms of his stride. Unlike the 3-year-old, who usually is able merely to jump up and down, the 4-year-old is able to make moderately good running and standing broad jumps. He can also skip, though he is still unable to hop. His new athletic feats are partially a function of greater independence of his leg musculature: "Here, as elsewhere, the principle of individuation is at work. There is less totality in his bodily responses; legs, trunk, shoulder, arms react somewhat less in unison. This makes his joints seem more mobile. Where at two and three, he would merely toss or hurl a ball in a propulsive manner (with much torso participation), he can now swing back a more independent arm and execute a strong, over-hand throw" (*31, 47*).

The average 4-year-old has gained sufficient spatial orientation and precision of movement to be able to trace on paper a diagonal-shaped pathway between parallel lines a centimeter apart, and can at last fold a piece of paper diagonally. He is still unable to copy a diamond from a model, however.

By 5 years of age, the average child has a fairly mature sense of balance, which is reflected in a more self-reliant abandon in his motor behavior. While still unable to hop, he skips and jumps more smoothly. Fine movements have also become better differentiated. Again according to Gesell, "he can pluck a dozen pellets one by one and drop them deftly into a bottle in about 20 seconds, typically with a preferred hand. In drawing, while the five-year-old still has some awkwardness in handling diagonal lines, he is capable of straight strokes in all directions; can copy a square and a triangle (though not a diamond); and can at last do a recognizable picture of a man" (*31, 52*).

LANGUAGE DEVELOPMENT

Like most complex skills, language is difficult to learn and cannot be mastered all at once. However, during the preschool years, the child's language development progresses rapidly.

The vocabularies of a large group of preschool children were studied by means of tests in which pictures of objects were presented (*77*). The child was credited with "knowing" a word if he named the object or answered questions which required understanding the word involved. The investigator's estimate of the increase in size of vocabulary (determined in this fashion) with advancing age is presented in Table 2. As may be seen from the table, while the average child of 2 has a vocabulary of only 272 words according to this test, his repertoire of available words has increased to well over 2000 words by the age of 5.

Increases in vocabulary size, however, provide only a limited basis for assessing the child's increased capacity to relate verbally to his environment. Between the ages of 2 and 5, he not only acquires more words, but he learns to use them far more efficiently and flexibly in communicating with others and in meeting his own needs. As the child advances through the preschool years, he talks more and his speech becomes more compre-

TABLE 2. Increase in Size of Vocabulary in Relation to Age [a]

Years	Months	N	Average number of words	Average gain
	8	13	0	
	10	17	1	1
1	0	52	3	2
1	3	19	19	16
1	6	14	22	3
1	9	14	118	96
2	0	25	272	154
2	6	14	446	174
3	0	20	896	450
3	6	26	1222	326
4	0	26	1540	318
4	6	32	1870	330
5	0	20	2072	202
5	6	27	2289	217
6	0	9	2562	273

[a] From (77) with permission State University of Iowa Press.

hensible, better articulated, and more complex in terms of grammatical structure (64). For example, one group of investigators (87), working with 204 preschool subjects, found a correlation of .80 between age and the ability to articulate sounds correctly. Thus, at 2 years, approximately 32 percent of the child's total number of basic speech sounds were given correctly; at 3 years 63 percent; and at 6 years, 89 percent. "The most marked increases in accuracy of articulation of all types of sounds appeared between two and three years of age" (64, 537). McCarthy found similar improvements with age in the comprehensibility of speech. Thus 67 percent of the 2-year-olds', 89 percent of the 2½-year-olds', 93 percent of 3-year-olds', and practically all of the 3½-year-olds' vocalizations were comprehensible (63).

Increments in sheer quantity of speech during this period are accompanied by greater complexity of grammatical structure. In one study of children's speech recorded during a one-hour free-play period, 2-year-olds averaged 78 words per hour, while 4-year-olds spoke 400 words (77). At 2 years of age, the average sentence length was 1.2 words, while by 5½ years, it had increased to about 5.1 words (78). Concomitantly, the children began to use more and more elaborate compound and complex sentences.

The 2-year-old child is at an "early sentence stage," characterized by a predominance of nouns and a lack of articles, auxiliaries and copulative verbs, prepositions and conjunctions. This stage gradually gives way to the "short-sentence stage," which consists of "sentences 3.5 to 4.5 words in length and having the same characteristics as the preceding stage, but to a lesser degree. Inflections have not yet been mastered, and only one or two sentences out of fifty are compound or complex." At about 4 years, the child enters the "complete sentence stage," consisting of 6- to 8-word sentences and "characterized by greater definiteness and complexity as shown by an increased use of relational words and a fairly good mastery of inflections" (64, 552).

Functions of Language During the Preschool Years

As soon as children begin to talk, they are likely to find that speech is often rewarded.

Apparently young children are motivated to use language in the beginning to satisfy their needs, wants, and desires and to control their environment in accordance with their needs and wants, for the category of emotionally toned responses including commands, requests, threats, and desires constitute a fairly large percentage of the responses of the youngest children (64, 571).

Since parents often respond to the child's verbal requests, he practices speech responses and becomes more skillful at them, just as he becomes more skillful at other techniques which lead to gratification.

As the child grows older and becomes increasingly aware of a wider world and his own relation to it, he finds that language is extremely useful in solving problems. This is reflected in changes in language during the nursery school period. Thus

. . . there is an increase with age in the number of remarks associated with the situation. The child is able to recall information, to bring his past experiences to bear on the present situation, to look ahead into the future, and to talk about related items as he grows older and gains in experience and in his ability to integrate his experiences and to verbalize about them (64, 571).

Moreover, children who have been rewarded for learning are, of course, interested in further learning, i.e., they are curious (cf. pp. 189–191). Three- and 4-year-olds seem to be asking questions endlessly, most frequently about causality, classification, and social relations. These are generally reflections of the child's curiosity, serving "as vehicles for securing a vast amount of information with a minimum of effort" (83, 359).

By nursery school age, the child has strong social needs and seeks to participate in social interchange. Many of his questions are probably motivated by these needs as well as by curiosity.

It gives the child pleasure to speak merely in order to be spoken to. Apparently children learn very early that they can gain the attention of adults and control others by the technique of asking questions. . . . Children often ask questions to which they already know the answers often because they are learning to make formulations of events and words and seek social sanctions for these formulations. In building up his system of knowledge the child is said to begin by making tentative statements, which, having an interrogative form, invite corroboration or rejection by others (*64, 573*).

Some of Piaget's studies of the functions of language in the child's life were concerned with age changes from egocentric to more sociocentric (socially oriented) speech. In egocentric speech, according to Piaget "the child does not bother to know to whom he is speaking or whether he is being listened to. He talks either for himself or for the pleasure of associating anyone who happens to be there with the activity of the moment. . . . He does not attempt to place himself at the point of view of his hearer" (*69*). In socialized speech, on the other hand, the child "addresses his hearer, considers his point of view, tries to influence him, or actually exchanges ideas with him" (*69*).

In one of his studies, 20 children between the ages of 2 and 11 were observed during free activity at the Rousseau Institute in Switzerland, and their verbalizations recorded. Analysis of these data showed that as children grew older, their speech became less egocentric and more sociocentric.

Undoubtedly the amount of egocentrism in young children's speech varies with the situation in which the responses are recorded and with the personality characteristics of the children being observed. Moreover, "even the highest estimates of egocentrism rarely exceed 50 percent, and hence the enthusiastic statements one occasionally finds regarding the *predominance* of egocentrism in the speech of young children are quite unfounded" (*64, 570*).

This change from egocentric to sociocentric speech must in part reflect the increasing socialization of the child. As he grows older, he finds that socially oriented speech is rewarded more frequently and more strongly and commands more attention than egocentric speech. The latter type of speech is probably being discouraged during this time and hence becomes less prominent.

Individual Differences in Language Development

General trends, such as those we have been discussing, and individual variations in language accomplishments are in part dependent on the vital roles of practice and reinforcement. Children whose speech responses are rewarded become proficient in language and communication rapidly. Goldfarb's studies (32, 33; cf. pp. 156–158) demonstrated that institutionalized children, who were not rewarded frequently or consistently for their speech responses, were handicapped in language development. Compared with children who lived in foster homes, those reared in an institutional environment displayed marked deficiencies in all areas measured—including speech sounds, intelligibility, and level of language organization (32, 33).

During the preschool years, girls maintain their early established superiority over boys in most aspects of language development (cf. p. 179). Children from upper socioeconomic class homes progress more rapidly than their lower-class peers (63, 64). Twins and triplets are markedly slower in speech than singletons, while of all groups studied, only children—especially only girls—are the most advanced in all aspects of language development (17, 18, 19, 20, 21). Children from bilingual homes have greater difficulty than those from monolingual homes in learning any language (78, 64).

These differences in verbal facility are probably related to variations in the learning situations encountered by different groups of children. For example, as we noted earlier, in our culture, girls and upper-class children probably experience greater and more frequent rewards for manifesting language skills than boys or lower-class children. Youngsters from bilingual homes are faced with much more complex learning problems than others. Twins and triplets are probably not so highly motivated to learn speech responses, since many of their needs (particularly social needs) are satisfied without verbal communication. Only children have great advantages in this respect, for they generally come from "environments . . . affording greater association with adults, broader experience, and greater opportunities for practice in the use of language under optimum conditions" (64, 589).

Language Difficulties in the Preschool Years

During the preschool years, the child often appears to have a hard time saying what he wants to say. Repetitions in speech are frequent, children between 2 and 5 repeating approximately one out of every four words, either in whole or in part (15, 16). Boys tend to repeat more than girls, and in both sexes, amount of repetition decreases with increasing age. It has been reported that 85 percent of all children 3 to 4 years of age show a hesitation in speech (62).

Such hesitations and repetitions may be attributed to the status of the child's language development at this time. The child is building up a hearing vocabulary faster than he can put it to use himself in connected discourse, and he is frequently forced to stall for time while he struggles with the proper mode of expression.

Speech difficulties may be regarded as normal during the preschool years. If the parents become tense and upset about their child's speech at this time, they are likely to convey their anxiety to the child and to lay the groundwork for real and chronic stuttering and stammering. One authority, Johnson (51), believes that children become chronic stutterers as a consequence of being so labeled by anxious parents. Other authors, particularly the more psychoanalytically oriented, tend to view stuttering as a reflection of more basic emotional tensions in the child, usually related to difficulties in parent-child relationships (10).

Available research evidence supports the hypothesis that emotional stress increases hesitancies and repetitions in speech during the preschool years. For example, several kinds of situational pressures—including excitement over activities; attempts to direct a peer's activities or to gain attention; and coercion by the teacher to change his activity—excite increases in speech hesitancies (15, 16).

Earlier we reviewed studies of the influence of parent-child relationships on the child's early speech development (cf. pp. 178–179). There is also impressive clinical evidence that language difficulties, particularly stammering and stuttering, during the preschool years are related to social and emotional adjustment.

One little boy began to stutter when a new baby sister was brought home from the hospital. He didn't show his jealousy outwardly. He never tried to hit or pinch her, he just became uneasy. A girl of two and one-half began to stutter when the maid who had been with the family a long time left and a new maid took her place. In two weeks when she became friendly with her, the stuttering stopped for the time being. When the family moved to a new house she was quite homesick and stuttered again for a period. Two months later the father was called into the Army. The family was upset, and the little girl started again. Mothers report that their children's stuttering is definitely worse when the mothers themselves are tense. I think children, who, during too much of the day are being talked to and told stories, urged to talk and recite, shown off, are especially liable. Stuttering may start when a father decides to be stricter in his discipline (79, 273).

Fortunately the vast majority of children who stutter between 2 and 3 and 4 years of age outgrow it in a few months. Since this speech difficulty seems to be related intimately to emotional stress, parents should attempt to find the sources of the child's disturbance. Parental anxiety about stuttering or urgent, high-pressure attempts to correct the child's speech may only serve to aggravate the problem.

If you think you have been talking at him or urging him to talk too much try to train yourself out of it. Play with him by *doing* things instead of always *talking* things. Is he having plenty of chance to play with other children with whom he gets along easily? Does he have toys and equipment enough, indoors and out, so that he can be inventing his own games without too much bossing? I don't mean that you should ignore or isolate him, but when you are with him be relaxed and let him take the lead. When he talks to you, give him your attention so that he doesn't get frantic. If jealousy is upsetting him, see whether you can do more to prevent it. Stuttering in most cases lasts a number of months with ups and downs. Don't expect it to go right away, be content with gradual progress (79, 274).

INTELLECTUAL DEVELOPMENT

As we pointed out earlier, intelligence tests given to infants under 2 sample functions which are very different from those tapped by the usual adult intelligence tests. Infant tests primarily involve measures of sensorimotor development, while adult intelligence tests emphasize verbal ability and abstract thinking. The correlations between infant (below 2) and adult intelligence test scores have been found to be insignificant (cf. pp. 179–182).

With the growth of language, however, it becomes possible to include on intelligence tests more items involving verbal ability and fewer dealing with relatively pure sensorimotor functions. And, in fact, this is what has been done. For example, the Stanford-Binet Intelligence Test (82), probably the best-known test of intelligence for young children, includes more and more verbal items with succeeding year levels of the test throughout the preschool period. According to the norms for this test, which includes both verbal and performance tasks, the average 2-year-old can place simple blocks properly in a 3-hole form board; identify models of common objects, such as a cup, by their use; identify major parts of a doll's body; and repeat two digits spoken together.

Four-year-level items include naming pictures of a variety of common objects; completing a drawing of a man; discriminating visual forms such as squares, circles, triangles; recalling (immediately) 9- and 10-word sentences; answering comprehension questions such as "Why do we have houses?" By 5½, the average child is able to define simple words such as ball; to copy a square successfully; and to count 4 objects (82).

Compared with infant intelligence tests, those given to preschool children are obviously much more heavily weighted with verbal items. In this sense, these tests are similar to tests given in later childhood or adulthood. As might be expected, scores on intelligence tests administered during the preschool period are better predictors of later intelligence than are scores on infant tests (42).

As part of an extensive longitudinal guidance study carried out at the University of California, subjects were given intelligence tests periodically beginning when they were 1 year 9 months old. During the preschool period the California Preschool Schedule was used, and the Stanford-Binet was administered to each child during later childhood and adolescence. At age 18, the subjects were given the Wechsler Adult Intelligence Scale. Table 3 shows the correlation between intelligence test scores at each of the preschool years and at ages 10 and 18. This table shows that as children advance in age through the preschool period, their test scores become increasingly more predictive of later performance.

TABLE 3. Correlations Between Intelligence Test Scores During the Preschool Years and I.Q. at Ages 10 and 18 [a]

Ages	N	Correlation with I.Q. (Stanford-Binet) at Age 10	Correlation with I.Q. (Wechsler) at Age 18
2	113	.37	.31
2½	114	.36	.24
3	229	.36	.35
3½	215	.59	.42
4	211	.66	.42

[a] After (42). With permission of Journal of Experimental Education.

It should be noted, however, that while these correlations are significant, and in some cases substantial, they are not high enough to preclude the possibility of large changes in the scores of individual children. Actually intelligence test scores of many children change markedly between the nursery school period and later childhood. As we shall see later, many factors may produce changes in intellectual performance (cf. pp. 377–380).

GENERAL ABILITIES

The developments of these years—physical, verbal, intellectual—are also reflected in changes in children's play and self-help activities, in emotional responses, and in social relationships. Doll (22, 23) has investigated progress in many aspects of behavior and has derived age norms of "social" behavior. The drawings and text on pp. 229–232, taken from his Vineland Scale of Social Maturity, indicate the typical behavior of children of the preschool years brought up under *average environmental circumstances in our culture* (23).

THE SOCIAL LEARNING SITUATION OF THE PRESCHOOL YEARS

All these advances in physical, motor, language, and intellectual abilities provide bases for further socialization training, and hence for important changes in personality. For example, many aspects of socialization are dependent upon proficiency in language.

When the child's language is not very useful as a means of social communication, he is still definitely an individualist, and it is probably significant that a marked degree of socialization of his behavior occurs during the later preschool period when language itself is becoming a more efficient means of intercommunication. Every nursery school teacher is familiar with the increased facility in controlling a child's behavior which comes as soon as his understanding of spoken language improves and with the marked change in social behavior which occurs when a child learns to make verbal instead of physical contacts with his playmates. A child who talks very little is often solitary even in a group situation, and a spurt in his linguistic development sometimes appears to facilitate his social contacts so that a previously solitary child may develop friendships as soon as he begins to talk and make verbal approaches to other children (64, 601).

At this time, the child's social world is constantly expanding and the opportunities for new social learning are becoming even more numerous. Before the age of 2, his social contacts were limited primarily to the members of his own family. But with further maturation, greater ability to take care of himself, and social pressures for increased independence, the child may be initiated into neighborhood groups, playgrounds, or nursery school.

Many of these new situations provide opportunities for practicing and strengthening responses learned at home and for learning new ones. As we shall see, this is a period during which the child changes from an individual who pays little attention to his peers—playing alongside, but not with them—to one who becomes involved in such complex personal interactions as forming friendships, having arguments, coöperating, compromising.

OCCUPIES self without "looking after" at own play such as drawing with crayon, building with blocks, dressing dolls, looking at pictures. Uses blunt-end scissors in cutting paper and cloth—is not destructive.

USES fork without much spilling, and eats solid food that does not require cutting. Can get drink of water unassisted, turning water tap on and off. Dries own hands if washed.

GIVES simple account of own experiences and tells stories that can be understood. By action or speech makes known desire to go to toilet — seldom has daytime "accidents."

AVOIDS simple hazards. "Comes in out of rain." Is careful about falling when on stairs and high places, avoids sharp edges, broken glass, etc., and should keep out of streets.

Courtesy, John Hancock Mutual Life Insurance Co.

WASHES hands acceptably without help and dries them without soiling towel. Puts on and buttons coat or dress, but may need help otherwise in dressing.

WALKS down stairs without help, one step at a time. Runs, skips, marches, and shows some sense of simple rhythm.

TAKES part in such group activities as simple kindergarten games; joins in simple play tea parties, and activities requiring no skill. "Performs" for others, upon request.

"HELPS" in small way about the house, such as running short errands, picking up things, feeding pets, dusting.

Courtesy, John Hancock Mutual Life Insurance Co.

DRESSES self except for tying laces, ribbons, or ties. Does all own buttoning, but clothing is laid out. May need help with muffler, rubbers, or overshoes, and with specially difficult or close-fitting clothes.

WASHES face, except ears (!) acceptably and dries his face without help. Goes to toilet alone and without help; unfastens own clothes: no daytime "accidents."

GOES about neighborhood unattended; may be restricted as to areas or "deadlines" so that his whereabouts are known, but is "on his own" within this limitation. Plays in small groups of children of same age such games as tag, hide-and-seek, jump-rope, hopscotch, marbles, etc.

DRAWS with pencil and crayon simple, but recognizable forms as man, house, animal, landscape.

Courtesy, John Hancock Mutual Life Insurance Co.

TAKES care of self unsupervised, outside own yard; manages roller skates, sled, wagon, velocipede, scooter, or other play vehicle.

PLAYS simple table games with others that require taking turns, observing rules, attaining goals, and does so without undue squabbling. (Games include tiddledywinks, parchesi, dominoes, etc.)

GOES to school unattended. He may go with friends, but no one is in direct charge of him. "On his own" outside his neighborhood. Learns to print simple words of three or four letters without copy—and his own first name. Does so without direction.

IS TRUSTED with small sums of money to make clearly-stated purchases. He carries out directions in returning purchases, but he may not be able to make change.

Courtesy, John Hancock Mutual Life Insurance Co.

In addition, emotional expression becomes more highly differentiated, complex, and adultlike during this period. Jealousy, sympathy, friendliness, coöperation, and rivalry become parts of the child's repertoire of emotional reactions. In some cases, severe emotional problems become apparent.

Maturation of intelligence and increased motor and perceptual ability, enabling finer discriminations among stimuli and more precise responses, may partially account for these changes. But important and pervasive changes are also largely attributable to the child's *social* experiences from which he learns that certain emotional responses are likely to bring tension reduction, while others, previously rewarded, now bring punishment.

The new situations to which the child is exposed in the preschool undoubtedly exert a tremendous influence, but in our culture, the home still remains the center of the child's world and the principal location of his social learning. The responses rewarded and learned there are probably those most readily available for application in social situations outside the home. It is therefore important to review some of the extensive theory and empirical findings concerning factors in the home situation which play a part in molding the preschool child's personality. Since psychoanalytic theory has proven to be a fruitful source of relevant concepts and hypotheses, it will be examined first.

PSYCHOANALYTIC HYPOTHESES CONCERNING THE PRESCHOOL PERIOD

Freud and his followers maintained that during the preschool years, crucial changes occur in the child's sexual interests and in his interpersonal relationships. Sometime during this period, usually in the fourth or fifth year, the child reaches the third stage of personality development, known as the *phallic phase*. It will be recalled that, according to psychoanalytic theory, in the first and second periods, oral and anal functioning are the chief sources of stimulation, interest, and pleasure for the child. During the third phase,

interest in the genitals becomes magnified and manifests itself behaviorally in the higher frequency of masturbation; greater desire for physical contact with others, particularly with members of the opposite sex; and the predominance of exhibitionistic tendencies. Apart from these behavioral manifestations, there are all sorts of sexual fantasies, usually associated with masturbation(9, 86).

The Oedipus Complex

The "central phenomenon" of this phase of personality development, according to the analytic theory, is the appearance of the *Oedipus complex*, which has broad and significant repercussions on familial relationships. This complex consists of the child's love for the opposite-sexed parent, together with hatred and jealousy of the parent of the same sex. "In its simplest form, the boy's already formed attachment to the mother unconsciously becomes tinged with the strongly emerging sexual impulses. To permit the gratification of these impulses, the father as an obstacle must be removed. This is accomplished by fantasying himself in the place of the rival father . . ." (9, 91).

Obviously, these feelings toward the parents cannot be maintained indefinitely. Resolving the Oedipus complex is "a prerequisite for normal adult sexuality, whereas unconscious clinging to [it] lays the cornerstone of neurosis" (9). Eventually most children resolve their Oedipus complex satisfactorily.

According to the psychoanalytic formulation, the male child represses his sexual feelings toward the mother because he fears castration if he does not do so. The complex is "smashed to pieces by the shock of threatened castration." Fear of castration (*castration anxiety*) may have its roots in the child's fantasies. However, it may be aroused or reinforced by certain of his experiences. "Many adults upon seeing a boy masturbate still threaten him with 'cutting it off.' Usually the threat is less direct, but other punishments are suggested, either seriously or jokingly, which the child interprets as threats of castration. But even experiences which objectively do not contain any threat may be misinterpreted . . . ; for example, the experience that there are really beings without a penis: the observation of female genitals. Sometimes this kind of observation lends a serious character to a previous threat that has not been taken seriously" (27, 78).

According to analytic theory, the "passing of the Oedipus complex" occurs somewhat differently in the case of the girl. She gives up her sensual desires toward her father and her hostility toward her mother because of her fear of punishment or of loss of love (9, 27).

In the cases of both boys and girls, Oedipal wishes are then replaced by *identification* (i.e., taking over the characteristics of the like-sexed parent). The child tries to be like the like-sexed parent, and in fantasy at least, to attain the same satisfactions.

IMPLICATIONS OF PSYCHOANALYTIC THEORY

These psychoanalytic hypotheses have been a major source of stimulation for students of personality development. Important aspects of the theory have been systematically investigated, and the broader implications of the hypotheses for such problems as sex training and parent-child relations have been explored. Investigation and further conceptualization have been concentrated on several aspects of this theory: infantile masturbation and sexual curiosity; sex training; the Oedipus complex; identification.

Infantile Masturbation

As we learned earlier, very young infants are capable of making reflex sexual responses. Erection of the penis in male infants may be a response to generalized bodily tensions, occurring most frequently when feeding is interrupted or when the bladder is full (cf. p. 91). Manipulation of the genitals seems to be rewarding, and becomes quite common among male babies after they have developed sufficient motor coördination to grasp their penis. In one study (54), over half of the 49 mothers interviewed had observed genital handling in their sons by the age of 3.

In another investigation of 320 problem children, almost half were reported by their mothers to have masturbated. Of these, over half were first known to have practiced the habit before they were 5 years old. As the author points out, "the findings are an understatement for they involve only those cases in which the parents had not forgotten the child's masturbation and how it was handled . . ." (46, 353).

These findings demonstrate that many children develop and maintain masturbatory habits. It may therefore be concluded that "there is some kind of reward associated with masturbating" (24, 141). Of course, masturbation in young children does not necessarily lead to orgasm. However, Kinsey's extensive data on sex behavior suggests that at least a small percentage of boys and girls under 4 have orgastic responses which appear to approximate those of adults (52, 53).

Sexual Curiosity

There is abundant evidence confirming Freud's contention that young children have a great deal of curiosity about sex. Analysis of mothers' recollections of the sex questions of 1790 children between 2 and 14 years of age indicated that many children asked sex questions before they were 5 years old. Between the ages of 2 and 5, the most common questions of this sort dealt with the origin of babies, and physical sex differences (*36*). Instances of exhibitionism (exposing genitals), voyeurism (looking at others' genitals) and persistent curiosity about the anatomy of the opposite sex have been observed frequently among nursery school children (*47*).

It can hardly be denied that in our culture shame and punishment become attached to sexual behavior and interests early in life. However, all the data indicate that despite these restrictions—or possibly partly because of them—young American and European children have considerable curiosity about sexual matters.

In more permissive and tolerant cultures, children may be much more open and spontaneous in their sexual behavior. For example, Malinowski observed that in the Trobriand Islands where sexual exploration is not punished or restricted, children of preschool age are highly active at a genital sexual level and a large proportion of their play is sexually oriented (*61*).

Sex Training

By calling attention to the sexual awareness and curiosity of young children, Freud challenged the prevalent puritanical notion that children are "innocent," "pure," and without sexual thoughts or feelings. Psychoanalytic theory clearly implies that parents' reactions to the child's earliest manifestations of sex behavior and curiosity may have important ramifications on his subsequent adjustment. The same prediction would be made on the basis of learning theory. Anthropological and clinical research provide evidence supporting this prediction.

In European and American cultures, masturbation, although quite usual among infants, often "evokes intense anxiety in the adults . . . and they promptly apply sanctions, ranging from persistently removing or jerking the child's hand away from its genital to slapping and spanking it. The result is to set up in the child the same sex-anxiety conflict which the adults have" (*24, 142*).

Severe punishment of masturbation may lead to reduction or elimination of this habit, but it may also have adverse influences on the child's future adjustment. The fear and anxiety elicited by punishment may become attached to masturbation and may generalize to all sexual behavior. If this is true, sex activity may be avoided in order to escape the intense anxiety and discomfort associated with it. Once learned, these generalized negative attitudes may, in extreme cases, be maintained even in adulthood, possibly preventing the individual from achieving satisfactory sexual adjustments.

Under normal conditions, childhood masturbation seldom becomes a problem. Psychiatrists and clinical psychologists feel that excessive masturbation is often a reflection of the child's general anxiety stemming from tensions in the home situation. It follows that the habit may, in that case, be reduced by alleviating the underlying conflicts. If the parents are worried and are unable to handle the problem themselves, they should seek professional help.

Like their handling of the child's masturbatory activities, parents' reactions to their youngster's sexual curiosity may affect significantly his general attitudes toward sex. If his questions meet with parental censure, silence, or embarrassment, the child may begin to associate anxiety, fear, or shame with his interest in sexual matters. As we have seen, such unfavorable reactions may become generalized, thus handicapping the individual in his subsequent sexual adjustments.

Parents who deal simply and realistically with sex questions are more likely to foster healthy attitudes toward sex in their child. Actually, this is not a complex problem.

When the child becomes interested in the problems pertaining to sex and birth, his questions should be answered frankly, truthfully, and without embarrassment as they come up. That is not so difficult a job as one might think because children need and want very little information at any one time. If children ask where they come from, and they are told that babies grow within the mother's body, that answer will satisfy most children for that particular day and, perhaps, for several weeks or months to come. They just do not get around to asking any more until something in connection with their play with other children or some event in the home life comes up which prompts a question for additional information. Very often parents make a problem for themselves by the feeling that when the child asks the first question about sex, they are obligated to tell him everything that has been written in a twelve volume treatise on sexuality. Obviously this is neither necessary nor advisable. Any parent who will put himself at ease on the subject of sex, not try to show how much he knows or be afraid of how little he knows, not be flustered with embarrassment but just answer what the child asks, will manage sex education in a very satisfactory manner (26, 72).

The Oedipus Complex

It is difficult to evaluate all aspects of a concept as broad and inclusive as the Oedipus complex. Undoubtedly the child of preschool age is still basically dependent upon his mother and prizes her affection and attention. Moreover, he has probably learned to enjoy the physical sensations which accompany her routine ministrations. However, it is difficult to test objectively the hypothesis that most boys of the age have specifically sexual desires for her, as the theory maintains.

CASTRATION THREATS. Objective data on the extent and importance of castration anxiety are also difficult to obtain. There is, however, evidence that, at least in some cases, parents behave in ways which may arouse or increase castration fears. For example, data from a study of masturbation indicated that many parents reacted to their child's masturbation in psychologically harmful ways, including threatening the child with physical punishment or bodily injury (46). About one-third of the parents reported specific threats of injury to the child's genitals (i.e., castration). How many more did so but did not report it, is, of course, unknown. It seems likely, however, that since cultural and moral values have changed in the direction of greater leniency, there are fewer threatening parents than there were in Freud's time.

This study does not, of course, provide direct evidence on the extent of castration anxiety among boys. On the one hand, it is possible that parental threats may not always lead to fear of castration. On the other hand, in the case of children who are not directly threatened, castration anxiety may still arise, as the theory maintains, from other sources.

UNIVERSALITY OF THE OEDIPUS COMPLEX. One of the major criticisms of the concept of the Oedipus complex is centered on Freud's assumption that it is universal and inevitable. Anthropologists have pointed out that its occurrence depends on the nature of family structure in the culture. For example, among the Melanesians, the father acts as a cheerful adult playmate of the children, while a maternal uncle functions more as teacher and punisher. Under these circumstances, the father could hardly be viewed as an object of hate or "a rival who stands in his way and whom [the child] would like to push aside" (29, 91).

Another anthropologist (25) reports that there is no evidence of an Oedipus complex among the Hopi Indians. In this group, diffuse affection is given to many relatives; hence there is no intense concern with the parent of the opposite sex.

Most social scientists reject the notion of a universal Oedipus complex. After reviewing a wealth of anthropological literature, Honigmann concludes that most workers in the field of culture and personality

. . . believe that hostility toward the father may well show up in *some* groups and may indeed be accompanied by rivalry for the affection and attention of the mother. Such behavior they expect is derived from social conditions, for example, in the small family where a child's affectional satisfactions are tightly dependent on only two adults. These adults become very precious. Lack of attention from one arouses ready jealousy. Hostility is more likely to attach to the father because dependence, for a variety of reasons, is more intense on the mother. It is in her that the child sees his security and safety bound up (*40, 67, italics ours*).

Thus, many writers (*81, 90*) maintain that intense, unresolved Oedipal conflicts are quite prevalent in our own society. No reliable statistical data are available, but mental hygiene workers agree that, in many cases, emotional maladjustments stem from excessive devotion to opposite-sexed parents and excessive hostility toward the same-sexed parent.

FAMILY RELATIONSHIPS AND OEDIPAL CONFLICTS. Certain kinds of family relationships appear to set the stage for the development of strong Oedipal conflicts which are difficult to resolve. A doting mother who fondles and caresses her son excessively and is overly solicitous is encouraging him to become strongly dependent upon her. If at the same time the father is "too busy" to spend time with the child and to satisfy some of his needs, favorable father-son relationships are not likely to develop. Moreover, by demanding some of the mother's attention, the father may prevent her from gratifying all the child's needs immediately. Perceiving this, the child may view the father as a frustrator, and hence as an object of resentment and hostility. Under these conditions, the fundamental components of the Oedipus complex, overattachment to the mother and hatred of the father, are present.

The most obvious consequents of unresolved Oedipal conflicts become apparent in adolescence and adulthood. For example, the boy who remains emotionally tied to his mother's apron strings does not make affectionate and love responses to others. When he becomes an adolescent or adult, he may still be unable to break his attachment to his mother; hence he will find it difficult or impossible to form any other relationships such as those required in heterosexual adjustment and marriage.

Freud's description of the Oedipus complex called attention to the problems children may face in learning to cope with complicated family relationships. In the adjustment of the 1- or 2-year-old, the nature of the mother-child interaction is paramount. However, children of preschool age must work out their relationships with everyone in the family. As we shall see presently, the role of the father in his son's socialization—and of the mother in her daughter's—is particularly crucial. Later we shall discuss the general family atmosphere and specific child-training practices which influence the child's adjustment during this period.

Identification

It will be recalled that, according to psychoanalytic theory, resolution of the Oedipus complex is followed by identification with the like-sexed parent. Identification generally refers to the child's adoption of the behavior, attitudes, values, motives, and taboos of others. For our purposes,

Courtesy LIFE Magazine © TIME, Inc.

Identification in Bechuanaland.

identification may be defined as a learned drive to imitate or be like another individual (or individuals) to whom one is emotionally attached. A child is said to identify with a parent when he gives that parent "emotional allegiance . . . and attempts to duplicate in its own life the ideals, attitudes, and behavior of the parent with whom it is identifying" (*80*, 163).

Whether or not they accept the Freudian hypothesis regarding the genesis of identification, almost all social scientists agree that it occurs universally and is important in all societies. In a sense, it is the fundamental mechanism of socialization. The parents are representatives of their culture. Hence the child's imitation of their responses, characteristics, attitudes, emotional reactions, and motives (i.e., his identification with them) helps him to acquire the behavior patterns appropriate to his sex and social class—in short, to his role in society.

Since identification is a special type of imitation (cf. pp. 131–133), it is a learning process, subject to the usual laws of learning. During the early part of the preschool period, the child's social contacts are largely restricted to the home, and he imitates and learns responses manifested by people there. Thus the members of the child's family serve as his earliest identification models.

Family identification is important in social learning, . . . because it leads the child's behavior in the direction which the reactions of his parents take. The boy who uses his father's words and inflections, or swaggers across the yard wearing his father's hat, is reacting to these characteristics and objects as if they were his. But in so doing he is also duplicating his father's reactions, and learning to act as his father acts. In more significant aspects of behavior it is the same. A child in cowering when his mother trembles at a brilliant lightning-flash, in rejecting food which his father does not like, or in viewing a visitor with the same alarm and suspicion his parents show, is reacting as if his parents' characteristics were also his. He is learning a family pattern of fear, aversion or suspicion which will one day indeed become his own (*12, 61*).

Superego Development

Identification with the parents and others also involves learning their —and the culture's—ideals, values, and morals.

Many tabus dealing with property, the proprieties, respect for authority, and general behavior are rigidly enforced in our culture; they are openly taken over, with full awareness, in the . . . [identification] processes of some two-year-olds, and can be seen to play a large role in the development of a well-defined conscience by two and a half or three years of age. It is quite true that when parental control is austere or violent, the frightened child may take over a violent self-censoring attitude . . . (*67, 543*).

Freud used the term *superego* "to describe the accumulation of ideals, attitudes, and behavior which one acquires in the process of identification and the agent which punishes us with a sense of guilt when we violate the codes which we have adopted" (*80, 163*). He spoke of it as "the representative of all moral restrictions, the advocate of the impulse toward perfection. In short it is as much as we have been able to apprehend psychologically of what people call the 'higher things in life'" (29, 94). Recognizing the role of learning, he maintained that superego development "can be traced back to the influence of parents, teachers, and so on" (29, 94).

The superego is one of the major products of identification. Once the child has learned his parents' evaluative processes he punishes himself "whenever he has done something for which he believes his parents would feel he should be punished" (89, 227). As Murphy phrases it, "through identification with the parent, he has taken over and incorporated within himself the attitudes of condemnation of those who transgress" (67, 541). "When, by this process of identification, he demands from himself conformity to a standard of conduct, the *superego* is said to be making its appearance" (67, 543).

Identification and superego formation are prolonged, and perhaps life-long, processes. As the child's social world expands, he will find other identification models—neighborhood children, teachers, fictional and movie heroes. He will attempt to emulate their behavior and characteristics, and their ideals will become his. Eventually, behavior learned from these sources may become more predominant than behavior in imitation of his parents.

Thus his personality, in the end, will be built upon the basis of a long series of identifications; in some respects he will be like his parents, in some respects like each of several admired or respected teachers, in some respects like the different heroes he has encountered in fiction, biographies, the movies, etc.; in some respects like ministers, doctors, or other respected people in his community, etc. Since his personality has been derived from so many different sources, it will be a complex and unique organization (71, 297).

Sex-Typing

In our culture, sex-typing (i.e., taking on behavior appropriate to one's own sex) begins early in life. There are, of course, universal, biologically determined sex differences in physical factors such as strength, motor capacity, and speed of reaction. But the personality traits, as well as the social and emotional behavior and attitudes, characteristic of males and females are largely dictated by cultural traditions and customs, and hence vary greatly among societies. Through identification with the like-sexed parent, the child learns the responses appropriate to his own sex in his particular culture.

Awareness of sex-appropriate conduct makes its early appearance in life through observation and imitation of models in the home. Some . . . observation . . . shows an increasing awareness of sex roles between the ages of two and three. . . . Sex models in the home must be appropriate *as long as society persists in stereotyping sex roles.* Domineering mothers and ineffectual fathers are likely to produce a younger generation of tomboys and sissies. . . . Deviant sexual orientation in later life may originate in the child's inability to identify himself with his like-sex parent. . . . Absence of the father or fear of him frequently results in a passivity in boys, and tendency on their part to imitate the attitudes, interests, and manners of the mother. Converse attachments may be built up in girls. In either sex, cross-parent identifications are often the cause of maladjustment in sex role and heterosexual inadequacy in adult life (76, 153).

The process of sexual identification has been summarized by Mowrer (65). He maintains that sex-typing is established by means of the parents' selective applications of reward and punishment for sex-appropriate and sex-inappropriate responses.

In the ideal family constellation, a little boy finds it very natural and highly rewarding to model himself in his father's image. The father is gratified to see this recreation of his own qualities, attitudes, and masculinity; and the mother, loving the father, finds such a course of development acceptable in her son. Tentative explorations, conscious and unconscious, in the direction of being "like mother" quickly convince the boy that this is not his proper or approved destiny; and he speedily reverts to his identification with father. In the well-ordered, psychologically healthy household, much the same picture, in reverse, holds for the little girl.

But where there is parental disharmony, all this is changed. If there is chronic antagonism between husband and wife, the boy discovers that if he identifies with his father it is at the price of losing his mother's love and approval; if she is antagonistic toward and disapproving of the husband, she will feel scant enthusiasm for seeing her son become "just like *him.*" If, on the other hand, the boy tries to take his mother as a personal model, he will almost certainly incur his father's displeasure and also risk the general opprobrium connected with being a "sissy."

For the little girl in such a household, very much the same type of dilemma arises. To be like her mother is to take a critical, unloving attitude toward her father; and if she tries to resolve her difficulties by being like father, she will lose the mother's support and possibly that of women generally (65, 596).

RESEARCH ON SEX-TYPING. The role of the like-sexed parent in the child's learning of sex-appropriate behavior was demonstrated in a study conducted by Sears, Pintler, and Sears (72, 73). These investigators assumed that the father supplies the primary pattern for, and rewards, masculine behavior patterns, such as aggression, in his son. Hence, they hypothesized that his absence from the home may delay the development of aggression in boys. On the other hand, since the father is not the model of sex-appropriate behavior for girls, it may be hypothesized that his presence or absence may have little influence on his daughter's aggressive expression.

In order to test the hypotheses, they studied the aggressive doll play of 22 boys and 20 girls at each of three age levels (3, 4, and 5 years). Within each age group, half of the subjects were from homes with both parents present, while the other half came from homes in which the father was absent, usually because of military service. Each child was observed as he participated in two 20-minute doll-play sessions, and all instances of physical and verbal aggression were recorded.

In general, the findings confirmed the original hypotheses. Girls from father-present homes did not differ significantly from girls whose fathers were absent in the amount of aggressive doll play. On the other hand, 3- and 4-year-old boys from father-absent homes manifested significantly *less* aggression in doll play than father-present boys of the same ages. Boys of this age were not as likely to learn typically masculine aggressive patterns if their fathers were not at home to serve as models and to reward these responses. Apparently father-absence has less influence on aggressive expression in older boys, for the two groups of 5-year-old boys did not differ significantly from each other in this measure of aggression. This result may be attributed to the broader social contacts of older boys. They can learn masculine behavior from peers and others outside the home.

Of course, the process of sex-typing continues long beyond the preschool period. As we shall see later, many factors influence the acquisition of sex-appropriate responses (cf. pp. 325–327; 421–423).

GENERAL FAMILY INFLUENCES ON PERSONALITY DEVELOPMENT

Like sex-typing, other aspects of personality are learned as a consequence of experiences in the total family setting. On the basis of the principle of generalization, it would be predicted that responses learned at home will be evoked in other situations which present stimuli similar to those encountered at home. Thus, careful analysis of parental behavior and attitudes toward the child should give us some basis for understanding which of the child's responses are likely to be rewarded, learned, and generalized. Furthermore, such analysis may provide the basis for making predictions about the kinds of responses which will become associated with fear and anxiety and thus be eliminated or considerably reduced. In short, analysis of the reward and punishment situations in the home (antecedents) should enable us to predict which responses will be expressed, and which will be inhibited, in situations outside the home.

Generalization of Social Responses

But all this depends on the applicability of the principle of generalization. Do children of this age actually transfer social responses learned in the home to other social interactions? Direct evidence on this problem comes from a study by Bishop (8). She observed the behavior of 34 children (17 boys and 17 girls between the ages of 40 and 67 months) interacting, first with their mothers, and later with a neutral adult.

During two half-hour sessions, each child was alone with his mother in a playroom containing toys and magazines. Mothers had been informed that they were participating in a study of children's behavior in the presence of adults. In order to investigate the extent of generalization of responses to the mother, each child was subsequently tested in this situation with an unfamiliar woman (neutral adult) who reacted to every child in a standardized manner. The reactions of the children to their mothers and to the neutral adult were observed and recorded in detail. All observations were made through a one-way mirror.

There were, of course, great differences in the responses displayed by both the child and mother subjects. In general, however, individuals were consistent in their behavior from one session to the next.

Subsequently, when the children were brought into the situation with a neutral adult, children reacted in the same way they had reacted to their mothers with respect to aggressive stimulation, inhibited and reluctant coöperation, noncoöperation, and resistance. Through generalization, earlier established responses were elicited in a new situation with an unfamiliar adult. The findings of this study are clearly consistent with the hypothesis that responses learned at home are likely to be carried over to other social situations. It follows that the child's reactions in his relationships with nursery school teachers and with peers may be largely dependent on the responses acquired at home. Hence a child's social behavior can be understood fully only if we know the conditions of learning in his home. More specifically, we must understand the kinds of relationships he encounters there, the social responses which are rewarded, and those which are punished.

Approaches to the Study of Home Atmosphere

There have been many investigations focusing attention on the impact of different kinds of maternal behavior and general home atmosphere on specific personality characteristics or on the general social and emotional adjustment of children. Some of these studies were developed to test specific hypotheses about the influences of reward and punishment on subsequent expression of clearly defined responses, such as aggression or dependency. Others have been concerned with broad aspects of the familial situation (e.g., democracy, permissiveness) and their consequents. Moreover, some of the studies have used normal children as subjects; others have involved clinic patients. In some cases, investigators have focused their attention on antecedent conditions, such as home environment, and then sought to determine the consequents. In other cases, some aspect of behavior (e.g., aggression, maladjustment) has been selected and an attempt made to discover the important antecedents of this behavior. Despite these discrepancies in the specific variables investigated, and in the methods and terminology employed, the bulk of the studies have yielded results which are, by and large, consistent with one another.

Antecedents of Aggression

THE EXPRESSION AND INHIBITION OF AGGRESSION.   The extent to which a child will express aggressive responses will depend on his previous history of rewards and punishments for such responses. As we noted earlier (cf. pp. 202–206), aggressive reactions to frustrating situations are likely to be reinforced during infancy. Hence aggressive drives develop early. Moreover, the greater the frequency with which aggressive responses are elicited and rewarded, the stronger the aggressive drive will be.

Subsequently the child may find that aggressive behavior brings punishment. On the basis of learning theory, it would be predicted that the child would then inhibit his aggressive responses in settings where fear and anxiety have become associated with these responses. Experimental confirmation of this prediction comes from a study by Hollenberg and Sperry (38). These investigators observed 23 nursery school children during four doll-play sessions and recorded and rated all instances of aggression. Ratings were made in two categories: *intense aggression* (physical punishment, injury, and destruction of equipment) and *attenuated aggression* (mischief, verbal aggression, and inducing discomfort).

During the second doll-play session, 12 children, the experimental group, were punished by verbal disapproval (statements such as "No, John, don't you know nice boys shouldn't do things like that?") every time they made an aggressive response. Members of the control group,

11 children, received no punishment and were allowed complete freedom to express aggression throughout the four sessions.

No one was punished during the third session. Nevertheless, the experimental subjects manifested significantly fewer and less intense aggressive responses in this session than they did during the first. The control group, on the other hand, increased regularly in both frequency and intensity of doll-play aggression from the first to the fourth sessions. In other words, as was predicted, punishment leads to an inhibition of aggression, while "permissiveness with respect to aggression reduces anticipation of punishment and/or increases anticipation of reward for aggression and thus results in an increase of aggression" (38, 42).

These findings seem quite applicable to the home situation. If aggressive expression is punished there, the child will learn to inhibit hostile responses in that setting.

Moreover, the fear and anxiety which become attached to hostile responses also generalize and become associated with aggressive expression in situations resembling the home situation. Hence the child learns to inhibit hostile behavior in these situations as well as at home. However, since the underlying aggressive *drives* have acquired considerable strength, they are *not* eliminated. Under these circumstances, aggressive responses may be "displaced," that is, they may be expressed in situations which are quite different from the home situation (e.g., in permissive doll play).

Specific predictions about the expression and inhibition of aggression may be derived from these theoretical considerations. For example, it may be predicted that children who are frequently frustrated at home develop strong aggressive drives and reactions. Moreover, those who are punished for the expression of aggression at home will "displace" their aggression, i.e., exhibit it in situations where there is little threat of punishment.

On the basis of their study dealing with the influences of *home punishment and frustration* on children's aggression in doll play, Hollenberg and Sperry (38) presented data relevant to these two predictions. The subjects were 30 nursery school children whose mothers were intensively interviewed and asked about such things as restrictive rules, responsiveness to the child's needs or requests, enforcement of compliance with mother's motivations, and maternal behavior during infant feeding, weaning, and toilet training. Measures of *home frustration* were derived from the answers to these questions. *Punishment* of aggression in the home was also rated on the basis of mothers' statements about the frequency, intensity, and duration of spanking, threatening, isolating, scolding.

The data generally confirmed the two predictions. Children who were in the highly frustrated group (above the median in *home frustration*) tended to be more aggressive in permissive doll play than mildly frustrated children. As was predicted, highly punished children (above the median in *home punishment*) exhibited more aggression in this situation (i.e., displaced aggression) than those who were mildly punished. Homes which rated high in both frustration and punishment produced children who manifested considerably more frequent and more intense expressions of doll-play aggression than children from homes rated low in both these variables.

INFLUENCE OF HOME PUNISHMENT AND FRUSTRATION ON AGGRESSION AND DEPENDENCY. The child who has been severely punished for aggression in the home may make aggressive responses in a permissive setting, such as the doll-play situations used in the Hollenberg and Sperry studies cited above. But such a child may inhibit aggressive behavior in social situations, such as those in nursery school, which resemble the home setting much more closely than the doll-play situation does. In other words, the inhibition of aggression, learned at home, may generalize to similar situations (such as the nursery school), but may not generalize to situations which are highly dissimilar (such as the doll-play situation).

Whiting (74) has hypothesized that while a *mild* degree of punishment for aggression may actually strengthen the aggressive drive, *severe* punishment may lead to general inhibition of aggressive responses. In other words, if the child is severely punished, fear and anxiety become attached to aggressive responses and may generalize widely.

Sears (74) has presented some data consistent with this hypothesis. He observed the aggressive responses of three groups of nursery school children in free-play situations. The first group had nonpunitive mothers. The second group had mildly punitive mothers; and the mothers of children in the third group were severely punitive. The second group, the mildly punished children, manifested the greatest number of aggressive responses. The first group had relatively few aggressive responses, presumably because they were seldom frustrated at home and hence did not have strong aggressive drives. The third group, the highly punished children, also made relatively few aggressive responses. In terms of the theory, the severe punishment these children had suffered led to inhibition of aggressive *responses,* and the inhibition generalized to the nursery school. However, this inhibition of *responses* did not indicate that the aggressive *drives* had been reduced. In permissive doll play, where there was little likelihood of punishment for aggressive responses, the children of highly punitive mothers exhibited more aggression than the children in either of the other two groups.

According to Sears, Whiting, Nowlis, and Sears (74), this same reasoning applies to dependency behavior. That is, in the case of both aggression and dependency, mild punishment of the responses may elevate the drives. On the other hand, severe punishment may lead to generalized inhibition of the responses.

In a well-designed and interesting study of the antecedents of dependency and aggression, these investigators focused attention on the relationship between the preschool child's home experiences and his aggressive and dependent behavior in nursery school.[1] On the basis of interviews with the mothers, three features of *current* maternal behavior were evaluated: (1) degree of punitiveness (use of spanking, scolding, deprivation in controlling aggression); (2) nurturance (gentleness of handling the child when the mother is busy or at bedtime and at night, and when the child is sick or injured; father's participation in taking care of the child); (3) degree of frustration (in eating and cleanliness training; overprotection in sickness or keeping the child away from danger). Nursery school teachers and trained observers rated each child on overt expressions of *dependence* in school (see p. 148 for description of the specific responses observed).

Analysis of the data showed that mothers who paid relatively little attention to their children (i.e., nonnurturant mothers) were likely to have children who sought to attract attention by whining, mischief, and annoying others. Probably these were the responses which were most likely to bring attention—and hence reward—from the nonnurturant mothers. Hence these responses were manifested in the nursery school.

According to these data, boys and girls reacted differently to maternal discipline. The sons of punitive and nonnurturant mothers tended to manifest greater than average dependency and high aggression. In contrast to this, daughters of punitive and nonnurturant mothers tended to be less dependent and less aggressive than average. In other words, boys

[1] It will be recalled that these investigators discovered that there was "a positive relation between infant feeding frustration and preschool dependency behavior, with severity of weaning contributing more than degree of scheduling" (74, 189). According to their data, infantile feeding frustration was not related to preschool aggression. Among the boys there was a slight (probably not very meaningful) correlation between severity of toilet training and over aggression in nursery school (74) (cf. pp. 148–149).

showed slightly positive frustration-aggression and frustration-dependency relationships, while girls showed slightly negative ones.

The authors reasoned that this sex difference in the direction of the correlations may be attributed to varying degrees of punishment inflicted on boys and girls. These writers hold that girls suffer more punishment for dependent and aggressive responses than their male peers. Since the girl has taken over (identified with) her mother's values to a greater extent, she is more likely to be self-punitive when her mother reprimands her. Hence girls "actually suffer more severe punishment [or frustration] than boys do from a given . . . amount of maternal punitiveness" (74, 220).

In terms of these investigators' theoretical formulation, the punishment the young boy receives from his mother may deter him from expressing these responses at home, but it may actually heighten his aggressive and dependent drives. Since these drives are strong, the boy is likely to displace them, i.e., to express them in his relations with peers and teachers in the nursery school. In contrast to this, the girl who is punished frequently is likely to be punished so severely that her aggressive and dependent responses become greatly reduced and she gives "more indications of generalized inhibition" (74, 220).

Influences of General Home Atmosphere

The basic postulates of learning theory should also be applicable in predicting the consequences of various types of home atmosphere on children's behavior. For example, if the child is rewarded for friendly, outgoing responses, for curiosity, and for self-expression at home, he may be expected to manifest these responses in other situations, such as in nursery school. On the other hand, if the child has been punished for self-expression and rewarded only for strict adherence to parental orders, he will probably be shy and timid in many social interactions. As we shall see presently, studies of the impacts of general home atmosphere on normal preschool children's behavior, although not specifically designed to test hypotheses based on learning theory, generally confirm these predictions.

The most systematic of these studies were conducted by Baldwin and his co-workers at the Fels Institute of Human Development (1, 2, 3, 4). In this research, a "home visitor," a highly trained woman, visited the children's homes, observed the general family atmosphere and parent-child interactions, wrote a critical summary of her findings, and rated the home on 30 carefully defined scales.

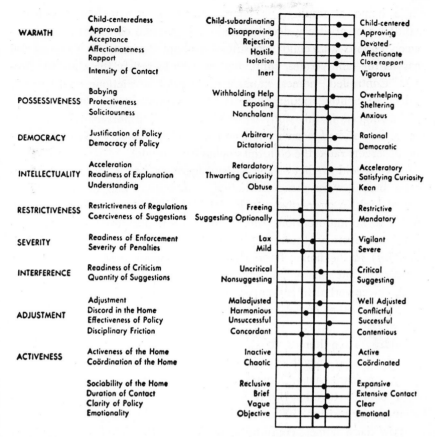

FIGURE 20. Ratings of a warm, democratic home on the Fels Parent Behavior Rating Scales. (After A. L. Baldwin, J. Kalhorn, and F. H. Breese, "Patterns of Parent Behavior." *Psych. Monogr.* (1945), 58:No. 3.)

These scales, called the Fels Parent Behavior Rating Scales, are shown in Figure 20. Taken together, they provide objective, well-rounded descriptions of the domestic situation. Moreover, they permit systematic examination of the relationships between home environment and children's characteristics.

Of course, the 30 scales are not entirely independent of each other: many of them are positively intercorrelated. Groups of related variables, called *clusters* or *constellations,* are assumed to measure some common aspect or area of parent behavior. In Figure 20, the scales are grouped into nine clusters listed in the left column (3).

DEMOCRATIC AND CONTROLLED ATMOSPHERES. Baldwin (1) has studied the relationships between two of these clusters, *democracy* and *control* in the home, and children's behavior in nursery school. The democratic home atmosphere is characterized by general permissiveness, avoidance of arbitrary decisions, and a high level of verbal contact between parents and child (consultation about decisions, explanations of reasons for family rules, supplying answers to satisfy the child's curiosity). "Controlled" homes emphasize clear-cut restrictions on behavior, and consequently, friction over disciplinary procedures is low.

The subjects in this study were 67 four-year-old nursery school pupils whose homes had been visited and evaluated. Nursery school teachers and observers rated the children's behavior in school.

As we would predict on the basis of learning theory, those from democratic homes were generally active, competitive, and outgoing. They ranked high in aggressiveness, leadership, planfulness, and cruelty, and tended to be more curious, disobedient, and nonconforming. If, in addition to democracy, there was a great deal of parent-child interaction (*activity*) in the home, these characteristics were most pronounced. In democratic, but relatively inactive, homes, characterized by more detachment, fewer verbal interchanges, and less leadership in the parent-child relationship, the consequences of democratic atmosphere were less marked.

Children from homes rated high in *control* showed relatively little quarrelsomeness, negativism, disobedience, aggression, planfulness, tenacity, or fearlessness. Homes characterized by *authoritarian control* (*high control* together with *low democracy*) produced quiet, well-behaved, nonresistant children who were socially unaggressive. Apparently in these homes, conformity, which was associated with restricted curiosity, originality, and fancifulness, was obtained at the expense of freedom of expression. Of course, democratic parents run the risk of producing too little conformity to cultural demands in their children. However, in the groups of homes investigated in this study, there was a positive correlation between democracy and control, i.e., most democratic parents practiced enough control to avoid the pitfalls of extreme nonconformity.

From the marked differences in behavior of children from democratic and controlled homes, the author concludes that "hereditary factors probably play a role, but in addition, an unresponsive environment can certainly stultify expressiveness and aggressiveness toward the world. The child requires not only freedom but response and encouragement if his wishes and his emotions are to be expressed actively, particularly in his relations to people" (*1, 135*).

In a supplementary study, this same investigator (*2*) described the consequents of three clusters of home variables—*democracy, warmth,* and *indulgence*—on children's personalities. The subjects were 56 nursery school children between the ages of 36 and 60 months who were rated on a battery of 45 behavior and personality variables.

Democracy in the home was found to be associated with *warmth*, i.e., most highly democratic families provided strong emotional support for the child. Children from these homes were socially outgoing in both friendly and hostile ways, participating actively in school events, expressing aggression, and generally asserting themselves quite strongly. Their bossing and aggressiveness seemed to be socially successful and they enjoyed superior status in their own group. Moreover, the democratic home environment seemed to promote intelligence, curiosity, originality, and constructiveness.

Indulgence (babying, protecting) appeared to foster the development of the opposite kinds of personality characteristics. Children from these homes were relatively inactive, unaggressive, lacking in originality, and of inferior social status. In addition, indulged children were apprehensive of physical activity and lacked skill in muscle activities.

Thus "the effect of the democratic home as contrasted to the non-democratic one is to stimulate the child in such a way that he is more actively engaged in peer-centered activities, that he is more successful in those activities, and that he is better able to contribute original creative ideas to the groups with which he interacts" (2, 62).

The general conclusions of these studies have major practical as well as theoretical significance. Apparently certain socially valuable behaviors and personality characteristics are created by the use of democratic child-rearing procedures. However, these techniques will probably be effective only if they are consistent with the parents' personalities and attitudes (4). If rigid, authoritarian parents attempt to employ democratic procedures they are likely to find them difficult and frustrating. This may produce a tense home situation which, as we shall see later, may be detrimental to the emotional health of the preschool child.

These research findings support predictions based on learning theory. In the permissive, democratic home the child is rewarded for participating in group decisions, doing things spontaneously, expressing opinions and feelings, attempting new ways of doing things, and asserting his rights, views, and ideas. These become his habitual responses at home and they are consequently generalized to other social situations, e.g., the nursery school. On the other hand, the child who is highly indulged, babied, and overprotected has not learned these responses. He is unlikely to have received many rewards for doing things independently, for expressing himself freely, or for trying out new activities. Fearing for the child's safety or threatened by his growing independence, his parents may punish (or at least discourage) outgoing responses, independent efforts, and activities involving physical manipulation. Consequently, the child displays timidity, awkwardness, and apprehension.

AUTOCRATIC AND DEMOCRATIC HOMES. Radke (70) used different research techniques in her investigation of the relationships between parental attitudes and child-rearing practices and the behavior of pre-school children. Her subjects, 19 boys and 24 girls between the ages of 3 years 10 months and 5 years 10 months, were enrolled in nursery school or kindergarten. Data on their behavior, attitudes, and adjustments were obtained through teacher ratings, interviews, doll-play sessions, and pictorial projective tests. Their mothers and fathers were interviewed and answered lengthy questionnaires dealing with many aspects of parent-child relations: autocratic or democratic control, restrictions on the child, severity of punishment, rapport, joint or individual parental responsibility for the child's discipline.

Compared with children from autocratic homes, those from democratic home atmospheres were rated as more stable emotionally and more successful in interpersonal relationships. They were inclined to be more competitive, more considerate of others, more sensitive to praise or blame, and less quarrelsome.

"Freedom-giving" homes—those in which parents exert relatively little control over the child's life, to a great extent allowing him to be on his own and to do what he likes—produced youngsters who were more competitive, less passive, and more popular than children of restrictive parents. Mild discipline in the home was related to rivalry, sensitivity to others' opinions, considerateness, popularity, affection, and talkativeness. Severe discipline was associated with the opposite kinds of characteristics, lack of rivalry, insensitivity, and unpopularity.

The "democratic" and "freedom-giving" homes in this study strongly resemble Baldwin's "democratic atmosphere" homes. Thus, despite the differences in subject populations and investigatory methods, the two studies reach conclusions which agree in most respects.

SIBLING RELATIONSHIPS. Radke's study was also concerned with the influence of sibling relationships on personality. Children who quarreled frequently with their siblings and displayed jealousy toward them were compared with others who got along well with their brothers and sisters. Of the two groups, the latter were characteristically more stable emotionally, and had better peer relationships in school. On the other hand, they were less energetic and rivalrous, more passive and compliant toward adults, less likely to be "regular fellows" (70). It may be inferred that their successful relationships with siblings were based on avoiding competition with them and reacting passively and compliantly in interactions in the family. These techniques, having been rewarded at home, were subsequently transferred to the nursery school situation.

OVERINDULGENCE. Other studies, although sometimes less comprehensive or less satisfactory from a methodological point of view, have yielded results essentially consistent with Baldwin's and Radke's. For example, in one study, 335 nursery school children were rated by their teachers on frequency of occurrence of 35 types of maladaptive behavior (e.g., jealousy, cries easily, shrinks from notice, wastes time, refuses to share, avoids play with others) (37). Their homes were visited by teachers who made ratings of 15 home factors, such as maternal oversolicitousness, negligence, nervousness, illness, family sharing of play and responsibility. Correlations between nursery school behavior ratings and home factors were determined. The results showed that children from overattentive (comparable with Baldwin's *indulged*) homes often displayed infantile behavior such as crying easily, dawdling, leaving tasks undone, probably because they lacked rewarded experience in behaving independently. These children withdrew from social relations (shrinking from notice, sulking, avoiding play) and remained highly dependent on adults, staying near them and often asking unnecessary help. Apparently these overindulged children, rewarded for infantile behavior and perhaps punished for independent responses at home, tried to use their immature techniques in their nursery school contacts. Here they were probably unsuccessful, and incurred punishment and rejection from other children. Since relations with others were unsuccessful, the overindulged children withdrew from interactions with their peers.

The children of negligent and irresponsible (nonnurturant) mothers were inclined to exhibit attention-getting mechanisms and behaviors reflecting "emotional tensions and insecurity" ("showing off," seeking praise, temper outbursts, aggressive tendencies, attacking others, refusing to share, breaking objects, lying, stealing, and cheating) (37).

Children from "calm, happy" homes tended to be more secure emotionally, and less negativistic, jealous, fearful, nervous, sulky, and less attention-demanding. Parents who worked and played with their children and allowed them to share domestic responsibilities promoted their children's emotional security and abandonment of infantile reactions.

Their youngsters were more coöperative and self-reliant, formed better work habits, established better interpersonal relations, and had more respect for the property of others. In general, children from "calm, happy" homes and those in which the family shared responsibilities had many characteristics in common with children from the "democratic-active" homes of Baldwin's study (cf. pp. 250–254). Very likely both investigations were concerned with similar parental responses, although different descriptive terms were used.

LEARNING MALADAPTIVE BEHAVIOR

The study of "abnormal" individuals contributes a great deal to the understanding of factors underlying "normal" behavior. Analogously, studies of "problem" children and "problem" behavior help to delineate the antecedents of good, as well as poor, adjustment.

As we shall see, parents are as instrumental in children's learning of maladaptive behavior as they are in the learning of good adjustment. A number of important studies have pointed up the relationships between parents' personal adjustments or parent-child interactions and (1) children's inadequate social and emotional adjustment or (2) the occurrence of "problem" behavior in normal children.

Maternal Overprotection

Levy (56) conducted intensive clinical studies of 20 children who had been subjected to maternal overprotection (cf. p. 192) for description of this treatment). In 11 cases, this was accompanied by *indulgence,* i.e., the mother consistently yielded to the desires of the child and submitted to extraordinary demands. At home, these children were disobedient, impudent, excessively demanding, and tyrannical in their relationships with their mothers. Their interactions with other children on the playground and in school were entirely consistent with their behavior at home. The techniques which had been successful in manipulating their parents (aggression, bossiness, and showing off) generalized to their relationships with peers.

In the other nine cases, maternal *domination, overdiscipline,* and *overcontrol* were associated with overprotection. Under these conditions, the child was frequently rewarded for complete submission and compliance. Spontaneous, outgoing responses were discouraged through discipline and punishment.

As would be anticipated, these children were shy, submissive, and somewhat withdrawn in interactions with their mothers, and these reactions generalized to their social contacts with neighborhood children. All the overprotected children (both the indulged and dominated groups) had great difficulty in maintaining friendships, since other children were not so tolerant of their behavior as their mothers were (56).

Tensions Between Parents

Interparental frictions may exert an adverse influence on children's adjustments. This was demonstrated in a comprehensive clinical study of 33 nursery school children and their parents (5). On the basis of the investigator's and the head teacher's ratings of each child's adjustment to himself, to his family, and to school groups, his general adjustment was evaluated as "poor" or "satisfactory." Data on the parents' general stability and domestic adjustment were obtained from intensive interviews with them.

Certain kinds of interparental friction were found to be significantly related to children's adjustments. Parental sex difficulties and ascendance-submission conflicts were most highly correlated with poor adjustments in the children. Children's emotional disturbances were also associated with other interparental tensions involving lack of consideration, lack of coöperation in the child's upbringing, extramarital relations, poor health, insufficient expression of affection, and conflicts about friends, work, or relatives. Inability to discuss their problems and dissatisfactions with each other often intensified the problems. Relatively minor arguments over such problems as leisure-time pursuits, finances, or differences in tastes, seemed to have little to do with their children's emotional status.

Unhappy and dissatisfied parents have difficulty in "teaching" their children good adjustments. Their tensions hinder them from providing relaxed, easygoing social situations in which the child can learn that interpersonal relationships are rewarding. Instead, they are likely to have tense, unpleasant interactions with their children, who may react by withdrawing. If this is true, the youngsters will be slow at learning adequate social techniques and may remain poorly adjusted to their families, and by generalization, to others, including peers.

Moreover, parents who are discontented with each other may reject the child whom they view as forcing them to continue in their marriage. If there is real rejection, the child is likely to be aware of it, and through identification with his parents, is likely to acquire unfavorable attitudes toward himself. Hence he would be "poorly adjusted to himself" (5).

PARENTAL BACKGROUNDS AND MARITAL MALADJUSTMENTS. In this

study, extensive clinical interviews revealed that the parents' marital maladjustments characteristically had their roots in their own family backgrounds. Parents who were attempting to prolong their childhood dependency status or to compensate for early deprivations of love and affection did not achieve good marital relationships. They experienced many tensions about sex adjustments, ascendance-submission, and co-operation in the child's upbringing. Women whose parents had not been happily married were much more likely to experience friction with their husbands, particularly in the areas of sexual adjustment and expressions of consideration and sympathy (5).

Thus a child's maladjustments may often be traced back at least a generation. His parents' emotional maladjustments, stemming from their early lives, may keep them from achieving a satisfactory marriage. These marital dissatisfactions and tensions, in turn, may preclude good relations with their children and thus keep the children from acquiring good techniques of personal and social adjustment.

Incidence of "Problem" Behavior in Preschool Children

Almost all children display some behavior "problems," fears, or anxieties. Hence a child should not be considered "neurotic" or a "problem" unless the frequency and/or intensity of these reactions interfere with effective functioning or the enjoyment of normal social interactions.

INCIDENCE OF PROBLEM BEHAVIOR IN NORMAL CHILDREN. As part of her extensive longitudinal study of 252 randomly selected children, Mac-farlane (58, 59) determined the incidence of each of 63 "problem" behaviors at each half-year interval during the preschool period. The average child of this age manifested between four and six problems.

Frequency was found to vary with age for most problems. Soiling and diurnal and nocturnal enuresis decreased with age and were eliminated in the order named. . . . Constipation, masturbation, and restlessness in sleep showed no trends with age for the preschool period. Thumbsucking decreased as nail biting increased. Overt tempers, fears, jealousy, and inferred over-sensitiveness increased to around four and four and one half years and then began subsiding. Since temper tantrums, fears, and overt jealousy occur at one age level in more than 50 percent of our children, they cannot sensibly be regarded as neurotic behavior when occurring in these early years, as so commonly assumed, but rather as evidence of tension or as adjustive devices (59, 313).

Certain of these problems tended to occur together, forming groups or clusters. For example, at year 5, four clusters could be detected. The first cluster, "suggesting a labile or disturbed" child consisted of: *quarrelsomeness, mood swings, negativism, irritability, temper tantrums, jealousy,* and *competitiveness.* The second cluster, involving psychological withdrawal and relatively poor physical health, included *withdrawal, introversion, submission, shyness, somberness, excessive reserve,* and *underactivity.* The third cluster was made up of *masturbation, unusual sex interest,* and *stammering;* while the fourth involved *diurnal* and *nocturnal enuresis* and *excessive modesty.* At this age, excessive modesty appeared to be more closely associated with eliminative processes than with masturbation (59).

FACTORS ASSOCIATED WITH "PROBLEM" BEHAVIOR. Any particular problem may have different meanings for different children. "For example, enuresis at five years in one child might be associated with poor muscle tonus, and in another with little or no attempts at toilet training; in a third it might appear symptomatic of marked tension and hostility following extremely drastic attempts at training before the child's psychomotor maturation permitted control" (59, 316).

Macfarlane also studied the relationship of familial variables, including economic status, parents' personalities, and marital discord to specific kinds of children's problems. Of all the familial variables studied, marital maladjustment of the parents was most consistently and highly correlated with problem behavior in children (59).

Attention demanding, temper tantrums, negativism, food finickiness, overdependence, and daytime enuresis showed more recruits from families with unhappy or difficult marital adjustment. With increasing age, tempers and negativism showed increasing relationships with marital maladjustment during this early preschool period. Thumbsucking and nocturnal enuresis, on the other hand, showed more recruits from happy and mutual supporting marital relationships (59, 323).

Among these families, unsatisfactory marital adjustment was also associated with parental disagreement on discipline. Compared with relaxed mothers, those who were tense and anxious in their relationships with their children engendered more behavior problems.

In summarizing these findings, Macfarlane notes that

. . . when a home was psychologically unfavorable in only one or two respects, the youngster could usually run his course without much disturbance, provided the parents were themselves secure enough to give the child adequate security and affection. But in homes with a large number of unfavorable aspects, the youngster was likely to give indications of being disturbed in his emotional development and habits. Affection and security between and from the parents was found to be a major need for the children (59, 324).

Although the child of this age is highly flexible and his behavior will change if his life circumstances shift, the child with many problems at this age is *more likely* than his peers to have many difficulties later on. Since the data of this study were longitudinal, Macfarlane and her colleagues (60) were able to compute the correlations between the children's total number of problems at one age with the total number at all other ages from 3 to 14. The correlations were for the most part positive and, in many instances, relatively high. These findings suggest that, among children who do not get special psychotherapeutic help, boys and girls who have high problem scores (i.e., many problems) during the preschool period are more likely to have a relatively large number of emotional difficulties later on (60).

Children's Fears

Every child learns a variety of fears. Some of these serve a "self-preservation" function; that is, fear and anxiety attached to certain kinds of stimuli (e.g., highways and moving automobiles) motivate the child to avoid these dangers. Moreover, as we noted earlier, fears may serve as a basis for new learning.

But extensive, overly intense, and unduly frequent fear responses (e.g., crying, retreating, withdrawing, cringing, trembling, protesting, appealing for help, cowering, clinging to parents) are incompatible with stable, effective behavior. For subsequent good emotional adjustment, many of these responses must be replaced by mature, purposeful reactions to previously fear-eliciting stimuli.

In their extensive study of children's fears, Jersild and Holmes (48) included 112 nursery school age children (cf. p. 207). For a period of 21 days, their parents recorded all the fears displayed by these children and the circumstances surrounding these.

In this group of normal children, fears of concrete and tangible stimuli (noises or objects, agents, and events associated with them; sudden unexpected movements, strange objects, situations, and persons) declined with age. On the other hand, fears of imaginary, anticipated, and supernatural dangers (e.g., events associated with the dark, dreams, robbers, imaginary creations, and the possibility of accidents) increased. In general, the frequency and intensity of the overt signs of fear decreased with age.

Childhood fears are highly unpredictable, and at all age levels, children vary greatly in their susceptibility to fear. The same stimulus may be extremely frightening to one child, but leave another completely unperturbed. Moreover, a child may be much disturbed by a particular stimulus in one situation, but pay no attention to it in another.

The parents of 30 of the subjects in this study were interviewed between 13 and 35 months after the original records had been made. By this time, more than half of the fears had dropped out, 36 percent persisted in their original form, and 11 percent were of the same class but modified in form (e.g., fear of the noise of a cleaner had generalized to all loud noises). Parents were able to supply examples of new fears growing out of older ones. For example, a child who feared a balloon used in administering the anesthetic during an operation became afraid of all balloons and objects resembling them. Another child, frightened by a mouse running through his bedroom, began to fear all scratching sounds at night. In brief, fears seem to spread by the process of stimulus generalization.

Intelligence may also influence the acquisition of fear. Among children between the ages of 2 and 5, "fear scores" correlated positively $(r = +.30)$ with I.Q., the relationship being most marked at the youngest age levels $(r = +.53$ at 24–35 months of age). Apparently more intelligent children were able to recognize "potential danger" more readily than duller ones. Sex differences were also apparent throughout the age range studied, a higher proportion of girls showing fear responses $(48, 49, 50)$.

These studies supply descriptive and normative data about fears characteristic of various age levels. They also make it clear that in the normal course of development, certain kinds of stimuli become less fear-eliciting, while others become more so. With greater maturity, the overt expressions of fear may be expected to become less frequent and intense. Such data may be useful diagnostically, for they provide standards for judging whether a particular child's fear behavior deviates markedly from the norms. Unfortunately, however, they tell us little about antecedent-consequent relationships in the development or modification of emotional behavior patterns.

Relationships Between Mothers' and Children's Fears

Since most fears appear to be learned, and since the child's most important learning at this age occurs in the home, it may be hypothesized that many of the young child's fears are acquired primarily from his parents. Some research by Hagman (34) tested this hypothesis. He interviewed the mothers of 40 boys and 30 girls between the ages of 23 and 70 months, asking questions about their own and their children's fears, and their techniques of handling them. The findings indicated a distinct tendency for a child to have the same fears as his mother, the relationship being particularly marked in the cases of fears of dogs, insects, and storms (34).

Through identification with the mother, the child acquires many of her fears. Moreover, if the mother is frightened in certain situations, she is probably unable to do anything to help modify her child's learned fear reactions. Consequently, he continues to view these stimuli as dangerous and to make withdrawal responses. These avoidance responses may be tension-reducing in the sense of removing him from the feared stimulus. Hence they are reinforced and tend to be repeated, thus preventing the learning of new, more mature reactions. For these reasons, fears which the child shares with his mother are particularly resistant to treatment and extinction.

Techniques of Eliminating Fears

In many cases, children do not automatically "outgrow" their fears. Unless they somehow learn new responses to fear-eliciting stimuli, fears are not eliminated. In the last chapter we discussed some means of reducing fears by pairing previously feared stimuli (such as an animal) with pleasant stimuli (desirable food). After several such pairings the child may begin to have more positive reactions to the object he had feared (cf. pp. 207–208).

It may be assumed that such techniques would continue to be effective with children of preschool age. In addition, as the child grows older and better able to use language, it becomes possible to supplement these techniques with verbal explanations.

According to mothers' reports of their attempts to reduce their children's fears, *explanation plus subjection* (intentionally confronting the child with the situation he fears), and *explanation plus gradual subjection* both facilitated the reduction of fears. *Explanation* alone was not found to be a useful method, since the child may not have learned to associate the words with the fear-provoking stimuli. On the other hand, when *subjection* was accompanied by *explanation*, the fear-eliciting stimuli became associated with the parent's calming presence, encouragement, and gentle words of explanation. Moreover, in this situation, the child was probably being rewarded for *inhibiting* fear responses. Under these conditions, new, positive (non-fear) responses to the stimuli may become dominant over fear responses in the hierarchy of responses (34).

Of course, in those cases where the child's fears are primarily a reflection of deep-lying psychological disturbances (as in the case of severe phobias) such relatively simple methods will probably not be effective and psychotherapy may be required. Available data indicate that among 5-year-old girls, for example, a high degree of fearfulness may be symptomatic of generalized anxiety which is also manifested in irritability, mood swings, somberness, and restless sleep (60).

Origins and Treatment of Jealousy

During the preschool period many children face the new, and often unpleasant, experience of having a new baby in the family. The new sibling requires much of the parents' time and care, and the older child is likely to be deprived of some of his accustomed attention. If this is upsetting, he may give evidence of "jealousy."

There is usually nothing "abnormal" about the young child's jealousy. In most cases, jealousy is "a normal response to actual, supposed, or threatened loss of affection" (85, 66). In some cases, however, the response may be overly severe or persistent and may affect the child's future adjustment adversely.

The tensions of jealousy may be discharged into a variety of reactions, such as aggression toward the younger infant, relapse into infantile behavior (e.g., refusal to eat solid foods; loss of bladder and bowel control), withdrawal from the mother or people generally, or repression (indifference or "I don't care" attitude).

Systematic comparisons of the case histories of 39 children displaying jealousy and 31 who did not have these reactions to their younger siblings have indicated that this characteristic is closely associated with dependence. Apparently, highly dependent children are likely to become severely jealous, since any loss of support is particularly painful to them (75).

Two-thirds of the jealous group were between 18 and 42 months older than the siblings who were the objects of their jealousy. This suggests that they were called upon to share their parents' attention and affection with this sibling at the time their dependency needs were strongest (cf. pp. 183–187). Since strong drives were being interfered with, these children became highly frustrated and hence emotionally insecure and upset. Furthermore, a large proportion of the jealous children were first-born children and had young, oversolicitous mothers. Probably these children had learned to associate their parents' unlimited attention with security and gratification of dependency needs. Moreover, they may have had little opportunity to develop independence. Consequently any loss of attention, signifying frustration of dependency drives, was traumatic.

On the other hand, if the new sibling did not arrive until the older child was 4 years old and had achieved some independence, the latter was less likely to manifest jealousy. In this case, the older child may find helping with the baby brings further recognition of his independent,

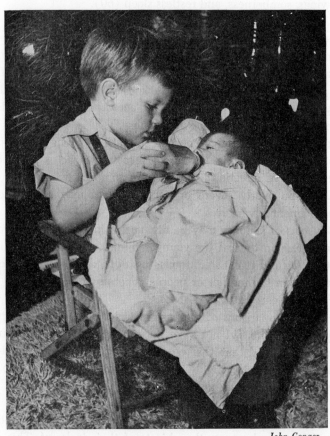

John Conger

Helping with the new baby.

"grown-up" status. As a consequence, feelings of resentment may be allayed.

Informing a child that he is to have a new brother or sister is not enough to prevent negative attitudes toward the new baby. Spending some time each day exclusively with the older child reassures him of the parents' affection and may help to reduce his jealousy. Good interpersonal relations in the home, consistency in discipline, reassuring affection, and continued gratification of the older child's basic needs (including dependency) are probably the most effective means of avoiding or alleviating jealousy (75).

Many psychiatrists believe that the child should be encouraged to express his jealous feelings rather than to suppress them. This may afford some relief from emotional distress and the tensions of repressed hostility. The jealous child may develop a negative self-evaluation and feelings of inadequacy if he feels that others consider him unworthy of their love. Parents must therefore take pains to assure him of their continued affection by satisfying his needs.

REFERENCES AND ADDITIONAL READING

1. Baldwin, A. L., Socialization and the parent-child relationship. *Child Develop.* (1948), *19*:127–136.
2. Baldwin, A. L., The effect of home environment on nursery school behavior. *Child Develop.* (1949), *20*:49–62.
3. Baldwin, A. L., Kalhorn, J., and Breese, F. H., Patterns of parent behavior. *Psych. Monogr.* (1945), *58*:No. 3.
4. Baldwin, A. L., Kalhorn, J., and Breese, F. H., The appraisal of parent behavior. *Psych. Monogr.* (1949), *63*:No. 299.
5. Baruch, D. W., A study of reported tension in interparental relationships as co-existent with behavior adjustment in young children. *J. exp. Educ.* (1937), *6*:187–204.
6. Bayley, N., Mental growth during the first three years, in R. G. Barker, J. S. Kounin, and H. F. Wright (eds.), *Child behavior and development.* New York: McGraw-Hill, 1943, pp. 87–105.
7. Bayley, N., Mental growth during the first three years: A developmental study of sixty-one children by repeated tests. *Genet. Psychol. Monogr.* (1933), *14*:No. 1.
8. Bishop, B. M., Mother-child interaction and the social behavior of children. *Psychol. Monogr.* (1951), *65*:No. 328.
9. Blum, G., *Psychoanalytic theories of personality.* New York: McGraw-Hill, 1953.
10. Buxbaum, E., The role of a second language in the formation of ego and superego. *Psychoanal. Quart.* (1949), *18*:279–289.
11. Cameron, N., *The psychology of behavior disorders.* Boston: Houghton Mifflin, 1947.
12. Cameron, N. and Margaret, A., *Behavior pathology.* Boston: Houghton Mifflin, 1951.
13. Conn, J. H., Children's reactions to the discovery of genital differences. *Am. J. Orthopsychiat.* (1940), *10*:747–755.
14. Davis, D. M., The relation of repetitions in the speech of young children to certain measures of language maturity and situational factors. Part I. *J. Speech Disorders* (1939), *4*:303–318.
15. Davis, D. M., The relation of repetitions in the speech of young children

to certain measures of language maturity and situational factors. Part II. *J. Speech Disorders* (1940), 5:235–241.

16. Davis, D. M., The relation of repetitions in the speech of young children to certain measures of language maturity and situational factors. Part III. *J. Speech Disorders* (1940), 5:242–246.

17. Davis, E. A., *The development of linguistic skill in twins, singletons with siblings, and only children from age five to ten years. Inst. Child Welfare Monogr. Ser.*, No. 14. Minneapolis: University of Minnesota Press, 1937.

18. Davis, E. A., Mean sentence length compared with long and short sentences as a reliable measure of language development. *Child Develop.* (1937), 8:69–79.

19. Davis, E. A., The mental and linguistic superiority of only girls. *Child Develop.* (1937), 8:139–143.

20. Day, E. J., The development of language in twins. I. A comparison of twins and single children. *Child Develop.* (1932), 3:179–199.

21. Day, E. J., The development of language in twins. II. The development of twins: their resemblances and differences. *Child Develop.* (1932), 3:298–316.

22. Doll, E. A., The Vineland Social Maturity Scale: revised condensed manual of directions. Vineland, N. J.: Smith Printing House, 1936.

23. Doll, E. A., *Your child grows up*. Boston: John Hancock Mutual Life Insurance Co., 1939.

24. Dollard, J. and Miller, N. E., *Personality and psychotherapy*. New York: McGraw-Hill, 1950.

25. Eggan, D., The general problem of Hopi adjustment, in C. Kluckholm and H. A. Murray (eds.), *Personality in nature, society, and culture*. New York: Knopf, 1953.

26. English, O. S., and Pearson, G. H. J., *Emotional problems of living*. New York: Norton, 1945.

27. Fenichel, O., *The psychoanalytic theory of neurosis*. New York: Norton, 1945.

28. Freud, S., *New introductory lectures on psychoanalysis*. New York: Norton, 1933.

29. Freud, S., *An outline of psychoanalysis*. New York: Norton, 1949.

30. Fromm, E., The Oedipus complex and the Oedipus myth, in R. N. Anshen (ed.), *The family: Its function and destiny. Vol. V*. New York: Harper, 1948.

31. Gesell, A., Halverson, H. M., Thompson, H., Ilg, F. L., Castner, B. M., Ames, L. B., and Amatruda, C. S., *The first five years of life: a guide to the study of the preschool child*. New York: Harper, 1940.

32. Goldfarb, W., The effects of early institutional care on adolescent personality. *J. exp. Educ.* (1943), 12:106–129.

33. Goldfarb, W., Psychological privation in infancy and subsequent adjustment. *Am. J. Orthopsychiat.* (1945), 15:247–255.

34. Hagman, R. R., A study of fears of children of preschool age. *J. exp. Educ.* (1932), 1:110–130.

35. Halverson, H. M., Infant sucking and tensional behavior. *J. genet. Psychol.* (1938), 53:365–430.

36. Hattendorf, K. W., A study of the questions of young children concerning sex: a phase of an experimental approach to parental education. *J. soc. Psychol.* (1932), 3:37–65.

37. Hattwick, B. W., Interrelations between the preschool child's behavior and certain factors in the home. *Child Develop.* (1936), 7:200–226.

38. Hollenberg, E., and Sperry, M., Some antecedents of aggression and effects of frustration on doll play. *Personality* (1950), 1:32–43.

39. Holmes, F. B., An experimental investigation of a method of overcoming children's fears. *Child Develop.* (1936), 7:6–30.

40. Honigmann, J. J., *Culture and personality.* New York: Harper, 1954.

41. Honzik, M. P., The constancy of mental test performance during the preschool periods. *J. genet. Psychol.* (1938), 52:285–302.

42. Honzik, M. P., Macfarlane, J. W., and Allen, L., The stability of mental test performance between two and eighteen years. *J. exp. Educ.* (1948), 17:309–324.

43. Horney, K., *The neurotic personality of our time.* New York: Norton, 1937.

44. Horney, K., *Our inner conflicts.* New York: Norton, 1945.

45. Hurlock, E. B., *Child development.* New York: McGraw-Hill, 1950.

46. Huschka, M., The incidence and character of masturbation threats in a group of problem children. *Psychoanal. Quart.* (1938), 7:338–356.

47. Isaacs, S., *Social development in young children: A study of beginnings.* New York: Harcourt, Brace, 1933.

48. Jersild, A. T., and Holmes, F. B., Children's fears. *Child Develop. Monogr.*, (1935) No. 20.

49. Jersild, A. T., and Holmes, F. B., Methods of overcoming children's fears. *J. Psychol.* (1935–36), 1:75–104.

50. Jersild, A. T., and Holmes, F. B., Some factors in the development in children's fears. *J. exp. Educ.* (1935), 4:133–141.

51. Johnson, W., *People in quandaries: the semantics of personal adjustment.* New York: Harper, 1946.

52. Kinsey, A. C., Pomeroy, W. B., and Martin, C. E., *Sexual behavior in the human male.* Philadelphia: Saunders, 1948.

53. Kinsey, A. C., Pomeroy, W. B., Martin, C. E., and Gebhard, P. H., *Sexual behavior in the human female.* Philadelphia: Saunders, 1953.

54. Levy, D. M., Fingersucking and accessory movements in early infancy. *Amer. J. Psychiat.* (1928), 7:881–918.

55. Levy, D. M., Studies in sibling rivalry. *Res. Monogr. Amer. Orthopsychiat. Assn.*, No. 2, 1937 .

56. Levy, D. M., *Maternal over-protection.* New York: Columbia University Press, 1943.

57. Lewis, M. M., *Infant speech: a study of the beginnings of language.* New York: Humanities Press, 1951.

58. Macfarlane, J. W., The relationships of environmental pressures to the

development of a child's personality and habit patterns. *J. Pediat.* (1939), *15*:142–154.

59. Macfarlane, J. W., Study of personality development, Chapter XVIII in R. G. Barker, J. S. Kounin, and H. F. Wright, *Child behavior and development.* New York: McGraw-Hill, 1943.

60. Macfarlane, J. W., Allen, L., and Honzik, M. P., A developmental study of the behavior problems of normal children between twenty-one months and fourteen years. *Univ. of Calif. Publications in Child Develop.*, 1954, No. 2.

61. Malinowski, B., Prenuptial intercourse between the sexes in the Trobriand Islands, N. W. Melanesia. *Psychoanal. Rev.* (1927), *14*:20–36.

62. Martin, W. E., and Stendler, C. B., *Child development: the process of growing up in society.* New York: Harcourt, Brace, 1953.

63. McCarthy, D., The language development of the preschool child. *Inst. Child Welfare Monogr. Series, No. 4.* Minneapolis: University of Minnesota Press, 1930.

64. McCarthy, D. *Language development in children,* in L. Carmichael (ed.), *Manual of child psychology* (2nd ed.) New York: Wiley, 1954, pp. 492–630.

65. Mowrer, O. H., *Learning theory and personality dynamics.* New York: Ronald, 1950.

66. Mowrer, O. H., and Kluckhohn, C., Dynamic theory of personality, in J. McV. Hunt (ed.), *Personality and the behavior disorders.* New York: Ronald, 1944, pp. 69–138.

67. Murphy, G., *Personality.* New York: Harper, 1947.

68. Nice, M. M., Length of sentences as a criterion of child's progress in speech. *J. educ. Psychol. 16*:370–379.

69. Piaget, J., *The language and thought of the child,* trans. by M. Warden. New York: Harcourt, Brace, 1926.

70. Radke, M. J., The relation of parental authority to children's behavior attitudes. *Univ. Minn. Child Welf. Monogr.*, No. 22, 1946.

71. Sappenfield, B. R., *Personality dynamics.* New York: Knopf, 1954.

72. Sears, P. S., Doll play aggression in normal young children: influence of sex, age, sibling status, father's absence. *Psychol. Monogr.* (1951), *65.*

73. Sears, R. R., Pintler, M. H., and Sears, P. S., Effect of father separation on preschool children's doll play aggression. *Child Develop.* (1946), *17*: 219–243.

74. Sears, R. R., Whiting, J. W. M., Nowlis, V., and Sears, P. S., Some child-rearing antecedents of aggression and dependency in young children. *Genet. Psychol. Monogr.* (1953), *47*:135–234.

75. Sewall, M., Two studies in sibling rivalry. I. Some causes of jealousy in young children. *Smith Coll. Stud. Soc. Wk.* (1930), *1*:6–22.

76. Seward, G. H., *Sex and the social order.* New York: McGraw-Hill, 1946.

77. Smith, M. E., An investigation of the development of the sentence and the extent of vocabulary in young children. *Univ. Iowa Stud. Child Welfare* (1926), *3*:No. 5.

78. Smith, M. E., A study of some factors influencing the development of the sentence in preschool children. *J. genet. Psychol.* (1935), *46*:182–212.
79. Spock, B., *The pocketbook of baby and child care.* New York: Pocket Books, 1946.
80. Stoke, S. M., An inquiry into the concept of identification. *J. genet. Psychol.* (1950), *76*:163–189.
81. Strecker, A., *Their mothers' sons.* Philadelphia: Lippincott, 1946.
82. Terman, L. M., and Merrill, M. A., *Measuring intelligence: a guide to the administration of the new revised Stanford-Binet tests of intelligence.* Boston: Houghton Mifflin, 1937.
83. Thompson, G. G., *Child psychology: growth trends in psychological adjustment.* Boston: Houghton Mifflin, 1952.
84. Thompson, H., Physical growth, in L. Carmichael (ed.), *Manual of child psychology* (2nd ed.) New York: Wiley, 1954, pp. 292–334.
85. Vollmer, H., Jealousy in children. *Am. J. Orthopsychiat.* (1946), *16*:660–671.
86. Watson, E. H., and Lowrey, G. H., *Growth and development of children.* Chicago: Year Book Publishers, 1954.
87. Wellman, B. L., Case, I. M., Mengert, I. G., and Bradbury, D. E., Speech sounds of young children. *Univ. Iowa Stud. Child Welfare* (1931), *5*:No. 2.
88. White House Conference on Child Health and Protection. *Growth and development of the child.* New York: Century, 1932–1933.
89. Whiting, J. W. M., and Child, I. L., *Child training and personality.* New Haven: Yale University Press, 1953.
90. Wylie, P., *Generation of vipers.* New York: Farrar and Rinehart, 1942.

Chapter 9

CHANGING SOCIAL RELATIONSHIPS IN THE PRESCHOOL YEARS

The most casual observation of a group of preschool children reveals that there are wide individual differences in personality and in social behavior. The last chapter emphasized the contributions of parental attitudes, disciplinary procedures, and general home atmosphere to the development of these characteristics. As we pointed out there, the basic qualities of the preschool child's social contacts with other children are, to a large extent, reflections of his learning in the home. Whatever patterns of behavior have been rewarded frequently there (whether outgoingness or withdrawal, dominance or submission, friendliness or hostility) gain ascendancy in the child's hierarchy of responses. Consequently, they are likely to be used in other social situations.

Into [the] wider community the child carries whatever behavior equipment he has succeeded in developing as a part of his growing personality, in the more intimate and protected home environment. . . . He will have learned at home some of the essential social techniques used in associating with other persons in group situations, and in behaving himself as one member of a group (13, 40). Cameron

This does not mean, however, that the social attitudes, behavior, and techniques of social interaction acquired in the home are fixed and unalterable. In his contacts in new social situations, such as nursery school, the child will undoubtedly find that many of the responses which his parents rewarded also bring rewards from others. Other parentally rewarded responses, however, may prove unacceptable elsewhere and may provoke punishment from teachers or other children. Such responses are likely to become reduced in strength or eliminated, and to be replaced

270

by new, more appropriate responses. In short, as a consequence of learning experiences in the wider community, the child's social repertoire becomes tremendously expanded, and many of his response hierarchies may undergo drastic revision.

The present chapter will be concerned with behavior changes of the preschool years and environmental influences which play an important part in producing them. Relevant systematic studies fall into three major categories. The first group, observational and descriptive investigations of youngsters' interactions, provides an overall picture of social development during the preschool period. The second category includes studies of situational factors as antecedent conditions influencing the child's responses. The third type of research is concerned with the outcomes of deliberate efforts to alter the child's personality. Systematic observational and clinical studies of the consequences of nursery school training and of psychotherapy are included in this last group of investigations.

CHANGES IN SOCIAL BEHAVIOR DURING THE PRESCHOOL YEARS

While it is usually true that the child's earliest learning occurs in relation to his mother, other family members and friends soon become involved. If the child's mother has fed, comforted, cuddled, caressed, smiled at, and petted him frequently in the presence of others, he will gradually learn to associate tension reduction and gratification with social situations. Such a child is quite likely to find participation in social groups rewarding, since his early experiences with groups of people were frequently associated with positive feelings generated by the mother's presence. In general, if the youngster has found relationships with his mother gratifying, the positive responses formed in relation to her may become generalized, and he is likely to seek social contacts with others.

In addition, social responses are likely to be reinforced directly from very early childhood. Within the family circle, the child's earliest affectionate, outgoing responses are likely to meet with obvious approval and rewards. This is particularly true in democratic, freedom-giving, and "calm, happy" homes (cf. pp. 250–256), where learning socially oriented responses is greatly encouraged. In such homes, group contacts are viewed as gratifying and desirable, and being a member of a social group acquires reward value early in the child's life.

By nursery school age, most children are socially outgoing and interested in establishing and maintaining relationships with other children.

In some cases, however, the child may find social interactions frequently associated with punishment and frustration. For example, a rejecting mother may be so severe in her treatment of her child that he learns to avoid her, and by generalization, to withdraw from social relationships generally, including those with other children. Hence he will experience great difficulties in interactions with his peers.

Under some circumstances, youngsters who have not experienced gratifications in their social contacts with adults may still learn that friendships with other children may be rewarding. This was dramatically illustrated in Freud and Dann's unusual study (22) of six German-Jewish orphans whose parents were killed in the gas chambers during World War II. Although their very early histories differed, all six children arrived at the same concentration camp when they were a few months old, and were always together as a group thereafter. Finally, when they were all between 3 and 4 years old, they were taken to live together in a large country house in England, where they were systematically observed for a year.

Obviously the experiences of these children were unusual. None of them had known any family life and all of them undoubtedly suffered extreme privations during early infancy. Beginning with their arrival at the same concentration camp, however, they experienced most of their satisfactions in each other's presence. Whereas the adults taking care of them varied from time to time, the other children represented a constant factor accompanying tension reduction. Hence being with them became associated with gratification and their presence acquired reward value. The dependence these children had on each other appeared to be similar to the kind of attachment normal children have toward their mothers.

> The children's positive feelings were centered exclusively in their own group. It was evident that they cared greatly for each other and not at all for anybody or anything else. They had no other wish than to be together and became upset when they were separated from each other, even for short moments. No child would consent to remain upstairs while the others were downstairs, or vice versa, and no child would be taken for a walk or on an errand without the others. . . . If anything of the kind happened, the single child would constantly ask for the other children while the group would fret for the missing child (22, 131).

> The children's unusual emotional dependence on each other was borne out further by the almost complete absence of jealousy, rivalry, and competition, such as normally develop between brothers and sisters or in a group of contemporaries who come from normal families. There was no occasion to urge the children to "take turns"; they did it spontaneously since they were eager that

everybody should have his share. Since the adults played no part in their emotional lives at the time, they did not compete with each other for favors or for recognition. They did not tell on each other and they stood up for each other automatically whenever they felt that a member of the group was unjustly treated or otherwise threatened by an outsider. They were extremely considerate of each other's feelings. They did not grudge each other their possessions, . . . on the contrary lending them to each other with pleasure. When one of them received a present from a shopkeeper, they demanded the same for each of the other children, even in their absence. On walks they were concerned for each other's safety in traffic, looked after children who lagged behind, helped each other over ditches, turned aside branches for each other to clear the passage in the woods, and carried each other's coats. In the nursery they picked up each other's toys. After they had learned to play, they assisted each other silently in building and admired each other's productions. At mealtimes handing food to the neighbor was of greater importance than eating oneself (22, 133).

Most children at first try to apply the social techniques which they have learned at home to their interactions with others, including peers. In contrast, these orphans reacted to the first adult with whom they had intimate contact as they had learned to react to their peers.

The children's first positive approaches to the adults were made on the basis of their group feelings and differed in quality from the usual demanding, possessive behavior which young children show toward their mothers or mother substitutes. The children began to insist that the members of the staff should have their turn or share; they became sensitive to their feelings, identified with their needs, and considerate of their comfort. They wanted to help the adults with their occupations, and in return, expected to be helped by them. They disliked it when any member of the staff was absent and wanted to know where the adults had been and what they had done during their absence. In short, they ceased to regard the adults as outsiders, included them in their group and, as the examples show, began to treat them in some ways as they treated each other (22, 142).

During the year's observation, the children never formed as close or strong ties with adults as they had with each other. It appears that the reward value of the children continued to be higher than that of adults. In the authors' words, "their companions of the same age were their real love objects. . . . This explains why the feelings of the six children toward each other show a warmth and spontaneity which is unheard of in ordinary relations between young contemporaries" (22, 166).

Increased Social Participation

The preschool child's physical and intellectual maturation provides a basis for more prolonged and complicated social interactions than he had

Solitary play.

Parallel play.

Coöperative play

when he was younger. However, the nature and extent of the child's social participation will be significantly influenced by his previous experience with rewards and punishments for social responses. The findings of several studies of social development in children are consistent with this hypothesis.

It will be recalled that social responsiveness increases between the ages of 6 and 25 months (*44;* cf. pp. 208–210). A study by Parten (*50*) demonstrates that further increments in social orientation occur throughout the preschool period. She made records of 20 one-minute observations of 42 nursery school children between the ages of 2 and 5. Social participation during each sample was classified and scored according to six categories: unoccupied behavior (-3), solitary play (-2), onlooker behavior (watches, but does not enter play) (-1), parallel play (plays alongside, but not with, other children using the same playthings) $(+1)$, associated play (plays with others and shares materials) $(+2)$, cooperative or organized play $(+3)$. A composite social participation score was computed for each child by summing the scores he obtained during all observation periods.

Only a small number of these children indulged in unoccupied behavior. Parallel play, the most rudimentary form of social behavior, was much more characteristic of younger than of older children. The latter, on the other hand, participated more frequently in associated or coöperative play. Composite social participation scores were highly correlated with chronological age $(r = +.61)$. This indicates that as they grow older, children generally spend more time in social interactions of an associated or coöperative sort and less time without activity, alone, or merely observing.

These changes in social behavior may be partially attributable to increased ability to get around and to participate in more complex, coöperative activities. In addition to this, however, the older child probably has had more experiences in which outgoing social responses have been rewarded. Attendance at nursery school and playgrounds gives him more opportunities to learn that group-centered behavior can bring gratifications. As a consequence of many experiences, socially oriented responses become stronger and the child is likely to engage in more group activities.

As social interactions become more frequent, they also become more complex. Between the ages of 2 and 5, the child forms his first friendships. This period is also marked by increments in many—often apparently opposite—types of interpersonal behaviors. For example, children may become not only more aggressive, "bossy," and competitive; but also more coöperative, friendly, and sympathetic (*34, 49*). In short, many aspects of social behavior change simultaneously.

Friendships

As they become generally more socially oriented, children are likely to become particularly closely attached to a few peers. In one study of the factors influencing the formation of friendships among preschool children, 33 boys and girls were observed during their free-play periods (*14*). Friendship indices were derived on the basis of the number of times children were members of the same play group. Teachers rated each of the subjects on sociality, physical activity, extroversion, attractiveness of personality, and frequency of laughter.

The findings indicated that children of preschool age formed friendships with members of their own sex much more frequently than with members of the opposite sex. Similarities in chronological age, sociality, and physical activity influenced friendships between boys. Girls who became friends were alike in social participation, chronological age, sociality, and physical activity. Resemblances in height, extroversion, attractiveness of personality, intelligence, and frequency of laughter did not appear to influence either boys' or girls' friendships.

These mutual attractions may be interpreted in terms of the rewards stemming from these associations. For example, at this age, association with—and copying the behavior of—individuals of the child's own sex are generally rewarded. Moreover, boys have to some extent developed masculine needs and interests, while girls have developed feminine ones. Like-sexed peers, having common needs and interests, are more likely to find each other's company satisfying.

Another investigator (*23, 24*) made records of all instances of preschool children playing and quarreling with each other during 40 half-minute observation periods. From these data, friendship indices, quarrelsomeness indices, and quarrelsomeness-friendship ratios (frequency of quarrels divided by frequency of playing together) were derived.

The data clearly support the hypothesis that friendship patterns change with age. For example, the average friendship index increased regularly with age. Between the ages of 2 and 3, there was generally an expansion in the *number* of playmates a child had. After this age, the primary increase was in *strength of friendship* for a few particular children, rather than in total number of friends (*24*). This shift in friendship patterns may be viewed a consequence of the child's learning in these new inter-personal situations. In his first experiences outside the home, the child may interact with many different children. Some of these early relation-ships do not bring rewards and may even bring punishment. With time, the child learns that relationships with certain children are more likely to be gratifying than others. Hence he forms closer attachments to these children. Moreover, the quarrelsomeness-friendship ratio decreases regularly with age, indicating that, with more social experience, children find that outgoing, friendly responses are more frequently associated with reward than hostile ones.

SYMPATHY. Responding to another's distress is closely related to friendship and is one of the important components of socially oriented and coöperative behavior. As they become more involved in social activities and in friendships, children begin to exhibit more sympathy toward their peers. Sympathetic approaches are rare among babies under 2, but they are common among preschool children.

Murphy (48) attempted to relate the amount of sympathy children displayed to their familial and cultural backgrounds. She observed and recorded instances of sympathetic and unsympathetic responses displayed by several groups of children during nursery school play periods. Interviews with parents were the source of data on background factors.

Lower-class children were freest in their expression of affection toward others. They frequently helped others or took responsibility in routine activities or on the playground. In their play with dolls, this group manifested many outgoing, affectionate interchanges between mothers and their imaginary babies. Apparently the families of these children expressed affection toward each other readily and rewarded the youngsters' friendly, coöperative responses frequently. These behaviors were subsequently transferred to relationships in nursery school. In general, more intelligent children also manifested more sympathetic behavior (48).

Immediate situational variables were important, too. For example, sympathetic behavior was more prominent in a group including both older and younger children than one made up of children of about the same age. In the former group, age differences probably reduced the amount of competition among the children, and, in the older children, may have stimulated protective, "big brother" responses. Competition for play materials probably accounted, at least in part, for the greater amount of conflict and less sympathetic behavior in the group of same-age children.

Friendship and Conflict

The increase in social responsiveness that takes place between 2 and 5 entails increases in conflicts as well as in sympathetic and friendly responses. As we saw earlier, preschool children from democratic homes are active socially in both friendly and hostile ways (cf. pp. 250–255). Murphy's study also indicated that among nursery school children, sympathetic and aggressive behaviors were positively correlated. Gregarious and sympathetic children were also likely to be aggressive and unsympathetic frequently. For example, in her study, the following pairs of behavior items were associated: *joining an attack on another child* and *defending children attacked by others; attempts to comfort other children* (pats, embraces, etc.) and *pushing or pulling other children; helping children out of painful situations* and *pummeling children who fall accidentally* (48).

In another study quarrelsomeness and friendship indices of 40 preschool children were found to be positively correlated (24). Mutual friends argued more than average, and correlatively, children who quarreled a great deal were also more likely to be friendly with each other.

Conflicts

Children's conflicts can, of course, take many forms. In a comprehensive study of 54 nursery school children in free-play situations, Jersild and Markey (35) made records of 1577 conflicts, noting each child's role, his attacks and defenses, and the outcome. Conflict was defined very broadly as "any instance in which one child attacks another . . . or by deed interferes with [his] activities or possessions . . . or threatens by word or gesture to do so, or endeavors by force or verbal demands to possess others' belongings, or direct another's activities in opposition to the apparent desires of the child against whom the aggression is made. These vary from severe encounters involving hitting, kicking, and crying to milder and more transient encounters in which the child tried to snatch another's toys or insist that another comply with his demands" (35). They found that overt or verbal aggression against a child's possessions and interference with freedom of movement were the two chief sources of conflict, although from the observer's point of view, much of the aggression seemed to be unprovoked.

On the average, children between the ages of 2 and 4 participated in a conflict every 5 minutes in nursery school, but there are tremendous individual differences. For example, during the course of the observations, one child engaged in 17 conflicts, while another was involved in

ance, the individual gives up his own desires and attempts to discover common goals that will be mutually satisfying to him and to others. Such behavior is demonstrated by such activities as showing common purpose by word or action, verbal requests or suggestions, or compliance with another's requests or suggestions.

The subjects of the study, 128 preschool children, were brought in pairs to an experimental room which contained a sandbox on a table and a few toys. Every child was involved in 5 pairings, each time with a different child. The behavior of each pair was observed for a 5-minute period through a one-way vision screen, and their reactions were recorded. *Dominance* and *integration* scores, consisting of the total frequency of these kinds of responses in the five pairings, were then computed.

It was discovered that domination evoked domination, and integration evoked integration on the part of the companion. For example, girls generally obtained higher dominance scores than boys; that is, girl-girl pairs displayed more dominance than boy-boy combinations. But when boys were paired with girls, their dominance scores increased, i.e., they approached the girl's dominance level.

When children with high dominance scores were paired with peers having lower scores, the latter increased greatly in dominance. The overall correlation between dominance scores of paired companions (based on over 500 pairings) was relatively high ($r = +.68$), while the integrative behavior scores of pairs of children were even more closely associated (2, 3). These findings suggest that children have learned that domination is the most effective technique for handling dominant children; and that integration yields the greatest rewards when playing with "integrative" peers.

TRAINING AND CHANGES IN CHILDREN'S BEHAVIOR

Learning principles may be applied directly in teaching children acceptable and adaptive social behavior. Through reinforcement, mature responses can acquire great habit strength and become higher in the child's social response hierarchies than less adequate behavior learned at an earlier developmental period. For example, composure, independent activity, attempts at problem solving, and systematic trial-and-error behavior can replace aggression or regressive behavior as reactions to failure. It may be predicted that if the child has been rewarded frequently for meeting difficulties calmly and independently, he will become more self-confident and will manifest fewer uncontrolled, inadequate responses to frustration.

Training for More Mature Reactions to Frustration

These predictions were confirmed in a study by Keister (38, 39). She trained children to overcome immature reactions to failure, to work independently, and to persevere in their efforts to solve frustrating problems. Her subjects, 82 preschool children, were observed while working individually on two difficult problems, one involving solution of a puzzle, and the other requiring great physical strength.

From this group, she selected 12 experimental subjects who made many immature responses to failure (e.g., retreating or giving up almost at once, crying, sulking). Each was given special training designed to teach him "to persist longer in the face of tasks that were difficult for him, to depend less on an adult for help in solving a problem, to give fewer rationalizations in the face of his failure, and to attack a problem and see it through with some composure" (38, 39). Another group of 12 children who gave slightly less evidence of immaturity in the test situations served as a control group. These children received no special training.

The training method consisted of introducing the child to a series of problems (picture puzzles and "block-boy" construction) of progressively increasing complexity. Subjects were given difficult problems only after they had experienced success at simpler ones.

During a 16-week training period, the experimenter met with each child in individual sessions lasting between 8 and 33 minutes, until the child was able to complete the training tasks. No direct assistance was given during these sessions, but independent behavior was praised by statements such as "That was fine! You are learning to try hard and not to have anyone help you. You did that one all by yourself" (38). In addition to this, the experimenter occasionally gave encouragement or direct suggestions for problem solutions.

The level of difficulty of the tasks increased regularly as training progressed. Nevertheless, the subjects showed continuous gains in independence and interest in the problems, requesting help less frequently and persisting longer in the more difficult tasks. Spontaneous verbalizations by the subjects also revealed increased self-confidence and ability to sustain effort. For example, after failing twice in the construction of a block-boy, one child said "I am sure havin' a hard time, but I'm making him better. I think it will be better this time" (39).

After completion of training, the children were tested again in a difficult puzzle-box experiment similar to the original one. In this situation, the trained group made significantly more "attempts to solve alone" and "interest" responses than they had in the original test. They manifested no exaggerated emotional responses such as crying, yelling, sulking, or destructive behavior in the retest. Rationalization (making excuses for failures), asking assistance, and whining were much less frequent than they had been in the first test, while statements reflecting more constructive reactions were more common. In short, the composed, mature, independent responses learned in training were transferred to other problem situations. In retest situations, the group who had no special training did not show any significant improvement in handling frustration (39).

Apparently socially immature and maladaptive reactions to frustration are amenable to change. Through training, young children can be guided to greater frustration tolerance (ability to handle frustration). Moreover, the techniques learned during training may generalize to other situations where composure, independence, and persistence are required for successful problem solution.

The Modification of Ascendant Behavior

Another group of experiments illustrates how learning principles may be applied to modify ascendance or dominance or to increase coöperation. In one experiment, each of the 18 subjects was paired with 10 other children for 5 minutes of play in an experimental room containing a sandbox and a few attractive toys (cars, trucks, shovels, and animals) (32). During this time, the interactions of the pair were observed and all ascendant reactions were recorded. Ascendance scores were based on the frequency of specifically defined responses indicating either "pursuing one's own purpose against interference" or "directing the behavior of one's companion."

Nursery school behavior records revealed that the six children who were most ascendant in the experimental situations were generally self-confident, while the six who were least ascendant lacked this characteristic. The investigator therefore reasoned that building up the child's confidence might raise his ascendance. To test this hypothesis, she chose the five least ascendant children as an experimental group and gave them special training designed to increase self-confidence. This consisted of a series of individual training sessions in which the subject was taught all the knowledge and skills necessary to master three tasks (making a cat with different colors and shapes of mosaics; a picture puzzle; recalling a story which had been read to him). A control group was composed of five other non-ascendant children who did not receive any special training.

Following these sessions, each child was observed in four pairings—each time with a different, originally more ascendant child—in situations resembling those used in training. In these interactions, the trained children were more ascendant than their companions (taking the lead in instructing them, demonstrating the use of materials, etc.).

As a final test, about ten weeks after the initial ascendance tests were made, the trained children were again paired with peers in the original experimental situation (sandbox and toys). They showed significantly greater gains in ascendance than untrained children did, four of the five showing marked changes. Ascendance scores of the control group did not change significantly between the initial and final experimental tests (32).

These findings support the investigator's hypothesis that a child may gain in ascendant behavior if his self-confidence is elevated. Moreover, this increase in confidence may transfer from the immediate situation in which the new learning occurs (in this case, the training situation) to other settings (such as the original test situation).

Other similar experiments reveal that moderately ascendant children may also profit from special training, making gains in ascendance both in situations similar to those used in training and in the original experimental setting (51). Training may affect the child's approach to many kinds of life situations, including routine nursery school interactions. Thus, in free-play activities following training, four originally non-ascendant children displayed as much ascendance as four untrained companions who had been much more ascendant initially.

Increases in ascendancy following training may be manifested in both socially desirable and socially disapproved behavior. In another experiment, seven non-ascendant youngsters were given training designed to increase their security and self-confidence (47). Afterward, they showed gains in many categories of ascendance, some of which were judged (by 41 experts) to be socially acceptable, others unacceptable. Heightened self-confidence was followed by increases in both selfish, hostile responses and constructive, self-assertive reactions. Moreover, the trained group made more attempts at ascendant behavior, and were much more frequently successful than they had been initially. In contrast, a control group of five untrained non-ascendant children changed little between the initial and final tests, showing no particular trend in either ascendant activity or successful ascendance.

Training for Increased Coöperation

Just as submissive children can be trained to be more ascendant, extremely dominating children can be trained to become more coöperative. In one experiment, each of 71 preschool children was paired with five other children for 5-minute periods in a room containing only one toy (15). *Domination* and *coöperation* scores were derived from records of behavior in this situation.

Of the 19 most dominating, uncoöperative children, ten were selected as an experimental group and given special help in understanding social situations and techniques of dealing with them. The other nine constituted a control group, which received no training or special attention.

The training program consisted of eleven 15-minute doll play periods during which the experimenter told the child a story involving two dolls who had social difficulties or conflicts. The child and the experimenter discussed and analyzed the situations together, attempting to decide upon the most desirable ways of resolving the problems. Occasionally the child was asked to work out a solution by himself. (Figure 23, p. 294).

After the training period, the experimental and control subjects were again tested in the original situation (i.e., paired with another child in a room with only one toy). Compared with their initial test behavior, the dominating behavior of trained children was considerably diminished, and they made more coöperative responses. On the other hand, the behavior of the controls was essentially unchanged. The decrease of domination in the trained group—which was still evidenced a month later—was not accompanied by either an increase in submission or a decrease in general social participation. Apparently, socially desirable behavior can be fostered without restricting the child's social activity or his ability to maintain his standing with his peers. Children can be helped to become more coöperative without becoming victims of the domination of others (15).

CONSEQUENTS OF NURSERY SCHOOL ATTENDANCE

The number of children attending nursery school is increasing continuously and at a rapid rate. Like most specialists on the subject, parents are becoming convinced that children benefit from nursery school attendance.

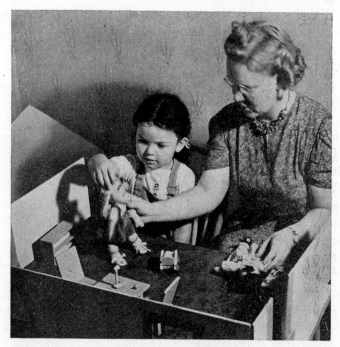

FIGURE 23. The training situation employed in Chittenden's
(15) study of the modification of assertive behavior. (With
permission of the Society for Research in Child Development.)

Social Adjustments

The objectives of the nursery school have been stated in various ways.
Some writers (4) consider an increase in "general security" to be the
basic goal. Others maintain that nursery school is "a social situation that
will constitute a real learning situation resulting in learning to adjust and
conform to others as well as maintaining [one's] own freedom as an individual in a group" (34). Furthermore, "successful adjustment to the
social situation may be considered one of the tool subjects in nursery
school" (34). Most workers in the field agree that the basic aims of the
nursery school include the promotion of personal adjustment and improvement of social relations. In many cases, the nursery school affords
the child his first contact with groups of peers, and thus marks the beginning of peer influences.

Some of the responses learned at home are likely to be reinforced
further in nursery school and hence to acquire greater habit strength.
Other responses are likely to be punished by peers or nursery school

teachers and hence to lose habit strength. It might therefore be anticipated that the child's behavior will change somewhat as a consequence
of nursery school experience.

There have been a number of studies attempting to evaluate either the
immediate or long-time consequents of nursery school attendance, and
we shall review some of the major ones presently. A word of caution in
interpreting the studies seems appropriate at the outset, however. Many
of the studies compare children who attend nursery school with those
who do not. In general the groups are matched with respect to a number
of important variables such as age, intelligence, and socioeconomic status.
But there are probably other important factors, such as parental attitudes,
on which the two groups cannot be matched. These factors may be intimately related to whether or not the child goes to nursery school at all.
Thus observed differences between children attending and those not
attending nursery school may not be attributable so much to the variable
of attendance as to differences in the family backgrounds.

In one of the earliest studies of the problem, 22 nursery school children
were compared with 21 youngsters matched in age, intelligence, physical
development, and socioeconomic background, who did not attend nursery school. All were rated on a series of behavior items at the beginning
of the school year and again six months later (58).

It was found that during the intervening period, the nursery school
children became less inhibited, more spontaneous, and more socialized.
They gained more than the other children in initiative, independence,
self-assertion, self-reliance, curiosity, and interest in the environment.
According to the investigator, these changes are "probably due to the
influence of the social force of a large group of children who had to
adjust to each other constantly" (58, 72).

In another study, systematic observations of the social behavior of 18
three-year-old nursery school children were made in the fall and again
in the spring (34). Nine of the children had attended the same school
during the previous year and knew each other, while the other nine were
new pupils. The investigators used a time-sampling technique, recording
all the child's verbalizations and social activities. Each child was
assigned a social participation score based on the time spent in coöperative play, sharing, and conversation.

During the fall observations, the children who had previously attended
nursery school were more sociable than the others, spending a significantly greater proportion of their time in social activities. However, most

of their social relationships were confined to children with whom they had been friendly during the preceding year.

The new children made rapid gains in social participation. As early as the latter part of the fall, they made 80 percent as many interpersonal contacts as the "older" group, and by the end of the school year, they were equal in social activity. Apparently these children discovered quickly that their peers could provide important gratifications and that social relationships could be rewarding. Moreover, the program in the nursery school probably included many group activities which were satisfying to all the children. It appears that the nursery school can be a social setting in which the child can learn to associate social participation with satisfactions and rewards. In this way, attendance may promote sociability and increase the child's interest in others.

Habit Patterns

Several studies (27, 36, 37) suggest that specific habit patterns may also change as a consequence of preschool experience. Observations and mothers' reports indicate that children attending nursery school eliminated more "undesirable," infantile and dependent habits during the year than a matched group of peers who did not go to preschool. Correlatively, they acquired a greater number of "desirable" habits, many of them indicative of emancipation from adults (37).

In a more extensive study, two matched groups of 106 children, one with an average of nine months attendance in nursery school, and a control group enrolled only a few weeks, served as subjects (27). Teachers rated each subject on 60 kinds of behavior involving routine habits, social adjustments, speech, nervous tendencies, and fears. Those who had attended nursery school longer showed fewer maladaptive reactions such as avoiding strangers, shrinking from notice, giving in easily, twisting their hair, tenseness, playing with fingers, wriggling, refusing food, enuresis, leaving tasks incomplete, and dawdling with food. Nursery school experience seems to facilitate social adjustment and the development of improved routine habits, at the same time reducing social inhibitions and nervous tendencies.

Preschool training did not affect manifestations of such "emotional" behaviors as *cries easily, fears animals, twitches, sulks, temper tantrums, thumbsucking.* This led the author to conclude that "the influence of nursery school may be greater for social behavior and routine adjustments than for emotional traits per se" (27, 188).

One study failed to demonstrate that children benefit from nursery school training (4). The investigators were concerned with the relationships between length of nursery school attendance and ratings on ten types of "insecurity" behavior (e.g., temper tantrums, nervous habits, physical inactivity, withdrawal into fantasy, oversensitivity to criticism). Total scores, based on all the ratings, were not significantly related to duration of nursery school experience, although increased physical activity and resistance to authority were somewhat associated with longer periods of attendance. In general, the findings were inconclusive, providing little evidence that children's insecurity feelings were influenced by preschool experience (4).

Except for this last, these studies are consistent in pointing out that youngsters benefit from nursery school attendance. The outstanding consequents seem to be advances in sociability, self-expression, independence, initiative, social adaptability, and interest in the environment. As we pointed out earlier, it is not always possible, in these studies on changes in behavior, to separate the influences of home atmosphere from the influences of nursery school attendance itself. Nevertheless, it seems reasonable to conclude that nursery school attendance itself may play an important part in strengthening such responses as social outgoingness, independence, and self-expression, for these are the responses which are highly rewarded in many such schools.

Influences of Different Nursery School Atmospheres

It should be pointed out that the nursery schools involved in the above studies very likely constituted a select sample of well-conducted schools with professionally trained personnel. Unfortunately, not all nursery schools are of this level. A well-designed experimental study shows how the impact of nursery school attendance on the child's personality and social adjustment varies with the general atmosphere, teaching techniques, and programs of the school (56). The investigator studied two groups of 4-year-olds—equated in I.Q., socioeconomic status, and general personality characteristics (judged by teachers)—who had different kinds of nursery school experiences. With one group of 12 subjects, the teachers were understanding and interested but somewhat detached, allowing the children to plan their own activities and assisting them only when they specifically requested help. With the other group, 11 subjects, these same teachers were warm, friendly, and coöperative, maintaining a great deal of personal contact with the children, guiding their activities, and spontaneously giving help and information.

After eight months of nursery school experience, the children who had a great deal of teacher guidance improved more in personal and social adjustment, became more ascendant, and participated more actively in social relationships than the others. They were also less hostile, rejecting, persecuting, threatening, attacking, and destructive. Frequent warm, friendly interactions with teachers also fostered more leadership, greater constructiveness when faced with possible failure, and a lower incidence of nervous habits. In short, from the points of view of the preschool child's social and emotional adjustment, active teacher guidance and participation are more beneficial than detachment. The favorable changes in children's behavior following nursery school training, noted in the studies cited above, may be attributable to the "high teacher guidance, active participation" qualities of the schools they attended.

Long-Range Consequents of Nursery School Experience

The nursery school's most important contributions to the socialization process and to personality development generally can be evaluated best in terms of ultimate consequents. In one study, report cards and anecdotal records of kindergarten children were analyzed. The data indicated that those who had attended preschool manifested more social poise and independence, but were not more "socially adaptable," than their peers without such training (26). Kindergarten teachers rated their nursery school trained pupils as somewhat superior to other children in general attitudes, but no better in specific characteristics (such as health habits, social adaptability, tenseness). According to teachers' and mothers' ratings of elementary school children, those with preschool experience displayed better than average emotional adjustment, more mature reactions to failure, greater independence of adult approval, and greater potentiality for leadership (57).

In general, the findings of these studies indicate that attendance at a good nursery school may have favorable consequences both immediately and over a longer period of time. However, the results must be interpreted cautiously, for, as we noted earlier, the influences of other factors cannot be isolated from the influence of nursery school attendance itself. In addition, the nursery schools studied may constitute a highly select sample. Less adequate, poorly conducted nursery schools may not produce the favorable consequences described in these studies. At any rate, all the evidence seems to contradict the notion that freedom, independence and habits of self-expression, acquired in a permissive nursery school, lead to adjustment difficulties in the more formal atmosphere of kindergarten and the primary grades.

Moreover, the data of one study indicated that there was a marked relationship between nursery school adjustment and subsequent emotional stability (57). The following characteristics of nursery school children were found to be predictive of poor emotional or social adjustment in elementary school: inflexibility, impulsiveness, negativism, moodiness, temper tantrums, jealousy, excessive fears, speech difficulties, uncoöperativeness, overassertiveness, and indifference to others. These problems, if present to an unusual degree in nursery school, may be regarded as warnings of subsequent danger.

On the other hand, children who were characterized in nursery school as self-controlled, optimistic, coöperative, able in leadership, and respectful of others' property rights were generally well adjusted in elementary school. Leadership ability in nursery school was prognostic of later leadership, active social participation, and sensitivity to the feelings of others. The investigators concluded that the "whole trend of the results shows how closely behavior in nursery schools parallels that of the upper grades" (57, 67).

PSYCHOTHERAPY

While special training and nursery school experience may modify certain personality and social characteristics, serious emotional problems may be more resistant to change. Since maladjustments are generally the consequents of complex, disturbed family relationships (cf. pp. 256–260), they often require special psychological treatment (psychotherapy) for their alleviation or elimination.

There are many different "schools" of psychotherapy, each of them making use of its own specific procedures and techniques. However, the most important aspect of all psychotherapy, shared by all "schools," is the establishment of a close relationship between the patient and a highly trained therapist (psychiatrist, clinical psychologist, social worker).

Psychotherapy is basically a learning process. Regardless of the specific techniques involved, all psychotherapeutic situations provide opportunities for learning new adaptive attitudes and behavior which may replace older, less adequate responses learned in the family setting.

If neurotic behavior is learned, it should be unlearned by some combination of the same principles by which it was taught. We believe this to be the case. Psychotherapy establishes a set of conditions by which neurotic habits may be unlearned and non-neurotic habits learned. Therefore, we view the therapist as a kind of teacher and the patient as a learner (*18, 7*). *Dollard & Miller*

Techniques of Therapy: Nondirective Approaches

Most child therapists use play as a therapeutic device, although, as we shall see, they use it in markedly different ways. Speaking of the rationale underlying the use of play, Axline, a leading authority in the field, says: "Play therapy is based upon the fact that play is the child's natural medium of self-expression. It is an opportunity which is given to the child to 'play out' his feelings and problems, just as in certain types of adult therapy, an individual 'talks out' his difficulties" (*6, 9*).

She classifies play therapy techniques into two broad categories, *directive*, in which "the therapist may assume responsibility for guidance and interpretation" and *nondirective,* in which "the therapist may leave responsibility and direction to the child." In nondirective play therapy, the child is allowed to do or say anything he wants in the playroom. Throughout the sessions, the therapist is friendly and interested but gives no direct suggestions. He remains alert to what the child is expressing in play and conversation and indicates his acceptance and understanding of his behavior. In this way "the child is given the opportunity to play out his accumulated feelings of tensions, frustration, insecurity, aggression, fear, bewilderment, and confusion" (*6, 16*).

By playing out these feelings he brings them to the surface, gets them out in the open, faces them, learns to control them, or abandons them. When he has achieved emotional relaxation, he begins to realize the power within himself to be an individual in his own right, to think for himself, to make his own decisions, to become psychologically more mature, and, by so doing, to realize selfhood.

The play-therapy room is good growing ground. In the security of this room where the *child* is the most important person, where he is in command of the situation and of himself, where no one tells him what to do, no one criticizes what he does, no one nags, or suggests, or goads him on or pries into his private world, he suddenly feels that here he can unfold his wings; he can look squarely at himself, for he is accepted completely; he can test out his ideas; he can express himself fully; for this is *his* world, and he no longer has to compete with such other forces as adult authority or rival contemporaries or situations where he is a human pawn in a game between bickering parents, or where he is the butt of someone else's frustrations and aggressions. He is an individual in his own right. He is treated with dignity and respect. He can say anything that he feels like saying—and he is accepted completely. He can play with the toys in any way that he likes to—and he is accepted completely. He can hate and he can love and he can be as indifferent as the Great Stone

FIGURE 24. A play therapy session. (Posed picture, courtesy of Harold E. Burtt, Ohio State University.)

Face—and he is still accepted completely. He can be as fast as a whirlwind or as slow as molasses in January—and he is neither restrained nor hurried.

It is a unique experience for a child suddenly to find adult suggestions, mandates, rebukes, restraints, criticisms, disapprovals, support, intrusions gone. They are all replaced by complete acceptance and permissiveness to be himself (6, 16).

As a consequence of this therapy, "the child gains the courage to move ahead, to become a more mature and independent individual" (6, 21).

Allen (1), a prominent child psychiatrist, is also nondirective in his techniques. Although he uses *free and spontaneous play* he involves the child in more discussion than Axline does. During treatment sessions, the emphasis is on the immediate situation, the child's present activities, statements, feelings, and emotions, rather than on past circumstances and events which have influenced his behavior. Difficulties and problems which arise during play are discussed in terms of what is happening at the moment. The sessions are regarded as "growth experiences," giving the child the opportunity to experience a unique emotional relationship in which he is completely accepted. Hence he may try new solutions to problems and learn to deal adequately with previously upsetting situations (1).

According to some therapists, spontaneous play techniques are particularly indicated with children whose neurotic traits are of long standing. They maintain that youngsters who are inhibited, repressed, extremely hostile, excessively timid, or overly meticulous are most likely to benefit from this kind of treatment (1, 50).

Directive Play Therapy

PSYCHOANALYTIC TECHNIQUES. The use of play as a therapeutic device originated in early attempts to apply psychoanalytic techniques to children. In psychoanalytic therapy with adults, free association and dream interpretation are among the principal techniques employed to uncover the patient's basic conflicts and sources of emotional maladjustment. Since these methods require a high degree of verbal facility and comprehension on the part of the patient, they have limited value for the treatment of children.

Anna Freud, the daughter of Sigmund Freud, was one of the first to recognize the therapeutic potential of play as a partial substitute for more verbal treatment methods (21). In her efforts to understand the child and his conflicts, she uses systematic observation of play, combined whenever possible with reports of dreams and daydreams, free associations, and direct discussion. While she may guide the child's play into certain areas of conflict, she seldom gives psychoanalytic interpretations. On these rare occasions, they are related to the child's personal experiences (21).

The techniques of Melanie Klein, an orthodox British psychoanalyst, differ from Anna Freud's. She frequently interprets the "symbolic meanings" of the child's play to him in terms of psychoanalytic concepts such as oral deprivation, Oedipal strivings, or castration anxiety (40).

CONTROLLED TECHNIQUES. Other play therapy techniques, at least partially derived from psychoanalytic theory and procedures, make use of "control" or standardized situations. In these approaches, "the therapist may select the material (dolls and other play material) and depict the plot, as in the sibling rivalry situation. The therapist supplies the main characters and the dramatic situation. The child is encouraged to work with the plot selected, add whatever other actors or scenes he wishes, and keep the play going" (42, 918).

David Levy, the leading exponent of this general approach, calls his technique *release therapy*. It is intended to relieve severe anxiety, fear reactions, or night terrors which have been precipitated by traumatic experiences, such as a surgical operation, accident, or divorce of the parents. He suggests that the use of the technique should be limited to children under 10, relatively new problems, and cases having "a definite symptom picture, precipitated by a specific event in the form of a frightening experience." Moreover,

. . . it is important that the child is suffering from something that happened in the past and not from a difficult situation going on at the time of treatment. Release therapy cannot be applied, for example, to a child suffering from the results of maternal rejection or overprotection. In such cases the mother and not the child is the primary or even the exclusive object of therapy (42, 916).

The following case illustrates the way in which release therapy may be used.

A boy aged 4 years, 1 month, the older of two children, was referred because of night terrors, timidity with children, negativism, and sibling rivalry. The symptoms were all of three weeks' duration (except sibling rivalry) and were precipitated by a fight with a companion in which the patient was licked. Night terrors had occurred a year previously and for one month following the birth of the younger sibling, a girl.

Patient was to leave for the country at the end of the week. There were daily sessions for six days, comprising sibling rivalry situations in which there was quick release of primitive hostility against mother, baby, and breasts. Anxiety of falling into the toilet and crushing a baby doll that fell in, occurred in the fourth interview.

Night terrors stopped after the second session. Follow-up interviews, 9 months, 22 months, and 4 years 5 months after treatment stopped, revealed a marked change in the sibling rivalry, first noted during treatment; a change from a jealous, hostile relationship to a protecting, friendly one. At school he became well adjusted, frequently exchanging home visits with children and showed good social initiative. School work was always superior. Negativism in the form of sulky disobedience and refusals were noted as modified in the first follow-up to amiable, reasonable attitude, which continued. Night terrors recurred for a period of about 5 weeks, three years after treatment, following a change of governesses and measles with delirium and high fever the first three days. They occurred nightly the first two weeks and gradually decreased in intensity and frequency (42, 922).

In Solomon's *active play therapy* (55), another controlled method, the child's play is limited to situations the therapist creates for him, although his interests are stimulated by statements such as "let's pretend" and "let's make up a game." It is assumed that the patient who describes the dolls as angry, sad, or happy in certain settings, reacts this way himself in real life situations. Throughout the sessions the therapist asks the child questions about his feelings and emotions. For example, if the child states that "the boy (doll) gets mad," the therapist would ask what makes him get mad and how he reacts when he is mad. According to Solomon, the child reaches an understanding of himself and his underlying problems and conflicts during the treatment sessions. He begins to have less fear of his hostility and guilt because he has been allowed to express them in permissive, non-threatening situations. Direct suggestions and help in solving problems are also used (e.g., "you don't have to feel badly about that"). As a consequence of all these factors, the child benefits from therapy.

The technique has been reported to be particularly effective with four categories of problems: aggressive-impulsive, anxiety-phobic (basically frightened, fearful children), regressive reaction (return to infantile behavior, wetting, thumbsucking, etc.) and schizoid-schizophrenic (withdrawn children who are more concerned with their fantasy life than with reality). Solomon does not claim that this technique is more successful than other methods, but feels that it may achieve important results in a shorter period of time (55).

These are only a few of the many kinds of play techniques employed in child therapy. Despite the wide differences among these approaches, adherents of every method report therapeutic successes.

Psychotherapy and Learning

As we pointed out earlier, therapy sessions provide learning settings in which the child may acquire new attitudes and feelings toward himself and others, as well as new overt responses. Patient-therapist relationships are social situations involving personal interactions which may be different from any the child has previously experienced. It may be the first prolonged contact with a person who does not restrain him or force him to do anything, but allows—even encourages—him to express himself completely spontaneously. Continued therapy means repeated experiences with rewarding social relationships. Personal interactions become associated with satisfaction and security rather than with upset feelings. The child may acquire new attitudes toward others and toward social relations, and these may generalize to everyday situations. Thus the initially shy, withdrawn child may develop more outgoing and sociable responses.

Inhibited, overly sensitive, and fearful children may also change following therapy. In their homes, they may have been punished for independent activities, and for self-expression, expression of hostility, and curiosity. Hence they may inhibit any responses not specifically approved by their parents.

The therapist, on the other hand, is tolerant of all kinds of behavior and the child—perhaps for the first time in his life—finds that he need not be afraid of expressing his own feelings. This promotes feelings of freedom and self-confidence, and concomitantly, reduces social fears and inhibition.

Specific fears and anxieties may also be eliminated through psychotherapy, especially using such techniques as those advocated by Levy and Solomon. In the therapy sessions, the child is confronted repeatedly with play situations resembling real settings which elicit fear responses. However, here he is in the presence of an individual with whom he feels secure, and the environment is protected and unthreatening. Although fear responses are not punished, more adequate reactions bring rewards from the therapist. During treatment, the child may try out new responses and those which are "good" and more mature will be reinforced by the therapist, and consequently will acquire greater habit strength. Subsequently, the newly formed, more adaptive reactions may become generalized to more important real-life situations.

One child psychiatrist, a practitioner of controlled play therapy, calls the play interview "a test situation" in which the child "not only learns what he has contributed to the total situation [i.e., his problems] but for the first time finds himself secure in a personal relationship. He can therefore begin to develop the courage that comes from self-criticism, a sense of freedom arising out of self-expression, and be helped in the direction of happy, healthy living" (16, 286).

Psychotherapy with Parents

By and large, the therapist's efforts can be successful only if the child lives in a home atmosphere which is favorable for maintaining the behavior changes achieved in the therapy sessions. Gains made in therapy can become general only if they are reinforced by other important individuals in the child's life. Parents supply most of the child's rewards and punishments. If adaptive responses, rewarded in therapy, are punished at home, they may be eliminated. Conversely, if maladaptive responses continue to be rewarded at home, they will not become reduced in spite of the therapist's efforts to alleviate them.

Almost all child therapists recognize this and agree that the fullest coöperation from the parents is essential if the child is to benefit from therapy. In many cases, the parents are also advised to have therapy while their child is being treated. When the therapist is consulted about a child's emotional problems, he must first direct his attention

. . . to the personalities of the parents and to ways and means with which he may improve their personalities. If their emotional problems are deeply ingrained and represent established neuroses or even psychoses it may then be necessary to spend a considerable period of time and effort in helping them. At times, however, parents have strayed from a proper role because of ignorance or mild emotional problems which are amenable to short-term psychotherapy easily carried out by a general practitioner or pediatrician. Obvious defects in the parental attitude may sometimes be removed by a few discussions. The overdemanding mother who has ritualized home routines may be sufficiently flexible to accept the physician's advice in the direction of more leniency. The father who spends little time with his children, feeling that his role in the family as far as they are concerned is unimportant, may be stimulated to greater activity by a physician's well-chosen comments (*19*, 137).

Removal from the Home

In some cases, the parents are so uncoöperative or incapable of change that their interactions with the child actually counteract the therapist's efforts. If, under these circumstances, the child's maladjustment is severe enough, he may be taken away from his own family and placed in a foster home or institution. However,

Removing children from their homes and placing them in an institution is generally considered one of the most drastic forms of treatment, one to be avoided whenever there are possible alternatives. In our society with its strong emphasis on the family unit and the traditional stigma of the kinds of institutions we have for children, this mode of dealing with children may possibly be more negative in its effects than in other societies. The fact remains, however, that in our society in most instances institutionalization creates more problems than it may solve for the child (*54*, 401).

There are no definite criteria to be applied in making decisions about institutionalization or foster home placement. Certainly all the factors in the child's life situation must be taken into account. However, most child therapists agree that this type of treatment is unadvisable "if there is a good chance of changing destructive family attitudes" (*53*, 168).

According to Rotter, "the most general rule is not to institutionalize except as a last resort or when all other avenues of treatment are blocked." Exceptions might be made in cases "where the institution is quite advanced in its treatment program and when the institutionalization itself is thought of as a temporary treatment measure rather than a technique of taking the child out of circulation" (*54*, 403).

Institutional Treatment

Unfortunately, only a few institutions have adequate psychological treatment programs. One of these is the therapy-oriented University of Chicago Sonia Shankman Orthogenic School which accommodates about 30 seriously disturbed—often extremely withdrawn—children between 6 and 14 years of age. During their 2- or 3-year residency at the school, the children have little contact with their homes. Trained staff members live with them 24 hours a day (11).

The school atmosphere is completely permissive. Children are allowed to eat as much and as frequently as they want, to soil themselves, and to express sex curiosity and hostility. There are no punishments and the staff tries to make all possibly threatening or anxiety-provoking routines (e.g., eating, going to the toilet, bathing) pleasurable and relaxed. In school and in social activities, children master simple tasks before being given more difficult ones. Thus failure and frustration are minimized, while success experiences are maximized, so that the child's self-confidence gradually increases. Gratifying interactions with adults and other children in the school promote new friendly feelings and attitudes toward others, and more outgoing, socially oriented behavior. These may then be transferred to other social situations outside the school.

In the school, contacts with kindly, tolerant adults are prolonged, and intimate child-counselor relationships are established. This may be the child's first opportunity to form a substantial identification with a stable individual. This "eventually challenges the child to change his personality at least in part in the image of the person or persons who are now so important to him. . . . Living day in and day out among adults who provide the child with images of reasonable and orderly living becomes a challenge to him to take up their pattern, first in his external, and then in his internal, life" (11, 28).

In summary, the social learning experiences in the school are both unique and immensely gratifying to the child. Hence he may leave the school considerably improved, more self-confident, more stable emotionally, and better adjusted socially.

REFERENCES AND ADDITIONAL READING

1. Allen, F., Psychotherapy with children. New York: Norton, 1942.
2. Anderson, H. H., Domination and integration in the social behavior of young children in an experimental play situation. Genet. Psychol. Monogr. (1937), 19:341–408.
3. Anderson, H. H., Domination and social integration in the behavior of

kindergarten children in an experimental play situation. *J. exp. Educ.* (1939), 8:123–131.

4. Andrus, R., and Horowitz, E. L., The effect of nursery school training: insecurity feeling. *Child Develop.* (1938), 9:169–174.

5. Arsenian, J. M., Young children in an insecure situation. *J. abnorm. soc. Psychol.* (1943), 38:225–249.

6. Axline, V. M., *Play therapy.* Boston: Houghton Mifflin, 1947.

7. Baldwin, A. L., Socialization and the parent-child relationship. *Child Develop.* (1948), 19:127–136.

8. Baldwin, A. L., The effect of home environment on nursery school behavior. *Child Develop.* (1949), 20:49–62.

9. Barker, R. G., Dembo, T., and Lewin, K., Frustration and regression: an experiment with young children. *Univer. Iowa Stud. Child Welf.* (1941), 18:No. 1, pp. 1–314.

10. Barker, R. G., Dembo, T., and Lewin, K., Frustration and regression, in R. G. Barker, J. S. Kounin, and H. F. Wright (eds.), *Child behavior and development.* New York: McGraw-Hill, 1943, pp. 441–458.

11. Bettelheim, B., *Love is not enough.* Glencoe, Ill.: The Free Press, 1951.

12. Burton, A., The aggression of young children following satiation. *Am. J. Orthopsychiat.* (1942), 12:262–267.

13. Cameron, N., *The psychology of behavior disorders.* Boston: Houghton Mifflin, 1947.

14. Challman, R. C., Factors influencing friendships among preschool children. *Child Develop.* (1932), 3:146–158.

15. Chittenden, G. E., An experimental study in measuring and modifying assertive behavior in young children. *Monogr. Soc. Res. Child Develop.* (1942), 7:No. 1.

16. Conn, J. H., The play interview as an investigative and therapeutic procedure. *Nerv. Child* (1948), 7:257–286.

17. Dawe, H. C., An analysis of two hundred quarrels of preschool children. *Child Develop.* (1934), 5:139–157.

18. Dollard, J., and Miller, N. E., *Personality and psychotherapy.* New York: McGraw-Hill, 1950.

19. English, O. S., and Finch, S. M., *Introduction to psychiatry.* New York: Norton, 1954.

20. Fite, M. D., Aggressive behavior in young children and children's attitude toward aggression. *Genet. Psychol. Monogr.* (1940), 22:151–319.

21. Freud, A., Introduction to the technique of child analysis. *Nerv. ment. dis. Monogr.,* 1928, No. 48.

22. Freud, A., and Dann, S., An experiment in group up-bringing, in R. Eisler, et al. (eds.), *The psychoanalytic study of the child.* Vol. 6. New York: International Universities Press, 1941, pp. 127–163.

23. Green, E. H., Friendships and quarrels among preschool children. *Child Develop.* (1933), 4:237–262.

24. Green, E. H., Group play and quarreling among preschool children. *Child Develop.* (1933), 4:302–307.

25. Greenberg, P. J., Competition in children: an experimental study. *Am. J. Psychol.* (1932), *44*:221–249.
26. Greene, K. B., Relations between kindergartens and nursery schools. *Childhood Educ.* (1930–1931), 7:352–355.
27. Hattwick, B. W., The influence of nursery school attendance upon the behavior and personality of the preschool child. *J. exp. Educ.* (1936), 5:180–190.
28. Hilgard, J. R., Sibling rivalry and social heredity. *Psychiatry* (1951), *14*: 375–385.
29. Honigmann, J. J., *Culture and personality.* New York: Harper, 1954.
30. Horney, K., *The neurotic personality of our time.* New York: Norton, 1937.
31. Horney, K., *Our inner conflicts.* New York: Norton, 1945.
32. Jack, L. M., An experimental study of ascendent behavior in preschool children. In L. M. Jack, E. M. Maxwell, I. G. Mengert, et al., Behavior of the preschool child. *Univ. Iowa Stud. Child Welf.*, No. 9 (1934), 3:7–65.
33. Jersild, A. T., *Child psychology,* 4th ed. New York: Prentice-Hall, 1954.
34. Jersild, A. T., and Fite, M. D., The influence of nursery school experience on children's social adjustments. *Child Develop. Monogr.*, 1939, No. 25.
35. Jersild, A. T., and Markey, F. V., Conflicts between preschool children. *Child Develop. Monogr.*, 1935, No. 21.
36. Joel, W., The influence of nursery school education upon behavior maturity. *J. exp. Educ.* (1939), 8:164–165.
37. Kawin, E., and Hoefer, C., *A comparative study of a nursery school* vs. *a non-nursery school group.* Chicago: University of Chicago Press, 1931.
38. Keister, M. E., and Updegraff, R., A study of children's reactions to failure and an experimental attempt to modify them. *Child Develop.* (1937), 8:241–248.
39. Keister, M. E., The behavior of young children in failure: an experimental attempt to discover and to modify undesirable responses of preschool children to failure. *Univer. Iowa Stud. Child Welf.* (1938), *14*:27–82.
40. Klein, M., *Psychoanalysis of children.* London: Hogarth, 1932.
41. Leuba, C., An experimental study of rivalry in young children. *J. comp. Psychol.* (1933), *16*:367–378.
42. Levy, D. M., Release therapy. *Am. J. Orthopsychiat.* (1939), 9:913–936.
43. Lewin, K., Behavior and development as a function of the total situation, in L. Carmichael (ed.), *Manual of child psychology,* 2nd ed. New York: Wiley, 1954, pp. 918–970.
44. Maudry, M., and Nekula, M., Social relations between children of the same age during the first two years of life. *J. genet. Psychol.* (1939), *54*: 193–215.
45. McKee, J. P., and Leader, F. B., The relationship of socioeconomic status to the competitive behavior of school children. *Child Develop.* (1955), *25*: 135–142.
46. Mengert, I. G., A preliminary study of the reactions of two-year old children to each other when paired in a semi-controlled situation. *J. genet. Psychol.* (1931), 39:393–398.

47. Mummery, D. V., An analytical study of ascendent behavior of preschool children. *Child Develop.* (1947), *18*:40–81.

48. Murphy, L. B., *Social behavior and child personality; an exploratory study of some roots of sympathy.* New York: Columbia University Press, 1937.

49. Muste, M. J., and Sharpe, D. F., Some influential factors in the determination of aggressive behavior in preschool children. *Child Develop.* (1947), *18*:11–28.

50. Newell, H. W., Play therapy in child psychiatry. *Am. J. Orthopsychiat.* (1941), *11*:245–251.

51. Page, M. L., The modification of ascendant behavior in preschool children. *Univer. Iowa Stud. Child Welf.* (1936), *12*:No. 3.

52. Parten, M. B., Social participation among preschool children. *J. abnorm. soc. Psychol.* (1932), *27*:243–269.

53. Rogers, C. R., *The clinical treatment of the problem child.* Boston: Houghton Mifflin, 1939.

54. Rotter, J. B., *Social learning and clinical psychology.* New York: Prentice-Hall, 1954.

55. Solomon, J. C., Play technique as a differential therapeutic medium. *Nerv. Child* (1948), *7*:296–300.

56. Thompson, G. G., The social and emotional development of preschool children under two types of educational program. *Psychol. Monogr.* (1944), *56*:No. 5.

57. Van Alstyne, D., and Hattwick, L. A., A follow-up study of the behavior of nursery school children. *Child Develop.* (1939), *19*:43–72.

58. Walsh, M. E., The relation of nursery school training to the development of certain personality traits. *Child Develop.* (1931), *2*:72–73.

59. Wright, M. E., Constrictiveness of play as affected by group organization and frustration. *Character and Personality* (1942), *11*:40–49.

60. Wright, M. E., The influence of frustration upon social relations of young children. *Character and Personality* (1943), *12*:111–122.

61. Yarrow, L. J., The effect of antecedent frustration on projective play. *Psychol. Monogr.* (1948), *62*, No. 6.

PART IV

Middle Childhood

Chapter 10

PERSONALITY DEVELOPMENT DURING THE MIDDLE CHILDHOOD YEARS

During the middle childhood years, the school begins to function as a major socialization agency. It supplements the family's teaching and provides opportunities for increased contacts with peers, and consequently, for stronger peer-group impacts on personality development.

Until he begins school, the child's adjustment and socialization are influenced primarily by his familial environment. The home is the center of his psychological world, and if his relationships with members of his family are stable, warm, and affectionate, he is likely to become well adjusted and well socialized.

The expanded environment to which the 6- and 7-year-old is exposed, however, requires new adjustments—to school itself, to school and neighborhood peers, and to his social-class group. The reactions of the child in new situations are to a large extent dependent on the kind of person he has already become as a consequence of his past learning at home, in the neighborhood, and in nursery school. As Murphy has pointed out, "the new experiences of this age level mean very different things to different kinds of children" (66, 678).

The psychoanalysts call the period between the fifth or sixth year and puberty the *latency* period, and according to orthodox analytic theory, it is characterized by a diminution of sexual interest and of sexual activity. Presumably, the resolution of the Oedipus complex (cf. pp. 234–240) involves a general repression of sexuality. Energy previously expended on sexual matters is channelized into new nonsexual activities, interests, and attitudes.

Some of the more biologically oriented psychoanalysts have viewed

The middle childhood years. Children's games in Bechuanaland and America.

latency as an inevitable phase of normal development. Others, particularly the neo-Freudians, feel that it is dependent on cultural factors. Our own thinking more closely parallels this latter view. There are many cultures in which children indulge in a great deal of sexual activity. In fact, where no cultural restraints are imposed—as among Marquesans, Trobrianders, Pukapukans, and Baiga—overt heterosexual behavior increases continuously throughout childhood.

The relative paucity of such activities in our culture may be interpreted in terms of superego development and increased social pressure to act in accordance with socially approved codes of behavior which forbid sexual expression in children. In some cases, children go through what appears to be a latency period simply because sexual behavior has been severely punished in the past, especially during the preschool period (77). Moreover, the emergence of new social interests and activities (see below) and the tendency of children of this age to prefer chums of their own sex may appear superficially to represent a loss of sexual interest.

Actually, preadolescents even in our culture manifest strong sexual interests and curiosity, though not so obviously or actively as children in the tribes mentioned above (46). Systematic observations of boys and girls between 5 and 16 years of age indicated that sex consciousness increased sharply between the ages of 9 and 11 (16). Kinsey reports that masturbation and sex play are quite common during this period of childhood (57).

A comprehensive review of the evidence concerning sexual latency in our culture led one author to conclude that "the relative de-emphasis in sexuality to which [some analysts] allude can probably be described more precisely as an increased emphasis on nonsexual behavior rather than any sharp decrease in underlying sexual concern" (3, 134).

GENERAL TRENDS IN PSYCHOLOGICAL DEVELOPMENT IN MIDDLE CHILDHOOD

Whether or not there is any real latency with respect to sex interests during this period, there is certainly no latency or quiescence in general psychological development between the ages of 5 or 6 and 12. As will become clearer later on, personality characteristics and social behavior are greatly modified during this period. Since physical changes occur relatively slowly and continuously during these years, they do not ordinarily present any serious personality problems, except where there are marked deviations in growth rate, health, or appearance. In these cases, problems can develop, as we shall see.

The major behavioral changes of this period are attributable to social learning experiences. In response to increased societal pressure, the child continues to learn behavior appropriate to his own sex and social class. Concomitantly, he develops more mature interests, assimilates more of the culture's moral values and beliefs, and is expected to assume greater personal responsibility for behaving in accordance with them. At the same time, he must learn to coöperate with others in complex personal interactions and must master skills basic to adjustment in his social group.

Development during this period must be understood not only in terms of how the child adjusts to new social experiences but also how his subsequent personality and behavior are influenced by them. The family, the school, the peer group, and the general community are the chief socialization agencies. These operate simultaneously—sometimes reinforcing, and sometimes opposing, each other—to mold the child's personality. In this and the following two chapters, we will examine the ways in which the child's adjustments at this time are, on the one hand, the *consequents* of other experiences, and on the other, the *antecedents* of later personality and social characteristics.

In reading these chapters it is important to bear in mind that various social factors are isolated and considered individually only for convenience of exposition. Actually, for the child, these are interrelated, interacting aspects of the environment. For example, the peer group is influencing him at the same time as he is being exposed to family, church, and school pressures. It is therefore difficult, in many cases, to separate particular antecedents from the total context of influences (except for purposes of discussion) and to evaluate their relative contributions to the child's overall personality development.

PHYSICAL FACTORS INFLUENCING ADJUSTMENT

General Trends in Physical Development

By the age of 6, physical growth, which has been proceeding at a remarkably fast pace, has begun to decelerate. The average child of this age in America stands about 46 inches tall, and weighs about 48 pounds (87). His height increases during the middle childhood years at the rate of about 5 or 6 percent a year, his weight at the rate of somewhat over 10 percent a year. By the time he reaches the age of 12, his height has increased to about 60 inches, and his weight to between 95 and 100 pounds (87).

Up until the tenth year, boys, on the average, are slightly taller than girls. However, from then until about 15, girls are, on the average, slightly taller than boys—as any dancing school instructor can testify (88) (see Figure 25). The pattern is similar with regard to weight. Until about 11 years of age, boys are slightly heavier than girls, but after that age girls weigh more (88).

FIGURE 25. Heights of boys and girls at various ages. (From *How Old Are You?* With permission of Metropolitan Life Insurance Co.)

The child's body proportions are already much like the adult's. The slight changes in build which occur in this period (cf. Figure 11, p. 83) (87) result largely from lengthening of the child's limbs.

Other changes occur too. Because of deposits of various mineral salts, especially calcium phosphate, the 12-year-old's bones are harder, but easier to break, than the 6-year-old's. At about 6, the average child loses his first teeth, but by 12, he has most of his permanent ones (11). With advancing age from 6 to 12, blood pressure increases, and pulse rate decreases (11). The child needs more to eat and he eats more. Concomitantly, muscle tissue increases proportionately, and the child grows stronger. For example, as judged by a number of physical measures, boys are twice as strong at 11 as they were at 6 (54). Girls also increase rapidly in strength, although they remain weaker than boys at all ages.

Neural conduction rates and reaction speeds both accelerate throughout this period (53). The child becomes better integrated and better coördinated, thus becoming capable of more complex motor and manipulative tasks. In general, boys surpass girls in speed of reaction (37) and coördination of gross bodily movements (53).

Although various aspects of growth (i.e., rates of development in dentition, height, weight, bone hardening) are generally correlated with one another, not all children develop in the same way or at the same rates. Some grow relatively more in height, others in weight, producing variations in general body types such as "tall, slender," or "short and stocky."

Physical Disease and Defect

These data on physical development apply only to representative samples of school children in the United States today. The figures would not have been the same 25 years ago in this country nor would they be the same for other countries today. In reviewing data on patterns of physical disease and defect among American school children, the lack of generality of such statistics must be emphasized. Changes in general economic conditions, cultural customs, medical and welfare facilities, educational and scientific development, and a host of other factors, affect the health status of the entire population.

DEATH RATES. Figure 26 (12) shows the remarkable decline in the death rate for children in recent years. This has been due in large part to medical progress in the treatment of infectious diseases. In the age range 5 to 9, deaths from tuberculosis, communicable diseases, pneumonia, and appendicitis have declined about 90 percent in only 25 years. Accidents now comprise the chief cause of death among children of this age (88).

INCIDENCE OF HEALTH PROBLEMS. Although the death rate has been markedly reduced, childhood disease and physical defects such as heart conditions, diabetes, crippling, and allergies, are still quite common. A recent study of elementary school children in seven California cities showed that absences from school were primarily due to: (1) respiratory diseases, including colds (46 percent); (2) common communicable diseases, like measles, chicken pox, scarlet fever (13 percent); (3) digestive disorders (6 percent); (4) miscellaneous medical causes (22 percent). These figures stand in sharp contrast to a total of only 13 percent absent for nonmedical reasons (50).

In addition, there are many children who are present in the schoolroom but are nevertheless suffering from a variety of physical ailments. For example, recent studies have shown that approximately 15 percent of school children suffer from defective vision (20/30 or worse), while over 4 percent have defective hearing (88).

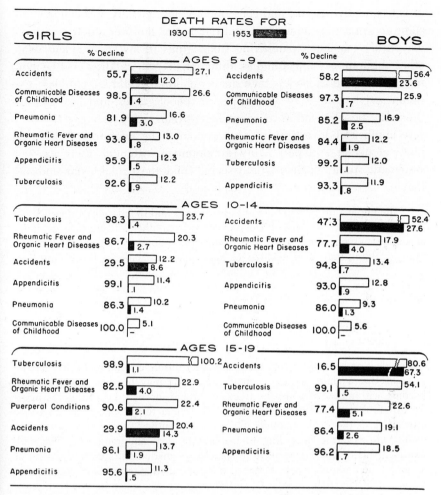

FIGURE 26. Death rates per 100,000 in school-age boys and girls from various causes, 1930 and 1953 compared. (After G. M. Wheatley and G. T. Hallock, H*ealth Observations of School Children.* New York: McGraw-Hill, 1951.)

Other conditions, such as poor nutrition and tooth decay, are also common among school children and, rather surprisingly, their incidence is almost as great among upper- as among lower-income groups (88). In addition, many children suffer from a variety of chronic diseases or defects, such as heart conditions, diabetes, crippling, and allergies.

Physical Defect and Personality

Obviously, the child's physical status can influence his emotional and social adjustment. Chronic illness may mean that the child tires easily or is frequently irritable and consequently has difficulty in social relationships and in academic work. A child's crippled limbs or a defective heart may bring too much pampering from adults in his environment while other children may reject him as "different." Bigger children may be more readily accepted as leaders than smaller children. Children with defective vision and hearing may receive poorer school grades, and healthy children may be regarded as more intelligent than their sickly peers.

A number of investigators have examined the relationships between physical defect and personality development. Although there are few systematic studies of the partially seeing child, the available data indicate that

. . . the unpleasant appearance of heavy glasses and the inability to participate in many games tend to cut off these children from others. There is a possibility of undue nervous tension resulting from trying to see with reduced vision. Many children may have feelings of inadequacy and inferiority because they are unable to keep pace with children of good vision. Visually handicapped children have been found to be more docile, less active, and to have less initiative than seeing children of corresponding ages (*11, 89*).

After reviewing the literature concerning hearing loss, Breckenridge and Vincent concluded that:

The deaf or hard-of-hearing child is often a misunderstood child. He may be mistaken for a child of poor mental ability. He may be then neglected and become withdrawn. Because he does not attend, he may be marked as indifferent, stubborn, careless, and impolite. The characteristics that are commonly attributed to the deaf, mentally sluggish, inattentive, suspicious, and melancholic, are not true according to teachers of deaf children (*81*). The very nature of his deafness may have in some cases made adults unduly critical of a child. The child may hear better at one time than another. Some voices may be more distinct than others. It can be easy for any other than a keenly observant and well-informed person to lay such a child's variable response to deficiencies in character. Deaf children can be misunderstood also, because they may misinterpret situations. Because they fail to hear all the facts, their conclusions and hence their behavior may seem strange to those who, because they can hear, can base their judgment on all the facts. Such children are often considered "dumb" or "queer" (*11*, 90).

A number of research workers have focused attention on the consequents of chronic disease or crippling. For example, in one study, groups of diabetic and nondiabetic children were compared (*13*). While the diabetics did not appear to be any more maladjusted than the others, they were more frequently

. . . careful, meticulous, earnest, and conscientious. This coupled with good school reports, was attributed . . . to the habit-training forced upon the diabetic child by the strict regime made necessary by the disease. School reports indicated a predominance of desirable traits, and few instances of feelings of inferiority and attention-seeking devices. Parents reported that the personality of these children had changed little since the onset of the disease. Excitability and irritability were the only traits that had increased considerably. There was some indication that these children had become somewhat more cautious and stubborn (11, 87).

However, changes such as these might reasonably be expected in children suffering from any chronic disease (11).

Most of the studies dealing with chronic illness, defect, or crippling are in agreement that these conditions themselves have no invariant effects on children's behavior. Crippled children, as a group, are only slightly more maladjusted than their noncrippled peers (55). If a child's handicap is treated sympathetically, but realistically, by his parents, teachers, and peers, his adjustment will probably not be seriously affected. However, inconsistent, rejecting, or overprotective parental behavior may have an adverse influence, leading to maladjustment and personality problems (1, 36). Spock (79) cites the example of a boy who was born with only a thumb and one finger on his left hand.

At two and one-half years the child was happy and could do almost as much with his left hand as with his right. His six year old sister was fond of him and proud of him, wanting to take him with her everywhere she went. The sister never seemed to worry about the boy's hand. The mother, however, was very conscious of the missing fingers. She winced when she saw a strange child catch sight of his hand and stare. She thought it fair to the child to keep him home where he wouldn't be subjected to curiosity and remarks, and made excuses when he wanted to go shopping with her (79, 468).

In this way, the child, who was not initially self-conscious about his defect, was made so by the parent's attitude.

If the parents from the beginning are unhappy or ashamed about a child's appearance, always wishing he were different, over-protecting him, keeping him from mingling with others, he is apt to grow up turned in on himself, dissatisfied, feeling that he is queer. But if they take his disfiguring birthmark or a deformed ear as of no great importance, act as if they consider him a normal child, let him go places like any one else, not worry about stares and whispered remarks—then the child gets the idea he is a regular guy and thinks little of his peculiarity (79, 469).

Physical Status, Personality, and Social Adjustment

Most children do not suffer from chronic illness, crippling, or serious physical defects. Does body type or physical status affect the normal child's personality characteristics? There is no definite answer to this question at present, but an exploratory study by Sanford and his associates (75) provides some interesting relevant data. It represents one of the few systematic attempts to study interrelationships among the many biological, social, emotional, and environmental variables which may influence the child's development. The subjects were 48 private school children, and as the authors themselves point out, cannot be regarded as a fair sample of all children. Hence, the findings, although interesting, must be considered suggestive rather than conclusive.

On the basis of a variety of personality tests, staff ratings, teacher interviews, and school reports, seven personality syndromes or broad, general patterns (collections of characteristics that go together) were isolated. The investigators then attempted to relate each of these patterns to physiological, illness, diet, and body build characteristics. The following is a highly condensed version of the relationships discovered.

The first pattern, *structured personality,* is made up of the following characteristics: orderliness, self-sufficiency, quiet dignity, satisfaction from the world of thoughts and feelings, coöperativeness, and strong conscience. This personality picture was characteristic of more children with tall, narrow, than with short, wide builds. These children had better than average diets, and displayed less muscular and verbal activity and more parasympathetic nervous system responses (i.e., flushing, sweating, etc.).

Children manifesting patterns two and three, the *active* and *inactive* child, differed markedly from each other in both psychological and physiological make-up. As a group, the former, characterized by "lively self-expression," playfulness, talkativeness, productivity, creativity, and originality, had good physical coördination, greater strength and energy, higher metabolic rates, and advanced osseous (bone) development. The *inactive children,* on the other hand, were sluggish, passive, and poorly coördinated. Neither activity or inactivity was associated with any particular type of body build.

Passivity, dependence on others, fearfulness, and worry were the major attributes of the *timid child,* the fourth syndrome. Physically these children tended to be "small in stature, poorly nourished, poorly coördinated, relatively weak, and apathetic" (75, 554). They also had more illnesses, and were absent from school more often than other children.

The *social being,* the child exhibiting the fifth personality syndrome, related actively to others and liked "to be affectionate with them, to play with them, to please and defer to them." He was generally a "good fellow," "assured and uninhibited, and able to express himself in a variety of ways." Physically, such a child was most likely to be short, stocky, and well coördinated and to have a high metabolic rate and advanced osseous development.

The last two personality syndromes, described as *sensitive creators* and *sensation seekers*, shared a desire for sensory impressions. But they also differed in several important respects. "In the sensation seeker syndrome, the dominant tendency is to seek for sensation and excitement, and the emphasis is upon sensuality or bodily sensations" (75, 568). In the sensitive creator, "The same tendencies are at work but on a higher level as it seems: there is more emphasis on esthetic sensitivity and taste. . . . [They] tend to create within themselves means for sensuous enjoyment" (75, 568).

Neither of these two personality constellations was significantly related to many physical characteristics, although both of these personality types had higher than average metabolism. There was an inverse (i.e., negative) relationship between the *sensitive creator* and the short, wide type of body build. The *sensitive creator* tended to have a better than average diet; while the *sensation seeker* had a poorer one (75).

Since the sample involved in this study was small and highly select, the observed relationships between physical and psychological characteristics cannot be considered definitive. Nevertheless, it is interesting to note that a number of these findings are consistent with the findings of studies of the relationship between the body builds and psychological characteristics of adolescents and young adults (17, 78).

It is possible to draw several kinds of conclusions from the findings of studies of this sort. For example, it might be concluded that genetic factors determine both particular physical attributes and personality characteristics. Or, the findings that *timid child* was correlated with *poor diet*, and *structured personality* with *good diet*, might lead one to infer that diet itself may influence personality directly. However, such inferences must be treated with great caution, as the investigators were well aware. For example, it is just as likely that certain types of family situations favor both a good diet *and* a structured type of personality development, as it is that "good diet gives rise to physiological processes, which in turn promote these kinds of psychological reactions" (75, 529).

Similarly, it is possible that both short, wide body build and a sociable outgoing personality are the results of specific constitutional factors. However, it is just as likely that children of different body structures may encounter different learning situations or be subjected to differential treatment by parents and peers. It may be hypothesized that the individual's physical characteristics may affect his behavior and personality "through modifying the conditions for learning" (*17*, 450). For example, the boy who is small in stature, poorly coördinated, or ill much of the time is unlikely to achieve success in physical tasks or in athletic games. Illness or physical weakness may prevent him from doing many things others can do. As a consequence, he is likely to have little prestige with his peers and he may learn to withdraw from them, as well as from many physical activities. Under the circumstances, he has little opportunity to be rewarded for social outgoingness or for independent, assertive responses. Hence he may appear to be timid, passive, and dependent. Similarly, the child of tall, thin build may be injured easily and may learn to avoid competitive games and athletics. Since his peers are likely to be much concerned with these activities, he may have relatively few social contacts with them and may learn instead to derive his satisfactions from the "world of thoughts and feelings." These are the characteristics of the child with *structured personality* (75) (cf. p. 322). These examples are hypothetical, but they illustrate one way in which physical characteristics may help determine certain conditions of learning, and thus influence the child's personality development.

FAMILY INFLUENCES DURING MIDDLE CHILDHOOD

Even though the child of this age is in school a large proportion of the time, he still looks to his home as the chief source of guidance and support. Parental behavior and attitudes continue to be important influences on his behavior at home, and also, as we shall see later, on his adjustments to school and to peers.

If a child is to get the most out of his social operations in the wider community, he must above all have a secure and dependable home base, one that he can leave without anxiety, one he can return to confidently for supplies, repairs and reassurance. . . . If he can be sure of his home, if life there provides emotional security and support when he needs them, the child can learn to absorb neighborhood reverses just as he learned to weather frustration and correction at home, and by using the same general techniques that he acquired there (*15*, 41).

It will be recalled that investigations of parent-child relationships usually employ either of two approaches: (1) focusing on particular home situation variables and determining their personality consequents; or (2) taking groups of maladjusted or neurotic children and studying them thoroughly, in an attempt to define the salient antecedents of their maladaptive behavior.

Reviews of both types of studies will make it clear that many of the factors influencing early personality development are also related to adjustment during the grade school years. Homes that provide social learning conditions conducive to the preschool child's acquisition of maladaptive or socially unacceptable behavior are likely to provide similar conditions during middle childhood. In most cases, the general familial climate remains consistent from one period of development to the next. Ordinarily the child keeps the same parents, and unless their basic attitudes and behavior toward him change, he receives essentially the same kind of treatment throughout his childhood.

Identification and Sex-Typing

During the school years the process of identification—acquiring the behavior, attitudes, and feelings of important figures in the child's life (cf. pp. 240–244)—continues. There are many identification models available to the school child: teachers, peers, Boy Scout leaders, clubmates, neighborhood leaders, characters in books, radio, movies, and television. However, the child's primary identifications are those he makes with members of his family.

Children of school age often consciously model their behavior after their parents. When children between the ages of 8 and 18 were asked to write an essay on "The Person I Would Most Like to Be," the older ones often named real or imaginary glamorous adults, but children below 10 most frequently wanted to emulate their parents (48).

Moreover, children of this age are generally aware of which parent can provide the best identification model for them. In response to the question: "Who do you think should be closest to the mother [or father], the boy or girl?", the vast majority of boys and girls between 5 and 14 said the girl should be closest to the mother, the boy to the father (30).

The methods used in training boys for sex-appropriate behavior may differ from the methods used in training girls. Moreover, the various social classes have divergent views as to what constitutes characteristic and adequate male and female behavior. They may also differ with respect to the age at which they train their children for sex-appropriate responses. Hence we would expect the sex of the child and his social-class background to affect his rate of acquisition of sex-appropriate responses.

Rabban (72) investigated these differences, using 300 children between 30 months and 8 years of age as subjects. Half of these children were from upper-lower, or working-class families, living in urban industrial areas, and half were from upper-middle-class suburban families (fathers in executive, business, or professional positions).

The examiner confronted the children individually with 16 interesting toys, eight conventionally considered appropriate for boys (gun, steamroller, dump truck, auto racers, fire truck, cement mixer), and eight for girls (high chair, baby buggy, beds, doll dishes, purse, baby doll, bathinette). Each child was asked to select the six toys he liked best.

The data revealed that boys generally showed earlier and clearer awareness of the behavior (choice of toys) appropriate for their sex. Both girls and boys of the lower class became aware of their sex-role patterns sooner than middle-class children. Thus, while lower-class boys reached a stable, high level of sex identification by the time they were 5, middle-class boys did not do so until they were 6. At the age of 6, lower-class girls made definite sex-appropriate choices, but middle-class girls did not show clear-cut acceptance of their role even by the age of 8 (72).

The earlier learning of masculine than of feminine roles in both classes suggests that there may be generally clearer standards of masculine behavior, and more rigorous rewarding and punishing of boys in accordance with these, in all strata of American society. The investigator also suggests several possible sources of the social-class differences. Perhaps the customs, traditions, and taboos of lower-class families provide early definitions and strong rewards for early sex-appropriate behavior and severe punishment for sex-inappropriate behavior. Middle-class families may be more permissive in this respect and not so likely to punish masculine behavior in girls or feminine behavior in boys. It is also possible that adult masculine and feminine roles are more clearly differentiated in lower-class families. These parents may provide more clear-cut models of sex-appropriate behavior, thus facilitating imitation of these responses. In addition to this, the middle-class father may more frequently spend much of his time away from home, and his son is consequently likely to be slower in learning to imitate his responses (72).

Failures in Sex-Typing

Unfortunately, many children fail to achieve appropriate sex identifications. In some cases, the child may learn to identify strongly with the opposite-sexed parent and fail to identify with the like-sexed one. The most extreme and dramatic failures in appropriate sex-typing are seen in the cases of homosexuals, individuals whose sexual interests are directed primarily to their own, rather than to the opposite, sex.

Homosexuality may be found even among young children. In one study, psychiatric examinations were given to 19 boys and 4 girls between the ages of 4 and 12 who were actively homosexual (2). No relationships between their sexual deviations and constitutional, endocrine, or intellectual status were discovered. There were no evidences of any basic physical "femininity" in homosexual boys or constitutional "masculinity" in homosexual girls. In all these cases, the children's maladjustments were judged to be rooted in early familial relationships which made appropriate sex identifications difficult or impossible.

According to these investigators, the major factors, or combination of factors, underlying homosexuality in these children included an absent, grossly abusive, or obviously ineffectual like-sexed parent, together with a dominant or oversolicitous opposite-sexed parent. Under these circumstances, which were characteristic of 90 percent of the cases studied, relationships with the like-sexed parent could not be secure, warm, or gratifying. The powerful, dominant opposite-sexed parent was more likely to be seen as the source of rewards. Consequently, the child identified with him, emulating his behavior. The investigators also found that the children's homosexual trends could be modified by intensive psychological treatment and removal from their home environments (2).

Family Influences on Superego Development

One of the corollaries of parental identification is the gradual development of conscience, or superego. The child learns his earliest, and probably most fundamental, lessons in ethical behavior in the family setting. As identification with the parents becomes more firmly established, more of their "evaluative responses" (89) are taken over. However, as the number of identification models expands, the child also assimilates other ethical standards, moral values, ideals, and scruples. Thus during the elementary school years, the child's superego becomes much more highly developed in scope and complexity.

As Piaget has shown, the young child's complete identification with his parents and his "unilateral respect" for them produce "moral realism," i.e., the absolute and unchallenging acceptance of their conceptions of what is good, moral, and proper (71). In the thinking of children below school age, violation of parental rules and prohibitions justifiably leads to punishments, and there can be no extenuating circumstances. Thus, when 4- or 5-year-old children were asked whether a child should be punished for breaking some dishes accidentally, they all replied affirmatively. Since at this age the child's social world has been restricted largely to his family, his "moral judgments" must be based primarily on parental rules.

With increased contacts with others, the child's moral concepts change (cf. pp. 425–429). The final content of a particular child's superego will vary not only according to the content of the evaluative systems of his parents, but also with those of other identification models such as teachers and peers.

The extent of the influence of these additional models may depend on the closeness of identification with parents. Thus the superego of the lower-class boy who is strongly identified with his law-abiding father would include taboos against imitating the behavior of delinquent peers. On the other hand, if the child has not achieved substantial identification with his father, he may not conform to social regulations and may learn that delinquent activities can lead to important rewards.

Compulsions

Psychoanalytic theory maintains that during the middle school years the superego tends to be especially severe. Conceptions of what is right and wrong are derived directly from the parents, and the child becomes highly self-critical, punishing himself whenever he feels he is not acting in conformity with their standards (3, 31).

Obsessive or compulsive symptoms (e.g., rigid following of repetitive patterns such as counting or stepping over cracks in the sidewalk, preferring even to odd numbers) are frequent during the early latency period (45). According to analytic thinking, these represent the child's attempts to regulate himself by rigid, inflexible standards and thus to ward off feelings of guilt and anxiety.

The hidden meaning of a compulsion pops out in the thoughtless childhood saying, 'Step on a crack, break your grandmother's back'. Everyone has hostile feelings at times toward the people who are close to him, but his conscience would be shocked at the idea of really harming them, and warns him to keep such thoughts out of his mind. And if a person's conscience becomes *excessively* stern, it keeps nagging him about such "bad" thoughts, even after he has succeeded in hiding them away in his subconscious mind. He still feels guilty, though he doesn't know what for. It eases his conscience to be extra careful and proper about such a senseless thing as how to navigate a crack in the sidewalk.

The reason a child is apt to show compulsions around the age of 9 is not that his thoughts are more wicked than previously, but that his conscience is

just naturally becoming stricter at this stage of development. He is now worry-
ing, perhaps, about his suppressed desire to hurt his brother or father or
grandmother when they irritate him. We know that this is an age when the
child is also trying to suppress thoughts about sex, and these sometimes play
a part in compulsions, too (79, 301).

Mild compulsions are so common around 8, 9, and 10 years of age that
they should not be considered "abnormal" (79). In most cases, they disappear readily with increasing age. However, overly strict parental
enforcement of taboos and restrictions may increase the severity of these
symptoms and tend to perpetuate them. The child, through identification
with the parents, may accept unusually strict standards for himself and
may become very harsh in self-criticism. If the child's compulsive symptoms become extreme, occupying too much of his time, psychiatric help
is indicated.

Family Relationships and "Character Traits"

The ways in which the child's superego develops and the specific character traits formed will depend largely upon the psychological climate
of the home. According to the principles of reinforcement learning
theory, we would expect the social responses which are rewarded there
to be generalized to social relationships outside the home. These social
responses may be manifestations of what are generally labeled "character
traits." If the child is frequently rewarded for helping others at home, he
is likely to be coöperative in his relationships with others. If helping
others at home is not found to be rewarding, he is likely to become
uncoöperative there and elsewhere.

The influence of the learning situation in the home on the development
of so-called character traits was demonstrated in a study in which a
Family Relations Questionnaire was administered to 105 ten-year-olds in
the schools of a small midwestern town (12). The questionnaire dealt
with six important aspects of parent-child relationships: (1) trust and
security in parents manifested in sharing confidences, (2) opportunity
for self-expression, (3) parental recognition of the child's work and play
activities, (4) parent-child sharing in work and play, (5) parents' sacri-
fice of own interests for welfare and security of children, (6) family solidarity or mutual loyalty.

Each subject's reputation was measured by several kinds of tests given
to teachers, youth-group leaders of the community, and peers, all of
whom were well acquainted with the children. For example, in one test,
these raters were asked to match a series of brief word pictures (e.g.,

Someone who goes out of his way to return anything he finds) with the names of all the subjects who fitted the description.

On the basis of peers' and adults' responses to such tests, each child was assigned scores on five character traits: *honesty, moral courage, friendliness, loyalty, responsibility*. These reputation scores, which were assumed to reflect the child's moral behavior in social situations, could also be considered measures of components of the superego. High scores indicated high moral principles and behavior in accordance with them.

Each aspect of superego development was significantly correlated with affectional family relationships (as determined by the Family Relations Questionnaire). In other words, in this group of 10-year-old subjects, *affectional parent-child interactions* were associated with high degrees of honesty (correlation of +.65), moral courage (correlation of +.51), friendliness (+.71), loyalty (+.69), and responsibility (+.79) (*12*).

Youngsters from families high in affectional relations are, by definition, involved in rewarding social interactions at home. They receive recognition and share with their parents in work and play. Consequently, they readily learn to make outgoing responses at home and these generalize to other social situations. This is reflected in the child's friendliness outside the home. In a similar way, if frankness, sharing confidences, and family loyalty are rewarded at home, the child is more likely to be *honest* and *loyal* in his relationships in the wider community. Learning to share actively in work and play in the domestic setting is conducive to taking *responsibility* in other social situations. Parents who encourage the child's self-expression, recognizing and rewarding his work efforts, promote self-confidence and the feeling that his ideas are worthwhile. Outside the home, such a child will be likely to manifest *moral courage*.

HOME ATMOSPHERE, CHILD BEHAVIOR, AND PERSONALITY

While the studies reported above deal specifically with problems of identification and superego development, others have been concerned with the influences of home background on a wide variety of personality characteristics. Unfortunately, there are no systematic investigations of school-age children comparable to Baldwin's direct observations of preschool children's interactions with their parents in the home (cf. pp. 250–254). However, salient general features of home atmosphere, evaluated by other less direct techniques, have been systematically related to personality and social behavior during middle childhood.

Acceptance-Rejection

It will be recalled that the studies of Baldwin and others were focused on the consequents of such familial variables as democracy, warmth, indulgence, and their opposites. Similar, though not identical, home conditions, and their influences on school-age children have also been investigated.

Symonds (84) compared the personality characteristics and social adjustments of 31 rejected and 31 accepted children.[1] Rejected children were those whose mothers and fathers failed to provide adequate care, protection, or affection. The two groups were carefully matched in sex, age, school grade, socioeconomic background, and intellectual level. Although the subjects ranged from 5 to 23 years in age, the average was 12.5, and the majority were of grammar school age. Experienced raters, familiar with the subjects and their families, filled out check lists dealing with the child's behavior, personality traits, neurotic attitudes, as well as with his parents' adjustments.

Children in the accepted group showed more socially acceptable behavior and appeared more coöperative, friendly, loyal, honest, straightforward, emotionally stable, calm, deliberate, enthusiastic, and cheerful. Children in the rejected group, on the other hand, were more often rated as emotionally unstable, restless, overactive, and given to attention-getting and trouble-making behavior. In general, they were more resentful of authority, including their parents, and more rebellious against society's rules and regulations. They manifested pronounced delinquent trends, frequently lying, truanting, running away from home, stealing, and quarreling.

In interpersonal relations, the accepted children were friendlier, more communicative, and more self-confident. These children generally did not dream frequently and were realistic and clear about their plans and ambitions. The few fantasies they reported were most often pleasant and represented rather obvious wishes.

In contrast to this, the rejected children felt insecure, inferior, and

---

[1] It should be pointed out that Symonds' work has one major methodological disadvantage. Since child and parent ratings were both made by the same investigator, they are not independent of one another. It is possible, for example, that if the investigator found the parent to be rejecting, he might tend to be selective in his perceptions of the child. That is, he might be inclined to see in the child only the personality characteristics he associates with rejection, neglecting to observe those which may be inconsistent with his notions of the consequences of rejection. Despite this source of possible bias, the findings are highly suggestive, and seem to agree quite well with other, less intensive studies, and with the impressions of clinical workers.

discontented, were confused and bewildered about future plans and goals. They often reported terrifying dreams or wish-fulfilling fantasies in which they occupied some prominent position of adulation and attention (*84*).

It appears that parental acceptance or rejection has broad ramifications on the child's personal and social adjustment. Rejected children are obviously more maladjusted emotionally, insecure, and unhappy. Moreover, their superegos are less likely to be well developed, i.e., they are less accepting of authority and less "moral" in their behavior. It may be inferred that rejecting parents do not establish close relationships with their children and do not provide good identification models. Consequently, their children are not so likely to learn mature, stable behavior or to assimilate socially approved behavior so readily.

Of course, no two children encounter "rejection" of quite the same quality or quantity, and none react to it in exactly the same way. Thus no two cases of rejection will present the same picture clinically. The child in the following case illustration, for example, undoubtedly would have reacted quite differently had her parents' rejection involved disinterest, actual neglect, or cruelty (*14*). Nevertheless, it serves as a living example of the way in which one child reacted to a particular form of perceived rejection.

Priscilla was about 14 when the climax of her difficulties was reached. From year to year she had become more stubborn and withdrawn. In school she sat with an air of complete detachment. Although of superior intelligence, her work was inadequate and often incomplete. She had few friends and participated in no social activity. Often she would give no reply to any questions and would sit biting her nails and sit staring truculently at people. ·

Priscilla was a graceful and attractive child who, had she been dressed in becoming clothes, might have been unusually charming. She had a small, sensitive face, but usually she had a hard and hostile expression. She seemed completely inaccessible and nobody really understood her.

Priscilla's parents were essentially well meaning, but completely lacked understanding. The father was a minister, the mother a former teacher. Both parents were educated and conscientious in their approach to life. They were sensitive, had high standards of duties and obligations, considered good manners and proper behavior important, and devoted themselves unselfishly to the upbringing of their two children, in whom they tried to instill their principles.

In spite of all these virtues, these parents were damaging to their daughter. Priscilla was a timid and fearful little girl who craved warmth and closeness which she never obtained, since both parents were rather distant. When at two years of age, Priscilla had a little brother who, different from the family pattern, was a gay and jolly baby, delighting his parents and everyone else with his cuteness, Priscilla felt utterly rejected and withdrew into a shell.

There is no doubt that her mother gave her much reason to feel that the brother was preferred. For one thing, mother lacked understanding to such a degree that, following her moral principles, she demanded that the defeated little daughter enjoy the baby as much as she did and later share things with him and not be jealous.

The unhappiness in which Priscilla lived, feeling rejected and also condemned for her jealousy, was increased by her unhappy school experiences. Priscilla went to school feeling that all the other children were happy and loved. Her feeling of isolation increased as she became aware of the awkwardness of her clothing. Her mother believed in practical, homemade dresses. Neither parent believed in vanities. Thus Priscilla always wore too-large, bulky dresses which the other children sometimes ridiculed.

Sullenness and a negative, stubborn antagonism toward the whole world became the mask beneath which Priscilla hid her hurt feelings. Her work was poor, although her intelligence was high. She had no friends. Her parents felt completely bewildered and outraged at their daughter's behavior. They tried everything they could think of—they admonished, scolded, punished, but to no avail. At twelve, Priscilla was fairly embittered, withdrawn, lonely, and unhappy (*14*, 132).

In the following case, the parental rejection is more readily apparent.

Connie is one of the rare cases in which a mother admitted being "not particularly fond of her child." The mother has "no use for women." She is frankly partial to her son, yet believes that she does not show this partiality. Connie is unfortunate enough to adore her mother. She is unhappy when she makes her mother unhappy. She retaliates by mistreating her brother.

Connie is unpopular in school. She says "A silliness gets into me, then I tickle the girls and pester them. I know I am not very well liked."

She does not know how to act with children, and in her insecurity she becomes aggressive. The baseball team is angry with her because she ruins their games.

She feels her mother does not understand her. Often she must lie because she is afraid of her mother scolding her or her father spanking her. She has no advocate (*14*, 135).

Domination-Submission

Using techniques similar to those employed in his study of acceptance and rejection, Symonds (*84*) compared the consequents of parental domination or submission upon children's personality structures. The subjects were 28 pairs of children, between 6 and 17 years of age, matched as in the other study. One member of each pair was the child of "dominating parents," the other of "submissive parents."

By dominating parents is meant those who exercise a great deal of control over the child, by being very strict and authoritative with him, who punish the child or threaten punishment, who are hard on the child and hold him to standards which are not suited to his age and development, who criticize a child, who unnecessarily frighten the child, who plan extensively for him, or, in some cases, who care for the child's needs to an unusual degree and give him unnecessary toys or advantages or special privileges (84, 105).

By submissive parents is meant those who permit the child a great deal of freedom, allow themselves to be dominated by the child and accede to the child's demands and wishes, who indulge the child and cannot refuse his requests or, on the other hand, who desert him or neglect the child, who do not give him proper training and leave him too much to his own resources (84, 108).

It should be noted that these "dominating parents" resemble the parents from Baldwin's "authoritarian home atmosphere" (cf. pp. 251–253), while part of the definition of "submissive parents" parallels Levy's description of overprotective, indulgent mothers (cf. p. 256).

Like Baldwin's nursery school subjects from "authoritarian control" homes, the children of "dominating parents" tended to be polite, inhibited, honest, careful, dependable, but submissive, docile, humble, shy, retiring, and self-conscious. As might be anticipated, they had greater difficulty in self-expression, and suffered more from feelings of inferiority, insecurity, confusion, and bewilderment than children who had more freedom (84).

The behaviors rewarded in dominating homes—submission to others, carrying out instructions faithfully, inhibition of aggression and independence strivings—were transferred to other social situations. Hence the children appeared to be highly socialized and to have strong superegos, achieved, however, at the cost of freedom of expression and spontaneity.

Children of "submissive parents," on the other hand, were rated as more disobedient, careless, irresponsible, stubborn, rebellious against authority, antagonistic, forward, and independent, but self-confident and spontaneous in forming friendships outside the family (84). These children had been rewarded for expressing their feelings freely and for making their needs and desires known. They had not learned to be obedient or submissive or to take responsibility at home, and hence did not appear to be highly conforming or socialized in the wider community.

Another extensive study, generally confirming Symonds' findings, compared the personality characteristics of children from "well-adjusted" and "overattentive" families (47). The latter correspond to the submissive parents of Symonds' study and their children were like those of Symonds' submissive parents. For example, compared with children from well-adjusted families, those from overattentive homes were judged to be socially maladjusted, and a greater proportion of them exhibited mal-adaptive characteristics such as social immaturity, no sense of responsi-bility, not dependable, nervousness, extreme dependency on adults, withdrawal, negativism, temper tantrums, oversensitivity, depression.

The ways in which these personality characteristics, rooted in the child's early learning in the family, affect the child's school adjustment will be discussed in detail in later sections (cf. pp. 387–391).

Parent-Child Relationships and Maladjustment

Studies of emotionally disturbed and neurotic children add further impressive evidence on the crucial role of parent-child relationships in molding personality. Comparisons of the family backgrounds of mal-adjusted and well-adjusted children supply information about conditions that promote, and conditions that hinder, the development of good social and emotional adjustment.

In Hardy's longitudinal investigation, the home environments of 110 well-adjusted and 144 poorly adjusted children from third grade to junior high school were studied. Teacher's records, objective ratings of the home and neighborhood surroundings, and annual psychological interviews with parents and children constituted the basic data of the study (41).

The maladjusted group consisted of children with markedly deviant classroom behavior and attitudes (as rated by their teachers) or with excessive fears, pugnacity, marked tendencies toward shyness, jealousy, worry, feelings of inferiority (revealed in their interviews). The criteria of satisfactory adjustment were friendliness, ability to win the esteem of the group, social recognition, and the absence of maladaptive behavior and attitudes.

From the larger group of subjects, the investigator selected two groups equated with respect to occupational status of the parents and ratings of various home conditions. This was done so that other differences which might emerge could not be attributed to differences in relative social and economic standing of the well-adjusted and poorly adjusted subjects. After this matching, the well-adjusted groups did *not* differ significantly from each other in: percent of foreign born and American parentage; formal schooling of parents; transiency of residence; sleeping arrange-ments; neatness of home and immediate surroundings; parents' partici-pation in social or civic organizations; signs of nervous instability in the family history; presence of relatives or stepparents in the home.

In certain other important respects, however, the two groups differed markedly. The poorly adjusted subjects had been reared in far less favorable familial environments. For example, poor health was reported by eight times as many fathers of the maladjusted as of well-adjusted children. This may be psychologically significant for the child, since a parent who is ill may be irritable and provoke much tension and friction in the home.

The maladjusted group included twice as many children from homes broken by divorce, legal separation, or desertion, and many more of their mothers were gainfully employed outside the home. It may be assumed that the broken homes were, or had been, characterized by emotional turmoil and that employed mothers were under a great deal of tension since they had to work at both job and household duties. For these reasons, these homes did not generally present a serene, happy atmosphere conducive to favorable emotional adjustment.

Furthermore, a relatively large proportion of the mothers of poorly adjusted children were very young when their children were born. Hence they were somewhat more likely to be too immature and inexperienced to give proper guidance and treatment during their early development. Wide disparity between the ages of the mother and father—and hence more frequent conflicts of interests and attitudes—was more often associated with poor adjustment of the children (41).

. . . when the economic and material features of the home were equally favorable for maladjusted and well-adjusted children; when their parents were equally well educated, when their hereditary background was equally free from the more obvious forms of mental instabilties; when all these conditions were ruled out there still were signs of parent incompatibilities, of family tensions, of reduced supervision, and of more complicating situations to wholesome development in the homes of the maladjusted children than in those of their schoolmates (41, 224).

All these differences in the home backgrounds and family situations of well-adjusted and poorly adjusted children indicate that tensions, unhappiness, and inharmonious family relationships are likely to produce poor adjustment in children. The well-adjusted child apparently experiences less frequent turmoil and tension in his family life. Consequently he has more opportunity to learn mature, socially adequate responses at home, and to transfer them to school and wider community settings.

In most cases the child's maladjustment seemed to be related to the cumulative effects of a number of adverse conditions.

Careful examination of the data with respect to the frequency with which unsatisfactory conditions operated conjointly suggests this conclusion. Combinations of two or more complicating situations were frequent occurrences among the maladjusted class and infrequent among the well adjusted. The daily experiences of the maladjusted class often include four or more of these conditions, those of the well adjusted rarely more than three and never more than four (*41, 223*).

Parental Tensions and Children's Maladjustments

Other investigators have attempted to relate school children's maladjustments more specifically to parental tensions. For example, analysis of extensive case history data on 25 behavior problem and neurotic children showed that almost all of them (23) had been rejected by their mothers, and most (16) by their fathers. In 16 cases, the children had been unwanted from the start and their mothers spoke of them as "bad from the beginning" (*33*).

None of the mothers was a "well-integrated" individual, all of them being diagnosed as either aggressive, submissive, neurotic, or infantile. Only two of the fathers in the group were judged to be emotionally stable. There were no "healthy" mother-child relationships in the group, but five fathers had good relationships with their children. The most common type of parent-child relationship was a combination of "under-love" and "overcontrol" (severe punishment, criticism, or unfavorable comparisons).

The mothers' maladjustments and unfavorable attitudes toward children were based on their backgrounds, which revealed a "general picture of weakness and unhappiness." Only two of the mothers expressed feelings of satisfaction about their own childhoods. The rest felt unhappy, unloved, and thwarted during that period.

The fathers had experienced somewhat more stable and satisfying childhoods, but on the whole, they too were immature and poorly prepared for adult relationships. In view of these factors, it is hardly surprising that in 17 of the 25 cases, one or both of the parents were dissatisfied with their marriage.

The parents' personalities, problems, and conflicts probably rendered them unable or unwilling to accept the responsibilities of parenthood. Consequently, they rejected their children and maintained only erratic or overcontrolling relationships with them (*33*).

In a related study, 75 rejected children, patients at a psychiatric clinic, were compared with a control group of normal children who presumably had not been rejected by their parents (*69, 70*). The groups were matched in average family size and ordinal position in the family. The rejected children were those whose mothers never wanted the children, or were predominantly hostile, severely punitive, indifferent, irritable, threatening, or suspicious in their relationships with them.

Analysis of the psychiatric social history and psychiatric interview data revealed that marital discord and maladjustment were much more common among the parents of the rejected children. For example, over half of the parents expressed disappointment with their mates and reported frequent quarrels, while only a small number of the controls' parents had such complaints. Maladjusted parents, lack of affection, broken homes, and cruelty of the husband were much more prevalent in the families of the rejected children. Over 30 percent of these children, but only 5 percent of the controls, had at least one parent who was neurotic, psychopathic, or psychotic. Unhappy childhoods and broken homes were important features of the backgrounds of many parents of rejected children, but relatively few parents of the controls.

In dealing with their children, the majority of the rejecting fathers were hostile, while 66 percent of the rejecting mothers were ambivalent, i.e., alternated between protective and hostile treatment. None of the rejecting mothers and only 9 percent of the rejecting fathers had "constructive" relationships with their children. On the other hand, fewer than 10 percent of the parents of the control group treated their children aggressively or inconsistently. The vast majority of them were judged to be "constructive" in parent-child relations.

All the rejected children were emotionally unstable and in need of psychological treatment. In contrast to this, almost all the children who were handled "constructively" were described as emotionally stable and popular, friendly, and obedient in school. On the basis of all these findings, the author concludes that rejection is

. . . primarily due to the mother's unhappy adjustment to marriage. This is usually the result of immaturity and emotional instability on the part of one or both parents. The mother's handling is frequently inconsistent, wavering between over-protective and hostile behavior. The children in turn showed mixtures of aggressive (quarreling, truancy, stealing), anti-social, as well as submissive, neurotic symptoms. Aggressive behavior occurred more frequently when parental handling was consistently hostile, submission when parental handling was consistently protective. The control group showed striking correspondence between constructive parental handling and stable behavior on the part of the children (70, 586).

It may be concluded from both of the above studies that a child's maladjustment frequently has its roots in unfavorable parental behavior and attitudes. These, in turn, may generally be traced back to the parents' own developmental histories, and consequently, their personalities.

It may be inferred that in unhappy, tense homes characterized by marital discord, children endure many upsets and frustrations, but few satisfying experiences. In many cases, their needs are probably satisfied only through such extreme behavior as violent aggression, complete submission, or neurotic symptoms. Under the circumstances, immature, socially maladaptive behavior is directly rewarded and learned. Also, in so far as these children identify with their parents, they probably adopt some of these adults' maladaptive and socially inadequate behavior. Children's neurotic symptoms and behavior problems may thus be interpreted as consequents of the home environment, or more specifically, lack of emotional warmth, healthy parent-child relationships, and good identification models. As we shall see in greater detail in Chapter 12, these home variables may also be important antecedents of delinquent behavior (cf. pp. 437–441).

Self-Perceptions and Attitudes Toward Family Among Maladjusted Children

Thus far we have considered primarily the influences of parent-child relationships on children's overt behavior and emotional disturbances. We have not taken account of the maladjusted child's self-perceptions, feelings, needs, emotions, and attitudes. Yet these are obviously of crucial importance. Are children aware of parental rejection and hostility? Do rejected children feel unwanted, unloved, unworthy, or unjustly punished? How do they regard themselves and their parents?

In order to examine these problems systematically, Jackson, a British psychologist, studied 70 maladjusted children—30 neurotics and 40 delinquents—and a control group of 40 normals (51, 52). Each subject told a story in response to each of six drawings depicting various kinds of family relationships (dependence on mother, exclusion from intimacy between parents, jealousy of siblings, disobedience, loneliness and guilt, fear of aggression, threats of punishment). Some of the subjects' ideas about himself, his family, and society in general were inferred from his responses to the test.

The maladjusted children's self-perceptions and attitudes differed markedly from those of normal children. In their projective stories, the normals generally described themselves (i.e., their heroes) as "good" or "nice," while the delinquent and neurotic children perceived themselves as naughty and disobedient. Emotionally stable youngsters were realistic enough to recognize that they misbehaved sometimes but did not feel that they were subjected to cruel or excessive punishments. They saw their parents as fond and accepting, giving them help and protection.

Neurotic and delinquent subjects, on the other hand, felt that their parents disliked, rejected, and maltreated them, and administered unjust punishment for their misdeeds. As would be anticipated on the basis of the principle of generalization, the maladjusted children viewed strangers with fear and mistrust, while the normal children saw others as generally good and kindly.

The neurotic children reacted to the injustices they felt they had suffered. They were hostile and rejecting of their parents, intensely jealous of their siblings, and fearful of aggression from older, more powerful brothers and sisters.

The delinquents did not show so much hatred of parents and siblings or so much anxiety or self-pity as the neurotics. The author points out that these children felt detached and "not belonging." Consequently, they were less emotionally involved with their families, and repressed all strong feelings about them (51, 52).

Clearly, the influences of healthy and unhealthy parent-child relationships are reflected in the child's attitudes toward himself and toward his family, as well as in his overt maladaptive behavior. The child who is punished and rejected is keenly aware of his parents' attitudes toward him. Moreover, he begins to view himself as unwanted and unworthy; that is, he may adopt his parents' attitudes toward him.

Relations with Siblings

More than 80 percent of American children have siblings. In the child's interactions with them, he may learn patterns of loyalty, helpfulness, and protection; or of conflict, domination, and competition, and these may be generalized to other social relationships. The number of siblings a child has and his relationship to them constitute an important aspect of the child's learning situation and hence may strongly affect what and how the child learns at home. A number of systematic studies have been concerned with the consequents of ordinal position (oldest, youngest, middle child), and "onliness" on the personality and behavior of the school-age child.

ORDINAL POSITION. The social learning situation encountered by the first-born child obviously differs from that of his younger siblings. For example, oldest children may be handicapped by the relative inexperience of their parents. They may be overstrained or pushed too hard to accomplish, or they may have to care for younger children before they are ready for such responsibility. They alone must face the difficult adjustment involved in losing "only child" status.

Youngest children, on the other hand, are more likely to be babied by parents, but to compete vigorously with older siblings for the satisfaction of their own needs. They are more likely to be bossed and punished by older siblings, but have the advantage over other siblings in never having to adjust to the competition of a newly arrived younger sibling. For reasons such as these we might predict that there would be personality differences related to ordinal position in the family.

Research studies of the problem show general agreement that oldest children are likely to be less aggressive and to have a higher incidence of problem behavior than their peers (19, 38, 56, 76). They tend to be less self-confident, and more sensitive, seclusive, introverted, passive, abusive, worrisome, and anxious to escape blame (19, 38). In general, they manifest less ability in leadership and less concentration and persistence in the face of difficulty (19, 73). Moreover, at least two independent studies show that there are disproportionately large numbers of first-born children among the patients at child guidance clinics (74, 90). Surveys of elementary school children also indicate that oldest children manifest greater numbers of nervous symptoms than either intermediate or youngest children (32, 56, 85).

A recent study of the problems of normal school children revealed that first-born boys and girls had more problems than their siblings, especially those indicating tension and withdrawal. Oldest boys had more withdrawing, internalizing problems (oversensitiveness, mood swings, fears); second-born boys had more overt competitive and aggressive patterns (63).

On the average, youngest children seem to present a sharply contrasting picture. Compared with other children, they appear to be highly striving (56, 73), more self-confident (56), more defiant (19), and more persevering in the face of difficulty (73). One survey revealed "a larger proportion of oldest children among the socially unadjusted, and a larger proportion of the youngest children among the well-adjusted group than in the other groups" (56).

Middle children have been found to be somewhat lacking in aggression, though not so markedly as oldest children. They are generally socially gregarious, rather easily influenced by suggestion, and eager for physical demonstrations of affection (8).

While the findings of these studies are generally consistent, they must be interpreted cautiously. For example, the differences between the ordinal position groups are small and there is a great deal of overlap on all traits. The influence of the child's ordinal position will certainly vary from one family to another, depending on many factors in the family situation.

NUMBER OF CHILDREN IN THE FAMILY. The social experiences of children from large families may differ from those of small-family children, but there is no evidence that family size itself has any uniform influence. Until recently, small families have been more typical of the middle than of the lower class, although there seems to be a trend toward larger families in the middle class at present.

Children from small families are likely to be subjected to pressures which differ from those exerted on children from large families. For example, sociological studies indicate that the parents of small families typically plan the number of children they will have, the child-rearing practices they will employ, and the attitudes they will take toward education, largely in terms of status achievement and promotion (10). Emphasis is placed on the child's development as an individual. The small-family child is more likely to be compared with other children with respect to accomplishment, and expectations for him are usually high. The mother in this type of family is more likely to be the main disciplinarian; the emotional climate of the family group is likely to be intense. Parents of large families, on the other hand, appear more typically to have a greater acceptance of fate, and to handle crises more flexibly. Discipline in large families tends to be undertaken more by siblings and less by parents (10).

It might be expected that these differences in family attitudes would affect the child's psychological development. For example, children of small families might be expected to learn stronger achievement needs, and to be less adaptable. Testing of such hypotheses is difficult, however, because family size may be correlated with social status, and the differences between large- and small-family attitudes may simply be reflections of social-class influences. However, it is possible that such relationships between family size and attitude would still appear even if the factor of social-class status were controlled.

THE ONLY CHILD. Investigations of the consequences of "onliness" have yielded somewhat contradictory results. There is general agreement among most studies that only children tend more than their peers to be self-confident, aggressive, and gregarious (32, 38). They also appear to be higher in initiative, originality, and conformity (40); more fond of physical demonstration of affection; and more inclined toward excitability, flightiness, and nervousness (38).

The implications of "onliness" for overall adjustment are much less clear, however. Some investigators have found the only child to be less popular with his peers; more conceited and bullying; and more inclined to such symptoms of emotional disturbance as temper tantrums, poor sleep, night terrors, feeding problems, fears, and enuresis (74, 90). Other authors have found him to be more popular than his peers; more coöperative, dependable, and courteous; and more obedient and manageable (40).

Such contradictions are probably attributable to sampling differences and, in many studies, to the failure to control for the influences of other important factors affecting adjustment. For example, only children generally come from homes of higher socioeconomic status, and this rather than "onliness" itself may have accounted for some of the results.

Even in characteristics where fairly consistent differences between only and other children have been found, the differences are small, and for this reason, any broad generalizations about only children seem unwarranted. It seems safe to conclude that "onliness" itself is not related to any specific type of personality structure or problem behavior. The child's familial background and his relationships with his parents probably influence his personality development much more than the presence or absence of siblings.

SOCIAL CLASS INFLUENCES ON BEHAVIOR

In the last section, we highlighted the crucial role of parent-child relationships in personality development, reëmphasizing the home and family as the primary sources of the child's social learning. To a certain extent, differences in family relationships result from the parents' unique developmental histories and personal adjustments. In great measure, however, they also reflect broad cultural influences. Each family belongs to subcultural groups (racial, religious, social-class, urban, or rural). Members of these groups share many attributes and differ in many ways from the members of other groups. In chapters 6 and 7, we reviewed studies indicating that middle- and lower-class families may differ in their infant training practices.

Subcultural influences continue to be effective during the middle childhood period. Within any particular community, members of a particular class attend the same schools, join the same clubs, have similar interests and attitudes, band together against outsiders from other classes, work together at the same kinds of jobs, and eventually marry each other. Consequently, their ideas about acceptable and unacceptable behavior—

including the techniques of child-rearing and discipline—are usually much alike (86).

Social-Class Differences in Child-Rearing Practices

Child behavior which is encouraged and rewarded by one social class may be disapproved and punished by another. Through an intricate system of selective rewards and punishments, parents teach their children the responses, values, and beliefs appropriate for their own social class.

Class training of the child ranges all the way from the control of the manner and ritual by which he eats his food to the control of his choice of playmates and of his educational and occupational goals. The times and places for his recreation, the chores required of him by his family, the rooms and articles in the house which he may use, the wearing of certain clothes at certain times, the amount of studying required of him, the economic control to which he is subjected by his parents, indeed his very conceptions of right and wrong, all vary according to the social class of the child in question (23, 609).

Davis and Havighurst analyzed interviews with 50 mothers in each of four groups (white middle class, white lower class, Negro middle class, and Negro lower class) (25; cf. pp. 163; 194). On the basis of their analysis, they concluded that "middle class children are subjected earlier and more consistently to the influences which make a child an orderly, conscientious, responsible, and tame person" (25, 707).

. . . the middle class mothers in general, expected their children to assume responsibility earlier in the home, to help with the younger children, and to cook and sew at an earlier age. . . . [This is surprising for] it seems obvious that there is more actual need of the children's help in lower class families, where the work of children to be cared for is greater and the mother has very little help with the housework. The explanation probably lies in a tendency on the part of middle class people to train their children early for achievement and responsibility, while lower class people train their children to take responsibility only after the child is old enough to make the effort of training pay substantial returns in the work the child will do. Middle class parents can afford to use time to train children to dress themselves, help around the home, sew, cook, and so on, at such an early age that the children cannot repay this training effort by their actual performance, although they may repay it by adopting attitudes of self-achievement and responsibility.

In addition to training their children to take responsibility early and to adopt attitudes favorable to self-achievement, middle-class families, attempt to curb those impulses of the child which would lead to poor health, waste of time, and bad moral habits according to middle class views. Therefore they require their children to take daytime naps longer, to come in to the house at night earlier, and they do not permit their children to go alone to movies at an early age. Nevertheless, they encourage their children to be venturesome in the more "constructive" activities, from the middle class point of view, of going down town alone to museums, department stores, dancing lessons, and the like (25, 708).

Focusing attention on related, but not identical aspects of child training practices, Maccoby et al. (60; cf. pp. 163; 195) interviewed 198 white upper-middle- and 178 upper-lower-class mothers of kindergarten children. Their findings are quite different from those of Davis and Havighurst, indicating that upper-middle-class mothers "are somewhat warmer and more demonstrative . . . than upper-lower mothers" (60, 395). Moreover, "upper-lower parents employed physical punishment, deprivation of privileges, and ridicule as techniques of controlling their children more commonly than do upper-middle parents. It appears likely that the upper-middle parents used reasoning and praise more often. . . ." (60, 395).

According to their data, parents of the higher socioeconomic group were less concerned with noise, neatness, and orderliness in the home and conformity in table manners. These parents also allowed their children more freedom to be aggressive toward them and toward other children.

This last finding seems contrary to some sociological observations of Davis (22, 23, 24) which suggest that lower-class parents encourage and reward aggression, while middle-class parents are less tolerant of it. This discrepancy may possibly be explained on the basis of differences in the populations studied. Maccoby et al. were concerned with the parents of kindergarten children while Davis focused his attention on older, pre-adolescent children. It is quite possible that middle-class mothers are more permissive of aggressive expression in young children, but punish aggression in preadolescents more strongly.

However, there appears to be a more fundamental disagreement between the findings of Davis and Havighurst and those of Maccoby et al. which is not so easily reconciled. The former concluded that "In the course of . . . training, middle class children probably suffer more frustration of their impulses" (25, 707). Maccoby et al., on the other hand, maintained that middle-class mothers were "more permissive and less severe in their child training than upper-lower mothers" (60, 395). These investigators concluded that "the most plausible explanation for . . . some of the differences between this study and that of Davis and Havighurst seems to be that somewhat different items were chosen for study, and that the findings have been interpreted differently" (60, 394).

We believe that this is true. For example, Davis and Havighurst based their interpretation largely on the observation that middle-class parents expect their children to assume responsibility relatively early. In contrast, the views of Maccoby et al. stem primarily from evidence that lower-class parents employ harsher disciplinary techniques. While the question is still open to argument, the available data leads us to believe that the emphasis of Maccoby et al. on the greater permissiveness of middle-class parents is more generally valid.

Class Differences in Children's Attitudes, Personality, and Adjustment

ATTITUDES TOWARD PARENTS. If the findings of Maccoby et al. are valid, lower-class children would be expected to perceive their parents' disciplinary procedures as harsh and punitive, while those in the middle class would see their parents as more lenient. Several investigations indicate that this is so. In one study, two groups of 21 fifth-grade children, one lower-class and one upper-middle-class, were asked to write compositions concerning a 10-year-old boy's reactions to his younger brother's misbehavior and interference. It was assumed that through the medium of the story, the child would reveal his perceptions of his parents' disciplinary procedures (28).

Twice as many lower- as middle-class children wrote stories involving nonconstructive solutions to the problem (e.g., appealing to authority). The vast majority of the solutions suggested by the higher social-class group, but only half of those given by the lower-class children, were constructive, amicable settlements. In general, children of low socioeconomic status were more inclined to use punishment and to avenge misdeeds.

Each subject in this study was also interviewed privately and asked ten questions relating to routine discipline problems in school, at home, or in the neighborhood (e.g., Should children ever talk back to their parents?). The socioeconomically more favored children revealed healthy attitudes toward their parents' treatment and toward authority in general. Lower-class children viewed authority, including their parents, as unreasonable and severe. Hence they revealed more rigid compliance and greater fear of deviating from fixed rules and regulations (28).

Somewhat similar results were obtained in another study of the influences of social-class variations in discipline procedures on children's attitudes toward parents. The subjects, three groups of 50 children each in grades V to VIII, were drawn from three schools representing upper-, middle-, and lower-class economic levels. Each child was seen individually, and after good rapport had been established, he was asked to speak out the first ten ideas (associations) that came to him when he thought of his mother and father. These data were analyzed to determine children's notions and descriptions of their parents; nature and degree of attachment and dependence; feeling tone, and degree of repression or expressiveness (64).

Although there was great variability in each group, children of different economic levels generally revealed fairly distinct attitudes toward their parents. For example, as a group, middle-class children manifested pleasant feelings, accepting and respecting their parents whom they regarded as helpful and permissive. Few of these children appeared to be overly dependent or hostile to their parents.

Lower-class children, on the other hand, had the greatest number of unfavorable reactions. Of the three groups, they were the most ambivalent (had mixed love and hostility) toward the parents and were the most insecure. Although they had relatively few feelings of rejection or overdependence, they felt that their parents were generally repressive and gave them little companionship. The upper-class group was the most variable, but as a group, they expressed the most feelings of rejection and overdependency. Hostility was less common in this group than among the lower-class subjects, but adoration and "blind love," together with fear and guilt, were more prevalent.

On practically all attitudes which are interpreted as indicators of mental health, or which in other ways are conducive to balanced personality development, the children from middle class parents rank first, the children from the highest economic level studied rank second, and the children from poorest parents rank last (64, 604).

CLASS DIFFERENCES IN ADJUSTMENT. If middle-class parents are actually warmer, more lenient, and more easygoing, we would predict that their children would be more stable than those of the lower class. Several studies of the relationship between children's adjustment and socio-economic status confirm this prediction. In spite of the fact that different test instruments were used, all the investigations agree in finding the middle-class group emotionally healthier.

For example, in one study, teachers' ratings of personality characteristics and problem behavior of a large group of slum-area children between the ages of 6 and 12 were compared with those of middle-class boys and girls of the same age and intelligence (80). Disinterest in school work, cheating, overactivity, unpopularity, and temper outbursts were more common among lower-class children. They also received poorer ratings in energy, persistence, cheerfulness, and self-control (80).

Analysis of personality test responses of sixth-grade children from high-, middle-, and lower-class backgrounds showed that, on the average, the upper-class groups had fewer personality problems and were better adjusted than their lower-class peers. However, the actual correlations between social status and personality, although positive, were low (39).

Economic privation during middle childhood may also be related to social maladjustment in later years. Personality tests administered to college students indicated that those who had suffered poverty during their grammar school years were more inclined to be introverted and seclusive and to feel inferior. "Poverty does not foster calm, unemotional personality, but rather nervousness, moods, depression, etc." (83).

Despite the consistency of the findings that middle-class children are better adjusted and have fewer emotional problems, interpretations must be made cautiously. There are several possible sources of error in these studies. For one thing, most teachers are middle-class people and may therefore rate their middle-class pupils more favorably than those of the lower class. Furthermore, if Davis' conclusions about lower-class approval of aggression are valid, hostility and temper outbursts prevalent in lower-class school children may be reflections of identification with their social group, rather than symptoms of maladjustment. It is also possible that middle-class children have greater knowledge of what constitutes socially approved and adaptive behavior, and hence are likely to answer personality tests and questionnaires "correctly."

In any case, the results of these studies, although suggestive, are not sufficiently definite to justify the conclusion that there is a *close* association between family social status and personal adjustment. While certain types of parental behavior and children's responses may be more prevalent in one social class than in another, there is a great deal of overlap between classes in both of these sets of variables. On the other hand, the slight relationships which have been discovered between these factors may be interpreted to mean that in the population at large, more lower-class than upper-class children are likely to be considered maladjusted.

Sources of Class Differences in Adjustment

If this is true, it is important to investigate which specific features of lower-class status contribute most to emotional maladjustment. To this end, Francis (34, 35) studied the relative impacts of physical surroundings, economic factors, and parental attitudes on the personality development of children. The subjects were 30 families, including 56 children, from each of two sections of a midwestern city. The suburban area was a typical solid, conservative, middle-class neighborhood, while the other was a poverty-stricken, degenerating area inhabited by lower-class people. There were great differences in real estate values, conditions and spacing of the homes, incomes of families, and recreational opportunities in the two areas.

On the basis of psychiatric interviews with children and parents, many individual features of the physical environment, parental behavior, and attitudes could be rated reliably as helpful (i.e., conducive to the child's emotional stability) or harmful (conducive to instability). Children's personality scores, derived from interviews and teacher ratings, were then correlated with each of the physical environment and parental variables.

Factors associated with the physical milieu, such as poverty, over-crowding, recreational space, and neighborhood appearance, were *not* found to be significantly related to personality development. However, a number of parental behavior and attitude variables—which reflect the learning situation the child encounters in his home—were associated with healthy adjustment in children. These were: care in the upkeep and furnishing of the home; knowledge of children's schoolmates; interest in child's school progress; allowing the child to go away from home with other children; giving freedom in recreational pursuits; allowing use of spending money as the child pleases; giving attention to religious upbringing; watchfulness over children's health; parents' attending entertainments. "Helpful" attitudes in all but two of these significant factors (religious training and watchfulness over health) were significantly more prevalent among middle-class than lower-class parents. It may be concluded that social-class differences in children's emotional adjustments are primarily dependent upon class-related attitudes and child-rearing practices (learning variables) rather than on differences in physical milieux.

In comparing the immediate physical environment of the children and the parental attitudes with their effect on the child's personality adjustment, the physical environment by itself is shown to be of comparatively little importance, where a number of the parent's attitudes appear to be significantly influential. Thus the factors originally thought to be important, namely, poor economic conditions, broken homes, foreign born parents, and physical sickness have little effect on their own account (35, 47).

Parental attitudes and practices are of vital importance in the child's development, and these are to some extent determined by social-class membership. In this sense, social-class influences may operate on the child indirectly, that is, as mediated through his family's behavior toward him.

Social-Class Influences on Recreational Activities

Peers also foster the learning of class-appropriate behavior, since most children's neighborhood and school companions are of their own social class. Moreover, children's preferences for leisure-time activities vary with their social-class membership. Thus, even if the child lives in a neighborhood or goes to a school having several social classes, recreational interests are likely to bring him into contact with peers of his own social group.

This was clearly illustrated in a study in which 241 children aged 10, 11, and 12 years from four social classes (upper-middle, lower-middle, upper-lower, lower-lower) kept daily activity diaries for two weeks (61). They all lived in a half-square-mile area and hence had equal access to the community churches, playgrounds, and clubs. Yet social-class groups differed sharply in their preferences for both group and individual activities. For example, about half of the upper-middle-class children belonged to the Scouts, but almost none of the lower-class children were members. Middle-class children went to church more, read more books, spent more time listening to the radio, but were somewhat restricted in movie attendance. Lower-class children, on the other hand, went to the movies frequently, but did relatively little reading or radio listening.

Many of the child's leisure-time activities bring him into contact primarily with others of the same social class. This enables children to influence each other and to reinforce class-appropriate behavior, ideas, and attitudes learned in the home. "When the findings of this study are interpreted in the light of a theory of social learning, it is seen that most of the children were learning the ways of behaving and believing of their own social class" (61, 512).

Social-Class Influences on Superego Formation

While all children's superegos become more complex and inclusive as development proceeds, social-class differences in moral and ethical behavior also become apparent. Thus Piaget found a general change in children's moral reasoning with increasing age from rigid authoritarian to more relative and equalitarian judgments (cf. pp. 426-429). However, as several investigators have found, these changes do not occur at the same rate in children of all social classes (42, 59). While lower-class children of 6 or 7 have absolute standards of right and wrong, middle-class children of this age tend to be more flexible and make fewer "arbitrary appeals to authority" in their moral judgments. Apparently, very young lower-class children tend to take over their parents' harsh, inflexible standards and do not allow for extenuating circumstances. On the other hand, the young middle-class child's background is more likely to include training in a more equalitarian philosophy.

IMMEDIATE OR DELAYED GRATIFICATION. Another social-class difference in superego development involves the capacity for delay in gratification of the child's needs. As Davis (22, 23) points out, lower-class children have little opportunity to learn that sacrificing immediate goals in favor of more substantial long-term objectives may be rewarding. Their lives are too filled with "peaks" and "depressions"; even the basic necessities of life such as heat, food, and shelter are not always assured from day to day. Consequently, the lower-class child is likely to adopt a philosophy that "a bird in the hand is worth two in the bush." The middle-class child's life, on the other hand, is more predictable, and long-term goals are more frequently rewarded.

These differences in the life experiences of the two social classes have obvious implications for superego development. The ability to delay satisfactions and to work for remote objectives are basic for working together to attain many valuable goals. Middle-class children are therefore more likely to act coöperatively and in accordance with long-time "ideals," while lower-class children are more likely to respond primarily to immediate rewards.

These differences in the gratification philosophies of the two social classes are reflected in many aspects of "moral behavior." For example, lower-class children are more likely than their middle-class peers to have heterosexual experiences (57), i.e., they are less likely to delay their sexual gratifications until adulthood. Also, since delinquent behavior offers some immediate gratifications, it is sanctioned in some lower-class families and neighborhoods.

AGGRESSIVE EXPRESSION. The taboos the middle-class child learns are not the same as those of his lower-class peers. Among lower-class preadolescents overt aggressive expression is encouraged, while middle-class children are more likely to be punished for displaying hostility (22, 23, 24). Consequently, the latter group is likely to inhibit aggression. Sanford (75) working with middle- and upper-class preadolescent subjects found that aggressive needs occurred frequently in their fantasies (projective stories) but, according to teachers' reports, were infrequently expressed overtly. Apparently general cultural pressures or their own superegos (internalized cultural pressure) prevent middle-class children from manifesting much aggression even though they have strong aggressive needs (as measured by the Thematic Apperception Test).

Since aggressive expression is more strongly approved in the lower-class preadolescent, it could be predicted that boys of this class would not inhibit their hostility. In one study, the aggressive needs and overt aggression of 29 lower-class boys, residents of a juvenile institution, were measured (68). The strength of each subject's needs was measured from stories he told in response to the TAT, while expression of aggression was evaluated by means of ratings and behavior reports submitted by attendants and teachers. As was predicted, aggressive needs and aggressive expression in this group were significantly related. That is, lower-class boys with intense aggressive needs manifested more hostile reactions than those who had few such needs.

In attempting to understand individual children, it is possible to place too much emphasis on class-typing of child-rearing and socialization practices. Although certain attitudes and procedures may be usual or modal in a particular class, many individual families within the social class may vary from the standards of their group. For example, many lower-class boys are forbidden to express overt hostility at home. Despite the lower-class mores, these particular children have learned to anticipate retaliation, and consequently they withhold aggressive expression. Those who have not learned to associate punishment with aggressive expression tend to express their hostility openly (68). In brief, aggressive behavior is more typically sanctioned in the lower than in the middle class, but the learning situation in individual families may counteract the general group influence.

Identification with Ethnic Groups

Ordinarily, the child's identification with his own social class occurs automatically as a by-product of his identifications with specific individuals, such as parents and peers. In a similar way, children learn to identify with the other subcultural groups (ethnic, religious, racial) to which they belong. Research studies indicate that these identifications develop gradually and usually become firmly established during the school years. In one of the few studies of the problem, 86 Protestant, Catholic, Jewish, and Negro children were interviewed and asked questions such as "What are you?" "What kinds of people live around your house?" "What is Daddy? Mommy?" (43, 44). The youngest children (3½ to 4½) typically identified themselves and others by referring to names. With advancing age, ethnic designations were used more frequently.

From the age of about 5½ on, the child's conception both of himself and others in terms of names is virtually abandoned. Reference to ethnic group membership becomes widespread, and, in a lesser degree, references to personal qualities are increasingly utilized. As exemplified by the responses secured in the 6½ to 8½ and 8½ to 10½ groups, both the child and his neighbors are most frequently viewed as "American," "Colored," "Jewish," "Catholic," "Italian," "Spanish" (43, 374).

Children generally describe their parents in the same ethnic identification terms they use for themselves.

Young children answered questions like "What does it take to be Catholic, Jewish?" "What does it mean to be Catholic, Jewish?" primarily in terms of concrete activities, e.g., "talking Jewish," "going to a synagogue," "making communion." Older children more frequently make use of abstractions. Thus a 10-year-old Jewish boy said, "Jewish is a religion just like Christian. You go to Hebrew (school) and you see the star in the Talmud Torah. It means to believe in these things, to respect your parents. You shouldn't steal" (44).

NEGRO CHILDREN'S IDENTIFICATIONS. The definition of who is Negro is, after all, a cultural one, dictated largely by the majority group. In our culture, anyone with even a small amount of Negro ancestry is defined as Negro. Hence identification with Negroes means acceptance of oneself as a member of a so-called "racial" group.

In one study of minority group identification, 253 Negro children between the ages of 3 and 7 were the subjects (18). In order to determine whether these children understood the word Negro, the examiner presented each child with Negro and white dolls and asked him to "give me the doll who looks like a Negro child." Apparently the word was not well understood in the early years, but by the age of 6, a substantial proportion (78 percent) of Negro children chose a brown-skinned doll.

Of course, the fact that a child is aware of the differences between Negroes and whites does not mean that he has made a personal identification with Negroes. In order to determine whether or not the children identified themselves with Negroes, the experimenter also requested each child to "give me the doll that looks like you." Again the youngest children were not certain of their identification. However, with increasing age, there was a marked rise in the percent of subjects who identified with the colored doll. Thus 36 percent of the 3-year-olds, 48 percent of the 5-year-olds, and 87 percent of the 7-year-olds chose the colored doll as the one "that looks like you."

Acceptance of himself as a member of the Negro group (as defined by our culture) seemed to be significantly influenced by the child's own skin color. Although all the children were aware of race differences, 81 percent of the dark Negroes, and 73 percent of the medium-colored group, but only 20 percent of the light-colored group identified themselves with the colored doll (18).

It may be concluded from both the above studies that identification with ethnic groups and ethnic-group symbols becomes well established early in the middle childhood years. Definitions and conceptions of the nature of the group change with age, and acceptance of group membership generally increases.

Influences of Minority-Group Status

Since individuals who belong to different social or cultural groups are subjected to varying pressures and make different kinds of identifications, they would be expected to differ in motives, values, attitudes, and outlooks. This expectation has been confirmed in a number of studies (20, 67).

In one of them, analysis of the Thematic Apperception Test responses of 50 white and 50 Negro preadolescent boys showed that the minority-group children interpreted the general environment as hostile more frequently than the others did (67). The heroes of their stories were often hated, scolded, reprimanded, or physically attacked.

Apparently they perceived others as basically inhospitable, unfriendly, and threatening. In addition, they had strong feelings of personal inferiority, helplessness, and indifference toward others. Relatively few Negro boys depicted their heroes (i.e., themselves) as leaders or as friendly and considerate individuals who respect others. They seemed to have little motivation for accomplishment and success but emphasized inactive pursuits such as thinking, reflecting, and speculating (67).

It is possible that these negative attitudes towards society primarily represented generalized feelings of hostility stemming from unstable family situations. However, the evidence indicated that Negro children felt more accepted and secure in their families than white children. Therefore it may be assumed that Negro boys' indifference to others, and their perceptions of the world as hostile, are largely attributable to other experiences—either to personal encounters with race prejudice or to general awareness of discrimination against Negroes.

REFERENCES AND ADDITIONAL READING

1. Allen, F. H., and Pearson, G. H. J., The emotions of the physically handicapped child. *Brit. J. Med. Psychol.* (1928), 8:212–235.

2. Bender, L., and Paster, S., Homosexual trends in children. *Am. J. Orthopsychiat.* (1941), 11:730–744.

3. Blum, G., *Psychoanalytic theories of personality.* New York: McGraw-Hill, 1953.

4. Bonney, M. E., A study of the relation of intelligence, family size, and sex differences with mutual friendships in the primary grades. *Child Develop.* (1942), 13:79–100.

5. Bonney, M. E., A study of social status on the second grade level. *J. genet. Psychol.* (1942), 60:271–305.

6. Bonney, M. E., The constancy of sociometric scores and their relationship to teacher judgments of social success and to personality self-ratings. *Sociometry* (1943), 6:409–424.

7. Bonney, M. E., Sex differences in social success and personality traits. *Child Develop.* (1944), 15:63–79.

8. Bonney, M. E., Relationships between social success, family size, socio-economic home background, and intelligence among school children in grades III and IV. *Sociometry* (1944), 7:26–39.

9. Bonney, M. E., A sociometric study of the relationship of some factors to mutual friendships on the elementary, secondary, and college levels. *Sociometry* (1946), 9:21–47.

10. Bossard, J. H. S., and Sanger, M., The large family. *Am. sociol. Rev.* (1952), 17:3–9.

11. Breckenridge, M. E., and Vincent, E. L., *Child development; physical and physiological growth through the school years.* Philadelphia: Saunders, 1949.

12. Brown, A. W., Morrison, J., and Couch, G. B., Influence of affectional family relationships on character development. *J. abnorm. soc. Psychol.* (1947), 42:422–428.

13. Brown, G. D., The development of diabetic children, with special reference to mental and personality comparisons. *Child Develop.* (1938), 9:175–183.

14. Buhler, C., Smitter, F., and Richardson, S., *Childhood problems and the teacher.* New York: Holt, 1952.

15. Cameron, N., *The psychology of behavior disorders.* Boston: Houghton Mifflin, 1947.

16. Campbell, E. H., The social-sex development of children. *Genet. Psychol. Monogr.* (1939), 21:No. 4, 461–552.

17. Child, I. L., The relation of somatotype to self-ratings on Sheldon's temperamental traits. *J. Personality* (1950), 18:440–453.

18. Clark, K. B., and Clark, M. P., Racial identification and preference in Negro children, in T. M. Newcomb and E. L. Hartley (eds.), *Readings in social psychology.* New York: Holt, 1947.

19. Cobb, E. A., Family press variables. *Monogr. Soc. Res. Child Develop.* (1943), 8:327–361.

20. Dai, B., Some problems of personality development among Negro children, in C. Kluckhohn and H. A. Murray (eds.), *Personality in nature, society, and culture.* New York: Knopf, 1953, pp. 545–566.

21. Damrin, D. E., Family size and sibling age, sex, and position as related to certain aspects of adjustment. *J. soc. Psychol.* (1949), 29:93–102.

22. Davis, A., American status systems and the socialization of the child. *Am. sociol. Rev.* (1941), 6:345–354.

23. Davis, A., Child training and social class, in R. G. Barker, J. S. Kounin, and H. F. Wright (eds.), *Child behavior and development.* New York: McGraw-Hill, 1943.

24. Davis, A., *Social class influences upon learning.* Cambridge: Harvard University Press, 1948.

25. Davis, A., and Havighurst, R. J., Social class and color differences in child-rearing. *Am. sociol. Rev.* (1946), 11:698–710.

26. Davis, E. A., The development of linguistic skill in twins, singletons with siblings, and only children from age five to ten years. *Inst. Child Welfare Monogr. Ser.,* No. 14. Minneapolis: University of Minnesota Press, 1937.

27. Davis, E. A., The mental and linguistic superiority of only girls. *Child Develop.* (1937), 8:139–143.

28. Dolger, L., and Ginandes, J., Children's attitudes toward discipline as related to socio-economic status. *J. exp. Educ.* (1946), 15:161–165.

29. Dyer, D. T., Are only children different? *J. educ. Psychol.* (1945), 36:297–302.

30. England, A. O., Cultural milieu and parental identification. *Nerv. Child* (1947), 6:301–305.

31. Fenichel, O., *The psychoanalytic theory of neurosis.* New York: Norton, 1945.

32. Fenton, N., The only child. *J. genet. Psychol.* (1928), 35:546–556.

33. Field, M., Maternal attitudes found in twenty-five cases of children with primary behavior disorders. *Am. J. Orthopsychiat.* (1940), 10: 293–312.

34. Francis, K. V., A study of the means of influence of socio-economic factors upon the personality of children. *J. juv. Res.* (1933), 17:70–77.

35. Francis, K. V., and Fillmore, E. A., The influence of the environment upon the personality of children. *Univ. Iowa Stud. Welf.* (1934), 9:No. 2.

36. Gates, M. F., A comparative study of some problems of social and emotional adjustment of crippled and non-crippled girls and boys. *J. genet. Psychol.* (1946), 68:219–244.

37. Goodenough, F. L., The development of the reactive process from early childhood to maturity. *J. exp. Psychol.* (1935), 18:431–450.

38. Goodenough, F. L., and Leahy, A. M., Effects of certain family relationships upon the development of personality. *Ped. Sem.* (1927), 34:45–71.

39. Gough, H. G., The relationship of socio-economic status to personality inventory and achievement test scores. *J. educ. Psychol.* (1946), 37:527–540.

40. Guilford, R. B., and Worcester, D. A., A comparative study of the only and non-only child. *J. genet. Psychol.* (1930), 38:411–426.
41. Hardy, M. C., Aspects of home environment in relation to behavior at the elementary school age. *J. juv. Res.* (1937), 21:206–225.
42. Harrower, M. R., Social status and the moral development of the child. *Brit. J. educ. Psychol.* (1934), 4:75–95.
43. Hartley, E. L., Rosenbaum, M., and Schwartz, S., Children's use of ethnic frames of reference: An exploratory study of children's conceptualization of multiple ethnic group membership. *J. Psychol.* (1948), 26:367–386.
44. Hartley, E. L., Rosenbaum, M., and Schwartz, S., Children's perception of ethnic group membership. *J. Psychol.* (1948), 26:387–398.
45. Hartmann, H., Kris, E., and Loewenstein, R. M., Comments on the formation of psychic structure. *Psychoanal. Study of the Child* (1947), 2:11–38.
46. Hattendorf, K. W., A study of the questions of young children concerning sex: a phase of an experimental approach to parental education. *J. soc. Psychol.* (1932), 3:37–65.
47. Hattwick, B. W., and Stowell, M., The relationship of over-attentiveness to children's work habits and social adjustment in kindergarten and the first six grades of school. *J. educ. Res.* (1936), 30:169–176.
48. Havighurst, R. J., Robinson, M. Z., and Dorr, M., The development of ideal self in childhood and adolescence. *J. educ. Res.* (1946), 40:241–257.
49. Hazard, C., The relation of reflex conduction rate in the patellar reflex to age in human beings. *Univer. Iowa Stud. Child Welf.* (1936), 12:No. 1.
50. *Health bulletin for teachers.* New York: Metropolitan Life Insurance Co., November, 1949.
51. Jackson, L. A. Emotional attitudes toward the family of normal, neurotic, and delinquent children. Part I. *Brit. J. Psychol.* (1950), 41:35–51.
52. Jackson, L. A., Emotional attitudes toward the family of normal, neurotic and delinquent children. Part II. *Brit. J. Psychol.* (1950), 41:173–185.
53. Jenkins, L. M., A comparative study of motor achievements of children of five, six, and seven years of age. *Teach. Coll. Contrib. Educ.* Columbia University, 1930, No. 14.
54. Jones, H. E., *The development of physical abilities,* in Adolescence, 43rd Yearbook, Natl. Soc. Stud. Educ., Part I. Chicago: University of Chicago Press, 1944.
55. Kammerer, R. C., An exploratory study of crippled children. *Psychol. Rec.* (1940), 4:47–100.
56. Kawin, E., *Children of the preschool age.* Chicago: University of Chicago Press, 1934.
57. Kinsey, A. C., Pomeroy, W. B., and Martin, C. E., *Sexual behavior in the human male.* Philadelphia: Saunders, 1948.
58. Krout, M. H., Typical behavior patterns in twenty-six ordinal positions. *J. genet. Psychol.* (1939), 55:3–30.
59. Lerner, E., *Constraint areas and moral judgment of children.* Menasha, Wisconsin: Banta, 1937.
60. Maccoby, E. E., Gibbs, P. K., and the Staff of the Laboratory of Human Development, Harvard University, Methods of child-rearing in two social

classes, in W. E. Martin and C. B. Stendler (eds.), *Readings in child development.* New York: Harcourt, Brace, 1954, pp. 380–396.

61. MacDonald, M., McGuire, C., and Havighurst, R. J., Leisure activities and the socio-economic status of children. *Am. J. Sociol.* (1949), *54*:505–519.

62. Maddy, N. R., Comparison of children's personality traits, attitudes, and intelligence with parental occupation. *Genet. Psychol. Monogr.* (1943), *27*:1–65.

63. Macfarlane, J. W., Allen, L., and Honzik, M. P., A developmental study of the behavior problems of normal children between twenty-one months and fourteen years. *Univ. of Calif. Publications in Child Develop.*, 1954, No. 2.

64. Meltzer, H., Economic security and children's attitude to parents. *Am. J. Orthopsychiat.* (1936), *6*:590–608.

65. Merry, R. V., *Problems in the education of visually handicapped children.* Cambridge: Harvard University Press, 1933.

66. Murphy, L. B., Childhood experience in relation to personality development, in J. McV. Hunt (ed.), *Personality and the behavior disorders.* Vol. 2. New York: Ronald, 1944, pp. 652–690.

67. Mussen, P. H., Differences between the TAT responses of Negro and white boys. *J. consult. Psychol.* (1953), *17*:373–376.

68. Mussen, P. H., and Naylor, H. K., The relationships between overt and fantasy aggression. *J. abn. soc. Psychol.* (1954), *49*:235–240.

69. Newell, H. W., The psycho-dynamics of maternal rejection. *Am. J. Orthopsychiat.* (1934), *4*:387–401.

70. Newell, H. W., A further study of maternal rejection. *Am. J. Orthopsychiat.* (1936), *6*:576–588.

71. Piaget, J., *The moral judgment of the child.* London: Kegan Paul, 1932.

72. Rabban, M., Sex-role identification in young children in two diverse social groups. *Genet. Psychol. Monogr.* (1950), *42*:81–158.

73. Roberts, C. S., Ordinal position and its relation to some aspects of personality. *J. genet. Psychol.* (1938), *53*:173–213.

74. Rosenow, C., and Whyte, A. H., The ordinal position of problem children. *Am. J. Orthopsychiat.* (1931), *1*:430–434.

75. Sanford, R. N., Adkins, N. M., Miller, R. B., Cobb, E. A., et al., Physique, personality, and scholarship: a cooperative study of school children. *Monogr. Soc. Res. Child Develop.* (1943), *8*:No. 1.

76. Sears, P. S., Doll play aggression in normal young children: influence of sex, age, sibling status, father's absence. *Psychol. Monogr.* (1951), *65*(6).

77. Sears, R. R., Survey of objective studies of psychoanalytic concepts. *Soc. Sci. Res. Council Bull. 51.* New York: 1943.

78. Sheldon, W. H. (with S. S. Stevens), *The varieties of temperament.* New York: Harper, 1942.

79. Spock, B., *Pocket book of baby and child care.* New York: Pocket Books, 1946.

80. Springer, N. N., The influence of general social status on the emotional stability of children. *J. genet. Psychol.* (1938), *53*:321–328.

81. Springer, N. N., A comparative study of behavior traits of deaf and hear-

ing children in New York City. Am. Annals of the Deaf (1938), 83:255–273.

82. Springer, N. N., The influence of general social status on school children's behavior. J. educ. Res. (1939), 32:583–591.

83. Stagner, R., Economic status and personality. School and Society (1935), 42:551–552.

84. Symonds, P. M., The psychology of parent-child relationships. New York: Appleton-Century, 1939.

85. Thurstone, L. L., and Jenkins, R. L., Order of birth, parent-age, and intelligence. Chicago: University of Chicago Press, 1931.

86. Warner, W. L., and Lunt, P. S., Social life of a modern community. New Haven: Yale University Press, 1941.

87. Watson, E. H., and Lowrey, G. H., Growth and development of children. Chicago: Yearbook Publishers, 1954.

88. Wheatley, G. M., and Hallock, G. T., Health observations of school children. New York: McGraw-Hill, 1951.

89. Whiting, J. W. M., and Child, I. L., Child training and personality. New Haven: Yale University Press, 1953.

90. Wile, I. S., and Jones, A. B., Ordinal position and the behavior disorders of young children. J. genet. Psychol. (1937), 51:61–93.

Chapter 11

ADJUSTMENT TO SCHOOL

We have already seen that differences in physical status, in parent-child relationships, and in social-class or caste background all help to produce differences in personality structure and emotional adjustment during middle childhood. There are, however, other factors which also influence development during this period. One of the most important of these, and the one with which we shall be chiefly concerned in this chapter, is the school. Once a child has entered kindergarten or first grade, school becomes for more than a decade the center of his extrafamilial world, occupying almost half of his waking hours.[1]

The importance of the school's role in the child's life would be difficult to overestimate. Not only does it serve as an additional source of reinforcement for the responses which the child's parents are teaching him; it also teaches him many new responses. The number, variety, and complexity of learned responses required of adults in our culture is so great that even the most remarkable of parents could hardly accomplish the task of instilling them in their children without assistance. As one of the principal socializing agents of our society, the school is uniquely qualified to supplement parental training. By teaching the child academic skills, by broadening his store of cultural information, and by giving him supervised practice in social relationships, it makes him better able to deal comfortably with the ever-widening range of problems that lie ahead of him on the road toward adulthood.

Of course, all schools do not do this job equally well for all pupils. As we shall see, the kind of teacher the child encounters, the educational philosophy of the school, and the opportunities for recreation or for indi-

[1] Another prominent influence at this age is, of course, the peer group, largely because school brings much greater contact with peers. Specific consideration of peer relations, will, however, be reserved for the following chapter.

360

vidual attention may each influence the child's psychological development profoundly. And the picture is not a simple one. The same school
influences will not affect all children in the same ways.

A child's school adjustment will depend not only on factors in the
school situation, but, probably even more importantly, on factors which
make him a unique individual (e.g., his physical status, parent-child relationships, intelligence, and class and caste status). Hence we shall consider the influences both of differences between children, and differences
in the school situation upon school adjustment.

Courtesy, American Red Cross

School as a socializing agency. Korean war orphans.

General Demands of the School Environment

As we have previously noted, the preschool child's existence generally
proceeds in a satisfactory manner if his relationships within the family
are happy. This becomes conspicuously less true when he enters school.
He is away from home for greater periods of time and can no longer turn
immediately to his parents for solace or advice when things go wrong.
In addition, he finds (perhaps for the first time in his life) sources of

authority which are independent of his family's authority, to which he must somehow adjust.

The school beginner also soon discovers that within his class, children occupy positions of different and recognizable prestige. It is true that these prestige hierarchies in the early grades are neither so stable nor so formalized as they become in later school years. The well-structured cliques of later childhood with their elaborate rituals, badges of belonging, and rules of admission are not important in this period. Nevertheless, it soon becomes apparent to the child that some children are favored over others by their peers and by their teachers. This again is a fact to which the child must somehow adjust.

While a child is learning to make such general social adjustments, he is, of course, also confronted with the more strictly academic demands of his new environment. Gradually at first, more intensively later, he must learn to read, to write, and to count. He must learn to retain facts: how the world began, the days of the week, the seasons of the year, his country's heroic individuals and events. From field trips, movies, and classroom discussion, he must begin to acquire the first rudiments of our socioeconomic structure: what the policeman does, and the postman; how railroads function, and stores and banks and factories. As time goes on, these lessons become even more complex: how governments are organized, why laws are necessary, how health is protected. Such academic requirements as these create new problems in adjustment for the child. But, as we noted at the outset, unless the child learns to meet the demands of the school situation as they arise, he will remain unprepared for the even greater demands of adult life. The practical problem faced by the teacher, therefore, is how to help the child to meet these socialization demands without being overwhelmed by them.

Children's Attitudes Toward Beginning School

In view of the formidable adjustments that the child must make upon entering school, the question of how children react to beginning school is of considerable interest. In one study (62, 63) of this problem, 212 mothers of first-grade children were given a series of three interviews. The first of these, conducted before the child entered school, dealt with children's attitudes toward beginning school. Almost all the mothers (197 out of 212) reported that their children had favorable anticipations of school. It appeared that parents, older siblings, and neighborhood chums had given them a great deal of information about school, and this pervasive "cultural dramatization" of the event had stimulated interest and eagerness to begin. After the children had attended school for two months, the mothers were again interviewed to determine the behavioral and attitudinal changes occurring in the intervening period. An overwhelming majority (86 percent) noted definite changes in the child's self-concept and behavior after two months of school attendance. These included enhanced feelings of self-importance and bigness, manifestations of increased independence (such as dressing self, and beginning work without special instructions), and a general improvement in behavior. For example, the children were found to be more responsible, helpful, coöperative, and reasonable; better-humored and more self-controlled; and less irritable and explosive.

The third interview was held eight months after the beginning of school. Mothers were asked to compare their children's behavior with what it had been before they went to school and to rate them as displaying more, equal, or less maturity, self-control, helpfulness, responsibility, patience, obedience, self-confidence, and ability to get along with playmates. An analysis of the data showed that most mothers felt that their children had improved significantly in all these traits with the exception of obedience and patience. From the point of view of ease of handling the child, only 14 percent of the mothers said that it had been a more trying year than the preceding one. Almost 60 percent said it was easier. These impressions may, of course, have been partly due to the fact that once the children were in school, their mothers had to handle them fewer hours a day. Furthermore, since no control group of like-age children who stayed at home was available for comparison, we cannot be sure how much the children's behavior might have improved without school, as the result of maturational and other environmental influences.

Nevertheless, it may be concluded that entry into school was eagerly anticipated and approached by most children, and it seems likely that school did promote more mature behavior. Improvements in personality characteristics and behavior were noted within the first two months and endured at least throughout the first year of school.

But while reactions to school were generally positive, the picture was not entirely blissful. For example, although 92 percent of the children in this study were reported to like school, 42 percent criticized both the school and teacher, and 39 percent occasionally did not want to go to school within the first two months. Obviously, all children did not react to school in the same way.

These findings suggest that although most children like school, the degree of liking varies considerably. Also there appears to be an important minority which finds the first few months of school at least occasionally a disturbing experience. These studies do not, of course, tell us why there are individual differences in school adjustment. This question demands an understanding of both of the personal and environmental factors involved. Let us begin by considering the personal factors first, since they have their roots deep in the child's preschool life.

PHYSICAL DEVELOPMENT, DEFECT, AND DISEASE IN RELATION TO SCHOOL ADJUSTMENT

We have already noted that variations in rates of physical development and in general health may be related to the child's social and emotional adjustment in the middle years. But are they also related specifically to school adjustment? For example, do handicapped children in fact receive poorer grades than their physically normal peers, as might be expected? Are they seen as special problems by their teachers? Do children with good general health perform better on school tasks than their less healthy peers?

A number of studies have investigated the relationship between physical development, defect, and disease, on the one hand, and measures of academic achievement and intelligence on the other. (As we shall see later, intelligence as measured by standard intelligence tests is closely related to success in school work.)

Physical Development, Intelligence, and Academic Success

It is well known that in certain types of mental deficiency such as cretinism, the arrested physical growth is accompanied by mental retardation. There also seems to be a slight relationship between physical and mental development among physically normal children (41). In two of the best studies in this area, positive relationships were obtained between intelligence and a number of physical measures at all ages from 2 to 17 years (1, 10). These correlations were not large, however, the greatest (between height and I.Q. of boys) being only .26. Intellectually gifted children tended to be superior throughout the growth period in physical development (height, weight, age of walking, and general health), and also in school grades and achievement test scores (66, 67, 69).

Positive relationships between physical status and intelligence may be explained in a number of ways. For example, it is possible that intelligence and development are positively correlated because they are both the result of the same genetic factors. It is also possible, however, that environmental factors such as a well-to-do home background may favor both superior intellectual performance and greater physical development (i.e., better diet, medical care, etc.). The child from such a home may have a better chance on intelligence tests, because of his cultural advantages. At the same time he may also have a superior physical development because of better diet, more sanitary living conditions, and better medical care.

Whatever their sources, it seems that within the normal range there are slight, but nevertheless statistically significant relationships between such physical measures as height and weight, and such academic measures as school grades, and achievement and intelligence scores.

Physical Defect and Disease in Relation to Academic Success

Several investigators (9, 41, 51) have demonstrated an inverse relationship between physical defect, disease, or nutritional deficiency and school achievement. One researcher (9) divided 3304 school children into three groups, on the basis of academic achievement: bright, normal, dull. Percentage incidence for physical defects for each group was then computed. The results are shown in Table 4 (9). As may be seen, the average number of defects per child is greatest among children with the poorest achievement.

TABLE 4. Percentage Incidence of Physical Defects in Three Groups (9)

	Bright	Normal	Dull
Defective teeth	34	40	42
Adenoids	6	10	15
Enlarged tonsils	12	19	26
Enlarged Glands	6	13	20
Defective breathing	9	11	15
Defective vision	29	25	24
Other defects	11	11	21
Average number of defects per child	1.07	1.30	1.65

Similar results have been found by other investigators. In one study (51), the relationship between average I.Q. at a number of schools in New York City and the percentage of students in each school having various physical defects was investigated. The subjects were fifth-grade children. Negative relationships between I.Q. and physical defects were found when school averages were compared ($-.50$ for defective teeth $-.40$ for visual defect, and $-.28$ for malnutrition).

Such results as these demonstrate that physical defect and poor general health tend to be associated with lowered school achievement. Again however, they do not establish that the relationship is a causal one. It has been found, for example, that children from lower socioeconomic groups tend both to have a higher incidence both of inadequate health and poor school progress. Thus it is possible that the negative relationships obtained between defect or disease and school achievement may not stem from the handicapping effect of the condition itself. Instead, both the defect or disease and the poor school progress may be functions of membership in a lower socioeconomic class, with its poorer conditions of diet and hygiene, and its cultural discouragement of school success. It is also possible that hereditary incapacity for learning may be more frequent in lower socioeconomic classes, and may lead to poorer school performance. This is at least a possibility in a culture like our own where a considerable degree of social mobility (i.e., improving or worsening one's socioeconomic condition) is possible.

Support for the hypothesis that social-class variables may be largely responsible for obtained relationships between defect or disease and intelligence may be gained from other studies in this area. In general, they indicate that when socioeconomic factors are controlled (i.e., by studying the effects of variations in health within each social class), impressive correlations between physical condition and intelligence tend to disappear. Thus it appears likely that defect and intellectual achievement tend to covary, not so much because one determines the other, but rather because both are the result of factors associated with social class.

An exception to this general conclusion appears in the case of markedly defective and severely undernourished children who, regardless of their social-class background, tend to perform more poorly on intelligence and achievement tests. In one ingenious investigation, the effects of nutritional status on achievement were studied experimentally (28). The subjects, 110 children in a Virginia orphanage, were divided into two groups of 55 each, carefully matched for sex, height, weight, length of residence in the orphanage, educational achievement, and intelligence test scores. The diet of one group was then supplemented by feeding them 2 milligrams of vitamin B-1 (thiamin) daily in tablet form. The other group received tablets of no nutritional value. The children themselves had no way of knowing whether they were receiving vitamins or not. Nevertheless, at the end of one year, the group receiving thiamin was significantly better than the control group in a number of measures, such as reading achievement, memorizing of new materials, and general educational progress. Thus, in this instance, improved nutritional status clearly resulted in academic progress. However, since we do not know the initial nutritional levels of these children, we cannot say with any certainty whether these results support the general finding that only marked deficiencies in diet affect achievement (70).

Summary

In viewing the multitude of research studies in this general area, several facts seem to stand out: (1) Relationships have been found between a number of physical measures (such as height, weight, disease, defect, or malnutrition) and the child's adjustment to school. (2) While in some cases these relationships may partly reflect the influence of the child's physical condition upon his behavior, in most cases they also indicate that other factors are at work, producing covariation of both physical and psychological measures. Several of the more important among these factors, such as genetic influence, socioeconomic status, and home background will be discussed at greater length later.

INTELLECTUAL DEVELOPMENT IN RELATION TO SCHOOL ACHIEVEMENT

With the beginning of school all children in our culture begin to be compared to one another with respect to a wide range of human abilities, aptitudes, and personality traits. Parents and others may have noted prior to this time that a particular child walked, talked, or was toilet-trained sooner than other children. Casual observations that one child appeared friendlier, more aggressive, brighter, or more handsome than his peers may also have been made.

But only with entrance to the first grade do such comparisons become an explicit part of our culture, affecting the welfare of all children. The explicit character of these comparisons is reflected by grades in academic subjects; ratings of physical prowess; marks for effort, interest or personality traits; and by health records, dealing with physical disease and defect.

In the last chapter, we noted that often gross impairment of vision, hearing, or available energy may not be picked up until after a child enters school. No doubt this may be attributed partly to the fact that the parents' standards are less rigorous than those of the school. But it may also be attributed partly to the individual parent's lack of comparative yardsticks with which to evaluate his ability, and partly to habituation. Johnny's defective vision may lead to squinting, to a perplexed manner, even to bumping into things at times. To the teacher or school nurse such symptoms may suggest impaired vision. To Johnny's mother they may just seem like Johnny acting his natural self.

For similar reasons, the topic of intelligence assumes major importance in the eyes of parents about the time their children begin school. Johnny's retarded or precocious intellectual ability is likely to be taken for granted by his parents until he starts school. Then suddenly it becomes for them "something" which Johnny has more or less of than his peers, something which spells future ease or difficulty in school achievement, something which leads to society's (i.e., the teacher's) approval, disapproval, or anxious concern.

As a result, the parent suddenly develops an interest in various problems of intellectual functioning. "What," he begins to ask, "do you actually mean by the term intelligence?" "What does an I.Q. of 80 mean?" "Can you tell whether a 6-year-old child will be able to go to college when he grows up?" "Does heredity play an important role in intelligence?" "How good are I.Q. tests anyway?" All of these are legitimate questions, and their answer is not simple, even for the specialist in psychological measurement.

The Meaning of Intelligence

Let us consider briefly the first of these questions, "What do we actually mean by the term intelligence?"

It is characteristic of people to think that because many words stand for *things*, that all words necessarily do. The idea is nevertheless false. Many words, such as the concepts of time and force in physics, are simply useful scientific fictions (i.e., hypothetical constructs) which help us to explain observable events. But they do not stand for objects, or classes of objects, in the way many other words, such as trees and chairs, do.

In the same way, no one has ever seen, heard or touched *intelligence*. It too is a scientific fiction which we invent because it helps us to explain and predict behavior.

The layman makes judgments about intelligence from observations of everyday behavior. For example, two boys may be in the habit of playing in a neighbor's yard. The neighbor hears that one of them is a good student in school, the other a poor one. She also observes that if she asks the "good student" to go to the store for her, he always remembers to bring home all the items she asks for; the other boy is likely to forget several items. Furthermore, she hears the boys playing counting games, or discussing the way in which various objects are made, and watches them as they go about their various activities. The same child always seems to do better. From this she concludes the one child is more "intelligent" than the other.

It can be seen from the above example that since intelligence is inferred from overt behavior, and since different individuals may choose to make their inferences from different kinds of overt behavior, there is no absolute or "true" definition of intelligence. The word may be defined in terms of the preferences of the individual doing the defining. For example, Terman, an American pioneer of mental testing and developer of the Stanford-Binet Intelligence Test for children, chose to define intelligence as an individual's ability to carry out abstract thinking, to use abstract symbols in the solution of all kinds of problems (68).

On the other hand, Wechsler, inventor of the widely employed Wechsler-Bellevue Intelligence Scales for children and adults, preferred to define intelligence as "the aggregate or global capacity of the individual to act purposefully, to think rationally, and to deal effectively with his environment" (71). Nevertheless, the definitions of most psychologists tend to be rather similar. In general most psychologists would agree with Goodenough that intelligence involves the "ability to profit by experience . . . in order to adjust to new situations" (24). They have often disagreed, however, about the proper selection of items to measure these abilities. The reasons for these arguments may be clarified by a discussion of the actual methods of constructing intelligence tests, and of their uses and limitations.

The Construction of Intelligence Tests

Intelligence testing had its real beginning in Paris in 1904, and evolved out of practical necessity. At that time:

The schools of Paris became concerned about their many non-learners and decided to remove the hopelessly feebleminded to a school where they would not be held to the standard curriculum. Aware of the errors in teacher judgment, they wished to avoid segregating the child of good potentiality who could learn if he tried and the trouble-making child whom the teacher wanted to be rid of. Moreover, they wished to identify all the dull from good families whom teachers might hesitate to rate low, and the dull with pleasant personalities who would be favored by the teacher. Therefore they asked Alfred Binet, a prominent French psychologist, to assist in producing a method for separating the genuinely dull from those who had adequate educability. The Binet Scale, which drew on his earlier studies, was published in collaboration with Simon in 1905. In 1909 a revision was published. The tests were arranged in order of difficulty so that a child passing those tests normally passed by ten-year-olds could be considered their mental equal in average performance. Still another revision was produced in 1911. The Binet Scale, as it stood then, differs only in detail from the individual tests for children in widest use today. (*19*, 103).

Probably the most widely used intelligence test for children at present is the Stanford-Binet, a revision of the earlier Binet test produced in 1916, and modified in 1937 by Lewis Terman and Maud Merrill of Stanford University. There have been several other revisions of the Binet Scale, but Terman's has proved the most fruitful. A discussion of the construction of the scale should serve to give us some insight into the construction of intelligence tests generally.

Construction of the Binet Scale

Binet did not start with a preconceived idea of an entity called intelligence. He started with the fact that on a number of kinds of tasks, some children seemed capable of doing better than others. He further observed that children who did better on one type of test were also likely to do better on others. From these observations he derived a generalized concept of intelligent behavior. He also assumed that individuals differed in their innate capacity for such behavior. His job was to find measures of intelligent behavior which were relatively independent of special training and experiences, and differences in motivation; and which would therefore reflect differences in native potential. An additional requirement of the job was to arrive at objective scores which would show the relative ranks of individuals on a continuum from bright to dull.

Selecting Test Items

In selecting items to differentiate bright from dull individuals, Binet and his successors were guided by several considerations:

1. Since mental ability presumably increases with age, a good test item should be one that is passed more frequently by older children than by younger ones. With this consideration in mind, potential test items were tried out by actually determining the percentage of children at each age level that could pass them. Figure 27 shows the results for an actual item, A, which was retained in the 1937 Stanford-Binet revision, and an imaginary item B which would have been eliminated. It may be seen that item A is a good item according to this criterion, since an increasing number of children are able to pass it with each increasing age level.

Item B, however, fails to discriminate significantly between younger and older children. Such an item would be thrown out as unrelated to the growth of mental ability (*19*).

2. Since Binet and his successors were interested in finding a generalized measure of intelligence, they felt that a good item was one that correlated highly with other items. Item A in the example above correlated .91 with total intelligence test score for 13-year-olds.

3. A number of other considerations employed in selecting items are cited by Terman in his discussion of the 1937 revision of the Binet (*68*):

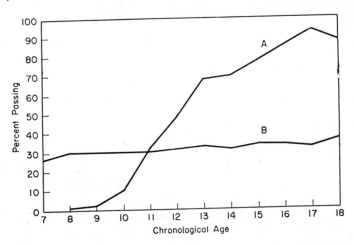

FIGURE 27. Percentage of children of each age passing two intelligence test items. A is an actual Stanford-Binet (*68*) of the year XIII level. B is an imaginary item which fails to discriminate between older and younger children. (After L. J. Cronbach, *Essentials of Psychological Testing*. New York: Harper, 1949.)

The test items should be reasonably easy to administer and score. They should sample a wide variety of tasks, so as to be representative of general ability, and, in so far as possible, they should reflect cultural experiences common to all children.

Items which meet the above criteria are then placed in the scale "according to their difficulty for children at each age. A test item which about 60 percent of 13-year-olds can pass is placed at year 13 on the scale" (*19*). Thus, item A in Figure 27 was placed at year 13.

The final form of the Stanford-Binet includes a wide variety of items, including measures of information and past learning, verbal ability, visual-motor coördination, memory, perception, and logical reasoning.

For example, at the sixth year level, the child is asked to define a number of words, such as orange, envelope, and puddle; to copy a chain of 7 different shaped beads; to find missing details in pictures; to count up to 9 blocks; to note similarities and differences in pictured objects; and to trace the correct path through a maze. (For sample test items at an earlier age level, see p. 226).

Administration and Scoring of the Binet

After establishing a comfortable relationship with the child to be tested, the examiner begins with items which are below the expected level of the child and gradually proceeds to those of greater difficulty.

The test is scored in terms of mental age, determined as follows: First, *a basal mental age* is established. This is the year level on the scale at which the child can pass all the test items. For example, a 10-year-old who passed all the items scaled at year 9, but failed some items at year 10, would receive a basal mental age of 9 years. The examiner would then proceed to add to this basal age when items of higher levels are passed. The amount added will depend on the total number of higher items correctly answered. The examiner stops when he reaches an age level at which all items are failed. To illustrate, if the 9-year-old in the above example passed half the items at year 10, one-fourth of the items at year 11, and no items at year 12, he would receive six months credit at year 10, three months credit at year 11, and zero months credit at year 12. Adding these scores to his basal age, he would receive an overall mental age of 9 years, plus 6 months, plus 3 months, or 9 years 9 months.

Since the particular items a child is given on the Binet will depend on the range of his ability, the same items are not given to all children. The test has been developed to cover the years from 2 to adulthood. While some of the items given normal 4- and 5-year-olds would overlap, normal 5- and 12-year-olds would be given completely different items.

Intelligence Quotients

We have already mentioned the term Intelligence Quotient, or I.Q. On the Binet the I.Q. is simply a ratio of mental age over chronological age multiplied by 100:

$$\text{I.Q.} = \frac{MA}{CA} \times 100$$

Thus a child of 10 years zero months who obtained a mental age of 10 years zero months on the Binet would be given a score of 10.0×100, or

$$\overline{10.0}$$

an I.Q. of 100. It can be seen that an I.Q. of 100 will be characteristic of the average child from the group on which the test is based. The 10-year-old previously described, whose mental age was 9 years 9 months, would receive an I.Q. of $\frac{9.75 \times 100}{10}$, or 97.5.

DISTRIBUTION OF I.Q.'s. Figure 28 shows the distribution of I.Q. scores for the population used in standardizing the Stanford-Binet. As may be seen, the distribution centers around I.Q. 100, with higher and lower I.Q.'s about equally common. Table 5 shows the percentage of individuals at each I.Q. level, and is probably the most helpful guide to understanding the meaning of a particular score.

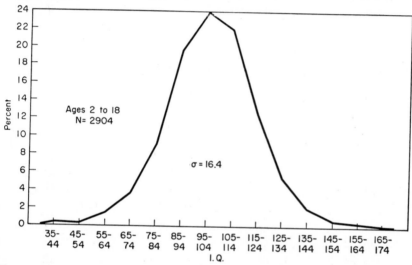

FIGURE 28.   Distribution of I.Q.'s in the Terman-Merrill standardization group.

CONSTANCY OF THE I.Q.   The practical utility of an intelligence test score will depend partly upon its stability or constancy; that is, upon its ability to yield similar scores on future retestings. How confidently can we predict that a child who obtains a superior score at one age will also obtain a comparable score at a later age? It will be recalled that tests given to infants under 2 have little value for the prediction of future intelligence scores (cf. pp. 181–182). Tests given to older children are more highly predictive (cf. pp. 226–227).

Table 6 shows the correlations between intelligence test scores during the middle childhood years and at ages 10 and 18. As may be seen, during the middle school years, the correlation between Stanford-Binet test scores given one or two years apart (for example, at ages 8 or 9, and

TABLE 5. The Meaning of Various I.Q.'s Obtained with the Revised Stanford-Binet Scale [a]

The child whose I.Q. is:	Is equaled or excelled by
160	1 out of 10,000
156	3 out of 10,000
152	8 out of 10,000
148	2 out of 1,000
144	4 out of 1,000
140	7 out of 1,000

The child whose I.Q. Is:	Equals or Exceeds	The child whose I.Q. Is:	Equals or Exceeds
136	99 percent	98	45 percent
135	98	97	43
134	98	96	40
133	98	95	38
132	97	94	36
131	97	93	34
130	97	92	31
129	96	91	29
128	96	90	27
127	95	89	25
126	94	88	23
125	94	87	21
124	93	86	20
123	92	85	18
122	91	84	16
121	90	83	15
120	89	82	14
119	88	81	12
118	86	80	11
117	85	79	10
116	84	78	9
115	82	77	8
114	80	76	8
113	79	75	6
112	77	74	6
111	75	73	5
110	73	72	4
109	71	71	4
108	69	70	3
107	66	69	3

[a] Reprinted from *Supplementary Guide for the Revised Stanford-Binet Scale* (Form L) by Rudolph Pintner, Anna Dragositz, and Rose Kushner. With permission of the Stanford University Press.

TABLE 5. The Meaning of Various I.Q.'s Obtained with the Revised Stanford-Binet Scale [a] (*Continued*)

106	64	68	3
105	62	67	2
104	60	66	2
103	57	65	2
102	55		
101	52	64	1
100	50	63	1
99	48	62	1

again at 10) is very high (around .90). Moreover, tests given during this period are fairly good predictors of intellectual status in early adulthood (age 18). Nevertheless, despite the fact that the I.Q. becomes more stable at later ages, we must be cautious in using test scores for predicting the future status of individual children, since "the correlations are not sufficiently high so that the possibility of marked changes in the I.Q.'s of individual children is precluded" (36). Repeated testings of a large group of children between the ages of 6 and 18 revealed that the I.Q. of over half the children "showed a variation of 15 or more points . . . at some time during the school years, and a third of the group varied as much as 20 points . . ." (36).

THE USEFULNESS OF I.Q.'s. What do we actually know when a child obtains an I.Q. of, for example, 132 on the Stanford-Binet? At the very least, we know that he can do the items on this test better than 97 percent (see Table 5) of the large group of persons of his age on whom the

TABLE 6. Correlations Between Stanford-Binet I.Q. During the Middle Childhood Years and I.Q. at Ages 10 and 18 (Wechsler-Bellevue) [a]

Ages	N	Correlation with I.Q. at Age 10	Correlation with I.Q. at Age 18
6	214	.76	.61
7	208	.78	.71
8	199	.88	.70
9	90	.90	.76
10	107	—	.70
12	92	.87	.76

[a] After (36). With permission of *Journal of Experimental Education*.

test was standardized. And we know that these items are probably representative of a large variety of tasks commonly met by people in their daily lives. In this sense, the authors of the test feel justified in calling it a measure of *general intelligence*. But how useful is such knowledge? Few teachers, for example, are particularly interested in whether a child can do the particular tasks on the Binet. They want to know if he will be able to do satisfactory work in reading, writing, and arithmetic.

The only way of settling the question is by examination of the actual relationship between I.Q. and school success. In general, I.Q. scores have been found to be fairly good predictors of academic performance. One investigator (*11*), for example, lists the following correlations between the Stanford-Binet Intelligence Test and school grades:

I.Q. and reading comprehension	.73
I.Q. and reading speed	.43
I.Q. and English usage	.59
I.Q. and history	.59
I.Q. and biology	.54
I.Q. and geometry	.48

Part of the fairly high relationship between school success and I.Q. scores has been attributed by some investigators to the similarity of the kinds of behavior measured in both cases. And indeed, when it comes to predicting success in less academic fields, such as mechanical trades, music, and art, the intelligence test does a much less adequate job.

Other Types of Intelligence Tests

Next to the Binet, the Wechsler Intelligence Scale for Children, or WISC (*73*), is probably the most frequently used test for older children. The I.Q.'s for children from 5 through 15 years may be derived from this test. While on the Binet children are given different items at the various age levels, on the WISC the items are the same for children of all ages. Also on the WISC, mental age is not used in deriving an I.Q. Instead the child's performance is compared with that of other children in his own age group. His I.Q. is merely a function of his percentile rank in comparison with his peers. To illustrate, let us say that a child of 6 obtains a WISC I.Q. of 79. This simply means (if one consults the appropriate table in the WISC manual) that this child has done better on the test than about 10 percent of 6-year-olds in the standardization group and less well than about 90 percent. Despite differences in method of computation, however, Binet and WISC I.Q.'s tend to be highly correlated (*56*). In general, the WISC is somewhat easier to administer and score than the Binet. Which of these two tests (if either) will ultimately prove more fruitful must await future research.

FIGURE 29. Administering the Wechsler Intelligence Scale for Children. (With permission of The Psychological Corporation.)

GROUP TESTS OF INTELLIGENCE. The intelligence tests described thus far must be individually administered. There are, however, a number of group tests available for use by teachers and others. Such tests have the advantages that they do not require intensive training to administer, and that they are economical of time.

On the other hand, they also have serious limitations. The results they yield are not so useful for prediction as those from individual tests administered by a skilled clinician. Practical decisions about children who deviate on these tests should not be made without individual follow-up testing by a competent psychologist, together with an investigation of other factors within the individual's life which may be affecting his performance (including his general health and sensory functioning). Too frequently erroneous diagnoses of mental deficiency have been made on the basis of low scores on group intelligence tests.

Criticism of Current Intelligence Test Practices

While intellectual functioning may be influenced by hereditary factors (cf. pp. 46–47), this does not mean that a person's score on an intelli-

gence test is a direct measure of his native capacity. Unfortunately, however, many people seem to think that it is. Such a process of reasoning
has serious practical implications. It may lead a teacher to lose interest
in a child who receives a low score on an I.Q. test, while concentrating
all her efforts on "bringing out the best" in the high-scoring child who
she thinks has greater "potentialities for development."

Such practices have recently come in for bitter attack from Davis,
Havighurst, and others (21, 31, 32). Davis points out that intelligence
can be inferred only from the specific "mental acts" which constitute the
pupil's responses to intelligence-test problems. And these mental acts in
turn will be a function, not only of an individual's heredity, but also of:

C— Cultural phenomena, involved in the pupil's degree of experience, in his
family or play-group, with that particular social environment which determines
both the content and the symbols of the test problem.

C—1 Training phenomena in school and home, involving more specific,
repetitive, and purposeful experience with cultural situations and symbols
which are closely related to the test-problem.

C—2 Cultural motivational phenomena, or "drives," those rewards and
punishments which exist at a level sufficient to impel a pupil to use his full
pattern of activities to solve a test problem.

S— The phenomena of speed, which are complex functions of (1) the hereditary factors, (2) the physical condition and stamina of the testee at the particular time, (3) his cultural habits of work, (4) his familiarity with the
cultural form and content of the problem, and (5) his previous experience or
training with this specific type of problem.

The relative success of two persons in solving a given problem, therefore,
depends not simply upon their hereditary equipment but also upon their relative familiarity with the cultural situations and symbols in the problem, their
relative degree of training with similar problems, and the relative strength of
their motivation. The factor of time may or may not be involved, depending
upon whether the test is a "speed" test or not (21).

Thus, as Davis points out, if an intelligence test is going to be used to
make inferences about the basic potentialities of individuals, the cultural
elements in the problems employed must be equalized. In Davis' opinion,
current test makers have not succeeded in doing this. He feels, for example, that in many instances the kinds of items selected for inclusion on
intelligence tests are likely to be more familiar to middle-class children
than to their lower-class peers, and are likely to appeal to them more.
Thus he feels that intelligence tests unduly penalize lower-class children.

In a systematic effort to determine the nature of social-class differences
in test responses on intelligence tests, Davis and Havighurst and their
associates (21) administered a variety of intelligence tests to all children

aged 9, 13, and 14 in a large midwestern city. The socioeconomic status of each pupil's family was also determined, by means of an objective index (21). It was found that a large proportion of the items in each of the intelligence tests discriminated between children from the highest and lowest socioeconomic levels, the latter passing a smaller percentage of items. Table 7 shows the percentage of items on each of the tests which showed a socioeconomic differential.

Davis feels that the way these social-class differences are distributed among the items supports his hypothesis of a cultural bias in the items employed. He notes that the items which were selected for these tests

TABLE 7. Percentage of Items on Various Intelligence Tests Discriminating Between High and Low Socioeconomic Groups [a]

| Test | Number of Pupils | | Percentage of Items Showing Socioeconomic Differential |
	High Socioeconomic Group	Low Socioeconomic Group	
Tests given to 9- and 10-year-old pupils			
Henmon-Nelson	226	322	93%
Otis Alpha (nonverbal)	223	316	46%
Otis Alpha (verbal)	223	326	70%
Kuhlmann-Anderson (Grade III)	225	327	56%
Kuhlmann-Anderson (Grade VI)	225	321	85%
Tests given to 13- and 14-year-old pupils			
Terman-McNemar	223	361	100%
Otis Beta	235	364	91%
California Mental Maturity	235	352	69%
Thurstone Spatial	235	352	84%
Thurstone Reasoning	232	358	100%

[a] From Davis (21). With permission of Harvard University Press.

tend to emphasize "only those types of mental behaviors in which the higher and middle socioeconomic groups are superior" (21), such as linguistic skill. And even in the items selected to measure these skills, the specific content is more likely to be familiar to upper-class socioeconomic groups. For example, Davis discusses two items from one of the tests in the above study. On one of these items, 78 percent of the pupils in the higher socioeconomic group answered the item correctly, but only 28 percent of the pupils of the lower group did so—a difference of 46 percentage in points. On the second item, the percentage answering the items correctly was practically identical for both socioeconomic groups. The content of these two items suggested to Davis the reason for the great variation in their socioeconomic differential: "The first item required the pupil to be familiar with the term 'sonata,' a word which will clearly be heard more often in the home in the higher socioeconomic brackets than in a family from the lower socioeconomic group. The second item, on the contrary, required the pupil to apply the concept of a 'cutting tool' so as to distinguish between this type and several other types of implements. Both the tools and the other implements are common to all socioeconomic groups" (21).

According to Davis, the poorer performance of lower-class children on these tests is attributable not only to a cultural bias in the selection of items, but also to lesser motivation to do well in school or in school-type tasks, such as achievement and intelligence tests (cf. pp. 382–387).

In addition to these broad cultural influences, there are also many other factors which may serve to deflate or inflate an individual's intelligence test scores. Among these are a child's emotional status, temporary illness, mental disorder, brain damage, and special abilities which a test either unduly emphasizes or ignores. For example, one of the authors recently tested an 8-year-old boy who was being evaluated by a welfare agency for adoptive purposes. This child had been physically and psychologically neglected by his mother from birth, and was finally removed from her custody by the welfare agency when he was 6 years old. At this time, he was tested by a psychologist and obtained an I.Q. of 51. Subsequently he was placed in the care of warm and understanding foster parents, and given good physical and psychological care. Two years later when he was retested, he obtained an I.Q. of 100. Apparently the child's deprived state at the time of the original testing adversely affected his performance. When his life circumstances improved, his test scores also improved.

Similarly, in one study of the constancy of children's I.Q.'s it was found that "children whose mental test scores showed the most marked fluctuations had like histories which showed unusual variations with respect to disturbing and stabilizing factors" (36).

Tests of Reading Readiness

There is another group of tests which deserve mention in connection with a discussion of children's intelligence and school adjustment; namely, tests of so-called "reading readiness" (19, 54, 55). While not in themselves measures of intelligence, the readiness tests correlate quite highly with I.Q. scores (52). They have been designed, however, for a much more specific purpose, namely, to gauge the proper time for the child to begin reading instruction, and also to detect possible difficulties which may be holding the child back in learning to read. These aims have been achieved remarkably well, and for this reason the tests have been widely adopted in elementary school programs. Parents are likely to hear a good deal about readiness tests at the time their children are beginning school.

The Reading Aptitude Tests (Primary Form) designed by Marion Munroe (55) will serve to illustrate the contents of readiness tests in general. Included in her battery are visual tests (designed to measure orientation of forms, ocular-motor control, and visual memory), auditory tests (including measures of pronunciation, discrimination of sounds, and auditory memory), language tests, articulation tests, and tests of motor skills (including both speed and steadiness).

From an overall knowledge of a child's competence in these basic skills, it is possible to establish with considerable accuracy how well the child will do in learning to read. Table 8 shows the relationship between readiness test scores and subsequent achievement in reading obtained in one study.

TABLE 8. Predictive Value of Monroe Reading Aptitude Tests [a]

| | Percent of Children Who Became | | |
Composite total percentile score on aptitude tests	Superior readers (upper quartile of reading tests)	Average readers (middle half of reading tests)	Inferior readers (lower quartile of reading tests)
90	100%	0%	0%
80	100	0	0
70	42	50	8
60	31	56	12
50	24	67	10
40	8	46	46
30	0	12	88
20	0	25	75
10	0	0	100
0	0	0	100

[a] From Monroe (54). With permission of Houghton Mifflin Co.

Like tests of general intelligence, reading readiness tests have proved their value. As in the case of intelligence tests, performance on reading readiness tests may be influenced by a wide variety of factors, ranging from heredity to socioeconomic status. For example, in one study Milner (52) found that children from the lower socioeconomic class tended to do more poorly on a first-grade reading readiness test than upper-class children. Milner attributed the results to cultural differences in practice and reward of related behavior. For example, the predominantly upper-class "high scorers" tended to engage in considerable two-way conversation with their families at breakfast, before school, and at supper. They were also the recipients of a good deal of overt affection from their parents. The "low scorers," on the other hand, did not characteristically eat breakfast with their parents, engaged in little conversation before school, and did not participate in two-way conversations at supper time. It seems likely that differences in background experience, such as greater encouragement of verbal accomplishment in the upper-class, play an important role in the lower reading potential of lower-class, as compared with upper-class children.

Thus reading readiness tests must be employed in a flexible fashion, with full awareness of the kinds of factors which may affect the scores obtained. It should not be automatically assumed that a child from an extremely deprived cultural background is incapable of learning to read, simply because he fails a reading readiness test.

SOCIOECONOMIC STATUS AND SCHOOL ACHIEVEMENT

Parental Rewards for School Achievement

Middle-class parents typically display marked interest in the child's reports of his school activities, praise him for his first stumbling attempts at reading, and may even provide more tangible rewards, in the form of movies, bicycles, or spending money, for school success. Furthermore, as he grows older, the middle- and upper-class child is able to see for himself the delayed rewards to which academic skills may lead, by noting the important part they play in the success of his doctor-father, his businessman-uncle, or his accountant-older brother. Of course, we would not expect these distantly anticipated rewards to be very effective if the child's immediate experiences were punishing, but when these latter are favorable, the prospects of additional future rewards may provide increased impetus for the child to do well in school.

Parental interest in the school is much less common among the lower socioeconomic groups. Upper-middle-class parents are great believers in education as the solution to many problems—economic, social, and personal. Lower-middle- and upper-lower-class parents tend to look upon school merely as a way of getting children ready for adulthood (*31, 32*). They are not great believers in education *per se*, but see it as necessary for vocational success. Nevertheless all these groups to some degree reinforce the value of school because they expect the school to do something for their children (*62*). In sharp contrast, lower-lower-class parents tend to be distrustful and suspicious of the school, and rejecting of its values.

Several factors seem to us to be meaningfully related to the more positive attitudes toward academic success shown by children and parents of the higher socioeconomic group.

For one thing, the school child's social-class identification tends to be strong (cf. p. 434), and threats to his membership status in a particular social class will be tremendously anxiety-producing. School success is much more important in maintaining class membership in the higher classes than in the lower, and consequently middle- and upper-class children will be more motivated to achieve it. They see that the kinds of jobs to which they and other members of their social class aspire depend heavily on the acquisition of academic skills. Obviously school success is much more important to the future banker, lawyer, or business executive than it is to the laborer or farm hand.

Moreover, upper- and middle-class parents are likely to encourage their children to apply themselves in school, because of their genuine interest in the child's happiness, and because of the threat to their own social status of having a child who "couldn't make the grade." In addition, parents of any class may desire to have their children *improve* their social status over their own. The school may provide the best route for social mobility, not only because it increases academic skills, but because it offers an opportunity for imitation of higher-class children (*21*).

Finally, parental attitudes toward school may be influenced by economic considerations. Lower-class parents may more often fail to encourage a child to set ambitious educational goals, since they feel that they will be unable to keep the child in school long enough to achieve them.

Of course, even within the various socioeconomic classes there are wide differences in attitudes toward education. A particular low-income family may make great financial sacrifices in order to provide for a child's education, while a particular middle-income family may be unwilling even to forego luxuries for this purpose. In families with a marginal level of subsistence, however, even great sacrifices may not provide enough money for a child's continued education.

Minority-Group Status and Parental Attitudes Toward School

Socioeconomic differences in parental attitudes toward school are not restricted to the white, native-born majority group in our culture. Social-class differences and attitudes seem to cut across racial and other minority-group lines. For example, Davis and Dollard (22) have shown that among middle-class Negroes in the South, the concern of parents for their child's scholastic success, and consequently their approval of responses in this direction are, if anything, stronger than among middle-class whites. The following comments of a middle-class Negro child are characteristic of their findings: "My mama even made me go to school the morning of the Mardi Gras. If it is raining hard and we say we are sick, we still got to go, if we have to go barefoot. A son of a friend of my mama's quit school and got married, and my mama is still lecturing on it." The mother herself stated, "One thing we are trying to do is bring all our girls up to be nice and decent, and get them a good education, so they can be somebody" (22).

Other middle-class children and their mothers made similar comments to the investigators in this study: "Because of my own educational background, and my husband's profession, I tell my children they have no excuse not to do well in school." "Even if I have to go out and work, I won't let my children stop school" (22).

On the other hand, Negro parents of the lower socioeconomic class seem even more pessimistic about the advantages of education for their children than lower-class white parents. Davis and Dollard (22) point out that the parents and teachers of the lower-class Negro child both realize that the child's chances of improving his social position are slight. Because of his discriminatory caste position as a Negro, few jobs are available in the broad middle range between laborer and professional person; and because of his family's economic status the chances of achieving professional status by finishing high school and college are remote. This realization, of course, is conveyed to the children. They learn that "the faster and surer ways to be socially mobile are to learn to tap dance, to box, to sing, or to play dance music" (22).

Peer-Group Influences on Motivation

As we have already seen, one of the pressing needs of school children is to gain acceptance by their peers. Depending upon the particular values of the peer group, the child's motivation for scholastic success may be either strengthened or reduced. In many middle- and upper-class groups, scholastic success—or at least the absence of scholastic failure—is positively valued and explicitly rewarded, not only by teachers and parents, but by the children themselves. Thus, in a number of studies involving primarily middle-class children (*12, 13*), for example, the children who were most popular in school were better students and were more conforming and coöperative. Lower-class, and particularly slum children are not likely to be rewarded either by parents or peers for scholastic achievement, as many discouraged teachers from marginal area schools can readily testify.

As Davis (*21*) points out, "Whereas the middle class child learns a socially adaptive fear of receiving poor grades in school, of being aggressive toward the teacher, of fighting, of cursing, and of having early sex relations, the slum child learns to fear quite different social acts. His gang teaches him to have a fear of being taken in by the teacher, of being a softie with her. To study homework seriously is literally a disgrace. Instead of boasting of good marks in school, one conceals them if he ever receives them" (*21*).

The Philosophy of Immediate Gratification

Davis argues that the most urgent problem before the public schools at the present time is "to learn the motivational structure of lower-class children and adolescents" (*21*). He points out that the majority of our elementary school pupils have been trained in lower-class families and neighborhoods; and that a sizable minority of our school population comes from the bottom group within the lower class, the slum culture.

Most teachers at least have an implicit recognition of the principles of learning. They realize that a child will not learn unless his needs are taken into account and unless he is rewarded when he makes the proper responses to the school situation. Unfortunately, however, many teachers assume that the fundamental needs in any group of 6- or 7- or 8-year-olds are pretty much the same for all children regardless of social class. Actually, of course, they are not.

Thus the kinds of universal needs that teachers are likely to attribute to all children will in most instances be their own middle-class needs, and hence appropriate to middle-class children. However, lower-class children are not likely to respond to appeals to middle-class needs in the way the teacher would predict. Hence she is likely to become hurt, bewildered, or angry.

Teachers frequently appeal to children on the basis of future rewards. To a certain extent, all education involves getting children to extinguish old ways of doing things in favor of new ones, through implicit assurance that these new ways will ultimately prove more rewarding. Such an approach may work well enough with middle-class children, because they have had prior opportunities to learn from their parents and from their own experience that moderation and foresight are ultimately rewarding. They are able to trust to the future because the future has for them been predictable.

But as we saw in Chapter 10, the past experiences of most lower-class children have done little to assure them that the future is predictable, and consequently they are likely to baffle and to frustrate their teachers by clinging to a philosophy of immediate gratification (cf. p. 385). Thus, given the choice between playing with the gang on a spring evening or studying so that they will receive a good grade in school (which will ultimately lead to other rewards), they are more likely to choose the playing.

Socioeconomic Status and the Curriculum

It has also been argued that lower-class children do more poorly in their studies because the curricula of our schools have been planned in a way that favors middle-class children. For example, educators may attempt to select reading matter in the primary grades that will relate to the daily life of the children, and thus be more interesting. But actually the activities discussed in these readings often typify the daily lives of middle-class and not of lower-class children. Many of the types of incidents depicted would be about as familiar to the average slum child as a description of Samoan boyhood to a middle-class New Yorker. Reading lessons in which the child's job is "to learn to decode someone's thoughts about a cat, a grandmother, a circus, or a trip to the country" are likely only to "seem foolish to the lower-class child because the experiences appear unreal, the words strange" (21).

Many stories dealing with typically middle-class experiences must seem equally unrealistic. Thus elaborate tales about extensive preparations for a new baby in the family, the mother's trip to the hospital, the long wait for a homecoming, and the fanfare which accompanies it, must seem quite bizarre to the slum child, who, the night before, has been briefly sent out of the house while his mother delivered her latest baby in her own bed. Moreover, much of the subject matter of these textbooks is easier for the middle-class child to master because of his greater experience with similar sorts of problems or content areas. Reading, counting, spelling, drawing, or the development of verbal fluency may come more easily to the middle-class child, because of his family's greater interest in and reward for these and related activities. Practical activities that lower-class children are more likely to be familiar with on the basis of previous experience are rarely stressed in most school curricula.

In brief, there seems little doubt that current academic curricula do favor the middle-class child. In addition, the fact that he cannot meet the demands of the school environment as easily as the middle-class child often makes the lower-class child feel discouraged about the whole matter of formal education.

PARENT-CHILD RELATIONSHIPS AND SCHOOL ADJUSTMENT

Earlier we saw how the specific attitudes that parents of various social classes have toward the school as an institution are transferred to their school-age children, with favorable or unfavorable results. There are, however, many other more generalized influences which parents exert upon the expanding personalities of their children—influences which directly affect the children's chances for successful school adjustment. While some of these influences appear to be correlated with social-class membership, many are at least partially independent of it. For example, we know that among all social classes and all economic levels, there are parents who are overprotective of their children and who baby them too much; parents who are cold and rejecting or neglectful; parents who are unduly dominating or submissive; parents who are happy and well adjusted, or miserable and maladjusted. As we saw in the last chapter, such variations in parental attitudes may profoundly affect the child's overall social adjustment during middle childhood, including, of course, his adjustment to his school peers. The specific question we would like to raise here is, do parental attitudes also affect the child's academic progress; and if so, how?

One of the most interesting approaches to this problem has been made by Kurtz and Swenson (42). They employed a series of interviews with parents, teachers, and children to study the home backgrounds of 40 underachievers and 40 overachievers in academic work. Overachievers were defined as children whose scholastic achievement was "well above" what would have been predicted from their intelligence test scores.

Underachievers were children whose achievement was "definitely below expectation" on the basis of their scores. In general, marked differences were found between the two groups.

Pride, confidence, affection, and interest of parents in their children as shown in instances in which parents read to their children, play with them, build for them, or attend school with them, appear to be in greater evidence for plus-achievers (overachievers) than for minus-achievers, (underachievers). On the part of children, there is a tendency among plus-achievers to respect their parents, to take them into their confidence, to be concerned about pleasing them, and to return the love their parents show.

Minus-achievers appear to have a comparatively limited place in the home. There does not appear to be so much exchange of affection, or mutual respect, desire to measure up to expectations. In fact even expectations appear limited for minus achievers . . . (42).

Somewhat similar results were obtained in an investigation of the home backgrounds of 30 children with reading disabilities. Twenty of these children came from homes where the mothers were overtly hostile, or were of a coercive, perfectionistic nature. In addition, the homes of nearly all the children were characterized by severe interpersonal tensions between at least some family members.

Another study dealt with the school work habits of 500 children from the Winnetka, Illinois, elementary schools (30). Confidential cumulative records of teachers having intimate contacts with parents were examined for evidences of (1) the child being babied by parents ("An only child whose mother admits she spoiled him"); (2) child being pushed by parents ("Parents have high standards of scholarship"; expect him to grow up over night and to show scholastic abilities which some relative did"); (3) home well-adjusted ("Serene home life. Home situation quite ideal—harmonious and coöperative").

Fifty-one instances of babying were found, 22 of excessive parental pressure, and 73 of good home adjustment.

In general it was found that the work habits of children pushed and children babied were predominantly poor. On the other hand, the work habits of children from "well-adjusted homes" were predominantly good. In addition, there was a tendency for poor work habits to increase as the child progressed in school in the case of children babied and to decrease in the case of children from well-adjusted homes.

This study is, of course, subject to the criticisms (1) that the teacher's estimates of home conditions may not have been entirely accurate, and (2) that the teacher's estimates of home conditions may have been in-

fluenced by the school behavior of the children and vice versa, thus producing a spuriously high relationship between the two. Nevertheless, the
findings are at the least suggestive, and it would be of considerable
interest to see this study repeated with more adequate controls.

The importance of preparing a child for the demands of the school
situation is emphasized in a study of the factors influencing changes in
school adjustment between kindergarten and second grade (26). The
investigators found a strong relationship between the harmoniousness of
a child's home and his chances of making a good social adjustment to
kindergarten. In addition, they found that a child's initial adjustment was
highly predictive of his school adjustment two years later. Furthermore,
in most cases, when favorable changes in adjustment did occur between
kindergarten and the second grade, favorable changes had also occurred
in the home.

Acceptance-Rejection

In previous chapters we have reviewed studies of the influence of
specific parental behaviors (e.g., overprotection, domination, submission,
etc.) on the child's overall adjustment. Many of these parental influences
also appear, not surprisingly, to affect the child's adjustment to school.
For example, the rejected children in Symonds' study (cf. pp. 331–
333) showed greater antagonism to the school as an institution, were
more often in rebellion against its rules and regulations, and truanted
more often. In their academic work, they were characterized to a greater
extent by a lack of sustained application, and by indifference and apathy.
More of them appeared to daydream in school, and to be confused and
bewildered about their goals.

Domination-Submission

It will be recalled (cf. pp. 333–335) that the children of dominant parents tended to be more polite, dependable, submissive and shy, whereas
children of submissive parents tended to be more independent, disobedient, overconfident, and rebellious. We might infer, therefore, that
the former group of children would give their teachers less trouble in the
classroom, and would be more compliant in carrying out assigned tasks.
The latter might be expected to display more independent thought, creativity, and initiative, though they would probably be more difficult to
handle. Research findings as to which group actually does better in academic performance are, however, lacking.

Overprotection

In Levy's study of 20 children of the overprotecting but loving mothers previously cited (cf. pp. 256–257), the academic progress of the children was also followed. Interestingly enough, while these children had, as we have already seen, considerable difficulty in adjusting socially, their academic progress did not seem particularly impaired. Levy attributes this, in the case of the overprotecting but dominating mothers, to an emphasis on submissive conformity which generalized from the home to the school situation. In the case of the overprotecting but indulgent mothers, he attributes it to "an exceptional and disciplinary attitude towards school work on the part of the mothers" (46).

In another study of these same children, it was found that as a group they tended to score low in mathematics but high in English and vocabulary relative to their peers (45). This was true both in school grades and on achievement tests. Levy feels that these results were due to the fact that overprotected children live in closer contact with adults, and that consequently they were more exposed to adult forms of speech. It is also probable that they are more often rewarded for making these adult speech responses themselves. Thus they found English and related subjects easier in the school situation and hence more rewarding. They then tended to concentrate on success in these subjects to the exclusion of others. Because of the small number of subjects employed in this study, and the questionable representativeness of the sample, it is difficult to estimate how typical such findings are of overprotected children in general.

In another study (53), a strong negative relationship (− .80) was obtained between persistence in a task and parental protectiveness. In other words, the more the child had been protected in the home, the less was his tendency to keep working away at the task. Since persistence is required of the child if he is to be able to go ahead and learn difficult new responses in the school situation, despite initial frustrations, it is obvious that the overprotected child will be at a marked disadvantage in comparison with his peers. The child who gets discouraged right from the start by failures in arithmetic, reading, or spelling is not likely to do well in these subjects.

Implications of These Studies

Many of the studies relating to the effects of specific parent behavior are not so well controlled as might be desired. Nevertheless, the total weight of the evidence seems to support the hypothesis that extreme domination, indulgence, or rejection by the parents is likely to cripple the child's chances of adjusting successfully in the school situation, either socially or scholastically.

All this seems to make excellent sense in terms of learning theory. To a great extent, the child is likely to generalize responses learned through interaction with his parents to key figures in the school situation. The child who has been rejected may generalize his resentment of parents to his teachers. Furthermore, if his parents are indifferent to intellectual growth he may continue to feel that intellectual accomplishment is unrewarding. Occasionally seeming contradictions occur. For example, a child who is submissive at home may be openly antagonistic at school. In such a case, however, the child may be displacing aggression acquired at home (cf. pp. 246–250). The contradictions are often more apparent than real.

Of course, it is always possible that the child may in fact react in new ways in the school situation. All responses to new situations are not simply generalizations or displacements of earlier responses. Discriminations may be learned. A rejected child who encounters a warm, understanding teacher may begin by reacting to her as he has learned to react to his cold, neglectful parents. But gradually he may learn that the teacher does not behave the same way his parents do—that, for example, expressions of trust will not be rebuffed by her. As a result, he may slowly learn new patterns of response.

One of the reasons that this happy consequence does not occur more often—that "a child's initial adjustment was highly predictive of his adjustment two years later"—is that the teacher in rewarding new responses is usually competing with the parents' continued reinforcement of old responses. Consequently, favorable changes in school behavior do not usually occur, unless they are accompanied by favorable changes in the home situation. The overall implication is that while good teachers may help the child to adjust to the school situation, the amount that a teacher can accomplish will be significantly influenced by conditions within the home.

EARLY SOCIAL EXPERIENCE WITH PEERS AND ACADEMIC PROGRESS

A number of authors have attempted to determine whether there is a relationship between prior contact with peers (e.g., in nursery school or with siblings) and school adjustment.

It may be expected that the child who has had more previous experience with peers should have learned more appropriate responses for getting along with them in ways that are mutually rewarding. This hypothesis fits in with popular notions that the only child is spoiled, and has not learned to take into account the needs of others in attempting to fulfill his own needs. It also fits in with educators' ideas that the primary purpose of nursery school is to teach the child to get along with peers before beginning the demanding academic work of grammar school. But is there support for this general hypothesis?

In Chapter 9, we reviewed several studies which suggested that children who had been to nursery school adjusted more easily to kindergarten and elementary school than their peers who had not had this experience. While the influences of both onliness and ordinal position on school adjustment have been investigated, there is little agreement among the various findings.

Several studies have reported that only children do not get along well in school and that more of them are delinquent (16, 17, 58). Other studies, however, indicate that only children receive better marks in school, have better health attitudes and habits, and are superior to non-only children in orderliness, initiative, self-control, industry, truthfulness, dependability, courtesy, coöperation, and conformity (12, 25, 27)—all traits often considered related to good school work. In one such study (25) the authors found that only children were more likely to show some instability of mood, to be more easily excited, and to display more flightiness and distractibility in their attention span.

Another interesting question concerns the consequences of varying ordinal position in the family. For example, do oldest children do better scholastically in a school situation than middle or youngest children? A number of studies have shown correlations between birth order, and both intelligence-test performance and academic achievement. For example, in one study of 5928 pairs of siblings (61) increases in intelligence-test scores with increasing order of birth through the eighth born child were reported (i.e., children born first had lower I.Q.'s). On the other hand, in another study of 156 girls, grades 9 through 12, it was found that as birth order increased, both I.Q. and academic achievement decreased (20). The correlations in both cases, though significant, were small.

It is obvious from the contradictory results obtained in these studies that no clear statement of the influences on school adjustment of previous peer experience in the family can be made. In our survey of the relationship of these same variables to personality development, we pointed out that in many of the relevant studies little effort was made to control for the effects of such extraneous variables as social class and family size (cf. pp. 340–343). The same criticisms apply here. The fact that other influences vary, often in unknown ways, from one study to the next, probably accounts for the discrepancies in the findings.

While adequate evidence is not currently available, our most likely guess is that where previous peer experience has been optimal, and has tended to result in the learning of responses which will be appropriate to the school situation (both academically and socially), then this experience will be a marked asset. On the other hand, it is perfectly possible that previous peer experience may result in learning response patterns which are incompatible with good school adjustment. Such experience will be a handicap. In short, the *kind* of previous peer experience is probably of more importance than its presence or absence in determining future school adjustment.

VARIATIONS IN SCHOOL EXPERIENCE

Thus far we have been discussing the relationships between the child's background and experiences, on the one hand, and differences in adjustment in the school situation, on the other. Equally important, however, are the ways in which variations in the child's school experience may influence his attitudes and behavior. These variations may be of two sorts —general and individualized.

In the first of these two categories would be included experiences which are common to an entire group. In this class would be placed what are usually called situational factors, such as school atmosphere, educational philosophy, physical facilities, class size, and recreational opportunities. In the second category would be included experiences which are common only to certain children in a particular group, such as experiences of failure or achievement in relation to the group as a whole. Situational factors will be discussed first.

General Variations in School Environment: Teacher-Child Relationships

Among the situational factors affecting school adjustment probably none is so important as the teacher-pupil relationship. Most adults can recall at least one teacher who, in their opinion, helped them a great deal in the business of growing up—who showed them better ways to get along with their peers, who made learning new things an exciting adventure, or who gave them comfort and solace when they were troubled. Unfortunately, most adults can also remember at least one teacher who made their school life miserable.

If we are not to be superficial in our consideration of the teacher-child relationship, we must realize that since both teacher and child vary in their personal adjustments, hopes, interests, values, assets, and liabilities, the relationship between them is bound to be complex. No two teachers will react to a particular child the same way. Conversely, no two children will react in identical fashion to the same teacher. There are as we shall see, certain kinds of teacher to whom most children in our culture will react favorably, others to whom they will react unfavorably. There are also general patterns of pupil behavior toward which most of our teachers will have positive or negative attitudes.

But, as we shall also see, the problem of predicting how a particular teacher and child will react to each other is complicated by the problem of individual differences in both.

Children's Preferences in Teacher Behavior

In a study of children's preferences in teacher behavior, Jersild (38) found that children in our culture tend to prefer teachers who possess the following characteristics: (1) *human qualities*—kind, cheerful, natural, even-tempered; (2) *disciplinary qualities*—fair, consistent, impartial, respected; (3) *physical appearance*—well groomed, nice voice, and generally attractive; (4) *teaching qualities*—helpful, democratic (give children voice in class affairs), interesting, and enthusiastic.

The same sorts of characteristics seem to be preferred by older as well as younger children (29, 44).

Teacher Behavior and Group Atmosphere

The view that dominating or hostile teachers will affect pupil adjustment adversely, while the nonpunitive, interested teacher will facilitate good adjustment, derives support from a number of studies of teacher behavior and group atmosphere. In a series of related studies (2, 3, 4, 5, 6, 7), Anderson and Anderson and their co-workers undertook to study "The nature and degree of relationship between . . . children's behavior . . . and . . . teacher's dominative and socially integrated contacts." These investigators were interested in testing two hypotheses which they felt could be applied to teacher-child relations. The first of these, referred to as "The Hypothesis of the Growth Circle" was that: "Integrative [i.e., give-and-take, democratic] behavior in one person tends to increase integrative behavior in others" (4). The second hypothesis, referred to as "Hypothesis of the Vicious Circle" was that: "Dominative [i.e., authoritarian] behavior in one person tends to incite domination in others" (4).

In their observations of teacher-pupil interactions, these investigators considered dominative behavior on the part of teachers to be evidenced by such behaviors as use of force, commands, threats, shame, blame, and rigid insistence upon conformity. Integrative behaviors, on the other hand, included approval, extending invitations to activity, questioning the child about his interests, sympathy, and mutual participation of children and teachers in activities (4).

In one of these studies the reactions of the pupils of two second-grade teachers from the same elementary school were observed (5). One of the teachers was found to be consistently more integrative or democratic, and less dominative; the other was consistently more dominative or authoritarian. The children in each of the teacher's groups had been assigned by lot in the first grade, and had been promoted as a room. Thus there was no reason to assume that the two classroom groups differed significantly in any important respects.

It was found that the children with the more integrative teacher tended to behave more integratively than did the children of the more dominative teacher. They displayed a significantly greater number of behaviors reflecting spontaneity, initiative, and constructive social attitudes relating to others. The findings "were consistent with the hypothesis that *integration in the teacher induces integrative behavior of the child*" (6).

On the other hand, the children with the more dominating teacher showed significantly higher frequencies of nonconforming behavior. This supported directly the hypothesis that domination incites resistance. In addition, the children with the more dominating teacher paid less attention to their work, engaging more in such activities as looking around and whispering to their companions (6). "If it is a pedagogical objective for a teacher to reduce the conflict and increase the harmony in her school room, then the study showed that [the dominating teacher] was defeating her own purpose" (6).

These same teachers and children were studied a year later (7). The children by this time were, of course, in the third grade. It was found that the teachers tended to behave in a similar manner year after year, regardless of the kinds of pupils they encountered. The children, on the other hand, did not. They showed far greater flexibility, reacting dominatively if they had a dominative teacher, but shifting readily to integrative behavior if their next teacher happened to be an integrative individual.

These studies suggest that the behavior of school children is highly dependent on the behavior of their teachers, and that teachers who use democratic (integrative) techniques with their children will be rewarded by greater coöperation, spontaneity, interest, and initiative on the part of their pupils. On the other hand, teachers who attempt to force compliance through aggressive dictatorial techniques will only be encouraging greater resistance on their pupils' part—whether manifested by whispering, doodling, lack of attention, or through more direct opposition.

These findings seem quite consistent with what we would expect on the basis of a reinforcement theory of learning. The integrative teacher, like the dominative one, has the responsibility for teaching the child to behave in a socially acceptable and constructive fashion. But the integrative teacher does so in ways which make socially constructive responses rewarding. As a consequence, the child is motivated to learn these responses because they also satisfy his own needs. Furthermore, the integrative teacher has a broader conception of what constitutes socially acceptable behavior than the dominative one. Thus she views fewer of the child's spontaneous responses as requiring elimination or modification than does the dominative, authoritarian type of teacher.

In short, the integrative teacher more often helps to satisfy the child's needs and less often frustrates him. This, of course, has many advantages, one of which is particularly noteworthy. There are times when even the most integrative of teachers must require socially constructive responses which run counter to some of the child's current drives. On a lovely spring day, the merits of a trip to the old swimming hole may seem considerably greater to the pupil than those of learning an arithmetic lesson. It might be argued that under such conditions the integrative teacher would have a much harder time controlling her students than the dominative one, because her pupils have been permitted to behave more spontaneously and with greater freedom. This does not appear to be the case, however, and there seems to be a good reason why it is not. Because she has so often been instrumental in meeting the child's needs in the past, the integrative teacher herself acquires learned reward value. As a result, doing something simply to please her will become rewarding to the pupil. And in many instances such a reward will be sufficient to offset the child's desire for other courses of action.

The dominative teacher, on the other hand, through her lack of concern for the child's needs and her narrower conception of socially acceptable behavior more frequently frustrates the child in his attempts to satisfy his needs. Since, as we have already seen (cf. pp. 202–206), frustration tends to produce aggression, the dominative teacher is likely to become a target for hostility, rather than a source of reward. Thus she is likely to encounter more difficulty in her attempts to instill socialized responses than the integrative teacher. She may be able to inhibit overtly aggressive responses on the part of her pupils through the use of fear and punishment, but she is not able to instill a positive desire for coöperation.

GROUP ATMOSPHERE. Somewhat similar conclusions were reached by Lewin, Lippitt, and White (47) in a study of "group atmosphere." While this study deals with the relations of boys' club members to adult leaders, rather than with those of pupils to a teacher, the situations are actually quite similar. Hence the study seems applicable to the school situation.

In this study, four recreational mask-making clubs, each consisting of five 11-year-old boys, were subjected to three different types of adult leadership and group atmosphere: democratic, authoritarian, and laissez-faire. In the authoritarian atmosphere, the adult leader determined all the club activities, policies, and procedures; assigned tasks and working partners; gave praise and reproof arbitrarily; and remained generally aloof from the group. Under democratic leadership, policy, group goals, individual responsibilities, and choice of working partners were all matters of group discussion and decision. The adult leader acted as a group member in spirit; assisted, encouraged, and gave advice about technical problems, and praised or criticized individual and group activities objectively. Laissez-faire leadership was essentially passive, and the group was completely free to make its own decisions about activities and procedures. The leader provided information and help only when asked and made no attempt to evaluate the behavior or the products of the individuals or the group.

The different groups were matched on intelligence, physical energy, and social behaviors, such as obedience, social participation, leadership, friendships, and quarreling. Since the investigators were interested in the consequents of shifts from one type of leadership to another within the same group, each group experienced seven weeks of each kind of leadership. For instance, in some groups democratic leadership followed laissez-faire, and in others the opposite order occurred.

Data collected included quantitative running accounts of the directive, compliant, and objective approaches and responses of leaders and children; minute-by-minute group structural analysis including activity subgroupings, goals, and initiator (child or leader); notations of significant member actions and changes in group atmospheres, and stenographic records of all conversations.

All the data indicated that the group atmosphere created by the leader affected many aspects of the children's behavior in interrelationships. Authoritarian leadership elicited either of two distinct kinds of reaction: passivity and apathy (extreme dependence on adult leader, relatively low levels of frustration, complete failure to initiate group actions) among the members of three clubs; and aggressive responses directed toward the authoritarian leader in the fourth club. Under this type of leadership, all groups were much more dependent upon the leader and demanding of his attention than in either the democratic or laissez-faire situations.

Rebellious feelings were expressed most frequently in the group which reacted to autocratic treatment with aggression. But in general, authoritarian leaders were approached submissively by their children. In the laissez-faire atmosphere, club members had no coöperative working relationships with their leaders and most frequently spoke to them only to ask for information. Personal, friendly, and confiding approaches to adult leaders were typical reactions in the democratic atmosphere, where there were few indications of feelings of discontent.

Interpersonal relations among the club members also varied with the social climate. Group-minded suggestions—connoting freedom, spontaneity, and interest in others—were most characteristic of the democratic social climate, and morale and coöperation were highest in this atmosphere. Friendly remarks and group-oriented statements (concerning "us" instead of "me") were most common under democratic, and least common under autocratic atmospheres. Moreover, free and easy sociability between the boys was apparently inhibited in the autocratic group, which had the smallest volume of conversation between children and little discussion about outside activities.

Irritability and aggression toward other club members were expressed more frequently in both authoritarian and laissez-faire climates than under democratic leadership. In a prior study, the group which reacted with great hostility to the authoritarian climate channelized its feelings on the leader and the members of other groups. In another related study (48), the aggression produced in the autocratic atmosphere was turned against two group members (scapegoats) whom the others treated so badly that they ceased coming to the club. When groups under autocratic domination were transferred to freer democratic or laissez-faire social atmospheres, there was a great deal of horseplay among the members, indicating a need to discharge pent-up aggressive tensions which had accumulated during their earlier experience.

Group goals and work achievements were affected by the social climate also. The masks made in the democratic atmosphere were of higher quality than those produced in the other two social climates.

When authoritarian leaders arrived late (intentionally) they found there was no group initiative to start new work or to continue with work already under way. On the other hand, in democratic climates, the groups became active in a productive way even if their leaders were not on time. When the authoritarian leader left the room, working time dropped to a minimum, while in the democratic atmosphere, absence of the leader did not affect the group productivity or intention to work.

At some point during the study each group was given hostile criticism by a stranger (a "janitor" sent by the experimenter) who entered while the leader was gone. In the authoritarian atmosphere, this criticism was passively accepted or led to aggression against an out-group. However, the democratic group showed a readiness to unite in rejecting the stranger's unjust comments.

It can hardly be denied that these experimental results are impressive and that behavior varies as the general social atmosphere changes. However, the finding that democratic treatment of the children resulted in greater coöperation, enjoyment, and productivity cannot automatically be generalized to apply to all children. It seems quite reasonable to believe that most of the subjects in this study came from democratic homes. Hence the cues presented in the democratic atmosphere were somewhat familiar to them. They had learned techniques for functioning effectively and coöperatively in such situations. They would consider the authoritarian atmosphere, and the experimenter's activities in particular, to be restricting and frustrating. Consequently they would be unhappy and behave in a disorganized, aggressive, ineffectual manner in such an atmosphere. Children from authoritarian homes who had been rewarded for submissive behavior might find the authoritarian situation easier to handle than the democratic. In brief, we cannot understand the child's behavior in any specific situation, such as the classroom, without considering his past history and learning, as well as the stimuli immediately present.

Teachers' Preferences in Pupil Behavior

We have previously discussed the fact that children prefer teachers who meet their social and emotional needs most adequately. Conversely, most teachers, since they are human beings (a fact often ignored by parents, pupils, and school boards) are likely to prefer students who either make their jobs easier or who give them a sense of accomplishment. The child who disturbs the smooth functioning of the class, or the child who gives the teacher a sense of failure, apparently either by refusing to learn, or by demonstrating inability to learn, is often likely to receive little consideration from the teacher.

In an excellent pioneer study of children's behavior and teachers' attitudes, Wickman (74) obtained the opinions of teachers as to the relative seriousness of 50 behavior problems of school children. The opinions of these teachers may be considered fairly typical for the era (the middle 1920's) in which they were obtained, since they represented the considered views of 511 teachers, distributed throughout the United States. In addition to obtaining teacher opinions, Wickman also asked 30 clinicians, all actually engaged in the study and treatment of behavior disorders in children, to rank the same 50 behavior problems.

The combined ratings obtained for each group were then compared. In general, the teachers viewed behaviors involving immorality, dishonesty, transgressions against authority, and classroom disturbances as the most serious problems. These included: heterosexual activity, stealing, masturbation, obscene talk, truancy, impertinence, cheating, and destroying school materials. Among the least serious problems, according to the teachers, were withdrawing personality characteristics, such as shyness, dreaminess, unsocialness, and sensitiveness.

The clinicians, on the other hand, viewed the latter characteristics, together with unhappiness, depression, resentfulness, and fearfulness, as among the most serious. In contrast to the teachers, the clinicians were least disturbed by violations of school procedures, such as tardiness, disorderliness in class, interrupting, destroying school materials, and disobedience; and by such socially disapproved behaviors as smoking, profanity, and masturbation.

It seems quite reasonable that there should have been these fairly consistent differences in the overall attitudes of the teachers and clinicians. After all, as already noted, the essential job of the teacher, at least as viewed at the time of this study, was to communicate the social values and basic skills of the culture to children. She could do this only in a reasonably orderly environment, and only with students who were able and motivated to learn. The child who was aggressive and attacking in his behavior naturally represented more of a threat to order than a withdrawing child. Though both may have had difficulty in school, the latter at least did not interfere with the learning opportunities of the other children. Therefore the teachers considered more serious those kinds of behavior which made teaching more difficult, challenged the social values that she had the responsibility for communicating, or threatened to undermine her authority.

The job of the clinician, on the other hand, was to promote individual adjustment. His function was only secondarily one of education. He would, therefore, consider most serious those problems which were most difficult to treat, or which posed the more serious threat to the individual's future mental health.

It should be pointed out in this connection that more recent studies have shown greater agreement between teachers' and mental hygienists' ratings of problem behavior. This probably reflects the greater emphasis currently being placed by teacher-training programs on the teacher's responsibility for the overall growth of the child, rather than merely on his academic progress. Unfortunately, there are still some teachers who either through lack of training or through personal inadequacy, see their function in the child's life as limited to teaching the three R's. They fail to recognize that the child has important emotional and social, as well as intellectual, needs, and that all are necessarily involved in adjusting to the complexities of life's demands—many of which are related only peripherally to academic proficiency. The present trend, however, is encouraging, and there can be little doubt that future generations of children will stand a better chance of becoming well-adjusted adults if it continues.

Individual Differences in Teacher Personality

Despite the fact that teachers as a group differed markedly from clinicians in Wickman's study, individual differences in teacher personality were clearly reflected in their ratings. Perhaps this is shown most clearly in a pilot study which preceded the work described here.

When teachers were asked to submit lists of school behavior problems that concerned them, some stressed primarily problems of obedience and honesty. Others concentrated almost exclusively on problems which offended their standards of morality. Still others were concerned with social difficulties with peers.

Obviously, individual differences in the attitudes of teachers may affect the social and emotional learning of their pupils. For example, the teacher who is concerned primarily with social adjustment will almost certainly reward and punish different behaviors than the teacher who is primarily concerned with moral transgressions. Of course, teachers' attitudes are, in turn, the consequents of many factors in their own lives: their experiences with pupils; their own childhood experiences with parents, teachers, and peers; and current frustrations or satisfactions in their everyday existences.

The effect of the teacher's personal satisfactions upon her adjustment, and the effects of this adjustment upon pupil development, are matters of particular importance today. There has been in the recent past, and there continues today, a tremendous increase in the size of the pupil population in this country. There has not been a commensurate growth in the number of qualified teachers (nor in fact in available physical facilities).

Part of the current shortage of qualified teachers may be due to a reluctance on the part of the public and of government officials to face the financial demands of increased enrollment realistically, with the result that new jobs are not created when they are needed. But part of the shortage must also be attributed to the lack of motivation of young people to go into teaching, and of experienced teachers to stay in their profession. The frustrations stemming from low pay scales, lack of community respect for the profession of teaching, and public interference in the personal lives of teachers have too frequently combined to make teaching an unrewarding profession.

INFLUENCE OF TEACHERS' GENERAL ADJUSTMENT. Are teachers' maladjustments likely to affect the emotional growth of their pupils?

One team of investigators (14) attempted to test the hypothesis that unstable teachers tend to have unstable pupils; while stable teachers tend to have stable pupils. Their subjects, 73 teachers and 1095 students, were given questionnaires dealing with emotional adjustment.

The teachers were divided into high- and low-stability groups on the basis of their scores on the questionnaire. The median scores of the children under the teachers from each group were then compared. In general, the children under the more stable teachers obtained better adjustment scores.

Such findings as these have led to a number of disputes among psychologists. Some have felt that they provide overwhelming evidence that maladjusted teachers produce maladjusted pupils (60). Others have argued that whether or not teacher maladjustment will adversely affect the pupil's emotional growth will depend on the nature of her maladjustment (23). The latter view seems more convincing to us.

Some lonely and unhappy teachers *do* make special efforts to lavish attention and love on some of their unhappy pupils. On the other hand, some maladjusted teachers release their pent-up aggressive tendencies by abusing the most defenseless children in their classrooms. It would appear that personally maladjusted teachers may or may not affect the personal and social adjustment of their pupils in an adverse way, depending on the type of overt behavior through which the teacher resolves his psychological frustrations. The maladjusted teacher who makes his adjustments through impunitive (non-punishing) and intrapunitive (self-punishing) patterns of behavior may be extremely unhappy himself, but have essentially no negative influence on his pupil's growth and adjustment. However, there is a high probability that the maladjusted teacher who employs extrapunitive (other-punishing) patterns of behavior to reduce his psychological tensions will have an undesirable effect on the psychological growth and adjustment in pupils. Children in his classroom will probably suffer intense frustration and pain as he vents his aggressive tendencies through sarcasm, threats, inconsistent episodes of anger, and corporal punishment. Although we do not wish to moralize, there seems to be little excuse in a democratic society for *forcing* children to suffer the taunts and jibes of a bitter teacher. This bleak picture of certain teacher-pupil relationships is only partially mitigated by the remarkable resiliency with which children respond to social pressure from all adults (70, 532).

Influences of Children's Textbooks

While the teacher's own attitudes and behavior undoubtedly exert a more profound effect on the school child's development than do the texts she uses, the latter also play an important role. It is, of course, obvious that textbooks contribute to the child's development of academic skills. It is probably less apparent that they may also influence his development of social and emotional attitudes.

In order to investigate the possible influence of children's readings on the socialization of the child, Child, Potter, and Levine (18) made an "analysis of certain content of the world of ideas which confront children in the process of education, from the point of view of the probable effect of that content on the motivation of their behavior." Specifically, all the stories in 30 general third-grade readers were analyzed with respect to: type of story, fictional characters, behavior displayed, circumstances surrounding behavior, and the consequences of behavior. These authors assumed that "when a sequence of behavior is seen as leading to rewards, the effects will be to increase the likelihood of the child behaving in that way under similar conditions in the future." "When, on the other hand, the sequence of behavior is shown as leading up to punishment, it is expected that the incident will contribute to the probability of the subject's avoidance of such behavior in the future."

These researchers found that "the treatment of various categories of behavior in children's readers can leave no doubt that this treatment tends to encourage the development of certain motives and to discourage others" (18).

The most frequently rewarded behaviors in the stories were: construction (creation of a material or intellectual production); sentience (enjoyment of and seeking after sensory pleasure); elation (joy, enthusiasm, and optimism); succorance (attempting to obtain protection, sympathy, or assistance from another person); affiliation (manifestation of friendliness and good will and the desire to do things in the company of others); nurturance (helpfulness and willingness to exert oneself to aid any creature that might be in need of assistance); achievement (ambition to succeed or a desire for a specific physical, intellectual, or social success).

On the other hand, displays of temper, flagrant disobedience, verbal and physical aggression, rejection (feelings of indifference, annoyance, or scorn toward other people; acts of avoidance and neglect) and infavoidance (self-consciousness, shyness, and social embarrassment) were most frequently punished in the stories. Despite an emphasis on learning there was little encouragement of intellectual activity as such or of original thinking.

The system of rewards and punishments in the stories obviously reflects and reinforces the general cultural norms of our society. They are "symptomatic of probable characteristics of other kinds of content in the world of ideas that reach children—what teachers say to them in classrooms, morals that their parents point up to them, the content of stories they read elsewhere" (18).

Generally speaking, the material of the readers "provides lessons to children encouraging or discouraging the development of motives in a way that is likely on the whole to lead to more satisfactory adjustment in our society" (18). However, the authors feel that the unrealistic optimism of many of the stories, and their failure to encourage independent, autonomous action on the part of the children may be regarded as defects.

The feelings, personal characteristics, and activities of the male and female characters in the stories were markedly different. Compared with males, females are more frequently portrayed as sociable, outgoing, kind, timid, easily frightened; but inactive, unambitious, and uncreative. "To the extent that boys identify with male characters and girls with female characters, this difference both in itself and as a reflection of facts that hold true of many sources of influences on children, must have a profound significance for the differential development of personality in the two sexes" (18).

The schools and educational methods align themselves with other familial and social forces in making clear distinctions between males and females with respect to appropriate behavior and personality. As the authors conclude, "there is clear evidence that the education [of the two sexes] is not the same, even at early levels of grammar school and even when boys and girls are mixed together, as they usually are, in the same classroom. Not only does the informal training of boys and girls at the home and in the community differ, but even the formal education they are receiving in the classroom differs" (18).

Competition and Coöperation

Any discussion of the effects of school experience upon children's behavior and adjustment must deal with the general problem of competition-coöperation. American school children appear to be rewarded for attempts to outdo others to a much greater extent than their peers in many primitive cultures. ". . . American education is at least partly a system of social relationships in which students are pitted to outdo each other. We sometimes talk of this as encouraging talent to come to the fore. Such education helps an American to feel most adequate in those tasks he can perform better than—or at least as well as—other individuals in his group" (34, 190).

As we saw earlier, research findings support the notion that young children are not particularly concerned with competition, but that they become progressively more competitive as they grow older (cf. pp. 280–283). These results probably reflect the growing child's awareness and consequent adoption of the competitive values which are so pervasive and so consistently rewarded in our culture. Different results probably would have been obtained if these studies had been conducted with children from less competitive cultures, such as the Hopi children studied by Asch (8). Consider, for example, this bit of Hopi classroom behavior.

. . . In order to introduce an incentive [the teacher], asked the children to turn their backs to the board as soon as they had finished [their work]. To her surprise she found that the quickest children, when they were through, waited and looked about furtively until another—and more mediocre child—had turned around, before turning himself or herself. Needless to say, the instructor was forced to abandon this practice.

The same instructor has experienced serious difficulty when she tried to appoint leaders to take care of the classroom. At first, she tried to designate the bright children as leaders, as a reward for their work. They quickly refused the "honor," for the same reasons that adults refuse to be foremen. She then hit upon the plan of designating leaders alphabetically. This method worked, because the children considered it a fair method of shouldering the unpleasant task of being leaders (8, 443).

As a group, children in our culture certainly appear to be more oriented toward individual competition than the Hopi children. However, there are great individual differences in degree of competitiveness within groups, and some children in our culture are undoubtedly as reluctant about individual competition as the Hopis.

Competition and coöperation are, of course, not mutually exclusive. In many activities, both coöperative and competitive responses may be reinforced simultaneously. For example, in team sports such as football, winning over the opposition team requires a high degree of coöperation among team members.

The problem of whether American children generally strive harder under conditions of individual competition or as members of competing groups was investigated in a series of experiments by Maller (50). He used an additions test to determine how hard children would strive for success under a variety of competitive and coöperative conditions. His subjects were 1538 students in the fifth through eighth grades of various eastern public schools. In general, it was found that children did consistently better on this test (more additions per 12 minutes) when working themselves for individual prizes than when working for a group prize based on an overall group score. Also, when children were offered the choice of working for themselves or for the group, the group was chosen in only 26 percent of cases and the self in 74 percent.

But while these children usually preferred individual competition to working with most kinds of competitive groups, this was not exclusively the rule. The following list shows the kinds of competitive and coöperative situations employed by Maller (50), and the children's relative preference for them (according to rank).

1. Sex groups.
2. Self.
3. Team: The children elected two captains; they in turn chose two teams which competed with one another in speed.
4. Partnership: Each pupil in the class was told to choose a partner; a contest between partnerships was then staged.
5. Classroom.
6. Arbitrary group: The examiner divided a class into two halves; the groups were then to compete with one another.

In general, this study suggests that American children generally prefer individual competitive situations, probably because this type of competition is more frequently rewarded in our culture than team competition requiring individual coöperation among team members. It is interesting to note that in this study participation as a member of a sex group was seen as more rewarding than individual competition. Unquestionably the tremendous amount of reward associated with playing one's sex role in our culture (cf. pp. 242–244), plus the increases in anxiety that accompany deviations from it, were in large measure responsible for this preference in Maller's experiment.

Personal factors may affect preferences for individual competition or group participation. In Maller's study, group-oriented children tended to be higher in "mental age, intelligence, moral knowledge, resistance to suggestibility, deportment in school, character ratings by teachers and classmates, tests of honesty and inhibition and neurotic index" (50). Fewer of them were only children, and more of them belonged to the boy or girl scouts. It seems likely that these children experience more parental and peer rewards for competing as members of coöperative groups.

A number of authors (37, 40), have challenged the wisdom of the American emphasis on individual competition as an end in itself. They have argued that competition is often an uneconomical, even at times an impossible way of attaining mutually beneficial goals. While at times people may work harder for individual as opposed to group rewards, this is often done at the expense of rewarding interpersonal relationships. For example, in one study (64), second-grade children were asked to paint murals under two conditions—for individual, and for group prizes. It was found that under the condition of individual competition, the children engaged in less positive and more negative behavior. Under the group conditions, the children "made more friendly remarks, shared materials, and helped one another more often than under competitive conditions" (64). Apparently undue emphasis on individual competition may have its negative aspects.

Of course, the problem is not simply one of the relative appropriateness of two kinds of competition—individual versus group (which also involves coöperation). In our society, children develop competitive needs early in life because competing is often rewarded. At the same time, however, they are often rewarded for coöperating with parents, siblings, or peers. Thus they develop needs for coöperating which are not necessarily associated with competitive goals. The problem of reconciling competitive and coöperative needs is often a difficult one. As Horney points out, "On the one hand everything is done to spur us toward success, which means that we must be not only assertive but aggressive, able to push others out of the way. On the other hand we are deeply imbued with Christian ideals which declare that it is selfish to want anything for ourselves, that we should be humble, turn the other cheek, be yielding" (37).

In other words, the culture not only reinforces one set of attitudes and behaviors, but also the opposite—often without providing clear cues as to the particular circumstances under which each may be appropriate. As a result, the child is unable to make proper discriminations, and may be in conflict as to whether to compete or coöperate.

Implications for Teacher Behavior

It might be hoped that the establishment of such discriminations could be aided by the teacher. But she can only do this if she, and the school of which she is a part, have themselves achieved a workable solution to the problem. Too often, however, the school not only fails to help the child solve preëxisting problems in this area but actually creates new problems or magnifies old ones.

In the light of the above considerations, Jersild's (40) warning as to the dangers of undue emphasis by the school on competition at all cost seems highly relevant. He points out that competitive pressures may be extremely unhealthy if they "force the judgment of failure and defeat even on those who do not of their own accord have a compulsion to compete" (40). As he says:

> The child who is interested and enterprising but who originally does not have a keen, competitive impulse might become doubtful of his worth when he notices that the school he attends is so ridden with competition that everything seems to require a rating, a mark, or a grade based on an external measure of achievement or success. When a child in such a situation notices the teachers seem to be slaves of the competitive system it will be difficult for him to see how a teacher could like him and respect him when the teacher knows he stands below the middle rank in his spelling, arithmetic, music, or some other occupation. The child has to be very sturdy if he is to keep his confidence in himself when called upon to face constant reminders of inferiority. Reminders of inferiority are inevitable in the school which stresses competitive standards, for it is of the essence of a competitive standard that only the one who wins top place or almost top place really has achieved something that counts. So a very able child, matched with many other able children, can get the impression of being a rather inferior character because competitive situations are usually so rigged that only a few can win. . . .
> Competitive standards give little recognition, if any, to the child who is not the first to cross the finish line but who entered the race even though he knew

he was handicapped. Yet if gameness were the criterion, he should get the prize. Competitive standards give a medal to the winner of the oratorical contest but they may quite ignore the one who, in joining the contest, scored a magnificent triumph over his shyness, even though he did not surpass someone else's skill! (40, 227).

Of course, competition cannot be avoided in the school, nor should it be, since the child must be prepared to exert himself in the struggle for existence when he steps out into the adult world. But competition solely for the sake of excelling others can be minimized. Competition with oneself in the sense of overcoming one's own handicaps can be stressed, with the credit given being proportional to the difficulties encountered in the struggle. So also can the real fact that often one can satisfy his own needs, not through competition with others, but only through mutual coöperation. In our complex society the individual who cannot coöperate will be just as frustrated in the satisfaction of his basic needs as the one who cannot compete.

Individual Variations in School Experience: School Success and Failure

As we have just noted, one of the unfortunate results of undue emphasis on competition may be to give many children feelings of failure. Of course, academic competition is not the only source of such feelings. Many other factors in the school situation may also contribute. The child may be made to feel inadequate either by teachers or peers because of his socioeconomic or caste status, his physical appearance or defects, his special interests, or his particular personality pattern. Regardless of the source of these feelings, however, they may have profound effects upon the child's school adjustment.

This is well illustrated in a study by Pauline Sears (59). She hypothesized that experiences of success or failure in a task would affect the child's self-confidence and would influence his future levels of aspiration (achievement goals) with respect to the tasks. She set out to test this hypothesis by selecting three groups of six children each, differing with regard to past experience in reading and arithmetic. A "success" group was made up of children who had shown objective evidence of success in reading and arithmetic, school grades and achievement scores, as well as subjective feelings of success during their entire school experience. A "failure" group was composed of children with the opposite experience. A third, or "differential" group was made up of children who had had successful experience with reading and unsuccessful experience with arithmetic. The three groups were matched on other factors which might conceivably have affected their performance in the experimental situation, such as chronological age, mental age, and sex. Each of these groups was then exposed to three experimental conditions—neutral, success, and failure.

NEUTRAL CONDITION. In the first of these, all children were given short speed tests in reading and arithmetic. After completion of a test, the child was told that he had completed it in so many seconds, and was asked how many seconds he was going to try to do the test in on a second trial. No comments about relative success or failure were made at this time: "After the first or neutral session, half of each group was given the reading material under success and the arithmetic under failure conditions; while the remaining half were given arithmetic under success and reading under failure conditions. All subjects performed on *both* *materials* in the first session under neutral conditions, and on subsequent days one material under success, and the other under failure conditions. The neutral, success, and failure sessions were each separated by two or three days" (59).

SUCCESS CONDITION. In the success session the subject was told that on the reading (or arithmetic test) which he had taken the other day, he had done well, and that the experimenter wanted him to take the test again to see if he was really that good. Twenty more trials were then given, and after each trial the child stated his new level of aspiration (i.e., in how many seconds he was going to try to do the next trial). On the whole the experimenter attempted to report times (scores) that showed progress and were more or less in accord with the child's most recently stated level of aspiration (regardless of the child's actual performance).

FAILURE CONDITION. In this session, the procedure was roughly opposite to that of the success condition. The subject was told how poorly he had done the other day, and during his twenty trials was reported to be getting progressively worse.

The measure adopted by Sears to study the relationship between level of aspiration and performance was a *discrepancy score*. A single discrepancy score was the difference (in time) between the performance score reported to a subject for a given trial (whether true or not) and the score the subject aspired to on the succeeding trial: "*a positive discrepancy score indicates a goal for achievement better than that of the preceding performance*" (59).

Sears made several interesting discoveries in analyzing her data. When all experimental conditions were lumped together and only groups with different school records were compared, the success group (those with histories of academic success) tended consistently to have low but positive discrepancy scores in the test situation. In other words, children who had previously been rewarded by success for improvement in certain areas (i.e., reading or arithmetic), kept on trying to improve in the experimental situation, though in a realistic fashion. The failure group, while also predominantly positive in their discrepancy scores, were much more variable, ranging from slightly *negative* to extremely (and unrealistically) positive. In short, children who had previously encountered only failure tended, in the experimental situation, to lower their goals, or to be altogether fanciful about their hope for improvement. The differential group (those with histories of success in reading and failure in arithmetic) responded like the success group on reading (in which they had always been good) and like the failure group on arithmetic (in which they had always been poor). Thus their level of aspiration showed the important influence of prior experience with success and failure in specific tasks.

In another phase of the study, the three groups of subjects with differing histories were *lumped* together, and only the various *experimental conditions* were compared. When this was done, it was found that induced failure tended to increase the discrepancy score and to make it more variable, while induced success tended to lower the discrepancy score and also to make it less variable.

In general, it was found in this study that subjects who had been successful in their past school work on such tasks tended to try to do better in the future but to be realistic about their goals, altering them in accord with the experimenter's statements as to their current level of performance. Failure subjects, on the other hand, appeared to react in a variety of ways. A few behaved much like the success subjects; but the majority either set unrealistically high goals in relation to their reported performance, or "played safe" by setting lower goals.

Sears' study suggests that experiences of success encourage children to adopt a relatively healthy approach to school work. Children with such experiences are self-confident and make attempts to improve because improvement responses have been rewarded, but their aims are realistic. On the other hand, children who are consistently confronted with failure tend to react either by setting unrealistically high goals which they cannot possibly accomplish, or by setting goals below their real level of ability, in an attempt to protect themselves from the anxiety of further failure.

In the light of such findings as these, it would appear important that the school should try to avoid giving any child repeated and consistent feelings of failure. Not only are such feelings likely to lead to extinction of responses aimed at improving in the particular task in which failure is experienced; they are also likely to generalize to other school tasks as well and to lead to the development of negative attitudes toward the school as a whole. Furthermore, such experiences are likely to influence negatively the child's overall appraisal of himself. In one study, children from the fourth grade through college were asked to write themes on *What I Dislike about Myself* (39). It was found that "at practically all levels (except at college) experiences pertaining to life at school were mentioned more often as a source of self-disparagement than as a source of confidence and good feeling toward the self" (40). Thus it appears that "in a great many instances the school does more to undermine than to encourage and support the average child's acceptance of himself" (40). Perhaps as Jersild suggests,

. . . the school constantly and perpetually, day in and day out, year after year, reminds great numbers of children that they are not much good. To a large number of children who do not happen to have the kind of intellectual and conformist tendencies which are praised in most institutions of learning the school dispenses unfavorable comparison, reminders of failure, and implied rejection on a colossal scale. . . . What often happens is that when a person fails in a given test in life, such as an important assignment at school, it is difficult for him not to view this as a test of him as a person, a total test rather than just a measure of a limited facet of his worth. When a child is deficient in arithmetic or in reading he will have a tendency, at least for the moment, to feel that he is just plain deficient in everything . . . . (40, 609).

While children need to be given realistic reminders of their deficiencies, this can be done without giving them the impression that they are failures in all respects. The teacher who can accept in herself the realization that there are some things in which she herself is not particularly talented without a loss of self-esteem, is in the best position to help the student face his own assets and liabilities without becoming discouraged (40).

REFERENCES AND ADDITIONAL READING

1. Abernethy, E. M., Relationships between mental and physical growth. *Monogr. Soc. Res. Child. Develop.* (1936), *1*:No. 7.
2. Anderson, H. H., An experimental study of dominative and integrative behavior in children of preschool age. *J. soc. Psychol.* (1937), 8:335–345.
3. Anderson, H. H., Domination and integration in the social behavior of

young children in an experimental play situation. *Genet. Psychol. Monogr.* (1937), *19*:341–408.

4. Anderson, H. H., and Anderson, G. L., Social development, in L. Carmichael, (ed.), *Manual of child psychology*. New York: Wiley, 1954.

5. Anderson, H. H., and Brewer, J. E., Studies of teachers' classroom personalities. I. Dominative and socially integrative behavior of kindergarten teachers. *Appl. Psychol. Monogr.* No. 6, 1945.

6. Anderson, H. H., and Brewer, J. E., Studies of teachers' classroom personalities. II. Effects of teachers' dominative and integrative contacts on children's classroom behavior. *Appl. Psychol. Monogr.* No. 8, 1946.

7. Anderson, H. H., Brewer, J. E., and Reed, M. F., Studies of teachers' classroom personalities. III. Follow-up studies of the effects of dominative and integrative contacts on children's behavior. *Appl. Psychol. Monogr.* No. 11, 1946.

8. Asch, S. E., Personality development of Hopi children, cited in G. Murphy, L. B. Murphy, and T. M. Newcomb, *Experimental social psychology*. New York: Harper, 1937.

9. Ayers, L. P., The effect of physical defects on school progress. *Psychol. Clin.* (1909), *3*:71–77.

10. Bayley, N., Factors influencing the growth of intelligence in young children. *Yearb. Nat. Soc. Stud. Educ.* (1940), *39*(II):49–79.

11. Bond, E. A., *Tenth grade abilities and achievements*. New York: Teachers College, Columbia University, 1940.

12. Bonney, M. E., A study of the relation of intelligence, family size, and sex differences with mutual friendships in the primary grades. *Child Develop.* (1942), *13*:79–100.

13. Bonney, M. E., Relationships between social success, family size, socioeconomic home background, and intelligence among school children in grades III to V. *Sociometry* (1944), 7:26–39.

14. Boynton, P., Dugger, H., and Turner, M., The emotional stability of teachers and pupils. *J. Juv. Res.* (1934), *18*:223–232.

15. Burks, B. S., Jensen, D. W., and Terman, L. M., *Genetic studies of genius: Vol. 3. The promise of youth; follow-up studies of a thousand gifted children.* Stanford University: Stanford University Press, 1930.

16. Burt, C., *The young delinquent.* Bickley, Kent: University London Press, 1948.

17. Busemann, A., Geschwisterschaft Schultuchtigkeit und Charakter. (Sibling status, school ability, and character.) *Z. Kinderforsch.* (1928), *34*:1–52.

18. Child, I. L., Potter, E. H., and Levine, E. M., Children's textbooks and personality development; an exploration in the social psychology of education. *Psychol. Monogr.* (1946), *60*:No. 3.

19. Cronbach, L. J., *Essentials of psychological testing.* New York: Harper, 1949.

20. Damrin, D. E., Family size and sibling age, sex, and position as related to certain aspects of adjustment. *J. soc. Psychol.* (1949), 29:93–102.

21. Davis, A., *Social class influences upon learning.* Cambridge: Harvard University Press, 1948.

22. Davis, A., and Dollard, J. *Children of bondage: the personality develop-ment of Negro youth in the urban South.* Washington: American Council on Education, 1940.

23. Gladstone, R., Do maladjusted teachers cause maladjustment? A re-review. *J. except. Child* (1948), *15*:65–70.

24. Goodenough, F. L., The measurement of mental growth in childhood, in L. Carmichael (ed.), *Manual of child psychology.* New York: Wiley, 1946.

25. Goodenough, F. L., and Leahy, A. M., Effects of certain family relation-ships upon the development of personality. *Ped. Sem.* (1927), *34*:45–71.

26. Griffiths, B., Stimson, M., and Witmer, H., Factors influencing changes in school adjustment between kindergarten and the second grade. *Smith Coll. Stud. soc. Wk.* (1941), *11*:191–284.

27. Guilford, R. B., and Worcester, D. A., A comparative study of the only and non-only child. *J. genet. Psychol.* (1930), *38*:411–426.

28. Harrell, R. P., Mental response to added thiamine. *J. Nut.* (1946), *31*:283–298.

29. Hart, F. W., Ten thousand high school seniors. In *Teachers and teaching,* New York: Macmillan, 1934.

30. Hattwick, B. W., and Stowell, M., The relation of parental over-attentiveness to children's work habits and social adjustments in kinder-garten and the first six grades of school. *J. educ. Res.* (1936), *30*:169–176.

31. Havighurst, R. J., and Breese, F. H., Relation between ability and social status in a midwestern community: III Primary mental abilities. *J. educ. Psychol.* (1947), *38*:241–247.

32. Havighurst, R. J., and Janke, L. L., Relations between ability and social status in midwestern community: I. Ten-year-old children. *J. educ. Psychol.* (1944), *35*:357–368.

33. Havighurst, R. J., and Taba, H., *Adolescent character and personality.* New York: Wiley, 1949.

34. Honigmann, J. J., *Culture and personality.* New York: Harper, 1954.

35. Honzik, M. P., and Jones, H. E., Mental-physical relationships during the preschool period. *J. exp. Educ.* (1937), *6*:139–146.

36. Honzik, M. P., Macfarlane, J. W., and Allen, L., The stability of mental test performance between two and eighteen years. *J. exp. Educ.* (1948), *17*:309–324.

37. Horney, K., *The neurotic personality of our time.* New York: Norton, 1937.

38. Jersild, A. T., Characteristics of teachers who are "liked best" and "dis-liked" most. *J. exp. Educ.* (1940), *9*:139–151.

39. Jersild, A. T., *In search of self.* New York: Teachers College, Columbia University, 1952.

40. Jersild, A. T., *Child psychology.* New York: Prentice-Hall, 1954.

41. Jones, H. E., The environment and mental development, in L. Carmichael (ed.), *Manual of child psychology.* New York: Wiley, 1954, pp. 631–696.

42. Kurtz, J. J., and Swenson, E. J., Factors related to over-achievement and under achievement in school. *Sch. Rev.* (1951), *59*:472–480.

43. Lee, I. M., et al., Measuring reading readiness. *Elem. Sch. J.* (1934), *34*:656–666.

44. Leeds, C. P., and Cook, W. W., The construction and differential value of a scale for determining teacher-pupil attitudes. *J. exp. Educ.* (1947), *16*: 149–159.
45. Levy, D. M., Relation of maternal overprotection to school grades and intelligence tests. *Am. J. Orthopsychiat.* (1933), *3*:26–34.
46. Levy, D. M., *Maternal overprotection.* New York: Columbia University Press, 1943.
47. Lewin, K., Lippitt, R., and White, R. K., Patterns of aggressive behavior in experimentally created "social climates." *J. soc. Psychol.* (1939), *10*: 271–299.
48. Lippitt, R., An experimental study of the effect of democratic and authoritarian group atmosphere. *Univ. Iowa Stud. Child Welf.* (1940), *16*:No. 3.
49. Lippitt, R., and White, R. K., The "social climate" of children's groups. In R. G. Barker, J. S. Kounin, and H. F. Wright (eds.), *Child behavior and development.* New York: McGraw-Hill, 1943, pp. 485–508.
50. Maller, J. B., Cooperation and competition: an experimental study in motivation. *Teach. Coll. Contrib. Educ.*, 1929.
51. Maller, J. B., Vital indices and their relations to psychological and social factors: A study of 310 health areas in New York City with reference to birth rate, death rate, juvenile delinquency, school progress, and intelligence. *Hum. Biol.* (1933), *5*:94–121.
52. Milner, E., A study of the relationship between reading readiness in grade one school children and patterns of parent-child interaction. *Child Develop.* (1951), *22*:95–112.
53. Morgan, J. J. B., and Banker, M. H., The relation of mental stamina to parental protection. *J. genet. Psychol.* (1938), *52*:347–360.
54. Munroe, M., Reading aptitude tests for the prediction of success and failure in beginning reading. *Education* (1935), *56*:7–17.
55. Munroe, M., *Reading aptitude tests, primary form.* Boston: Houghton Mifflin, 1935.
56. Mussen, P., Dean, S., and Rosenberg, M., Some further evidence on the validity of the WISC. *J. consult. Psychol.* (1952), *16*:410–411.
57. Page, J. D., The effect of nursery school attendance upon subsequent I.Q. *J. Psychol.* (1940), *10*:221–230.
58. Parsley, M., The delinquent girl in Chicago. III. The influence of ordinal position and size of family. *Smith Coll. Stud. soc. Wk.* (1933), *3*:274–283.
59. Sears, P. S., Levels of aspiration in academically successful and unsuccessful children. *J. abnorm. soc. Psychol.* (1940), *35*:498–536.
60. Snyder, W. U., Do teachers cause maladjustment? *J. except. Child.* (1947), *14*:40–46.
61. Stekel, M. A., Intelligence and birth order in family. Cited in L. L. Thurstone, and R. L. Jenkins, *Order of birth, parent-age, and intelligence.* Chicago: University Chicago Press, 1931.
62. Stendler, C. B., Social class differences in parental attitudes toward school at Grade I level. *Child develop.* (1951), *22*:36–46.
63. Stendler, C. B., and Young, N., Impact of first-grade entrance upon the

socialization of the child: changes after eight months of school. *Child Develop.* (1951), 22:113–122.

64. Stendler, C. B., Damrin, D., and Haines, A. C., Studies in coöperation and competition: I. The effects of working for group and individual rewards on the social climate of children's groups. *J. genet. Psychol.* (1951), 79:173–197.

65. Stendler, C. B., and Young, N., The impact of beginning first grade upon socialization as reported by mothers. *Child Develop.* (1950), 21:241–260.

66. Terman, L. M., The gifted student and his academic environment. *Sch. & Soc.* (1939), 49:65–73.

67. Terman, L. M., et al., *Genetic studies of genius: Vol. 1. Mental and physical traits of a thousand gifted children.* Stanford: Stanford University Press, 1925.

68. Terman, L. M., and Merrill, M. A. *Measuring intelligence: a guide to the administration of the new revised Stanford-Binet tests of intelligence.* Boston: Houghton Mifflin, 1937.

69. Terman, L. M., and Oden, M. H., *The gifted child grows up: twenty-five years' follow-up of a superior group.* Stanford: Stanford University Press, 1947.

70. Thompson, G. G., *Child psychology; growth trends in psychological adjustment.* Boston: Houghton Mifflin, 1952.

71. Warner, W. L., Havighurst, R. J., and Loeb, M. D., The social role of the teacher, in W. L. Warner, et al., *Who shall be educated?, the challenge of unequal opportunity.* New York: Harper, 1944.

72. Wechsler, D., *The measurement of adult intelligence.* Baltimore: Williams and Wilkins, 1944.

73. Wechsler, D., *Wechsler intelligence scale for children.* New York: Psychological Corporation, 1952.

74. Wickman, E. K., *Children's behavior and teacher's attitudes.* New York: Commonwealth Fund, 1928.

Chapter 12

THE MIDDLE CHILDHOOD YEARS: ADJUSTMENT TO PEERS

The teaching functions of the school are not restricted to the inculcation of academic skills. As a major agent of socialization, the school must be concerned with the child's overall development. It must help him to acquire "a growing awareness of, and interest in, other persons, together with an appreciation of their rights and desires and a willingness to subordinate personal wishes to the greater good of the greater number" (21, 87).

Of course, parents and teachers can help the child to achieve these goals by serving as models for constructive social behavior. But many of the skills required for adequate social adjustment can be learned only through intensive and varied interactions with peers. One of the school's most important functions is to provide opportunities for such contacts.

The nature of the child's interactions with his peers will depend partly on his personality and earlier social learning. Obviously the behavior patterns, identifications, and superego structure (i.e., "character," morals, ideals) he has already developed will influence his relationships with other children. But the nature and intensity of the new stimuli he encounters will also play an important role. The peer group itself exerts many social pressures on the child, and these increase as the child grows older. In this social setting, the child learns new interpersonal behavior patterns, establishes new identifications, and acquires new interests, attitudes, and values.

It will be our purpose in this chapter to examine the child's social behavior during the school years from a number of points of view: the adjustments required by increased peer-group contact; children's ways of relating to one another; the physical, personality, and background factors involved in acceptance by the group; formation of friendships; leadership; and the factors which lead to rejection by peers.

We will also be concerned with the ways in which the peer group may foster the child's socialization by helping him to develop new skills and interests, to learn more about sex-appropriate behavior, and to gain experience in getting along with others. Peer-group rejection (or the absence of peer-group contacts) may result not only in immediate unhappiness, but also in subsequent difficulties in interpersonal relationships.

Following our discussion of peer-group influences, we will turn our attention to two major social problems arising during middle childhood—minority-group prejudice and juvenile delinquency. These phenomena are of course tremendously interesting and important in their own right. In addition, however, they offer dramatic demonstrations of the principle that the major factors influencing personality development—family, social class or caste, school, peers—all operate simultaneously and interact in complicated ways. For purposes of exposition, we have been forced to discuss them separately; in reality, none of them functions in isolation from others. As we shall see, delinquency and prejudice are clearly the consequents of complex combinations of pathological influences.

Integration into New Peer Groups

The child of this age quickly discovers that many of his satisfactions are dependent on establishing himself as a member of a peer group. His opportunities for companionship, and his chances of being asked to play favored roles—or even to participate in various play activities—vary with the degree of his acceptance by the group. Furthermore, physical retreat from the peer-group situation is practically impossible now. In the past, if the child failed to enjoy playing with his peers, he could always "pick up his marbles and go home," but now no such solution is available. Happy or not, he must remain in school.

It is therefore not surprising to find that most children of school age are intensely motivated to gain peer-group acceptance. At the same time, they are rather tentative and cautious in their initial attempts to become group members. A new social situation has a great deal of potential for both reward and punishment. Yet, in most instances, children have little prior knowledge of what will be considered the correct and incorrect responses in the new setting and hence must rely to a great extent on trial and error.

In an attempt to study the process of assimilation into peer society, one team of investigators (38) introduced four 6- and 7-year-old children individually into well-established, "nucleus" play groups of three children their own age. The new child did not know the other children or the experimenter.

They found that the newcomers made real efforts to relate to the nucleus group and to become part of it "on a par with other members." Apparently, most of them had already learned that group activities (being a member of a group) may be very rewarding, and they were therefore eager to play with the others.

In these groups, the new arrival had to take the initiative in interacting with other children. Established members of the group rarely tried to solicit his interests, put him at ease, or take him into account in their activities. The same sort of behavior has often been observed in the schoolroom where "new" children often seek the teacher's aid in dealing with other pupils before they initiate direct social contacts.

The usual technique of relating to the group consisted of imitating the remarks, actions, and gestures of the most active member. Progress in becoming integrated was gradual and continuous. For example, only 5 percent of the average newcomer's responses during his first meeting with the group were classified as "successful initiation and direction of group activities." Four sessions later, he made almost as many contacts of this type as "nucleus" members did (25 percent of his contacts) (38).

The children who had been together longer knew how to interact successfully, i.e., they had learned the important cues and the responses which were likely to be reinforced by their peers. The new child did not know what behavior would be rewarded by these strangers, and hence was at a tremendous disadvantage. Under the circumstances, he turned to an adult for help, probably because parents or teachers had been helpful in such situations previously. In short, he may have generalized earlier rewarded responses of looking to adults for help. Where this was not possible and where there were no specific instructions, the child's best tactics were to observe the behavior patterns of successful children and to imitate these.

Varieties of Children's Groups

The nature of children's groups varies somewhat with age. During the early years of middle childhood, informal groups, formed by the children themselves, predominate. While the adolescent speaks in rather formal and exclusive terms of "my crowd," the school-age child is more likely to refer to "the gang." The gang has few formal rules for governing itself, and there is a rapid turnover in membership. Expediency plays a large role in determining group membership. Factors such as social class,

The early school years: children of both sexes play freely together.

Department of Photography, Ohio State University

The middle school years: sex segregation is at its highest.

Department of Photography, Ohio State University

The high school years: interest in the opposite sex becomes stronger.

Department of Photography, Ohio State University

specialized interest, and physical appearance play less of a part than they will in the future.

Later, however, between 10 and 14, there is a tendency for children's groups to become more highly structured. Aspects of formal organization, such as special membership requirements and elaborate rituals for conducting meetings, appear. Even so, the personnel may change frequently and the group itself may not last long. At this time, formal organizations such as the Boy Scouts, Girl Scouts, or Campfire Girls become more important, especially with middle-class children.

FUNCTIONS OF THE PEER GROUP

The peer group obviously provides an opportunity for the child to gain many immediate satisfactions. Here he finds companions who can keep up with his restless energy in a way that tired fathers with aching joints never could. He finds others of his own level of intellectual and social development with whom to talk and to compare notes. He finds the personnel necessary for group sports and games.

It would be a mistake, however, to dismiss the peer group as simply a way of keeping the child happy during this period of his life, for it serves much more extensive purposes in the child's socialization. The school carries out its educational objectives, not only through formal class work, but also by bringing children together so that they may learn from one another. It affords "an opportunity for experience in the kind of social skills in extra-family group relationships which the child will eventually require as an adult" (*31*, 445). Let us turn our attention to the specific influences of the peer group, i.e., what peers teach each other.

Further Training in Sex-Typing

Observational studies of children's interactions and studies of preferences among playmates reveal a sharp social separation between the sexes during the latter part of middle childhood (after the eighth or ninth year). In the early school years boys associate freely with girls, playing or fighting with them without consciousness of sex. The vast majority of 6- and 8-year-old boys observed in one investigation played freely with girls. After this age, however, they had fewer associations with members of the opposite sex. Between 10 and 14, the so-called "gang age," most boys showed a distaste for girls and played only with other boys (*13*).

Data from a 3-year follow-up study of recreational clubs at the Merrill-Palmer School in Detroit corroborated these conclusions about sex segregation and extended them to girls (*10*). In this study, 53 girls and 56 boys from kindergarten to high school age, were observed as they met weekly in free-play club meetings, and their behavior was objectively recorded.

The youngest group, aged five to about seven, seemed to ignore sex in choosing play groups. Boys chose girls in their dramatics, or on their "sides" as freely as they chose boys. At eight years, however, the picture began to change, and by 10 or 11 boys and girls almost completely segregated themselves from each other. This stage of segregation began with haughty aloofness, became apparent contempt, and active hostility, and then changed to shy withdrawal which seemed to mark the end of this period and the beginning of adolescent heterosexuality after puberty (*10*, 465).

Children in all grades favor members of their own sex as close associates, but the tendency is most marked in the upper (sixth, seventh, and eighth) grades of elementary school. In one study by Moreno (*33*), children were asked to name the classmates they wanted to have in their classrooms or in the next seat. Intersexual attractions (boys choosing girls and vice versa) were highest in kindergarten and the first and second grades (25, 27, and 17 percent of the total choices, respectively). The percentage of choices for members of the opposite sex dropped markedly in the third grade (9 percent) and decreased still further (to about 3 percent) in the fourth to seventh grades.

When pupils from nursery school through high school were asked to indicate the preferred member of all possible pairs of classmates, children at all grade levels favored their own sex. As in the other studies, the bias was most pronounced in the upper grammar school grades (*24*).

The segregation between the sexes, noted in all these studies, seems clearly related to the continuing process of sex-typing. As has already been noted, many cultural pressures are exerted throughout the child's development to mold his behavior into sex-appropriate patterns (cf. pp. 242–244). The process begins in the home, but as the child grows older, the school plays an increasingly important role in sex-typing. School and neighborhood peers contribute further to the achievement of proper sex identification.

As a consequence of all these forces, children of school age are highly sensitive to "male" and "female" personality characteristics, activities, and interests. For example, they have fairly clear-cut conceptions of "boy traits" and "girl traits." In one study, a large number of California children in Grades I, III, and V responded to the Reputation Test (*51*, *52*). This test consists of a series of brief word pictures, and subjects are instructed to match these descriptions with the names of classmates who best fit them. The items are arranged in pairs, one item designating the positive extreme of a dimension and the other, the negative. For example, one pair, labeled Popular–Not Many Friends, has the items: Who are the ones everybody likes? and Who are the ones nobody likes?

These children characterized the typical girl as quiet, popular, full of fun, not quarrelsome, good sport, a little lady, good-looking, not a show-off, tidy, and friendly. The typical boy, on the other hand, was judged to be wiggly, quarrelsome, bossy, and a show-off, inclined to take chances, not bashful, good at games, and a "real boy" (51).

The picture of the typical boy and girl as conceived by children even in the primary grades seems to be almost a photostat of the common identification by adults in our society of aggressiveness, restlessness, and daring with masculinity, and amiability, docility, and timidity with femininity (51, 19).

The child's peers will probably reward responses which are consistent with their conceptions of sex-appropriate behavior, and they will punish those which they consider sex-inappropriate behavior. Hence it may be predicted that children will modify their behavior to conform with these peer conceptions. Some evidence confirming this prediction comes from a study of popularity among school children (52). In this study, it was observed that *quarrelsomeness* and *lack of quietness* were negatively associated with popularity in girls, but had little to do with prestige status among boys. Apparently, aggression and loudness in girls were punished by unpopularity, while their opposites' lack of aggression and quietness, were rewarded by popularity. *Daring* and *lack of bashfulness* were found to be associated with popularity in boys (i.e., the manifestations of these characteristics were rewarded by popularity) (cf. pp. 242–244) (52). Since the peers' influences are strong and may lead to modifications in a child's behavior, the peer group plays a direct role in sex-typing, and more generally, in personality formation.

Sex Differences in Interests and Activities

Like the school, the peer group itself reinforces the boy's acting like a "real boy" and the girl's being a "real girl," while it punishes his "sissy" and her "tomboy" behavior. Thus sex-appropriate responses become progressively more firmly established (i.e., acquire greater habit strength), and consequently, boys and girls become more disparate in their activities, interests, and attitudes. Even in the first grade, "boys are beginning to formulate roles in accordance with the differentiated positions they must look forward to occupying" (49). At this age, sex differences in interest are reflected in the finding that play activities constitute boys' primary concern, while helping adults with their work is essentially a girl's interest (53).

Between the ages of 9 and 13, many activities become clearly designated as masculine or feminine (10). The marked contrast between the

FIGURE 30. Play interests are clearly sex-linked by the fourth grade. (Courtesy of Department of Photography and University School, The Ohio State University.)

sexes in interests at this age is reflected in children's play, reading, movie, and radio preferences, and in vocational choices.

PLAY INTERESTS. In an extensive study of children's play, Lehman and Witty (26) questioned thousands of urban and rural children. Their data showed that games became clearly sex-linked between the ages of 6 and 12, boys playing active, vigorous, competitive games involving muscular dexterity and skill; and girls engaging in more quiet, sedentary games. Interestingly enough, the most marked sex differences in play interests occurred between the ages of 8½ and 10½, the period during which the social distance between the sexes is greatest.

READING INTERESTS. Until they are 8 or 9 years old, boys and girls are attracted to the same kinds of reading, preferring fairy tales, and stories about nature and foreign lands. After this age, sex differences in reading interests become apparent, boys choosing more adventure, mystery, and science stories. Girls continue to show some liking for fairy tales and animal stories, but become more interested in romance and domestic affairs (48).

The divergence in reading interests becomes even greater in the sixth, seventh, and eighth grades. Boys of this age prefer books of adventure, exploration, travel, and biographies of great men. Love and romance, feminine activities, mild adventure, and biographies of women are the topics which appeal most to girls (50).

ENTERTAINMENT INTERESTS. Boys read more magazines than girls, preferring detective and mystery stories (25). Their favorite comic strips feature adventure and mystery with strong masculine heroes (Superman, Dick Tracy, Joe Palooka). Girls of this age liked comics about women, children, and animals (Winnie Winkle, Blondie, Little Orphan Annie) (47).

Sex differences in movie and radio preferences are comparable with those in reading interests. The questionnaire responses of a large group of children, grades V to VIII, indicated that comedy-variety and crime drama were most popular radio programs for both sexes. Other program preferences were more sex-linked. Sports, anti-crime, and daily adventure were more appealing to boys, while girls found drama, soap opera, and popular music more attractive (44).

Investigation of third- to eleventh-grade children's preferences in "the content of mass media as a whole" (reading, radio listening, and movies) uncovered three major patterns of interest: adventure and violence; love, private life, and glamor; "educational" content (29). There was considerable consistency in preference from one medium to another. Thus, interest in all adventure and violence categories (radio, magazines, books, and movies) was characteristically masculine. Preferences for love, private life, and glamor stories in all media were more typically feminine.

Both of these investigations of preferences in entertainment were conducted before television became as popular as it is today. While television may now occupy more of the average child's time than either of the other media, it seems safe to assume that there are equally definite masculine and feminine patterns of program interest in this entertainment field.

VOCATIONAL INTERESTS. Young children's vocational interests are unstable, but sex-appropriate occupational choices are recognized early. When children in the first six grades of elementary school were asked what they planned to be when they were adults, girls most frequently chose teaching. Getting married and keeping house, nursing, and working in a beauty parlor were also named often. Boys manifested a wider range of choices, but were primarily interested in aviation, carpentry, railroad engineering, and chauffeuring (9).

These sex differences in interests, activities, and occupational preferences throw some light on the characteristic ways boys and girls view their sex roles in our society (49). In addition, they indicate that the peer group has a tremendous impact on the child's socialization.

The unisexual peer groups of this age provide the most appropriate outlets for already developed sex-typed interests. Others of the same sex are more likely to have the same needs and interests, and hence to make satisfying, rewarding companions. Furthermore, social pressures in the same-sex group foster the further development of sex-typed interests, attitudes, and behavior. For example, the child's choices of extracurricular games, reading, movies, radio and television programs, are probably most strongly swayed by his peers' opinions and suggestions. Since these media may provide new identification models, they may affect the child's personality in the same way textbooks do (cf. pp. 403–405). Thus, by influencing the child's recreational interests, peers may also contribute to shaping his personality.

Peer-Group Influences on Superego Development

In addition to promoting sex-typing of personality attributes, interests, activities, and values, the peer group augments the socialization process by helping to mold the child's superego or conscience. As we noted earlier, children's original concepts of ethical and "moral" behavior stem largely from learning within the family. Youngsters take over their parents' codes of behavior without questioning them, as though these were inherently and absolutely correct ("moral realism") (cf. pp. 327–328). While learning is restricted largely to the home, children have little opportunity to learn moral values which differ from those of their parents. Subsequently, however, associations with peers and others outside the home stimulate the learning of new concepts of right and wrong.

The findings from some of Piaget's ingenious work on age changes in children's moral ideas and judgments illustrate this phenomenon (39). His techniques of investigation included conversing with children and asking them questions about moral issues or about the ethics of charac- ters and events in short stories. For instance, in a conversation with a child he would ask "Why shouldn't you cheat in a game?" Or, after tell- ing a story about a mother who gives the biggest piece of cake to her most obedient child, he would question the subject about the justice of her action.

Many of Piaget's observations demonstrate that as the child becomes a member of larger, more varied peer groups, rules and moral judgments become less absolute and authoritarian, more dependent on the needs and desires of the group. "Moral relativism," based on coöperation and respect for others eventually replaces "moral realism": "For very young children, a rule is a sacred reality because it is traditional; for the older ones it depends upon mutual agreement" (39, 96). For example, 150 children between the ages of 6 and 12 were told stories involving a con- flict between obedience to parents and a sense of justice or equality, and were asked to solve the conflict. The percentage of children who chose solutions involving "obedience to adults" decreased steadily with advanc- ing age. Thus 95 percent of the 6-year-olds, but only 5 percent of the 11-year-olds, and none of the 12-year-olds, favored this type of solution.

In another phase of this investigation, children were asked to give examples of what they regarded as unfair. "Behaviors forbidden by parents" were mentioned by 64 percent of the children between 6 and 8 years of age, but only by 7 percent of those in the 9- to 12-year-old group. On the other hand, inequality in punishment and treatment were mentioned by 73 percent of the 9- to 12-year-olds but only 27 percent of those 6 to 8 years of age.

On the basis of numerous studies of this sort, Piaget concluded that:

. . . there are three great periods in the development of the sense of justice in the child. One period, lasting up to the age of 7–8 during which justice is sub- ordinated to adult authority; a period contained approximately between 8–11, and which is that of progressive equalitarianism; and finally a period which sets in toward 11–12, and during which purely equalitarian justice is tempered by considerations of equity (39, 314).

Using both American and Swiss children as subjects, Lerner (27, 28) confirmed Piaget's findings regarding age changes in moral judgments, especially among children of a lower socioeconomic status. He found a progressive decline in suggestions for solving conflicts by subordination to adult demands or acceptance of authority (including majority opinion) between the ages of 6 and 13. During the same period, solutions based on moral relativism, reciprocity, and equality increased.

Summarizing these changes in moral concepts, Murphy says:

Moral realism yields gradually during childhood to an ethics of reciprocity; what is right is now defined not in terms of self-evident and inherent necessity but in terms of a sense of balance or justice. Rightness is a matter of the mutual consideration of needs (34, 386).

With expanded social contacts, the child begins to identify with more people and hence to understand others' concepts. In Lerner's terms, he develops "reciprocal points of view," and "moral perspective." Through association and identification with members of the peer group, the child learns new ways of reacting in interpersonal situations. He finds that consideration for others and acknowledging their rights, prerogatives, and feelings bring him rewards. Hence coöperative and sympathetic responses, as well as corresponding attitudes, gain in habit strength.

One investigator attempted to test directly the relationship between the nature of the child's moral concepts and his interactions with parents and peers (30). Moral judgment tests, and questionnaires about parents and peers, were administered to 244 American boys between 5 and 14 years of age. From the boys' answers to the questionnaire items, the invesgator derived measures of several aspects of authority and peer relations.

These data, like Piaget's and Lerner's, showed that "a child's morality changes as he grows older, from strict and specific moral rules deriving force from parental authority to more general principles supported by groups of equals" (30, 14).

Moreover, analysis of the questionnaire data revealed that boys who were strictly controlled by their parents, currently or in the past, tended to conform rigidly to adult dictated regulations. Compared with the children of less strict parents, these boys were more likely to make moral judgments primarily on the basis of "such moral prescriptions as . . . respect for property, obedience to teachers, and veracity" (30, 17). They were less likely than the other boys to be influenced by the obligations of friendship and peer-group membership.

As we saw earlier, children from authoritarian, highly disciplined homes do not ordinarily have friendly, relaxed, give-and-take relationships with their peers. They do not find interactions with their fellows rewarding, and hence they are not so likely to become loyal to them, to identify strongly with them, or to learn their ways of perceiving things. On the other hand, relaxed, democratic parent-child relationships seem to produce children who have freer, more rewarding relationships with their peers. Hence these children are more likely to identify with their friends, to learn other children's points of view, and to acquire stronger patterns of group loyalty. In making moral judgments, these children may at times appear to be independent of their parents' conceptions of right and wrong, and more likely to be influenced by their peers' opinions.

FACTORS AFFECTING GROUP ACCEPTANCE AND STATUS

From our discussion thus far, it is apparent that the peer group plays an important role during middle childhood, not simply in providing the child with immediate satisfactions, but in implementing his integration into the broader social world. It can help to train him to become a competent and knowledgeable individual, secure in his sex identifications, and possessed of the interests, attitudes, and skills expected of his sex group. In addition, relationships with peers teach him to work coöperatively toward the achievement of mutually rewarding goals.

When we consider the scope of these functions, we can appreciate the advantages that accrue to the youngster who is accepted by his peers, and the penalties to which the rejected child is subject. It is therefore important to understand both the factors which promote and those which militate against peer-group acceptance. What determines whether a child will be popular in his group, treated indifferently, or avoided by others? On what basis are friendships among children formed? What variables are related to leadership? What are the consequents of high or low social standing in the group?

Social Status

Several techniques of measurement have been used in studies of the social status of children. In the sociometric approach, youngsters are asked to list their preferences and rejections among the other children of the group with respect to some definite criterion. For example, each child in a camp cabin might be asked to name three children he would like to have as team mates, as swimming buddies, or as neighbors at home. From these data, a composite diagram of all the children's choices, known as a *sociogram*, can be constructed. This shows the relative social status of each child from the most popular (i.e., most frequently chosen) to the "social isolates" (never chosen).

Bonney (6, 7, 8) used the technique to differentiate socially successful and unsuccessful fourth-grade children in three schools. On the basis of his classmates' responses to a series of sociometric questions (e.g., whom would you like to serve with on committees?), each child received a composite social acceptance score.

Classmates and teachers rated the 20 most popular (i.e., highest in social acceptance) and 20 least popular children on a battery of 20 personality variables. Popular children were rated much higher in socially aggressive and outgoing characteristics. In general, they manifested either of two personality syndromes (groups of characteristics which go together). The first was composed of strong, positive, aggressive characteristics such as leadership, enthusiasm, and active participation in recitations. The second, which was less definite, involved cheerful disposition and friendly attitudes (tidy, good-looking, frequent laughter, happy, and friendly) (6, 7). By and large, the characteristics associated with popularity showed a great resemblance to those which have been found to be the consequents of gratifying and rewarding early interactions in the family setting.

Personality variables related to popularity have also been investigated by analyzing responses of a large number of first-, third-, and fifth-grade boys and girls to the Reputation Test (cf. pp. 422–423) (52). In this test, the subject lists the children in his class who "have many friends," are "good sports," "good-looking," etc. Popularity scores, the number of votes received on "Has Many Friends" minus the "Not Many Friends" votes, were then correlated with scores on all other personality variables. Data were analyzed separately for boys and girls in each grade.

Popularity scores were found to be positively correlated with all other favorable personality variables. Popular children in most groups were considered good-looking, friendly, good sports, and best friends. The relationships of other attributes to popularity varied with sex and age. For example, among first-grade girls, popularity was closely associated with the characteristics "acting like a little lady," "being quiet," "not quarrelsome," and "not bossy." The importance of "acting like a little lady" declined as girls grew older, until by the fifth grade this trait had little to do with social prestige. At this age, good looks, good sportsmanship, friendliness, tidiness, and lack of quarrelsomeness were most highly correlated with girls' popularity.

The most highly esteemed first-grade boys were those whom their peers considered good sports, good at games, "real boys," not bashful, and daring. Fairness in play and leadership ability were the most important correlates of popularity among third-grade boys. Prestigeful fifth-grade boys received many votes as best friends, good-looking, not bashful, and "real boy." In this group, friendliness, good sportsmanship, and tidiness were somewhat less closely linked to popularity; characteristics such as "not bossy," "doesn't get mad," "not quarrelsome," and "doesn't fight" had little to do with prestige position (52).

It may be concluded that the responses and characteristics most likely to be rewarded by social acceptance vary according to age and sex. In general, however, the characteristics which conform to the cultural stereotypes of masculine behavior—athletic skills, leadership, and daring —are associated with popularity in boys, while typically feminine characteristics, such as docility and unassertiveness, are associated with popularity in girls. From this, it may be inferred that high prestige with peers is at least partially a product of adequate sex-typing.

UNPOPULARITY. Unpopular children, on the other hand, appear to be those who have never learned adequate techniques for relating to peers. Intensive clinical studies of the 20 least socially accepted children (according to sociometric tests) in the fifth and sixth grades of a public school in Canada showed that these "outsiders" could be differentiated into three distinct groups (37). Six children, called *recessives*, were described as listless, lacking vitality, under par physically, careless in appearance, unintelligent, and unconcerned with people or events. The second group, the *socially uninterested*, consisted of nine children who superficially resembled the recessives in being shy, passive, and retiring. Actually, however, they were children who were primarily interested in personal rather than social activities, e.g., art or music. The third group, five children, were *socially ineffective*: noisy, rebellious, delinquent, and arrogant. Although desirous of social relationships, they did not know how to establish them and often made conspicuous, foolish, and futile attempts to be recognized and accepted by the other children.

The investigator felt that the behavior of the extremely introverted *recessives* could probably be modified only by means of psychotherapy. However, case histories of the children showed that teachers could help other unpopular children to achieve greater social acceptance. For example, redirection of the child's personal interests into social channels— e.g., getting him to use his musical ability in group activities—was often useful in helping him to discover that social participation can be rewarding. Thus he became more outgoing and more concerned with interpersonal relationships. Efforts to extinguish the attention-getting responses of *socially ineffective* children by not rewarding them also proved effective frequently. Group discussions of desirable and undesirable characteristics also helped these children to improve their social behavior (*36, 37*).

Social Class and Peer-Group Status

As we might expect, peer-group status is related to social class. In one study of 63 children in two school classes, social acceptance (as defined by sociometric questions) was found to be highly related to objective measures of family socioeconomic status (*3, 4, 7*). The child's social-class background was apparently of major importance in determining his social prestige among peers.

Other findings from sociometric studies indicate that lower-class children are more likely to have poor reputations among their peers of all social classes, including their own. They are likely to have few friends and are generally considered poorly dressed, plain-looking, unpopular, aggressive, not liking school, dirty, bad-mannered, unhappy, and unfair in play (*6, 7*).

Economic factors may partially account for the relatively poor social standing of lower-class children. Poverty may mean poor health, poor clothes, and little participation in social activity. Any of these factors may reduce the child's opportunities for establishing stable peer relationships, and may thus handicap him in learning good social techniques. Moreover, the lower-class child's awareness of his lack of social know-how may produce feelings of inferiority and inadequacy and hence withdrawal from social interactions.

Social Prestige and Social Behavior

It is our thesis that the child's social prestige, which depends to a great extent on his personality and class background, strongly affects the course of his socialization. More specifically, what the child learns and how he learns it are both related to his status in the group. An interesting social psychological study illuminates the relationship between the child's prestige position among his peers and his ability to exercise influence over others as well as his proneness to be influenced by others (*40*).

The subjects of the investigation were 8 groups of boys and 8 groups of girls (with from 7 to 9 members each), ages 11 to 15, in a summer camp. Observers recorded all interactions involving attempts to influence others either indirectly or directly (by demanding, using force or threats, pleading, suggesting). They also noted all instances of *behavior contagion*—spreading of behavior—initiated by one of the children, even though the initiator did not communicate any intention to be imitated.

Each child's *group influence* was assessed in terms of frequencies of both *initiation of contagion* and *successful direct attempts to influence others*. The frequency of his compliance with the attempts of others at direct influence and the number of contagion incidents he "picked up" were used as measures of *susceptibility to social influence*. Counselors rated the children on *feeling of acceptance in the group, adult relatedness, group relatedness, group belongingness need*. Prestige position was evaluated directly by means of cabinmates' rankings on strength and ability in athletics; independence of adults; having ideas for fun; sex sophistication ("knowing the score"); independence of social pressure.

Status position correlated significantly with ratings on *feelings of acceptance in the group, contagion initiation, and successful direct influence attempts*. In other words, children who were accorded high status felt more secure and accepted in the group and were able to sway the behavior of others by means of both direct and indirect techniques. Others responded by following their leads, thus rewarding their leadership activities.

Prestigeful children were less likely to accept others' commands and suggestions, but were more susceptible than the average to behavior contagion. Since they were secure in their group, they were free to "pick up" contagion if they wished but could also resist direct attempts at influencing them. Their peers, aware of the high-status children's position in the social hierarchy, more frequently made indirect, rather than direct, approaches to them when attempting to influence their behavior.

By and large, those children to whom prestige position is attributed are aware of the fact; their awareness is facilitated by the behavior of others toward them in a variety of ways including, among other things, a readiness to be influenced either directly or "contagiously." They tend to act on the basis of this awareness by making more direct attempts at influencing, and by other behavior indicative of freedom to act spontaneously in the group (40, 334).

Several inferences may be drawn from these studies of social status among peers. Whether the child is prestigeful or not is largely dependent on the social position of his family and on personality characteristics which have their roots in his early development. Other children respond to the child in accordance with his prestige position. For example, as we noted above, the highly esteemed child's outgoing leadership responses are reinforced by his peers' deference toward him and by their imitation of his behavior. Hence responses that originally helped him win popularity gain habit strength and are repeated and he is likely to maintain his status. Sociometric studies indicate that school children tend to retain their relative prestige positions from one year to the next (5).

Friendships

Of all his peers, the child's close friends are probably his most important "teachers," exerting the most potent and direct influences on his development and behavior. Hence it is important to understand how he selects them.

When asked to name their best friends, children of school age choose others of their own sex almost exclusively (51). This is hardly surprising in view of the sex-segregation characteristic of this period (cf. pp. 421–423). Propinquity is also an important situational determinant of friendship choice. Most pairs of friends live in the same neighborhood or are in the same classroom at school (13).

Furthermore, personal characteristics appear to play a significant part in the formation of friendships. In one study, data on 62 pairs of boy chums were analyzed to determine the ways in which friends resemble each other (13). Pairs of friends resembled each other most in "developmental age" (a measure of social maturity) and were also somewhat alike in chronological age, height, weight, and intelligence. The investigator concluded that resemblances in non-intellectual traits are probably more crucial in friendship ties than similarities in intelligence (13).

In a series of studies of grammar school children, mutual and unreciprocated pairs of friends were compared (4, 8). Mutual friendships were those in which two children named each other frequently in response to sociometric questions such as: Who would you like as a partner for a trip to the zoo? In unreciprocated pairs, one child showed attraction for another who practically ignored him.

In general, mutual friendship had little relationship to academic achievement, but mutual friends resembled each other in socioeconomic background and in general intelligence. "Only" children, who generally came from families of higher socioeconomic status, were more successful in maintaining reciprocated relationships than those from large (four or more children) or medium-sized (two or three children) families. In the lower grades of elementary school, girls appeared to be more sociable than boys. They chose more companions for the suggested activities, and were involved in more mutual friendships (4).

Among fourth-graders, mutual friends tended to possess strong, positive, aggressive personality traits and to be outstanding in leadership and class recitation. In at least half of the pairs of mutual friends, both members were rated above average by their classmates in quietness, tidiness, daring, leadership, friendliness, desirability as companions, good looks, enthusiasm, frequent laughter, and activity in recitations (8).

Apparently, capable, alert, energetic, responsive children are ordinarily attracted to each other. This may be attributed to their ability to understand and satisfy each other's needs. Associations with listless, unresponsive children are not rewarding to them, and they do not generally form friendships with such children. Other children are often attracted to those with more positive traits, but their friendship is usually rejected (8).

In another study, 400 sixth-grade children were asked to list the names of their three best friends, together with their reasons for choosing them (2). Frequent associations (for example: living near by; selling papers together), similarity of interests or tastes (such as reading books together; having the same hobbies), cheerful ("have fun with him"; good-natured), nice and friendly ("nice guy"; "swell girl") were the four most frequently mentioned reasons.

Friendships were quite unstable at this age. A few weeks after the initial lists were made, these subjects were again asked to name their best friends. Sixty percent of the subjects rejected at least one of the children they had chosen originally, usually giving lack of recent contact ("don't see him very much") or a quarrel as the reason for the changed relationship (2).

The instability of friendships is probably related to rapid fluctations in interest at this age. Two children with similar interests are likely to form an alliance, for they can understand and satisfy each other's needs, and their relationship is rewarding to both children. However, when interests change, they no longer provide mutual gratifications and their friendship is likely to be discontinued.

With increasing age, interests generally become more crystallized, and as we would expect, friendships become more enduring (22). Persisting mutual interests give a substantial basis for maintaining friendship. Like any other learned behavior, friendship responses are repeated if they are continually reinforced.

SPECIAL SOCIAL PROBLEMS

In an organized democratic society, juvenile delinquency and minority-group prejudice may be regarded as problems in pathology. Contrary to much popular literature and thought, these phenomena are not the consequents of single factors like poverty, parental rejection, neurotic tendencies, or prevalent social attitudes. Any or all of these may contribute, but it requires a combination of unfavorable influences to produce delinquent behavior and intolerance of minorities.

DELINQUENCY

Juvenile delinquency is basically a legal concept, defined in different ways in different times and places. In our culture, the term *juvenile delinquent* is generally applied to children under 16 or 18 who exhibit behavior which is punishable by law.

Delinquency may be viewed as a failure to acquire socially acceptable responses or the moral and ethical standards typical of the general culture. In some instances this failure may be related to unique problems in the child's psychological development which prevent him from becoming properly socialized or developing an adequate superego. In other instances, failure to adopt generally accepted standards may have other sources. For example, the child may come from a subcultural group which condones certain kinds of behavior which the broader community considers delinquent. Thus if a child lives in a slum area where gang warfare and petty theft are accepted or even encouraged by peers, he may readily adopt these practices.

Although most delinquents are adolescents when they come to the attention of the authorities, they generally begin their criminal activities during middle childhood. About 60 percent commit their first offenses before they are 10 years old (*11, 14, 15*). Moreover, as we shall see, a vast amount of research indicates that early childhood environment and family variables, particularly parent-child relationships, loom large in the etiology of juvenile delinquency.

General Environmental Factors

Ecological studies (analyses of the spatial distribution of social phenomena) (*14, 15, 45, 46*) have made it clear that delinquency rates vary from one part of a city to another. Most offenders come from deteriorated neighborhoods near the center of the city, which are adjacent to business and heavy industry and are characterized by economic privation, rapid population turnover, and general social disorganization. In these areas, delinquency is often an approved tradition and there are many opportunities for learning antisocial behavior from delinquent peers. An overwhelming majority of 1000 male offenders studied at the Boston juvenile court associated with undesirable companions, hung around the streets, and had no affiliations with organizations such as Boy Scouts, settlement houses, or boys' clubs (15).

Many delinquents come from broken or economically substandard homes. Moreover, delinquency is about twice as frequent among the children of immigrant as among those of native-born parents. Children of immigrant parents may experience a great deal of conflict produced by the contrasting standards of their homes, on the one hand, and the neighborhood and school, on the other. Moreover, the prestige of these children in the community may be relatively low. In addition to this, compared with native-born families, immigrant families are more likely to live in deteriorated neighborhoods, and hence their children are more likely to become delinquent.

Intelligence of Delinquents

Although there is a somewhat larger proportion of mentally deficient children among juvenile delinquents than among the population at large, there is a wide range of intelligence in the delinquent group. A comparison of the Stanford-Binet Intelligence Test scores of 500 juvenile delinquents and a representative sample of 3000 children showed similar distributions for the two groups, although the average I.Q. of the delinquents was 92.5 as compared with 101.8 for the nondelinquents (32). Since the average difference between the two groups is not a large one, and since there is a great deal of overlap between the delinquent and nondelinquent groups, low intelligence itself cannot be considered a major factor in determining most cases of juvenile delinquency.

Personality and Delinquency

Any of the above factors—poverty, poor neighborhoods, foreign parents, low intelligence—may be related to a particular child's delinquency, but no single variable can be interpreted as a sufficient antecedent condition for delinquent behavior. Of the total number of children who are mentally retarded, reside in high delinquency areas, or experience broken or economically impoverished homes, only a fraction become delinquent.

Comparisons between delinquents and nondelinquents who come from the same general social backgrounds offer the best approach to understanding the personal motivations underlying delinquent behavior. Basically we are concerned with discovering how the individual's unique developmental history and personality are related to "the way in which

[he] will be influenced by social disorganization, culture conflict, and the growing-pains of the city" (15, 6).

In their classic study of the personality structures and motivations of delinquents, Healy and Bronner (18) obtained extensive case history data on 105 juvenile offenders by means of psychiatric, psychological, and social-work interviews. Each of the subjects had a nondelinquent brother or sister near his own age who served as a control and was studied in the same way.

Despite the fact that they had the same parents and came from identical family backgrounds and environmental milieux, delinquents and controls differed markedly in their personality characteristics, attitudes, and interpersonal relationships. More delinquents than controls manifested neurotic tendencies, "personality deviations," and symptoms indicative of maladjustment (food and sleep idiosyncrasies, excessive nailbiting, thumbsucking, excessive masturbation, excessive smoking). Fewer of them were judged to have "normal emotional control," and most of them expressed strong antipathy for school. Their academic records were inferior to their brothers' and sisters', and they felt they were unpopular with schoolmates (18).

The most striking difference between the two groups, however, involved "familial attitudes and emotional experiences." The investigators were "tremendously impressed by the prevalence of profoundly felt emotional disturbances among the delinquents. These disturbances indubitably played a large part in the origin and growth of their delinquent tendencies" (18, 121).

It finally appears that no less than *91 percent of the delinquents* [96 cases] gave clear evidence of being or having been very unhappy and discontented in their life circumstances or extremely disturbed because of emotion-provoking situations or experiences. In great contradistinction we found similar evidences of inner stresses at the most in *only 13 per cent of the controls* (18, 122).

The authors list the following as the major types of emotional disturbances in the delinquent group. Many subjects showed more than one type of maladjustment.

1. Feeling keenly either *rejected, deprived, insecure, not understood* in affectional relationships, unloved, or that love has been withdrawn.

2. Deep feeling of being *thwarted* other than affectionally; either (a) in normal impulses or desires for self-expression or other self-satisfactions, (b) in unusual desires because earlier spoiled, or (c) in adolescent urges and desires— even when (as in 5 cases) desire for emancipation had been blocked only by the individual's counteractive pleasure in remaining childishly attached.

3. Feeling strongly either real or fancied *inadequacies or inferiorities* in the home life, in school, or in relation to companionship or to sports.

4. Intense feelings of *discomfort about family disharmonies,* parental misconduct, the conditions of family life, or parental errors in management and discipline.

5. Bitter feelings of *jealousy* toward one or more siblings, or feelings of being markedly discriminated against because another in the family circle more favored.

6. Feelings of confused unhappiness due to some deep-seated, often repressed, *internal mental conflict*—expressed in various kinds of delinquent acts which often are seemingly unreasonable.

7. Conscious or unconscious *sense of guilt* about earlier delinquencies or about behavior which technically was not delinquency; the guilt sense directly or indirectly activating delinquency through the individual's feeling of the need of punishment (in nearly every instance this overlaps with the last category) (*18*, 128).

There were only 9 delinquents who gave no strong evidence of emotional maladjustment. In these cases,

. . . there were various factors playing a part in the drama of causation—mainly social pressures deriving from poverty, poor family standards, lack of supervision, ideas of delinquency received from companions, etc.—with very little to counterbalance on the positive or constructive side (*18*, 129).

There were also 14 controls

. . . who evidently had experienced some considerable degree of emotional discomfort, but in every instance, they were able to find counterbalancing satisfactions. Either they found some other affectional relationship which substituted for the one barred to them, or their feeling of inadequacy in some direction was compensated for by satisfactory achievement in other ways, or distress about a family situation was made more tolerable for them by active allegiance to one of the parents. It might be thought that the delinquents also had opportunities for achieving satisfactions to offset emotional stress, but the ascertainable fact was that either circumstances totally prevented compensatory adjustments or that the established reactive tendencies of the delinquent individual or of others in the family circle did not permit satisfying emotional responses (*18*, 130).

The presence in this study of emotionally stable delinquents and highly disturbed controls again emphasizes that no single factor can be interpreted as *the* explanation of delinquency.

Another extensive study made use of a staff representing several disciplines (psychologists, psychiatrists, sociologists, anthropologists, and social workers) (*15*). These workers made detailed examinations of 500 delinquent boys "most of whom had court records reflecting persistent delinquency" and 500 control subjects matched in age, ethnic origins, intelligence (as measured by standard tests), and general socioeconomic background.

All the available data indicated that the nondelinquent controls were better handled by their parents. For instance, the early disciplinary techniques to which the delinquents had been subjected were typically "lax" and "erratic" (swinging from overstrictness to laxity without any consistency). Fathers of delinquents were more frequently "overstrict" and a smaller proportion of them were considered "firm but kindly." Physical punishment was the favorite disciplinary method of delinquent boys' parents, while the controls' parents more frequently reasoned with the boy about his misconduct (15).

In general, the delinquents' parents were less affectionate, more indifferent and hostile toward them, and correlatively, showed less warmth, sympathy, and affection. Compared with the control group, relatively few of the delinquents had close ties to their fathers and more of them expressed open hostility toward both parents. Many of them felt that their fathers were wholly unacceptable as models for their conduct. Obviously, they must have found it difficult to identify with them, or to learn acceptable patterns of social behavior from them.

In brief, "the delinquent boys, far more than the nondelinquents, grew up in a family atmosphere not conducive to the development of emotionally well-integrated, happy youngsters, conditioned to obedience to legitimate authority" (15, 133).

All subjects were given the Rorschach, a projective personality test in which the subject describes what he sees in each of a series of 10 ink blots. Analysis of the test responses suggested that, as a group, the delinquents were much more socially assertive, defiant, ambivalent to authority, resentful, hostile, suspicious and destructive, impulsive, vivacious, independent, and extraverted. At the same time, they were significantly less self-controlled, less submissive to authority, less conventional in ideas and behavior, less coöperative, and less fearful of failure and defeat. "Even a simple review of the traits and tendencies under consideration shows that they are of a nature to facilitate uncontrolled, antisocial self-expression" (15, 241).

Viewed in perspective, research on delinquncy indicates that emotional maladjustment, frustration, feelings of inadequacy, and rejection are extremely significant in predisposing the child to crime. However, by themselves, they are not sufficient to produce delinquency. A child does not become a delinquent unless he learns antisocial behavior, and he does not persist in this behavior unless some rewards are associated with it. Delinquent parents or peers may supply both the patterns and rewards for delinquent behavior.

MINORITY-GROUP PREJUDICE

Minority-group attitudes may be considered integral parts of the American social scene since "the general cultural pattern . . . includes racial, national, and religious affiliations as significant attributes relevant to the consideration and description of the individual" (*19*, 184).

The Development of Prejudice

Studies indicate that by kindergarten, many children have developed hostile attitudes toward minority groups. During the early school years, these become more crystallized and conform more closely to adult patterns of prejudice. Radke and her colleagues (*41, 42, 43*) interviewed 251 lower-middle-class children, ages 5 to 8, in kindergarten and the first two grades of six public schools in the Philadelphia area. Each subject was asked to interpret several pictures showing children of different groups in simple social situations in school, on the street, and on the playground. For example, in one picture, a Negro boy is watching some white children play ball; in another, several boys are watching two Jewish boys coming out of a synagogue. The racial and religious identifications of the individuals depicted are defined by the tester if the child does not acknowledge them immediately, and the child is then asked to interpret the picture by telling a story about it. The child's attitudes toward minority groups were assessed from the content of his stories.

The stories revealed, not "childish imaginative content, but . . . a more or less faithful reproduction of patterns of group prejudices in the adult culture" (*41*, 363). Even the youngest children studied had anti-minority group attitudes and with advancing age, the percentage of children expressing prejudice and awareness of group tensions in society increased. Thus, from kindergarten to the second grade, the proportion of white children who rejected Negroes rose sharply.

Among the religious groups, the Jews were most frequently rejected, and hostility toward them also increased with age. In many stories told by gentile children, Jewish children were excluded from a play group because of their religious affiliation. Anti-Semitism was strongest in schools located in areas with heightened intergroup tensions, but group hierarchies and race attitudes were basically similar in all neighborhoods studied. Older children applied group labels much more frequently and freely than younger ones, stating their attitudes with greater feeling and conviction.

Qualitative analysis of the data of this study indicated that the children's prejudices were rarely based on their own experiences. Their verbalizations about minorities obviously reflected negative attitudes learned from the direct or indirect teaching of adults (41, 42).

In a second investigation, the mothers of many of these children were interviewed about their own attitudes toward, and perceptions of, minority groups (43). In general, these parents made statements in support of democratic values and intercultural education, and opposed to racial or religious segregation in the schools. However, they had little insight into their own underlying feelings toward minority groups or the implications of their own group membership, and made no direct or planned attempts to teach their children ethnic attitudes. Instead, these were conveyed to the children by restricting social relationships in the home, neighborhood, and school, and by disapproving of friendships with members of certain groups.

Background and Personality of Prejudiced Children

Children may acquire the prejudices of those with whom they identify —parents, peers, their social group. Children of prejudiced parents may become bigoted, while those emulating tolerant parents may develop democratic attitudes. However, more is involved in the development of prejudice than simple imitation of attitudes. Studies of anti-Semitic and anti-Negro adults show that their prejudices are components of broader patterns of attitudes and are related to basic personality structure. Compared with tolerant people, prejudiced adults tend to be rigid, authoritarian, highly conforming, and overly moralistic (1).

An excellent study by Frenkel-Brunswik "designed to throw light on the determinants of susceptibility to racial or ethnic prejudice and allied forms of undemocratic opinions and attitudes" (12, 295) demonstrates that children's ethnic prejudices are also related to general personality structure. About 1500 California boys and girls between the ages of 11 and 16 were given tests measuring attitudes toward Jews, Negroes, Japanese, Mexicans, and out-groups in general. A series of statements about these groups were presented and the subjects were asked to express their agreement or disagreement with each. Some contained stereotypical accusations: Japanese cruelty, Negro laziness, Jewish radicalism and money-mindedness, etc. Others involved sharing activities with minority group members (e.g., eating in the same restaurants, living in the same neighborhood, socializing together). From the larger group, the 120 most and least prejudiced children were selected for further study, including personality tests and interviews.

Ethnocentric (prejudiced) children revealed selfish orientations toward America and indifference toward other countries. They agreed with generally intolerant statements (e.g., "Only people who are like myself have the right to be happy"; "We should not send any of our food to foreign countries, but should think of America first") much more frequently than unprejudiced children did.

Other generalized attitudes typical of the prejudiced child, but not the unprejudiced, were: rejection of all that is weak or different; rigid conceptions of appropriate sex roles, together with intolerance of passive or feminine behavior in boys and masculine or tomboyish behavior in girls; admiration of the strong, tough, powerful, and in the boys, a fear of weakness in themselves; rigid conformity to approved social values and moralistic condemnation of others; feelings of helplessness in a world thought to be full of chaos and destruction. All these attitudes were considered indicative of "narrow and rigid personality" (12).

In discussing relationships with parents, the tolerant children frequently mentioned affection, coöperation, and companionship, while the prejudiced children complained of lack of affection and submission to stern, harsh, punitive treatment. Interviews with the parents offered evidence that the tolerant child "learns at home the equalitarian and individualized approach to people, as the ethnocentric child learns the authoritarian and hierarchical way of thinking" (12, 302).

From these data, Frenkel-Brunswik concluded:

From the point of view of society as a whole, the most important problem . . . seems to be the child's attitude toward authority. Forced submission to authority produces only surface conformity countermanded by violent underlying destructiveness, dangerous to the very society to which there seems to be conformity. Only a frightened and frustrated child will tend to gain safety and security by oversimplified black-white schematizations and categorizations on the basis of crude, external characteristics. Deliberately planned democratic participation in school and family, individualized approach to the child, and the right proportion of permissiveness and guidance may be instrumental in bringing about the attitude necessary for a genuine identification with society and thus for international understanding (12, 306).

In another investigation of the relationship between personality and ethnic attitudes, a variety of tests were given to 242 fourth-, fifth-, and sixth-grade subjects (16). Subjects were asked to indicate agreement or disagreement with each of: (1) eighteen statements regarding Negroes (e.g., "They are pretty dumb"; "They are always honest"); (2) nine items concerning social distance or acceptance of Negroes and Jews ("I would let them go to my school"; "I would let them be my best friends"); (3) eight general intolerance statements taken from the Frenkel-Brunswik study summarized above ("A dance hall should allow all kinds of people from all races"; "People from all races should be allowed to stay in the same hotels"). In addition, there were 24 statements which tapped aspects of personality presumably related to prejudice (for example, "There are only two kinds of people; the weak and the strong"; "I have often been punished unfairly"; "Most people hate it when they have to help someone else"). The high correlations obtained between general intolerance and attitudes toward Jews and Negroes, indicate that there is a generalized prejudiced attitude.

Compared with the tolerant children,

. . . the more prejudiced child favors his own immediate group over any larger society, he thinks categorically of "weak" and "strong," he declares himself in favor of authoritarianism on the part of teachers, he is suspicious of integrity of others. . . . In general, the picture one gets of the prejudiced child . . . suggests fear and distrust of others, lack of confidence in himself, feelings of guilt and uneasiness, insecurities and doubts about the larger physical and social world and possibly a reactive hostility toward people who are "weak" or "different" (16, 89).

"Moreover, intolerant children . . . have cynical, distrustful opinions of others, have fears of being exploited or duped, or have feelings of having been treated unfairly" (16, 91).

These two investigations are in essential agreement about the nature of the personality structure of the prejudiced child. In general, as Frenkel-Brunswik's study indicates, personality characteristics associated with intolerance are established in early parent-child relationships.

In a further study of the antecedents of children's prejudices, one team of investigators (17) made a direct test of the hypothesis that "authoritarian and disciplinary attitudes of parents concerning child training practices would be related to a greater incidence of ethnic bias in the children of these parents" (17, 170).

The subjects were 154 mothers of children whose attitudes toward minority groups had been tested. The mothers answered questionnaires consisting of 81 items grouped into five scales: authoritarian attitudes and practices; permissiveness; parent-child integration (evidence of a close, affective emotional parent-child relationship); parental rigidity or fussiness; general good judgment. The correlations between the parental behavior scales and children's attitudes scores generally substantiated the original hypothesis. There was a distinct tendency for more of the mothers of prejudiced children (as contrasted with mothers of non-prejudiced children) to score in the higher ranges of the authoritarian and rigidity scales. Correspondingly, fewer of the mothers of low-prejudice children scored low on permissiveness, parent-child integration, and "good judgment" (17).

Prejudice in children appears to be associated with the complex of parental attitudes which is involved in authoritarian handling of control and with lack of tolerance of children's "annoyance value." It appears that attitudes of tolerance and good judgment in child rearing are possibly part of a personality and attitude complex on the parents' part which is associated with freedom from ethnic prejudice in children (17, 180).

What children learn is not a specific attitude, but a whole "complex of attitudes and personality characteristics, which reveal themselves in interpersonal relationships of various sorts" (17, 180).

Modification of Racial Attitudes

Since intolerance is related to firmly established characteristics, it might be inferred that it could be reduced only by changing the basic personality structure of the prejudiced person. This, of course, would require intensive clinical treatment.

It would be a serious mistake, however, to assume that there is a one-to-one correspondence between personality and prejudice. If they live among bigoted people, well-adjusted children may learn to behave intolerantly, i.e., in accordance with the standard or accepted attitudes of their own social group. In such cases, prejudice might be viewed as a reflection of the child's identification with his group, rather than as displacement of his hostility toward his parents. Perhaps those whose prejudice has this kind of basis, but who in general are well adjusted and not essentially hostile, would become more tolerant if they were transferred to an environment that promoted "democratic living" and an equalitarian philosophy. On the other hand, those who *need* scapegoats as an outlet for deep-lying aggressive feelings may not be able to relinquish their prejudices, even in a democratic setting. To test these hypotheses, one investigator (35) studied changes in boys' attitudes toward Negroes after a four-week vacation at an interracial camp where Negroes and whites lived, ate, and played together. The subjects were 106 white New York City boys ranging from 8 to 14 years of age.

An indirect test of prejudice was administered to each boy less than 24 hours before he left home, that is, before intimate contact with Negro boys at camp. In this test the child was given 12 photographs of boys' faces, eight of them Negro, four of them white. In the first part of the test, the child simply indicated his order of preference for these faces. In the second part, he selected the pictures of boys he would like to go to the movies with, invite home to lunch, etc. The extent of discrimination against the pictures of Negroes constituted the measure of prejudice. This test was given again just before the children left the camp.

Personality structure was evaluated by analyzing objectively responses to a picture-story test (the Thematic Apperception Test) in which the subject's underlying needs and attitudes were reflected in the kinds of stories he told. Data about personal and social adjustment at camp were collected from two sources: a brief interview with each child and a camp social worker's report.

Following the camp experience, some of the boys increased significantly in prejudice whereas others decreased. As hypothesized, these changes were related to personality structure. In general, the boys who increased in prejudice were hostile, defiant youngsters who perceived the world as cruel and unpleasant and felt they were frequent victims of aggression. Since, for them, the expression of aggression led to punishment, retaliation, and restraint, they probably did not "act out" their hostile feelings. Hence they had greater needs to displace their aggression by means of anti-Negro prejudice.

Moreover, these boys were dissatisfied with the camp itself, the other campers, and interpersonal relations there. The child who was poorly socially adjusted in the situation and did not find the experience rewarding probably did not identify with the camp or accept its attitudes. Under the circumstances, he may have felt more frustrated, and may have become more, rather than less, prejudiced against Negroes.

Children who decreased in prejudice presented a sharply contrasting picture. They manifested fewer aggressive needs, less hostility toward their parents, fewer feelings of restraint, and generally favorable attitudes toward society. Consequently, they had little need to displace aggression through prejudice.

In the camp, they were well accepted by their peers, and their counselors judged them to be high in "ability to relate to others." They complained less about interpersonal relations, were more satisfied with the camp experience and their fellow campers, and probably formed more intimate friendships (35). It may be assumed that they found the experience rewarding and consequently identified more closely with the camp, accepting its tolerant and equalitarian philosophy.

Apparently both personality and social situational factors are involved in changes in race attitudes. The study suggests that prejudice may be reduced by educational measures, such as encouraging contacts between members of various races. Such measures may often be effective with well-adjusted children whose prejudices are simply a reflection of prevalent stereotypes. On the other hand, where prejudice is a function of deep-seated psychological disturbances, such measures will not be effective, or may even strengthen the prejudice.

REFERENCES AND ADDITIONAL READING

1. Adorno, T. W., Frenkel-Brunswik, E., Levinson, D. J., and Sanford, R. N., *The authoritarian personality*. New York: Harper, 1950.
2. Austin, M. C., and Thompson, G. G., Children's friendships: a study of the bases on which children select and reject their best friends. *J. educ. Psychol.* (1948), *39*:101–116.
3. Bonney, M. E., A study of social status on the second grade level. *J. genet. Psychol.* (1942), *60*:271–305.
4. Bonney, M. E., A study of the relation of intelligence, family size, and sex differences with mutual friendships in the primary grades. *Child Develop.* (1942), *13*:79–100.
5. Bonney, M. E., The constancy of sociometric scores and their relationship to teacher judgments of social success and to personality self-ratings. *Sociometry* (1943), *6*:409–424.
6. Bonney, M. E., Sex differences in social success and personality traits. *Child Develop.* (1944), *15*:63–79.
7. Bonney, M. E., Relationships between social success, family size, socio-economic home background, and intelligence among school children in grades III and IV. *Sociometry* (1944), *7*:26–39.
8. Bonney, M. E., A sociometric study of the relationship of some factors to mutual friendships on the elementary, secondary, and college levels. *Sociometry* (1946), *9*:21–47.
9. Boynton, P. L., The vocational preferences of school children. *J. genet. Psychol.* (1936), *49*:411–425.
10. Campbell, E. H., The social-sex development of children. *Genet. Psychol. Monogr.* (1939), *21*:No. 4, pp. 461–552.
11. Fenton, N., and others, *The delinquent boy and the correctional school*. Claremont, Calif.: Claremont College Guidance Center, 1935.
12. Frenkel-Brunswik, E., A study of prejudice in children. *Human Relations* (1948), *1*:295–306.
13. Furfey, P. H., Some factors influencing the selection of boys' chums. *J. appl. Psychol.* (1927), *11*:47–51.
14. Glueck, S., and Glueck, E. T., *One thousand juvenile delinquents*. Cambridge: Harvard University Press, 1934.

15. Glueck, S., and Glueck, E. T., *Unraveling juvenile delinquency*. New York: Commonwealth Fund, 1950.
16. Gough, H. G., Harris, D. B., Martin, W. E., and Edwards, M., Children's ethnic attitudes: I. Relationship to certain personality factors. *Child Develop.* (1950), *21*:83–91.
17. Harris, D. B., Gough, H. G., and Martin, W. E., Children's ethnic attitudes: II. Relationship to parental beliefs concerning child training. *Child Develop.* (1950), *21*:169–181.
18. Healy, W., and Bronner, A. F., *New light on delinquency and its treatment*. New Haven: Yale University Press, 1936.
19. Horowitz, E. L., Race attitudes, in O. Klineberg (ed.), *Characteristics of the American Negro*. New York: Harper, 1944.
20. Horowitz, E. L., and Horowitz, R. E., Development of social attitudes in children. *Sociometry* (1938), *1*:301–338.
21. Horrocks, J. E., *The psychology of adolescence*. Boston: Houghton Mifflin, 1951.
22. Horrocks, J. E., and Buker, M. E., A study of the friendship fluctuations of preadolescents. *J. genet. Psychol.* (1951), 78:131–144.
23. Jennings, H. H., *Leadership and isolation: a study of personality in interpersonal relations*. New York: Longmans, Green, 1943.
24. Koch, H. L., A study of some factors conditioning the social distance between the sexes. *J. soc. Psychol.* (1944), *20*:79–107.
25. Lazar, M., *Reading interests, activities, and opportunities of bright, average, and dull children. Contributions to Education, No. 707.* New York: Bureau of Publications, Teachers College, Columbia University, 1937.
26. Lehman, H. C., and Witty, P. A., *The psychology of play activities*. New York: Barnes, 1927.
27. Lerner, E., *Constraint areas and moral judgement of children*. Menasha, Wis.: Banta, 1937.
28. Lerner, E., The problem of perspective in moral reasoning. *Am. J. Sociol.* (1937), *43*:249–269.
29. Lyness, P. I., The place of the mass media in the lives of boys and girls. *Journalism Quart.* (1952), *29*:43–54.
30. MacRae, D., A test of Piaget's theories of moral development. *J. abnorm. soc. Psychol.* (1954), *49*:14–18.
31. Martin, W. E., and Stendler, C. B., *Child development: the process of growing up in society*. New York: Harcourt, Brace, 1953.
32. Merrill, M. A., *Problems of child delinquency*. Boston: Houghton Mifflin, 1947.
33. Moreno, J. L., *Who shall survive?* Washington: Nervous and Mental Disease Publishing Co., 1934.
34. Murphy, G., *Personality*. New York: Harper, 1947.
35. Mussen, P. H., Some personality and social factors related to changes in children's attitudes toward Negroes. *J. abnorm. soc. Psychol.* (1950), *45*: 423–441.
36. Northway, M. L., Children with few friends. *School* (1944), *32*:380–384.

37. Northway, M. L., Outsiders; a study of personality patterns of children least acceptable to their age mates. *Sociometry* (1944), 7:10–26.
38. Phillips, E. L., Shenker, S., and Revitz, P., The assimilation of the new child into the group. *Psychiatry* (1951), 14:319–325.
39. Piaget, J., *The moral judgment of the child.* London: Kegan Paul, 1932.
40. Polansky, N., Lippitt, R., and Redl, F., An investigation of behavorial contagion in groups. *Human Relations* (1950), 3:319–348.
41. Radke, M. J., Trager, H. G., and Davis, H., Social perceptions and attitudes of children. *Genet. Psychol. Monogr.* (1949), 40:327–447.
42. Radke, M. J., and Trager, H. G., Children's perception of the social roles of Negroes and whites. *J. Psychol.* (1950), 29:3–33.
43. Radke-Yarrow, M., Trager, H. G., and Miller, J., The role of parents in the development of children's ethnic attitudes. *Child Develop.* (1952), 23:13–53.
44. Ricciuti, E. A., Children and radio; a study of listeners and nonlisteners to various types of radio programs in terms of selected ability, attitude, and behavior measures. *Genet. Psychol. Monogr.* (1941), 44:69–143.
45. Shaw, C. R., *Delinquency areas.* Chicago: University of Chicago Press, 1929.
46. Shaw, C. R., McKay, H. D., and others, *Juvenile delinquency and urban areas.* Chicago: University of Chicago Press, 1942.
47. Strang, R., Why children read the comics. *Elem. Sch. J.* (1942–1943), 43:336–342.
48. Terman, L. M., and Lima, M., *Children's readings,* 1st ed. New York: Appleton, 1926.
49. Terman, L. M., and Tyler, L. E., Psychological sex differences, in L. Carmichael (ed.), *Manual of child psychology,* 2nd ed. New York: Wiley, 1954, pp. 1064–1114.
50. Thorndike, R. L., and Henry, F., Differences in reading interests related to differences in sex and intelligence level. *Elem. Sch. J.* (1940), 40:751–763.
51. Tuddenham, R. D., Studies in reputation: I. Sex and grade differences in school children's evaluation of their peers. II. The diagnosis of social adjustment. *Psychol. Monogr.* (1952), 66:No. 333.
52. Tuddenham, R. D., Studies in reputation: III. Correlates of popularity among elementary-school children. *J. educ. Psychol.* (1951), 42:257–276.
53. Tyler, L. E., The relationship of interests to abilities and reputation among first-grade children. *Educ. Psychol. Meas.* (1951), 11:255–264.

PART V

Adolescence

Chapter 13

PHYSICAL DEVELOPMENT IN ADOLESCENCE

Adolescence is generally viewed, at least in American culture, as a period of unusual difficulty in adjustment. Actually adolescence merely means the process of becoming an adult, growing into maturity. However, ". . . the term has gained other less favorable meanings. These are implied when we speak of adolescent 'stress and strain,' 'growing pains,' 'teen-age troubles,' 'the silly phase,' and other phenomena to which we attach the adjective 'adolescent' (sometimes in a resigned mood and sometimes in exasperation" (27). The "storm and stress" (22) of these years have been described with sensitivity and considerable insight by poets, dramatists, and novelists (9). They have been described in less inspired, if more succinct terms, by psychologists, sociologists, anthropologists, and psychoanalysts. One analyst, for example, describes adolescence as a period often marked by contradictory psychological expressions: "Egoism and altruism, pettiness and generosity, sociability and loneliness, cheerfulness and sadness, silly jocularity and overseriousness, intensive loves and sudden abandonment of those loves, submission and rebellion, rudeness and tender consideration—all are typical" (16).

The adjustment difficulties of American adolescents have been explained in a variety of ways by biologists and social scientists, depending on their theoretical orientation. For example, some biologists are likely to attribute the adolescent's difficulties to such things as changes in hormone secretion, changes in the rate of skeletal growth, and temporary imbalances of body structure and function. It is these imbalances, they are likely to maintain, which are the immediate source of adolescent maladjustment (27).

In classical psychoanalytic theory, the physiological changes of puberty are viewed as disrupting forces requiring new psychological adjustments on the part of the adolescent. According to Fenichel, a prominent psychoanalyst:

The relative equilibrium of the latency period lasts until puberty. Then there is a biological intensification of sexual impulses. . . . All the mental phenomena characteristic of puberty may be regarded as attempts to reëstablish the disturbed equilibrium. Normal maturation proceeds in such a way that upon attainment of genital primacy the ego [self] accepts sexuality as the important component of his personality and learns to adjust to it.

This is not simple in societies with our cultural conditions. The psychological task in puberty is the adaptation of the personality to new conditions which have been brought about by physical changes (16, 110).

Both of the above viewpoints tend to emphasize the role of biological factors in producing adolescent adjustment difficulties. The cultural anthropologist, on the other hand, is likely to hold the culture responsible, pointing out that adolescent adjustment varies from one society to another, and that adolescence is not considered a difficult period in all cultures (6, 27).

It has been maintained throughout this book that psychological development proceeds as the result of complex and continuous interactions between a biological organism and its environment. We think that it is important to emphasize our argument again at this point, since adolescent behavior cannot adequately be explained in one-sided terms, whether physiological, cultural, or specifically sexual.

There can be little doubt that the sudden physiological changes that accompany the onset of adolescence require new adjustments. Sudden spurts in height and weight, changes in body structure and function, increased sexual drive all have their effects, as we shall see shortly.

Nevertheless it would be an oversimplification to ascribe the fact that adolescence in our culture emerges as a period of "storm and stress" solely to physical maturation. If physical factors alone were responsible, we would expect this phenomenon to characterize adolescence in all cultures, since the physiological changes of puberty are common to mankind everywhere. Anthropological evidence, however, indicates that adolescence is not viewed as stressful in all societies. For example, among the Samoans, it is seen as a time of considerable happiness (6).

Furthermore, even in those societies which do recognize a period of difficulty in adjustment comparable to adolescent "storm and stress" in our society, this period does not necessarily coincide with biological puberty. Thus the adjustment difficulty cannot be simply the result of the biological changes of puberty. As Benedict notes:

The most casual survey of the way in which different societies have handled adolescence makes one fact inescapable: Even in those cultures which have made most of the trait [adolescent adjustment difficulty], the age upon which they focused their attention varies over a great range of years. At the outset, therefore, it is clear that the so-called puberty institutions are a misnomer if we continue to think of biological puberty. The puberty they recognize is social, and the ceremonies are a recognition in some fashion or other of the child's new status of adulthood. This investiture with new occupations and obligations is in consequence as various and as culturally conditioned as the occupations and the obligations themselves. If the sole honorable duty of manhood is conceived to be deeds of war, the investiture of the warrior is later and of a different sort from that in a society where adulthood gives chiefly the privilege of dancing in a representation of masked gods. In order to understand puberty institutions, we do not most need analyses of the necessary nature of *rites de passage* [formal ceremonies acknowledging the achievement of adult status]: we need rather to know what is identified in different cultures with the beginning of adulthood and their methods of admitting to the new status. Not biological puberty, but what adulthood means in that culture conditions the puberty ceremony (6, 23).

But if exclusively maturational explanations of adolescent adjustment difficulties can be ruled out, how can we account for the fact that in our society adolescence is viewed as a well-defined stressful period while in other cultures it is not? The answer to this question seems to be that there are cultural differences in the number and extent of the demands made upon the adolescent. For example, among the Samoans the adolescent is not required to inhibit sexual expression, and this fact may help to make adolescent adjustment easier in Samoan culture (34). In American middle-class culture, it is demanded (though not too successfully, as Kinsey's data show) that the adolescent avoid sexual expression.

There are of course many other societal demands which may affect the American adolescent's adjustment. The adolescent must also prepare himself for a job; for changed political and social status as a citizen; for marriage; for relatively complete separation from the parents and the setting up of an independent household; and for a mature philosophy of life. When we consider that in most cases the American adolescent has had little previous training for any of these tasks prior to puberty, it is not surprising that he should have difficulty in learning them completely and easily in the few short years between puberty and nominal adulthood.

The problem is further complicated by the fact that, despite the crucial importance of coping successfully with social demands, the adolescent finds little consistent guidance from the culture to help him. In fact, becoming aware of, and learning to adjust to the contradictory values, goals, and methods of adults constitute added problems.

Many American adolescents are in the position of knowing that it is important for them to get somewhere in a hurry, but they know only roughly where, and have an even poorer idea of how to proceed. Furthermore, as Lewin (32) has pointed out, they have no real status in our society during this period. The adolescent has renounced childhood, but has not yet been fully accepted as an adult. Partly accepted and partly rejected by the privileged adult group, he "has a position somewhat similar to what is called in sociology the 'marginal [i.e., underprivileged] man.' To some extent behavior symptomatic for the marginal man can be found in the adolescent. He too is oversensitive, easily shifted from one extreme to the other, and particularly sensitive to the shortcomings of his younger fellows. Indeed, his position is sociologically the same as that of the marginal man; he does not wish to belong any longer to a group which is, after all, less privileged than the group of adults; but at the same time he knows that he is not fully accepted by the adult" (34).

A prominent psychiatrist recently made a similar comment when he referred to the adolescent as being in the "not quite stage"—not quite an adult, not quite a child, and not quite sure of himself (33).

As we shall see later, in a number of other cultures, the types of adolescent demands cited above either do not exist, or are spread out over larger periods of time. In these cultures, adolescence tends to be less stressful. On the other hand, in some other cultures the demands of adolescence are greater in number than ours or more severe. Needless to say, adolescence in these cultures tends to be rather stressful.

In summary, we do not believe it is possible to gain a proper understanding of adolescent development, in our own or any other culture, without a full awareness both of the biological changes occurring at this time and also of the cultural influences to which the individual is subjected. Although the two usually work together in complex ways, for purposes of exposition our primary emphasis in this chapter will be upon the physical and intellectual changes of puberty and adolescence, and the psychological problems associated directly with these. In the next chapter, we will turn our attention to the special socialization demands made upon the adolescent in the American culture and the ways in which they compare to those of other cultures.

PHYSICAL CHANGES IN PUBERTY AND ADOLESCENCE

The term puberty has been derived from the Latin word *pubertas*, or "age of manhood" (*24*). It refers to the first phase of adolescence, the phase during which the individual is maturing sexually as a result of complex hormonal changes in his body. Most frequently, puberty is dated from the beginning of menstruation (the menarche) in girls, and the emergence of pigmented pubic hair in boys (*11*). Puberty is considered to begin with these two events only because they offer convenient lines of demarcation on which it is possible to obtain data.

Age of Menarche

According to various studies, the average age at which American girls begin menstruation is between 13 and 14 years (*47*). These same studies, however, have revealed considerable individual variation. "Women of excellent health may reach puberty as early as the 9th year and as late as the 20th" (*11*). Most American girls, however, reach menarche between 11 and 15 years of age, with only about 3 percent falling below, and 3 percent above this range (*49*). Within the United States, different racial and socioeconomic groups do not appear to differ significantly in age at menarche. In some cases of precocious puberty, menstruation occurs regularly from birth. There are other cases in which menstruation does not begin until the third or fourth decade. Such cases, however, are extremely rare, and in most instances can be attributed to some definitely pathological condition (*11*).

There is a persistent popular belief that girls in tropical countries reach puberty earlier than girls in the more temperate zones, such as the United States. Available research data, however, do not support this notion. The average age of menarche for various tropical and semitropical countries ranges from 13.5 to 14.5 years (*11*).

On the other hand, far northern girls, such as the Greenland and Labrador eskimos, do appear to mature quite late (around age 16). Northern European girls also appear to reach the menarche somewhat later than American girls (from 14½ to almost 16 years). There is also some evidence to suggest that the average menarchial age is decreasing slightly in a number of countries, including the United States (*11*).

The various hypotheses which have been developed to account for variations in menarchial age are beyond the scope of this book. However, it should be emphasized that the menarche should be viewed only as a reflection of the individual's general physiological state (*49*). As such, it is subject to a wide variety of influences ranging from genetic factors to nutritional conditions. For example, girls who have had rickets mature later than others.

Pubertal Age in Boys

Information about the onset of puberty is not so extensive in the case of boys as it is for girls. However, in a relatively complete study (43), the status of primary and secondary sexual development in 1475 normal, representative New York males, ranging in age from birth to 25 years was investigated. Each subject was classified as either (1) prepubescent; (2) in one of four stages of pubescence (progressively greater pubic hair development, increase in size of penis and testes); or (3) fully mature. Marked individual variations were noted in the rates at which normal boys mature sexually. For example, while 17 percent of the 20- to 21-year-old males were still in the last stage of pubescence, 7 percent of the 14-year-olds were already fully mature. Similarly while 6 percent of the 14-year-olds had not yet reached pubescence, 4 percent of the 10-year-olds were already pubescent.

The limited number of other studies of pubertal age available are in essential agreement with these findings. In general, they show that boys develop noticeable pubic hair about the same time that girls begin their menses—again between 13 and 14 years, on the average; and that they show the same sorts of individual variations in age of pubescence as girls (a range from 10 to 15 years) (2, 11, 12). If we were to assume that the development of pigmented pubic hair in boys is really equivalent to the menarche in girls, it would appear that both boys and girls reach comparable stages of adolescence at approximately the same age. But as we have already emphasized, the selection of these two events as criteria of puberty has arisen mostly from convenience, and there is no necessary reason for assuming their equivalence.

Adolescent Fertility

Perhaps the age at which the adolescent achieves fertility (i.e., the ability to have children) might be considered a more convincing criterion of maturity. Unfortunately, however, such data are extremely difficult to obtain. There is some evidence to suggest that both boys and girls tend to remain sterile for a considerable period after the development of pubescent hair or the menarche, but precise information is lacking, particularly in the case of boys (49). One team of investigators (36) recorded the ages of the menarche and of the first conception in various groups among which promiscuity was frequent from an early age. They found that "conception is extremely unlikely to occur during the first year following the menarche, and that for a period of four to six years it is less likely than after full maturity but does occur with increasing frequency. This period of adolescent physiologic sterility progressively shortens as the menarche is delayed. Conception can occur very early, but it seldom does so before the age of 16, regardless of the age at the menarche" (36).

Physical Growth and Development

Actually, most people's notions that girls mature earlier than boys are not derived from statistics on pubescent hair, menstruation, or fertility. They stem from the valid observation that girls attain adult standards of height and weight earlier than boys (45).

As several investigators have shown, girls tend to reach the prepubescent stage of most rapid growth in height about two years before boys. The findings of one investigation, summarized in Figure 31, indicate that

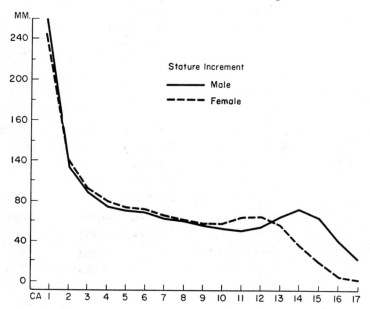

FIGURE 31. Stature increment according to chronological age. (Reproduced from K. Simmons, "The Brush Foundation Study of Child Growth and Development. II. Physical Growth and Development." *Monogr. Soc. Res. Child Develop.* (1944), 9:No. 1. By permission of the author and Society for Research in Child Development.)

while, in general, girls tend to gain height at an accelerated rate from 9 to 12 years, boys do so from 11 to 14 years (*49*).

The average 9-year-old girl in our culture stands about 4 feet 2½ inches tall, and weighs about 57 pounds. These figures reflect a leisurely increase both in height and weight in the early years of middle childhood. As a result of her ensuing growth spurt, however, by the age of 12 she will stand about 4 feet 9 inches tall and weigh about 100 pounds (*51*).

At the beginning of his growth spurt the average 11-year-old boy stands about 4 feet 10 inches, and weighs about 86 pounds. By age 14, his height will have increased to about 5 feet 4 inches, and his weight to about 119 pounds (*51*).

"From 13 years in girls and 15 years in boys the rate of growth in height decelerates rapidly, and after about three years ceases. According to these yearly averages, the 12th year in girls and the 14th year in boys appear to be those of maximum growth" (*49*). These are also roughly the years of maximum weight increment.

As puberty approaches, the body proportions of both boys and girls undergo change also, though again the change is later among boys. The baby face of childhood begins to disappear. The low forehead becomes higher and wider. The mouth widens and the flat lips become fuller. The slightly receding chin of childhood begins to jut out. Moreover, the relatively large head characteristic of childhood becomes smaller in proportion to total body length. This is due in large measure to the fact that during this period the extremities are growing at a faster rate than the head. By age 10, the average child's head has achieved 90 percent of its mature length, and by age 15 it has practically reached adult size. During these years the extremities are still growing rapidly.

Along with the increases in height and weight during this period, less obvious physical changes are occurring too. As we have already seen (cf. pp. 171; 218), not only do the bones change in size, proportion, and shape as the child grows older, but they change internally also. It will be recalled that in early childhood the composition of the bones is such that there is a preponderance of cartilage and fibrous tissues, with less mineral matter than is found later. This makes the bones somewhat spongy and soft. Because of this they are liable to deformity. But as the bones increase in size, the cartilage begins to calcify, making the bones harder, denser, and more brittle. This process of ossification speeds up at puberty. By the age of 17 the average girl's bones "should be mature not only in size, but also in ossification" (*24*).

Just as in the case of the growth spurt, the average boy's skeletal development is relatively delayed. For example, the average boy of 9 is about 1 year behind the average girl in osseous development. By 11 he is about 18 months behind, and after 12 about 2 years. This relative situation persists until the girl has reached maturity in her osseous development (51). The average boy's skeletal development is not completed until around 19 years of age.

A similar situation exists with regard to muscular development. During adolescence, both boys and girls show marked increases in the percentage of body weight occupied by muscles. In the average 8-year-old child, the weight of the muscles makes up about 20 percent of gross body weight. By 15, however, the percentage has increased to 32 percent, and by 16, to 44 percent. After 16, little increase in the size or weight of muscles takes place. These are average figures which mask sex differences, however. Again the boy's development tends to be more delayed. In girls, the most pronounced increase in muscle tissue in relation to total body weight comes between 12 and 15 years of age; in boys it does not occur until around 15 or 16 years (24). Of course, the ultimate development of the girl's muscles is not so great as the boy's, so that girls are not as strong as boys at maturity.

As might be expected, motor performance improves as these changes are occurring. It has been found that among girls, measures of coördination, strength, speed, and accuracy all improve with age up until about age 14. After that, they either fail to improve or decline. In contrast, the mean performance of boys on all these tests increases steadily up to 17 years. Despite marked individual differences on these tests, boys generally do better than girls on all the measures, and this superiority increases with age.

There are fairly clear relationships between the various aspects of pubertal development described above. For example, there appears to be a close correspondence between the age at which an individual reaches his maximum rate of growth in height and weight, and the age at which puberty is reached (11, 44, 46). Even before the maximum growth rate is achieved, measures of skeletal activity can be used to predict whether girls will be likely to have an early, average, or late menarche (46). Similar relationships seem to hold among other aspects of growth and primary and secondary sexual development. In other words, there tends to be a general "going togetherness" of various maturational factors involved at this period of the individual's life (37).

Despite this general tendency, however, individual exceptions do occur. For example, bones and muscles may have differential growth rates, and these may serve as a basis for some of the complaints of adolescents. When muscle growth forges ahead of osseous development, looseness of the muscles occurs, resulting in some incoördination and clumsiness. However, when the bones develop faster than the muscles, cramps and "growing" pains are common experiences (24).

In addition, early or late maturation may be related to the kind of physique the individual ultimately develops. Boas (21, 22) found that among individuals who had the same stature at an early age, those whose period of maximum growth rate was earlier, tended to be shorter as adults. These differences, however, were not great. It appears that while individuals with an early age of maximum growth rate tend to have longer periods of increased growth rate (and hence can be expected to reach a greater adult height), such individuals seem at the same time to have less intense growth rates. Thus the effect of the longer period of growth in these people is pretty much canceled out by their generally less intense growth.

Boys who mature early tend to have broader hips, narrower shoulders, and shorter legs than those who mature late. "The typical masculine figure with its slender hips and broad shoulders seems to be that of the late maturing boy" (24). In girls there is no such marked correlate of early or late maturing, although late-maturing girls tend to have somewhat broader shoulders and hips (3).

PRIMARY AND SECONDARY SEX CHARACTERISTICS IN GIRLS. As the girl's body changes in size, strength, and proportion in the prepubertal period, secondary sex characteristics begin to appear. X-ray examinations show that:

During the prepubescent period the (girl's) pelvis grows slowly and symmetrically. During pubescence, however, it not only grows much more rapidly, but changes in shape and undergoes considerable remodeling. During this time the pelvis increases more rapidly in width and depth. . . . This period of rapid growth and fundamental changes in character of the pelvis usually requires about 18 months for its accomplishment. The changes described ordinarily begin after the first signs of breast development have appeared, are well along at the time of the menarche, and end shortly thereafter. During the postpubescent period there is apparently a slight further growth of the pelvis but not much further change in its shape. The earliest changes in the appearance of the breasts are usually noticeable before any pubic hair is seen (49, 103).

The first stage of pubescent development of the breast is characterized by a small conical elevation of the area (called the areola) immediately surrounding the nipple. The rest of the chest remains flat. This stage, known as the "single-bud" stage, generally develops in the eleventh year but not infrequently does so in the tenth to twelfth years. The second stage is primarily brought about by an infiltration of fat under and surrounding the areola, referred to as the "primary breast," which causes a further elevation of the areola. The third stage involves further enlargement of the breast itself with incorporation of the former areola, so that only the nipple remains elevated. This is the so-called "secondary" or "mature" breast, but its size at maturity varies widely. The breast is most frequently in the primary stage at the time of the first menstrual period, but it may still be in the bud stage and occasionally has attained the form of the mature breast (49).

The vagina and uterus begin to mature rapidly in the period between the onset of the growth spurt and the menarche (38, 49). The growth rate of the ovaries, on the other hand, does not begin to accelerate markedly until after the menarche has occurred, and becomes really rapid only between the seventeenth and twentieth years (20, 49).

PRIMARY AND SECONDARY SEX CHARACTERISTICS IN BOYS. In boys, the more conspicuous secondary sex characteristics make their first appearance only after the rapid growth of the primary characteristics associated with reproduction has begun (43, 49). These primary characteristics consist, of course, of the testicles or testes, where the sperm are manufactured; of the penis, the external male organ through which the sperm are ejaculated; and of a number of intercurrent body organs which serve to collect the sperm, to lubricate them, and to convey them from the testes to the penis.

Both the testes and penis grow very slowly during the early years of life (43, 49). However, beginning with the preadolescent growth spurt, they develop rapidly, usually reaching maturity at about age 17 (43, 49).

At about the time that growth of the genitals begins, the pubic hair starts to become somewhat coarser and to show pigmentation, the traditional landmark of puberty. By maturity, this pubic hair is markedly dense, coarse, deeply pigmented, long, and in some locations curly. The development of pubic hair is followed by hair in the axillae, the face, and finally, in certain areas of the trunk, arms, and legs (21, 49).

Voice change is another aspect of the development of male secondary sex characteristics. According to one study, 13.4 years is the median age for the first indication of the deepening of the voice. However, in many cases the process is not completed until from 2 to 4 years later (40).

Intellectual Growth in Adolescence

We have already seen that throughout the adolescent years, the individual continues to develop physically. But what about his intellectual capacities? Does intellectual capacity continue to expand as physical growth in adolescence proceeds, or does it mature more quickly than physical characteristics?

The reader is probably familiar with the conclusions reached on the basis of the mental testing of our Armed Forces personnel in World War I, namely, that the average white adult in the United States possessed a "mental age of 13 years and that mental growth was usually complete by

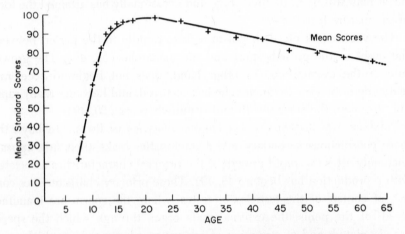

FIGURE 32.   Curve of mental growth and decline. Wechsler-Bellevue Intelligence Scale. Ages 7–65. (From D. Wechsler, *The Measurement of Adult Intelligence*. Baltimore: Williams and Wilkins, 1944. With permission of Williams and Wilkins Co.)

the time the person attained the age of 13 or 14" (*23*). However, these findings have not stood the test of further research. More recent findings consistently support the hypothesis that mental ability continues to increase throughout adolescence and into early adulthood (*26*, *52*).

For example, it has been found that performance on the Wechsler-Bellevue Scale of Intelligence (*52*) continues to improve throughout adolescence, reaching a maximum in the age range 20 to 25 years (see Figure 32).

Findings such as these indicate that by the time the adolescent is 18, he has already reached his intellectual peak, or will show only a slight increase from that point on.

Under the circumstances, his learning ability is potentially as great as it will be during his adult years, and he may profitably be subjected to learning experiences that will challenge his capacities. The reason for withholding certain types of learning experience from an adolescent is not that he is not potentially capable of profiting from them, but that he may have had insufficient previous experience or training. Thus an intelligent eleventh-grader would be capable of learning the calculus providing he had previously studied preliminary mathematics. The process of curriculum development is that of providing essential preliminary learning experiences to children so that they may be capable of profiting from advanced learning experiences as soon as they are capable of being subjected to these experiences. The curriculum maker will, of course, remember that individuals differ in intelligence and that an effective school program is one that individualizes its instruction on the basis of the intellectual capacities of the various children who attend the school . . . (23, 225).

FACTORS RELATED TO INTELLECTUAL ABILITY IN ADOLESCENCE. In general, the factors which are related to intellectual ability in adolescence are no different from those related to it at earlier ages. The adolescent's intelligence is related to such factors as parents' intelligence, parental education, socioeconomic status of the family, schooling, and general cultural opportunities. In fact, in many cases, the correlations are somewhat higher than in earlier years. Thus, Bayley (4) studied the relationship at successive ages between mental test scores of children and the average amount of their parents' education. She found that the correlations continued to improve from infancy through age 18 (i.e., from close to zero in infancy to plus .60 at 18 years): "For such findings the most obvious interpretation is that better educated parents provide environments more stimulating to mental growth and that in general children tend to acquire the intellectual status characteristic of the environment to which they are exposed. Equally reasonable, however, is an interpretation based primarily on the maturing of hereditary potentialities" (29).

PSYCHOLOGICAL PROBLEMS ASSOCIATED WITH PHYSICAL DEVELOPMENT

We have been concerned thus far with physical changes during puberty and adolescence. It seems appropriate at this point to inquire as to the implications of these changes for personality development. In so doing, however, it is important to emphasize again that not all the psychological problems of adolescence are the result of physical change. As we shall see in some detail in the next chapter, many of the adjustment problems of puberty and later adolescence are primarily functions of prior psychological experiences and of the special cultural demands made upon the individual at this time. Even many of the problems which seem to us most directly related to physiological change—for example, sexual adjustment (cf. pp. 470–483)—appear to pose no special problems in some other cultures. But there seems no doubt that while many of these problems emerge only in particular cultural backgrounds, they are nevertheless precipitated by physiological changes requiring new adaptations. The argument should become clearer in the following discussion of some of the specific psychological problems associated with the physical changes of adolescence.

Adolescent Awkwardness

There is little doubt that many adolescents go through a period of awkwardness, and that this difficulty depends upon both biological and social forces. As we noted earlier, faster growth in muscles than in bones may produce incoördination. There are, however, other possible biological sources of awkwardness. Muscle development in adolescence is constantly increasing, making the individual stronger; but skillful use of this new muscular potential must await practice. In addition, the adolescent faces the problem of readjusting the movements of his body in space to compensate for his changed physical dimensions (1). For example, where previously he may have had to extend his arm fully to reach an object a given distance away, he may now only have to extend it to four-fifths of its length, as a result of growth in arm length. Adjusting his movements to his changing physical dimensions may create few problems for the younger child, since the change is gradual. But it may result in real difficulty for the pubescent child, because he is growing rapidly at this time.

Social factors magnify the problem of adolescent awkwardness in our culture. For one thing, American adults tend to tease adolescents a good deal, not only in daily life but in plays, movies, radio series of the Henry Aldrich variety, and in books. The result is quite likely to be an increase in self-consciousness and consequently an increased awkwardness. In addition, as we shall see in Chapter 14, the sheer number of demands for new social adjustments which our culture imposes on the adolescent is great. His uncertainty about his ability to meet these demands may lead to anxiety and self-consciousness, and consequently to increases in "adolescent awkwardness."

Age of Maturation

Individual differences in age of maturation may often be disturbing to conformity-conscious adolescents (1). Early or delayed growth spurts in height, weight, and strength, and in the development of primary and secondary sex characteristics all may be sources of serious concern. Although personality factors are clearly involved, the amount of concern is likely also to be a function of the degree and conspicuousness of the deviation. In most cases, delayed development appears to cause more concern than early development. For example, in a study of 590 tenth-grade boys and girls, 17 percent of boys and 13 percent of girls described themselves as developing late (19). Of these, almost half of both boys and girls expressed concern about the matter. In contrast, 19 percent of the boys and 24 percent of the girls described themselves as developing early, but relatively few of either sex expressed concern about it.

It is not hard to see why delayed development may lead to more concern than early development. The child who matures early (especially if he is very deviant) may become somewhat anxious about it. He may feel out of place in his own age group. Because of his size, adults may subject him to premature demands for social maturity. But since both he and his peers can perceive that his development is progressing in the direction of adulthood with its higher social status, the child's own concern and the taunting of his peers is likely to be minimal. On the other hand, the slow maturer is likely to suffer "greater disadvantage because of the uncertainty of his situation and the limited time perspective characteristic of adolescence. He has no way of knowing when his pubescence will eventually occur. In the meantime, he begins to wonder if he is a biological anomaly and frequently entertains serious doubts that he will ever mature'" (1).

In addition, the slow maturer is likely to be at a disadvantage socially. For example, being shorter, lighter, and weaker than his peers, he is often handicapped in the pursuit of athletic recognition.

Farnham (15) describes the case of a youngster who was brought in for examination because he was inattentive in school, often quite insolent, and difficult to manage.

He was bright enough by all tests, and was quite able to do his work when he put his mind to it, which most of the time he failed to do. Punishment had not the slightest effect on him and he seemed almost blandly indifferent to his teachers' and parents' frantic attempts to make him conform. One glance at him gave a pointer at least. He was a small, almost bird-like boy who looked ridiculous in the long trousers and bow tie which his associates were wearing and which he, too, insisted on wearing. He was talkative and apparently self-assured. When he was examined it was found that he was markedly under-sized and his large parents were chagrined and unhappy about it. Treatment soon showed that he felt so small, so unimportant, and so unmanly that he was almost overcome by the realities of the school room and the playground. He either escaped into day dreams where he was always a large and powerful man, or denied his plight by insolent boldness which seemed to substitute for his manly size (15, 3).

In one intensive study of the relation of physical maturing among boys to behavior, skeletal age was used as an index of maturity (28). The subjects included 16 boys, ages 12 to 17, who were currently accelerated, and 16 boys who were currently retarded in maturing. Using social observational data and peer group ratings as measures of behavior, the investigators found that the later maturers tended to engage in more attention-getting behaviors, and were rated more restless, talkative, and bossy. They were also less popular than the early maturers, fewer of them were leaders, fewer were able to laugh at themselves, and fewer were considered matter-of-fact and unaffected. The authors conclude that:

Those who are physically accelerated are usually accepted and treated by adults and other children as more mature. They appear to have relatively little need to strive for status. From their ranks come the outstanding student-body leaders in senior high school. In contrast, the physically retarded boys exhibit many forms of relatively immature behavior: this may be in part because others tend to treat them as the little boys they appear to be. Furthermore, a fair proportion of these boys give evidence of needing to counteract their physical disadvantage in some way—usually by greater activity in striving for attention, although in some cases by withdrawing (28, 148).

Early- and late-maturing boys and girls also appear to differ in theii interests. In a study of pre- and postmenarchial girls of matched ages, Stone and Barker (48) found that the postmenarchial girls were more interested in social activities with the opposite sex, in personal adorn-ment, display of person, and in daydreaming. On the other hand, menar-chial girls were less interested in games and sports requiring vigorous activity. On a test of masculinity-femininity, early maturing boys obtain more masculine interest scores, and early-maturing girls more feminine interest scores than their later-maturing peers. Similarly, a study of adolescent boys revealed a relatively high correlation (.51) between amount of male hormone in the urine and maturity of interests and atti-tudes (47).

While late maturing generally appears to have a handicapping effect, we must not forget that many other factors will also affect the individual adolescent's social and emotional adjustment. As we shall see, the early maturer who is nagged by skin blemishes or other physical disturbances, by membership in a minority group, by unusually uneven growth, or by adverse factors in the home may have a more difficult time adjusting socially than the slightly late maturer, who is more fortunate in other respects.

During the years of relatively leisurely growth, such as middle childhood, most children are not particularly concerned with their bodily appearance and functioning. But when a period of marked change in external appearance comes, as at puberty, they are likely to become very conscious of their bodies. When our arms and legs do what we expect, we take them for granted. When they do not, we suddenly become intensely aware of them.

The same thing applies to our inner conceptions of ourselves. Part of the feeling of "selfness" arises from the pressure of familiar and persistent internal physiological stimuli. When these change rapidly, as the result of major shifts in adolescent physiology, revisions of the self-concept also become necessary. Heightened emotionality, new sensory experiences from developing sexual organs, changes in kinesthetic stimulation all serve to augment the adolescent's consciousness of his body.

But increased awareness of one's physical self is not precipitated by physiological change alone. It is also fostered by:

. . . increasing identification with culturally determined ideals concerning appropriate physical characteristics for men and women.

Since the peer group becomes the chief source of his status and prestige, the adolescent desires to conform to the specific norms of body proportions and growth prevailing in his own limited circle. Now, for the first time, physical attractiveness becomes a crucial determinant of the girl's sociometric status among her peers of both sexes. In similar fashion, the boy's sociometric status is largely governed by his relative degree of masculinity in athletic prowess (1, 161).

The important role of physical characteristics in the adolescent's self-evaluation was demonstrated in a study by Jersild (25). When junior high school students were asked what they did and did not like about themselves, they mentioned physical characteristics more often than either intellectual or social characteristics. This trend was much less marked in senior high school.

Furthermore, there is evidence to suggest that when they compare themselves with the stereotyped ideal of their own peer groups, most adolescents are not entirely satisfied with the results. When tenth-grade boys and girls were asked whether they desired a change in their physical selves, the majority of both sexes replied that they did (19).

The commonest complaint among both boys and girls concerned facial defects, principally skin disturbances. Other desired changes reflected quite clearly stereotyped masculine and feminine ideals. Boys of the group wanted to have broader shoulders, more rugged builds, and larger chests. Those who were short wanted to be taller.

Many girls wanted slimmer hips, smaller feet, smaller waist, and a "good shape." Tall girls wanted to be shorter. Girls on the whole were more concerned with complexion problems than with being pretty; boys were more concerned about stature and physical strength.

It is often painful for parents to watch their children suffering from real or imagined somatic deviations from the peer-group ideal. Fortunately, they can comfort themselves with the realization that as maturity approaches both the peer group and the individual himself will have become much more tolerant of somatic deviations.

SEXUAL RESPONSES IN ADOLESCENCE

The complex changes in hormonal balance which accompany puberty produce modifications in the individual's motivational structure and in his behavior, through their effects upon sexual drive. While sexual behavior does not necessarily begin with puberty, the increased production of the so-called male and female hormones, as the result of stimulation in puberty by the gonadotrophins (anterior pituitary hormones), produces a marked increase in sexual drive. Physiological deficiencies in sex hormones may result in a deficiency in sexual drive, and hence a lack of sexual responsiveness, as the following illustrates.

The . . . case was that of a young man of 22 whose testes had been destroyed before he had attained puberty. He presented a picture of physical immaturity with psychological concomitants. He was keenly aware of his sexual shortcomings, despaired of ever possessing a wife, sex life, and marriage. He was depressed and frequently wept. One month of medication by means of testosterol proprianate induced dramatic changes. Hirsuital development took place; the voice became deeper. He experienced marked libido (sexual urge) with erections, masturbation with orgasm, and later, satisfactory coitus. In mental outlook he became happy and hopeful and contemplated early marriage (11, 658).

While this case represents an extreme deviation in both physiology and behavior, lesser variations in hormonal and other physiological factors may also affect sexual drive level.

Increases in drive are likely, as we have already seen, to increase trial-and-error behavior, thus magnifying the chances that drive-reducing responses will be hit upon. Such responses in turn will be learned.

This is essentially what seems to happen in human sex behavior around the time of puberty. Individuals who have previously practiced few specifically sexual responses prior to puberty are likely at this time to try out a number of such responses, adopting those which lead to a decrease in sexual drive without producing an overly great increase in other drives, such as anxiety.

Because of the important role of learning in determining sexual responses, it would be an error to infer an individual's hormonal levels directly from his behavior (17). Experience plays a vital part in determining what kinds of sexual responses will be learned and expressed. For example, while many boys in their teens may have learned that masturbatory responses can be tension-reducing, they may not practice these responses frequently, simply because they have been taught to be anxious about them.

In summary, it appears reasonable to conclude that for an explanation of the changing sexual patterns of boys and girls during puberty and adolescence, we must look primarily (1) to physiological changes in the individual as the source of increases in sexual drive; and (2) to the learning experiences of the individual as determiners of the types of sexual responses which will be adopted to reduce this drive.

CULTURAL DIFFERENCES IN SEXUAL ATTITUDES AND BEHAVIOR

In light of the role that learning plays in determining the sexual response patterns which are adopted as ways of reducing sexual drive, it is not surprising to find that sexual behavior during adolescence varies markedly from one culture to another. There are important differences between cultures, not only in the amount and type of sexual behavior which receives social acceptance, but also in the consistency of the society's sexual standards as development proceeds. A culture may be restrictive with regard to sexual activity throughout childhood, adolescence, and even to some extent in adulthood. It may be fairly permissive at all ages. Or it may be highly restrictive during childhood and adolescence, and then suddenly become much more permissive about, and, of course, in many cases demand, sexual activity in adulthood. Our own society falls pretty much into this latter category. From the standpoint of reinforcement learning theory, it seems as though we spend a great many years teaching the individual to avoid sexual responses in order to prepare him for a time when he will be expected to make these responses. We teach him to respond to sex with anxiety, and then demand that he not respond anxiously after he is married. "The man or woman who learned during childhood and adolescence that it was 'wrong' to examine or stimulate his or her own genitals, that it was 'even worse' to have any contact with those of another person, and, particularly, that attempts at heterosexual relations were immoral, is expected to reverse completely at least some of these attitudes on the wedding night or shortly thereafter. This expectation is difficult to fulfill. If the initial lessons have been well learned, the unlearning is bound to take a long time and may never be completed" (17, 195).

It would be a mistake to assume that such contradictory cultural expectations are confined to our own society. For example, "in sexual matters the Manus boy is in much the same position as our middle-class adolescent male" (1). While the male physiological sex drive is recognized as natural in this New Guinea tribe, sexual behavior is strongly tabooed until marriage. Apparently such release of tension as does occur is achieved primarily through covert homosexual activity and through solitary masturbation "surrounded by shame" (1). The Manus girl's position is highly reminiscent of that of a female of the Victorian era. She is taught that sex is not gratifying to women, and, in fact, that it is "loathsome, shameful, and repugnant" (1). The consequent difficulties in adjusting to intercourse after marriage can easily be imagined.

In some nonliterate societies, the inconsistencies of social attitudes toward sex are even more extreme than in our own. For example, among the Ashanti, sexual intercourse with a girl who has not undergone the puberty ceremony is considered so harmful to the community that the offense is punishable by death for both parties (17).

In contrast, there are many cultures, such as the Hopi, the Siriono, and the Alorese, which are highly tolerant of sexual behavior in childhood. In most cases, this tolerance persists into adolescence and adulthood. Under such conditions, sex play increases in both sexes, beginning with casual masturbation and extending, as the child grows older, to handling the genitals of the same and opposite sex, and to intercourse (17).

Among the Ila-speaking people of Africa, "childhood is regarded as a time of preparation for adult life and mature sexual functions. At harvest time, each girl is given a house to which she takes a boy of her choice, and there they play as man and wife. It is reported that there are no virgins among these people after the age of 10" (17). The Lepcha of India "believe that girls will not mature without benefit of sexual intercourse. Early sex play among boys and girls characteristically involves many forms of mutual masturbation and usually ends with attempted copulation. By the time they are 11 or 12 years old, most girls regularly engage in full intercourse" (*17*).

Obviously, adolescent sexual attitudes and practices vary widely from one culture to another. These attitudes and practices, in turn, will have a marked influence on the ease with which the adolescent is able to adjust to adult heterosexuality.

Sexual Attitudes in Relation to the Total Culture

The type of sexual training an individual receives during childhood and adolescence helps to determine whether he will show great or little interest in sexual behavior, and whether he will tend to view sex as a pleasant and matter of fact affair; as sinful and dangerous; extremely exciting; or as a matter of aggressive conquest, or even rape. Sex-training practices in turn are intimately related to broad cultural attitudes. Among the Zuni, for example, the relations—sexual and otherwise—between husband and wife tend to be pleasant, coöperative, and untainted by feelings of guilt. And this is true not simply because of cultural attitudes toward sex, but because of cultural attitudes toward living generally. The sense of sin, for example, is not absent only with regard to sexual behavior. As Benedict says, "It is unfamiliar to them not only in sex but in any experience" (*6*). Sexual intercourse is a coöperative, rather than a competitive matter to the Zunis, "not simply because of specific sex training, but because coöperation is an integral part of the whole Zuni way of life" (*6*).

In other societies, such as the Mundugumor, aggression and competition play an important part in the individual's sexual relations largely because they pervade the whole Mundugumor way of life.

The data on cultural variations in sexual behavior presented in the preceding sections provide impressive evidence of the modifiability of human sexual behavior. These data also demonstrate the tremendously important role of cultural influences in determining both the frequency and direction of an individual's sexual responses and the degree of anxiety associated with them.

SEXUAL PATTERNS IN AMERICAN CULTURE

As already pointed out, in comparison with other cultures, the attitude of American culture toward sexual behavior among children and adolescents is highly restrictive—though there are other cultures which are even more severe.

Sexual Responses of American Boys

Despite these social pressures, however, adolescent boys (and girls) do engage in a wide variety of sexual behaviors.[1] Kissing, necking, and petting are extremely common. According to Kinsey (30), 95 percent of boys have had their first orgasm by the age of 15. Other authors give similar estimates. Of these orgasms, two-thirds were obtained through masturbation, one-eighth through heterosexual intercourse, and one-twentieth through homosexual contacts.

As adolescence progresses, the average boy's frequency of orgasm increases, reaching a lifetime peak of about 3.4 per week between 16 and 17 years of age (30). This frequency tends to persist with only slight diminution until the age of 30, after which there is a gradual tapering off (30). For most boys during the early adolescent period, the major source of orgasm is masturbation (about 60 percent of the total outlet). Almost all adolescent boys (over 90 percent) engage in masturbation. In the years from 16 to 20, masturbation is replaced by intercourse as the major source of orgasm, although masturbation is still common. During this period masturbation accounts for about 38 percent, and intercourse for about 42 percent of total outlet. Premarital intercourse increases in frequency as adolescence progresses, so that by the late teens, nearly three-fourths of American males have had such experience (30). Other sources of outlet during adolescence include (in order of frequency at ages 16 to 20) homosexual outlet, about 8 percent; nocturnal emissions, 7 percent; and petting to climax 2.5 percent (30).

Sexual Responses of Girls

The available evidence strongly suggests that adolescent girls engage in considerably less sexual behavior than boys. According to Kinsey, petting, masturbation, and intercourse are all less frequent among teen-age

[1] Much of the evidence in this matter has been obtained by Kinsey and his associates (30, 31). It is necessary, therefore, to point out that a number of legitimate criticisms of Kinsey's findings have been raised by various authors. In the main, these deal with (1) the representativeness of his sample of U.S. males and females, and (2) the dependability of the information volunteered by his subjects. It is our position, that while deficiencies in these respects probably produce some distortion of the data, these distortions are probably not marked. Therefore, in the absence of more dependable data from any other sources, we have decided to make use of his findings. It should also be noted with regard to the particular data cited here, that most other investigators in this field have reached similar conclusions on the basis of more limited samples.

girls (*31*). For example, by age 20, 71 percent of males and 40 percent of females have engaged in intercourse; by the same age, less than half as many females as males have masturbated.

Furthermore, sexual behavior leads to orgasm in many fewer adolescent girls than boys. Even at age 20, only 53 percent of girls have achieved orgasm, and the incidence does not reach a lifetime maximum of around 90 percent until age 35 (*31*).

There are also marked sex differences in the source of first orgasms. Only 37 percent of girls appear to reach their first orgasm through masturbating, as compared with approximately two-thirds of boys. On the other hand, while premarital petting to climax is an insignificant source of first orgasm in boys, it accounts for 18 percent of such orgasms in girls. Again, while marital intercourse is a minor source of first orgasms in boys, it accounts for 30 percent of such orgasms in girls. Other sources of sexual outlet account for a minor proportion of girls' initial orgasms (*31*).

While frequency of orgasm in boys increases sharply in adolescence, reaching a peak at 16 to 17 years (3.3 per week), the maximum mean frequency for girls (1.8 per week) does not occur until the period of 26 to 30 years (*30, 31*). While nearly 100 percent of boys have reached orgasm by the time of marriage, only 30 percent of females have done so.

As might be anticipated from their overt behavior, girls also seem to have more restrictive attitudes toward sexual behavior than boys in our society. More girls than boys believe that adolescent sexual behavior is deserving of social condemnation (*1*).

Factors Influencing the Type and Frequency of Sexual Responses

SEX DIFFERENCES. There are a number of factors which bear important relationships to adolescent sexual behavior. Obviously from our discussion thus far, one of these is sex membership. Overall sexual activity is far more abundant in adolescent males than in females. The question of why this should be so is clearly an important one. The answers, however, are far from certain. Several theories have, however, been advanced —some primarily physiological in nature, others primarily cultural.

One possibility is that females are less likely than males to discover sexual responses spontaneously, because the girl's sexual organs are less prominent. Some authors have advanced such an argument to account partially for the greater incidence of masturbation among adolescent males than among females. As Mead says, "The human female shows a lesser capacity for sexual stimulation, and it might be argued that the lesser frequency of masturbation among young females that is reported in our own society, and characteristic of all South Sea societies I have studied is merely a structural matter. The female child's genitals are less exposed, subject to less maternal manipulation and self-manipulation. If masturbation is not socially recognized and taught either by parents to children or by older children to younger, it may escape the spontaneous learning of the female child" (35).

It is also possible that there may be basic physiological differences in sex drives among male and female adolescents as some authors have suggested (30). However, it seems probable to us that the lesser sexual responsiveness of female adolescents is attributable in large measure to our more restrictive social attitudes toward sex in the case of girls.

SOCIOECONOMIC DIFFERENCES. In addition to differences between adolescent males and females in sexual responsiveness, there are also differences in responsiveness related to social-class membership. In this instance, the sources of the variation are considerably easier to trace. Since we may assume that fundamental differences in sexual anatomy and physiological functioning are not correlated with social class, the variations in sexual responses may be attributed to psychological and cultural influences peculiar to each of these levels. On the basis of the social-class literature which we have considered throughout this book (which shows marked differences in learning experience among the various social levels) this explanation seems highly plausible.

It is interesting to note that the effects of social-class membership apparently are considerably less for females than for males. In their report of female sex behavior, Kinsey and his associates (31) point out: "There seems to have been no correlation at all between occupational classes of the parental homes in which the females in the sample have been raised and the incidences and frequencies of their total (sexual) outlet." There also appeared to be little relationship between social-class background of females, and incidence or frequency of most types of sexual response.

In contrast to the rather negligible influences of social-class membership upon sexual behavior in females, religious affiliations seem to play a strong role, both during adolescence and in later life. Kinsey found regularly that inactive members of the Protestant, Jewish, and Catholic faiths were consistently more sexually active both before and after marriage than were moderately active church members. Devout members, in turn, were consistently least active sexually. Kinsey comments that: "Among all the cultural and biological factors which might affect their sexual activity, and which in actuality had considerably affected the sexual activity of the male in the sample, only the religious backgrounds of the unmarried (and married) females had had any material relationship to their acceptance of either solitary or socio-sexual contacts" (31).

Among boys, on the other hand, Kinsey has shown that implicit standards of acceptable sexual behavior vary widely from one social class level to another. For example, among higher-level boys, masturbation and petting to climax, while not specifically approved, are generally viewed as more acceptable than actual intercourse. As a result, both of these practices are far more common among the higher social levels than the lower. In fact, there is a general tendency among lower-class individuals to consider these practices both abnormal and immoral (30).

On the other hand, actual intercourse, which is considered so dangerous by upper- and middle-class boys, is considered entirely normal by those of lower status: "They have nothing like the strong [higher-level] tabu against premarital intercourse, and, on the contrary, accept it as natural and inevitable and as a desirable thing. Lower-level tabus are more often turned against an avoidance of intercourse and against any substitution for simple and direct coitus" (30).

As a reflection of these disparate attitudes, we find that by age 15 nearly half of lower-class boys and only 10 percent of higher-status boys have engaged in intercourse (30).

PARENTAL ATTITUDES TOWARD SEXUALITY

As Frank (18) points out, "Until recently, save in some exceptional families, it has been customary to regard matters involving sex as more or less shameful. It was considered depraved and perverse for children to be curious about biological processes and anatomical differences; adults were confirmed in these attitudes by the church and other social influences."

Viewed in this light, it is not simply fortuitous that in the past children have obtained a greater part of their information about sex largely from their peers. One investigator (41), for example, studied the sources of information on various sexual topics in a group of 291 adolescent boys, in a large middle western city in the early '40's.

He found that for all sexual topics studied, the primary source of information was the male peer group. The mother was responsible for first knowledge of the origin of babies in 27.5 percent of cases, and of menstruation in 20.2 percent. First knowledge on other topics did not come from either parent in more than 5 percent of the cases studied.

Another study (5) of both boys and girls, conducted during the middle 1930's, yielded similar results. Moreover, it showed that more girls than boys, and more white than Negro adolescents, received sex information from their parents. The greater frequency of parental instruction among girls probably has several origins. Girls are likely to have closer emotional relationships with their mothers than boys with their fathers; also boys talk more freely among themselves than do girls. In addition, it is possible that parents may feel that a girl should be given sex information to protect her from victimization by sexually aggressive males. In the case of the boy, they may feel that so long as he does not know about sex, he is less likely to become involved in sexual activity.

In recent years, parents may have begun to take a more active role in sex instruction. In at least one recent study of high school youth (42), parents, rather than friends, were the most frequently mentioned source of sex instruction for the higher socioeconomic group. If this actually is a trend toward more instruction by parents, it would suggest that parents are developing a less guilty attitude toward sex. This would certainly be desirable. It seems clear that if adolescents are to achieve a healthy adjustment to the sexual changes at puberty, they need more than specific sexual information from their parents. They need to learn healthy attitudes. These are necessary if the adolescent is to satisfactorily integrate his sexual attitudes and behavior into his overall philosophy of life. We are reminded of the transatlantic airplane map inserted by Thurber and White in the middle of a discussion of sex in their satirical little volume, *Is Sex Necessary?* The authors admit that it is customary in such discussions to include a schematic diagram of the male and female genitalia. However, they say, they did not have any such diagram available, and hence included the airplane map. They go on to comment that while people might argue that a transatlantic airplane map may be of little help to the sexual novice; on the other hand, so is a schematic diagram of the male and female genitalia.

While the adolescent may need some specific sexual information, he is more likely to need to learn about the role sex plays in the individual's general adjustment. As Frank says: "Teaching about procreation is the last thing they are really concerned about. They want to know, not about babies, but what you do about sex, what you can give and receive from the other, what love means!" (18).

In other words, adolescents want to learn how to fit sex meaningfully and without anxiety into their lives.

In the next chapter, we will discuss the problems which the adolescent faces in his efforts to integrate the psychosexual changes of puberty into his general social development, and the ways in which parents may facilitate or hinder him in this task. For the moment, however, we would like to confine our discussion to the ways in which parents can help or hinder adolescent adjustment through their reactions to some of the more troublesome problems related to sexual maturation.

Menstruation

Menstruation means much more to the adolescent girl than just a simple physiological readjustment. It is a symbol of sexual maturity—of her future role as a wife and mother. Since the reactions of the girl to menstruation may generalize so broadly, it is vital that her initial experience with this phenomenon be as favorable as possible.

Many girls do look forward calmly to the onset of menstruation, and receive it proudly, as a sign of increased status. Unfortunately, since many notions [2] concerning the shamefulness or even dangerousness of menstruation have persisted in our time, there are other girls who fear and hate it. In a study of the emotional reactions of 475 girls to the onset of their menses, it was found that 51 percent reported their reaction as one of indifference; 4 percent said they were curious and interested; 12 percent were chagrined; 1 percent were terrified; and only 6 percent were delighted and proud (10).

Probably one of the main reasons that girls may react negatively to menstruation is that they are influenced by the negative attitudes of others. Thus, if a menstruating girl's parents and friends act as though she requires sympathy for her "plight"—an attitude implied in such prevalent euphemisms for menstruation as "the curse," "being unwell," etc.—the girl herself is likely to adopt similar attitudes toward her menstruation.

Negative reactions to menstruation may also stem in part from physical discomfort. During the early years of menstruation, when the menses are

[2] Strong tabus still attend menstruation in many of the world's societies. In Bali, menstruation is considered so shameful that its significance is not even socially recognized. The Manus equate menstruation with injury. Among many tribes, such as the Arapesh, the menstruating woman is assumed to have special and dangerous powers. As a result, women may be isolated in special huts during their periods, or prevented from preparing food for their families, since it is thought they may magically poison them. In some tribes, menstruating women may not tend gardens because it is believed that the plants will wither and die (35).

likely to be quite irregular, a number of girls experience disturbing symptoms in relation to their menstrual period. Among the more common of these are: headaches, backaches, cramps, and severe abdominal pain (1, 24). However, in most cases where such initial disturbances occur, they tend to disappear as puberty progresses and menstruation becomes more regular.

Another factor which may adversely affect the girl's reaction to her first menstruation arises from the similarity between menstruation and other physical reactions. Since the menstrual flow may be similar to other types of bleeding, the girl who has been inadequately prepared for menstruation may, and too frequently does, gain the impression that she has been injured (13).

There are, of course, other reasons why the adolescent girl may react negatively to menstruation. For example, if she has been unable to establish a satisfactory feminine identification, she may be disturbed by having her attention bluntly directed by the onset of menstruation to the fact that she is a woman and can do nothing about it.

Many of these negative reactions could be avoided or alleviated, if the parent employed a wise and understanding approach to the problem. By seeing that the girl receives adequate medical care in the case of physical difficulties; by explaining to her the naturalness of the phenomenon; and by showing pride and pleasure in her greater maturity, the parents—particularly the mother—can help to make the onset of menstruation a happy, rather than a feared or hated event. This of course will have consequent benefits for the girl's whole future sexual and social role as a woman.

Nocturnal Emission

Just as the onset of menstruation may cause concern to the pubescent girl, so may the appearance of nocturnal emissions surprise and worry the pubescent boy. By nocturnal emission is meant ejaculation of the seminal fluid during sleep. According to Kinsey (30), approximately 83 percent of males report experiencing nocturnal emissions at some time in their lives. Frequently, but by no means always, these emissions are accompanied by erotic dreams.

It seems to be true that boys as a group worry less about nocturnal emissions than girls do about menstruation, perhaps partly because boys are more often able to talk freely among themselves about such matters. Nevertheless, many boys do not gain proper instruction from their peers or parents, and torture themselves with unnecessary fears.

Masturbation

While masturbation at one time or another during adolescence is admitted by virtually all boys and many girls (cf. pp. 474–475), it is still a frequent source of worry to them. In a study (39) of the beliefs of 75 college freshmen concerning the effects of masturbation, conducted during the late 1930's, it was found that the great majority felt that masturbation would lead to some type of serious damage, whether physical, mental, moral, or social. Thus it is highly probable that many of these boys engaged in masturbation *in spite* of their fears of the results. Such a conflict is obviously potentially damaging psychologically. Not only may it lead to current unhappiness and reduced efficiency, but also to long-term attitudes of fear or disgust, which may adversely affect future sex adjustment. Fortunately, a much more realistic attitude toward masturbation seems to be developing, especially among the middle class (1), and it is unlikely that figures as disturbing as these would be found among most college males today. Nevertheless, as any psychotherapist can readily testify, many boys and girls still suffer considerable conflict over masturbation.

Since masturbation is a common accompaniment of normal sexual growth, parents should not ordinarily become worried about it, since they may only be creating a problem where none exists. However, if the child seems unduly preoccupied with masturbation, or is losing interest in the world about him, the situation may be more serious. In such a case, the child's excessive masturbation is probably a symptom of a more profound underlying disturbance. Hence his basic emotional difficulties, rather than the symptom itself, should be the focus of parental or professional attention.

Homosexual Behavior—a Special Problem

According to Kinsey, approximately 3 percent of girls and about 27 percent of boys experience orgasm as a result of homosexual contacts during adolescence, usually through mutual masturbation (30, 31). It is important to note that in most instances, neither overt homosexual behavior during early adolescence, nor the intense emotional relations involved in crushes (cf. pp. 511–512) necessarily leads to the adoption of a homosexual way of life in adulthood. Many later-adolescents and adults trouble themselves unnecessarily with fears of their presumed perverseness because of earlier experiences of mutual masturbation with same-sexed peers or because of a realization that sexual feelings were involved in an adolescent crush.

Of course, it is true that not all adolescents do go on to achieve a successful heterosexual adjustment. As we saw previously, some may already have too strongly adopted cross-sex identifications as the result of unfortunate parental influences (cf. pp. 326–327). It should be stressed, however, that persisting homosexual patterns stem from the individual's learning experiences (cf. pp. 470–471), rather than from hormonal factors.

When large amounts of androgen [male hormone] have been administered to male patients diagnosed as exclusively homosexual, the result has been an intensification of the sex drive with no alteration in direction. Homosexual patients treated in this manner desired and achieved increased frequency of homosexual contacts. The fundamental error involved in this type of therapy is the unjustified assumption that gonadal hormones determine the character of the sexual drive in human beings. This is not the case. The reproductive hormones may intensify the drive but they do not organize the behavior through which it finds expression (17, 236).

As we saw earlier in this book, the best guarantees against the development of a primarily homosexual orientation in later life appear to be: (1) a lack of highly punitive and frightening experiences with sexuality; (2) a same-sexed parent who loves and accepts the child and who is himself a good sex-role model—one which the child will be rewarded for imitating; and (3) an opposite-sex parent who also loves and accepts the child, and who rewards the child for imitating the same sex parent in his responses.

Sex Education

It should be obvious from the previous discussion that sex education is an important parental function. But sex education does not mean thrusting a pamphlet into the hands of a 14-year-old boy or girl with embarrassed instructions to read it. For one thing, even for the purpose of disseminating sex information, the time is likely to be too late (41). If parents are going to be able to take the place of peers as sources of sex information, they must begin earlier than some of them do.

But as we have already emphasized, the sexual attitudes which parents convey to their children are more important than the dissemination of specific biological information. If parents can demonstrate to the child that for them sex has a rightful place as an integrated part of human experience—not divorced from love, courtship, religion, and ideals, then there is little reason to fear that the child will be overwhelmed by the sexual adjustments of adolescence. Thus the most important part of sex education depends not on biological instruction *per se,* but upon the demonstration of healthy attitudes on the part of parents, teachers, and other influential adults.

No amount of information or reassurance in preadolescence or adolescence will enable the child to adopt a healthy attitude toward sexuality if in the preceding years he has been taught to fear sexual responses. We have already reviewed many of the ways in which such fears can be instilled (cf. pp. 236–237). He can discover that for his parents, sex is whispered about, joked about, denounced or avoided, but never referred to directly (or indirectly) as good, as normal, or as healthy. He (or she) can be taught that it is something that he will have to endure rather than something to which he can look forward. Clinicians have found that when unfavorable sexual attitudes have been built up as a consequence of such experiences, it is extremely difficult, and sometimes impossible, to shift them through the use of rational advice given in adolescence. Even extensive psychotherapy may fail to change attitudes which have become too deeply ingrained.

REFERENCES AND ADDITIONAL READING

1. Ausubel, D. P., *Theory and problems of adolescent development.* New York: Grune and Stratton, 1954.
2. Baldwin, B. T., A measuring scale for physical growth and physiological age. *Yearb. Nat. Soc. Stud. Educ.* (1916), *15*(I), pp. 11–23.
3. Bayley, N., Size and body build of adolescents in relation to rate of skeletal maturing. *Child Develop.* (1943), *14*:51–89.
4. Bayley, N., Some increasing parent-child similarities during the growth of children. *J. educ. Psychol.* (1954), *45*:1–24.
5. Bell, H. M., *Youth tell their story.* Washington: Am. Council on Educ., 1938.
6. Benedict, R., *Patterns of culture.* Boston: Houghton Mifflin, 1934.
7. Boas, F., Observations on the growth of children. *Science* (1930), *72*: 44–48.
8. Boas, F., Studies in human growth. *Human Biol.* (1932), *4*:307–350.
9. Cole, L., *Psychology of adolescence.* New York: Rinehart, 1948.
10. Conklin, E. S., *Principles of adolescent psychology.* New York: Holt, 1933.
11. Dennis, W., The adolescent, in L. Carmichael (ed.), *Manual of child psychology.* New York: Wiley, 1946, pp. 633–666.
12. Dimock, H. S., *Rediscovering the adolescent.* New York: Association Press, 1937.
13. English, O. S., and Pearson, G. H. J., *Emotional problems of living.* New York: Norton, 1955.
14. Espenschade, A., Motor performance in adolescence. *Monogr. Soc. Res. Child Develop.* (1940), *5*:No. 1.
15. Farnham, M. L., *The adolescent.* New York: Harper, 1951.

16. Fenichel, O., *The psychoanalytic theory of neurosis*. New York: Norton, 1945.

17. Ford, C. S., and Beach, F. H., *Patterns of sexual behavior*. New York: Harper, 1951.

18. Frank, L. K., Adolescence as a period of transition. In *Adolescence*, 43rd Yearbook, Natl. Soc. Stud. Educ., Part I. Chicago: University of Chicago Press, 1944.

19. Frazier, A., and Lisonbee, L. K., Adolescent concerns with physique. *Sch. Rev.* (1950), 58:397–405.

20. Greulich, W. W. et al., A handbook of methods for the study of adolescent children. *Monogr. Soc. Res. Child Develop.* (1938), 3:No. 2.

21. Greulich, W. W. et al., Somatic and endocrine studies of puberal and adolescent boys. *Monogr. Soc. Res. Child Develop.* (1942), 7:No. 3.

22. Hall, G. S., *Adolescence; its psychology and its relations to physiology, anthropology, sociology, sex, crime, religion, and education*, Vol. 1. New York: Appleton, 1904.

23. Horrocks, J. E., *The psychology of adolescence; behavior and development*. Boston: Houghton Mifflin, 1951.

24. Hurlock, E. B., *Adolescent development*. New York: McGraw-Hill, 1949.

25. Jersild, A. T., *In search of self*. New York: Teachers College, Columbia University, 1952.

26. Jones, H. E., and Conrad, H. S., The growth and decline of intelligence. *Genet. Psychol. Monogr.* (1933), 13:223–298.

27. Jones, H. E., Adolescence in our society. In *The family in a democratic society*, Anniversary papers of the Community Service Society of New York. New York: Columbia University Press, 1949, pp. 70–82.

28. Jones, H. E., The environment and mental development, in L. Carmichael (ed.), *Manual of Child Psychology*. New York: Wiley, 1954, pp. 631–696.

29. Jones, M. C., and Bayley, N., Physical maturing among boys as related to behavior, *J. educ. Psychol.* (1950), 41:129–148.

30. Kinsey, A. C., Pomeroy, W. B., Martin, C. E., *Sexual behavior in the human male*. Philadelphia: Saunders, 1948.

31. Kinsey, A. C., Pomeroy, W. B., Martin, C. E., and Gebhard, P. H., *Sexual behavior in the human female*. Philadelphia: Saunders, 1953.

32. Lewin, K., Field theory and experiment in social psychology. *Am. J. Sociol.* (1939), 44:868–897.

33. Lowrey, L. G., "Not quite" age. *Science News Letter* (1952), 62:356.

34. Mead, M., *From the south seas*. New York: Morrow, 1939.

35. Mead, M., *Male and female*. New York: Morrow, 1949.

36. Mills, C. A., and Ogle, C., Physiologic sterility of adolescence. *Human Biol.* (1936), 8:607–615.

37. Olson, W. C., and Hughes, B. O., Growth of the child as a whole. In R. G. Barker, et al. (eds.), *Child behavior and development*. New York: McGraw-Hill, 1943, pp. 199–208.

38. Pilcher, J. D., and Tuchewicz, H., Premenstrual state in young girls. *Am. J. Dis. Child.* (1943), 65:296–304.

39. Pullius, E. V., Masturbation as a mental hygiene problem—a study of the beliefs of seventy-five men. *J. abnorm. soc. Psychol.* (1937), *32*:216–222.

40. Ramsey, G. V., The sexual development of boys. *Am. J. Psychol.* (1943), *56*:217–233.

41. Ramsey, G. V., The sex information of younger boys. *Am. J. Orthopsychiat.* (1943), *13*:347–352.

42. Remmers, H. H., Drucker, A. J., and Christenson, H. T., Courtship conduct as viewed by high school youth. *Purdue Opin. Panel*, X, No. 2 Report No. 27), 1950.

43. Schonfeld, W. A., Primary and secondary sexual characteristics: study of their development in males from birth through maturity, with biometric study of penis and testes. *Am. J. Dis. Child.* (1943), *65*:535–549.

44. Shuttleworth, F. K., The physical and mental growth of girls and boys, age six to nineteen, in relation to age at maximum growth. *Monogr. Soc. Res. Child Develop.* (1939), 4:No. 3.

45. Simmons, K., and Greulich, W. W., Menarcheal age and height, weight, and skeletal age of girls age 7 to 17 years. *J. Pediat.* (1943), *22*:518–548.

46. Simmons, K., The Brush Foundation study of child growth and development. II. Physical growth and development. *Monogr. Soc. Res. Child Develop.* (1944), 9:No. 1.

47. Sollenberger, R. T., Some relationships between the urinary excretion of male hormone by maturing boys and their expressed interests and attitudes. *J. Psychol.* (1940), 9:179–189.

48. Stone, C. P., and Barker, R. G., The attitudes and interests of premenarcheal and postmenarcheal girls. *J. genet. Psychol.* (1939), *54*:27–71.

49. Stuart, H. C., Normal growth and development during adolescence. *New Engl. J. Med.*, 1946, pp. 234, 666–672, 693–700, 732–738.

50. Terman, L. M., and Miles, C. C., *Sex and personality.* New York: McGraw-Hill, 1936.

51. Watson, E. H., and Lowrey, G. H., *Growth and development of children,* 2nd ed. Chicago: Year Book Publishers, 1954.

52. Wechsler, D., *The measurement of adult intelligence.* Baltimore: Williams and Wilkins, 1944.

Chapter 14

ADOLESCENT ADJUSTMENT IN AMERICAN CULTURE

We have already discussed at some length the biological changes of puberty, and we have seen that these changes within the organism may affect adolescent learning and adjustment. But learning and adjustment are dependent also on the environmental influences to which the organism is subjected. For example, while the emergence of strong sexual drive is a consequence of increased hormonal production in puberty, it poses different adjustment problems in a society that views adolescence as a time of carefree experimentation with sexual responses, than it does in a society that views any form of sexual responsiveness as shameful, abnormal, or dangerous. Thus we cannot hope to gain insight into adolescent development without considering the individual's cultural milieu.

In this chapter we shall attempt to gain a better understanding of adolescent adjustment in our society through an examination of some of the more important problems faced by the American adolescent. We have maintained that adolescence in our own culture is often a time of "storm and stress," at least partially because so many cultural demands tend to be concentrated within a relatively short period of time. It seems likely that the sheer amount of pressure exerted by these demands—pressure for the simultaneous learning of many new responses and the extinguishing of many old ones—is sufficient in itself to produce a great deal of stress.

THE ESTABLISHMENT OF INDEPENDENCE

One of the most prominent of these cultural demands involves the establishment of independence from the family, which often also includes preparation for the setting up of a separate household. There can be little doubt that this demand constitutes a major adjustment problem in our society, requiring the learning of many new response patterns. Strong conflicts are likely to be set up between the wish to remain secure, dependent, and free of responsibility, on the one hand, and the wish to be free to determine one's own destiny, on the other hand.

Establishment of Independence in Other Cultures

In a number of primitive societies the task of establishing independence may be less difficult for several reasons. In some societies, the child may be prepared more gradually for independence, being given increasing freedom from early childhood on, with no discernible spurt at puberty. In others, true independence from the parents may be postponed until long after puberty, and may occur slowly. Among the Arapesh people of New Guinea, for example, the adolescent takes over much of the responsibility for supporting and managing the household, but there are few marked changes in basic family relationships at this time. The Arapesh girl does not suddenly leave home during adolescence to go to live in a strange household with strange people, in order to undergo the joint uncertainties of married life, sex, and childbearing. In this culture, the girl has been chosen as a wife by her husband's parents many years prior to the consummation of the marriage, and she has been allowed during the interim to wander confidently back and forth between her own home and her future husband's. By the time her marriage is consummated she has come to think of her parents-in-law as an additional mother and father. She has known her husband almost as an older brother, whose responsibility it has been to look after her, to feed her, to help her grow up. Neither the girl nor the boy in Arapesh culture is rushed into consummation of their marriage. According to Mead:

After the first menstruation ceremony, the betrothed girl's life goes on as before. The parents-in-law will continue their slight, unobtrusive chaperonage. She still sleeps in their hut, and if one of the daughters of the house is at home, the young sisters-in-law may sleep together. Just below the surface of articulate recognition by the community is the knowledge that sometime soon now, in a few months, in a year, this marriage will be consummated. Meanwhile, the girl makes herself a lovely grass skirt; with young wives a little older than she is, she spends many hours plaiting the sago-shoot shreds that she has wheedled some old woman into dyeing a beautiful red. She keeps her skin bathed and shining, and wears her necklace of opossum-teeth or dog's teeth every day. No one is fairer or gayer in the whole of Arapesh than these young girls waiting, in lovely attire, for life at last to catch up with them. No definite date is set; as the months pass, the parents relax their chaperonage more and more. The girl is fully mature now. The boy is tall and well developed. Some day the two, who are now allowed to go about alone, together in the bush, will consummate their marriage, without haste, without a due date to harry them with its inevitableness, with no one to know or to comment, in response to a situation in which they have lived comfortably for years in the knowledge that they belong to each other (*49, 97*).

As time goes on, the Arapesh girl takes on increasing responsibility in her new home. However, many of the problems which occur frequently in American marriages do not exist in Arapesh culture. There is none of the atmosphere of confusion, of sudden complete separation from parents, of moving into a new house and beginning a separate existence with a relatively unknown male, and of bearing and caring for her babies by herself.

Similarly, the independence problems faced by the Arapesh boy are likely to be less severe than those faced by American boys. Once the Arapesh youth has passed through the initiation ceremony following pubescence, he assumes added responsibility. "From one who has been grown by the daily carefulness and hard work of others, he now passes into the class of those who care for others' growth" (*49*). He takes on new responsibilities toward those "who after years of devotion to his growth are now growing old themselves, and toward his brothers and sisters, and his young betrothed wife" (*49*). But he does not need to go out into a new community on his own, somehow obtain an unfamiliar job, and complete his emotional independence from his parents. He continues, but with new responsibility, to till the family's garden. He still sees his parents daily, and when at last he consummates his marriage, it is with a girl he has known, whom he has cared for, and to whom he has had to adjust his personality over a long period of time.

There is another factor which helps the Arapesh boy, and boys in some other primitive societies, to avoid some of the independence conflicts so characteristic of our own culture. Independence appears most difficult to establish where the parent-child relationship has been a superior-inferior one, where the parent was a strong authoritarian figure demanding complete submission to parental dictates (cf. pp. 333–335). Such a parent seldom rewards independent action, and gives the child little opportunity to develop confidence in his own judgment. Furthermore, the child's adjustment is likely to be complicated by the development of an uncomfortable ambivalence in his attitudes toward his parents. He is likely to show mixtures of dependence on, and resentment of, their authority. In Arapesh culture, however, "there is no feeling on the part of the boy that he is subservient to those older than himself, and that he chafes beneath the power of those stronger than himself. Instead, the oldest and the youngest, the aging parent and the little child, are placed together in

Arapesh feeling, in contrast to those who from puberty to middle age are specially concerned with sex and child-rearing" (49).

The Arapesh father makes no attempt to dictate to his son. He is glad of the opportunity to help his son grow up strong and healthy. When the son becomes old enough to take on adult responsibilities, the situation is reversed—"as the young wax strong, the old retire more and more" (49). This is not done in a spirit of competition, however. The son is grateful for the opportunity to repay his father for his years of tender care. In Arapesh culture, the young man takes great pains never to speak rudely or harshly to those of his father's generation (49).

In contrast to the Arapesh youth, the Mundugumor adolescent finds the problem of orderly transition from dependence on the parents to the setting up of an independent household infinitely more difficult. This increased difficulty is at least partially attributable to the fact that "Mundugumor social organization is based on a theory of a natural hostility between all members of the same sex . . ." (49). Fathers and sons view each other almost as natural enemies, as do mothers and daughters. Moreover, relations between husband and wife are notably poor. Fathers band together with daughters, while mothers band together with sons. Between the two subfamily groups rivalry and distrust are characteristic.

Consequently, it seems likely that the Mundugumor boy approaches adolescence close psychologically only to his mother, hostile toward his father, and distrustful of girls his own age. The girl, on the other hand, has strong ties to her father, resentment toward her mother, and distrust of her male contemporaries. Furthermore, the girl's problem is magnified because of the jealous father's attempts to keep his hold on her as long as possible (49).

Mundugumor adolescence is not viewed by the father as a time when the sons he has so carefully nurtured can now help to care for him, as in Arapesh culture. Rather it is viewed as a threatening period in which his sons are becoming strong enough to aggress against him, as he has aggressed against them. His sons are becoming able to demand the father's prerogatives, and to leave him with little protection for his old age.

There seems little doubt that Mundugumor children, who grow up in a culture that contains so much hostility and so little tenderness, early develop a kind of hardy independence that prepares them somewhat for the demands they must face in adolescence. But this advantage is virtually negated by the fact that the independence demanded of the Mundugumor adolescent is so much more extreme than in most cultures. The prospect of establishing independence is unpleasant, and in many ways threatening. In fact its only really attractive aspect seems to be escape from the hostility of the same-sexed parent.

Problems of Independence in American Culture

In setting up his own household the American adolescent certainly encounters more stress than the Arapesh youth, though he is spared much of the violence of the Mundugumor's independence struggles.

In contrast to the Arapesh adolescent and those in many other primitive cultures (79), the American adolescent is expected, in the years between puberty and adulthood, to pass from a state of relatively great dependence on his family to one of considerable independence. Middle-class Americans begin independence training somewhat earlier than most primitive societies (79). However, they generally complete this training relatively late, requiring a high degree of continued dependence into adolescence (79).

Not until the adolescent is nearing adulthood do the demands for true independence become really strong. In other words, the American adolescent is asked to assume real independence suddenly after having developed strongly rewarded dependence responses over a long period of time. As a consequence of strong societal demands for independence, in the face of incompatible and well-established dependence responses, the adolescent is likely to be in conflict. And the fact that this conflict is timed to coincide with so many other demands related to puberty and adolescence only increases its stressfulness.

Moreover, no clear pattern of transition from dependence to independence is spelled out for the adolescent by our society as a whole. There is little agreement as to the forms this greater independence should be allowed to take. We have no formalized procedures in our culture comparable to the puberty ceremonies or *rites de passage* of many primitive cultures which can serve as guides both to the parents and to the adolescent as to when and how independence should be granted and assumed.

In our society, children do not achieve adult status through the succession of rituals and observances . . . that mark development in many societies. In some contemporary primitive societies certain culturally valued individual accomplishments are recognized with feasts and ceremonies, and new, more clearly adult privileges and responsibilities are thereafter accorded the boy or girl. In other words, the beginning and the end of various culturally described stages of development are observed with similar ceremonies and rituals, followed for the individual by a new status. In this way, individuals or groups of individuals are inducted into their adult roles (70, 237).

About all our culture has in the way of institutionalized forms of recognizing the adolescent's increasing independence are a number of laws, often internally inconsistent and varying a great deal in their content from one area of our culture to another. For example, there are sizable variations from state to state in the age at which the child becomes legally responsible for his own actions, and at which the parent is no longer held responsible. There are differences, too, in the ages at which the adolescent is considered competent to drive a car, to marry, to own property, to carry firearms, to drink alcoholic beverages, and to purchase tobacco.

Thus the adolescent who must face the problems of transition from childish dependency to adult independency is likely to be impressed, not with the solidarity of the expectations of the adults in this regard, but with their divisiveness. In one instance, or with one set of people, he is likely to find that independency responses are rewarded. In other instances, or with other people, he may just as easily find that they are punished. The church, the school, the members of the various social classes, even the adolescent's own parents may have different notions as to the time when adult protection and guidance should be relinquished in favor of greater individual responsibility.

The adolescent is likely to observe that one of his peers is allowed by his parents to decide how to spend his money, to use the family car, to date, to choose his own vocation, to do part-time work, to choose his own companions, to go off on trips by himself or with his friends. Another adolescent, even of the same age and social group, may be allowed to do none of these things.

Moreover, the adolescent finds numerous inconsistencies in the ways in which people react to him as an individual. The young high school student's employer usually expects him to be independent and responsible more often than do his parents. The same thing usually holds true for his male peers and his sweetheart. It is also true of the law in most instances.

A mother and father may have differing independence expectations with regard to their child. In addition, either or both parents may possess mixed feelings over their child's growing independence. These mixed feelings are likely to be reflected in inconsistent patterns of parental behavior—as, for example, demanding independence and at the same time punishing it when it occurs (cf. pp. 497–500).

The adolescent himself is likely to be uncertain and confused about the problem of achieving independence. He may desire to be a free agent, but he may just as truly want the security and lack of responsibility that are associated with continuing dependence. As a result, he may suffer personal conflict over independence needs. When all the above environmental inconsistencies with regard to independency-dependency expectations are added to the adolescent's own uncertainties, it is not surprising to find that the adolescent's path to independence should often be a stormy one both for the adolescent himself and for his parents.

Farnham (22) has given an excellent picture of the way in which an adolescent's conflicts over independence and the parents' own mixed feelings may affect the family in the middle-class American home.

In the years between babyhood and adolescence . . . the youngster has been safely contained within the family circle. Now he must begin the process of breaking out of that circle. At first he is apt to display not much more than a determined opposition, where formerly he showed compliance. The relied-upon family dishwasher may suddenly develop a vast indifference to his family routines. Many are the bewildered mothers who wail, "I can't get that child to do a thing in the house." Mother's little helper has given way to someone who appears to have never heard of such a thing as family coöperation. He or she now much prefers matters of such singular importance as club meetings, lolling in a comfortable chair, talking over the telephone interminably, to the drab and uninteresting concerns of the household. Attempts to remedy this situation by the formerly reliable methods of persuasion and discipline may not bear the expected fruit. Evasion and delay are useful tools. The watchword of this method is "just a minute" or "I'll do it when I've finished." The tally of the verbal ways to avoid going along with a parental request is almost endless. Some parents themselves are driven to distraction by a noticeable tendency on the part of the youngster to develop deafness at convenient moments. To make a request half a dozen times and then be met with an apparently surprised, "Were you talking to me?" has been known to flurry the calm of even the "best-tempered." Naturally, "I'm busy" is again but of such an ordinary quality that it is rarely used and then only in extreme cases. Homework may become a fascinating undertaking if only because it interferes with doing what the parent requires. This high devotion to intellectual labor is a common method of escape. Not infrequently when the parent has bowed his head to the obvious necessity of following the call to higher endeavor, he has later discovered the "homework" to consist of elaborate manicuring, shoe-polishing, bemused gazing in the mirror, or just plain sitting and doodling. Brought to book, the child takes recourse in the esoteric "I'm thinking." Parents may wonder at times why all the "thinking" done by adolescent youngsters "has not by now solved the problems of the universe." It has done a lot toward it.

If such methods as these do not avail, it is probable that the child will display some open hostility. It is safe to say that at some time during adolescence parents may expect to encounter real enmity from their youngster (22, 60).

As Farnham points out, however, this kind of antagonism is not continual. It is likely to alternate with reasonable compliance to the demands of family living. At times, it is even likely to be followed by periods of almost infantile dependence, so that the parents, instead of fearing reckless independence, begin to wonder if the child will ever stand on his own feet.

SPECIFIC PARENT-CHILD CONFLICTS. Not surprisingly, in light of the above discussion, parent-child conflicts during adolescence tend to fall into two main categories: (1) issues involving greater adolescent demands for independence than the parents are willing to grant; (2) issues involving more dependent, or childish, behavior on the part of the adolescent than the parents feel able to tolerate (9, 28, 48). In the first category would be included arguments over such topics as: time the child gets in at night, use of the family car, and freedom to choose own friends among boys and girls (28, 48). In the second category would fall parental objections to: noisiness and untidiness, teasing of siblings, silliness, and shirking of home duties (28, 48).

Block's study (9) is fairly typical of investigations in this area. Her subjects were 528 junior and senior high school boys and girls. Using a questionnaire approach, she derived a list of the 50 problems of parent-child relationships most frequently mentioned by these students. These sources of conflict and the percentage of students reporting them are shown in Table 9.

It should be stressed that such conflicts may stem from more basic problems of parent-child relationships. All such conflicts are not going to be resolved by reaching agreement about the use of the family car, or making some new technical arrangement about allowance, or by deciding that lipstick is all right for the girl to use.

INDEPENDENCE CONFLICTS AND PREVIOUS PARENT-CHILD RELATIONSHIPS. The severity of the adolescent's conflicts over independence-dependence, and the ease with which they are resolved in the direction of greater independence will depend to a large extent on previous parent-child relationships.

For example, we have already seen (cf. pp. 333–335) that the child whose parents have been overly dominant tends to become overly dependent and submissive to authority, since these are the types of responses which such parents reward. By adolescence, these responses are likely to have acquired such great habit strength that the individual will have great difficulty in eliminating them and substituting the more independent responses which the society demands.

According to one author, "if the dominated child is at the same time wanted or accepted, and if the domination is steady, deliberate, and probably not harsh, the result is continued attachment to parents along with a lack of normal social development outside the family" (52). He may even retreat into more dependent behavior. Even where he is able to change, it is only with considerable effort, and often after highly turbulent parent-adolescent conflicts.

TABLE 9. Percent of High School Boys and Girls Reporting Each of 50 Sources of Parent-Child Conflicts [a]

Problem	Percent reporting	
	boys	girls
1. Insists upon nagging me regarding what I wear and how I dress.	26.3	50.9
2. Complains about how I comb my hair.	24.3	26.0
3. Fusses because I use lipstick.	0.0	64.6
4. Refuses to let me buy the clothes I like.	12.7	55.6
5. Complains about my hands or neck or fingernails being dirty.	55.7	10.5
6. Pesters me about my table manners.	74.8	63.9
7. Pesters me about my personal manners and habits.	68.5	70.0
8. Objects to my smoking.	0.8	13.4
9. Objects to my going with boys or girls she doesn't like.	19.1	40.4
10. Makes me go to bed at the same time that my younger brothers and sisters do.	30.6	45.1
11. Objects to the books and magazines I read.	17.9	32.5
12. Objects to my going to dances.	0.0	58.8
13. Insists that I eat foods which I dislike, but which are good for me.	82.4	83.8
14. Won't let me attend the church I want to attend.	4.4	53.4
15. Urges me to make friends with children of important people in town.	9.6	13.4
16. Won't let me take subjects I want in school.	32.9	56.1
17. Won't let me follow a vocation in which I am interested.	64.5	34.3
18. Insists that I go with friends of her choice.	20.3	69.7
19. Won't let me spend the night with any of my friends.	15.1	42.6
20. Nags about any little thing.	26.3	66.4
21. Insists upon interfering in settling any difficulties I may have with friends or teachers.	20.3	23.1
22. Talks baby talk to me.	33.4	10.5
23. Teases me about my girl friends.	51.3	0.0
24. Teases me about my boy friends.	0.0	65.7
25. Brags about me to other people.	50.1	22.7
26. Holds my sister or brother up as a model to me.	66.9	75.8

Problem	Percent reporting boys	girls
27. Spends most of her time at bridge parties, etc., and is rarely ever at home.	28.7	78.0
28. Tells her friends things about me that I tell her confidentially.	13.5	16.2
29. Insists that I be a goody-goody.	32.2	57.8
30. Shows favoritism to my brother or sister.	30.6	44.4
31. Embarrasses me by telling my friends what a good son or daughter I am.	49.8	26.4
32. Is cold to friends of mine she doesn't like.	19.9	45.1
33. Makes a huge fuss over friends of mine whom she likes.	34.3	36.8
34. Scolds if my school marks aren't as high as other people's.	82.4	85.9
35. Gets angry if I don't spend most of my time with her.	28.3	34.7
36. Talks against my father and wants me to agree with her.	8.4	16.6
37. Treats me as if I were a child.	5.2	16.3
38. Objects to my going automobile riding at night with boys.	65.7	87.4
39. Objects to my going automobile riding during the day with boys.	49.0	66.4
40. Insists that I tell her for exactly what I spend my money.	80.0	81.2
41. Won't give me a regular allowance.	54.1	52.3
42. Accompanies me to parties, movies, etc.	3.2	30.3
43. Insists that I take my sister or brother wherever I go.	50.5	82.3
44. Investigates places when I go to parties, etc., before I go.	15.1	44.4
45. Worries about my physical health.	26.7	58.8
46. Won't let me use the car.	85.7	70.8
47. Urges me to beat the next fellow in school work.	3.6	13.0
48. Urges me to outdo others socially, which I hate to do.	0.0	28.2
49. Won't ever let me go to the movies or dancing.	7.6	13.4
50. Won't let me entertain at home.	9.2	53.1

a From Block (9). With permission of the American Psychological Association.

Farnham (22) has described the case of a parent who came to her in alarm when her 13-year-old daughter announced in icy terms one day, "I hate you." It became obvious upon investigation that while the girl had always been a model child from her parent's point of view, the whole relationship had been based on a system of parental dominance and filial submission. During the past year the child had attempted to assert herself in an effort to achieve independent feminine status. This was resisted by the mother, until finally the issue was brought to a head by an apparently trivial argument having to do with "hours and limitations on her freedom." It was then that the daughter announced her hatred.

Fortunately this child was able to assert some independence (though at considerable emotional cost) despite a long history of having been rewarded primarily for dependent responses. Other children, however, are often so strongly rewarded for dependency responses and so severely punished for independent responses, that such rebellion is not possible for them. They remain hopelessly dependent. Furthermore, as cultural demands for independence increase, this dependent behavior becomes progressively more inappropriate.

While the overly dependent child faces special problems of adolescent emancipation, it should not be assumed that all children who approach adolescence with well-developed independency responses will necessarily establish a successful adjustment. For example, the rejected child may have been forced to develop a certain amount of independence; but as a result of his rejection, he may develop a strong resentment toward his parents for their behavior. He may then generalize this resentment to the society at large. The other side of the coin of emancipation from parents is successful integration into the wider community. While the overly dependent child may have difficulty with the emancipation aspects, the relatively independent, but rejected and resentful youngster may have trouble fitting himself coöperatively into the adult social order. As a result of stimulus generalization, his attitudes toward the society may become permanently fixed (just as they have toward his parents) in the form of hostility and suspicion.

On the other hand, the child who has already attained some status within his family as an independent person by adolescence, whose opinions are considered worth respect, who is given responsibility, and who is loved by his parents, may be expected to weather the storms of adolescence reasonably well. Independence-dependence problems will still exist, and they will no doubt produce minor crises at times within the family structure. But they will not assume unmanageable proportions, and they will eventually resolve themselves as adult status is gained.

The relation between early parent-child interactions and the successful resolution of the independence conflicts of adolescence is shown in a recent study by Ausubel (5). From a group of 20 individuals who had in the past suffered from serious conflicts with their parents over emancipation, he compared 10 individuals who showed little residual conflict as adults with 10 other individuals who showed considerable residual conflicts. He found that both groups manifested significantly greater conflict with parents during childhood than the general population. However, in the case of the group that did not improve, the conflicts were much more severe than in the improving group. Furthermore, once adolescence was past, the parent-child relationships of the improving group tended to become stabilized and more satisfying. The author concludes that parents can therefore "be given assurance that if their relationships with their children have been established on the basis of mutual respect and affection, it is reasonably certain that this same relationship will be reëstablished when the turbulent period of adolescence is over" (5).

PARENTAL ATTITUDES TOWARD ADOLESCENT INDEPENDENCE. We have already seen that there are likely to be contradictions in attitudes toward adolescent independence, not only *between* various agents of the adult culture, but also *within* the individual parent. It is this second type of contradiction which is likely to be most difficult for the adolescent to cope with because of its elusiveness. When one voice of the culture, such as the church, issues a particular set of directives for adolescent behavior, and another voice, such as the peer group, issues another, the adolescent may be in conflict, and he will be forced to choose between them. But at least in this situation he has a clear recognition of the attitudes with which he is dealing. On the other hand, when a parent proclaims, for example, that he wants his son to be independent, but covertly does everything he can to prolong dependency, the result is likely to be confusion for the adolescent. His position becomes similar to Alice's in her encounter with the Mad Hatter—nothing is ever quite what it seems. Because of the difficulty of identifying and labeling parental attitudes correctly, he finds it almost impossible to deal with them rationally.

Parental inconsistencies with regard to emancipation may simply reflect confusion on the part of the parent as to the role society expects him to play. (When *should* he permit a child to date, to have his own spending money, to drive a car, to make his own decisions?) If so, the problem of helping the parent to achieve consistency may be merely one of education. More often, however, a parent's inconsistencies seem to result from his own contradictory needs—needs that are deeply rooted and not infrequently unconscious. Many parents, for example, genuinely want their children to become able to handle their own affairs because they realize that ultimately this will be necessary. But at the same time, they are likely to want to continue to protect their children from the unpleasant realities of existence—an impossible task (21).

There are of course many other possible sources of a parent's inconsistencies. A parent with strong needs to be all-powerful and all-wise in the eyes of others may in reality have gained little recognition from the world at large. As a result, he may be unwilling to grant his child independence, since an inevitable corollary of independence is a renunciation of the idea that any one, including one's parents, is always right and can be trusted to run one's life adequately.

Similarly those parents who feel unloved by their marriage partners or their friends may be reluctant to see their children begin leading their own lives. For they realize, either consciously or unconsciously, that another of the inevitable consequences of independence is a shift in primary affectional goals from parents to other important life figures—whether sweetheart, marriage partner, or one's own offspring. As Meyers states, "Allowing a child to achieve emancipation, will be difficult in proportion as the parent has achieved satisfaction, knowingly or not, for his own wants by loving and controlling his child. If the child is providing gratification and compensation for frustrations arising elsewhere, he will be surrendered reluctantly, surrendered at a cost, or not surrendered at all" (21).

The parent who possesses secret needs for sexual delinquency may project these desires on to the child, and hence become fearful of what the child may do if left to his or her own devices. As a result, the parents may become unduly repressive in controlling the child's activities.

English and Pearson (21) point out that many parents, while consciously desirous that their children lead a happy and rewarding life, often keep them tied to their parental apron strings through jealousy. Unconsciously, they do not want their children to enjoy good times that they themselves have missed.

There are, of course, many other reasons why parents may be reluctant to grant their children independence, such as fearing that they may marry too young and thus require a longer period of financial support. Parents may also fear that a young person will marry unwisely, or marry the wrong person, or someone beneath him—whatever that may mean to the particular family. Moreover, they fear there is a real danger of sexual indulgence before marriage and that this friendly proximity is going to be a temptation to sexual intercourse, with the resultant danger of illegitimate pregnancy or disease and the consequent disgrace (21).

In general, it appears that the most common source of parental ambivalence (mixed feelings) toward the child's assumption of independence is the realization on the one hand that the child must someday stand on his own feet; but the coexistent fear that in learning to do so he will be deeply hurt. A great many of these fears, however, are unfounded.

Children will, of course, make mistakes, and they may even be hurt.

This is unfortunate. But the chances of their being seriously harmed seem to us much less if they are allowed to learn independency responses gradually, while they are still able to turn to their parents for support, than if they are suddenly thrust out into the world at the age of twenty-one, totally unprepared to act independently.

Horrocks offers a worth-while caution, however, in regard to parents' attempts to help their children achieve emancipation: He points out that extremes can be exceedingly dangerous, and that while it is necessary for the parent to promote independence, "there is danger that a child may be emancipated too early, or that emancipation may be too vigorously or too harshly promoted" (33). He adds that, "Emancipation cannot be achieved overnight and the wise parent will make it a gradual process of induction over a period of time so that the adolescent will not lose his sense of security, or misunderstand the motives of his parents. . . . The problem seems to be that of striking a golden mean between overprotection and overrestriction on the one hand, and absolute independence on the other" (33).

OTHER FACTORS AFFECTING EASE OF EMANCIPATION. In addition to parent-child relationships, there are a number of other factors which can facilitate or retard emancipation from the family. It is not enough for the parents to reward responses of greater responsibility, to encourage independence, to withdraw their emotional protectiveness gradually—while at the same time continuing to show their love and acceptance of the child. The adolescent must also be given an opportunity by the society to act like an adult, to put independency responses into practice. He must find enough security in his contacts with peers and nonparental adults to compensate for the loosening of family ties, and in addition, he must be motivated by the society to want to be an adult. In other words, he must be shown that society will reward independent, adultlike behavior, as, for example, by granting him increased prestige and greater privileges.

Other factors, such as the child's general approach to experience, the rate at which he matures physically, and his sex membership will also play an important role. Outgoing children are less likely to have difficulty in emancipation than their more sensitive, introspective peers, since they are more likely to try out the aggressive, self-assertive responses which lead to social rewards. Physical growth is also an important factor in determining the speed of emancipation, since adults tend to base their expectations of mature behavior more on the child's size than on his actual age (7). It has been found, for example, that taller, heavier, stronger children tend to be rated as more highly emancipated than their peers (*17*). Moreover, there is evidence that in dealing with same-age children, parents and teachers tend to treat those who are more advanced physically more maturely (*7*).

Another study indicates that among college students, boys tended to be more emancipated from their families than girls (*63*). Much of the difficulty adolescent girls experience tends to focus in the home because parental attitudes have not kept pace with social changes in the status of women (*4*). Parents tend to take their son's emancipations for granted, but they appear unwilling to "acknowledge the same emancipation needs in their daughters; instead of relinquishing some control at adolescence, they seem to impose more rather than less supervision" (*4*).

PEER RELATIONSHIPS IN ADOLESCENCE

One of the most striking characteristics of the adolescent in our society is his great dependence on peer groups. While, as we have just seen, dependence on the family gradually weakens, peer-group dependence undergoes a corresponding increase, at least in the early years of adolescence. Acceptance by his peers brings elation; rejection brings despair. The momentary values of the peer group become his values, as do also the fashions and the fads.

It is of course true that the child's ties to his peers have been steadily becoming stronger during the school years. However, during adolescence, the child's outside attachments become stronger and far more crucial to his overall adjustment. Perhaps nowhere is this more clearly demonstrated than in the slavish conformity of many adolescents to peer-group norms. Wearing the same clothes the same way, speaking the same special vocabulary, preferring the same foods, keeping the same hours, enjoying the same sorts of recreation, following the same rules of heterosexual conduct—all are extremely important to the members of an adolescent group (*22*). In many cases, adolescents will go to great lengths to gain status among their peers, and will accept considerable abuse from them if necessary in order to maintain group membership. One may well ask why group conformity responses seem to be so satisfying to the adolescent, and why it is that conformity needs some more urgent in adolescence than at earlier age levels.

There are certainly no simple answers to these questions. The needs of adolescents are numerous and complex. In addition, there is great variation from one individual to another. Nevertheless, certain characteristics seem to stand out.

As we have previously pointed out, the adolescent is faced with severe demands from the society with regard to what he must accomplish; but he is given little indication of how this is to be done. The anxiety engendered by such a situation as this is further magnified by the gradual loss of parents as acceptable sources of gratification for his dependency needs. Anxiety is also increased by his social status as a "marginal man"—rejecting of childhood, but not yet fully accepted by adults (cf. p. 456). It is hardly surprising that in such a situation the adolescent should turn to his peers, since there are many ways in which they can help him to make the transition from childhood to adulthood more readily.

1. Possibly the most important role played by the peer group is that of a teacher. Faced by uncertainty as to how to reach adult status safely, he is likely to operate on the familiar principle that "fifty million Frenchmen can't be wrong"—that if he does as other adolescents do, he will probably reach adulthood safely, since most other adolescents do. This is, of course, particularly likely to occur if he has been rewarded for imitative responses in his past life.

Furthermore, such imitative behavior serves an extremely practical purpose. In fact, several authors (5, 70) maintain that the peer group is *the* major training institution for adolescents in our society. They see the school's role in adolescent development as stemming chiefly from the opportunities it provides for adolescents to come into contact with one another. Through such contacts the adolescent may learn many important attitudes, beliefs, and techniques of social interaction that he cannot learn from his parents or teachers (24). Sex roles become further clarified, competitive and coöperative responses and social skills are developed. The child who, for one reason or another, is deprived of peer contact at this period may miss important opportunities to learn many significant aspects of socialization.

2. Identification with his peer group also seems to play an important role in the adolescent's achievement of independence from his family. Not only can peers provide a substitute source of reinforcement for persisting dependency needs, as dependence on his parents decreases; but they can also provide him with moral backing in his demands for independence (5).

"By pooling their resistance in groups and throwing up barriers of one kind and another against adult authority and interference," adolescents can "exclude adults and protect themselves from . . . the coercions that (adults) are prone to use" (70).

3. The peer group also provides opportunities for adolescents to

acquire sex information, to learn to relate socially to members of the opposite sex, and to acquire standards of sexual behavior (5, 70). In this general area, the teaching function of the peer group assumes special importance because the adult culture provides so little consistent guidance.

4. Finally, the peer group provides a much needed source of status and prestige to the adolescent. As Farnham says, "no group is more susceptible to the need for status and prestige than are the adolescents. Unsure of themselves and their values, requiring above all things the approval and acceptance of those around them, they are always urgently seeking ways of finding these things" (22). In their status as "marginal men," who have renounced childhood, but who are not yet fully accepted by adults, adolescents are forced to turn for status and support to their peers. In brief, the peer group acts as a potent agent of reward. Hence, as we would expect on the basis of a reinforcement theory of learning, the peer group exerts a tremendous influence on the adolescent. Furthermore, since the peer group usually makes these rewards contingent upon conformity to the rules of the group, the adolescent tends to learn to conform to his group's ways of thinking and acting. Thus he learns a wide variety of responses, many of which will also be rewarded in his future contacts with the world outside his immediate peer group—in work, social life, or marriage.

General Changes in Peer Relations During Adolescence

At the beginning of adolescence, the youth's relationships with his peers are quite similar to those of younger children. The changes that occur as adolescence proceeds are probably best seen in the context of the general social development that takes place during this period. Several of the more important of these changes will be discussed in some detail:

Changing Patterns of Group Identification

As he grows older, the adolescent shifts from a desire for identification with the herd to one of identification with a small, select group (35). Having the right kind of friends becomes more important than their number (15). As a result the old, loose-knit "gang" of childhood begins to be replaced by the more selective "crowd" and the even more select and exclusive "clique."

When the mother of an adolescent boy or girl asks her child where she is going, the answer is likely to be "just out with the crowd." A few years earlier the reply is "just out with the gang." From the adult point of view, the "gang" and the "crowd" may be more or less synonymous, but the adolescent uses the terms to denote somewhat different groups. The gang is typically a spontaneous social unit of late childhood. Its members are generally of the same sex, and it is relatively small. The activities of a gang are, of course, influenced by the outlets provided in a given neighborhood, but its general objective is to seek adventure and excitement. The crowd, on the other hand, is typically composed of both boys and girls, preferably an equal number of each. It contains from six to a dozen members who usually live within two or three blocks of each other, attend the same school, and have much the same socioeconomic background. Its chief activities consist of talking, listening to the radio, watching television, eating, and dancing at home to radio or phonograph.

In the summer the crowd sits around on someone's porch, with occasional excursions to the neighborhood drugstore. In winter it sits around in someone's house, plays the radio, and makes raids on the icebox. None of these come under the heading of adventure as seen through the eyes of late childhood, but it is apparently exciting to the adolescent. It is adventure, not into the world of things, but into the world of social relationships (15, 261).

The "clique" is even more selective than the crowd and reflects the need for even more intimate contact than the crowd provides. The crowd needs only to be similar in background, interests, and ideals; a clique on the other hand, requires not merely shared purposes, interests, and social class values, but in addition, personal compatibility, congeniality, close ties of mutual admiration and affection (15).

FACTORS AFFECTING CLIQUE FORMATION. Girls tend to form cliques earlier than boys and continue to operate them in a more exclusive, tightly knit fashion. This greater tendency for clique formation among girls may indicate that they have less opportunity than boys to establish independent status in the adolescent peer culture (5).

As already pointed out, selection of clique mates first involves similarity in broad sociological characteristics such as socioeconomic status, ethnic origin, family background, and propinquity. In one study (29), three-fourths of "best friends," as rated by high school boys and girls in a midwestern town, were of the same social class. In another investigation (64), 68 percent of close friends were found to live within a block or two of each other. These associations probably result from more than mere availability. Individuals who have learned similar attitudes and goals as the result of class-conditioned home training find their needs better met by one another than by persons with differing backgrounds.

Within the limits of these general requirements for same-clique membership, more individual factors come into play. It has been found, for example, that similar degrees of social maturity play an important role in the formation of mutual friendships (37). In early adolescence, this is often correlated with degree of physical maturity. Various studies of junior high school students suggest that similarities in other characteristics also influence the choice of mutual friends. These include similarities in mental age; interests; moral knowledge and standards; personality traits, such as degree of sociability in play, of criticalness of self or others, of neuroticism, of extroversion, and of social intelligence (17, 28, 35, 54).

THE SATURDAY EVENING POST

Saturday Evening Post, courtesy of Don Tobin

May I borrow the phone for the evening?

Some shifts in standards for selecting companions occur as adolescence progresses, particularly with regard to interest. In early adolescence, students appear to be strongly influenced by similar preferences in games and sports, by ability to think of and to do exciting things, and by duration of acquaintance (17, 28). In later adolescence, such factors as acceptability of friends to members of the opposite sex (particularly among girls) become important (35).

In addition to the influence of specific similarities between individuals in the formation of friendships and cliques, there are a number of general personal characteristics which appear to be social assets generally in many kinds of peer groups, and also a number which appear to be liabilities. For example, according to the data of one study, boys tended to like peers who were coöperative, helpful, considerate of others, courteous, honest, unselfish, and self-controlled. They tended to dislike peers who showed off, bluffed, bullied, quarreled, carried grudges, thought they were 'picked on,' alibied, made excuses, acted superior or domineering, or showed overdependence on others (32). It seems quite obvious that boys who had personal characteristics which were likely to make contact with them rewarding to their peers were viewed as more acceptable.

SOCIAL-CLASS DIFFERENCES IN PEER PREFERENCES. Preferences in peer associations also reflect, as one might expect, the effect of broad social variables such as social-class membership. Anastasi and Miller (2) found that high school students as a group preferred the following characteristics in friends: is friendly, well-mannered, coöperative in a group, enjoys hearing or telling jokes, and is loyal to friends. There were some differences in preferences between those of higher socioeconomic status who were planning to go to college and those of lower status who were not. The college-preparatory group chose the following characteristics with greater frequency: serious-minded, talkative, talented in arts and crafts, enjoys working on his own hobbies, is enthusiastic. The noncollege group more frequently chose: good listener, athletic, enjoys practical jokes, peppy, neat in appearance, grown-up, hale-fellow-well-met. These results appear to reflect differences between the two groups in the kinds of interests which brought rewards in the past and in those which were expected to be rewarding in the future.

Changes in Group Structure and Function

Not only does youth in our society seem to prefer identification with smaller groups as adolescence progresses, but the structure and functions of these groups also change. For one thing, their composition becomes less changeable. In this connection, it is interesting to note that boys maintain a greater number of stable long-term friendships than girls (37); on the other hand, girls maintain a greater number of stable friendships over short periods of time (69). In addition, peer relationships become more intimate. This is particularly true of girls, who spend more time with their close friends, and prefer smaller groups of friends (5). Also, girls' choices of friends tend more than boys' to be reciprocal, as measured by sociometric choices (5, 23).

Many friendships in adolescence are extremely intimate. As one author notes: "Two youngsters of this age often give the appearance of being mutually absolutely dependent. They play together, work together, and would live together if circumstances would allow them. At times they seem to be almost one and the same person, the lines between them are so fuzzy and indefinite. They wear each other's clothes, exchange possessions in a casual way, talk in the same manner with the same inflections. Not infrequently they go to such extremes in this indiscriminate exchange that when one meets one of them, he or she is scarcely recognizable because of being dressed entirely in the other's clothes" (22).

As this greater intimacy in peer relations increases, there is a qualitative change in the types of needs satisfied by these relationships. Whereas the more extroverted preadolescent is usually content to *participate* in group activities, the adolescent is much more concerned with the subjective analysis of group experience. He is very much aware of the "subtle overtones and elusive undercurrents in interpersonal relations, and attempts through introspection to conceptualize them more precisely" (5). He is no longer content just to be a member of the group. He must be intimately accepted as an individual, and he is keenly aware of any slight evidences of acceptance or rejection by his peers.

As might be expected, communication between peers becomes a matter of urgent necessity at this time. The adolescent uses the constant interchange of ideas and experience as a means of reassuring himself that he is still liked and understood. By this means, he also maintains an awareness of the subtle cues on which appropriate behavior in his social group must be based.

Changing Patterns of Leadership

The characteristics demanded of the leader will be a function of the situation in which he is to lead. The behavior of the leader will be tolerated only in so far as it helps to meet the needs of the group. Thus it might be expected that the qualities of leaders will change as the needs of the peer group change during the adolescent period. In addition, different kinds of persons may be expected to emerge as leaders in different peer subgroups having different purposes. Such indeed seems to be the case.

In early childhood the child is led by domination. The aggressive type of individual is generally the leader. At this age individuals transfer from parental domination to the authority of the child whose personality is domineering or bossy. Toward the latter part of childhood the bully or tyrant loses favor with the group. The resistance to domination that appears in parent-child relation-ships is also felt in relationship with peers. The newly expressed self-assertiveness of the older child makes him rebel against the aggressive leader. He now wants a new type of leader who coöperates, rather than dominates, in leader-group relationships.

With the increase in variety of activity that developed during adolescence, the demand for a new type of leader is even stronger. There is now a need for leaders who are equipped to lead in these different types of activities. This differs from childhood, when the activities are not so varied and when different leadership ability for different activities is not so important. Awakening of heterosexual interests likewise brings about a new requirement for the adoles-cent leader. He must be presentable and make a good appearance if he is to represent the group (35, 195).

Apparently among adolescents, the individual who takes into account the needs and wishes of his group is likely to be most successful as a leader, although he must be comparatively subtle in his methods and not deviate too far from accepted patterns of adolescent behavior (33).

The qualities of leaders will vary at different stages of adolescence and also according to the specific purposes of various peer subgroups (ath-letic, social, vocational, academic, etc.). Nevertheless, it appears that cer-tain characteristics have more leadership value than others in most adolescent peer-group situations in our culture.

Research findings agree that the adolescent leader surpasses the non-leader in five broad areas of personality that are self-evidently related to leadership functions: (a) *physical appearance:* height, weight, strength, and athletic prowess; (b) *intelligence;* (c) *decision-making ability:* discriminating judg-ment, firmness of decision, low suggestibility, self-confidence, and imagination; (d) *interests:* maturity and breadth of interests, and participation in social and leisure-time activities; (e) *socially relevant aspects of temperament:* extro-version, dominance, liveliness, and good sportsmanship (5, 372).

INTEREST PATTERNS IN ADOLESCENCE

Following puberty, significant changes occur in the interests and activ-ities of adolescents. During the early years of adolescence there is a marked shift toward any activities which provide an opportunity for learning responses needed in social interaction. As already noted, "hang-ing around with the crowd" is of paramount importance: the particular activities of the crowd, if any, are of secondary significance. As the adolescent approaches maturity, however, simply being with the crowd is not enough. Its activities must be individually satisfying. At this age the adolescent becomes more interested in specialized subgroups, based upon his own particular interests (50). Also he is more likely to go steady, and in doing so is more likely to date alone (50, 59).

These changes in activity reflect the adolescent's decreasing concern with the mechanics of social intercourse and with the previously paramount issue of belonging to, and being accepted by, the peer group. They also show his increasing concern with the responses which he will be expected to be able to perform as an adult, in business, as a marriage partner, parent, or citizen. Along with these changes, there occurs a growing freedom from slavish conformity to peer-group practices shown by younger adolescents, and a growing tolerance for nonconformist behavior in others (5, 50, 70, 71).

Sex Differences in Adolescent Interest

While the general trends described above apply both to boys and girls, there are, of course, also sex differences in interests. These differences seem to reflect either variations of the sex-typing influences of the culture, or differences in physical structure, or both. For example, girls are likely to engage more than boys in sedentary activities, such as reading, and quiet hobbies, or talking with one another; while boys engage more in individual and team sports (8). Boys show more interest in organized activity than girls. In addition, girls show less fluctuation in their interests from one year to the next (32, 44, 53).

In one investigation of the scholastic interests of adolescents, high school boys and girls were asked to name the subjects they thought to be of most future value (57). Boys felt mathematics to be most useful, followed by English and occupational training. Girls, on the other hand, named English first, followed by commerce and home economics. Again it may be seen that these interest patterns reflect a growing concern among the members of each sex with the roles they will be expected to play as adults.

In a study of the written wishes of adolescents, Washburn (77) studied differences in the wishes of boys and girls. Boys far exceeded girls in expressed wishes for such things as autos, airplanes, speedboats, etc.; wealth, sporting goods; health; and long life; always having family near; marriage; and athletic skill. On the other hand, girls far exceeded boys in wishes for: clothes; good looks; possessing or playing a musical instrument; travel; being a teacher; having brothers and sisters; skill in school; and visiting and going to parties.

Other Factors Related to Adolescent Interests

Differences in interests are also related to differences in educational background. For example, in one study the principal leisure-time activities of out-of-school youth having different amounts of education were compared. The findings revealed increases with greater education in such activities as reading and individual sports. On the other hand, dancing, dating, loafing, and team games *decreased* with greater education (8).

Differences in the living conditions of rural and urban youth also produce differences in interests and activities. Group activities, particularly those involving only the individual's own age and sex group, appeal more to city youth (33). Rural youth, on the other hand, tend to have better-developed interests in solitary or adult-child activities.

Differences in intelligence also play a role in determining interests. More intelligent youth tend to have a greater number and variety of interests than the less intelligent. Not surprisingly, they also tend to have more sedentary, intellectual types of interests, such as reading (33).

The above group differences in interests seem to reflect the influences of past rewards, the social expectations of others in the society, practical opportunities, and individual differences in capacity. Activities at which an individual is unable to do well, or which are discouraged by others when they are performed, tend to be dropped; those which are possible and which are encouraged tend to persist.

RELATIONS WITH OPPOSITE-SEX PEERS

In the previous chapter, we saw that the ease with which heterosexual adjustments are made during adolescence will be in large measure a function of cultural influences. In some primitive societies, such as the Samoans or the Alorese, heterosexual adjustment proceeds naturally and easily, with few sudden changes. In other societies, such as the Manus, the culture seems almost to conspire to make heterosexual adjustment as difficult as possible. While our own culture's attitudes are somewhat more permissive than those of the Manus, it is still true that one of the most profound adjustments which the adolescent must make in our society involves his relationship with opposite-sexed peers. As we saw earlier, during preadolescence most boys and girls in our society not only confine their social activities primarily to members of their own sex, but manifest in addition a marked aversion or antagonism toward members of the opposite sex (cf. pp. 421–422).

Between the age of 12 and adulthood, these same children are expected to learn to relate socially and with ease to members of the opposite sex. They are expected to cope with problems of what to do about increases in sex drive (as discussed in the previous chapter)—whether or not to engage in masturbation, necking, petting, or intercourse; and if so, to what extent and at what age. They are supposed to switch to obtaining a greater part of their satisfactions in interpersonal relations with one member of the opposite sex, rather than as in the past with a primarily same-sexed gang. Furthermore, they are expected to develop strong interests in becoming marriage partners, parents, and managers of independent households. They are expected after marriage to be capable of enjoying sexual activity with their spouses, and only with their spouses. Lastly, they are also expected to enjoy life with their marriage partners enough to compensate for the inevitable limitations on personal freedom that marriage brings.

Factors Affecting Attitudes Toward Opposite-Sex Peers

In view of the extent of these demands, it is not surprising that some adolescents have trouble making satisfactory heterosexual adjustments. The ease with which the child will be able to progress from antagonism to a positive interest in the opposite sex will depend largely on his previous parent-child relationships. The attitudes which the child develops in his early relations with his mother and father may persist into adolescence and may be generalized to other males and females. For example, as a child a girl may have learned to expect love and admiration from her father. She may have been rewarded by her mother for exhibiting feminine traits. Such a girl will tend to grow up expecting that relations with males in general can also lead to love and admiration. She will not be ashamed of playing a feminine role in relation to male contemporaries during adolescence and adulthood.

On the other hand, the girl whose father has rejected her is likely, also on the basis of generalization, to anticipate rejection from all men. Similarly, the boy whose mother has exploited him or dominated him is likely to anticipate exploitation and domination from all women.

The above, of course, are simply examples of the ways in which attitudes developed in relation to parents are likely to be generalized to same- or opposite-sex contemporaries in adolescence, with either a facilitating or damaging effect upon the child's chances for reaching an adequate heterosexual adjustment.

Antagonism toward the opposite sex, stemming from the differential treatment of boys and girls, is another factor which may handicap the adolescent in his heterosexual relationships. The adolescent who finds members of the opposite sex able to do things he is unable to do, or receiving rewards he does not receive, may become resentful of them.

This is probably more true among girls than among boys, since in our society boys seem to have a preferred status which is tacitly acknowledged by both sexes. In one study, it was found that while boys seldom if ever wished they were girls, girls were not infrequently envious of and wished they were boys (78). On the other hand, girls are more likely to receive preferential treatment at home, and this may lead boys to resent them (5).

Factors which may further magnify this sex antagonism and prolong it, possibly permanently, include learned fears of sexuality, shyness, fear of social relationships, and of course as already mentioned, poor parental identification patterns.

Adolescent Crushes

With the onset of puberty, adolescent "crushes" are likely to occur. Crushes involve a strong attraction to and admiration of a peer of the same sex, or an older person of either sex. The first sort may be manifested by constant attempts to be with the loved one; by despondency when even short absences occur; by evidence of emotional excitement in the presence of the loved one, by ardent protestations of affection and undying devotions; and by imitation of the loved one's speech, mannerisms, and activity (35).

On the other hand, a crush toward an older person is characterized more by romantic idealization and hero worship; and is most likely to be expressed as silent adoration (35).

There is good evidence that both these types of crushes are extremely common, particularly among girls (34, 42). Crushes are most frequent between 14 and 18 years of age, and according to one study, usually last between one and six months (34). Girls are more likely to have crushes on same-sexed peers, while boys' crushes tend more to center on an older person of the opposite sex (11).

Because of the similarity of crushes to romantic behavior generally, crushes on same-sexed individuals have been interpreted by some authors as evidence that the child passes through a homosexual stage before achieving adult heterosexuality. It should be pointed out, however, that while crushes often seem to involve some physical affection, they rarely involve specifically sexual responses. Moreover, they tend to be easily dropped as new interests are aroused, and seldom lead to any difficulty in forming later heterosexual attachments (42).

Crushes may serve as substitute sexual outlets at a time when boys and girls are shy and self-conscious about relating to one another (5). But they may also serve a variety of other important adolescent needs. For example, they may help to fulfill the adolescent's needs for status, through identification with successful persons in his environment, whether teachers, older friends, or popular peers.

Boy-Girl Relationships

As they mature, boys and girls begin to pay more attention to one another. Earlier sex antagonisms and crushes begin to wane, and frankly heterosexual interests begin to predominate. The amount of time that boys and girls spend talking about problems of relationships with the opposite sex, and the number of worries they go through in connection with them, are probably partly due to the effects of preceding periods of culturally induced segregation. Since early childhood the child has had only limited opportunity to develop appropriate responses for social interaction with the opposite sex. Hence many of these responses must now be learned in a short period. Furthermore, strong emergence of sexual drive following puberty, and the lack of readily available responses for dealing adequately with it, complicate the matter. And, as previously noted, the adult culture in most instances provides little really useful guidance to the adolescent in these matters. Consequently, topics dealing with heterosexual relationships (e.g., dates, marriage, ideal person of the opposite sex, sexual relations, dancing, and love) occupy what may seem to adults like an inordinate percentage of the conversational repertoire of most high school and college students.

In the earlier years of adolescence topics of major concern (particularly to middle-class youngsters) include: whether to date alone or to double date, and whether to permit kissing on dates; what clothes to wear; what conversational topics to pursue; even how to have conversation at all with those strange beings of the opposite sex (12).

In later adolescence, more urgent questions of sex mores inject themselves. An extensive study of college fraternity members, sorority members, and dormitory women, revealed that between 21 and 30 percent of all topics discussed in "bull sessions" dealt with some aspect of sex (66). Using an anonymous questionnaire technique with adolescent young people's groups, another investigator (12) found that among the important topics discussed at this age are moral questions relating to petting,

Reproduced courtesy of LADIES' HOME JOURNAL © C. O. Co. 1955

Pete, I'm worried. This stuff doesn't seem nearly as stupid as it used to.

trial marriage, the nature of true love, birth control, the wisdom of marrying someone of a different cultural, religious, or racial background.

In view of the fact that there is little agreement among adults in our culture as to what constitutes permissible adolescent heterosexual behavior, one would expect individual adolescents to vary widely in their sexual practices. A study of the current sex behavior of 582 college students (19), indicated that among boys, approximately 4 percent were not dating at all. Of the remainder, about 4 percent engaged in no physical contact or only holding hands; 23 percent stopped at kissing and hugging; 32 percent engaged in "heavy petting"; 37 percent went as far as sexual intercourse. Among the girls, 1 percent were not dating currently. Three percent went no further than hand holding; about 46 percent stopped at hugging and kissing, 40 percent engaged in "heavy petting"; and 10 percent went as far as sexual intercourse.

College students, of course, fall primarily in the middle class. Comparable figures for lower-class youths are, unfortunately, not so available, although Kinsey's data suggest that lower-class males engage in actual intercourse more frequently than their middle-class peers, and in other forms of heterosexual stimulation less frequently (cf. pp. 476–477).

Bases for Heterosexual Attraction and Rejection

One of the most painful experiences for an adolescent is to be rejected by members of the opposite sex. What characteristics do boys and girls of this age admire in each other? One investigator (68) asked eleventh-grade high school boys and girls to name the characteristics they considered desirable in opposite-sexed peers. His findings, listed in order of importance to the students, are given in Table 10. As may be seen,

TABLE 10. Desired Qualities of Opposite-Sexed Peers [a]

What eleventh-grade high-school girls want in boys	What eleventh-grade high-school boys want in girls
1. Personality.	1. Personality.
2. One who gets on well with all kinds of people including parents.	2. Nice-looking.
3. Good physique.	3. One who is considerate.
4. Good conversation (variety—both small talk and serious).	4. Good conversation (variety—both small talk and serious).
5. Good listener.	5. Good listener.
6. Intelligent.	6. Both feminine and a pal.
7. Not conceited.	7. Can do many things, such as swimming, hiking, skating.
8. Good sense of humor (fun but not silly).	8. Intelligent.
9. Looks neat and clean.	9. Good sense of humor.
10. Polite.	10. The kind that makes one want to be polite.
11. Good dancer.	11. Not too much make-up.

[a] From Taylor (68). With permission of Appleton-Century-Crofts, Inc.

boys place more emphasis on physical appearance than girls. Girls place more emphasis on ability to get along with people. This finding is supported by another study (6), in which it was found that 68 percent of college males said they would not marry girls who were not good-looking, while only 21 percent of college females considered good looks essential in their future hubands. Among both male and female college students, however, there is a high correlation between peer ratings of general physical attractiveness and appeal to the opposite sex (55).

It is also interesting to note that intelligence as a desirable opposite-sex characteristic is rated higher by boys than by girls (68). Several studies of college females (39, 75) indicate that, correctly or incorrectly, many girls feel that they should occasionally pretend to be inferior to men, even though they might feel equal (or superior) to them (75). Thus, in one study, to the question, "In general do you have any hesitation about revealing your equality or superiority to men in intellectual, artistic, or athletic competence?" 35 percent of girls replied that they had at least some hesitation. Over half of the girls reported advice, primarily from mothers and fathers, to the effect that they should act more "feminine" (75).

Apparently many college girls tend to overemphasize the importance of "playing dumb," for actually the majority of college males say that they want mates who are at least their equal in intelligence and education (61). In our opinion, the probable truth is that while adolescent males want their girls to be feminine, and do not want to be threatened or dominated by them intellectually, they are not particularly interested in establishing long-term relationships with girls who are clearly inferior to them mentally.

Among the characteristics adolescent boys dislike in girls, the following have been found to be prominent: is a "golddigger," always has to be taken some place, is self-centered, wears too much make-up, is fickle, talks baby talk, tells shady stories, swears, talks about other dates, sulks and pouts. Girls, on the other hand, objected to a boy who: is "vulgar minded," drinks, is conceited, brags, swears in front of girls, sponges off other boys, and "waits till the last minute to ask you for a date, especially if he knew about the occasion earlier" (82).

Preferences for Marriage Partners

In a study of courtship conduct as viewed by high school youths, boys and girls displayed preferences for somewhat similar characteristics in prospective mates (60). Among the characteristics emphasized were physical and mental fitness, desire for a normal family with children, dependability and trustworthiness, compatible interests, good personal appearance and manner, pleasant disposition, and a sense of humor. Many of the boys stressed the importance of their future mates' knowing how to cook and keep house, and a majority of the girls spontaneously expressed concern with their future mates' chances of making money and getting ahead. The boys placed more emphasis on physical attractiveness, whereas girls placed greater stress on their parents' approval of their choice and on the traits of dependability and considerateness. In another study (61), the majority of high school girls said that they would prefer marriage partners who were one to two years older than themselves. Boys seemed to agree—they preferred their future wives to be one or two years younger than themselves.

Relation of Family Background to Dating and Courtship Behavior

A survey of several studies (74, 80, 81) relating family background to dating and courtship behavior indicated that whenever there had been prior disturbances in parent-child relationship, adolescents had more difficulty with dating and courtship during high school. The sources of disturbances included: absence of one parent in the family group, loss of both parents—due to death or desertion, foreign nativity of the parents, open revolt of the children against parental authority, and serious tension of any kind (15).

These studies demonstrate clearly the importance of good previous parent-child relationships in making heterosexual adjustments.

VOCATIONAL ADJUSTMENT IN ADOLESCENCE

Vocational Adjustment in Other Cultures

In many primitive societies, the vocational problems of the adolescent are much simpler than in our own culture. The number of vocations supported by the culture are fewer, and the adolescent is already likely to be familiar with them—either through observation or apprenticeship.

Among the Arapesh, for example, children know from an early age the vocational demands they will have to face as adults, and begin to learn responses which will be useful in meeting them. The Arapesh boy knows that when he becomes a man, the garden that he has been helping his father to attend will finally become his own responsibility, and he will then have the duty of seeing that his parents are fed, just as they have in childhood had the duty of feeding him. He knows that on hunting trips, or expeditions into the bush to gather herbs or to cut wood for the house building, it will be his responsibility to see that the job is done correctly. Instead of being a little boy tagging along behind his father or older brother, he will become the leader, and his own little brother or son will be tagging along after him (49). The vocational future of the Arapesh boy is highly predictable; he is not troubled by the possibility that there will be a flood of yam growers or lizard hunters on the labor market which will throw him out of work. He will simply go on to do what his father had done before him, and what, in childish ways, he has been preparing himself to do since early childhood (49).

Similarly, the Arapesh girl begins to assume domestic duties at an early age, first in her parents' home, and by the age of 9 or 10 in her future husband's home (49). She learns to carry small bundles on her head in leisurely preparation for the day when as an adult she will carry large ones. She learns to help in harvesting the family's crops, and to assist with the cooking and other household chores.

Throughout Arapesh culture there is a gradual transition from the life of the child to the life of the adult, in work as well as social relations. Because the child learns his vocational role gradually, little frustration occurs at any one time, and the disorganizing anxiety that comes from finding that one's old responses no longer lead to reward is kept to a minimum.

On the other hand, the vocational problems of the adolescent in some cultures are more complex than those in our own society. The Manus adolescent, for example, probably faces more severe demands in adolescence than does the youth in our own culture, and is probably less prepared to meet them. In his early years the Manus child lives a happy and carefree existence (5). At adolescence, however, he is suddenly thrust into a ruthlessly aggressive and competitive adult society based largely on material values (5).

The Manus adolescent can expect no genuine assistance from family, friends, or society in getting started in adult life; nor can he join in any communal economic enterprise. He has no choice but to become an independent entrepreneur, and to surrender his self-respect by borrowing from . . . "big men" in the village the wherewithal to do so. Release from this humiliating dependence can be accomplished only be emulating the culturally valued traits of unrelenting industry, acquisitiveness, and ruthless unconcern for human values. In this way he may himself become a successful and prosperous man of property on whom others in turn become dependent (5, 19).

Vocational Adjustment in American Culture

The typical adolescent in our own society, while spared the severe vocational problems of the Manus adolescent, does not share the advantages of the Arapesh youth. He knows that many of his important satisfactions will depend on his ability to find and keep a job, including his chances for full emancipation from his parents, for acceptance as an equal by his peers, for getting married and maintaining a home.

But despite the importance of vocational adjustment for the American adolescent, he typically has only a vague idea of the nature of the various jobs available in the society. He does not know which he would be able to do successfully and would enjoy doing, the prior training required for a specific job, or the present or future demands for workers in the various occupations.

Ordinarily, as the adolescent leaves his childhood behind, and the time when he must support himself approaches, he begins to spend more of his time thinking about vocational goals.

He also becomes progressively more realistic about these goals. As a child, he is likely to have preferred occupations which seemed active and exciting to him, such as those of cowboy, fireman, airplane pilot, or detective. The social status of his preferred occupation is not likely to have had much influence on him. However, as he grows older, he is likely to begin to prefer occupations of marked prestige in the adult world—being a famous doctor, scientist, or lawyer. Finally, as adulthood approaches, he is likely to settle upon some occupation that represents a realistic reconciliation between what he would like to do and what he thinks he might actually be able to do.

As the child's vocational interests become progressively more realistic, more influenced by status and less by glamour and excitement, they also become more stable. For example, it has been shown that the older the adolescent, the more stable (i.e., the less changeable) his vocational interests become (as measured by vocational interest tests repeated after a given interval of time) (14). By middle adolescence, vocational interest has become fairly stable, though changes may still occur. By age 25, practically complete stability is achieved.

Despite the increasing stability and realism of the adolescent's vocational interests, there is considerable evidence that he cannot be left to his own devices in dealing with his vocational problems. In a complex society such as ours, where the actual requirements of most jobs and their availability in the labor market are not matters of common knowledge, the adolescent needs help.

In our culture, the young person's vocational interests usually develop in a rather unsystematic fashion, guided by such influences as parental desires, accidental contact with various occupations, the kinds of jobs his friends are going into. Class- and sex-conditioned influences in general play a role, as we shall see in more detail shortly. For the moment, however, let us contrast these standards for selecting an occupation with the kinds of criteria cited by Hoppock (30) as forming a more realistic basis for occupational choice:

Employment prospects:

Are workers in demand today? Is employment in this occupation expected to increase or decrease?

Nature of the work:

What is the work of a typical day, week, month, year? What are all the things a worker may have to do in this occupation, the pleasant things, the unpleasant things, the big and little tasks, the important responsibilities, and the less glamorous details?

Qualifications:

Age. What are the upper and lower age limits for entrance and retirement?

Sex:

Is this predominantly a male or female occupation? Are there reasonable opportunities for both? Is there any more active demand for one than for the other?

Height and weight:

Are there any minimum or maximum requirements? What are they?

Other physical requirements:

Are there any other measurable physical requirements, e.g. 20/20 vision, freedom from color-blindness, average or superior hearing, physical strength, etc.?

Aptitude:

Has there been any research on aptitude required, e.g., minimum or maximum intelligence quotient, percentile, rank on specific tests of mechanical aptitude, clerical aptitude, finger dexterity, pitch determination, reaction time, etc.?

Interests:

Have any vocational interests tests been validated against workers in this occupation?

Tools and equipment:

Must these be supplied to the worker at his own expense? What is the average cost?

Legal requirements:

Is a license or certificate required? What are the requirements for getting it?

Unions:

Is the closed shop common or predominant? If so, what are the requirements for entrance to the union? Initiation fees? Dues? Does the union limit the number admitted?

Discrimination:

Do employees, unions, or training institutions discriminate against Negroes, Jews, others?

Preparation:

Distinguish clearly between what is desirable and what is indispensable. How much and what kind of preparation is required to meet legal requirements and employers' standards?

How long does it take? What does it cost? What does it include? How much elimination is there during training?

Where can one get a list of approved schools?

What kind of high school or college program should precede entrance into the professional schools? What subjects must or should be chosen?

What provisions, if any, are made for apprenticeship or other training on the job?

Is experience of some kind prerequisite to entrance? Is the completion of a part of the course of any value, or must one finish the training in order to derive benefit from it?

Entrance:

How does one get his first job? By taking an examination? By applying to employers? By joining a union? By registering with employment agencies? By saving to acquire capital and opening his own business? How much capital is required?

Advancement:

What proportion of workers advance? To what? After how long and after what additional preparation or experience?

What are the related occupations to which this may lead, if any?

Earnings:

What are the most dependable average figures on earnings by week, month, or year?

What is the range of the middle 50 percent?

Are earnings higher or lower in certain parts of the United States, or in certain branches of the occupation?

Number and distribution of workers:

Are the workers evenly distributed over the United States in proportion, or concentrated in certain areas? Where? Why?

Can a person practice the occupation anywhere he may wish to live?

Do conditions in small towns and rural areas differ materially from those in urban centers? How?

Advantages and disadvantages:

What do workers say they like best and dislike most about their jobs?

Are hours regular or irregular, long or short? Is there frequent overtime or night work? Sunday or holiday work?

What about vacations?

Is employment steady, seasonal, or irregular? Does one earn more or less with advancing age?

Is the working lifetime shorter than average, e.g., professional athletics?

Are the skills acquired transferable to other occupations?

Is the work hazardous? What about accidents, occupational disease?

In comparison with other occupations requiring about the same level of ability and training, in what ways is this one more or less attractive (30)?

When we contrast the haphazard ways in which many adolescents find their jobs with the systematic approach to job selection described above, it is small wonder that many youths decide upon vocations for which they are not fitted, which they do not really want to do, or which are unavailable. Consequently, many of them become dissatisfied in an activity that occupies the major portion of their waking hours.

Vocational Ambitions and Probabilities of Employment

Practically all investigations of the vocational goals of adolescents reveal that they are out of line with the actual economic needs of the time (5). A study of male Michigan high school students conducted in 1948,

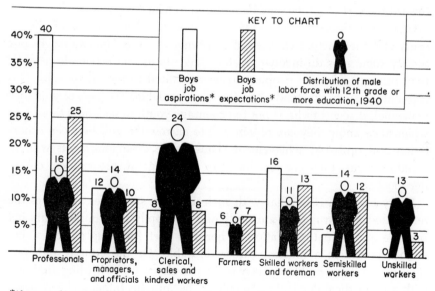

*14 percent did not indicate aspirations; 22 percent did not indicate expectations

FIGURE 33. Aspirations and expectations of Michigan high school seniors compared to work world opportunities. (Based on *Sixteenth Census of the United States,* pp. 89 and 91. With permission of Social Research Service, Michigan State College.)

a prosperous year, can be considered rather typical. Figure 33 shows the distribution of (1) boys' job aspirations (what they would *like* to do), (2) their actual expectations, (3) the distribution of the male labor force with twelfth-grade or more education (83). These findings demonstrate that both the boy's aspirations and his expectations are often out of line with economic realities. The discrepancy between *aspiration* and *expectation* is probably not too serious, since it involves an adjustment to the fact that it is not always possible to do what one wants. The discrepancy between *expectations* and *actual job availability* appears more disturbing, since it suggests that many youths receive rude and sudden shocks when they discover that they cannot do even what they had expected to do.

To a large extent, the discrepancy between aspiration and job availability stems from the fact that too many adolescents desire the small number of professional and technical jobs available. Too few want to enter the general labor force, where the greatest need exists (8).

There appears to be a need for more systematic vocational guidance of students in high school. Such a program could provide the student with information concerning the actual needs of the labor market. It could also help in preventing the adolescent from developing scornful attitudes toward the sort of job he may be required to take.

Of course, discrepancies between the vocational aspirations of adolescents and their actual chances of satisfying them are inevitable. In our society some jobs do involve greater social status and economic rewards than others, and more people will be motivated to seek these jobs. Unfortunately, such jobs tend to be the least available. The task of guidance personnel, it seems to us, is not to encourage youth to seek only those jobs which they know they can obtain, but to narrow the gulf between expectation and probable achievement. Thus, while disappointments will inevitably occur, they are less likely to be too great, too sudden, or too unexpected.

Every clinician is familiar with such unhappy spectacles as that of the untalented girl struggling anxiously and unhappily to be a musician, not because of any real motivation on her own part, but simply because her mother considers a musical career desirable. Or the equally unhappy sight of the boy who likes poetry and hates chemistry struggling aimlessly with a premedical curriculum in college, because his father has convinced him that he should become a doctor. As Landis (43) remarks, "The admonition of the Talmud is appropriate counsel to such parents: 'Limit not thy children to thine own desire. They are born in a different time.'"

Unfortunately, too many parents are too absorbed in satisfying their own unfulfilled ambitions through their children, or too convinced that the satisfactions they feel in their own occupation must inevitably be shared by their offspring, to listen to such advice.

The vocational counselor may encounter adolescents who have adopted very unsuitable career goals as a result of family pressures. In the case of a self-reliant youngster, showing him that he is really carrying out his parents' desires rather than his own may not be too difficult. In the case of dependent, insecure, submissive children fearful of losing parental approval, the task may present serious problems and may sometimes require the specialized help of a psychiatrist or clinical psychologist. That the task can be rewarding, however, if tackled early, is seen in the following case.

Earl S. was a freshman in engineering who had just failed both mathematics and mechanical drawing. By contrast, his work in English had been outstandingly good. When Earl first talked with the counselor he refused to so much as consider changing from engineering into some other course of study. He refused to take any aptitude tests although the counselor suggested that the results might be useful to him. He was quite unable to accept the idea that he might actually need help.

About a week before the end of the following semester Earl returned to the counselor in a state bordering on panic. It appeared that he was now failing everything, even his English. Gradually Earl was able to bring out the main outline of his difficulties. He had always done well in linguistic studies and badly in both mathematics and science. He was, however, convinced that he "ought" to take things that were hard for him in order to improve his mind. He had entered engineering at the urging of his father, who had always regretted that he had not taken an engineering course. Earl had a great admiration for his father but at the same time stood somewhat in awe of him, and he did not see how he could love him after the complete failure of his second semester's work. The counselor tried to talk the lad into a more cheerful mood and managed to relieve his worst apprehensions by offering to break the news to the father and to discuss with him a possible future for Earl, now that the engineering school was about to dismiss him. The father turned out to be a man who was deeply devoted to his son, but who was an extroverted, overactive, talkative individual who expressed his own ideas so continually that he never did learn what other people thought or felt. He was genuinely surprised to discover that Earl did not like engineering. Apparently it had never crossed his mind that his son was not merely a younger edition of himself. It was also clear to the counselor that all the talk about the fascination of engineering was merely an outlet for the father whenever he happened to be bored with his work as a lawyer—an occupation in which he was far better adapted than to engineering. As a fantasy it did no harm, but when he tried to influence his son into living out his own fantasy, the trouble began. The man was bright enough to see the situation and perfectly willing to take the major blame for his son's academic maladjustment. His devotion seemed genuine, and he did not even resent the advice to talk less and listen more!

The following year Earl transferred to a small arts college, where he majored in English literature. Since his early failure in engineering seemed still to rankle a bit, he returned to the university from which he had been dismissed and took his Ph.D. there, doing most of the work in Old English. Earl is now a professor in a small college, and his father is extremely proud of him (V, 15, 628).

Individual Differences and Occupational Requirements

Another of the important functions of a vocational guidance program is to help the adolescent select an occupation which is appropriate to his

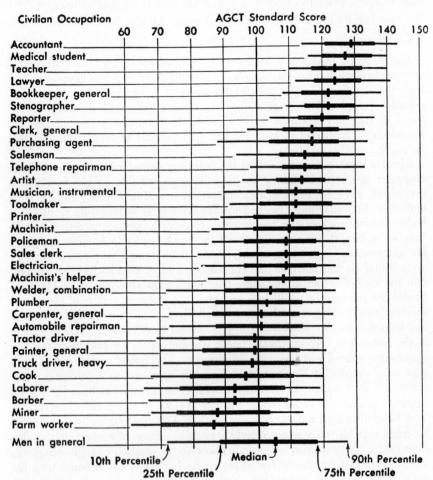

FIGURE 34.   Army General Classification Test scores for various occupational groups. (After N. Stewart, "ACGT Scores of Army Personnel Grouped by Occupation." *Occupations* (1947), *26*:5–41. From L. J. Cronbach, *Essentials of Psychological Testing*. New York: Harper, 1949. With permission of Harper & Brothers.)

aptitude, special abilities, and intelligence. It is all very well to find that a youngster is genuinely interested in a field, and that the field is not hopelessly overcrowded. But there is little point in encouraging him to pursue this interest unless one knows that there is some possibility of his being able to do the job. For example, all occupations obviously do not require the same intelligence level. Figure 34 shows the distribution of scores on one form of intelligence test for various occupational groups (16, 65). Obviously there is little point in encouraging a man with a score of 70 on this test to try to become an accountant—he would be hopelessly outdistanced by his peers. Conversely, the chances are that most persons with an AGCT score of 140 would feel dissatisfied and bored serving as heavy-truck drivers.

Fortunately, as we have already seen, well-standardized intelligence tests are available for use in vocational counseling. There are also a variety of tests of special abilities and aptitudes (e.g., tests of clerical aptitude or musical ability). This too is important, since two persons may well have the same intelligence level, but may have their particular aptitudes and abilities quite differently distributed. One adolescent with an I.Q. of 120 may be excellent at tasks involving mechanical ability but may be only fair at those requiring verbal proficiency. Another boy of the same I.Q. may be extremely talented in expressing himself verbally, but may be all thumbs in motor tasks. It is impossible here to survey the field of vocational testing, but excellent summaries are available elsewhere (16). At any rate, it should be obvious that by a careful matching of an adolescent's talents with the demands of the various jobs in which he is interested, vocational maladjustment, with its attendant bitterness and frustration, can be avoided.

Figure 35 compares one student's performance on a variety of tasks with the level of proficiency required for teaching. Obviously, this student should be encouraged to seek some other occupation than teaching —one in which his particular talents will be more useful, and his liabilities less troublesome. In this particular instance, the job ought to be one in which clerical, mechanical, or scientific abilities are important, but verbal abilities are not. In short, the adolescent's needs should be taken into account in helping him to choose a job which will prove rewarding. But he should not be encouraged to aspire to goals he cannot hope to achieve, either because of his own inability to learn the responses required by the job, or because the job is simply unavailable.

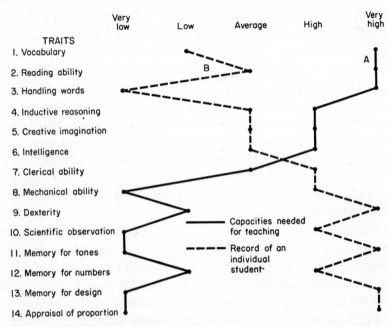

FIGURE 35.   Comparison of test scores needed for teaching with those of an individual student. (From L. Cole, *Psychology of Adolescence.* New York: Rinehart, 1948. With permission of Rinehart & Company, Inc.)

Subcultural Influences on Vocational Choice

Up to this point in the discussion, we have been dealing with broad problems of vocational choice as they affect adolescents in our culture. There are, however, two subcultural influences which affect vocational goals differentially, and which seem to us important enough to merit special consideration.

SOCIOECONOMIC FACTORS AND VOCATIONAL GOALS.   Social-class membership operates to influence vocational goals in a variety of ways. For one thing, it helps to determine the kinds of occupations with which the individual will be familiar, and hence which he will be likely to consider in formulating his occupational aims. In addition, it plays an important role in determining the social acceptability (i.e., the reward value) of a given occupation to the young person and to his peers. As pointed out previously (see Chapter 12), the individual's social-class status is related to his occupation. Certain types of occupations are considered appropriate to the members of a particular social class, others inappropriate. The individual who deviates from class expectancies for occupational choice is likely to be subjected to anxiety-producing disapproval from his peers, particularly if this deviation is in the direction of jobs associated with lower-class status. The very young upper-class child who wants to be an iceman, or fireman, or policeman, may be indulged or even encouraged. After the attainment of adolescence, however, when the problem of vocational choice becomes a serious one with practical implications, the child's parents are not likely to find such notions amusing (5).

Choices of lower-status occupations run counter to the parents' ideas about appropriate behavior for a member of their social class, and consequently are likely to be discouraged. The parents may also fear that such a choice will lead to general social disapproval both of their child and indirectly to themselves. Also where economic rewards are involved in the occupation chosen, they may fear that the child will not be able to live in the same neighborhood as other members of his social class, to afford the same social, recreational and educational advantages for himself and his family. As Levin (46) states, "occupations must be selected, consciously or otherwise, in terms of their value in either maintaining the present class membership, if that is adequate to the individual's level of class aspiration, or in terms of their value in facilitating the individual's climb to the class considered higher, if he is motivated to do so" (40).

Aspirations toward higher-social-status occupations may also lead to social disapproval (particularly if they are flaunted openly), since such aspirations may be viewed as a threat by other members of the individual's social class. In this case, however, the disapproval is likely to be much less strong and, in the child's view, may be more than outweighed by the prospect of increased rewards associated with higher-class status. This observation is supported by the fact that actually most young people wish for jobs having a somewhat higher socioeconomic status than those of their parents (40).

The relation of social class membership to vocational aspiration is clearly demonstrated in a study by Hollingshead (29). Adolescents in a small midwestern city were asked to list the occupations they would like to follow as adults. The results, subdivided according to social-class membership, are shown in Figure 36. As may be seen, while 77 percent of the children of the highest two social classes listed business and professional occupations, only 7 percent of the children in the lowest social class made these choices. Similarly, while only 1 percent of Class I and II (higher social class) members listed the various services and trades, 25 percent of class V (lower social class) did. It is interesting to note that the number of youths undecided about their vocational aspirations increased regularly as socioeconomic class decreased.

There are other important factors associated with social class which affect vocational aims. While adolescents may be somewhat unrealistic about their vocational goals, they possess some awareness of practical obstacles which may modify their vocational aspirations.

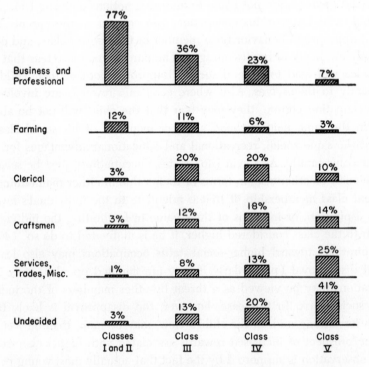

FIGURE 36. Vocational aspirations of adolescents of different social classes. (From K. C. Garrison, *Psychology of Adolescence.* New York: Prentice-Hall, 1951. After A. B. Hollingshead. *Elmtown's Youth: The Impact of Social Classes on Youth.* New York: Wiley, 1949. With permission of Prentice-Hall, Inc.)

The boy whose parents are unwilling or unable to help him go to college, much less to medical school, is less likely to aspire to be a doctor than one whose parents encourage such a vocational choice. Similarly, the boy whose parents expect him to go to work upon completion of the ninth grade is not likely to spend much time contemplating the idea of being an engineer.

In addition to limiting the adolescent's opportunity for training in a particular occupation, social-class factors are also likely to influence his chances of obtaining some jobs, even if qualified. As anthropological studies (76) have shown, persons in a particular social class tend to pick others from the same social class as their colleagues and successors. While this is often done without conscious awareness, it is done nevertheless. The employer may say that a person from another social class does not have the right sort of personality for a particular job, when he means that he does not have the same sets of class-learned social traits as others holding that position.

"It would not even be rash to assume that many of the emotional and personality requirements of various occupations are fundamentally based on class-status factors and not on job requirements, as such. Thus the professional is expected to appear, behave, feel, and think quite differently than the skilled worker, and even more differently than the semi-skilled or unskilled worker. The stereotyped hierarchical classification of vocations is essentially a reflection of their class-conferring character" (46).

To a certain extent, such attitudes may be justified in that people with similar social backgrounds may find it easier to deal with one another in the job situation. But it appears that the importance of socially derived personality characteristics is often exaggerated by employers. This may be attributable in part to their need to maintain their own status as members of a particular social class.

Apart from social-class membership, there are a number of other general socioeconomic conditions which influence the adolescent's vocational aspirations.

"Such conditions include the general occupational outlook as determined by a war-time economy or by economic depression and prosperity, as well as more specific regional or industry-wide fluctuations and job demand. They affect not only the relative attractiveness of different occupations, but also the degree of social mobility and the disposition of the adolescent to aspire to higher levels of vocational status" (5).

Sex-Differences in Vocational Adjustment. Cultural demands in regard to preparation for a vocation differ significantly for boys and girls in our society. In the case of the boy, the society appears to say: You must prepare yourself adequately for a vocation, since your success in work will largely determine your ability to feed yourself and others, your readiness to marry, and to a significant extent, the social status of your family. For these reasons, vocational success acquires great reward value for boys at all socioeconomic levels as adolescence progresses.

With girls, however, the position is somewhat different. Most girls expect, and are expected by society, to prepare themselves for a vocation. For example, a study of 6000 Michigan teen-agers (83) showed that most adolescent girls think they should work for at least a year or two before marrying. Most of them, however, also feel that their primary goal is marriage. And it is certainly true that such attitudes are reinforced by the society generally. For while a man's status in the socioeconomic hierarchy stems largely from his job, that of the average woman is derived primarily from their husband's position. To the extent that she has

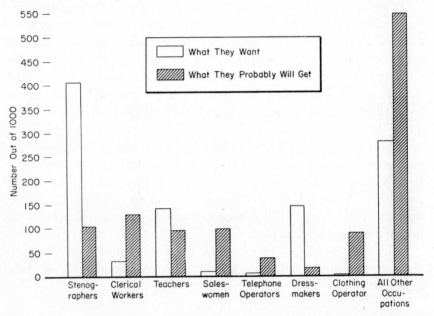

FIGURE 37. Girls' vocational ambitions and probabilities for employment. (From H. M. Bell, *Youth Tell Their Story.* Washington: American Council on Education, 1938. With permission of the American Council on Education.)

independent status, it is based, not so much on her vocational competency, as on her success as a wife, mother, and manager of the home. It is on such criteria that her adequacy as a female is most often judged by society.

Probably for these reasons, most girls are willing to settle for more subordinate kinds of jobs than their male peers. They need a job only to tide them over until they marry, or as a supplemental source of income. They do not need it as a primary source of social status.

Like boys, girls are often unrealistic about their vocational plans, as evidenced by Figure 37, which shows the discrepancy between the vocational hopes of 1000 New York junior high school girls and the actual distribution of available jobs. However, the problem of differences in social status between probable and desired jobs is not so acute as it is for boys. In general, girls' probable and hoped-for jobs tend more to be at the same socioeconomic level than is the case with boys. Thus they are less likely to encounter disappointment or frustration in their pursuit of a vocation.

In another respect, however, the vocational problems of girls appear more complicated than those of boys. For while few girls would prefer a job to marriage, many girls feel that outside jobs are more rewarding and more interesting than housekeeping. This is particularly likely to be true of girls with higher education, who are more likely than their less-educated sisters to have been taught to view vocational success as important. Such girls may also see a greater discrepancy between what they are capable of doing (in a job) and what they must do in taking care of a home. This is not surprising when we consider that most of these girls receive more training in outside vocations than in home care prior to marriage. In our educational system the talent required for professional success is often emphasized, while the talent required for creating and maintaining a successful home is frequently ignored.

In the light of these realities, the agents of higher education in our culture—teachers, deans, administrators, as well as parents—might do well to consider placing a greater emphasis on the creative character of homemaking and on the skills necessary for doing it well. Thus they might help many girls to avoid building up vocational ambitions which will prove incompatible with the demands of marriage and a home. We are not challenging here the girl's right to equal professional status with men, but we are questioning the tendency in some educational circles to overemphasize professional success for women, as compared with success as a wife, mother, and homemaker. Furthermore it is not a matter of inventing pretty phrases to make the woman feel important in a necessary but actually unimportant role. For as we have already seen throughout this book, in most cases it is the woman, who, as a mother, is the most significant influence in determining whether the lives of other human beings, her children, will be happy or unhappy.

MORAL AND RELIGIOUS PROBLEMS OF ADOLESCENTS

In our culture, adolescence is commonly viewed as a time of great moral confusion and conflict, of changing values, of religious conversion or disenchantment. The popularity of this view is undoubtedly partly due to novels about, or autobiographical writings by, disturbed adolescents. Some children, of course, do undergo a complete shift in their moral and religious value systems during adolescence, hence experiencing more emotional strain than their peers. However, most adolescents do not renounce the faith of their fathers, with or without personal agony. And most tend to maintain views somewhat similar to those of their parents, with regard to such matters as political philosophy and sex morality (5). For example, in a study of almost 10,000 young people it was found that 81 percent of those who had some church affiliation had adopted the faith of both their parents, whether Protestant, Catholic, or Jewish. Only a small percentage adopted a faith different from that of either parent (8).

Nevertheless, many adolescents do encounter emotional stresses in regard to moral and religious values. For the most part, however, these stresses do not involve marked changes in moral or religious orientation, but rather changes in the basis on which moral values are accepted. As we saw earlier (cf. pp. 427–428), with increasing age there is a decrease in moral absolutism, an increase in doubt, and generally, a greater liberality, tolerance, and flexibility of moral outlook (5).

It will be our purpose here, first to examine the general developmental basis for adolescent conflicts with regard to moral problems, and then to survey the factors which are likely to precipitate these conflicts in adolescence.

Superego Problems

We have already reviewed, in some detail, the gradual emergence of conscience, or superego in the child (see pp. 241–242). It seems worth while, however, to review this process briefly here. As we noted, the very young child does not possess complex adult notions of right and wrong. He simply wants "what he wants," and he wants it now, regardless of ethical or even practical considerations. As development proceeds, however, impulsive behavior becomes modified through experience. The child begins to learn that he cannot always have what he wants at any particular moment. Some things he can never have. He learns that certain of his responses will be rewarded, while others will be punished.

This does not mean, however, that at this age he is also guided by moral considerations, by a "conscience" or "superego." It is true that the child may learn to avoid responses which his parents refer to as "wrong" or "bad." But he is likely to avoid them less out of moral considerations than out of expediency. He may avoid hitting his baby brother, or knocking over lamps; but he is likely to do so not so much because he would feel guilty violating his own ethical beliefs, but rather because he has no desire to be spanked.

As he grows older, however, all this changes. The responses which previously he avoided in large measure because they led to punishment by the environment he now avoids because to carry them out would lead to increases in anxiety and other painful drives. In psychoanalytic terminology, the values of the environment have been internalized and have become his own values. An internal policeman of conscience, or superego, has been substituted for the cop on the corner. In other words, the thought of carrying out a tabooed response now leads to anxiety without the need any longer for external reinforcement. As a result, the child now makes avoidant responses, not to avoid external punishment but simply to avoid increases in his own anxiety.

By the time the American child reaches adolescence, his conscience has had a good many years in which to develop. Anxiety has become associated with a great number of responses. As long as he can continue to avoid making such responses, all is reasonably well. But when incompatible drives are aroused—drives which can be reduced only through making responses previously associated with increases in anxiety—then conflict and tension must inevitably result. For example, a child may have learned to associate anxiety with sexual responses. As long as the child's sexual needs are not too strong, little conflict may result, since the child may simply avoid these responses. However, with increases in sex drive at puberty, strong conflicts may be precipitated, since the responses which are necessary to reduce sex drive will also lead to increases in anxiety. The adolescent would encounter minimal emotional strain if the society consistently demanded that certain responses be carried out, and always rewarded them; and also that certain other responses *not* be carried out, and always punished them. Unfortunately, our society is not nearly so consistent. In many cases, as we have repeatedly seen, it demands simultaneously that responses, such as competition, be both carried out and avoided. Or it insists that responses *not* be carried out at one stage of the individual's life, but that they be performed *enthusiastically* at a later stage (e.g., independence responses, sexual behavior).

In general, we would expect that adolescents who encounter the fewest contradictory demands from their environment would have the least conflict over moral values and behavior.

Differences Between Parents and Peer Groups

There are, of course, a number of sources of conflicting pressures on the adolescent. For one thing, the standards of the child's parents and those of his peers may be in conflict. Such discrepancies may have a variety of origins. As we have already pointed out, parents may attempt to make the adolescent conform to the kinds of behavior which were expected of them in their own youths, but which are no longer characteristic of the culture. To illustrate, approved patterns of social relationships between boys and girls have changed markedly in the last 25 years. So have attitudes towards many kinds of feminine behavior, such as working, traveling alone, and smoking—especially in the middle class. The parent who attempts to make his children conform to the social norms of a previous generation is bound to precipitate conflicts in the adolescent, since his peers will have different expectations of him.

Furthermore, if the social-class allegiances of the adolescent's parents are different from those of his peers, strong conflicts between a whole host of social attitudes may be precipitated in the adolescent. When forced to choose between parental and peer values, the adolescent may decide in favor of the peer group, since he is more dependent on them for satisfaction of his needs. Of course, such a choice will produce emotional strain not only because of the necessity of choosing between conflicting loyalties, but often also because the youth may have to become aware that he is relinquishing the comfort of dependence on his parents. He may also become more aware that his behavior is being determined by a rather crude sort of expediency aimed at peer-group acceptance. Since many adolescents are idealistic and perfectionistic in their goals for themselves, this latter sort of awareness may be difficult to tolerate.

In most cases, however, the adolescent will associate primarily with peers of his parents' (and his own) social class. In this case, the consistencies of parental and peer-group attitudes may be expected to help keep parent-child differences in viewpoint to a minimum. In fact it is largely because of these consistencies that most adolescents do not make major shifts in their general moral beliefs even when their primary loyalties are shifted from the parents to the peer group. In other words, the same general moral beliefs and behavior tend to be rewarded both by parents and by peers.

Finally, it should be noted that parent-child conflicts may develop even where they are not associated with such broad sociological conditions as age or social-class differences, as a result of idiosyncrasies in the parent's or the child's personality and behavior. Thus the child whose parents cling to restrictive notions with regard to smoking, drinking, or dating, or other forms of social activity when other parents are displaying a more liberal attitude is placed in a difficult position. Not only is he led to doubt the rightness of his parents' views; but he is also likely to bear them many hard feelings for the restrictions they impose upon him. Furthermore, when this resentment is personally unacceptable to the child, he may have to hide his resentment even from himself and may undergo considerable emotional strain.

The child whose parents possess religious beliefs deviant from those of their subgroups faces similar problems. The child whose parents are Catholic and who comes into contact primarily with other Catholic adults and peer-group members is not given much impetus for reconsidering his Catholic religious beliefs. The same cannot be said of a Catholic or Orthodox Jew, growing up in a Protestant community, or going to a Protestant school or college.

Differences Between Professed Beliefs and Behavior in the Adult Culture

The adolescent may also experience conflict if he finds adults (including his parents) behaving differently from the ways in which they have led him to believe that they act, and the ways in which they have taught him to act. This is especially likely to happen, it seems to us, in the case of the middle-class child, whose parents are more likely to have rewarded strict codes of behavior in childhood; who have succeeded in making the child more anxious about violations of strict moral codes than lower-class children; and who, in addition, have tended to protect the child more from viewing the adult world as it really exists. As Frank (24) expresses it:

But the adolescent's distress arises not merely from the family situation. If he or she has grown up with the usual fanciful picture of society, so characteristic of the well-protected, middle-class child, then his exposure to the actual life of the outer world may be devastating. It may be difficult for the adult who has forgotten his or her adolescence to recall or realize the turmoil and confusion which sometimes occurs. What outcome is to be expected when the adolescent finds his romantic ideal of marriage impaired by the discovery of marital discord, divorce, and infidelity; when his vision of government as the wise guardian of social order is displaced by the picture of political chicane and graft and the other aspects of machine administration; or when business is, in some quarters, disclosed as a hard and ungenerous struggle for the defeat of others, quite lacking in the glamour of the publicized success stories?

It is obvious that such revelations may be for some adolescents, a profoundly disillusioning experience. The individual boy or girl, especially the boy, may react rather strongly to his disillusionment. He may suddenly repudiate many of his previous beliefs and ideals, scorn the church and all official religions, become hard-boiled and cynical, and decide to play the adult game like the others. If he does follow this path, he may then be reproached by his elders for lack of idealism, often by the very people whose conduct has been most disillusioning. Other adolescents may respond to these disclosures of the actual social life by a burning ambition to remake the world, to reform society and clean up the mess—and then they are denounced for . . . [threatening the] social order! (24, 251).

Traditional Problems of Adolescents and Shifting Standards of Moral Behavior

There is, as we have seen in our discussion of sexual behavior, considerable difference in the moral beliefs and behavior expected of the child at different ages. In our discussion of psychosexual development we stressed the difficulty the child may have in eliminating old responses in order to establish new and markedly different responses necessary for meeting changes in the expectations of the adult culture. Such developmental inconsistencies do not occur only in the area of sexual behavior, however; they occur also in many other areas. A child may be expected, for example, to believe in Santa Claus, in the code of doing unto others as he would have others do unto him. He is expected to believe in a personal God. He may often be taught that it is wrong to be aggressive, to compete, to question authority, to play cards, to smoke, to swear, and to lie. And yet when the same child grows up, he is often expected suddenly to change and to be sexually responsive; "one of the boys" with respect to smoking, swearing, card playing, and similar activities; not to be too "naïve" in his religious beliefs; and "when necessary," to be aggressive and competitive regardless of the consequences to others, and even at times to lie and cheat a bit. Having once adopted at face value the parable of the Good Samaritan, he is faced with the task of renouncing this belief with the newer dictum that "business is business." Where previously he was exhorted to be an idealist, he is now exhorted with equal vigor to be "practical." Hence the adolescent may at times have difficulty in adjusting to such shifting mores.

The above represent simply some of the sources of conflicting demands which may confront the adolescent with regard to moral beliefs and behavior. There are, of course, others, such as conflicts between the standards of society as a whole and those of particular cultural subgroups or institutions, and between these various sub-elements of the society themselves. Thus there may occur conflicts between church and state; between racial and religious groups; or between geographical regions, such as New England and the deep South.

Areas of Conflict in Moral Beliefs and Behavior

All these contradictory influences may lead to troublesome conflicts over moral values in adolescence. Also, as might be anticipated, when one or another influence becomes stronger, values change.

CHANGES IN RELIGIOUS BELIEFS DURING ADOLESCENCE. General religious beliefs in adolescence tend to become more abstract and less literal between the ages of 12 and 18 (41). In addition, God is more frequently seen as an abstract power rather than as a fatherly human being. Religious views also become more tolerant and less dogmatic (41).

In an attempt to determine the nature of changes in religious beliefs during adolescence, one team of investigators prepared a list of 70 statements dealing with religious issues, and asked a group of 547 twelve-, fifteen- and eighteen-year-old students to indicate, for each statement, whether they believed it, didn't believe it, or wondered about it (41). A number of these statements about which opinions changed between 12 and 18 years are shown in Table 11. The results indicate that many adolescents do change at least some aspects of their religious beliefs.

In a somewhat similar study of college youths (36), freshmen and seniors were asked to rate each of a number of statements dealing with religion, according to the extent of their agreement or disagreement with them. Seniors were far more liberal in their beliefs than the freshmen. The older students were skeptical on the question of life after death, while most freshmen were convinced that there was considerable justification for such a belief. Freshmen tended to doubt evolution, while seniors tended to accept it. Women students were distinctly more conservative in their attitudes than the men.

Various studies reveal that according to adolescents themselves the most important influences producing changes in their religious beliefs are: teachers, peer-group contacts, individual reading, ministers, various organizations, such as YMCA (38), personal experiences, such as the loss of a relative or close friend or seeing injustice done (10), and contact with other faiths or creeds (10, 38).

How disturbing to the adolescent are these changing values? It is not possible to say with any certainty, but various studies (38, 45) seem to indicate that only a minority of adolescents see the experience of change as seriously disturbing. In one study of college students, for example, only about 7 percent of the students said that they felt that changes in

TABLE 11. Age Differences in the Religious Beliefs of Adolescents. [a]

	"Believe" Percent			"Not Believe" Percent			"Wonder About" Percent		
	12 Years	15 Years	18 Years	12 Years	15 Years	18 Years	12 Years	15 Years	18 Years
God is a strange power working for good rather than a person.	46	49	57	31	33	21	20	14	15
God is someone who watches you to see that you behave yourself and who punishes you if you are not good.	70	49	33	18	37	48	11	13	18
I know there is a God.	94	80	79	3	5	2	2	14	16
Catholics, Jews, and Protestants are equally good.	67	79	86	9	9	7	24	11	7
There is a heaven.	82	78	74	4	5	5	13	16	20
Only good people go to heaven.	72	45	33	15	27	32	13	27	34
Hell is a place where you are punished for your sins on earth.	70	49	35	16	21	30	13	27	34
Heaven is here on earth.	12	13	14	69	57	52	18	28	32
People who go to church are better than people who do not go to church.	46	26	15	37	53	74	17	21	11
Young people should belong to the same church as their parents.	77	56	43	13	33	46	10	11	11
The main reason for going to church is to worship God.	88	80	79	6	12	15	4	7	6
It is not necessary to attend church to be a Christian.	42	62	67	38	23	24	18	15	8
Only our soul lives after death.	72	63	61	9	11	6	18	25	31
Good people say prayers regularly.	78	57	47	9	29	26	13	13	27
Prayers are answered.	76	69	65	3	5	8	21	25	27
Prayers are a source of help in times of trouble.	74	80	83	11	8	7	15	10	9
Prayers are to make up for something that you have done that is wrong.	47	24	21	35	58	69	18	17	9
Every word in the Bible is true.	79	51	34	6	16	23	15	31	43
It is sinful to doubt the Bible.	62	42	27	18	31	44	20	26	28

538

religious belief had taken away something of vital importance and had left nothing but doubt and anxiety about the problems of life (38). One investigator (45) felt that the outstanding finding in her study of adolescents was widespread indifference.

Thus, while some adolescents undergo considerable personal stress as a result of conflicting pressures with regard to religious belief, most adolescents do not seem to undergo any profound disillusionment. As we noted earlier, the majority of adolescents "belong to a church, usually the same church as their parents, attend church service once a month or more, have a favorable attitude toward the church, rely upon prayer, and believe in a personal, omnipotent, omniscient God, who, although bodyless, participated in the writing of the Bible and guided the affairs of men and nations" (5).

CHANGES IN MORAL BELIEFS IN ADOLESCENCE. As in the case of religious beliefs, there do not appear to be any profound shifts in the moral codes of behavior of most young people during adolescence. Expediency plays a greater part in determining moral conduct and beliefs, and there tends to be somewhat less moral absolutism, less rigidity and naïveté, more tolerance of deviation from the ideal, and a more abstract approach to moral questions, as maturity approaches. A number of studies illustrate these points. For example, Stone and Barker (67) found that, compared with premenarchial girls, postmenarchial girls exhibited more tolerance of such things as smoking, playing cards, dancing, playing hookey, anger, fussiness, and quarreling. Several investigations (27, 72) have found a rapid increase in the frequency of lying, as adolescence progresses. A decrease in superstition as a basis for moral beliefs also occurs (13, 18, 47, 73).

While ethnic prejudices are already well formed in most cases by the time of adolescence (cf. pp. 441–442), the reasons given for prejudice become more sophisticated and more skillfully rationalized with increasing age (5, 51).

Havighurst and Taba (27) investigated the moral beliefs of 16-year-olds in Prairie City, a typical small city in the middle west. Using questionnaires and personal interviews, they attempted to study the ideas of these adolescents with regard to honesty, responsibility, moral courage, loyalty, and friendliness.

These students seemed to be most certain of the need for being honest and responsible, which they interpreted largely in terms of following correct rules of accepted conduct. They also tended to place a good deal of value on the need for being friendly and accommodating to all people.

For example, 75 percent of the students believed in "not saying unkind things, taking time to cheer up unhappy persons, and making strangers feel at home at a party, and in having many friends" (27).

These adolescents were most confused when it came to their beliefs about loyalty and moral courage. They seemed particularly uncertain about issues involving conflict of several loyalties, or conflict of loyalty with other values, such as defending the family against criticism or dropping a friendship if one's reputation is in danger.

With respect to moral courage, it was found that doubt and anxiety tended to be expressed about any opinions or actions which were likely to arouse the displeasure of authority figures or to jeopardize the adolescent's popularity with his peers. These adolescents tended to avoid criticizing peers, even if they felt them to be wrong, for fear of rejection.

The authors also cite a number of general characteristics which they regard as common to these adolescents' beliefs. Among these they include accepting familiar stereotypes: "High agreement usually occurs on statements which express the obvious middle-class codes of conduct in stereotyped language requiring little thought or analysis" (27). Inconsistencies appear, however, where these general values are tested in specific situations.

Adolescents seemed to fear and avoid peers holding beliefs in any way deviant from those of the group, even when they felt that they were right. In other words, desires to be accepted by peers frequently triumphed over moral conviction.

A third characteristic was that of evading a conflict of moral choices whenever possible. For example, there was hesitancy in taking positions when conflicting loyalties (e.g., between family and friends) were involved. These adolescents felt most sure of beliefs on which families, teachers, and friends were in agreement.

EMOTIONAL MATURITY

It should be possible at this juncture to cast a long look backward over the whole course of the child's development. Such a longitudinal survey should certainly serve to convince us that no man's behavior can be explained by easy platitudes. As we maintained at the outset, people do not behave as they do simply because "their mothers spoiled them," because "they were born that way," because "they are underprivileged," or because "they are suffering from an Oedipus complex." Our personalities

are the result of too many complex interacting forces ever to be adequately explained in terms of any one of them.

In the course of this book, we have reviewed many of the kinds of
forces that, taken together, determine the unique personality that the
individual will develop. We have seen that his development is bound to
be affected, for good or ill, by his genetic inheritance; by his prenatal
environment; by his physical and psychological environment; by the
attitudes and behavior of his parents, teachers, and peers; by the
"alarums and excursions" of his own particular era in history; and by his
culture and subculture—economic, religious, or social.

When one attempts to translate this breathtaking expanse of possible
developmental influences into personal terms, one question seems most
like to arise: What do we want our children to "get out of it all"?

Every parent will have his own answer, determined largely by his own
unique set of life experiences. The parent who has himself fought against
great economic odds may want financial security for his children. The
parent who was unloved or rejected may want affection and love. The
parent who had to leave school at 14 in order to go to work may feel that
a proper education is all-important. Specific frustrations may play a role
too. How many parents want their children to realize their own unfulfilled dreams: to be an artist, or banker, or doctor, or general, or states-
man, or movie actress?

It does not seem a naïve oversimplification, however, to state that probably most of all, most parents want their children "to be happy." But
wherein lies the key to happiness; and how can we gain it for our children? By helping them to become financially secure? By looking out for
their health? By protecting them from tragedy and misfortune? Certainly
we can make efforts in these directions; but we cannot, in this most unpredictable of worlds, be sure of success. In spite of our efforts, fortunes
may crumble, health may fail, tragedy—at one time or another—will
surely strike.

When we look unsparingly at reality, it seems that the best insurance
that we can try to pass on to our children is what the minister probably
would call "inner strength" and what the psychologist and psychiatrist
would term "emotional maturity." Life brings many crises and disappointments to all of us, but the emotionally mature person will at the least be
better prepared to cope with them than the immature, the rigid and inflexible, or the neurotic.

But what actually do we mean by "emotional maturity"? According to
English and Finch, ". . . a person with a mature personality has worked

out a harmonious relationship between his basic needs, his conscience and ideals, and the environment which enables him to make maximum use of his psychic energies in constructive work, heterosexual adjustment, and altruistic living" (20).

The first responsibility of those who are entrusted with the task of socialization—parents, teachers, or others—is to understand the structure of the adult society which the child is to enter. Without such knowledge, the process of socialization becomes a hit-or-miss affair. With such knowledge, intelligent training can be undertaken.

No individual can avoid encountering conflicts between his needs and the demands of reality, and between opposing needs within himself. Nor would such a state of affairs probably be desirable, even if it were possible, since a reasonable degree of conflict often provides the impetus for the further development of the individual. One of the useful functions parents can perform is to help their children learn to tolerate conflict and frustration, and to deal with them effectively. However, through proper parental guidance, the child can be helped to avoid learning conflicting needs which are too strong and which, instead of promoting maturity, tend to handicap the individual's adjustment. Thus the child may be helped to avoid conflicts based on extreme needs for both dependency and independency, on intense desires for social or sexual contact and paralyzing fears of them, on wishes to exploit others and to serve them. The child can also be taught those responses in the form of knowledge, social and performance skills, and cultural attitudes, which are likely to lead in his particular culture to satisfaction of his existing needs, both primary and learned.

In the present chapter, we have reviewed many of the needs and response patterns which are necessary for successful adaptation to adult life in American culture. We have seen, for example, that the individual must have learned to be reasonably independent and capable of foresightful planning. He must have been motivated to gain satisfaction from fulfilling the roles he must play in his own society. He must have developed the skills necessary for performance of a vocation which is needed by the culture. He must have learned to compete and to coöperate; to assert himself when necessary without paralyzing fear, and to gain satisfaction from being helpful to others. He must have learned to tolerate frustration and anxiety—for no individual's life is without painful stress and at times seemingly insurmountable obstacles. And he must be flexible, able to try out new responses when old ones fail as environmental situations change—for change is inevitable.

Probably more than anything else, he needs to have developed a realistic knowledge of himself, his capabilities and limitations, his predominant needs, his fears, his sources of conflict. For without a reasonable degree of such knowledge, he is like a man trying to put together a jigsaw puzzle when several of the most important parts are missing. He may attempt goal responses of which he is incapable, thus wasting his energy and becoming discouraged or defeated. Conversely, he may neglect to try out those responses of which he is capable, and which could lead to the satisfaction of his basic needs.

He may also deny to himself the existence of needs that he actually has, because he has been taught that they are wrong. But since denying that one has needs does not lead to their extinction, he may learn to cope with them in maladaptive or neurotic, rather than in realistic ways. Thus, instead of admitting and expressing his anger toward his boss, a young man may displace his angry feelings to his sweetheart, thus unnecessarily alienating her. The young person with extreme dependency needs may run from friendship to friendship, always concluding that "people are no damn good," simply because they have not been able to meet his insatiable needs for dependence. The individual with secret needs for status may deny them to himself, but he may become an antiminority hate monger in an effort to achieve some kind of prestige. In Alexander's words: "The Greek maxim, 'Know yourself,' may once have been a luxury. Today it is a necessity. Man can adjust himself to his changing environment only by knowing himself, his desires, impulses, motives, and needs. He must become wiser, more judicious and self-reliant; in one word, more mature" (1).

The task of guiding the child's development so that he will be able to meet the demands of life maturely is not an easy one. For one thing, as we have repeatedly seen, our culture itself is often inconsistent in its expectations. The parent or teacher has to contend with the fact that the society as a whole frequently demands responses of the child which are wholly incompatible with those which will be expected of him as an adult. In addition, the culture often rewards incompatible responses simultaneously, both in childhood and in adult life. Horney has called attention to several of the more important contradictions implicit in our culture (31). She points out, for example, the contradiction between rewards for "competition and success on the one hand, and brotherly love and humility on the other" (31). She also mentions the conflict between stimulation of the individual's needs and the frustrations he encounters in trying to satisfy them. The individual is constantly being encouraged to develop learned needs which he will never be able to satisfy. Finally, Horney notes the contradiction between our emphasis on "freedom of the individual"—being told that one is free, and that the "great game of life" is open to him, on the one hand, and on the other, finding that actually for the majority of people the possibilities are quite limited (*31*).

Even without such cultural difficulties, however, no parent or teacher could, or would want to, prepare a child completely for all the problems he must face. One of the authors is reminded of a question he was once asked while addressing a mothers' group. He had made the point that parents should look forward to the kinds of responses which would be expected of their children at later stages of development; and then try to help the children to become ready to meet them. One of the mothers interrupted to inquire how she was going to know what these expected responses would be. "For example," she said, "I've been reading in Kinsey's books that the sexual responses of college-educated people are different from those of people with grade school educations. Suppose that I prepare my child to make college-level sexual responses and then he flunks out of school?"

While specific preparation for all of life's problems is obviously impossible as well as undesirable, the basic skills involved in satisfactory social relationships can be taught. Even more importantly, as we have already implied, the acquisition of favorable emotional attitudes and personality traits can be fostered. Upon the development of such characteristics will depend the child's chances for a happy and effective existence.

Throughout this book, we have tried to stress the ways in which the child's early social learning affects his ultimate psychological adjustment. It is our hope that in the process we have helped to show that much of the personal misery, and thus part of the social unrest abroad in the world today, is not inevitable. For since maladjusted or neurotic behavior, like emotionally mature behavior is learned, it is at least potentially avoidable or modifiable.

Present-day youth are living in a difficult era—an "age of anxiety." Upon their collective display of emotional maturity may rest not only their individual chances for achieving satisfaction from living, but also the survival of the world. The task of helping as many of our youngsters as possible to become mature—responsible, independent, and self-reliant —must be a primary concern of all of us, whether as parents, teachers, psychologists, doctors, ministers, employers, government officials, or even simply as neighbors. As Alexander points out, probably more than anything else, the achievement of emotional maturity depends on "knowing ourselves." On the contribution that it can make to this end rests the ultimate justification, not merely for such a book as this, but for our whole field—the still embryonic science of child psychology.

REFERENCES AND ADDITIONAL READING

1. Alexander, F., From adolescence to adulthood. *Ment. Health Bull.* Illinois Society for Mental Hygiene (1948), 26:1–4.
2. Anastasi, A., and Miller, S., Adolescent "prestige factors" in relation to scholastic and socioeconomic variables. *J. soc. Psychol.* (1949), 29:43–50.
3. Ausubel, D. P., Problems of adolescent adjustment. *Bulletin, Natl. Assn. Secondary School Principals* (1950), 34:1–84.
4. Ausubel, D. P., *Ego development and the personality disorders.* New York: Grune and Stratton, 1952.
5. Ausubel, D. P., *Theory and problems of adolescent development.* New York: Grune and Stratton, 1954.
6. Baber, R. E., Some mate selection standards of college students and their parents. *J. soc. Hyg.* (1936), 22:115–125.
7. Barker, R. G., Wright, B. A., and Gonick, M. R., *Adjustment to physical handicap and illness, Bulletin No. 55.* New York: Social Science Research Council, 1946.
8. Bell, H. M., *Youth tell their story.* Washington: American Council on Education, 1938.
9. Block, V. L., Conflicts of adolescents with their mothers. *J. abnorm. soc. Psychol.* (1937), 32:193–206.
10. Brown, F. J., *The sociology of childhood.* New York: Prentice-Hall, 1939.
11. Buhler, C., The social behavior of children, in C. Murchison (ed.), *A handbook of child psychology,* 2nd ed. Worcester: Clark University Press, 1933.
12. Butterfield, O. M., Love problems of adolescents. *Teach. Coll. Contr. Educ.,* 1939, No. 7.
13. Caldwell, O. W., and Lundeen, G. E., Further study of unfounded beliefs among junior-high-school pupils. *Teach. Coll. Rec.,* (1934), 36:35–52.
14. Carter, H. D., The development of interest in vocations. In *Adolescence,* 43rd Yearbook, Natl. Soc. Stud. Educ., Part I. Chicago: University of Chicago Press, 1944.
15. Cole, L., *Psychology of adolescence.* New York: Rinehart, 1948.
16. Cronbach, L. J., *Essentials of psychological testing.* New York: Harper, 1949.
17. Dimock, H. S., *Rediscovering the adolescent.* New York: Association Press, 1937.
18. Dudycha, G. J., The superstitious beliefs of college students. *J. appl. Psychol.* (1933), 17:586–603.
19. Ehrmann, W. W., Dating behavior of college students. *Marriage Fam. Living* (1952), 14:322–326.
20. English, O. S., and Finch, S. M., *Introduction to psychiatry.* New York: Norton, 1954.

21. English, O. S., and Pearson, G. H. S., *Emotional problems of living*. New York: Norton, 1955.
22. Farnham, M. L., *The adolescent*. New York: Harper, 1951.
23. Flemming, E. G., Best friends. *J. soc. Psychol.* (1932), 3:385–390.
24. Frank, L. K., The adolescent and the family. In *Adolescence*, 43rd Yearbook, Natl. Soc. Stud. Educ., Part I. Chicago: University of Chicago Press, 1944, pp. 240–254.
25. Garrison, K. C., *Psychology of adolescence*. New York: Prentice-Hall, 1951.
26. Havighurst, R. J., Robison, M. Z., and Dorr, M., The development of the ideal self in childhood and adolescence. *J. educ. Res.* (1946), 40:241–257.
27. Havighurst, R. J., and Taba, H., *Adolescent character and personality*. New York: Wiley, 1949.
28. Hicks, J. A., and Hayes, M., Study of the characteristics of 250 junior-high-school children. *Child Develop.* (1938), 9:219–242.
29. Hollingshead, A. B., *Elmtown's youth: the impact of social classes on youth*. New York: Wiley, 1949.
30. Hoppock, R., A check list of factors about jobs for use in vocational guidance. *Am. Psychologist* (1948), 8:417–418.
31. Horney, K., *The neurotic personality of our time*. New York: Norton, 1937.
32. Horrocks, J. E., The adolescent, in L. Carmichael (ed.), *Manual of child psychology*. New York: Wiley, 1946, pp. 697–734.
33. Horrocks, J. E., *The psychology of adolescence*. Boston: Houghton Mifflin, 1951.
34. Hurlock, E. B., and Klein, E. R., Adolescent "crushes." *Child Develop.* (1934), 5:63–80.
35. Hurlock, E. B., *Adolescent development*. New York: McGraw-Hill, 1949.
36. Jones, E. S., The opinions of college students. *J. appl. Psychol.* (1926), 10: 427–436.
37. Jones, M. C., Adolescent friendships. *Am. Psychologist* (1948), 3:352 (abstract).
38. Katz, D., and Allport, F. H., *Students' attitudes*. Syracuse, N.Y.: Craftsman Press, 1931.
39. Komarovsky, M., Cultural contradictions and sex roles. *Am. J. Sociol.* (1946), 52:184–187.
40. Kroger, R., and Louttit, C. M., The influence of father's occupation on the vocational choices of high-school boys. *J. appl. Psychol.* (1935), 19: 203–212.
41. Kuhlen, R. G., and Arnold, M., Age differences in religious beliefs and problems during adolescence. *J. genet. Psychol.* (1944), 65:291–300.
42. Landis, C., et al., *Sex in development*. New York: Hoeber, 1940.
43. Landis, P. H., *Adolescence and youth: the process of maturing*. New York: McGraw-Hill, 1952.
44. Lehman, H. C., and Witty, P. A., *The psychology of play activities*. New York: Barnes, 1927.
45. Leonard, E. A., Problems of freshman college girls. *Child Develop. Monogr.* 1932, No. 9.

46. Levin, M. M., Status anxiety and occupational choice. *Educ. psychol. Measmt.* (1949), 9:29–38.
47. Lundeen, G. E., and Caldwell, O. W., A study of unfounded beliefs among high-school seniors. *J. educ. Res.* (1930), 22:257–273.
48. Lynd, R. S., and Lynd, H. M., *Middletown.* New York: Harcourt, Brace, 1929.
49. Mead, M., *From the south seas,* Part III, *Sex and temperament in three primitive societies.* New York: Morrow, 1939.
50. Meek, L. H., *The personal-social development of boys and girls with implications for secondary education.* New York: Progressive Education Association, 1940.
51. Meltzer, H., The development of children's nationality preferences, concepts, and attitudes. *J. Psychol.* (1941), 11:343–358.
52. Meyers, C. E., Emancipation of adolescents from parental control. *Nerv. Child* (1946), 5:251–262.
53. Parkham, Y. C., Out-of-school environment and activities of junior high school pupils. *Soc. Educ.* (1942), 6:27–30.
54. Partridge, E. D., A study of friendships among adolescent boys. *J. genet. Psychol.* (1933), 43:472–477.
55. Perrin, F. A. C., Physical attractiveness and repulsiveness. *J. exp. Psychol.* (1921), 4:203–217.
56. Piaget, J., *Moral judgment of the child.* New York: Harcourt, Brace, 1932.
57. Poll No. 13, Institute of Student Opinion, *Scholastic Magazine,* 1946.
58. Pressey, S. L., and Robinson, F. P., *Psychology and the new education.* New York: Harper, 1944.
59. Punke, H. H., Dating practices of high school youth. *Bulletin, Natl. Assn. Secondary School Principals* (1944), 28:47–54.
60. Remmers, H. H., Drucker, A. J., and Christenson, H. T., Courtship conduct as viewed by high school youths. *Purdue Opin. Panel,* X, No. 2 (Report No. 27), 1950.
61. Rockwood, L. D., and Ford, M. E. N., *Youth, marriage, and parenthood.* New York, Wiley, 1945.
62. Rosander, H. C., Age and sex patterns of social attitudes. *J. educ. Psychol.* (1939), 30:481–496.
63. Sherman, A. W., Emancipation status of college students. *J. genet. Psychol.* (1933), 43:422–437.
64. Smith, M., Some factors in friendship selections of high-school students. *Sociometry* (1944), 7:303–310.
65. Stewart, N., AGCT scores of Army personnel grouped by occupation. *Occupations* (1947), 26:5–41.
66. Stoke, S. M., and West, E. D., Sex differences in conversational interests. *J. soc. Psychol.* (1931), 2:120–166.
67. Stone, C. P., and Barker, R. G., The attitudes and interests of premenarcheal girls. *J. genet. Psychol.* (1939), 54:27–71.
68. Taylor, K. W., *Do adolescents need parents?* New York: Appleton-Century, 1938.

69. Thompson, G. G., and Horrocks, J. E., A study of friendship of urban boys and girls. *J. genet. Psychol.* (1947), 70:53–63.

70. Tryon, C. M., Evaluation of adolescent personality by adolescents. *Monogr. Soc. Res. Child Develop.* (1939), 4:No. 4.

71. Tryon, C. M., The adolescent peer culture. In *Adolescence*, 43rd yearbook, Natl. Soc. Stud. Educ. Part I, Chicago: University of Chicago Press, 1944, pp. 217–239.

72. Tudor-Hart, B. E., Are there cases where lies are necessary? *J. genet. Psychol.* (1926), 33:586–641.

73. Valentine, W. L., Common misconceptions of college students. *J. appl. Psychol.* (1936), 20:633–658.

74. Walford, O. P., How early background affects dating behavior. *J. Home Econ.* (1948), 40:505–506.

75. Wallin, P., Cultural contradictions and sex roles: a repeat study. *Am. social Rev.* (1950), 15:288–293.

76. Warner, W. L., and Lunt, P. S., *The social life of a modern community.* New Haven: Yale University Press, 1941.

77. Washburn, J. N., The impulsions of adolescents as revealed by their written wishes. *J. juv. Res.* (1932), 16:193–212.

78. West, J., *Plainville, U.S.A.* New York: Columbia University Press, 1945.

79. Whiting, J. W. M., and Child, I., *Child training and personality: a cross-cultural study.* New Haven: Yale University Press, 1953.

80. Winch, R. F., Interrelationship between certain social background and parent-son factors in the study of courtship among college men. *Am. sociol. Rev.* (1946), 11:333–343.

81. Winch, R. F., The relation between the loss of parents and progress in courtship. *J. soc. Psychol.* (1949), 29:51–56.

82. Wood, N. W., *Living together in the family.* Washington: American Home Economics Association, 1946.

83. *Youth and the world of work.* East Lansing, Michigan: Social Research Service, Michigan State College, 1949.

INDEXES

Index of Names

Abernethy, E. M., 364, 412
Abraham, K., 143, 166
Adkins, N. M., 322, 323, 324, 351, 358
Adorno, T. W., 442, 447
Alcott, B., 9
Alcott, L. M., 9
Aldrich, C. A., 140, 166
Alexander, F., 543, 545
Allen, L., 199, 201, 212, 219, 227, 260, 263, 267, 268, 284, 301, 302, 307, 341, 358, 375, 380, 414
Allport, F. H., 537, 546
Allport, G., 21, 22, 34, 35, 121, 134
Amatruda, C. S., 58, 86, 87, 93, 105, 106, 173, 181, 211, 219, 220, 266
Ames, L. B., 82, 86, 87, 93, 94, 104, 106, 210, 219, 220, 266
Ames, V. C., 210
Anastasi, A., 505, 545
Anderson, G. L., 394, 395, 413
Anderson, H. H., 284, 288, 289, 307, 394, 395, 412, 413
Anderson, J. E., 182, 210
Anderson, M., 186, 213, 214
Andrus, R., 294, 297, 308
Arnold, M., 537, 538, 546
Arsenian, J. M., 187, 188, 189, 208, 210
Asch, S. E., 405, 406, 413
Austin, M. C., 435, 447
Ausubel, D. P., 466, 467, 469, 475, 479, 481, 483, 496, 497, 500, 501, 503, 505, 506, 507, 508, 511, 512, 517, 521, 527, 529, 532
Axline, V. M., 300, 301, 308
Ayers, L. P., 365, 413

Baber, R. E., 514, 545
Bakwin, H., 82, 104, 105
Bakwin, R. M., 82, 104, 105
Baldwin, A. L., 250, 251, 252, 253, 255, 256, 265, 282, 306, 308
Baldwin, B. T., 458, 483

Banker, M. H., 390, 415
Barker, R. G., 23, 212, 268, 285, 287, 288, 300, 308, 468, 485, 499, 500, 539, 545, 547
Baruch, D. W., 257, 258, 265
Bowlby, J., 183, 184, 185, 186, 187, 213
Bayley, N., 93, 172, 181, 182, 210, 265, 364, 413, 462, 465, 468, 483, 484
Beach, F. A., 471, 472, 473, 481, 484
Beckey, R. E., 179, 210
Bell, H. M., 478, 483, 508, 522, 530, 532, 545
Bell, M., 62
Benedict, R., 131, 134, 454, 455, 473, 483
Bender, L., 327, 355
Benjamin, J. D., 147, 166
Bettelheim, B., 307, 308
Bishop, B. M., 245, 265
Block, V. L., 493, 494, 495, 545
Blum, G., 52, 70, 141, 166, 196, 210, 233, 234, 315, 328, 355
Boas, F., 40, 49, 462, 483
Bolles, M. M., 44, 45, 50
Bond, E. A., 376, 413
Bonney, M. E., 341, 355, 385, 392, 413, 429, 432, 434, 435, 447
Bossard, J. H. S., 342, 355
Bossik, 17, 19
Boyle, R., 18
Boynton, P., 402, 413, 426, 427
Bradbury, D. E., 221, 269
Breckenridge, M. E., 84, 105, 317, 320, 321, 355
Breese, F. H., 250, 251, 253, 265, 378, 383, 414
Brewer, J. E., 394, 395, 413
Bridges, K. M. B., 103, 104, 105
Brodbeck, A. J., 111, 134, 141, 157, 166, 167
Brody, S., 83
Bronner, A. F., 438, 439, 448

551

Index of Subjects

Academic achievement, see School

Acceptance-rejection, consequents of, 330–333; by parents, and school adjustment, 389

Acquired characteristics, inheritance of, 56–57

Adjustment, in relation to early feeding practices, 145–148; role of parent-child relations in, 152–162, 189–193, 244–256, 324–343; of institution reared children, 154–159; and toilet training, 199–202; and nursery school attendance, 293–298; social class differences in, 347–350; to school, 360–412; to peers in middle childhood, 417–447; of juvenile delinquents, 437–441; and prejudice, 442–445; and physical development in adolescence, 465–470; and sexual development in adolescence, 470–473; of adolescent, 486–500; independence-dependence as problems of, 486–500; peer relations and adolescent, 500–507; adolescent heterosexual, 509–516; vocational, 516–531; moral problems in, 531–540; emotionally mature, 540–545
See also Maladjustment

Adolescence, physical growth and development in, 453–483; development of sex characteristics in, 462–463; intellectual growth in, 464–465; psychological problems and physical development in, 465–470; sexual responses during, 470–473; 473–477; parental attitudes toward sexuality during, 477–483; sexual adjustment problems in, 479–483; sex education in, 482–483; independency-dependency problems in, 486–500; peer relationships in, 500–507, interest patterns during, 507–509; relations

with opposite-sex peers during, 509–516; vocational adjustment in, 516–531; moral and religious problems in, 531–540; and emotional maturity, 540–545

Aggression, and early feeding experiences, 148–149; as a consequent of severe toilet training, 201; early development of, 202–206; learning of, 202–203; and sex-typing in preschool boys, 244, 279; antecedents of, 246–250; as a consequent of home punishment, 247–249; inhibition of, 246–247; as reaction to frustration, 246–247, 284–285; and situational factors, 278, 284, 285; among preschool children, 278–280; and social class, 345, 351–352; and school adjustment, 389; and teacher behavior, 383–397; and group atmosphere, 397–399; and juvenile deliquency, 437–441; and prejudice, 442–447

Alcohol, 56

Alorese, 509

Amnion, 55

Anal character, see Psychoanalysis

Anal phase, see Psychoanalysis

Anger, early development and manifestations of, 202–206
See also Aggression

Anoxia, 72

Anthropology, and child psychology, 7

Anticipatory response, 117

Anti-Semitism, see Prejudice

Anxiety, of mother during pregnancy, 66–70; primal or birth, 70–72; as learned drive, 124–126; pain as determinant of, 124–125; an example of learned, 125–126; and insecurity, 187–189; and self-confidence, 192–193; as a consequent of severe toilet

Health, *see* Illness
Hearing, in neonate, 89; defects and personality, 318, 320
Height, of neonates, 82; sex differences in, 82, 217–218, 316–317; during first year, 82; during second year, 170; during preschool years, 217–218; during middle childhood, 316–318; during adolescence, 459–460
  See also Physical development
Hereditary transmission, 28–34
Heredity, *see* Genetics; Genetic factors
Heredity versus environment, *see* Genetics; Nature-nurture controversy
Home, atmosphere in, 245–246, 250–256; democracy in, 251–253; control in, 251–253; frustration in, and behavior, 247–250; autocratic, 254, 334; removal from, in therapy, 306
  See also Family; Parent-child relationships
Homosexual behavior, development of, 325–326, 481–482; during adolescence, 481
Hopi, 111, 405, 472
Hormones, sex, 470–471, 482
Hospitalism, *see* Marasmus
Hostility, *see* Aggression
Hunger, in neonate, 87; during first year, 87; role in early learning of, 136
  See also Feeding
Hypertension, 42
Hypothesis, in scientific procedure, 13; testing of, 14

Ideals, *see* Superego
Identification, 234
  defined, 234, 240–241; and learning, 241; and imitation, 241; familial influences on, 243–244, 325–327; with ethnic groups, 352–353; with peers in middle childhood, 421–423; with peers in adolescence, 501–507
  See also Psychoanalysis; Sex-typing
Idiographic approach, 21
Illness, and locomotion, 172; incidence during middle childhood, 317–318; and personality, 319–321
  See also Disease
Imitation, as example of learning, 131–133; matched-dependent, 132; copying, 132–133
  See also Identification
Impersonal care, consequents of, in infancy, 152–156; in later childhood, 156–158
  See also Institutionalization

Independence, beginning of, 183; and parental attitudes, 189–193; and learning, 290–291; establishment of adolescent, 486–500
Indulgence, consequents of, 253, 255–256, 334
Inhibition, of aggression, 246–250
Initial response hierarchy, *see* Response hierarchies
Innate response hierarchy, *see* Response hierarchies
Insecurity, reactions to, 184–189
Institutionalization, early, consequents of, 154–158, 160; for psychotherapy, 307
Instrumental conditioning, 126
Integration, in social interactions of preschool children, 288–289; in behavior, 394–397
Intellectual development, early stages, 179–180; during preschool period, 226–227; and school adjustment, 367–380; and physical development, 364–365; and physical defect and disease, 365–367; in adolescence, 464–465
Intelligence, genetic factors in, 37–38, 46–48; effects of premature birth on, 73–75; of institution-reared children, 154–155, 157; infant tests of, 180–182; relationship of preschool test scores to later performance, 227; related to sympathy, 277; meaning of, 368–369; tests of, 376–377; criticisms of current tests of, 377–380; and juvenile delinquency, 437
Intelligence quotients, computation of, 372–373; distribution of, 373; constancy of, 373–375; usefulness of, 375–376
Intelligence tests, *see* Intelligence
Interests, in middle childhood, 423–426; sex differences in, 423–426; during adolescence, 507–509
Interview, as method of observation, 13
Irradiation (x-ray), effects on fetus of, 64

Japanese, 442
Jealousy, origin and treatment of, 263–265
  See also Siblings
Jews, and minority-group prejudice, 441–445
Juvenile deliquency, *see* Deliquency

Kinesthetic sensitivity, in neonate, 90

Mental retardation, *see* Mental deficiency
Mesoderm, 55
Mexicans, 442
Microcephaly, 64
Minority group prejudice, *see* Prejudice
Minority groups, identification with, 352–353; membership in, 354
Mitosis, 27
Mongolism, 66
   See also Mental deficiency
Moral judgment, in middle childhood, 327–328, 426–429
Moral problems of adolescents, 531–540; influence of parents and peers in, 534–535; role of adult culture in, 535–537; areas of conflict in, 537–540
   See also Religion
Moral realism, 327
Morals, *see* Superego
Mother, age of, and fetal development, 65–66; role of, in socialization of child, 137; early treatment of child by, 152–162; and feeding practices, 163–165; as source of security, 187–189; permissive, 189–191; rejecting, 191; overprotecting, 192; overmeticulous, 192–193
   See also Mother-child relationships
Mother-child relationships, effects of maternal emotional states on fetus, 66–67, 69–70
   See also "Mothering"; Parent-child relationships
"Mothering," "warm," in feeding, 152–158; defined, 152; consequences of "good" and "poor," 152–162
   See also Impersonal care; Mother; Parent-child relationships
Motivation, *see* Drives; Learning; Needs
Motor development, genetic factors in, 43; prenatal, 58–61; during first year, 93–98; cephalo-caudal, proximo-distal, mass-specific trends in, 98; during second year, 173–174; maturation and, 174; learning and, 174; during preschool years, 219–220; during middle childhood, 317; during adolescence, 461
Movies, 425
Mundugumor, 489–490
Muscle development, during first year, 84; during second year, 171; during preschool years, 218; during middle childhood, 317; during adolescence, 461
Myelinization, 171, 218

Nature-nurture controversy, 34–36
   See also Genetics
Needs, physiological, during first year, 83–87; in relation to drive, 114
   See also Drive
Negativism, in infants, 153; as a consequence of severe toilet training, 200; and overattention, 335
Negroes, identifications of, 353–354; motives and attitudes of, 354; attitudes toward education of, 384; and minority-group prejudice, 441–447
Neonate, physical characteristics of, 81–84; skeletal development of, 83–84; physiological needs of, 84–87; muscular development of, 84; sensory development of, 88–91; reflexes of, 91–92; responses of, 91–92; learning in, 119–120; primary drives in, 119–120
Nervous system, development of, 55, 171
Neurosis, genetic factors in, 45; in children, *see* Maladjustment
Nomethetic approach or method, 21–22
Nondirective techniques in psychotherapy, 300–302
Nursery school, consequents of attendance at, 293–298; variations in atmosphere of, 297–298
Nurturance, 249–250, 255–256
Nystagmus, in neonate, 90

Observation, in scientific procedure, 13; in child psychology, 15–16
Oedipus complex, 234, 237–239
   and castration threats, 238; universality of, 238; and family relationships, 239; consequents of unresolved, 239
   See also Psychoanalysis
Olfaction, in neonate, 89
Only child, personality and adjustment of, 342–343; and friendships in middle childhood, 342–343; academic progress of, 392–393
Oral fixation, *see* Psychoanalysis
Oral phase, *see* Psychoanalysis
Ordinal position, influence on personality and adjustment of, 340–342; and school success, 393–399
Orgasm, *see* Sex responses
Ossification, *see* Skeletal development
Overattention, consequents of, 334–335
Overprotection, and obesity, 40–41; of premature infants, 74–75; and prevention of independent behavior, 192; consequents of, 192, 256–257, 334; and school adjustment, 390